PAUL
Apostle of God's Glory in Christ

A PAULINE THEOLOGY

THOMAS R. SCHREINER

IVP Academic

An imprint of InterVarsity Press
Downers Grove, Illinois

Apollos
Leicester, England

InterVarsity Press, USA
P.O. Box 1400, Downers Grove, IL 60515-1426, USA
World Wide Web: www.ivpress.com
Email: email@ivpress.com

APOLLOS (an imprint of Inter-Varsity Press, England)
38 De Montfort Street, Leicester LE1 7GP, England
Website: www.ivpbooks.com
Email: ivp@ivp-editorial.co.uk

InterVarsity Press®, USA, is the book-publishing division of InterVarsity Christian Fellowship/USA®, a movement of students and faculty active on campus at hundreds of universities, colleges and schools of nursing in the United States of America, and a member movement of the International Fellowship of Evangelical Students. For information about local and regional activities, visit intervarsity.org.

Inter-Varsity Press, England, is the publishing division of the Universities and Colleges Christian Fellowship (formerly the Inter-Varsity Fellowship), a student movement linking Christian Unions in universities and colleges throughout Great Britain, and a member movement of the International Fellowship of Evangelical Students. For information about local and national activities write to UCCF, 38 De Montfort Street, Leicester LE1 7GP, email us at email@uccf.org.uk, or visit the UCCF website at www.uccf.org.uk.

All Scripture quotations, unless otherwise indicated, are the author's translation.

Image: ©sedmak/iStockphoto

USA 978-0-8308-2825-8
UK 978-1-84474-139-7

Printed in the United Kingdom ∞

Library of Congress Cataloging-in-Publication Data

Schreiner, Thomas R.
  Paul, Apostle of God's glory in Christ: a Pauline theology / Thomas
R. Schreiner.
     p. cm.
  Includes bibliographical references and indexes.
  ISBN 0-8308-2651-3 (cloth: alk. paper)—ISBN 0-85111-777-5 (cloth
  : alk. paper)—ISBN 0-8308-2825-7 (pbk.: alk. paper)
  1. Bible. N.T. Epistles of Paul—Theology. I. Title.
  BS2651.S277 2006
  277'.06—dc22
2005028341

British Library Cataloguing in Publication Data

A catalogue record for this book is available from the British Library.

P	25	24	23	22	21	20	19	18	17	16	15	14	13	12	11	10	9	8
Y	31	30	29	28	27	26	25	24	23	22	21	20	19	18	17	16	15	

To my children—
Daniel, Patrick, John and Anna—
sources of unspeakable joy

CONTENTS

Preface

My goal in writing this book was to write a textbook on Pauline theology for students at both the college and seminary level. I do not intend, therefore, to interact extensively with other scholars, though I dialogue enough with them to demonstrate that I am conversant with what is happening in Pauline studies. Some books provide a genuine service by sketching in the landscape provided by secondary sources. My fundamental aim, however, is to explain the biblical text since students need to see that the primary sources are foundational for doing Pauline theology. My intention is to set forth and defend my particular understanding of Pauline theology. I acknowledge at the outset that I have not written the definitive Pauline theology, but I hope that others can profit from my own wrestling with the text.

When one compares my work with the recent and excellent Pauline theology by James Dunn, at least three major differences are evident. First, Dunn's theology is a mammoth work that both examines the biblical text and interacts with the secondary sources. Such an enterprise is extremely helpful, but because I do not dialogue as extensively with secondary sources here, I limited the size of my book. Second, I have tried to organize my book in a fresh way. Dunn uses Romans as the template to organize Pauline theology, and this is a valuable way to proceed. Yet I do not believe that there *is only one way* to structure a Pauline theology. I think my approach opens some new windows into Paul's theology by focusing on Paul as a missionary and on his apostolic sufferings—two topics that are often neglected in Pauline theologies. I also argue that God's work in Christ is the foundation and goal of Paul's theology. I think it is a mistake to identify some aspect of salvation, whether it is justification or salvation history, as the key to Paul's thinking. Third, Dunn excludes Ephesians and the Pastoral Letters from his study, and he thinks Colossians was written by Timothy while Paul was still living. I am persuaded, however, that all thirteen letters are authentic. I do not argue the case for authenticity in my theology; instead I refer the readers to others who have made the case effectively.[1] The Pauline theology offered here is distinctive in that all thirteen letters ascribed to Paul are mined to decipher his theology.

Finally, I want to thank those who have assisted me in the writing of this book. I am grateful to Dan Reid, the academic reference editor at InterVarsity Press, for his encouragement and assistance in the writing of this work. Dan is himself an expert in Pauline studies, and hence he made numerous suggestions that have been incorporated into the book so that it is better than it would otherwise be. Frank Thielman, professor of New Testament at the Beeson Divinity School, read the entire manuscript, pointed out some deficiencies that needed correction and was a great encouragement to me. Boyd Luter, the dean at Criswell College, offered to read the entire work in a short time period, corrected a number of mistakes and commented helpfully at a number of places. Justin Taylor read the entire manuscript, corrected a number of errors and made many helpful suggestions. Five students at the Southern Baptist Theological Seminary helped me significantly. My Garrett fellow and longtime friend Philemon Yong chased down references, copied needed articles and proofed the manuscript carefully. Jeff Evans and Jim Hamilton proofed the book under a tight deadline, and I am thankful for their help in spotting errors. I also am grateful to Randall Tan and Brian Vickers, who serve as editors at *The Southern Baptist Journal of Theology*. Randall Tan read the manuscript with a sharp eye and made many suggestions for improvement. A special thanks goes to Brian Vickers for his labor of love in reading the manuscript so diligently and for his numerous stylistic suggestions. Every reader made the book better than it was before, for which I am thankful. I also want to thank my wife, Diane, for her love. Her faithfulness to me over twenty-five years of marriage has been a wellspring of life to me. I dedicate this book to our children—Daniel, Patrick, John and Anna. They have been sources of unspeakable joy to me. Finally, I pray that God would be magnified and praised through Jesus Christ by what I have written here. The grace of our glorious God sustained me as I wrote.

---

[1]Recent commentators who have defended the authenticity of the Pastoral Letters include J. N. D. Kelly, Joachim Jeremias, Donald Guthrie, Gordon Fee, George Knight III, Philip H. Towner, Luke Johnson and William Mounce. Compare also E. Earle Ellis, "Pseudonymity and Canonicity of New Testament Documents," in *Worship, Theology and Ministry in the Early Church: Essays in Honor of Ralph P. Martin,* JSNTSup 87, ed. M. J. Wilkins and T. Paige (Sheffield: JSOT, 1992), pp. 212-24.

Abbreviations

AB	Anchor Bible
AGJU	Arbeiten zur Geschichte des antiken Judentums und des Urchristentums
AnBib	Analecta biblica
BBB	Bonner biblische Beiträge
BBR	*Bulletin for Biblical Research*
BECNT	Baker Exegetical Commentaries on the New Testament
BETL	Bibliotheca ephemeridum theologicarum lovaniensium
Bib	*Biblica*
BJRL	*Bulletin of the John Rylands University Library of Manchester*
BSac	*Bibliotheca sacra*
BZ	*Biblische Zeitschrift*
BZNW	Beihefte zur Zeitschrift für die neutestamentliche Wissenschaft
CBQ	*Catholic Biblical Quarterly*
Chm	*Churchman*
EvQ	*Evangelical Quarterly*
ExAud	*Ex auditu*
FRLANT	Forschungen zur Religion und Literatur des Alten und Neuen Testaments
HBT	*Horizons in Biblical Theology*
HTR	*Harvard Theological Review*
ICC	International Critical Commentary
Int	*Interpretation*

JBL	*Journal of Biblical Literature*
JETS	*Journal of the Evangelical Theological Society*
JSNT	*Journal for the Study of the New Testament*
JSNTSup	*Journal for the Study of the New Testament* Supplement Series
JTS	*Journal of Theological Studies*
LEC	Library of Early Christianity
Mart. Pol.	*Martyrdom of Polycarp*
NICNT	New International Commentary on the New Testament
NIGTC	New International Greek Testament Commentary
NIVAC	NIV Application Commentary Series
NovT	*Novum Testamentum*
NovTSup	*Novum Testamentum* Supplements
NTAbh	Neutestamentliche Abhandlungen
NTS	*New Testament Studies*
PSBSup	*Princeton Seminary Bulletin* Supplement
PTMS	Pittsburgh Theological Monograph Series
RTR	*Reformed Theological Review*
SBG	Studies in Biblical Greek
SBLDS	Society of Biblical Literature Dissertation Series
SBLMS	Society of Biblical Literature Monograph Series
SBT	Studies in Biblical Theology
SJLA	Studies in Judaism in Late Antiquity
SJT	*Scottish Journal of Theology*
SNT	Studien zum Neuen Testament
SNTSMS	Society for New Testament Studies Monograph Series
StudBibT	*Studia Biblica et Theologica*
TBei	*Theologische Beiträge*
Them	*Themelios*
TJ	*Trinity Journal*
TynBul	*Tyndale Bulletin*
TZ	*Theologische Zeitschrift*
USQR	*Union Seminary Quarterly Review*
WBC	Word Biblical Commentary
WEC	Wycliffe Evangelical Commentary

WTJ	*Westminster Theological Journal*
WUNT	Wissenschaftliche Untersuchungen zum Neuen Testament
ZNW	*Zeitschrift für die neutestamentliche Wissenschaft und die Kunde der älteren Kirche*

1

INTRODUCTION
The Centrality of God in Christ
in Paul's Theology

T he goal in writing a Pauline theology is to unearth Paul's worldview and to present it to contemporaries. The task is not merely to reproduce Paul's thinking on various topics, but to rightly estimate what is most important in his thinking and to set forth the inner connections between the various themes. Such a task is difficult since Paul's theology is complex and presented in occasional letters written to churches. If scholars debate the nature of John Calvin's theology, even though he wrote an organized summary of his theology in the *Institutes of the Christian Religion,* how much more challenging is it to discern Paul's theology since we lack a systematic explanation of his thought. It would be naive and pretentious to assert that I have discovered the key to Paul's theology. Nonetheless, I believe that I have detected some themes that are insufficiently appreciated in most standard works on Paul. The goal in this work is not to interact point by point with other scholars who have investigated Pauline thought.[1] Such a task would make this

---

[1]For the two most recent and helpful analyses of Paul's thought, see Ben Witherington III, *Paul's Narrative Thought World: The Tapestry of Tragedy and Triumph* (Louisville, Ky.: West-

book far too long (and boring!). It should be evident, on the other hand, that this work has not been done in a vacuum and that the contributions of other scholars form the backdrop for what is discussed. The footnotes in each chapter either provide the source for a citation or point to works that should be consulted for further research.

The goal in the present work is to see what Paul says and to see it in the right proportions. Adolf Schlatter has rightly commented that the hardest thing to observe is often right in front of our eyes, for we may think we have understood when we actually only have a superficial acquaintance with reality. He perceptively remarks:

> The first task of New Testament theology consists in perceiving the facts of the case, and it would be childish to worry that there is no more work for us to do since countless scholars have been observing the New Testament for a long time now. That would show how little we were aware of the size of the task posed by the formula "observation." What has happened exceeds in its fullness and depth our capacity for seeing, and there is no question of an end being reached even of the first and most simple function of New Testament study; namely, seeing what is there.[2]

Schlatter is correct when he says that the task is so large that no one can claim to have seen all that is present in the documents before us. And yet I hope that I can introduce a fresh vision of Paul to students in a relatively nontechnical way.

The Center of Paul's Thought

Scholars have been attempting to perceive the central theme in Paul's thought ever since biblical theology became a discipline in its own right.[3]

---

minster John Knox, 1994); and James D. G. Dunn, *The Theology of Paul the Apostle* (Grand Rapids, Mich.: Eerdmans, 1998). For my review of the latter, see *Trinity Journal* 20 (1999): 95-100. Any reader who compares my work with Witherington and Dunn will see that I differ with them at a number of significant points. For a briefer analysis, see N. T. Wright, *What St. Paul Really Said: Was Paul of Tarsus the Real Founder of Christianity?* (Grand Rapids, Mich.: Eerdmans, 1997).

[2] Adolf Schlatter, "The Theology of the New Testament and Dogmatics," in *The Nature of New Testament Theology,* ed. Robert Morgan, SBT 25 (Naperville, Ill.: SCM Press, 1973), p. 136.

[3] A number of works have been written on the history and nature of New Testament theology. The work edited by Morgan cited in n. 2 above is a useful resource in this regard. The work that is the most helpful in charting one's way in contemporary discussions of New Testament theology is Gerhard Hasel, *New Testament Theology: Basic Issues in the Current Debate* (Grand Rapids, Mich.: Eerdmans, 1978). Hasel summarizes the history of the movement, major works that have been written and the various methodologies employed, and he discusses the attempt to identify a single center. Interestingly, Hasel maintains that only "God" is a large enough theme to constitute the center of New Testament theology.

The sheer number of proposals has led some to doubt that any center can be identified at all. The very search for a center is dismissed as an attempt to capture the uncapturable. It smacks of an enlightenment pretension that claims the ability to summarize everything under one main idea. Anything that conflicts with the central theme is swept aside or domesticated. In the process the genuine Paul, the Paul with rough edges and sides, is planed down to fit a prefabricated theory. The danger of imposing an alien center on Paul is a real one, and it may be the case that no single theme embraces the whole of Paul's thought. One of the problems here is with the word *center* itself. If one theme is in the center, then we may form an image or picture in our minds of other teachings in Paul radiating out from that center. If we conceive of the center as a bull's-eye and of other Pauline themes as circles around the center, then we could get the impression that some Pauline teachings are crucial since they are near the center whereas others are peripheral and insignificant since they are far from the center. We may be tempted, therefore, to erect a "canon within the canon" in which the core represents Paul's "real" convictions and in which other themes (which do fit with "our" center) are dismissed as secondary and unimportant. The image of a center could lead to a static conception of Pauline theology where one theme is given hegemony and other themes are slotted in accordingly. No vital connection is established between the various themes, and the whole enterprise appears startlingly subjective.

Some centers proposed, however, have struck a chord with many Pauline scholars. Scholars have sensed that these themes are comprehensive enough to warrant further scrutiny or even to be accepted as "the center." We think of themes like justification, defended by Ernst Käsemann, Peter Stuhlmacher and Karl Kertelge;[4] reconciliation, which has been proposed by Ralph Mar-

---

[4]For Ernst Käsemann's understanding of righteousness, see his *Commentary on Romans* (Grand Rapids, Mich.: Eerdmans, 1980), and his essay, "God's Righteousness in Paul," *Journal of Theology and Church* 1 (1965): 100-110. For Peter Stuhlmacher, see *Gerechtigkeit Gottes bei Paulus*, FRLANT 87 (Göttingen: Vandenhoeck & Ruprecht, 1965), and his essay, "The Apostle Paul's View of Righteousness," in *Reconciliation, Law and Righteousness: Essays in Biblical Theology* (Philadelphia: Fortress, 1986), pp. 68-93. Karl Kertelge is a Roman Catholic scholar who has emphasized the centrality of justification. See his *Rechtfertigung bei Paulus: Studien zur Struktur und sum Bedeutungsgehalt des paulinischen Rechtfertigungsbegriffs*, 2nd ed., NTAbh 3 (Münster in Westfalen: Aschendorff, 1967). For a recent defense of the centrality of justification that moves in a different orbit from Käsemann and Stuhlmacher, see Mark A. Seifrid, *Justification by Faith: The Origin and Development of a Central Pauline Theme*, NovTSup 68 (Leiden: Brill, 1992), and his *Christ, Our Righteousness:Paul's Theology of Justification* (Downers Grove, Ill.: InterVarsity Press, 2001).

tin;[5] the mystical doctrine of being "in Christ," as it is set forth by Albert
Schweitzer, or participation in Christ, as explained by E. P. Sanders;[6] salvation
history, supported by Herman Ridderbos and Marvin Pate;[7] or the imminent
apocalyptic triumph of God, as defended by J. Christiaan Beker.[8] It is not the
intention of this work to discuss the merits and demerits of each of these proposals individually. They would not have exercised such appeal if they were
secondary motifs in Paul. Their obvious importance has provoked some
scholars to propose, and some to ratify, them as the center. And yet others
have, just as emphatically, denied that these various themes serve as the center of Paul's thought, for in each case there are some Pauline themes that sit
awkwardly with the proposed center.

I would like to suggest that each theme fails as the "center" for the same
reason. Every proposed center suppresses part of the Pauline gospel. Identifying the center as, say, justification exalts the gift given above the giver. The
gift of righteousness is not more important in Paul's thinking than the person
who gave the gift. A similar objection could be directed against the idea that
reconciliation should have pride of place. Nor does salvation history or apocalyptic fare any better. In these instances the fulfillment of God's promises in
the history of redemption is featured. Jesus Christ is acknowledged as the ful-
crum of history, but the focus is fixed on salvation history, reconciliation or
apocalyptic instead of on God and Jesus Christ. God's unfolding plan in history cannot be more central than the person who generates and sustains the
plan. The fulfillment of God's saving promises is of massive importance. It
would be a mistake, though, if the promises received more attention than the
one who made and fulfilled them. Now some may object that I have already
imposed on Paul my own "center." They may think that I have placed a pre-
formed grid over the Pauline materials so that my preferred theme emerges
as victorious. We must all beware of preformatting Paul in such a way that
his voice is not heard. I can only say at this juncture that I will attempt to
demonstrate in this chapter that the centrality of God in Christ is not imposed

---

[5]Ralph P. Martin, *Reconciliation: A Study of Paul's Theology*, rev. ed. (Grand Rapids, Mich.:
Zondervan, 1989).

[6]Albert Schweitzer, *The Mysticism of Paul the Apostle* (New York: Henry Holt, 1931); E. P.
Sanders, *Paul and Palestinian Judaism: A Comparison of Patterns of Religion* (Philadelphia: Fortress, 1977).

[7]Herman Ridderbos, *Paul: An Outline of His Theology* (Grand Rapids, Mich.: Eerdmans,
1975); C. Marvin Pate, *The End of the Age Has Come: The Theology of Paul* (Grand Rapids,
Mich.: Zondervan, 1995).

[8]J. Christiaan Beker, *Paul the Apostle: The Triumph of God in Life and Thought* (Philadelphia:
Fortress, 1980).

from without but is vindicated by an *inductive* study of his letters.

The Image of a House

The image of a house may help us visualize the heart and soul of Pauline theology. I am not using the illustration of the house in the same way Paul himself does, where the house functions as an illustration of the church. For instance, Paul describes Apollos and himself as workers in God's house, that is, in the church of Jesus Christ (1 Cor 3:5-9). Paul plays the vital role of the one laying the foundation of the house (i.e., the church), and he warns that those who work on the house must be careful to build on the foundation (1 Cor 3:9-15). The foundation of the building is Jesus Christ himself (1 Cor 3:11). Similarly, in Ephesians 2:20-22 Paul also conceives of the church as God's temple, though here the foundation is the apostles and prophets and Jesus Christ is the cornerstone. The illustration of a house is used here because it is suggestive in conceiving of Paul's theology, not because Paul himself supplies such an illustration. No analogy fits perfectly when we try to communicate the Pauline gospel. Visualizing Paul's thought in terms of the building of a house provides an entry point into Paul's thought, a doorway through which we can enter into his worldview.

The foundation of the house is God himself. From him the house takes its shape, and it is utterly dependent on him for its growth. The house in this illustration represents God's saving plan in history, and that plan includes the role of the church in history. God is the foundation for all that occurs, "because from him and through him and for him are all things. May the glory be his forever" (Rom 11:36).[9] The words we wish to highlight here are *from him (ex autou):* God is the source of all things—he is the foundation. This verse is not wrenched out of context, for Paul introduces this thought *after* explaining in Romans 9—11 God's *saving plan* by which both Jews and Gentiles will be beneficiaries of God's saving mercy. God has constructed history so as to pour his lavish mercy on both Jews and Gentiles. That God is the origin of all things is confirmed in 1 Corinthians 8:6, "But for us there is one God, the Father, from whom are all things." One advantage of thinking of God as the foundation is that the other teachings of Paul are not then conceived as concentric circles that are farther and farther from the center. Whether Paul thinks of justification, reconciliation or sin, they are all based on the foundation; they are not separate from the foundation, nor are they far removed

---

[9]The Scripture translations throughout this book are my own unless otherwise noted.

from it. They are themes that frame the house and give it detail, but all these themes depend on the foundation. Since God is the foundation of the house and it depends on him for its survival, he deserves honor for the building of the house. Paul draws this very conclusion in Romans 11:36. Since God is the one *from whom all things come*, he is therefore the one who receives glory.

Such an illustration also highlights the importance of salvation history, what is often called the "already but not yet" dimension of Pauline theology. When we speak of salvation history, we think of the fulfillment of God's saving plan and promises. The fulfillment of God's plan in history is announced in the Pauline gospel. The promises made to Israel in the Old Testament have now become a reality in and through the ministry, death and resurrection of Jesus Christ. God's saving promises are already a reality for the believer in Jesus Christ—in this sense God's plan is "already" being fulfilled. The gift of the Holy Spirit, for example, demonstrates that God's covenant promises are now a reality for those who have faith. On the other hand, believers still await the consummation of salvation history; in this sense we do "not yet" enjoy all that God has promised. Believers who have the gift of the Spirit still struggle with sin and await the day when their bodies will be resurrected (Rom 8:18-25). Salvation history, then, could represent the remodeling of the house, for the new covenant fulfills what was promised in the old (Jer 31:31-34; 2 Cor 3:4-18). The image of "remodeling" is misleading if it suggests that God "starts over" with the church. Perhaps we should think of the Old Testament as the framing of the house and think of the fulfillment of salvation history as the completion of the inside of the house. We could also say that the theme of salvation history is the gospel of God (Rom 1:1). Hence, the image of the house nicely captures various dimensions of Paul's theology—the foundation is God and Christ, salvation history portrays the progress being made on the house, and the theme of the house is the gospel.

God and Christ

God is not only the *foundation* of the house; he and his Son, Jesus the Messiah, are the *means* by which the house is built. They are the architects, the contractors and the workers who build the house. Saying that God is the one who builds the house does not deny the role of human beings in the house's construction. It has already been noted that Paul lays the foundation of the house (i.e., the church) and others build on the foundation (1 Cor 3:9-15). But the work accomplished by Paul and others is ultimately ascribed to God (1 Cor 3:5). One plants and another waters, "but God is the one who gives the growth" (1 Cor 3:7). And the foundation laid for the house is none other than Jesus Christ (1 Cor 3:11).

One should not conceive of God (or Christ) merely as a static foundation of the house; he is actively building the house now. Once again, both Romans 11:36 and 1 Corinthians 8:6 are germane. The house is not only from God but also "through him" (Rom 11:36). Paul often describes Jesus Christ as God's agent. In 1 Corinthians 8:6 he says that there "is one Lord, Jesus the Messiah, through whom are all things and we exist through him." Jesus is the agent through which all things, without exception, exist. A similar theme is sounded in Colossians. Everything in the universe is created "in Christ," whether earthly or heavenly beings. In other words, "all things have been created through him and for him" (Col 1:16). Nothing exists in the universe apart from the mediating, creative work of Christ. Nor is it right to think of Christ's work in the past only, as if he brought the world into being and then it continues on its own power. Colossians 1:17 clarifies that "all things in him hold together." The natural world endures and continues because of the dynamic work of the Son who continually sustains and preserves it. Suffice it to say that there is ample evidence that the building, whether it is conceived of as the people of God or the universe, would not remain without the sustaining and preserving work of the Father and the Son.

To continue the illustration, what is the ultimate goal of the building of the house? The goal is not the building itself, whether it is conceived in terms of God's righteousness, reconciliation, salvation history or apocalyptic. All of these themes constitute the house, but they are not the end for which the house was made. Fulfilling salvation history cannot itself be the goal of salvation history, for that would be redundant. Instead God has built the house to bring honor and praise to himself. Romans 11:36 again surfaces as a crucial text: "Because from him and through him and for him are all things. May the glory be his forever." Not only do all things have their source and agency in God, he is also the one "for whom" *(eis auton)* all things exist. Similarly, in 1 Corinthians 8:6, after Paul says that all things are from the Father, he reaches a climax by saying that "we exist for him" *(hymeis eis auton)*. Nor is such language restricted to the Father, for not only were all things created by means of the Son's agency, but also "all things were created for him" (Col 1:16). The ultimate reason for the creation of the world and for the fulfillment of salvation history (see Rom 11:36) was for the sake of the Father and the Son. Doubtless the metaphor of the house is imperfect since, for example, the Father is both the foundation of the house and the reason the house was made. But it conveys the dynamic interaction of the various themes better than the term *center*, and it also provides a visual image by which the various Pauline themes are laid on the superstructure of the ultimate foundation, that is, God himself. He is the source, the means and the goal of all things. Thus, to return to the image of the center, God is the center of Pauline theology. But to say that God is the center of Pauline theology is not to diminish the centrality of Christ, for, as we shall see, the exaltation of Jesus the Messiah brings glory and praise to God. Perhaps we can say that *God in Christ* is the foundation of Pauline theology.

When we want to assess what is foundational for a writer, we can learn by paying attention to what surfaces as he discusses a variety of subjects. In Paul's case the priority of God and Christ emerge again and again as that which dominates his thinking. We might be tempted, for example, to think that the gospel is Paul's foundational motif.[10] After all, Paul was called as an apostle for the sake of the gospel (Rom 1:1). He devoted the bulk of his life to preaching the gospel and planting churches, and he is filled with joy when his converts stay true to the gospel (1 Thess 3) and deeply grieved when they abandon it (Gal 1:6-9). The gospel, however, is "the gospel of God" (Rom 1:1), indicating that the gospel cannot be prized over the God who makes it a reality. The gospel is good news because it proclaims the saving message *about God and from God*, and this gospel centers on God's Son, who fulfills the ancient prophecies (Rom 1:2-3). We note how easily Paul glides from the gospel of "God" to the gospel "concerning the Son," since in his mind the centrality of Christ and the centrality of God are of a piece. As noted earlier, the gospel can be conceived of as the theme of the house, while the glory of God and Christ constitute its foundation.

The Gospel of God in Christ

The centrality of Christ is evident in the letter to the Galatians. The reason Paul is so deeply distressed about the Galatians' defection from the gospel is that it undermines the person and work of Jesus Christ. They have forsaken the "grace of Christ for another gospel" (Gal 1:6). The Torah, according to Paul's adversaries, is the determinative issue for one's salvation. But, if the Torah is so crucial, then faith in Jesus Christ becomes secondary (Gal 2:16-21). The essence of Christian living is "faith in the Son of God" (Gal 2:20), but this is undermined if the Torah is the gateway into the people of God. Indeed, those who lobbied so fiercely for circumcision turned the clock back in salva-

---

[10]Joseph A. Fitzmyer (*Paul and His Theology: A Brief Sketch* [Englewood Cliffs, N.J.: Prentice Hall, 1989], pp. 37-38) says that christology and the gospel are the center of Paul's theology, and hence his center is quite close to my own.

tion history. In effect, they installed the law as the climax of salvation history instead of seeing that the Messiah, Jesus, was the fulfillment of Abraham's promise and is the fulfillment of God's saving promises (Gal 3:15—4:7). The centrality of Christ emerges because he is the *only* seed of Abraham (Gal 3:16), and thus entrance into Abraham's family is only through him. The law was a temporary expedient until the coming of Christ (Gal 3:24). Now all people, both Jews and Gentiles, can be part of the family of Abraham in Christ Jesus through faith (Gal 3:26). The issue is not whether one has had a physical operation on a part of one's body; the issue is whether one has been clothed with Christ and immersed into Christ.

Indeed, if one's eternal destiny turns on the acceptance or rejection of circumcision (Gal 5:2-6), then Christ died for nothing (Gal 2:21). If those who agitate for circumcision are on target, then Christ's death is not the pathway for entrance into the people of God. In Galatians circumcision and the cross of Christ are polar: one lives under the banner of either the one or the other. If one adopts circumcision, then Christ cannot profit for salvation (Gal 5:2). Those who desire to be righteous before God by virtue of the law are cut off from Christ and have fallen from grace (Gal 5:4). Either people receive the marks of circumcision, or—like Paul—they bear on their body the marks of Christ's death (Gal 6:17) by accepting the suffering that comes when one forsakes circumcision and trusts Christ for eschatological salvation. Christ's death (not circumcision) delivers people from the evil age (Gal 1:4). His death is evacuated of all meaning if righteousness is available through the law (Gal 2:21; cf. Gal 3:1). Apparently, the Galatians, by succumbing to circumcision, believe that the curse of the law can be removed by keeping the law (Gal 3:10-12), but Paul counters that it can only be removed through the curse-bearing work of Christ on the cross (Gal 3:13). Liberation from the power of the law and sin is due to Christ's redeeming work (Gal 4:4-5). If circumcision is accepted as salvific, the scandal of the cross is nullified (Gal 5:11). And those who subscribe to circumcision do so to avoid the persecution of the cross (Gal 6:12-13), for only through the cross of Christ is allegiance to the old world order severed (Gal 6:14-15), and that old world order includes circumcision!

The priority of Christ manifests itself in another situation that is remarkably different from what happened in Galatia. In 1 Corinthians 1—4 we see that the church is plagued with divisions over ministers. The long discussion on wisdom (1 Cor 1:18—2:16) suggests that the quarreling over ministers (Paul, Apollos, Peter, etc.) centered on the Corinthians' estimation of the wisdom of the various ministers. Many suggestions have been advanced to explain the nature of the divisions in Corinth, and we can hardly resolve the debate here. The most likely theory is that the debate over the wisdom of the ministers was not an argument over the theology of the various leaders. Rhetorical skills, not false teaching, fomented the debate. Duane Litfin and Bruce Winter argue this thesis persuasively.[11] The Greco-Roman world highly prized rhetoric, and speakers were estimated in accordance with their ability to dazzle audiences with their artistry, skill and persuasive power. What is striking about Paul's response is his conclusion that, if the Corinthians are entranced by the rhetorical ability of the various ministers, then they have misunderstood the cross of Christ. Devotion to human rhetoric and skill panders to human pride, and anything that exalts human wisdom undercuts the cross of Christ, for the preaching of the cross underscores the truth that believers are utterly dependent on God for everything. Human wisdom is not the path to life (1 Cor 1:18-25), nor does God call those who are wise, strong and residents of the upper class (1 Cor 1:26-31). Paul renounces rhetorical artistry in preaching the gospel so that faith depends on God instead of the strength and wisdom of human beings (1 Cor 2:1-5). What troubles Paul is that devotion to various human ministers nullifies the cross of Christ, the very center of the gospel. The Corinthians are transfixed by either Paul or Apollos, and they have forgotten that *God* is the one who gives the growth (1 Cor 3:7). The underlying problem in promoting the various human ministers is pride (1 Cor 1:29, 31; 3:21; 4:6-7). By exalting human ministers the Corin-

---

[11]Scholars continue to debate the nature of the divisions present in 1 Cor 1—4. F. C. Baur inaugurated critical study of the text with his distinction between the Petrine and Pauline factions. See his *Paul the Apostle of Jesus Christ: His Life and Work, His Epistles and His Teachings. A Contribution to a Critical History of Primitive Christianity*, 2 vols. (London: Williams & Norgate, 1873). Baur's view is no longer in favor today, though his ghost still exerts an influence on New Testament studies. Many other proposals have since been advanced, but they will not be examined here. For a summary of the various proposals in the history of scholarship, it is useful to consult Duane Litfin's *St. Paul's Theology of Proclamation: 1 Corinthians 1-4 and Greco-Roman Rhetoric*, SNTSMS 79 (Cambridge: Cambridge University Press, 1994). In my estimation, Litfin is correct when he argues that the divisions cannot be traced to theological differences between Peter, Paul and Apollos. The divisions among the Corinthians stemmed from their estimation of the "wisdom" of the various ministers, and they assessed the "wisdom" of Paul and Apollos on the basis of their rhetorical ability. Some of the Corinthians criticized Paul and sided with Apollos because they deemed Paul's rhetorical ability to be inferior. I do not believe, however, that Litfin is convincing when he says that Paul's rhetorical style is unique in the sense that he surrendered all attempts to persuade others. Paul endeavored to persuade others of the legitimacy of his view, but he did not rely on the artifices of rhetoric and human eloquence in order to do so. For a confirmation and development of Liftin's view, see Bruce W. Winter, *Philo and Paul Among the Sophists*, SNTSMS 96 (Cambridge: Cambridge University Press, 1997).

thians have forgotten God! The Corinthians are satisfied with too little, for they boast in human ministers and have forgotten that they have something greater—namely, God and Christ. In having God and Christ they have all things, including human ministers (1 Cor 3:21-23). The reason Paul brings in the cross as a counter to human wisdom is so people will boast in God and keep him central (1 Cor 1:29, 31). When Paul learns of divisions in the church, he perceives that the church has abandoned the core of its message: the cross of Christ and the centrality of God in all things. This in turn suggests that such themes were the foundation of Paul's preaching.

Unity and Living for Christ

When we turn to Philippians we again find indications of tensions in the community.[12] Euodia and Syntyche are at odds (Phil 4:2-3), and the long summons to unity (Phil 1:27—2:30) suggests that disharmony plagued the church. Paul calls the church back to the gospel of Christ as its uniting cause. Paul himself was harassed by fellow believers who preached the gospel of Christ but had a personal animus against him (Phil 1:12-18). Their message was in accord with the truth, but their personal motives were self-seeking and injurious. Presenting himself as a model to the Philippians, Paul informs them how he reacts to his envious detractors. He rejoices in the message preached—even though the motive of the messengers is flawed—because "Christ is preached" by his competitors (Phil 1:18). The way to triumph over petty squabbles, Paul informs the Philippians, is to keep the missionary mandate firmly before one's eyes. Since Paul's greatest joy was in Jesus Christ, he could overlook the antagonists who wanted to bring him grief. Paul informs the Philippians (Phil 1:19-26) that his goal, whether he lives or dies, is for "Christ to be magnified in his body" (Phil 1:20). The Christ-saturated vision of Paul is expressed in his famous statement, "For to me to live is Christ and to die is gain" (Phil 1:21). Thus, he is willing, as Christ's slave (cf. Phil 1:1), to die now and be with him or to have his life extended so that he can minister to others. In either instance, Jesus Christ and the mission to proclaim his gospel are the animating principles that drive Paul.

When he exhorts the church to be united, it is not a call to unity "for the sake of unity" (Phil 1:27—2:4). They are to live "worthily of the gospel," to

---

[12]The idea that the Philippians were fractured by disunity has been argued by a number of scholars recently. Davorin Peterlin (*Paul's Letter to the Philippians in Light of Disunity in the Church,* NovTSup 79 [Leiden: Brill, 1995]) makes a sustained case for this theory, though he overstates his case at a number of places.

stand united "for the faith of the gospel" (Phil 1:27). The cause of the gospel of Christ and its extension in the world are the reasons unity is prized. He appeals here to the example of Christ Jesus himself (Phil 2:5-11), who did not take advantage of his equality with God but endured a humiliating death on a cross because God had called him to do so. In response to Jesus' obedience God exalted him as the universal Lord who is to be confessed as such by all beings. The centrality of Christ emerges in his death, resurrection and exaltation. Does the exaltation of Jesus Christ threaten the supremacy of the Father? By no means, for Christ's humiliation, resurrection and exaltation were "for the glory of God the Father" (Phil 2:11). The Father's glory is not diminished but enhanced by the work of Christ on the cross.

This fits with 2 Corinthians as well. Jesus Christ is the fulfillment of salvation history, for all "the promises of God are yes in him" (2 Cor 1:20). But Paul specifically proceeds to say that the fulfillment of the promises in Christ brings glory to God (2 Cor 1:20). The new covenant is superior to the old, for the glory of Christ outshines the glory of Moses (2 Cor 3:10-11). The gospel is nothing less than "the glory of Christ" (2 Cor 4:4). But the stunning radiance of Christ's glory does not diminish the glory of God the Father, for the glory of Christ is not in conflict with the glory of God. God "has shone in our hearts to give the light of the knowledge of the glory of God in the face of Christ" (2 Cor 4:6). We observe here that the glory of God is revealed in "the face of Christ." It is not the case that the splendor of Christ blinds our vision to God's glory or that his glory is dimmed by Christ's glory. God's glory is enhanced and manifested when his Son is glorified.

The Christ-exalting passion of Timothy and Epaphroditus is the primary reason Paul commends them (Phil 2:19-30). People live for many things, but Timothy stands out because he is worried about the faith of the Philippians (Phil 2:20). Others seek their own interests, but Timothy seeks "the things of Jesus Christ" (Phil 2:21). Timothy's joy is fulfilled in Christ, and in turn he wants to share that joy with others. Epaphroditus, similarly, is so devoted to the work of Christ that he risked his life on behalf of the cause of the gospel (Phil 2:25-30). And we see in chapter 3, once again, why Paul reacted so vehemently to those who demanded circumcision. Instead of boasting in Christ, they were boasting in the flesh (Phil 3:3). Adherence to circumcision robs Christ of his glory and ascribes it to the person submitting to the rite. For Paul the heart of his new faith is personal devotion to Christ (Phil 3:7-11). He counted his past religious accomplishments as worthless and meaningless compared to the supreme joy of knowing the Messiah Jesus as his Lord. The goal of his life is to know him better, to have his righteousness, to participate in his sufferings and to obtain the resurrection of the dead. Even though he has not yet attained perfection (Phil 3:12-16), he exerts his energy to reach the prize of perfection, which awaits him at the eschaton. Thus, those who oppose the message of the gospel are to be avoided as enemies, while those who live like Paul are to be imitated as coworkers and friends (Phil 3:17—4:1). In a sense, Paul's message in Philippians can be summarized in the words, "Rejoice in the Lord" (Phil 4:4). One's greatest joy lies in one's greatest treasure, and Paul's treasure was the Lord.

The Preeminence of Christ

The preeminence of Christ breathes through all of Colossians. Apparently, the church was influenced by certain teachers who contended for a different path to divine fullness. We need not determine here the precise contours of what is often called "the Colossian heresy." The details are obscure, but the main picture is reasonably clear. The teachers advocated divine fullness through asceticism and devotion to angels (Col 2:8-23). Paul emphatically repudiates this teaching because it robs Christ of his supremacy. The magnificent hymn of Colossians 1:15-20 emphasizes the person of Christ. He is the image of God, the firstborn, the agent of creation and the purpose of creation. The created order is sustained and preserved by him, and he is "before all things" (Col 1:17). Not only is he the ruler of creation, but he is also the ruler of the church (Col 1:18). He was resurrected "in order that he should be preeminent in all things" (Col 1:18). The divine fullness is in him, and reconciliation of all things is via his cross (Col 1:19-20). The rival teachers may claim to have the "mystery" that is the secret to vitality and growth, but they should be summarily dismissed. The "mystery" is "Christ in you" (Col 1:27), God's mystery is "Christ" (Col 2:2), and "in him are all the treasures of wisdom and knowledge hidden" (Col 2:3). Seeking to find wisdom through any other source than Christ is folly. The philosophy offered by the teachers is deficient because "it is not according to Christ" (Col 2:8). Growth in the Christian life comes by walking in him (Col 2:6-7), not by following some ascetic regime where certain foods are forbidden and special festival days are observed (Col 2:16-17, 21-23). These things are "shadows," and the substance is Christ (Col 2:17). Nor will people discover fullness by pandering to angels or worshiping them (Col 2:10, 15, 18). The angels are subordinated to Christ because he created them (Col 1:16), defeated them at the cross (Col 2:15) and reigns over them (Col 2:10). Since all of God's fullness resides in Christ, believers will experience fullness only in him (Col 2:9-10). Believers should hold fast to the head, who is Christ himself (Col 2:19), and realize that in him they have all they need: their sins are forgiven (Col 2:11-14), they have died to the elements of the world (Col 2:20), and they have been raised up with Christ (Col 3:1). "Christ is your life" (Col 3:4), and believers await future glory with him.

Righteous Living and the Priority of God in Christ

Thus far the supremacy of God and Christ has been traced in particular Pauline letters. If we cast the net thematically, similar conclusions emerge. In Colossians, for instance, the recipients are exhorted to put off sin and be clothed with righteousness (Col 3:5-17). The exhortations are punctuated with the words, "And everything, whatever you do, whether in speech or work, do all things in the name of the Lord Jesus, giving thanks to God the Father through him" (Col 3:17). We could scarcely claim, therefore, that ethics can be sundered from the preeminence of Christ, for everything done by believers is to be done in the name of Jesus and for his honor. There is no conception here of doing what is right simply because it is the right thing to do, or of duty for duty's sake. A similar statement comes near the end of Paul's discussion of food offered to idols in 1 Corinthians 8—10. He sums up by saying, "Whether then you eat or drink or whatever you do, do all things for the glory of God" (1 Cor 10:31). In Colossians the animating motive is the name of Jesus; here it is the glory of God. These two are not in conflict but are compatible for Paul. We simply observe here that there is no activity in life, no realm of existence that is outside the sphere of God's rule. Even the ordinary actions of eating and drinking should be done to honor God. That honoring God should be the goal of ethics is unsurprising once we grasp that dishonoring him is the root of all sin. The wrath of God is visited on the world (Rom 1:18-25) because people have rejected him. They know he is God but they refuse "to glorify him as God or give thanks" (Rom 1:21). They abandon the glory of God and turn to the worship of idols (Rom 1:23). They "worshiped the creature rather than the creator" (Rom 1:25). Because God has been rejected as God, he hands human beings over to all the other sins that blight human existence (Rom 1:24, 26, 28). The fundamental sin, however—which is the root of all others—is the failure to honor, praise and glorify the one and only true God. It is fitting, then, that a life pleasing to God is marked by doing all things in his name, by the desire to honor him in all things.

Once we grasp that the origin of all sin is failure to serve and worship

God, we also understand why "whatever is not of faith is sin" (Rom 14:23). Most commentators argue against applying this text universally to all situations, but I have argued in my Romans commentary that such exegesis is mistaken.[13] Paul does conceive of ordinary actions like eating and drinking being done for God's glory! Conversely, he says that anything that is not animated by faith is sin. The best commentary on this is the depiction of Abraham's faith in Romans 4. Abraham was asked to believe the impossible, that he and his wife—though beyond the age of bearing children—would indeed have a child. Abraham was keenly aware of the inadequacy of both Sarah and himself (Rom 4:19); his faith did not consist in his denying the facts of life. His faith was directed to God's promise, for he "was fully assured that he was able to do what he had promised" (Rom 4:21). Despite the impossibility of the situation, "he grew strong in faith, giving glory to God" (Rom 4:20). The essence of faith, then, is that it grants glory to God. God is glorified in faith because he is honored as the all-sufficient one who can meet every need. He is conceived of as the one who can raise the dead and create out of nothing (Rom 4:17). Thus, trust and honor are inevitably intertwined. The one who is trusted is also the one whom we honor as trustworthy. That which is done outside the realm of faith is sin because such actions are done outside the realm of God's lordship.

Paul's call to honor God in our everyday existence is not restricted to the few texts cited above. Though Paul uses various terms, the notion that God and Christ are the center and circumference of the ethical life permeates Paul's writings. A few examples will suffice. Paul warns the Corinthians about the dangers of sexual immorality, employing a number of arguments against sexual license (1 Cor 6:12-20). He concludes, though, by reminding the Corinthians that their lives are not their own. They have been purchased with the price of Christ's blood. He draws the final conclusion in verse 20, "Therefore glorify God with your body." The fundamental reason for sexual purity is that such a life honors God, showing that the person who lives chastely trusts that following God's will is the path to joy. The Corinthians are exhorted to give generously so that thanksgiving might be rendered to God (2 Cor 9:11-12) and so that he will be honored and glorified (2 Cor 9:13). Similarly, Paul thanks the Philippians for their generosity to the gospel cause in Philippians 4:10-20. Paul is exceedingly careful here, for he does not want the Philippians to think that they put God in their debt, and yet at the same

---

[13]See Thomas R. Schreiner, *Romans*, BECNT (Grand Rapids, Mich.: Baker, 1998), pp. 738-39.

time he is genuinely grateful for their assistance. He reminds them that God will supply all their needs, and thus "to our God and Father belongs the glory for all the ages, amen" (Phil 4:20). The ultimate source of every gift is the one who is to be praised for his lavish generosity.

The centrality of God and Christ in the warp and woof of life is woven into the fabric of Pauline ethics. Believers are to live worthily of the Lord (Col 1:10) and give thanks to the Father for their liberation from sin (Col 1:12). They should avoid the vain and licentious behavior of Gentiles, for they did not learn of Jesus in such a way (Eph 4:20). Tensions surfaced between the weak and strong in Rome (Rom 14:1—15:6). Paul calls on them to accept one another and wants them to worship in harmony instead of being rent by mutual recriminations. The reason he wants them to accept each other is that such acceptance brings glory to God (Rom 15:7).

In the concrete circumstances of life, the particulars that constitute every-day existence, Paul directs his readers' minds Godward. The household code in Ephesians 5:21—6:9 is a case in point. Husbands and wives (Eph 5:22-33) are not merely to follow social conventions, though the extent to which social conventions are reflected is debated. Wives are to submit to husbands "as to the Lord" (Eph 5:22). They are to submit in the same way the church subordi-nates itself to Christ her Lord (Eph 5:24). Some commentators detect the par-allels in Paul's advice to other secular writers of his day, but, amazingly, they often give short shrift to what is distinctive in the exhortations. The wife is not to subordinate herself to the husband, finally and ultimately, because of social convention or because society will run smoothly. She is to do so in honor of her Lord, Jesus the Messiah. Similarly, and perhaps even more radi-cally, husbands are summoned to love their wives "as Christ loved the church and gave himself for it" (Eph 5:25). Surely Paul could have exhorted hus-bands to treat their wives with kindness and affection and to look out for their wives' interests. There was no need to invest his exhortation with the great themes of Christ's redemptive work. Nonetheless, when he calls on husbands to love their wives, he summons them to reflect on Christ's redemptive work for the church and to model it in their treatment of their wives. Even if Paul appropriates the cultural ethic of his day, he does not appropriate it without transmuting it through the refinery of the gospel. We will return in due course to what Paul says about slavery. Here it should sim-ply be observed that the obedience rendered by slaves is suffused with the Christ-centered vision of Paul. Slaves should render their service to please the Lord and not to receive commendation from their human masters (Eph

6:5-8; Col 3:22-25). The primary issue for slaves is how their earthly lives relate to their Lord Christ. The estimation of human masters is secondary.

The Centrality of God in Christ in History

When human beings reflect on their lives, the fundamental issue, according to Paul, is not their social status but whether they are in Adam or in Christ. For Paul these two persons (Rom 5:12-19) are the key individuals in human history. If people are in Adam, then they are under the reign of sin and death. If they are in Christ, they have been freed from these tyrannical powers. The "old person" *(palaios anthrōpos)* "has been crucified with" Christ (Rom 6:6). That is, the old Adam has been slain for those who are baptized into Christ. In the midst of Paul's exhortations in Colossians 3:5-11, he reminds believers that they have put off the old person and put on the new (Col 3:9-10). The new Adam is none other than Christ himself, for he represents the new humanity, and all those who are in him are incorporated into the people of God. Thus, Paul can say that "where" *(hopou)* the new Adam exists—namely, Christ—social distinctions are irrelevant (Col 3:11). Whether one is Greek or Jewish, circumcised or uncircumcised, barbarian or Scythian, slave or free is immaterial because ethnic identity constitutes no advantage relative to salvation. Christ alone is sufficient for salvation, and in that sense Christ is all. The centrality of Christ and the new humanity formed in him signifies that all other human classes, organizations and distinctions are outmoded.

During the present evil age believers face suffering, pressures and afflictions. Such sufferings, however, are designed to bring thanksgiving to God who so powerfully rescues his people in and through the painful circumstances of life (2 Cor 1:3-11). Being led to death in suffering is a means by which the fragrance of the gospel of Christ is wafted into the world (2 Cor 2:14-16). The treasure of the gospel is encapsulated in weak and suffering vessels so that all will see that the power comes from God and not Paul (2 Cor 4:7). Paul does not preach himself, after all, but Jesus Christ as Lord (2 Cor 4:5). The life of Jesus is manifested most powerfully when his servants are suffering (2 Cor 4:10-11). His power shines in Paul's weakness (2 Cor 12:9). If Paul and the others who proclaimed the gospel were glorious and strong, then they would be praised for their wisdom and strength. The advance of the gospel would be attributed to the quality of the messengers. When the gospel advances through weak and suffering messengers, however, people are provoked to thank God for its advance and triumph and thus the glory goes to him rather than those who proclaim the message (2 Cor 4:15).

When the Corinthians are asked to reflect on their calling (1 Cor 1:26), it becomes evident that their ranks are not composed of intellectuals, the mighty and the ruling class. Those whom "God has chosen" (1 Cor 1:27-28) are deemed as foolish, weak and of ill-repute in the world. God has selected the insignificant in the world "so that no flesh should boast in his presence" (1 Cor 1:29). Indeed, God's saving work is from start to finish a miracle of grace: "Because *of him [ex autou]* you are in Christ Jesus" (1 Cor 1:30). And Jesus is the wisdom from God on behalf of believers. Indeed, righteousness, sanctification and redemption are all his work (1 Cor 1:30). Ascribing ultimacy to God's saving righteousness, sanctification or redemption would be a massive mistake, for verse 31 indicates the purpose *(hina)* for the bestowal of these gifts. God has lavished his grace on believers "so that the one who boasts should boast in the Lord" (1 Cor 1:31). God's ultimate goal, according to Paul, is not redemption, righteousness or sanctification. He grants these saving gifts to his people so that they will exult in him and praise his name. We are reminded of Romans 5:1-11, where Paul proclaims the tremendous hope that is ours because of God's saving righteousness. The climax of the paragraph is reached with the words, "And not only this, but we also boast in God through our Lord Jesus Christ through whom we have now received reconciliation" (Rom 5:11). The capstone of the experience of believers is not reconciliation or the gift of righteousness (Rom 5:9); it is the exultation in God that becomes ours *through Jesus the Christ.* We also see that boasting in God is inseparable from boasting in Jesus Christ the Lord.

A text with a similar theme is Ephesians 1:3-14. Paul recounts the spiritual blessings that belong to believers in Christ. They are chosen to be holy and blameless before the foundation of the world and are predestined to be adopted as his sons (Eph 1:4-5). Why has God lavished such blessings on his people? He did so "for the praise of the glory of his grace" (Eph 1:6). Through Christ believers are redeemed and forgiven of their sins (Eph 1:7). They know the mystery of his will, which centers on Jesus Christ himself (Eph 1:9-10). They have received the predestined inheritance (Eph 1:11). Why are these gifts ours? "So that we who have previously hoped in Christ might be to the praise of his glory" (Eph 1:12). Believers have been sealed with the Spirit who is the promised down payment of the eschatological inheritance (Eph 1:13-14). They are guaranteed that their body will be redeemed on the day of the Lord. God grants these blessings "for the praise of his glory" (Eph 1:14). It could scarcely be clearer that redemption is penultimate and the praise of God is ultimate. Three times Paul clarifies the reason God lavishes his merciful grace on his children. Indeed, the same theme heads up the paragraph as Paul exclaims, "Blessed be the God and Father our Lord Jesus Christ" (Eph 1:3). Paul begins the paragraph by praising God for his inestimable blessings, and then he explains three times that his saving gifts were given so that we would praise his grace.

Nor is it the case that God is exalted and Christ is diminished. Paul emphasizes repeatedly that all these blessings are ours "in Christ." Indeed, on eleven occasions in Ephesians 1:3-14 God's gracious work is said to have been bestowed on us either in or through Christ. The work of Christ cannot be relegated to a sidebar or an excursus. The mystery of God's will (Eph 1:9; cf. the discussion of Colossians above) centers on Jesus Christ and God's decision to sum up (anakephalaiōsasthai) all of human history in him. "The fullness of times" (Eph 1:10), that is, the completion of salvation history, does not occur apart from Jesus Christ. God planned that history would only reach its consummated goal in and through him. Thereby, he honors his Son by showing that the fulfillment of all things cannot occur apart from him.

The centrality of Christ permeates the letter to the Ephesians. God has enthroned Christ above all spiritual powers and names, and the sovereignty that has been given to Christ will be his not only in this age but also in the age to come (Eph 1:20-21). Everything has been put under the feet of Jesus the Messiah, and he also reigns as head over the church (Eph 1:22). In chapter 2 Paul returns again to the salvation that was accomplished for believers. They were dead in sins, under the dominion of the ruler of the air and enslaved by the social patterns of their society (Eph 2:1-3). God in his merciful love awakened his people out of their slumber; he breathed his life into them and granted them life with Christ; and he raised them with him and seated them with him in the heavenlies (Eph 2:4-6). Why did he do all this? Ephesians 2:7 communicates the answer in a purpose clause (hina), "so that he could show in the coming ages the surpassing riches of his grace in kindness upon us in Christ Jesus." Once again we see that the salvific work of God's grace on our behalf is not God's ultimate concern, though, of course, the latter theme should not be minimized as insignificant. God's supreme aim is to display for the coming ages the stunning nature of his grace.

The centrality of Christ is preserved in accomplishing this aim because the unity of Jews and Gentiles in God's plan only occurs through his work on the cross (Eph 2:11-22). The Gentiles did not become the people of God apart from the cross. The cross is the means by which God extended peace to those who were both far and near. The mystery that was veiled from previous generations was the coparticipation and coequality of Jews and Gentiles in the people of God (Eph 3:5-6). The mystery has become a reality only through the gospel, and the very center of the gospel is the atoning work of Christ by which both Jews and Gentiles are reconciled to God. The summing up of all things in Christ (Eph 1:10) embraces the inclusion of the Gentiles *at this juncture of history* into the people of God. Since Gentiles participate in covenant membership only through Christ, Christ is honored as the one through whom God's promises are realized. God's plan is such "that he has now made known to the rulers and authorities in the heavenlies through the church the multifaceted wisdom of God" (Eph 3:10). The rulers and authorities here probably refer to both good and evil angels. The existence of the church and the revelation of the mystery, namely, the unity of Jews and Gentiles in the church, redound to the wisdom of God. His saving plan is featured in a climactic way in the church of Christ Jesus. The purpose of the church's existence, in the final analysis, is to bring glory to God. Paul's prayer at the conclusion of Ephesians 3 bears this out: "To him be the glory in the church and in Christ Jesus for all the generations of the ages of ages, amen" (Eph 3:21). God instituted the church to bring glory to his name forever.

Paul also prays that the church, which has received such mercy and grace, would experience the boundless greatness of Christ's love "so that you would be filled to all the fullness of God" (Eph 3:19). "The fullness of God" is another way of designating the God-permeated vision of Paul. Being filled with God's fullness is the climactic experience for believers, and this occurs when his love seizes and grasps them. The fullness of God becomes a reality in the world through the work of Christ. His incarnation and ascension were designed "so that he might fill all things" (Eph 4:10). The church is to be the "perfect man" *(andra teleion)*, and this "perfect man" is nothing less than "the measure of the stature of the fullness of Christ" (Eph 4:13). He is the head to which the body grows (Eph 4:15). We have already seen that he is the new Adam (Eph 4:24) with which believers are to adorn themselves.

Conclusion

When Paul prays for Christians to grow strong in the faith, he does so "for the glory and praise of God" (Phil 1:9-11). When he thinks of the coming of the Lord, he says that "he will be glorified among his holy ones and be marveled at among all those who have believed" (2 Thess 1:10). When he considers God's merciful grace in calling him as the chief of sinners to salvation (1 Tim 1:12-16), he breaks into praise, saying, "Now to the king of the ages, incorruptible, invisible, to the only God, be honor and glory for the ages of ages, amen" (1 Tim 1:17).[14] When he considers his call to bring about the obedience of faith among the nations, he says that this is done "for the sake of his name" (Rom 1:5). When he concludes his greatest letter and returns to the theme of bringing about the obedience of faith among the nations (Rom 16:25-26), he again breaks into prayer: "To the only wise God, through Jesus Christ, to him be the glory for the ages, amen" (Rom 16:27). The passion of Paul's life, the foundation and capstone of his vision, and the animating motive of his mission was the supremacy of God in and through the Lord Jesus Christ.[15]

---

[14]For the centrality of God in the Pastorals, see Greg A. Couser, "God and Christian Existence in the Pastoral Epistles: Toward *Theological* Method and Meaning," *NovT* 42 (2000): 262-83.

[15]I am indebted to John Piper for my understanding of Paul and of biblical theology as a whole. Readers should consult his many books.

2

PROCLAIMING A MAGNIFICENT GOD

The Pauline Mission

Magnifying God in Christ was the animating principle of Paul's life and the foundational principle of his theology. Scholars rarely, however, consider Paul's missionary focus when explaining his theology.[1] Perhaps the missionary focus of the Pauline writings is not attractive because most scholars are not missionaries. We tend to seize on themes that interest us, and most scholars are not inclined to missions. Paul, on the other hand, was first and foremost a missionary. He was not a systematic theologian who wrote treatises in which the various parts of his theology were logically related and explained. I am not suggesting, incidentally, that such a systematic task is fundamentally flawed, for the only way to discern Paul's theology is to engage in some kind of systematic task. Nor am I denying that Paul had a coherent theology that informed his thinking. A book like this would be superfluous (or at least largely negative in intention) if Paul was a not coherent thinker. Some scholars believe that Paul ultimately was either incoherent

---

[1] A few scholars have considered the role of Paul as a missionary. Peter T. O'Brien's work is especially insightful, and he briefly reviews other scholars who have reflected on Paul as a missionary in his book *Gospel and Mission in the Writings of Paul: An Exegetical and Theological Analysis* (Grand Rapids, Mich.: Baker, 1995).

or contradictory. For them, one could no sooner systematize Paul's thought than square a circle.[2] I would concur with J. Christiaan Beker that Paul had a coherent theology, but his coherent thinking can only be gleaned by seeing how he addressed particular situations.[3] In any case, Paul's primary aim was not to leave an epistolary legacy in which subsequent generations would marvel at his theological system. He was a missionary who wrote letters to churches in order to sustain his converts in their newfound faith.[4] He saw himself as a missionary commissioned by God to extend the saving message of the gospel to all nations. Thus, he was fulfilling the covenantal promise given to Abraham that all nations would be blessed through Israel.[5]

Nor was Paul primarily a pastor who exercised leadership over his churches. Paul appointed elders or overseers for that task (Phil 1:1; 1 Tim 3:1-7; 5:17-25; Tit 1:5-9) after the churches were established. Certainly, Paul functioned in a pastoral role in his churches by visiting them after they were planted and by writing them letters to instruct, admonish and encourage them. Viewing his letters and subsequent visits fundamentally through a pastoral lens, however, is distorting. If we want to get a clear angle of vision as to how Paul conceived of his relationship to the churches, then we need to consider Paul as a missionary. His letters were addressed to churches that he planted on his missionary journeys. Of course, Paul was not an ordinary missionary either. He was an *apostolic* missionary who had received a unique

---

[2]Heikki Räisänen is the most notable recent example of a scholar who maintains that Paul's theology is logically incoherent and inconsistent. See his *Paul and the Law* (Philadelphia: Fortress, 1983).

[3]J. Christiaan Beker articulates the distinction between Paul's coherent theology and the contingent situations he faced in his book on Pauline theology, *Paul the Apostle: The Triumph of God in Life and Thought* (Philadelphia: Fortress, 1980), pp. 11-17. Beker, however, also argues that Paul is not completely consistent and that some contradictions exist in his thought. See his essay "Romans 9—11 in the Context of the Early Church," PSBSup (1990): 40-55.

[4]My purpose in this book is not to write a life of Paul. For an excellent and lucid life of Paul, see John B. Polhill, *Paul and His Letters* (Nashville: Broadman & Holman, 1999). Polhill rightly argues that Paul is the author of all thirteen letters ascribed to him.

[5]Some scholars have postulated the theory that Paul developed in his theology. See for instance C. H. Dodd, "The Mind of Paul: A Psychological Approach," *BJRL* 17 (1933): 91-105; Dodd, "The Mind of Paul: Change and Development," *BJRL* 18 (1934): 69-110; John W. Drane, *Libertine or Legalist? A Study of the Theology of the Major Pauline Epistles* (London: SPCK, 1975); Hans Hübner, *Law in Paul's Thought* (Edinburgh: T & T Clark, 1984). Nonetheless, the notion that Paul's theology underwent development is not really convincing. See J. Lowe, "An Examination of Attempts to Detect Developments in St. Paul's Theology," *JTS* 42 (1941): 129-42; Richard N. Longenecker, "On the Concept of Development in Pauline Thought," in *Perspectives on Evangelical Theology,* ed. K. S. Kantzer and S. N. Gundry (Grand Rapids, Mich.: Zondervan, 1979), pp. 195-207.

commission and call to establish churches. Since Paul wrote letters to churches that he established (with the exception of Romans) to help them through concrete circumstances that troubled them, we should not expect a comprehensive treatment of the various subjects he addressed. Of course, Paul did not personally establish the church at Colossae, but it is quite probable that one of his coworkers, Epaphras (Col 1:7; 4:12), planted the church under Paul's aegis.

Nor should we assume that we have every piece of Paul's theology in his letters. We have a number of pieces, to be sure, and enough to see that Paul was a fascinating, deep and (I believe) coherent thinker. It would be rash to conclude that we have enough material for a comprehensive Pauline theology. Some important Pauline themes may be mentioned briefly or not at all because he had already explained them in his evangelistic preaching. For example, the Davidic sonship of Jesus was probably proclaimed at some length in his preaching (cf. Acts 13:22-23, 32-37), but he only mentions it twice in his letters (Rom 1:3; 2 Tim 2:8). Similarly, if it were not for 1 Corinthians 10—11, we would not even know that Paul practiced the Lord's Supper! The partiality of our information is never clearer than in 2 Thessalonians 2:5-7, where he fails to identify the restrainer since the readers know what he is talking about, whereas modern scholars find the identity of the restrainer to be tantalizingly obscure.

Perceiving that Paul was a missionary helps us understand his letters. They serve as pastoral words to churches he established to ensure that they would stand in the faith. Paul did not conceive of his mission as successful if his converts initially believed his gospel and then lapsed. His work was in vain unless his converts persisted in the faith (1 Thess 3:1-10). Thus, his letters were part of his missionary work, written to encourage believers to continue in their newfound faith. The strengthening function of his letters does not imply that the letters were hastily written instructions lacking any organization or coherence. Nor does the fact that he addressed specific circumstances suggest that Paul tacked this way and that, offering any advice that appeared to help his churches at the moment. What made Paul such an effective missionary is that he wrote his letters out of deeply held and thoroughly thought-through convictions. These convictions anchored him and his churches as they passed through storms in which false teaching and immoral behavior threatened the churches' survival. Paul made a lasting impact precisely because he tackled the specific circumstances in the churches from a worldview that was powerfully coherent.

Indeed, a number of recent scholars are convinced that Paul wrote his letters and employed the pattern of Greek rhetoric in doing so.[6] Hans Dieter Betz's analysis of Galatians stands out in this regard, but a continuing stream of studies since Betz's work explicate the rhetorical structure of the Pauline letters.[7] I remain unconvinced that the Pauline letters reflect a knowledge of or adherence to the Greek rhetorical handbooks, for they depart in too many respects from the forms prescribed in the handbooks. And yet the thesis that Paul wrote in accord with Greek rhetoric, even though mistaken, indicates that the letters were carefully written, because such a thesis would never be advanced by so many scholars if the letters were composed in a slapdash pattern. Paul's letters continue to be studied (and believed!) to this day because they reflect the thinking of a brilliant man who responded thoughtfully and passionately to issues arising in churches.

God's Grace in Paul's Calling

When Paul reflects on his calling as a missionary, he invariably attributes it to God's grace and mercy. He considers himself the least of the apostles and unworthy to be an apostle because of his persecution of the church (1 Cor 15:9). He was "formerly a blasphemer and persecutor and violent man" (1 Tim 1:13), and he estimates himself as "the chief of sinners" (1 Tim 1:15) and "the least of all the saints" (Eph 3:8). Nonetheless, he *is* an apostle and asserts that "by the grace of God I am what I am" (1 Cor 15:10). When he considers his call (and conversion), he considers it as a testimony to divine mercy (1 Tim 1:13, 16) and attributes his transformation to the stupendous grace of God (1 Tim 1:14). Mercy has been bestowed on him "because he acted ignorantly in unbelief" (1 Tim 1:13). The stewardship of grace entrusted to him is a divine gift (Eph 3:2), and God graciously revealed to him the content of the mystery of the gospel, so that his insight into the mystery should not be ascribed to his own wisdom but God's beneficence (Eph 3:3-5). Paul is emphatic in stating that his ministry is a product of grace, for in Ephesians 3:7 he explains that his ministry is "according to the gift of grace which was given to me according to the working of his power."

---

[6]For a brief evaluation of rhetorical criticism in Paul's letters, see my *Interpreting the Pauline Epistles* (Grand Rapids, Mich.: Baker, 1990), pp. 31-36. For a thorough analysis, see S. E. Porter and T. H. Olbricht, eds., *Rhetoric and the New Testament: Essays from the 1992 Heidelberg Conference* (Sheffield: JSOT, 1993).

[7]Hans Dieter Betz, *Galatians: A Commentary on Paul's Letter to the Churches in Galatia*, Hermeneia (Philadelphia: Fortress, 1979). For an introduction to other works on rhetorical criticism, see Porter and Olbricht, *Rhetoric and the New Testament*.

So too, in Colossians 1:25 he says that his task of fulfilling the word of God "was given to him." Even though he is the least of the saints, he received the privilege of proclaiming the gospel to the Gentiles, and the gospel is defined as "the unsearchable riches of Christ" (Eph 3:8). Not only does Paul disseminate the gospel among the Gentiles, but he also helps them to "see" (*phōtisai,* "to illumine") and "understand" the mystery that he proclaims (Eph 3:9). The notion that Paul's ministry is due to God's grace is confirmed by Galatians 1:15-16, a passage that we shall look at more closely in a moment. What we want to emphasize here is that God is the one who "called" *(kalesas)* Paul as an apostle, and he was "pleased" *(eudokēsen)* to "reveal" *(apokalypsai)* his Son to him. The words *calling* and *called* in Paul regularly denote effective initiative in summoning people to salvation (cf. e.g., Rom 8:28, 30; 9:12, 24; 1 Cor 1:9, 24, 26; Gal 1:6; 5:13; 2 Tim 1:9). Similarly, the word *pleased (eudokēsen)* signifies God's sovereignty and delight in choosing Paul as an apostolic messenger.

Though Paul consistently features God's grace as the foundation for his apostleship and reminds the readers of his unworthiness, he also emphasizes his untiring effort and work as an apostle. After stressing his unworthiness and God's grace in 1 Corinthians 15:9-10, he says, "But I labored more than them all, and yet not I, but the grace of God which was with me." Paul does not wallow in his past but sees grace as effective in his current ministry. He is a debtor to all, both Jews and Greeks, and is eager to proclaim his gospel in Rome (Rom 1:14-15), and his ministry is a testimony to his untiring efforts to spread the gospel. Though necessity—that is, a divine call—impinges on him so that he must preach the gospel (1 Cor 9:16), yet his "reward" is to preach the gospel without charge (1 Cor 9:15-18), thereby distinguishing himself from the false apostles in Corinth (2 Cor 11:12-15). Paul's effort is conveyed by athletic metaphors. He labors as a wrestler, runner and boxer (Col 1:28—2:3; 1 Cor 9:24-27) to bring all to completion in Christ and in Christian maturity. Concerted discipline and painful exertion characterize his ministry. The apostolic ministry is not one of serenity in the sense that the nitty-gritty nature of everyday life is transcended. Labor, exertion and effort are part and parcel of Paul's ministry. His toil, though, is traced back to God, for he is the one "working in me in power" (Col 1:29). Paul commends his ministry by rehearsing the evidence of God's work in him as he recounts the many difficulties he experienced in the course of his ministry (1 Cor 4:11-13; 2 Cor 6:3-10; 2 Cor 11:22-29). His ministry is due to God's grace, and that grace provides the impetus for his work.

Paul's Calling Challenged by Opponents

We would probably lack any account of Paul's own reflections on his apostolic call if it were not challenged by some of his opponents. Of course, we do possess the Lukan account of Paul's call in Acts 9, 22 and 26, in which Luke summarizes what Paul said about his conversion and call. Despite the protestations of some scholars, there is no reason to doubt the accuracy of what is recounted in Acts.[8] What we have in Acts is the portrayal of Paul's conversion from another perspective. In Paul's letters he provides his own portrait of his conversion. The accounts in Acts and the epistles are not contradictory but complementary. Indeed, the accounts in Acts match Paul's own letters in that they emphasize his call to preach the gospel *to the Gentiles.*

We know from Paul's letter to the Galatians that the legitimacy of the Pauline gospel was under attack.[9] As a corollary, the legitimacy of Paul's apostleship was questioned fiercely as well. The adversaries probably suggested that Paul preached a circumcision-free gospel to please people rather than God (Gal 1:10). Perhaps they even went so far as to say that in other contexts Paul demanded circumcision (Gal 5:11), but the meaning of this verse is notoriously uncertain. Nor would they have been slow to point out that Paul was not part of the original Twelve. He was not appointed by Jesus the Messiah during his earthly ministry, and any authority he had must be ratified by the Twelve. The pure gospel must be drawn from the wells of Jerusalem, and the Pauline gospel, according to the opposition, was *dependent* on the Twelve in Jerusalem. As long as Paul agreed with the Twelve, his teaching should be followed. The agitators probably also claimed that Paul *distorted* the teaching of the Twelve by discounting the necessity of circumcision (Gal 5:2-6; 6:12-13).

Paul, on the other hand, considered the message of the adversaries to be a false gospel, a gospel that would receive God's curse (Gal 1:6-9). He could

[8]Throughout this book I will feel free to use Acts as a reliable historical source. Thus, the accounts of Paul's conversion in Acts 9, 22 and 26 should be viewed as independent and reliable descriptions of that event. For a thorough and modern defense of the historical accuracy of Acts, see Colin J. Hemer, *The Book of Acts in the Setting of Hellenistic History,* ed. Conrad H. Gempf, WUNT 49 (Tübingen: J. C. B. Mohr, 1989). The six-volume series *The Book of Acts in Its First-Century Setting,* published by Eerdmans, also supports the historical veracity of Acts. For a history of Acts research and a defense of its historical reliability, see also W. Ward Gasque, *A History of the Interpretation of the Acts of the Apostles* (Peabody, Mass.: Hendrickson, 1989). For a very positive assessment of the historical accuracy of Acts, see Martin Hengel, *Acts and the History of Earliest Christianity* (Philadelphia: Fortress, 1979). C. K. Barrett ("The Historicity of Acts," *JTS* 50 [1999]: 515-34), though not dismissing the accuracy of Acts altogether, questions its reliability in its representation of Paul.
[9]Most scholars continue to agree that Paul defends his apostleship in Galatians 1—2. See, e.g., Richard N. Longenecker, *Galatians,* WBC (Dallas: Word, 1990), pp. lxxxiii-c.

hardly criticize their "gospel," however, when his own apostleship was under attack. Thus, in Galatians 1—2 Paul defends his apostolic legitimacy and explains his apostolic call before he wages a full-scale attack on the opponents' theology in Galatians 3—6. In the very first verse a defensive tone peeks through: "Paul, an apostle, not from human beings nor through human beings but through Jesus Christ and God the Father who raised him from the dead" (Gal 1:1). He immediately counters the notion that his authority stems from any human source or agency. The same theme is reiterated in Galatians 1:11-12. His gospel cannot be traced to any human source; he received it through a revelation of Jesus Christ. Paul proceeds, in the subsequent verses, to defend the claim that his gospel stems from Jesus Christ instead of from people (Gal 1:13-17). The substance of his argument is that only God's intervention explains his proclamation of the gospel. If his motivation were to please people, he would have continued to be devoted to and insist on the ancestral traditions of Judaism. He received accolades from his contemporaries because his fervor was such that he outstripped others of his day in his knowledge of and devotion to the traditions. He was thoroughly convinced that the church of Jesus the Christ was dangerous and to be resisted, and thus he persecuted it and attempted to stamp it out. Paul believed his resistance to the church, in his pre-Christian days, was honorable and that it manifested his zeal for God and his law (Gal 1:14; Phil 3:6; cf. Acts 22:3). It is virtually certain that Paul saw himself as following in the footsteps of Phinehas, who demonstrated his zeal for God by killing the Israelite man and Moabite woman who cohabited in blatant disregard of the Torah (Num 25:1-9). He was like Mattathias, who showed his zeal by slaying the man who would compromise by offering sacrifice to a foreign god (1 Macc 2:23-26) and who exhorted those who were zealous for the Torah to follow him in guerrilla activity (1 Macc 2:27-28).

Paul's Calling and Conversion

How then did Paul come to be a proclaimer of the gospel of Christ? Scholars have occasionally resorted to psychological explanations, suggesting that the pressure of living under the Jewish law was gnawing at him or that his conscience was wounded over the slaying of Stephen (Acts 7:57—8:1). We have already seen that Paul was not troubled by the death of Stephen. The execution of Christians did not torment his conscience but was a testimony of his zeal for God since he was following in the footsteps of Phinehas and Mattathias in stamping out heresy. The flaw in psychological

explanations is that they depart from Paul's letters and indulge in speculation, since Paul gives no hint of psychological distress before his conversion. It is certainly possible that hidden psychological insecurities and fears
troubled Paul before his conversion, for he was an ordinary human being.
Gerd Theissen has performed a valuable service in reminding us that psychological dimensions cannot be jettisoned in studying Paul.[10] But it is
extraordinarily easy to engage in projection while reading Paul, for we
must admit that most psychological theories about his conversion are speculative fancies that cannot be demonstrated from any reading of Paul. Psychological analyses of Paul remain in the area of conjecture, and in doing
Pauline theology we must restrict ourselves to Paul's conception of his call,
instead of imposing our psychological analyses on the data.

Paul conceives of his call in prophetic terms, hearkening back to the language of the call of the prophets to delineate his own summons to proclaim
the gospel.[11] The separation from his mother's womb (Gal 1:15) and his calling (Rom 1:1) echo the call to prophetic ministry given to Isaiah (Is 49:1) and
Jeremiah (Jer 1:5), suggesting that Paul was invested with authority from God
himself. What is striking is the emphasis on God's sovereignty in the calling
of Paul. Serving as an apostle was scarcely Paul's idea; he was a bright shin-
ing light in Pharisaism, outshining his contemporaries (Gal 1:14). His devotion to the oral law, that is, to the ancestral traditions, was well-known, and
he was doubtless praised for his perspicacity. How can we explain Paul's
turnaround, his abandonment of Pharisaism and his devotion to Jesus of
Nazareth? Paul's own appraisal does not attribute his change to a psychological crisis. If anything, he should have remained in Judaism, for there he
received accolades from his contemporaries. The remarkable change of
course is ascribed to God himself; his induction into the ministry was due to
God's "good pleasure" (*eudokēsen*), God's "separating" (*aphorisas*), God's
"calling" (*kalesas*) and God's "revealing" (*apokalypsai*, Gal 1:15-16). In other
words, the radical change in Paul's allegiance can only be attributed to God
himself. Like Jeremiah he was arrested by God and summoned into service
(Jer 1:4-19). God commissioned him to preach the gospel, and thus Paul was
not dependent on any human being for the content of his gospel. Hence, he
did not consult any other human beings or proceed to Jerusalem to receive

---

[10]Gerd Theissen, *Psychological Aspects of Pauline Theology* (Philadelphia: Fortress, 1987).
[11]The notion that Paul should be considered in prophetic terms is well defended by Karl O.
Sandnes, *Paul—One of the Prophets? A Contribution to the Apostle's Self-Understanding*,
WUNT 2/43 (Tübingen: J. C. B. Mohr, 1991).

validation or instruction (Gal 1:17-24). He proceeded to preach the gospel that was sovereignly revealed to him by Jesus the Messiah.

Recently, some scholars have maintained that Paul was *called, not converted,* on the Damascus Road.[12] In other words, Paul did not conceive of himself as forsaking Judaism and joining a new religion called Christianity when he was summoned to be an apostle. We must be exceedingly careful here, for the imposition of modern categories could easily lead us astray. For example, the use of the term *religion* as an abstract entity is not the best term with which to approach the whole discussion, and it is also anachronistic to speak of *Christianity.* However, those who try to segregate Paul's call from his conversion are clearly mistaken, for the two are inseparable; it is apropos to speak of *a call and a conversion.* As Paul reflects on his past, he says that he was "formerly in Judaism" (Gal 1:13). The word *formerly (pote)* surely implies that he is no longer part of Judaism. Indeed, it is telling that the term *Judaism* (Gal 1:13-14) is used twice to depict Paul's allegiance before his calling. He never uses this term in his letters to describe his faith in Christ. He could easily speak of his calling as an apostle as a fulfillment of his "Judaism," but he never does. In fact, he characterizes the mode of life practiced by Peter and himself as "not living Jewishly" (Gal 2:14). While living in Judaism he was devoted to "the ancestral traditions" (Gal 1:14), but—again—this expression is never used elsewhere to describe his life as an apostle. It is quite clear that Paul has abandoned these traditions.

Of course, Paul conceived of his faith in Christ as the *fulfillment* of the Old Testament scriptures, and *in that sense* he did not abandon his heritage. The gospel fulfills the prophetic promises in the Old Testament (Rom 1:2). Previously, Paul thought that the covenantal promises contained in the Old Testament would be fulfilled through devotion to the Torah. Likewise, many of his adversaries opposed him because they were devoted to "the ancestral traditions," believing that only through keeping such traditions could the salvation promised in the prophets be realized. Thus, they demanded that Gentiles observe circumcision and purity laws to belong to the people of God. Paul, after his revelation on the road to Damascus, moved in a dramatically new

---

[12]The notion that Paul was called but not converted has been most eloquently argued by Krister Stendahl, *Paul Among Jews and Gentiles and Other Essays* (Philadelphia: Fortress, 1976). For a recent defense of a similar view, see James D. G. Dunn, "The Justice of God: A Renewed Perspective on Justification by Faith," *JTS* 43 (1992): 1-22. Alan F. Segal, however, argues convincingly that Paul was both called and converted. See his *Paul the Convert: The Apostolate and Apostasy of Saul the Pharisee* (New Haven: Yale University Press, 1990).

direction. He now grasped that the covenantal promises of the Old Testament were fulfilled in Jesus (more on this later). The new age of salvation had begun in which the promises of salvation were now being fulfilled. The new exodus promised in Isaiah was now a reality, and not only Israel but also Gentiles were being redeemed. Thus, the segments of the law that divided Jews from Gentiles—circumcision, food laws and sabbath—were no longer normative. The fulfillment of the promises also introduced a redemptive historical discontinuity. Thus, Paul maintains that those who insisted on circumcision for righteousness were preaching another gospel and were under God's curse (Gal 1:6-9). They were "false brothers" (Gal 2:4; 5:10) who were to be resisted fiercely, and succumbing to their pressure would nullify the truth of the gospel (Gal 2:5). Compromise is impossible; one must side with either Christ or circumcision as the path to salvation (Gal 5:2-4). If righteousness can be obtained through the law, then Christ's death is useless (Gal 2:21). Paul as a Pharisee persecuted the church for *theological reasons*. He believed that it was blasphemy to proclaim a crucified man (Deut 21:23; cf. Gal 3:13) as God's Messiah, and he perceived clearly that if Jesus were the way to salvation, then the law's centrality was compromised. When Paul was converted, Jesus took center stage and the law was demoted accordingly. Any notion that Paul believed that the Judaism from which he emerged was compatible with his newfound faith in Christ cannot be sustained by the evidence.

Paul's reflections on his past and present existence in Philippians 3:2-11 yield a similar conclusion. He recounts all the advantages of his past among which are his circumcision, Jewish heritage, Pharisaic training and extraordinary devotion to the law (Phil 3:5-6). All these advantages are dismissed as worthless refuse for Christ's sake (Phil 3:7-8). If he clings to his past as *gain (kerdos)*, then he *loses (zēmia)* Christ. If he *gains* Christ, then he *loses* the advantages of his previous adherence to the law. The language of gain and loss is probably shaped by the Jesus tradition (Mk 8:36 and par.). The contrast ultimately is between "my own righteousness which is from the law" and righteousness "through faith in Christ" (Phil 3:9). Paul does not argue tolerantly that some believe the law is the way to righteousness while others believe in Jesus as the Messiah, and that both should be fully convinced in their own minds (Rom 14:5). He characterizes those who espouse circumcision and the law as rapacious dogs and mutilators who must be rejected and avoided. The heart of their religion is egoism and self-promotion, for they put confidence in the flesh (Phil 3:3). We can scarcely dismiss these words as those of an armchair theologian because the theology that Paul criticizes so vehemently is the theology he once held! Some scholars argue that Paul adopted a two-covenant view of salvation, so that Jews and Gentiles are saved by different covenantal structures.[13] We will return to such an issue in due course. What we must see here is that Paul understood his own calling as a conversion as well. He does not estimate his past as a valid and acceptable way to escape God's wrath on the day of judgment. He rejects his past with passion and vehemence and says that those who advocate such a theology stand under God's curse. This is the language of a man who is called and converted.

The Prophetic Dimension of Paul's Call

We have already noted that Paul frames his apostolic calling in terms that echo the call of the prophets. Like Isaiah and Jeremiah he was summoned to service from the womb (Is 49:1, 5; Jer 1:5; Gal 1:15). Also like Isaiah and Jeremiah, Paul was appointed by God to his distinctive ministry (Is 49:1, 5; Jer 1:5; Gal 1:15). Another instructive connection emerges when we consider the suffering of Jeremiah and the servant of the Lord. Both Jeremiah and the servant of the Lord endure suffering in their proclamation of the word (Is 50:4-11; 52:13-53:12; Jer 8:18—9:1; 11:18—12:6; 15:10-21; 17:14-18; 18:18-23; 20:7-18). Similarly, Paul, as we shall see in a later chapter, conceived of the word spreading through his suffering. Indeed, there is significant evidence that Paul understood his ministry in terms of the "servant of the Lord" of Isaiah (Is 42:1-9; 49:1-6; 50:4-11; 52:13—53:12). Jesus himself was supremely the servant of the Lord, and Paul almost certainly perceived the death of Jesus as a fulfillment of the suffering-servant texts (cf. Is 53:3 with Phil 2:7; Is 53:5 with Rom 4:25; Is 53:5-6, 8, 12 with 1 Cor 15:3; Is 53:11-12 with Rom 5:15, 19; Phil 2:7; Is 53:12 with Rom 4:24). When Paul portrays himself as the servant of the Lord, he is not arrogating to himself the same position as he ascribes to Jesus. Nevertheless, since he is "in Christ" and commissioned as an apostle, he plays a servant role as well. Even in Isaiah, the servant is identified with the prophet Isaiah and yet transcends Isaiah. Similarly, Paul is the servant of the Lord, and yet the servant of the Lord transcends Paul and reaches its ultimate fulfillment in Jesus himself. The servant was to be "a light to the nations, to open the eyes that are blind, to bring out the prisoners from the dungeon, from the prison those who sit in darkness" (Is 49:6-7 RSV). When Paul explains his role and calling to King Agrippa, his language resonates with the role of

---

[13]So, e.g., Lloyd Gaston, *Paul and the Torah* (Vancouver: University of British Columbia Press, 1987); John G. Gager, *The Origins of Anti-Semitism: Attitudes Toward Judaism in Pagan and Christian Antiquity* (New York: Oxford University Press, 1983).

the servant. Paul's task "is to open their eyes, to turn them from darkness to light and from the authority of Satan to God" (Acts 26:18). It is likely that Paul understood the imprisoning darkness of Isaiah 42:7 to refer to the incarceration of sinners by Satan. The servant in Isaiah is instrumental in the realization of the new exodus, which involved the liberation from Babylon and the realization of God's promises to Abraham (Is 11:15-16; 40:3-11; 42:16; 43:2, 5-7, 16-19; 48:20-21; 49:6-11; 51:10). So too, Paul celebrates the new exodus by which believers have been given the inheritance promised to the people of God, have been liberated from the domain of darkness and transferred into the Son's kingdom and have experienced the new exodus (or redemption) in the forgiveness of their sins (Col 1:12-14).

That Paul saw himself as the servant is confirmed by Acts 13:47, for when he and Barnabas bring the message of the gospel to the Gentiles, they vindicate this decision by appealing to Isaiah 49:6, "I have appointed you as a light to the Gentiles, so that you might bring salvation to the ends of the earth." In the Old Testament context this role belongs to the servant, but Paul now perceives his ministry in this light. Similarly, in Romans 15:21, a passage in which Paul explains his missionary strategy, Paul cites Isaiah 52:15, "for that which has not been told them they shall see, and that which they have not heard they shall understand" (RSV). In Isaiah such a task is assigned to the servant who will be exalted after suffering (Is 52:13—53:12), and his message will reach out to the nations. Paul discerns that the nations' seeing and hearing the truth is fulfilled through his proclamation of the gospel. His pioneer mission work brings to fruition the promises of salvation, deliverance and a new exodus found in Isaiah. That we are on the right track is confirmed by Romans 10:16—a verse that appears in another crucial missionary text in Paul (Rom 10:14-17). Here Paul cites Isaiah 53:1 ("Lord, who has believed our message?"), signaling that Isaiah's prophecy is being fulfilled in his ministry. The other link in this text is Paul's claim to be preaching the good news of Isaiah 52:7. It is evident to all scholars that the "gospel" *(euangelion)* is crucial in Pauline theology, and some, as noted, even designate it as the central theme. It is likely that Paul's use of the term *gospel* has its origins in Isaiah 40:9 and 52:7. In context both of these passages speak of the final salvation and deliverance God would bring, the new exodus in which Israel's enemies would be defeated and God's reign would be restored. Apparently, Paul conceived of his ministry as playing a vital role in fulfilling these promises.

Another connection between the servant and Paul is found in 2 Corinthians 6:2, which cites Isaiah 49:8, "at the acceptable time I heard you and in the day of salvation I helped you." In Isaiah the second exodus is clearly in view, for Israel returns to the land and is released from her imprisonment in Babylon (Is 49:8-13). Paul maintains that this day of salvation is actualized in and through his ministry. The inheritance is ready (Gal 4:7), and believers are now free from Satan's imprisonment (Col 1:12-14). Indeed, Greg Beale has persuasively argued that the whole context of 2 Corinthians 5:11—6:10 is suffused by themes relating to the new exodus.[14] When Paul was in Corinth, he faced significant opposition and wondered if he should remain in the city. The Lord appeared to him and assured him of his presence, saying, "Do not fear, but speak and do not be silent, for I am with you and no one will lay a hand upon you to harm you, for I have many people in this city" (Acts 18:9-10). Perhaps this promise alludes to Isaiah 43:5, another context that features the second exodus, where Yahweh assures Israel by saying, "Fear not, for I am with you; I will bring your offspring from the east, and from the west I will gather you" (RSV).

In saying that Paul is the servant of the Lord, I am not claiming that he is "the" servant of the Lord. Paul probably saw his ministry as patterned after and a replication of the ministry of the servant of the Lord, of Jesus the Messiah. Of course, there are discontinuities between the ministry of Paul and Jesus, and Paul does not equate himself with Jesus, as if his ministry is of equal stature. The uniqueness and centrality of Christ is maintained in his theology. He sees himself continuing and advancing the work of Christ in his servant role. The careful reader will have noted that Paul never refers to himself as the *agent* of redemption. The saving work on the cross was accomplished by Jesus himself and is the basis of Paul's servant ministry. We shall see in chapter four that Paul argues something rather similar: his suffering is a corollary of the suffering of Christ. So too, his servant role is modeled after the servant role of Christ.

The Commission to Preach to the Gentiles Defended in Galatians

Now we return to Paul's call and its distinctive feature. God called and revealed his Son to Paul "in order that I should preach him among the Gentiles" (Gal 1:16). The other apostles were also called and commissioned by Jesus Christ, but only Paul received the specific call of bringing the gospel to

---

[14]Greg K. Beale, "The Old Testament Background of Reconciliation in 2 Corinthians 5—7 and Its Bearing on the Literary Problem of 2 Corinthians 6:14—7:1," *NTS* 35 (1989): 550-81; see also William J. Webb, *Returning Home: New Covenant and Second Exodus as the Context for 2 Corinthians 6.14—7.1*, JSNTSup 85 (Sheffield: JSOT, 1993).

the Gentiles. The apostolic council in Galatians 2:7-9 verifies this insight. We noted above that Paul's opponents at Galatia charged him with being *dependent* on the pillars and *distorting* their message. We have examined briefly Paul's argument in Galatians 1:11-21, where he contests the idea that he is dependent on the Jerusalem apostles. His gospel was independently received from Jesus Christ. Even though Paul's gospel is not derived from the Jerusalem apostles, he is well aware that his work will be practically nullified and in vain if the pillars repudiate his gospel (Gal 2:1-2). Paul walks a fine line here, for he must maintain his independence from the pillars; yet at the same time he realizes that if he does not have the support of the pillars, he can hardly expect success in his mission, for everywhere he travels detractors would be close behind informing Pauline converts that the authorities in Jerusalem disagree with Paul. Thus, in Galatians 2:1-10 Paul relays to the church in Galatia the response of the pillars to his gospel. Peter, James and John ratified and agreed with Paul's gospel, concluding that God had called him specially to go to the Gentiles (Gal 2:7-9). Thus, Paul had not *distorted* the gospel proclaimed by the pillars. Rather, he had a unique commission that they *recognized*. The word *recognized* (*gnontes* in Gal 2:9) is crucial, for the pillars did not *grant* Paul legitimacy; they simply recognized the legitimacy of the apostleship God had already given him. And the unique element in his call was the bringing of the gospel to the Gentiles.

It is imperative to recognize precisely here the insight of F. C. Baur's reconstruction, even though he exaggerated his own thesis. Bringing the gospel to the Gentiles was a distinctive advance in the mission of early Christianity, and Paul perceived the theological implications of the gospel more clearly than did the pillars and the other apostles in Jerusalem. A difference in perception is evident, because otherwise Paul would not fear that his own ministry might possibly be for naught (Gal 2:2). Paul realized that the pillars ministered mainly to Jews and saw matters a bit differently. The world James inhabited, for instance, was distinct from Paul's since James ministered in Palestine and seems to have restricted his ministry to Jewish Christians until his death in A.D. 62. It does not follow from this that Paul obscures the opposition of the pillars in Galatians; nor, in the end, is their fundamental perspective at variance with his. They recognize the truth of his gospel and affirm that circumcision is not a prerequisite for salvation. But Paul was launching out on new frontiers, and his missionary work provoked new questions, which were resolved only after much debate, discussion and, presumably, prayer.

Paul refers to the pillars—James, Cephas and John—in a nuanced way. On the one hand, he recognizes their stature as pillars of the church, knowing that if they disagree with him, his gospel to the Gentiles has been proclaimed in vain (Gal 2:2). Paul is scarcely conceding, on the other hand, that he might be wrong on the circumcision question. He recognizes that his gospel will not endure practically if opponents follow in his train announcing that Jerusalem disagrees with him. On this point Paul is more insightful than those contemporary scholars who believe that Jerusalem disagreed with Paul yet think that the Pauline gospel ultimately triumphed over the gospel preached in Jerusalem. Such a scenario is historically implausible, and Paul realized at the outset that his gospel would not survive without the agreement of the pillars. Paul must also maintain, however, his independence of the pillars. To do otherwise would sacrifice the truth of the gospel and the legitimacy of his apostolic commission. He was firmly convinced that God had entrusted him with the gospel for the Gentile world (Gal 2:7, 9). So, in one sense, it was irrelevant what the pillars believed, for they are merely human beings and God is not impressed by human status (Gal 2:6). Paul was all too familiar with the prestige and pride that accompanied authority, and he had left this world behind when he encountered Christ on the Damascus Road. Paul's remarks on the pillars are not intended to criticize them directly. It is the Galatians, not the apostles, who are in danger of ascribing an authority to James, Peter and John that surpasses a commitment to the gospel. The authority of the pillars is relativized for the sake of the Galatians, not in an attempt to cast any aspersions on James, Peter and John, though Paul may be criticizing any notion that the Jerusalem apostles should be thought of as pillars or venerated because of their position. For Paul recognizes that the same gospel was revealed to the other apostles and that they had a special commission to proclaim the gospel to the Jews (Gal 2:7-9).

The outcome of the discussion and debate in Galatians 2:1-10 is a ratification of the freedom of the gospel (Gal 2:4). The pillars concur with Paul and not with the false brothers, maintaining that circumcision is not an entrance requirement for induction into the people of God. The account in Acts 15:1-29 points to the same conclusion, and hence we should probably see Acts 15 and Galatians 2:1-10 as referring to the same incident.[15] What precipitates the con-

---

[15]There is not space here to examine all the theological and historical questions raised by the account in Acts 15. Scholars debate whether Gal 2:1-10 represents the same event as the account in Acts 15. For a recent discussion of the relationship between Acts and Galatians, and its implications for the addressees of Galatians, see Longenecker, *Galatians,* pp. lxi-lxxxviii.

troversy is the same: the success of the Pauline mission among the Gentiles. The subject of the controversy is the same: should circumcision be required for entrance into the people of God? The place of the controversy is the same: Jerusalem. The actors in the controversy are the same: Paul and the Jerusalem apostles, especially Peter and James, the brother of the Lord. The conclusion of the controversy is the same: circumcision is not required for entrance into the people of God.

At this juncture we must examine the encounter with Peter at Antioch since so many scholars use this event as a platform to construct a continuing hostility between Peter and Paul.[16] Indeed, some scholars claim that this text reveals that the agreement in Galatians 2:1-10 was short-lived, for when Peter in Galatians 2:11-14 actually understands the implications of Paul's gospel he moves in another direction. Some conclude that from this time on Paul lost his base at Antioch, that he was severed from Jerusalem and the pillars and that he struck out on his own. We can understand why such a view has arisen, since Paul and Peter probably had different inclinations relative to Jewish Christians. Peter was more inclined than Paul to live according to the Jewish law, simply because he often ministered among the Jews. But the idea that Antioch was a major turning point in the Pauline mission reads more into the text than is warranted.

Before becoming entranced with theories that attempt to explain the relationship between Paul and the other apostles, we need to grasp the function of Galatians 2:11-14 *rhetorically* in its context. The paragraph was not included to chronicle Paul's relationship with Peter, for Paul does not even bother to record Peter's reaction to his words. Paul includes his words to Peter not because they were directed to Peter but because they were the words *the Galatians needed to hear.*[17] Two other observations should be made relative to this account. First, it is hardly likely that Paul, in writing this passage to the Gala-

---

J. B. Lightfoot is probably correct when he argues that Gal 2:1-10 and Acts 15 represent the same event from the perspective of different writers, viz., Luke and Paul. See Lightfoot, *The Epistle of St. Paul to the Galatians* (reprint, Grand Rapids, Mich.: Zondervan, 1967), pp. 18-35. Not all of Lightfoot's arguments are equally plausible, nor am I suggesting that the North Galatian hypothesis is correct. I concur with those who identify Gal 2:1-10 and Acts 15:1-29 and believe that the letter was written to South Galatia. The differences between the accounts should be attributed to the difference of perspective that naturally occurs when two different authors relay the same events. See also Robert H. Stein, "Relationship of Galatians 2:1-10 and Acts 15:1-35: Two Neglected Arguments, "*JETS* 17 (1974): 239-42.

[16]For a representative and influential advocate of this view, see James D. G. Dunn, "The Incident at Antioch (Gal. 2:11-18)," *JSNT* 18 (1983): 3-57.

[17]Because Paul's addressees are the Galatians, it is unclear where the words directed to Peter end in the text. For examples, the NIV gives all of Gal 2:14-21 as Paul's speech to Peter whereas the NRSV gives only Gal 2:14.

tians, believed that the incident at Antioch voided the agreement recorded between him and the pillars in Galatians 2:1-10. We have already seen that the recognition of his gospel in Jerusalem was important for his ongoing mission. It would be useless for him to include such an account in Galatians if the incident at Antioch rendered the prior agreement invalid or if what happened at Antioch revealed that the pillars misunderstood Paul in the first place. If Paul and the pillars really disagreed, then the news of such would reach Galatia no matter how smoothly Paul tried to paper over their differences. Thus, Paul did not understand the events at Antioch as revoking or qualifying the agreement at Jerusalem, nor is it likely that Peter responded to the Antioch conflict by withdrawing his support from the Pauline mission. The primary reason Paul includes Galatians 2:11-14 is to validate his authority as the apostle to the Gentiles. Even Peter had to bend to Paul's authority when he acted contrary to the gospel. Second, Paul explains that the behavior of Peter and his cohorts was marked by hypocrisy and fear (Gal 2:12-13). They did not act from their *convictions;* they deviated from what they knew was right because they feared those who came from James. At this point, many scholars depart from Paul, claiming that Peter actually had different convictions from Paul. Such reconstructions are fascinating, but they depart from the realm of exegesis. No warrant is given in the text for the theory that Paul and Peter had contrary convictions on the matter. Such a theory can only be sustained by suggesting that Paul was mistaken in saying that Peter was motivated by hypocrisy and that we can discern what really happened by reading between the lines. Is this any more speculative than the view held by some in the early church that Peter was pretending to disagree with Paul so that the church would learn a lesson, or that the person attacked was another Peter besides Peter the apostle? Both deviate from the text to shore up an appealing historical theory.[18]

This fairly long discussion on Galatians 1—2 is relevant because it indicates the lengths to which Paul goes to defend his authority as the apostle to the Gentiles (cf. 1 Tim 2:7). His missionary mandate to the Gentiles was from Jesus Christ himself and was defended against all detractors. We need not delve into the theology behind Paul's mission here, but we must see that Paul defended the inclusion of the Gentiles into the people of God apart from cir-

---

[18]What makes the text more complicated is the identity of "certain ones from James" and "those of the circumcision" (Gal 2:12). The latter phrase probably designates non-Christian Jews, and "certain ones from James" likely warned Peter that his behavior put at risk the standing of Christian Jews in Palestine. Under such pressure Peter capitulated.

cumcision. Gentiles are inducted into the family of Abraham by faith, not by adhering to circumcision and the Old Testament law (Gal 3:7, 9, 14, 29). If circumcision were required of the Gentiles, then the very basis of Paul's unique mission and calling to the Gentiles would be compromised and the centrality of Christ would be diminished. It is not the case that Paul jettisoned circumcision because it made preaching the gospel to the Gentiles *easier*, as some have suggested.[19] Paul did not resist the imposition of circumcision on Gentiles first and foremost because it would have hindered his mission; he resisted it because it was contrary to "the truth of the gospel" (Gal 2:5). Nor did Paul think avoiding circumcision made life easier, for by rejecting circumcision he exposed himself to persecution (Gal 5:11; 6:17). About two hundred years before Paul, Jews were put to death for practicing circumcision by Antiochus Epiphanes (1 Macc 1:60-63). Hence, for Paul now to say that circumcision was insignificant was outrageous to many Jews, and it is even possible that a zealot-type movement threatened the lives of Jewish Christians who taught that circumcision was unnecessary.[20] On the contrary, Paul charges that the adversaries want to impose circumcision to make their own lives easier and to avoid persecution (Gal 6:12), and there are hints that the Galatians may have been contemplating circumcision to escape harassment (Gal 3:3; 4:29).

From Galatians and Romans we see that Paul had to be a theologian to function successfully as the apostle and missionary to the Gentiles, for he had to explain how it was that Gentiles did not need to receive circumcision or observe Torah to be members of the family of Abraham. Indeed, any apostle or missionary has to think theologically; what marks Paul is that he was an exceedingly good theologian. The pillars recognized that Paul had received a special gifting from God to advance the gospel among the Gentiles (Gal 2:7-9). His distinctive call to preach the gospel to the Gentiles—a gospel that does not involve submission to the law but freedom from it—is likely what Paul has in mind when he refers to "my gospel" (Rom 2:16; 16:25). We shall see in chapter four that Paul's missionary mandate is inextricably joined with the call to suffer and that he endured such suffering because he preached a gospel that did not require submission to the Torah. Interestingly, even the

---

[19]See, e.g., the view of Daniel P. Fuller, *Unity of the Bible: Unfolding God's Plan for Humanity* (Grand Rapids, Mich.: Zondervan, 1992), pp. 369-70. Fuller thinks one reason circumcision was dispensed with was because it was so difficult for Gentiles to accept it. This explanation seems quite improbable to me and overlooks the centrality of salvation history in Paul.

[20]See Robert Jewett, "Agitators in the Galatian Congregation," *NTS* 17 (1971): 198-212.

account of his commissioning in Acts 9:15-16 unites his call to preach the gospel to the Gentiles with suffering. In Galatians, Paul also traces his suffering to his refusal to demand circumcision for salvation. Instead, he preaches the cross of Christ (Gal 5:11; 6:17). Paul saw more clearly than the other apostles the implications of the gospel relative to the Torah.

The Commission to Preach to the Gentiles Explained in Ephesians and Colossians

The theological underpinnings of Paul's mission are also clarified in Ephesians 2—3 and Colossians 1:24—2:3. The standard Jewish view, one that Paul shared, was that the Jews were God's elect people and that Gentiles joined the people of God by becoming proselytes to Judaism. The status of Gentiles before the coming of Christ is described in this way: "You were at that time without Christ, separated from the commonwealth of Israel and strangers to the covenants of promise, having no hope and without God in the world" (Eph 2:12). If we engage in a thought experiment, we can imagine Paul, as an apostle of Jesus Christ, repudiating the Old Testament teaching that featured Israel as God's elect nation and placed the Gentiles outside God's covenantal mercy. He could have argued that the Old Testament was fundamentally flawed in presenting Israel as God's chosen and unique people, and he could have maintained that the only rational position is the view that all peoples have always been part of the people of God. But Paul did not resort to the expedient of dismissing or contradicting Old Testament revelation to support his view that Gentile believers were equal members in the people of God with the Jews. He understands salvation history in a way that is compatible with most Jews of his day: namely, the Gentiles, by virtue of being alienated from Israel, were estranged from God and Christ. Paul is privileged to serve as the apostle to the Gentiles because he lives at a unique juncture in salvation history. Though in the past the Gentiles on the whole were severed from the people of God, "now" (nyni) they have been brought "near by the blood of Christ" (Eph 2:13).

God has planned history in such a way that the unity of the Jews and Gentiles would occur through the work of his Messiah on the cross. Enmity marked the relations between Jews and Gentiles before the arrival of the new covenant (Eph 2:14-19). Peace between these factions has been accomplished through the cross of Jesus the Messiah. Now both Jews and Gentiles have access to the Father through the Spirit. Social hostility between Jews and Gentiles was certainly a hallmark of their relations. Paul's gospel is not merely that they should now get along, that they should cease being enemies and work at being friends since a new era has dawned. Nor does Paul say that the Jews and Gentiles were equally at fault in the disruption between them. The Jews, despite their sinfulness, were God's elect people. They had access to God through the covenant. They were not without hope and without God and alienated from his saving promises, as were the Gentiles. They were the recipients of God's law, which taught them how to serve and worship their God (Eph 2:15). We should not conclude from this, however, that the Jews were saved by virtue of being Jews, for the cross of Christ is also the means of their inclusion into the people of God.

Paul conceives of Jews and Gentiles as at enmity with one another. The wall of hostility between them (Eph 2:14) may be symbolized by the inscription in the temple that prohibited Gentiles from going beyond the Court of Gentiles at the pain of death. Gentiles, after all, were uncircumcised and separated from God's people. The separation of Jews from Gentiles was evident in the Greco-Roman world because Gentiles did not observe the sabbath, receive circumcision or practice the food laws. These differences reminded Jews that Gentiles were not a part of God's people. The laws and commands that segregated Jews from Gentiles have been abolished in Christ Jesus, so that the religious and social hostility between Jews and Gentiles on the basis of specific Jewish practices has ended. Paul does not argue only that the social barriers between Jews and Gentiles have been torn down, though this is a major theme in the text. He locates the hostility of Jews and Gentiles to their relationship with God. Both Jews and Gentiles need to be reconciled to God through Christ.

Now it is not the purpose here to explain the salvation-historical role of the Jews in detail, but when the new era of salvation history arrived, they were already "near" (Eph 2:17) to God. After all, they were his covenantal people (Eph 2:11-12). However, in Paul's mind it is vital that they respond to the message of peace proclaimed relative to Jesus the Messiah (Eph 2:17). If they reject this message, they are alienated from God. Clinging to the old covenantal arrangement will not suffice now that what was promised in the Old Testament scriptures has been fulfilled.

Understanding this text is crucial to discern rightly Paul's mission to the Gentiles. Paul does not merely exhort all peoples everywhere to live peaceably one with another. He locates the disharmony between Jews and Gentiles *in enmity against God*. Only by their being vertically reconciled to God through Christ will the horizontal enmity between Jews and Gentiles be resolved. Paul functions as the apostle to the Gentiles because the turning of the ages has occurred. Those Gentiles who believe in Christ are no longer excluded from the people of God. They are "no longer strangers and aliens but are fellow citizens of the saints and members of God's household" (Eph 2:19). Paul emphasizes in Ephesians 3 that his role in proclaiming the unity of Jews and Gentiles in the church is a divine gift. The "mystery" has been entrusted to him as the apostle to the Gentiles. The word *mystery* refers to something that was previously hidden and is now revealed. This definition is borne out by Ephesians 3:5, for Paul says that the mystery "was not made known to other generations of the sons of men as it has now been revealed to his holy apostles and prophets in the Spirit." Similarly, Colossians 1:26-27 says that the "mystery *was hidden* from the ages and generations, but is *now manifested* to his saints, to whom God *wanted to make known* what is the riches of the glory of this mystery." The mystery involves the revelation of something that was previously obscured. What was previously hidden was the Gentiles' equal status in the people of God. The Old Testament could be read to say that Gentiles will be members of the people of God but that they will be subordinate to the Jews (Ps 72:10-11; Is 2:2-4; 45:14; 49:23; 60:10-14; Mic 7:17; Zech 14:17). With the fulfillment of salvation history it is now clear that Gentiles are "fellow heirs and members of the same body and fellow sharers of the promise in Christ Jesus through the gospel" (Eph 3:6). God willed that Gentile participation become a reality "in Christ Jesus" so that he would be magnified as the means by which his great saving plan was accomplished. Thereby the multifaceted wisdom of God is communicated for the coming ages (Eph 3:10-11). The "mystery" is defined in a similar way in Colossians relative to the *Gentiles*. It is "Christ in you, the hope of glory" (Col 1:27). The mystery is not merely that Christ resides in people generally but that he resides *in Gentiles*. The revelation of the mystery at this juncture in salvation history is due to God's desire to magnify Christ. He is God's mystery according to Colossians 2:2, and "all the treasures of wisdom and knowledge are hidden in him" (Col 2:3). The mission to the Gentiles at this time in salvation history brings honor to Jesus the Messiah, and it is through his death that Jews and Gentiles are reconciled into one people of God.

The Inclusion of the Gentiles: A Mystery Revealed and a Prophecy Foretold

We have seen how Paul as a missionary emphasized that the inclusion of Gentiles into the people of God was a *mystery*, that is, it was hidden from those who lived in the former periods of salvation history. But how does this square with another Pauline theme—the idea that the gospel fulfilled what was prophesied in the Old Testament (Rom 1:2; 16:26; Tit 1:2)? Indeed, many Old Testament texts look forward to the future and proclaim that the Gentiles will be included within the orbit of God's saving purposes (e.g., Ps 47:9; 87:6; Is 11:10; 19:16-25; 25:6-7; 49:6; 55:5; 56:6-7). Other texts look forward to the inclusion of the Gentiles but seem to assign an inferior status to the Gentiles (Is 60:10-14; 61:5-7; Zech 2:11-12; 8:22-23; see also texts above). The salvation of the Gentiles, in Paul's mind, was both a mystery revealed and a prophecy fulfilled. But how can it be both? We must preserve the tension Paul maintains in his writings. The salvation of the Gentiles was not a mystery in the sense that it was unheard of in the Old Testament, for the Old Testament prophesied a future salvation for Gentiles, as we have noted previously. The mystery, therefore, could scarcely be the fact that Gentiles would be saved. If this were the case, Paul could not credibly maintain that his gospel was *prophesied* in the Old Testament. On the other hand, it will not do to say that Paul's understanding of the future inclusion of the Gentiles in the people of God was patently clear to anyone reading the Old Testament. If this were the case, Paul would not be justified in referring to his understanding of the inclusion of the Gentiles as a *mystery* that was now revealed. Since the salvation of the Gentiles was also a mystery, there must be a sense in which it was obscure to readers of the Old Testament revelation.

How can we bring together the themes that the salvation of the Gentiles fulfilled Old Testament prophecy and that their salvation was only now disclosed, hidden from former generations? The texts we cited above are of some assistance here, for when we read the Old Testament it is unclear as to whether the Gentiles will enter the people of God with the same status as the Jews. The Old Testament clearly proclaims a future salvation for Gentiles, but one may receive the impression from the Old Testament that Gentiles will always be inferior to the Jews and that the Jews will maintain a special prerogative and supremacy. Paul's gospel functions both as prophecy fulfilled and mystery revealed because it explains both these aspects. The Old Testament prophecies that the Gentiles would be saved are fulfilled through the death and resurrection of Jesus the Messiah. Paul's gospel, however, clarifies how these prophecies are fulfilled. The promises of God are fulfilled through the Messiah, Jesus Christ. It is not the case that Jews and Gentiles have a different status in the people of God. Now that the mystery is revealed, it is clear that Jews and Gentiles are equal members in God's household (Eph 2:19) and fellow members of the same body (Eph 3:6). We understand the import of Old Testament prophecies more clearly because now we read them in light of the fulfillment accomplished by Jesus the Messiah. When Paul speaks of the mystery being revealed, his point is that certain dimensions of the Old Testament revelation are only clarified in light of the fulfillment accomplished through Jesus Christ. In particular, the equality of the Gentiles with the Jews in the church is a truth that is not prominently featured in the Old Testament. When we think of the mystery of God's work relative to Jews and Gentiles, Paul's discussion of the whole matter in Romans 9—11 inevitably comes to mind, but we shall postpone the discussion of these chapters until chapter sixteen.

When Paul reflected on his mission to the Gentiles, he considered his role *theologically.* His mission is only possible because the Messiah has come and inaugurated a new era in the history of salvation. Paul was given a unique understanding of the implications of the redemptive historical shift for the inclusion of the Gentiles into the people of God.[21]

One of the striking elements in Paul's writing is his self-consciousness

---

[21]Terence L. Donaldson (*Paul and the Gentiles: Remapping the Apostle's Convictional World* [Minneapolis: Fortress, 1997]) attempts to explain why Paul contended for a mission to the Gentiles that did not include keeping the Torah. Donaldson accepts the new perspective on Paul, which argues that the fundamental problem with the law should not be explained in terms of legalism or failure to keep the law. Instead, the basic problem that Paul attacks is the ethnocentricism and exclusivism of Jews, who are trying to compel Gentiles to become Jews to enter the people of God. Hence, Donaldson feels compelled to offer a new paradigm to explain why Torah was not mandated for the Gentiles. He suggests Paul believed that Gentiles were required to become full proselytes (i.e., circumcised) in order to be saved during his days as a Pharisee. Paul persecuted the church in his pre-Christian life because he was convinced that the Christian movement displaced Torah's central role in entering the people of God. Therefore, when Christ appeared to Paul on the Damascus Road, Paul became convinced that Christ (not Torah) was the exclusive means to enter the people of God. In other words, Paul did not surrender the notion of exclusivity but only the means by which Gentiles could enter the people of God. Gentiles who believed, therefore, became part of Israel that was christologically redefined. Paul believed that there was a short interval of time before the parousia in which the Gentiles could become part of the people of God. At the second coming of Christ, all Israel would be saved and the era of salvation would terminate for the Gentiles.

Much of Donaldson's paradigm is helpful and insightful. His acceptance of the new perspective, however, lands him in a problem. No real explanation for the abandonment of Torah is given. Donaldson does not successfully explain why Paul did not opt for Christ *and* Torah as the pathway to salvation. Nor has Donaldson grasped fully Paul's understanding of Jews and Gentiles in salvation history, as is evident in his claim that Paul's discussion in Rom 9—11 leads inevitably to the displacement of Israel (unless Christ would have returned in Paul's generation). For an alternate explanation of the logic of Rom 9—11, see chapter sixteen of this book.

about his commission. We see it not only when he is under attack as in Galatians or 2 Corinthians, but also in more peaceful circumstances when he contemplates his role. He is the "prisoner of Christ Jesus on behalf *of the Gentiles*" (Eph 3:1). The administration of God's grace to the Gentiles has been vouchsafed to him (Rom 15:15-16; Eph 3:2; Col 1:25), for the mystery of Gentile inclusion has been revealed to him (Eph 3:3). God has given him this ministry according to his grace, and even though Paul is unworthy, he has the task of preaching the riches of Christ to the Gentiles (Eph 3:8-9; Col 1:28-29). He is a specially appointed "minister *[leitourgos]* of Christ Jesus for the Gentiles," and he functions as priest in his proclamation of the gospel (Rom 15:16). The offering that he brings to the altar is the Gentiles themselves: the conversion of the Gentiles is the sacrifice. Of course, Paul never claims that his apostolic ministry is due to his own greatness. Any good work he has done is rooted in the powerful grace of God and the work of the Spirit (Rom 15:17-19). Paul was conscious that he enjoyed the privilege of preaching the fulfillment of God's saving promises to the Gentiles.

Paul's Distinctive Ministry of Planting New Churches

Not only did Paul have a special commission as the apostle to the Gentiles, but he carried out the mission in a unique way. When Paul wrote his letter to the Romans he desired to extend the mission to Spain (Rom 15:22-24, 28). In the process a window is opened on what animates Paul in his mission to the Gentiles. He claims to have "fulfilled" the gospel of Christ from Jerusalem to Illyricum (Rom 15:19). The specific geographical questions that arise are not of interest to us here, and scholars adduce various explanations for Paul's language. Paul probably is saying that in a large region extending roughly from Jerusalem to Illyricum the gospel has been proclaimed. A similar sentiment is conveyed in Romans 15:23, where Paul says he "no longer has a place in these regions." How can Paul possibly think that he has completed preaching the gospel in such a large region since numerous people had not yet heard the gospel in the area? The answer to this query is found in Romans 15:20-21. Paul's goal was to preach the gospel where Christ was not proclaimed previously to avoid building on another's foundation. Thereby he fulfills the prophecy of Isaiah 52:15 by proclaiming Christ to those who have not seen or heard him. When Paul says he has "fulfilled the gospel of Christ from Jerusalem to Illyricum," he does not mean that the gospel has been proclaimed to every person individually; he means that he has accomplished his goal of establishing churches in virgin territories. Paul has systematically planted churches in strategic centers so that Gentiles who had not yet heard the gospel would now hear it proclaimed. Paul presumably feels that no further work awaits him in the east because the foundation has been laid there. By establishing churches in strategic centers from Jerusalem to Illyricum, the base has been laid, and Paul leaves to others the task of moving from these centers to the hinterlands. Apparently, Paul believes that there are others who will continue to proclaim the gospel in the east, but he sees no one who is planning to preach in Spain. Spain is virgin territory as far as the gospel is concerned. The interpretation proposed for Romans 15 is confirmed in 2 Corinthians 10:13-18. Paul's work in Corinth is distinguished from the false apostles' work (2 Cor 11:13-15) because he planted the church in Corinth, whereas these interlopers create havoc in churches already planted. Indeed, Paul hopes that the faith of the Corinthians will grow so that they will support him in the preaching of the gospel in regions beyond Corinth, regions in which the gospel has not yet been proclaimed (2 Cor 10:15-16).[22]

Romans 15 and 2 Corinthians 10 are of crucial importance in understanding Paul, for they explain how he understood his mission. Not only was he specially commissioned as the apostle to the Gentiles, but he also had a passion to establish churches in virgin Gentile territory, in areas where Christ was not previously proclaimed. In other words, he conceived of himself first and foremost as a missionary apostle, not as a theologian or a pastor. His theological and pastoral work were all designed to buttress his mission. Much controversy exists over why Paul wrote the letter to the Romans, and the answer to this question might enlighten our understanding of his view of his mission.[23] The verses we have just examined in Romans 15, however, must be included in formulating the purpose of the letter. The church in

---

[22]James M. Scott suggests that Paul was convinced from the Old Testament (Ezek 5:5; 38:12) that Jerusalem was the center, or "navel," of the world (*Paul and the Nations: The Old Testament Jewish Background of Paul's Mission to the Nations with Special Reference to the Destination of Galatians*, WUNT 84 [Tübingen: J. C. B. Mohr, 1995]). His mission to the Gentiles began in Jerusalem and from there extended to the nations of the world. Scott emphasizes that Paul was influenced by the Table of Nations in Genesis 10, so that his distinctive mission was to reach the Japhethites. Indeed, Scott thinks that Paul longed to travel to Spain since they were the last portion of the Japhethites who had to believe in order for the fullness of the Gentiles to be completed (Rom 11:25). Scott's thesis is intriguing and deserves further research. I have some reservations since Paul does not emphasize a distinctive ministry to the Japhethites but to the Gentiles. One wonders whether Scott reads too much into the text here. Nor is there any clear evidence that Paul believed that his ministry to the Japhethites would be concluded when Spain was converted.

[23]For a discussion of the purposes of Romans, see Thomas R. Schreiner, *Romans*, BECNT (Grand Rapids, Mich.: Baker, 1998), pp. 10-23.

Rome was experiencing tensions between Jews and Gentiles (Rom 9—11, 14—15). Paul wrote to bring unity to a fractious situation so that Jews and Gentiles would glorify God together in worship (Rom 15:7-13; see below). Paul also knew that questions had surfaced in Rome about the validity of the Pauline gospel, particularly of his understanding of the law and the role of the Jewish people in God's saving plan. Paul desired that the Roman church support him in his Spanish venture. In order to garner their support, though, the church needed to rally behind the Pauline gospel. Thus, he explains and defends his gospel in some detail so that the Romans would understand and embrace it and then proceed to support his mission to Spain. Paul's greatest letter, therefore, fits with the missionary ambition that drove him in his ministry.

Paul's desire to bring the gospel to the Gentiles, without forsaking a witness to the Jews, provoked him to flexibility relative to the law (1 Cor 9:19-23). When he was only with the Jews he practiced Jewish customs and the Torah to win the Jews. But when he was with Gentiles he abandoned Jewish distinctives, such as observance of food and purity laws, to win Gentiles for the gospel of Christ. Such "flexibility," of course, could easily be seen as hypocrisy, and Paul's critics could obviously charge him with inconsistency.[24] Paul's defense was that his adaptability was designed to bring as many people to salvation as possible: "I have become all things to all people, so that by all means I should save some" (1 Cor 9:22). We should observe that "winning" (kerdainō) or "saving" (sōzō) in this text cannot be limited to initial conversion, for the text refers to "winning the weak," but the weak have already made a profession of faith, and thus Paul has in mind both the idea of an initial commitment to Christ and continuing to follow him. The use of the word *save* communicates the same idea, since salvation for Paul is primarily a future reality (e.g., Rom 5:9; 13:11). This is not to say that the original experience of salvation is excluded. The idea is that salvation also includes adhering to the faith until the end. The principle enunciated in 1 Corinthians 9:19-23 is also stated in a different way in 1 Corinthians 10:33, "Just as I endeavor to please all, not seeking my own profit but that of the many, that they might be saved." This follows on the heels of the

---

[24]Some scholars claim that Paul's variable stance relative to the law landed him in inconsistency. Of course, what this "inconsistency" involved is controversial. For one perspective, see Peter Richardson, "Pauline Inconsistency: 1 Corinthians 9.9-13 and Galatians 2.11-14," NTS 26 (1979-1980): 347-62. For a convincing response to Richardson, see David (sic D. A.) Carson, "Pauline Inconsistency: Reflections on 1 Corinthians 9.19-23 and Galatians 2.11-14," Chm 100 (1986): 6-45.

admonition not to cause the church of God to stumble, and thus salvation is to be construed as eschatological salvation.

The Pauline principle of flexibility explains why Paul refused to circumcise Titus as a Gentile (Gal 2:3-5) but consented to circumcise Timothy. The latter as the son of a Jewish mother would be considered a Jew (Acts 16:3).[25] Circumcising Titus would compromise the principle that salvation was available to Gentiles apart from the observance of the Torah, and thus Paul adamantly refused to circumcise him in order to preserve "the truth of the gospel" (Gal 2:5). Paul agreed to circumcise Timothy, however, to regularize his status as a Jew so that he and Timothy could minister together in Jewish settings. Paul did not have an animus against circumcision per se (cf. 1 Cor 7:19; Gal 5:6; 6:15). He resisted it fiercely when it was imposed as a requirement for salvation, but he was willing to circumcise Timothy to promote the furtherance of the gospel among Jews. The situations of Titus and Timothy, then, were dramatically different. Timothy, as a Jew, was circumcised for cultural reasons to advance the gospel among the Jews, whereas the circumcision of Titus as a Gentile would nullify a fundamental principle of the Pauline gospel. Paul's flexible stance toward the law when among Jews explains how he could participate in temple sacrifice when he returned to Jerusalem in Acts 21:21-26, for his intention was not to alienate the Jews who were committed to the Torah. His goal was to vary his practice so that as many as possible would be saved. Of course, there were situations in which no compromise was possible. Thus Paul rebukes Peter for abandoning table fellowship with Gentiles, which, in effect, compelled them to observe purity laws (Gal 2:11-14). But if the situation permitted it, Paul would alter his observance of the Torah, depending on whether he was with Jews or Gentiles. This "inconsistency" in practice was all geared toward a higher goal and aim: to reach as many as possible with the saving message of the gospel. Paul's adaptability was not designed to avoid suffering so that he was well accepted among those to whom he ministered. Peter, on the other hand, discontinued eating with Gentiles (Gal 2:11-14) precisely because he feared persecution from fellow Jews. Paul's motive, on the contrary, was not to secure the acceptance of other people so that they would praise him as a faithful Jew. On the contrary, his flexible stance relative to law inevitably led to opposition, so that, for instance, he received the thirty-nine lashes from the Jews on five occasions (2 Cor 11:24). Such a pun-

---

[25]For further discussion on this text, see Thomas R. Schreiner, "Circumcision," in *Dictionary of Paul and His Letters* (Downers Grove, Ill.: InterVarsity Press, 1993), pp. 137-39.

ishment would have been administered in the synagogue and may have been inflicted because Paul violated some precept of the Torah. The reason for Paul's flexibility was not his own comfort and security but the salvation of others. He was so concerned about the good of others that he was willing to be called "inconsistent" to win them for the gospel.

Advancing by Prayer and the Word

With the exception of Romans most of Paul's remaining letters were written to maintain the faith of those who had joined the new community, for persistence in faith was the mark of a successful mission. Encouragement to pray for his mission also marks his letters. He asks the Thessalonians to pray "that the word of the Lord would run and be glorified just as it did in your case" (2 Thess 3:1; cf. 1 Thess 5:25). The Thessalonians are urged to support Paul's apostolic mission, and they do this by praying for the advancement of the *word of the gospel.* Such an exhortation is apparently rather typical, for Paul summons the Colossians and Ephesians to pray for him. In particular, they are to pray for an *open door for the word* so that Paul has the opportunity to speak the mystery of Christ and to speak it in a fitting and bold manner (Eph 6:19-20; Col 4:2-3). Paul has no conception of his mission advancing apart from the proclamation of the gospel, and thus we see again that the missionary and theological task of Paul are indissoluble. Once we grasp that the Pauline mission advances in and through the preached word, we understand why the fundamental prayer was for opportunities to proclaim the word in new regions. The preached "gospel is the power of God unto salvation" (Rom 1:16). This concept of the power of God's word is no innovation with Paul; he derives it from the Old Testament and other Second Temple literature (Gen 1:3, 6; Ps 147:15; Is 40:8; 55:10-11; Jer 23:29; Wis 18:15). The transforming power of the proclaimed word of the gospel renders Paul unashamed. The "word of the cross" is "God's power for those who are being saved" (1 Cor 1:18). The message of Christ crucified is considered to be offensive by Jews and foolishness by Gentiles, but it is God's power and wisdom toward those who have been called (1 Cor 1:23-24). Paul intentionally refused to rely on the rhetorical artistry that was common in the Greco-Roman world of his day (1 Cor 2:1-5). A dependence on rhetoric would evacuate the gospel of its power, for the proclamation of Christ crucified ensures that faith is based on God's power instead of human wisdom. Paul was confident that the gospel was so powerful that it would certainly bear fruit. The gospel proclaimed among the

Colossians "in all the world is bearing fruit and increasing just as it did in your case" (Col 1:5-6). Wherever the gospel is preached, fruit is the inevitable consequence, for the proclaimed word is a performative word, accomplishing what it demands. When Paul preached in Thessalonica, his "gospel did not come to you in word only but also in power and in the Holy Spirit and in full assurance" (1 Thess 1:5). Wherever Paul preached, the word invaded the lives of some, begetting belief in and obedience to the gospel of Christ.

One of the emphases in Paul's thought is that righteousness comes by faith. Faith, however, does not become a reality apart from hearing the word. Faith is not a private reality that arises from inner reflection or as a result of philosophical investigation. People receive the Spirit "by hearing with faith" (Gal 3:2, 5). When human beings hear the word of the gospel and believe, they are saved. The oral proclamation of the word is necessary for faith. We have already seen in Ephesians 2:11-12 that Paul conceives of Gentiles as separated from God's covenantal promises given to Israel. They are without God, without Christ and without hope, and they are separated from God's saving promises and his covenant people. In other words, Gentiles become part of the people of God only by believing in Christ. Paul does not gaze back on the place of Gentiles in redemptive history and see them as included in God's saving plan. He believes that they were not part of God's people and that their only hope of salvation is the gospel. Thus, the proclamation of the word is essential for their salvation. Paul argues similarly in Romans 1:18-32 that God's revelation through the created order is not salvific, for people universally (cf. Rom 3:9-20!) reject the revelation of God through nature and turn toward idolatry. The exclusive path of salvation, then, is a believing response to the gospel of Christ (Rom 3:21-26). This fits with Romans 10:14-17, where Paul forges a logical chain of argumentation. Those who call on the Lord will be saved (Rom 10:13), but one will not invoke the Lord for salvation unless one *believes* in him. And yet one will not believe in him if one has not *heard* of him. And one will not hear about him unless someone *proclaims* him. And no one will proclaim him unless he or she is *sent*. Paul sums up the flow of thought in Romans 10:17: Faith in Christ stems from hearing the preached message about Christ. Paul's mission is vital, therefore, because it is the means by which people will hear the gospel of Christ and be saved. Hence, it is scarcely surprising that Paul exhorts Timothy to proclaim the word fearlessly and regularly (1 Tim 4:6-16; 2 Tim 2:15; 4:1-5).

Paul does not contemplate some mysterious and private interaction between people and God. It is necessary to hear a spoken and articulated word in order to become right with God. In both Colossians and Ephesians Paul prays for boldness, for the spoken word is often offensive. And Paul does not only pray for opportunities to proclaim the message; he also prays that people will be saved. Examples of praying for the salvation of others are scarce in the Pauline letters, but they do exist. In Romans 10:1 Paul prays for the salvation of the Jews. He solicits prayer for leaders in 1 Timothy 2:1-2. Perhaps prayer for governmental leaders is offered solely so that peace and tranquillity will be maintained in society (1 Tim 2:2). Paul also emphasizes, however, God's salvific intention for all people in 1 Timothy 2:1-7. The emphasis on universal salvation suggests that prayer for the salvation of leaders and all people is intended. Since salvation is of the Lord, Paul asks believers to pray that God will intervene and save others.

Maintaining the Faith of Converts

Paul was called as an apostle and was set apart for the gospel (Rom 1:1). His passion as an apostle was to bring about the obedience of faith among the Gentiles (Rom 1:5; 16:26). The obedience of faith cannot be confined to the initial decision to join the Christian community. Paul often insists that perseverance to the end is necessary for salvation—for entering the kingdom of God (e.g., Rom 8:13; 1 Cor 6:9-11; 15:1-2; Gal 5:21; 6:8-9; Col 1:21-23). This theme will be explored in chapter eleven. It surfaces at this juncture because it helps us realize that for Paul, the initial preaching of the gospel was not all that was necessary to plant a church successfully. Of course, as we have already noted, Paul had a unique vocation to preach the gospel in areas where it had not yet been proclaimed. As Peter O'Brien says, Paul describes this work in terms of "planting (1 Cor 3:6-9; 9:7, 10, 11), laying foundations (Rom 15:20; 1 Cor 3:10), giving birth (1 Cor 4:15; Philem 10) and betrothing (2 Cor 11:2)."[26] However, the Pauline emphasis on perseverance indicates that simply laying a foundation was not sufficient.[27] He did not believe his work as an apostle was accomplished unless both the churches were *estab-*

---

[26]O'Brien, *Gospel and Mission*, p. 42.

[27]O'Brien (ibid., pp. 38-45, 62-65) and Paul Bowers ("Fulfilling the Gospel: The Scope of the Pauline Mission," *JETS* 30 [1987]: 185-98) have convinced me that the gospel involves more than just the original proclamation of the message. Paul's restriction of his work to "planting" and "laying the foundation" in 1 Cor 3:5-15 does not contradict this notion since (as Bowers observes) this is a historical description of what Paul actually accomplished in Corinth, not a prescription of his task. Indeed, the two letters to the Corinthians demonstrate that Paul did not restrict his work in Corinth to "planting."

lished and they *persevered*. Thus, after establishing the Thessalonian church, he sent Timothy to discern whether his work was in vain, for if the Thessalonians had jettisoned the faith, then his apostolic work was nullified (1 Thess 3:1-10). He rejoiced when Timothy brought the good news of the Thessalonians' continuance in the gospel. He knew a church was firmly entrenched when they endured trials and sufferings for the sake of the gospel. How important the persistence of faith in his converts was to Paul is indicated by his reflections on what will happen in the presence of God in the last day. The churches are his joy, hope, glory and crown of boasting in the day of the Lord (1 Thess 2:19-20). Paul really lives if believers "stand in the Lord" (1 Thess 3:8), and his joy over the authenticity of their faith knows no bounds (1 Thess 3:9). Since he knows tenacity is crucial, he prays incessantly that he can visit the Thessalonians and complete what is deficient in their faith (1 Thess 3:10). He prays so ardently because he wants them to be blameless before God on the last day (1 Thess 3:13; 5:23). The parallels in Philippians are instructive. Paul overflows with emotion, addressing the community as "my beloved and longed for brothers, my joy and my crown" (Phil 4:1). He then summons them to "stand in the Lord." His joy in them will not be complete unless they persist to the end. Only if they "hold fast the word of life" will there be "boasting for me on the day of Christ"; otherwise, Paul would have labored and run in vain (Phil 2:16). It is not an exaggeration to conclude that all of Paul's letters were written to ensure that his churches continue in the faith, since "we are your boasting just as you also are ours on the day of our Lord Jesus" (2 Cor 1:14).

The discussion here helps us understand Paul's missionary activity. His work of preaching the gospel is not complete with the initial proclamation of the message; the church must also be firmly established to withstand the vicissitudes of persecution and afflictions. It is likely, therefore, that preaching the gospel *(euangelizomai)* and "gospel" *(euangelion)* in Paul cannot be confined to the initial proclamation of the message.[28] We have already seen that the gospel involves the obedience of faith (Rom 1:1-5; 16:25-27); and this obedience of faith cannot be restricted to conversion but is borne out by perseverance. Under the umbrella of the gospel is every aspect of Christian existence, for Philippians 1:27 calls on believers "to live in a manner worthy of *the gospel* of Christ." Believers will be saved if they adhere to the gospel until the end (1

---

[28]So Bowers, "Fulfilling the Gospel," pp. 196-98; O'Brien, *Gospel and Mission*, pp. 38-45, 61-65.

Cor 15:2). And the proclamation of the gospel is not complete until believers are perfected in Christ at the last day (Col 1:28-29). Paul's distinctive role, of course, was to bring this gospel to the Gentiles.

The Spread of the Gospel by Other Believers

Paul was not the only one spreading the gospel. The Pauline churches, as we have already seen, participated in mission by praying for the expansion of the gospel through Paul. It is somewhat surprising that more specific exhortations to proclaim the gospel are not directed to believers in the Pauline letters. And yet when seen together, a number of smaller pieces of evidence indicate that the dissemination of the gospel is expected of all believers.[29] Apparently some believers were considered to be specifically gifted in the proclamation of the gospel since some are "evangelists" (Eph 4:11; cf. 2 Tim 4:5). Those who are so gifted would have the responsibility and privilege of proclaiming the gospel. We think here as well of Euodia and Syntyche who labored together with Paul in the gospel (Phil 4:3). Presumably, this means that they also preached the gospel (perhaps particularly to women, for in the ancient world they may have had freer access to women). When Paul contemplates the role of servants of the Lord (2 Tim 2:22-26), he exhorts them to live godly lives, to avoid needless quarrels and to pursue a life of patience. Such gentleness does not rule out instruction but includes it, for the goal is the salvation of opponents. Through the gentle demeanor and instruction of the Lord's servant, God might even grant repentance and salvation to unbelievers. Unbelievers have been anesthetized by the devil so that they are impervious to the gospel. Satan has captured their minds and hearts so that they are his lackeys (cf. Eph 2:2). But God can free them from their slumber and bondage, and the means he uses to do so is the gentle instruction of his servants. These various texts reveal that Paul was convinced that other believers could play a crucial role in the salvation of others, and they also suggest that such ministries were important to him, part of the fabric of early Christian existence.

The moral excellence of believers' lives also plays a role in bringing people

---

[29]Contra the thesis of W. Paul Bowers, "Church and Mission in Paul," JSNT 44 (1991): 89-111. For the view that Paul expected his churches to be involved in evangelism, see Robert L. Plummer, "The Church's Missionary Nature: The Apostle Paul and His Churches" (Ph.D. diss., The Southern Baptist Theological Seminary, 2001). Plummer's dissertation was completed at a stage in which I could not incorporate his arguments. For instance, he presents a cogent argument for 1 Thess 1:8 representing the mission of the Thessalonian church, contrary to what I have written in this chapter. He especially emphasizes the dynamic and effective quality of God's word in the spread of the gospel.

to faith. Instead of participating in evil, believers are to bring it to light and expose it (Eph 5:11). When evil is exposed to the light, then salvation for those in darkness may occur (Eph 5:13-14). Paul cites what is apparently an early Christian hymn, "Arise, O Sleeper, and Rise from the dead, and Christ shall shine on you" (Eph 5:14). Almost certainly this relates to the conversion of those who are slumbering in the darkness of evil and who have risen to life in Christ when he shines on them in his grace. The means of their conversion is apparently the moral excellence of Christians. Ephesians 5:15-16 may also relate to mission. The word *therefore (oun)* links Ephesians 5:14-15, suggesting that Christians are urged to live wisely (Eph 5:15) precisely because that is the means by which nonbelievers escape the clutches of darkness. It may also follow that "buying up the time" (Eph 5:16) involves using the opportunity to expose evil and see others transformed by the light.

A passage that is parallel in some respects is Colossians 4:5-6. Believers are commanded to use wisdom (cf. Eph 5:15) with outsiders, and the outsiders here are surely unbelievers. They are to make use of opportunities as they arise, "buying up the time" (Col 4:5; cf. Eph 5:16). It is just possible that "buying up the time" refers generally to relations with outsiders. Two factors, however, suggest that evangelism is in view. First, in the immediately preceding verses Paul requests prayer for his mission. The subject has probably not diverged radically here, and opportunities to share the gospel with unbelievers are to be snatched up. Second, the parallel text in Ephesians 5:11-16, as noted above, likely relates to evangelism. Thus, the same conclusion should be drawn here as well. Paul avoids formulating a specific pattern for relating to unbelievers. Life is too complex and situations are too varied to enforce preset formulas. Accordingly, he prays for wisdom in relating to unbelievers. One crucial dimension is the believers' speech. Their speech is to be gracious and winsome (Col 4:6). In this way they will know how to respond to each person, whether by way of explanation or defense. A harsh or caustic spirit is to be avoided, for the character of believers is foundational in the dissemination of the gospel.

Perhaps a missionary thrust also underlies the parenetic instructions in Titus 2—3.[30] Older and younger women are encouraged to live in a godly and submissive way so that "the word of God will not be reviled" (Tit 2:3-5).

---

[30]For the view that mission is pervasive in the Pastoral Epistles, see Philip H. Towner, *The Goal of Our Instruction: The Structure of Theology and Ethics in the Pastoral Epistles*, JSNTSup 34 (Sheffield: JSOT, 1989). Towner probably overemphasizes the mission theme in the Pastorals, but he rightly discerns its presence.

Younger men and Titus are to live exemplary lives to prevent any evil from being spread about believers (Tit 2:6-8). Slaves are to be honest and submissive "in order to adorn the teaching of God our Savior in all things" (Tit 2:9-10). Each one of these purpose clauses probably relates to salvation, for the saving intention of the gospel is then detailed in Titus 2:11-14. Similarly, the call to obey the government and to treat all people with gentleness is based on the fact that believers were formerly foolish and enslaved to evil (Tit 3:1-7). If mercy has been extended to us, then surely we ought to live in such a way that others can see the beauty of what we have received, so that they too will share in God's kindness. Paul is not merely concerned about the lives of believers because he wants them to be respectable in the eyes of society, as if a bourgeois way of life is the endpoint of his concern. The confessional statements in Titus 2:11-14 and 3:3-7 reveal that the salvation of others is also in view. Believers who live unremarkable or even evil lives instead of adorning the gospel not only detract from it but also hinder its progress in the world.

Paul does not specifically command the Thessalonians to proclaim the gospel, but he does commend them because their conversion and joy under persecution was provocative enough to disseminate "the word of the Lord . . . in every place" (1 Thess 1:8; cf. Rom 1:8). It is doubtful that the Thessalonians sent out missionaries and heralded the gospel. The message of the gospel resounded through the transformation of their lives. No direct injunction to spread the gospel exists here, and yet the spread of the gospel is surely important for Paul, for he commends the Thessalonians precisely because the gospel is being disseminated through their lives.

Perhaps there is also a reference to spreading the gospel in Ephesians 6:15. Proper footwear is needed to fight the battle against spiritual powers. Armies lacking proper shoes or boots were in serious danger, for after long marches soldiers would be sore and hurting instead of prepared to engage in battle. Believers are to have the proper equipment on their feet "in preparation for the gospel of peace." The word *preparation (hetoimasia)* suggests that believers are to be alert, standing ready to proclaim the gospel of peace. Opportunities, like battles, may spring up at the most unlikely times. Believers, then, must be vigilant and light on their feet, prepared to share at any time the good news of the gospel.

One way in which the Philippian believers helped advance the gospel was through giving (Phil 1:5; 4:10-19). When donors make financial contributions, of course, they are not directly preaching the gospel. The Philippians' giving, however, did support and extend Paul's ministry. Evidently, they did not conclude that proclaiming the gospel was solely Paul's affair, one in which they shared no responsibility. They were moved to support Paul financially, and thereby they played a role in the extension of the gospel.

An account shared for another purpose also indicates, at least indirectly, that proclaiming the gospel was not confined to Paul. Paul relates his imprisonment and the good effect it had for the progress of the gospel, extending even to the whole Praetorian Guard (Phil 1:12-18). Another happy consequence of Paul's confinement was that other believers were emboldened, seeing Paul's courageous response to suffering, to proclaim the gospel. Some preached Christ with good intentions but others were malicious, hoping to dash Paul's spirits during his imprisonment. Paul rejoices in both instances because they are "proclaiming Christ" (Phil 1:17-18). What interests us here is not the situation that Paul recounts but the fact that other believers proclaim Christ and the gospel. This suggests that it is incumbent on other believers to do their part in disseminating the gospel.

The Ultimate Goal of Paul's Mission

Paul's ultimate goal, however, was not his mission. He was commissioned to bring about "the obedience of faith among all the Gentiles for the sake of his name" (Rom 1:5). The reason he engaged in mission was for the sake of the name of Jesus Christ, to see him exalted so that every knee would bow and every tongue confess him as Lord (Phil 2:10-11). And in the conclusion of Romans the revelation of Paul's gospel is again linked with the obedience of faith among the Gentiles (Rom 16:25-26). In addition, the motive for the spread of the gospel among the Gentiles is to bring glory "to the only wise God through Jesus Christ" (Rom 16:27). We see in a more extended passage in Romans a similar emphasis. Tensions existed between the weak and strong in Rome, for the weak in conscience and conviction believed that one should adhere to Old Testament food laws and observe the sabbath (Rom 14:1-6, 14, 20). The strong, on the other hand, were convinced that these things were unnecessary. Paul sides theologically with the strong, but he summons all to unity and acceptance of one another. The weak were probably composed primarily of Jewish believers, while the strong were made up primarily of Gentile Christians. Paul calls them to harmonious acceptance, but the exhortation for unity is not his highest goal. He calls them to unity "for the glory of God" (Rom 15:7). Moreover, the dissension between the weak and strong causes him to reflect on Christ's mission in Romans 15:8-13. Christ specially ministered to the circumcision to fulfill and establish God's saving and covenantal promises, which were made to the Jews. But his intention was also to show covenantal mercy to the Gentiles so that they too would glorify and praise God. In the subsequent verses Paul cites texts from the Old Testament (Deut 32:43; 2 Sam 22:50; Ps 117:1; Is 11:10) that mainly emphasize the united *worship* of Jews and Gentiles in the people of God. Paul's ultimate aim is not the horizontal reconciliation of Jews and Gentiles, important as that is. Nor is his missionary ambition satisfied when God's saving promises come to fruition among Jews and Gentiles, though he devoted his life to bringing God's saving message to Gentiles. The ultimate goal of Paul's mission was to see God glorified, and this reaches its zenith when Jews and Gentiles together worship and praise God. Such united worship begins on earth and will last forever.

3

THE BASIS OF MISSION

The Fulfillment of
the Promise to Abraham

T hus far we have seen that Paul was called to mission as an apostle to the Gentiles and that his aim was to honor God and Christ in his mission. We have also touched on the theme of salvation history in our discussion. Paul was privileged to serve as the apostle to the Gentiles because he lived at the turning of the ages, the era in which God's saving promises were being realized. The gospel of Christ fulfills what was written in the Old Testament scriptures, and believers inherit the promises made to Abraham. Thus, we can only grasp Paul's mission adequately if we see that he believed that the promises given to Abraham came to fruition in Christ.

The History of Israel

To understand Paul's conception of redemptive history we must try to view the Old Testament scriptures through his eyes, and thus an all too brief survey will follow.[1] God promised to Abraham land, seed and blessing (Gen

---

[1] My summary of the Old Testament is exceedingly brief. For a thorough and mainly convincing portrayal of Judaism, see N. T. Wright, *The New Testament and the People of God*, vol. 1 of *Christian Origins and the Question of God* (Minneapolis: Fortress, 1992), pp. 147-338. Insofar as Wright adopts the new perspective, however, he goes astray. For an alternate

12:1-3; cf. Gen 15:4-5; 17:1-8; 18:18-19; 22:16-18). The blessing was not simply confined to Abraham; *all people groups* throughout the earth would be blessed through Abraham. The promise made to Abraham was confirmed to his sons Isaac and Jacob (Gen 26:3-5; 28:13-15; 35:9-12). The promise of a seed was fulfilled in a miraculous way in the case both of Isaac and of Jacob and Esau. The multiplication of the seed began to be a reality through the children of Jacob, and when the book of Exodus opens the Jews were growing so rapidly that the Egyptians feared them. The promise of the land was not yet fulfilled, however, since Israel was in Egypt. Through the agency of Moses, Yahweh delivered his people from Egypt. A covenant was enacted with Israel at Sinai, and God gave Israel his law. If the Israelites responded to the law in obedience, they would be blessed. If they flouted God's law and turned their back on him, they would be cursed. The wilderness generation immediately turned its back on God and worshiped the golden calf (Ex 32—34). God had mercy on his people and did not destroy them utterly, and under the leadership of Joshua they were established in the land of promise. The promises of land and seed were substantially fulfilled at this juncture, but there was little evidence that all nations would be blessed through Abraham. In the generations following Joshua's victory, Israel compromised with surrounding nations, worshiped their gods and suffered defeat (see the book of Judges). God rescued the people when they repented, but Israel was weak, divided and one step away from national disaster.

To bring some unity to the nation a king was appointed by the name of Saul (1 Sam 8—12). His dynasty was removed from him since he was unfaithful to Yahweh's commands, and God raised up a new king by the name of David. Because of David's faithfulness God promised him an eternal dynasty (2 Sam 7). The people of Israel reached their glory days under David and his son Solomon, and yet the promise of universal blessing through Abraham was not realized. After Solomon's reign the Jewish people divided into two factions, Judah in the south and Israel in the north. The north was plagued by idolatry from its inception and was exiled to Assyria in 722 B.C. because of its sin. Though the southern kingdom was blessed with some righteous kings, the trajectory of the nation as a whole was

---

view, see Mark A. Elliott, *The Survivors of Israel: A Reconsideration of the Theology of Pre-Christian Judaism* (Grand Rapids, Mich.: Eerdmans, 2000). For an overview of the theme of mission in Scripture, see Andreas J. Köstenberger and Peter T. O'Brien, *Salvation to the Ends of the Earth: A Biblical Theology of Mission*, New Studies in Biblical Theology (Downers Grove, Ill.: InterVarsity Press, 2001).

toward evil. Judah transgressed the stipulations of the Sinai covenant and was exiled by Babylon (586 B.C.) as a punishment for its sins.

The prophetic movement flowered during the northern and southern kingdoms. The prophets threatened judgment on the day of the Lord for those who forsook Yahweh and his law, but they promised that ultimately the Lord would reveal his saving righteousness and fulfill his promises to Israel. A new covenant would be enacted in which Israel would be given the desire and ability to keep God's law (Jer 31:31-34; Ezek 11:19-20; 36:26-27); his law would be written on their hearts, and God would remove their inflexible stony hearts and put his Spirit in his people so that they would keep his law. The prophets (and the psalmists) did not confine their promises to Israel. They looked forward to the day when God would bring to pass the universal blessing promised to Abraham (Ps 22:27; 47:1-9; 72:17; 86:9; 96:1-13). Even Egypt and Assyria would participate in God's saving blessings in the future (Is 19:16-25). The covenantal mercies pledged to David would also include Gentiles (Is 55:3-5). Israel continued to look forward to the day when the promises of God's worldwide blessing would be theirs through a future descendant of David (Is 9:2-7; 11:1-10; 55:3; Jer 23:5-6; 30:9; Ezek 34:23-24; 37:24-25; Hos 3:5; Mic 5:2-4; Zech 9:9; cf. *Pss. Sol.* 17—18).

In the days of Jesus and Paul, Israel still awaited the fulfillment of God's saving promises, the coming of his kingdom and the worldwide blessing that was pledged to Abraham. Some (e.g., the Qumran community and the circles producing the Psalms of Solomon) may have believed that the coming of the kingdom was imminent. There was general agreement, in any case, that the promises were not yet fulfilled since Israel was under the thumb of Rome. It is also clear from reading the Old Testament that Israel's failure to attain the promises was due to their violation of the Sinai covenant. Some circles in Israel, such as the Pharisees and the Qumran community, devoted themselves assiduously to keeping the law, presumably to facilitate the fulfillment of what God promised to Israel long ago. The Qumran sect expected the promises to be realized soon, but the hoped for golden age had not yet arrived. When it did, the covenanters would have control of the temple and its cult, and the Romans would be ousted.

Jesus as Messiah in Paul

Paul fiercely persecuted a new sect in Judaism that declared Jesus of Nazareth as Messiah, probably because he understood this sect as renouncing the Torah. A man crucified on the cross could hardly be the Messiah (Deut 21:23). Moreover, the demotion of the law in the Christian sect threatened the fulfillment of God's saving promises. By promoting deviation from the law, the Christian sect, Paul likely reasoned, continued to bring God's curse on Israel. Perhaps Paul also thought it was obvious that Jesus could not be the Messiah since the promises of God were obviously not yet fulfilled in history. Rome was still in charge, and the situation of Israel had scarcely changed at all. The small ragtag sect claiming that the promises were being accomplished through a crucified man could scarcely be right, and yet they had to be resisted since some in Israel were so desperate that they were capitulating to the new movement.

When Paul was called and converted, he came to believe that the promises in the Old Testament were being fulfilled through Jesus of Nazareth and the gospel. Paul's conversion did not involve a repudiation of the Old Testament scriptures. He maintained that the gospel was the fulfillment of what was promised in the Prophets (Rom 1:2; 16:25-26). One of the remarkable omissions in the Pauline letters is a sustained defense of the Messianic status of Jesus of Nazareth. Some have concluded from this that Paul was uninterested in the historical Jesus. Rudolf Bultmann, for instance, drew this conclusion from his interpretation of 2 Corinthians 5:16: "So then, from now on we know no one according to the flesh, even if we have known Christ according to flesh, but now we know him no longer."[2] Others have noted how rarely Paul appeals to the Davidic descent of Jesus (Rom 1:3; 2 Tim 2:8), or have observed that Paul seldom appeals explicitly to the teaching of Jesus. Even though Paul rarely cites the sayings of Jesus explicitly, Michael Thompson's careful work on Romans demonstrates that there are numerous allusions to Jesus' teaching in Paul's writings.[3] Moreover, David Wenham has illustrated that Jesus' teaching is compatible with and exerted an influence on Paul's theology.[4] Paul's failure to provide an exten-

---

[2] For Rudolf Bultmann's interpretation of 2 Cor 5:16, which he used to support the thesis that Paul had no interest in the historical Jesus, see his *Primitive Christianity in Its Contemporary Setting* (New York: Meridian, 1956), p. 197. For a convincing criticism of Bultmann's view, see Victor P. Furnish, *II Corinthians*, AB (Garden City, N.Y.: Doubleday, 1984), pp. 312, 330.

[3] Michael Thompson, *Clothed with Christ: The Example and Teaching of Jesus in Romans 12.1—15.13*, JSNTSup 59 (Sheffield: JSOT, 1991). See also the essays by Peter Stuhlmacher, "Jesus-tradition im Römerbrief: Eine Skizze," *TBei* 14 (1983): 240-50; and Dale Allison, "The Pauline Epistles and the Synoptic Gospels: The Pattern of the Parallels," *NTS* 28 (1982): 1-32. For a contrary view, see F. Neirynck, "Paul and the Sayings of Jesus," in *L'Apôtre Paul: Personnalité, style et conception du ministère,* ed. A. Vanhoye, BETL 73 (Leuven: University Press), pp. 265-321.

[4] David Wenham, *Paul: Follower of Jesus or Founder of Christianity?* (Grand Rapids, Mich.: Eerdmans, 1995). I would not endorse all of Wenham's conclusions, but his basic thesis is correct in my opinion.

sive defense of Jesus' messianic status could be interpreted variously. The omission could be construed as evidence for Paul's lack of interest in the subject. On the other hand, Paul often refers to "Jesus Christ" or "Christ Jesus." Scholars have customarily maintained that the term *Christ* has lost its titular force in Paul, so that it has virtually become a last name for Jesus instead of serving as a title to designate his messiahship. N. T. Wright has demonstrated, on the contrary, that the title "Christ" is still important to Paul.[5] As a Jew, Paul would continue to recognize the titular associations of the term. He speaks of "Jesus Christ" and "Christ Jesus" so often because one of the foundations of Paul's worldview is that Jesus is the promised Messiah. No extended defense of such a view was needed since the messianic status of Jesus was apparently well accepted in all his churches. Divisions and arguments arose over many matters in the churches, but apparently no serious debate erupted over whether Jesus was the Messiah. This was an accepted datum in all the Pauline churches.

When did the Pauline churches come to the conviction that Jesus was the Messiah? Obviously they did not embrace this view through the Pauline letters, for the letters assume he is David's promised heir. The natural answer is that Paul argued extensively that Jesus was the promised Messiah when he evangelized the churches. We have only one account in Acts in which Paul proclaims the gospel to Jews and Gentiles familiar with the Old Testament (cf. Acts 13:16-41). According to this text, Paul defends the notion that Jesus is David's promised heir. Such a view seems to be confirmed by the letter to the Romans. It is telling that when writing to the one church that was not established by Paul or one of his coworkers, he establishes his orthodox credentials by appealing to what was the common confession in the churches, and this confession included the idea that Jesus was the seed of David (Rom 1:3). Paul wanted to assure the Romans that the gospel he preached was the gospel commonly held by all Christians everywhere. We are reminded again of the occasional nature of Paul's letters. Not every part of his theology receives equal emphasis due to the circumstances that precipitated the various letters. Paul's constant references to Jesus as Messiah—which in his letters are to "Jesus Christ" or "Christ Jesus"—demonstrate that this was a central feature of his theology, even though no detailed defense or discussion ensues. A new age in salvation history had arrived, for the promised Messiah had come.

---

[5]See N. T. Wright, *The Climax of the Covenant: Christ and the Law in Pauline Theology* (Minneapolis: Fortress, 1992), pp. 41-55.

The Promise of Blessing for the Nations

Promised in the Old Testament. The coming of the Messiah was crucial for the Pauline mission, for Paul understood the Old Testament to teach that the Messiah, when he came, would bring salvation to the Gentiles (Ps 22:22-31; 72:1-20; Is 11:1-10; 49:6; 55:3-5). In other words, the coming of the Messiah signified that a new era in redemptive history had begun, for the covenant with Abraham, which promised blessing to all nations, was now being fulfilled. The Gentiles are not shunted off to the side in a secondary way. Through faith in Christ they become part of the family of Abraham, for as Paul says, "those of faith, these are the sons of Abraham" (Gal 3:7). The Abrahamic blessing of Genesis 12:3 is realized when Gentiles exercise faith in the same way as Abraham (Gal 3:8-9). Gentiles are not required to observe Torah to be part of Abraham's family. Devotion to Torah is not merely unnecessary; it is also dangerous, because those who attempt to secure the blessing of Abraham through Torah are cursed (Gal 3:10). The exclusive way to participate in the blessing of Abraham is to have the faith of Abraham (Gal 3:11-12). The curse that lies on humanity is removed only by Christ in his curse-bearing work on the cross (Deut 21:23).

Marked by the gift of the Spirit. The blessing of Abraham is defined by Paul in Galatians 3:14 as the gift of the Spirit. Christ redeemed believers from the curse "so that the blessing of Abraham might come to the Gentiles in Christ Jesus, so that we should receive the promise of the Spirit by faith." The two purpose clauses in the verse are coordinate and mutually interpret one another. "The promise of the Spirit" is the eschatological Spirit promised in the Old Testament scriptures (Is 44:3; Ezek 11:19-20; 36:26-27; Joel 2:28-32). We should especially note Isaiah 44:3: "For I will pour water on the thirsty land, and streams on the dry ground; I will pour my spirit upon your descendants, and my blessing on your offspring" (NRSV). We should note that the "Spirit" and the "blessing" are parallel in Isaiah 44:3. Doubtless Paul was reflecting on this verse as he composed Galatians. Indeed, he was probably seeing a fulfillment of the second exodus promised in Isaiah since Isaiah predicts that God is going to accomplish a new exodus in delivering his people from Babylon (Is 11:15-16; 40:3-11; 42:16; 43:2, 5-7, 16-19; 48:20-21; 49:6-11; 51:10). With the coming of Jesus the new exodus is a reality, and God's people are being delivered from the exile imposed by sin.[6] The

---

[6]Scholarly discussion continues on whether the return from exile is featured in Paul. Mark A. Seifrid doubts that such a theme is legitimately read into Paul's letters. See Seifrid, "Blind Alleys in the Controversy over the Paul of History," *TynBul* 45 (1994): 73-95; Seifrid,

Pauline assertion that Gentiles were participating in the blessing of the new exodus is not a misreading of Isaiah, since Isaiah himself emphasizes that the Gentiles will share in the salvation God brings. God verifies the inclusion of the Gentiles by giving them the "blessing" of the covenant of Abraham, namely, the Holy Spirit. The scriptural connection between the "blessing" and the gift of the "Spirit" in Isaiah 44:3 suggests that it is misleading to characterize the argument of Galatians 3:1-5 as experiential, especially if by "experiential" the theological dimensions of Paul's argument are slighted. Paul is arguing both experientially and theologically in Galatians 3:1-5, for the Galatians' receiving the Spirit demonstrates that the promise to Abraham is being fulfilled since the Spirit is the blessing of Abraham (Gal 3:14; Is 44:3).

Jesus as the seed of Abraham. One of Paul's more puzzling statements is the claim that Jesus is the singular seed of Abraham: "Now the promises were to Abraham and to his seed *[spermati]*. He does not say, 'and to his seeds *[spermasin],*' as a reference to many, but as to one, 'and to your seed *[spermati],*' who is Christ" (Gal 3:16). We can scarcely say that Paul was unfamiliar with the plural dimensions of the singular *seed.* He says in Galatians 3:29, "And if you belong to Christ, then you are the seed *[sperma]* of Abraham, heirs according to promise." He uses the singular with a plural sense just a few verses later! The English word *sheep* provides a fitting analogy, for the term can have both a singular or plural referent. Nor would Paul claim that no one after Abraham lived righteously, and so we cannot reasonably say that his point is that Jesus was the only righteous seed of Abraham— though, of course, Jesus was the only seed of Abraham who was sinless. Paul was well aware of the remnant and of righteous people such as Joseph and Daniel. Paul may be arguing in a typically rabbinic way here, but such an observation is unsatisfying in that it does not explain the meaning of the statement. It often seems as if those who appeal to "rabbinic" categories are suggesting that any explanation for Paul's theology is beyond us in such

---

"The 'New Perspective on Paul' and Its Problems," *Them* 25 (2000): 8-12. Seifrid raises some cautions that must be seriously considered. A number of scholars, on the other hand, have argued that such a theme is in Paul. For a detailed examination of the exile theme, see J. M. Scott, ed., *Exile: Old Testament, Jewish and Christian Conceptions* (Leiden: Brill, 1997). See also James M. Scott, "Paul's Use of Deuteronomic Tradition," *JBL* 112 (1993): 645-65; William J. Webb, *Returning Home: New Covenant and Second Exodus as the Context for 2 Corinthians 6.14—7.1,* JSNTSup 85 (Sheffield: JSOT, 1993). The crucial point is that Paul sees the promises recounted in Isaiah (esp. Is 40-66) as being fulfilled in Christ. Whether the notion of "return from exile" is the best wording to capture this theme is debatable, but the idea that God is now fulfilling the promises made in Isaiah seems clear.

instances. Paul probably has in mind the idea that Jesus is the corporate head of God's people, just as Adam was the head of all humanity (cf. Rom 5:12-19). In Genesis itself the coming ruler is a descendant of Judah, who is himself the seed of Abraham (Gen 49:10). Jesus—as the singular seed of Abraham—is the representative and head of all those who belong to the *redeemed* people of God. After all, only Jesus lived a life that was perfectly devoted to God, a life that was unstained by any sin (2 Cor 5:21). David and others trusted God for their salvation, but they were also sinners who violated God's law. Only Jesus as the Messiah lived a life that was always pleasing to God. Paul probably also identified Jesus as the seed of Abraham because Jesus was singularly endowed with the Spirit. God anointed Jesus with the Spirit during his ministry, and Jesus in turn poured out the blessing of the Spirit on his people.

Whatever we make of the reasoning that provoked Paul to identify Jesus as Abraham's sole seed, the function of Jesus as the seed of Abraham is of massive significance for the inclusion of the Gentiles. The way into Abraham's family is not dependent on circumcision and Torah. That path belonged to an interim period that has now ended (Gal 3:15-25). The Sinai covenant should not be considered as the climax of God's covenants, but instead as a temporary covenant that pointed to and was replaced by the new covenant. Supporting the transitory nature of the law is the history of Abraham. When we consider Abraham as the paradigmatic believer, it must be observed that he was righteous by faith *before he was circumcised* (Rom 4:9-12). Thereby he functions as the father both of Gentile believers who are uncircumcised and of Jewish believers who are circumcised. Circumcision was not vital for his righteousness before God. Abraham's history shows that circumcision is a matter of indifference. Now that Christ has come, the era in which Israel lived under the pedagogue is complete (Gal 3:23-25). Now all are "sons of God," adult children in God's family in Christ Jesus (Gal 3:26) through faith. Abraham is the universal father of both Jewish and Gentile believers because all enter his family by faith (Rom 4:16-17). What matters is not whether one has submitted to the knife of circumcision but whether one has been baptized into Christ Jesus (Gal 3:27). Those who have been baptized into Christ are clothed with Christ, and thus ethnic background, social class and gender are irrelevant in terms of participation in Abraham's family. Those who belong to Christ Jesus are one new family. To be a member of Abraham's family one need only belong to Christ (Gal 3:29). The "fullness of time" has come (Gal 4:4), a new era of redemptive history has dawned, and those who are Christ's—those who believe in him, whether Jew or Gentile—are part of the new people of God. They are his sons and daughters.

Gentiles as the children of Abraham. Paul identifies Gentile believers as "sons of Abraham" (Gal 3:7) and the "seed of Abraham" (Gal 3:29). Abraham is the *father* of both Jews and Gentiles who believe in Christ (Rom 4:9-12, 16-17). It is instructive to see that the same line of thinking is established relative to circumcision. Israel was circumcised physically in the Old Testament, but physical circumcision was never sufficient; Israel was also called on to circumcise their hearts (Deut 10:16; Jer 4:4; 9:25-26). Moses looked forward to the day when this would be a reality (Deut 30:6), and Jeremiah's call to circumcise the heart is surely fulfilled in his new-covenant prophecy (Jer 31:31-34). The author of Jubilees forges a link between the circumcision of the heart and the gift of the Spirit (*Jub.* 1:23). In Romans 2:25-29 Paul considers the benefits of circumcision. He dismisses circumcision if it is viewed as some kind of magical talisman that saves simply by virtue of being applied to the body. Those who are circumcised but transgress God's law are not members of God's covenant people. The Jews cannot appeal to their circumcision, violate God's law and expect to receive praise from God on the last day (Rom 2:29). On the other hand, Gentiles who keep God's law are to be considered as spiritually circumcised, even if they are physically uncircumcised. In other words, such Gentiles are part of the people of God. Paul explains how this can be in Romans 2:28-29. Genuine Jewishness and true circumcision are not outward and external matters. The true Jew is one inside, and circumcision is a matter of the heart. It is the work, Paul says, *of the Spirit.* We observed above that the circumcising of the heart by the Spirit was considered to be an eschatological work that would occur in the days when redemptive history was being fulfilled. The circumcision of the heart by the Holy Spirit signifies the inauguration of redemptive history. God is now fulfilling his saving promises. That which physical circumcision anticipated, the circumcision of the heart, is now a reality through the Holy Spirit. Since true circumcision and genuine Jewishness are not external matters but the result of the Spirit's work, it follows that Gentiles are part of God's people—true Jews! God's saving promises made to Abraham are now becoming a reality.

A similar idea is found in Philippians 3:2-3. Those agitators who insist on circumcision for entrance into the people of God are "dogs," and what they call circumcision is nothing less than physical mutilation. Believers are the true circumcision because they worship in the Holy Spirit and boast in Christ Jesus alone. Circumcision, rightly understood, anticipates God's work by which he removes the power of sin in the lives of his people. When it is turned into an external sign that one boasts in, then it is misapplied and its true intention reversed. Believers are to boast only in the cross (Gal 6:14) and not in circumcision. This fits with Colossians 2:11 as well, where "the circumcision of the Christ" probably refers to his being "cut off" at his death. The "removal of the body of the flesh" in the same verse should probably be understood as a designation for the old Adam, who dominated the Colossians' lives before they came to faith.[7] If this exegesis is correct, then Paul locates the stripping away of the flesh's power in the cutting off of Christ at the cross. The only circumcision believers need is the circumcision of the heart accomplished by Christ and applied by the Spirit. Those still insisting on physical circumcision cling to the shadows even while the sun dawns on a new era (cf. Col 2:17). Believers in Christ are the sons of Abraham, the seed of Abraham and the true circumcision. Participation in the family of Abraham does not require observance of Torah, food laws or sabbath. Faith in Jesus Christ marks the people of God.

The identity of the "Israel of God" in Galatians 6:16 remains controversial. Some interpreters confine the reference to ethnic Israel, and this is certainly a possible reading of the text. The debate will probably not be resolved by considering the syntax of the verse itself, for syntactically a plausible case can be made for a reference to ethnic Israel or the church. A weighing of the context, however, suggests that the Israel of God refers to all believers in Christ, whether Jews or Gentiles. Paul criticizes the motives and practices of those advocating circumcision (Gal 6:12-13), thus confirming and reinforcing his disavowal of physical circumcision. The only boasting that counts is boasting in the cross of Christ (Gal 6:14). Preoccupying oneself with circumcision or becoming entranced with uncircumcision is extraneous. What matters is the "new creation" (Gal 6:15). The reference to the new creation indicates that the fulfillment of God's promises to bless the whole world is now a reality. A new world has arrived in which the promises of Abraham are being realized. Focusing on physical circumcision or uncircumcision indicates that one is living under the old order. So too, restricting the Israel of God to ethnic Israel misses the connection between Galatians 6:15-16. Those who walk by the rule

---

[7]The meaning of this verse (Col 2:11) is disputed. For the various options, see Peter T. O'Brien, *Colossians, Philemon*, WBC (Waco: Word, 1982), pp. 116-17.

articulated in Galatians 6:15, that is, the new creation, perceive that being a physical descendant of Abraham is not the crucial question. All who boast in the cross of Christ are part of the Israel of God. All those who have experienced the power of the new creation are members of the Israel of God. Understanding the "Israel of God" as referring to both Jews and Gentiles who believe in Christ fits well with the entire letter of Galatians. Paul has argued that believers are sons of Abraham and the seed of Abraham and that circumcision is unnecessary to enter the people of God. Paul's emphasis on the inclusion of Gentiles throughout the letter makes it doubtful that he would conclude the letter by restricting the Israel of God to ethnic Israel. Most likely, the conclusion of the letter reflects one of the central themes of the letter. The true people of God cannot be restricted to those who are ethnic descendants of Abraham. The family of Abraham is now made up of both Jews and Gentiles who believe in Christ. In other words, the new creation has dawned and a new Israel of God has been formed, fulfilling the promise to Abraham that all nations would be blessed through him.

The inclusion of the Gentiles into God's people. That Jews and Gentiles are one people of God fits with Paul's argument in Ephesians 2:11—3:13, which we surveyed in chapter two. In the previous era of salvation history the Gentiles were separated from God's people, Israel. The Gentiles were not the recipients of his saving promises and were separated from God and Christ. In the new age of redemptive history, however, they have been inducted into the people of God through the death of Christ. Now Gentiles are fellow citizens with the Jews in the people of God. There are not two peoples of God but one people of God in which the Gentiles are "fellow heirs and members of the same body and fellow partakers of the same promise in Christ Jesus through the gospel" (Eph 3:6). This unity between Jews and Gentiles was not revealed in the former ages of redemptive history, but it has now been clarified by God's authoritative apostolic messengers. We should not understand Ephesians to say that the significance of ethnic Israel has been nullified altogether, for we shall see in chapter sixteen that Paul believes in a future salvation for ethnic Israel. On the other hand, one's view of the future of Israel should not suppress the emphasis on the new people of God that permeates Paul's writings. Jews and Gentiles together compose one people of God, and they are the family of Abraham. Such a unity has occurred because God's saving promises to Abraham are becoming a reality.

Another piece of evidence confirms the inclusion of the Gentiles into the people of God: designations used to describe Israel in the Old Testament are applied to the church of Christ. We begin with the word *ekklēsia* (assembly, church). The *qāhāl* (assembly) of Yahweh, often translated *ekklēsia* in the LXX, was Israel in the Old Testament (Judg 20:2; 1 Kings 8:14, 22, 55; 12:3). Paul regularly applies the term *ekklēsia* to his Gentile readers (Rom 16:1, 4; 1 Cor 1:2; 4:17; 11:16; 14:33-34; 16:1; 2 Cor 1:1; 8:1; Gal 1:2; Col 4:15-16; 1 Thess 1:1; 2 Thess 1:1; Philem 2). The new assembly of God comprises Jews and Gentiles. Similarly, in the Old Testament, Israel was "holy" (*hagios*—Ex 19:6; Deut 7:6; 14:2, 21; 28:9), "elect" (*eklektos*—1 Chron 16:13; Ps 89:3; 106:5; Lam 1:15 LXX), "beloved" (*agapētoi*—Ps 60:5; 108:6) and "called" (*kaleō*—Is 41:9; 42:6; 43:1, 22). All these terms are now applied to Gentiles in Christ. They are God's "holy ones" (e.g., Rom 1:7; 1 Cor 1:2; 2 Cor 1:1; Eph 1:1; Phil 1:1; Col 1:2; 3:12; Philem 5), "chosen" (Rom 8:33; Col 3:12; 2 Tim 2:10; Tit 1:1), "beloved" (Rom 1:7; Eph 5:1) and "called" (Rom 1:6-7; 8:28; 1 Cor 1:2, 24). The transfer of terms to the church that applied to Israel signifies that the church is the new people of God, the fulfillment of the promises made to Israel.

Paul's discussion of Israel and the Gentiles in Romans 9—11 also casts light on his understanding of the fulfillment of the promises made to Abraham. These chapters, naturally, raise many questions, most of which will be explored later. The primary issue in these chapters is whether the saving promises made to ethnic Israel will be fulfilled, whether God is faithful to his covenantal promises. At this point, however, we will confine ourselves to some observations that are made relative to the Gentiles. For example, Paul understands that the prophecies of Hosea—where God promises that he will call a people who were formerly not his people to be his own (Hos 1:9; 2:23)—though made originally to Israel, are fulfilled in the calling of the Gentiles (Rom 9:24-26). The promises made to Israel are not merely applied to Gentiles; it seems that Paul envisions the promises made to Israel as fulfilled in the church of Christ. Thus, the church of Christ is the people of God. It is likely that Paul envisioned a fulfillment of the promise made to Abraham here in which all peoples are blessed in him. The illustration of the olive tree in Romans 11:17-24 is also instructive. The identity of the olive tree is disputed, but it probably designates the true people of God. In the Old Testament the olive tree referred to Israel as God's people (Jer 11:16; Hos 14:5-6). In Romans the olive tree is composed of both Jews and Gentiles who belong to the church of Christ. Indeed, the tree at the time Paul wrote was composed primarily of Gentiles, and thus Paul admonishes them not to boast over the Jews. What we want to observe, though, is that Gentiles are part of the true people of God. God's people are no longer marked out specially by ethnic identity. The promises of Abraham are in the process of being fulfilled, and the people of God is composed of both Jews and Gentiles.

Conclusion

When Paul contemplated his mission, he recognized God's grace because he was commissioned to serve as an apostle to the Gentiles at the point in history when God was fulfilling his saving promises. The prophecy that the Gentiles would be blessed in Abraham was not fulfilled in the days of David, Isaiah or Jeremiah. Now that the Messiah, Jesus, had come, these prophecies were being fulfilled. Paul was called by God to advance God's mission in the world, particularly by extending God's saving grace to Gentiles. In order to sustain his mission Paul had to demonstrate theologically that his mission to the Gentiles was a fulfillment of the scriptures. Paul's mission to reach Gentiles cannot be attributed to his tolerant and inclusive personality. In his view the promises of redemptive history were being fulfilled, and these promises included salvific blessings for the Gentiles. His mission to include Gentiles in the promise was *theologically* grounded, and it had to be theologically defended. He also believed that the mission to the Gentiles was the only means by which ethnic Israel would be saved. But that is a story for chapter sixteen.

4

SUFFERING & THE PAULINE MISSION

The Means of Spreading the Gospel

B ooks on Pauline theology do not typically have a separate chapter on his suffering. A chapter on suffering is included here because Paul's suffering is vital to his mission as the apostle to the Gentiles. We should not conceive of Paul as engaging in mission and experiencing the unfortunate consequence of suffering in the process, as if his difficulties were unrelated to his mission. On the contrary, the pain Paul endured was the means by which the message of the gospel was extended to the nations. Suffering was not a side effect of the Pauline mission; rather it was at the very center of his apostolic evangelism. His distress validated and legitimated his message, demonstrating the truth of the gospel. This is not to say that sufferings in and of themselves ratify the truth of the Pauline gospel. Rather, Paul's sufferings provide evidence of the truth of his gospel. Indeed, his sufferings are a corollary of the sufferings of Jesus. Obviously Paul's anguish was not atoning, nor did he bear the sins of God's people in a substitutionary death as Jesus did. His suffering was, however, central to his apostolic calling. Hence, an understanding of Pauline theology and the Pauline mission must investigate Pauline suffering. Paul's life as a missionary was marked by suffering from its inception. God promised him at his call that his mission and suffering would be intertwined (Acts 9:15-16), showing that suffering was central to the Pauline mission.

Paul Attacked Because of His Suffering

What Paul may not have expected was that his suffering would be used against him by his opponents. The false apostles in Corinth (2 Cor 11:13-15) denounced the validity of Paul's apostleship because of his suffering and weakness (see 2 Cor 10—13). His adversaries believed that genuine apostles performed signs, wonders and miracles. Of course, signs and wonders were characteristic of Paul's ministry (2 Cor 12:12), but Paul believed that strength *in weakness* was even more distinctive of an apostolic ministry. We cannot be certain about every detail of the opponents' attack on Paul in 2 Corinthians, but the clues we have suggest that their attack against him was multifaceted.[1] They accused Paul of being a vacillator since he promised to visit Corinth twice and then reneged on his promise (2 Cor 1:12-22). Surely someone who violates their promises, they alleged, cannot be a legitimate apostle! They probably also criticized Paul for his lack of success in evangelism (2 Cor 2:14-16; 4:3-4), complaining that an apostle who was truly empowered by the Spirit would have more converts to show for his efforts. They may also have suggested that Paul needed letters of recommendation (2 Cor 3:1; 5:12). Paul, after all, was not part of the original Twelve, and his relations to Jerusalem were suspect (cf. Gal 2:1-14). If he were truly legitimate, he would have credentials and references that placed his status beyond dispute. They also charged Paul with hypocrisy. When he was present with the Corinthians, he was deferential and humble, and his speaking ability was—in their view—lamentable; but when absent he would write bold and fiery letters (2 Cor 10:1, 10; 11:5-6; 12:11). A proof of Paul's inferiority, in the eyes of his detractors, was his failure to take pay for his work (2 Cor 11:7-11; 12:13-18). If Paul were truly worth supporting, he would not be hesitant to ask for money. They probably reasoned that those who offer something truly worth having are not afraid to be supported financially. Those who know that they are inferior, like Paul, are reluctant to ask for funding. Indeed, Paul sent messengers, like Titus, to extract the money craftily from the Corinthians. He lacked the courage and integrity to demand the money up front. Nevertheless, the root of all the disquiet and doubt about Paul's apostolic legitimacy was his weakness and suffering (2 Cor 12:8-10; 13:3-4). This particular charge against Paul informs the entire letter, and his response to the charge constitutes the heart

---

[1]For a useful method for discerning opponents and their teaching in Paul, see Jerry Sumney, *Identifying Paul's Opponents: The Question of Method in 2 Corinthians*, JSNTSup 40 (Sheffield: JSOT, 1990). See also John M. G. Barclay, "Mirror-Reading a Polemical Letter: Galatians as a Test Case," *JSNT* 31 (1987): 73-93.

of the letter. Paradoxically, Paul's suffering increased because his opponents in Corinth argued that his suffering disqualified him as an apostle.

The letter in which Paul explains in some detail the role of his suffering as an apostle is, given the opposition traced above, 2 Corinthians. It is not the case, though, that the place of suffering in his apostolic mission is confined to 2 Corinthians. The connection between suffering and his apostolic ministry surfaces on a number of occasions in his letters. The prominence of this topic in Paul also says something about typical Pauline theologies, for seldom do they contain an extended discussion of suffering. Such an omission suggests that certain systematic categories, which interest contemporary authors, may cause them to overlook a theme that permeates his letters. In a biblical-theology approach, suffering must be examined since it is a topic that Paul discusses at some length and it is vital to the Pauline mission.

The Role of Pauline Suffering According to 1 Thessalonians

After Paul established the Thessalonian church, he was worried about its stability because he knew afflictions were coming and he was unsure about how the church would respond (1 Thess 3:1-5). He rejoiced, however, when he heard that they were persisting in the faith and that they remembered him with love (1 Thess 3:6-10). Paul recounts in some detail the integrity of his own ministry in 1 Thessalonians 2:1-12, and scholars debate whether this defense constitutes a response to attacks from opponents. It is certainly possible that Paul defends himself against attacks made by his enemies, but it seems probable that Paul features the integrity of his ministry for rhetorical purposes.[2] No other evidence exists in the letter that Paul was under suspicion by the Thessalonians, but we do know that the Thessalonians' faith was severely tested by their own sufferings. Paul recounts his own perseverance and integrity while suffering to show that he serves as a model and pattern for the Thessalonians. For instance, in 1 Thessalonians 1:6 he says that the Thessalonians "have become imitators of us and of the Lord, by receiving the word in much affliction with the joy that comes from the Holy Spirit." Just as Paul has become an example for the Thessalonians through his suffering, so they have become a model for others by their own suffering (1 Thess 1:7). What is particularly interesting is that Paul links together the power of his

---

[2]In defense of this view, see two articles by Abraham Malherbe, " 'Gentle as a Nurse': The Cynic Background to 1 Thess. 2," *NT* 12 (1970): 203-13; and "Exhortation in 1 Thessalonians," *NT* 25 (1983): 238-56. I am less convinced about the plausibility of a Cynic background.

word with the integrity of his ministry: "Our gospel did not come to you in word only but also in power and in the Holy Spirit and in full assurance, because [taking *kathōs* as causal] you know what sort of people we were among you for your sake" (1 Thess 1:5). The word of the gospel had such effectiveness because of the kind of people Paul, Silas and Timothy were. The integrity of Paul and his colleagues was reflected in their response to suffering, in that they responded to afflictions with the joy that comes from the Holy Spirit (1 Thess 1:6). Before 2 Corinthians was written, then, Paul was already arguing that suffering did not *disqualify* him from ministry. Instead, his suffering *legitimated* his ministry, for his response to his afflictions showed that he was empowered by the Spirit.

The brief comments made about the integrity of Paul's ministry while suffering (1 Thess 1:5-6) are expanded on in 1 Thessalonians 2:1-12. He reminds the Thessalonians that he boldly proclaimed the gospel among them, even though fierce opposition plagued him in Thessalonica (Acts 17:1-9) and despite the fact that he and Silas had been beaten with rods just previously in Philippi (Acts 16:16-40). The "for" *(gar)* in 1 Thessalonians 2:3 provides the reason for his boldness despite suffering and opposition. What Paul emphasizes is the *integrity* of his ministry. His message, unlike the messages of some of the itinerants of his day, was not full of guile and trickery. His motive was not to please people, win their praise and then solicit money from them. He was a minister approved by God (1 Thess 2:4), and God's approval was probably gained through Paul's suffering. Nor did Paul use his authority in a tyrannical and burdensome way. His ministry was marked by a tender concern, affection and love for the Thessalonians. In 2 Thessalonians 2:9 Paul appeals to the secular employment in which he engaged so that he did not have to solicit any money from the Thessalonians. Ronald Hock has demonstrated that by plying a trade Paul exposed himself to the suffering of working as an artisan and that the difficulties of such a job were common knowledge in Paul's day.[3] What was striking about Paul is that he endured such indignities voluntarily so that the gospel could be preached to the Thessalonians without charge. The effectiveness of the message of the cross is evacuated if the messengers are hucksters. On the other hand, proclaiming the gospel with integrity in the midst of suffering commends the gospel to the hearers.

---

[3]See Ronald F. Hock, *The Social Context of Paul's Ministry: Tentmaking and Apostleship* (Philadelphia: Fortress, 1980), pp. 31-37.

Suffering and the Gospel in 1 Corinthians

A common view is that Paul defends his apostleship against detractors in both 1 and 2 Corinthians. No one doubts that Paul responds to opponents in 2 Corinthians, but the evidence for a self-defense in 1 Corinthians is not as persuasive.[4] For example, 1 Corinthians 9 contains a long defense of Paul's right to receive financial support for his apostolic ministry. This is often seen as an attempt to *defend* his right for support and as an *explanation* of his reasons for refusing it. It is doubtful, though, that such an explanation is correct since it does not adequately account for the context of 1 Corinthians 8—10. Paul's aim in these chapters is to persuade those who freely eat sacrificed food to forgo their rights to eat it for the sake of the weak, whose consciences are defiled by eating such food. In the midst of this discussion (1 Cor 9) he uses his *right* to receive financial support as an illustration of a case in which one has a right and refuses to use it for the benefit of others. Such an illustration would scarcely work if Paul's refusal to accept money were controversial in Corinth. The illustration would lose its punch if it brought to the forefront *another controversy*, namely, whether Paul should or should not receive money from the Corinthians. The illustration works precisely because it removes the debate from the issue presently under contention (i.e., food offered to idols) and offers an example from another realm (financial support) that is currently not under dispute. Of course, we know that by the time he wrote 2 Corinthians the situation had changed radically and Paul's refusal to accept support was criticized fiercely. We must beware of imposing the situation from 2 Corinthians into the epistolary situation of 1 Corinthians.

Similarly, it is a mistake to conclude from 1 Corinthians 1:10—4:21 that some Corinthians disputed Paul's apostolic authority or teaching. The strife pervading Corinth was due to varying estimations of the rhetorical abilities of Paul and Apollos and Cephas. No significant quarrel was raised with the *apostolic authority* of Paul. Some of the Corinthians simply believed that he was less effective rhetorically than Apollos and Peter. Thus, Paul nowhere in these early chapters defends his unique authority as the apostle to the Gentiles. As the apostle to the Gentiles, he explains how the gospel he preaches relates to the quarrels in Corinth, demonstrating that their strife over minis-

---

[4]Contrary to the view of Gordon D. Fee, *The First Epistle to the Corinthians*, NICNT (Grand Rapids, Mich.: Eerdmans, 1987), pp. 393-94. For a persuasive critique of Fee's view, see Scott J. Hafemann, *Suffering and the Spirit: An Exegetical Study of II Cor. 2:14—3:3 Within the Context of the Corinthian Correspondence*, WUNT 2/19 (Tübingen: J. C. B. Mohr, 1986), pp. 127-33.

ters is rooted in a secular worldview that denies the message of the cross.

The Corinthians' entrancement with the rhetorical marvels of certain speakers betrayed their fascination with the wisdom of this world. Why did they take sides and parcel out their affections to Peter, Apollos, Paul or even Christ? Paul identifies their root sin as pride (1 Cor 1:29, 31; 2:5; 3:21; 4:6-7, 18). Behind their advocacy of Paul or Apollos is a spirit of self-promotion. Paul counters with the theology of the cross because it is an antidote to the conceit that boasts in ministers rather than in God. The theology of the cross reminds readers that salvation was accomplished through the suffering and death of Jesus of Nazareth. He did not bring salvation by coming to the earth as king but by taking upon himself the degradation of the cross. Associated with the pride of the Corinthians was their overrealized eschatology.[5] They believed that they were enjoying on earth now the life reserved for heaven. Perhaps they distorted Paul's theology of the inauguration of the kingdom and drew the conclusion that the consummation of Christ's reign was now realized (1 Cor 4:8). Some of the Corinthians apparently concluded that there was no future resurrection for believers (1 Cor 15). Perhaps they maintained that they were *already* raised with Christ, and therefore they scorned the notion of a future physical resurrection. Perhaps they maintained that the only resurrection which mattered was spiritual, in which believers were exalted to heaven, so that they enjoyed the presence of God even now. We lack enough information to explain in depth how the Corinthians' overrealized eschatology affected other issues broached in the letter. It may be the case, however, that some of them justified sexual sin by appealing to the abolition of marriage in the coming age (1 Cor 6:12-20; cf. Mt 22:23-33 and par). Perhaps some of the women invoked the same line of thought to support the idea that any distinctions between males and females were passé (1 Cor 11:2-16; 14:33-36). The avid use of spiritual gifts, especially the gift of tongues, may have persuaded some that the age to come was fully realized now (1 Cor 12-14).

Paul responds to the Corinthians' pride by emphasizing the weakness of the apostles in 1 Corinthians 4:8-13.[6] The Corinthians may think they reign now, but Paul emphasizes that the kingdom will be consummated in the *future*. Unfortunately, the Corinthians have forgotten the "not yet" element relative to the kingdom of God. In the present age God has not exalted the

---

[5]See Anthony C. Thiselton, "Realized Eschatology at Corinth," *NTS* 24 (1977-1978): 510-26.
[6]My understanding of the role of Paul's sufferings, especially in 2 Corinthians, has been influenced at many points by the crucial work of Hafemann, *Suffering and the Spirit*.

apostles but instead has displayed them as last. *God* has delivered them over to the "arena" *(theatron)*, the place where people are condemned to death. The Corinthians conceived of themselves as wise, strong and beautiful. But apostolic existence and, yes, Christian existence as well are characterized by foolishness (in the eyes of the world), weakness and dishonor. Paul recounts the indignities he suffers as an apostle in 1 Corinthians 4:11-13. The "not yet" dimension of the kingdom shines through, for Paul is thirsty, hungry, poorly clothed, beaten and homeless. In this catalog of sufferings Paul also mentions the manual labor by which he supports himself. This strengthens the suggestion that his supporting himself financially constituted part of his sufferings since it is included in this list of woes. Paul is criticized mercilessly, he is persecuted, and he is considered as the dregs of the world. The Corinthians conceived of high status and success as an indication that they were under God's favor. Paul counters that the opposite is the case; those who are condemned by the world and rejected as nobodies are God's genuine messengers. Paul's suffering does not undercut the legitimacy of his message; it testifies to its authenticity and truth.

That suffering characterizes this age instead of the age to come is also communicated in 1 Corinthians 15:30-32, where Paul indicates that enduring suffering and pain is senseless if there is no future resurrection. He might as well pursue happiness in this world and try to escape all pain if the resurrection is untrue. And yet it is through such weakness and suffering that the powerful gospel was manifested, for Paul is the one who gave birth to the Corinthian church (1 Cor 4:15). The power of the kingdom is not absent but manifested through Paul (1 Cor 4:20). Indeed, Paul renounces rhetorical artistry in his preaching, and weakness and fear characterize his presence so that the Corinthians' faith does not rest on human wisdom but divine power (1 Cor 2:3-5). The manifest power of the kingdom, therefore, is expressed in and through the weakness and suffering of Paul. The manner in which Paul preaches, then, replicates the cross of Christ, for the message of the cross is foolish and weak in the eyes of those who are dazzled by human wisdom and signs and wonders (1 Cor 1:18-25). If the preaching of the cross is presented by speakers who impress others with their rhetorical brilliance, the cross is robbed of its power (1 Cor 1:17) and attention is fixed on, and glory given to, the human speaker. Paul eschewed rhetorical artistry and endured suffering so that his manner and message would function as a corollary to the cross of Christ.

The Corinthians were impressed by the credentials and ability of human messengers, and thus factions sprang up in support of Paul, Apollos, Peter and even Christ. They were convinced that they were people of the Spirit. But Paul counters that their preoccupation with and quarreling over human ministers reveal that they are acting like those of the flesh (1 Cor 3:1-4). The Corinthians believed that they were experiencing the powers of the coming age in an unprecedented way, but their strife over human ministers reflected their subjugation to the old age. Paul refuses to accommodate their vanity by comparing his effectiveness to that of Apollos. To be entranced by Paul or Apollos betrays an astounding lack of wisdom, for these men are simply servants and all growth comes from God (1 Cor 3:5-9). Boasting in human ministers is foolish, and it is a manifestation of the wisdom of the present world because it loses sight of God and the truth that all things are gifts to believers (1 Cor 3:18-23). Paul's suffering and weakness, then, are not incidental to his ministry but constitutive of it. His suffering reminded his hearers that the glory and power belonged to God rather than Paul. Any cultlike devotion to Paul or Apollos was fundamentally misguided since it detracted from the glory of God and honored servants rather than the only Lord.

Pauline Suffering According to 2 Corinthians

Since Paul was attacked by opponents for his weakness and suffering, it is not surprising that the most extended explanation of and apologetic for his suffering is found in 2 Corinthians. The integrity of 2 Corinthians is a matter of spirited debate. Many scholars think a number of different letters of Paul have been stitched together. Others think that at least chapters 10-13 were composed after chapters 1-9.[7] I am persuaded of the integrity of the entire letter, and I believe the letter is structured carefully, so that even chapters 10-13 were in Paul's mind from the inception of the letter.[8] Paul begins the letter by explaining his apostolic sufferings. God brings afflictions into his life and strengthens him in these afflictions, so that he, as an apostle, can in turn strengthen others suffering pain (2 Cor 1:3-7). Paul explains that God "comforts us in affliction" so that he can "comfort those in every affliction through the comfort with which we ourselves are comforted by God" (2 Cor 1:4). Paul's afflictions are for their "comfort and salvation" (2 Cor 1:6). We must notice here that Paul does not argue that he and the Corinthians both experi-

---

[7]For the view that chapters 10-13 were composed after chapters 1-9, see Victor P. Furnish, *II Corinthians*, AB (Garden City, N.Y.: Doubleday, 1984), pp. 30-54; Ralph P. Martin, *2 Corinthians*, WBC (Waco, Tex.: Word, 1986), pp. xl-xlvi.

[8]For a defense of this view, see Scott J. Hafemann, *2 Corinthians*, NIVAC (Grand Rapids, Mich.: Zondervan, 2000), pp. 31-32.

ence afflictions and mutually comfort one another.[9] God comforts *Paul* in his
sufferings, and in turn Paul comforts the Corinthians. He does not say that
the Corinthians also comfort Paul. Paul as an apostle fills a unique role in
transmitting comfort and salvation to his converts through his suffering.
Hence, his sufferings do not disqualify him from his apostolic office but are
the means by which God's Spirit is poured out in the lives of his converts.

The agitators complain that Paul's sufferings disqualify him from apostolic office, but Paul explains that his sufferings are the means by which the
Corinthians receive divine comfort and salvation. We see that Paul functions
as a corollary of the cross of Christ, in that his suffering is the path of salvation for the Corinthians, just as Christ's suffering is the way God's saving
power is released: "For he was crucified out of weakness, but he lives by the
power of God" (2 Cor 13:4). Paul boldly appropriates the image of the triumphal procession in 2 Corinthians 2:14 to convey the nature of his ministry.[10]
"Thanks be to God who always leads us to death in Christ and manifests
through him the fragrance of the knowledge of him in every place." After
winning a war, the Romans would conduct a triumphal procession in which
they would parade through the streets the booty captured from their enemies. They would also feature in the procession some of the people captured,
especially those who were taken from the upper classes. At the end of the
procession those enemies who were led in triumph were executed. The image
of the triumphal procession is used in Colossians 2:15, where God's victory
over the angelic powers in Christ is proclaimed. These enemies were routed
and executed at the cross. What is astonishing about 2 Corinthians 2:14 is that
Paul places *himself* as the object of the triumphal procession. Most English
versions, following the lead of Calvin, find it hard to believe that Paul could
make himself the object of the triumphal procession, and thus they make Paul
the subject.[11] The verse then reads that Paul is always triumphing through
Christ. They hesitate to identify Paul as the object, for how could Paul possibly be led to death in Christ? Nonetheless, identifying Paul as the subject of
the participle *(thriambeuonti)* is grammatically impossible. The verse *does* say
that God leads Paul to a triumphal procession in which he is being led to his

---

[9]For this view see Hafemann, *2 Corinthians,* pp. 62-63.

[10]My understanding of the triumphal procession depends on the work of Hafemann, *Suffering and the Spirit,* pp. 18-39.

[11]For John Calvin's interpretation of 2 Cor 2:14, see D. W. Torrance and T. F. Torrance, eds.,
*The Second Epistle of Paul the Apostle to the Corinthians and the Epistles to Timothy, Titus and
Philemon* (Grand Rapids, Mich.: Eerdmans, 1964), pp. 33-34.

death. Can a sensible meaning be attached to such an image? The metaphor is illuminating if Paul refers to his suffering as an apostle. The adversaries charged that Paul's sufferings disqualified him. Paul responds that his sufferings are chartered by God himself. Not only are his afflictions planned by God, they are the means by which the fragrance of the knowledge of Christ is emitted to the world. It is instructive that Paul shifts from the image of the triumphal procession to sacrificial imagery (2 Cor 2:14-16), for sacrificial language evokes the theme of suffering as well. The fragrant aroma that reaches the world is emitted from Paul as the suffering apostle.

The theme in 2 Corinthians 4:7-15 is remarkably similar. The treasure of the gospel is intentionally located in clay pots so that it will be evident to all that power resides in God rather than human messengers. Paul catalogues some of the sufferings he endures (2 Cor 4:8-9) to testify that God is the one who delivers him (2 Cor 1:8-11) from situations and experiences in which he is helpless. He carries about in his body the dying of Jesus by experiencing suffering on behalf of his Lord. The parallel in Galatians 6:17 is instructive ("For I bear on my body the marks of Jesus"), for the marks that Paul bears on his body were inflicted because he refused to submit to the mark of circumcision. In 2 Corinthians 4:10 the emphasis is on Paul's *decision* to carry in his body the dying of Jesus, and in doing so the life of Jesus is revealed in his body—"always carrying about the death of Jesus in the body, so that also the life of Jesus should be manifested in our body." The word for "death" (*nekrōsis*) refers to the process of being put to death, the decision to die with Jesus daily. Paul's commitment to suffer and die for Christ is the means by which the strength of Jesus and his life are revealed through Paul. The opponents insisted that signs and wonders were indications that God's Spirit was working, but Paul maintains that one must suffer for the life of Jesus to be revealed. Signs and wonders are not evil, but in themselves they do not provide a basis for legitimacy since those who are evil can also perform the miraculous (2 Thess 2:9). If 2 Corinthians 4:10 stresses Paul's *decision* to undergo suffering, then 2 Corinthians 4:11 focuses on *God's* role, in that he hands Paul over to suffering so Jesus' life will be manifested: "For we who live are always being handed over to death for Jesus' sake, so that also the life of Jesus should be manifested in our mortal flesh." The death that is operative in Paul's life through suffering is the means by which life is produced in the Corinthians (2 Cor 4:12). Paul is again, therefore, the corollary of Jesus, for just as Jesus died to convey life to his people, so too Paul must suffer for the life of God to be communicated to others. The "already but not yet" dimension of his theology is also apparent. The fullness of the kingdom has not yet come since Paul suffers and is destined to death; and yet the new era has been inaugurated, for in and through such suffering the life of God is revealed. The age to come has penetrated this age, and thus God brings life where there is death.

Nor is it persuasive for opponents to charge that Paul's sufferings disqualify him as an apostle. Paul counters with the opposite thesis. He does not argue that his sufferings have been minimal or that he is not as weak as it seems. Rather, he insists that his endurance of sufferings *commends* his ministry (2 Cor 6:3-10; 11:22-33). The catalog in 2 Corinthians 6:3-10 introduces a theme that we already noted in 1 Thessalonians: suffering alone does not commend Paul's ministry; his ethical integrity in the midst of such afflictions demonstrates that he is authentically from God. Thus Paul boasts in his weaknesses and sufferings because these are the means by which the power of Christ and his grace are communicated (2 Cor 12:7-10). As 2 Corinthians 12:9 says, God's "power is perfected in weakness." Paul's boasting in his accomplishments is, therefore, foolish (2 Cor 11:1—12:10), but not because boasting itself is wrong. Boasting in God and Christ is legitimate (Rom 5:11; 1 Cor 1:31), and rejoicing in weakness is also commended (2 Cor 12:10). Boasting in accomplishments is foolish because the focus shifts from the power of Christ to the ability of human beings. Paul reckons his boasting as foolish because it suggests that his own wisdom, strength or capacities somehow qualify him for the ministry. The fundamental error of the Corinthians is that they believe miracles, revelations and human ability commend one for ministry. By failing to understand that God works through human weakness the Corinthians have not progressed much beyond the issues in 1 Corinthians, for the message of the cross teaches that God's power is revealed in and through weakness (2 Cor 13:3-4). This explains partially why Paul refuses financial support from the Corinthians (2 Cor 11:7-15). His financial independence demonstrates that he preaches the gospel because of his love for the Corinthians, for love is willing to endure deprivation for the good of others. The false apostles, on the other hand, are pursuing the Corinthians for their own financial comfort (cf. 2 Cor 2:17; 11:12-15).

Paul is determined to be financially independent so that the opponents are demonstrated to be on a different plane from Paul. He refuses financial support "so that" the false apostles cannot boast that they are "just like" he is (2 Cor 11:12). He cuts off any "bridgehead" *(aphormē)* of opportunity (v. 12)— the word is used to describe the base of operations from which to launch an attack—from the opponents, so that they will have no grounds to compare themselves to Paul. Paul rejects these so-called leaders as "false apostles, deceitful workers, who disguise themselves as apostles of Christ" (2 Cor 11:13). Once again, Paul's integrity is featured in the way he conducts himself financially. He is keenly conscious that his sufferings and gospel are of no value if he does not live out the message with probity. This explains why he must rebut the charge that he made an idle promise to visit Corinth, a promise that he later reneged on. He insists that he behaved in an ethical manner in his relations to the Corinthians, and his refusal to visit cannot be chalked up to fleshly behavior (2 Cor 1:12). Paul affirms that the trustworthiness of the message he proclaims is bound up with his own ethical behavior (2 Cor 1:17-22). If he says yes when he really means no, then this would imply that God's word to human beings is both yes and no at the same time. But this is impossible, for all of God's saving promises are yes in Jesus Christ. The same God who validated (*bebaiōn*—2 Cor 1:21) and anointed *(chrisas)* Paul for ministry is the God who always stands true to his promises. If the messenger (Paul!) is flawed, then so is the message.

Paul invites his readers to examine his conduct, confident that he will be vindicated, thereby indicating how sure he was of his apostolic call (cf. 2 Cor 3:4, 12; 4:1). He explains (2 Cor 1:23—2:4) why he did not follow through on his initial plans to visit Corinth. The fundamental reason is that he does not enjoy disciplining those whom he loves but enjoys rejoicing with them over their progress in the faith. If he is compelled by the evil behavior of his converts, he will come in a stern and disciplinary mode (1 Cor 4:21; 2 Cor 12:19—13:4). Hence, in 2 Corinthians 10—13 Paul threatens the stubborn minority who have not repented that he will come in judgment if they do not repent. Nonetheless, he begins by emphasizing the "meekness and gentleness of Christ" (2 Cor 10:1), because like Christ he is giving them an opportunity to turn from their sin before he enforces judgment.[12] Paul does not perceive his fundamental role, however, in terms of a stern taskmaster and disciplinarian. He was called to build his converts up in the faith and not to tear them down (2 Cor 10:8; 12:19; 13:10). Even though his behavior appears on first glance to be inconsistent, his motives and actions have been dictated by the gospel in all his contacts with the Corinthians. Like Christ he offers salvation before pronouncing judgment.

Even Paul's apologetic on his behalf in 2 Corinthians is not ultimately

---

[12]So Hafemann, *2 Corinthians*, p. 393.

designed to protect his own reputation (2 Cor 12:19). He knows that the only way the Corinthians can be reconciled to God is if they are reconciled to his ministry (2 Cor 5:20—6:2; 6:11—7:2). If they throw their lot in with the false apostles (2 Cor 6:14—7:1), they have abandoned the gospel of Christ (2 Cor 11:2-4), for Paul's ministry is a corollary of Christ's suffering on their behalf (2 Cor 13:3-4).[13] Of course, the atonement of Christ was unique (2 Cor 5:18-21) and unrepeatable. And yet Paul's ministry mirrors Christ's, and thus to reject Paul is to repudiate the saving message of the cross.

Imprisonment and the Advance of the Gospel

The advance of Paul's mission, that is, the progress of the gospel, occurred through his suffering. This explains why Paul could rejoice in weakness (2 Cor 12:7-10), for he understood that weakness was the means by which the powerful word of the cross took effect in people's lives (1 Cor 2:3-5). As God led Paul to death, the fragrant aroma of the gospel was spread through the world. The death working in Paul led to life for others (2 Cor 4:12). When Paul inquires whether the Galatians have had a spell cast over them since they fail to see Jesus as the crucified one (Gal 3:1), he probably has in mind his own suffering as a corollary to Christ's. If they reject his gospel, which he announced as the suffering apostle, then they will also reject the crucified one. The Galatians embraced the gospel despite, or perhaps even because of, Paul's suffering (Gal 4:12-14). Their falling prey to circumcision signals that they are exulting in the flesh rather than God and that they are in danger of succumbing to circumcision to avoid suffering. Paul has the scars on his body that show he has followed the pathway of the cross (Gal 6:17). Indeed, the word "bear" (*bastazō*) is the same term used of Christ's carrying his cross (Jn 19:17) and is contained in Jesus' demand that disciples carry their cross daily (Lk 14:27). The Galatians' renunciation of the salvific efficacy of circumcision has brought suffering to Paul (Gal 1:10-17; 5:11). They must participate in such suffering if they are to stay true to the gospel (Gal 3:3; 4:29).

Paul's reflection on his suffering helps us understand how he can say in Ephesians that he is a prisoner of Christ for the sake of the Gentiles (Eph 3:1;

---

[13]Most scholars do not understand 2 Cor 6:14—7:1 as referring to the false apostles. The text is notoriously difficult, for some think it belongs to a different Pauline letter, while others think it is an interpolation. I think that the text is authentic and that it fits within the context of 2 Corinthians. For a defense of these two views and a history of interpretation, see William J. Webb, *Returning Home: New Covenant and Second Exodus as the Context for 2 Corinthians 6.14—7.1*, JSNTSup 85 (Sheffield: JSOT, 1993), pp. 16-30, 159-75, 184-99. For the view that the false apostles are indicted here, see Hafemann, *2 Corinthians*, pp. 279-88.

cf. Phil 1:7) and that his sufferings are for their glory (Eph 3:13), for Paul understands his afflictions as God's appointed means for the salvation of the Gentiles. Similarly, in 2 Timothy 2:9-10 Paul writes that he is not discouraged by his imprisonment because "the word of God is not bound" because of his incarceration; on the contrary, he "endures all things for the sake of the elect" that they might be saved. Apparently he views his suffering as the bridge-head for the advance of the gospel. His suffering is the means by which the Gentiles are saved. Such sufferings, then, are not to be interpreted as an irritating side effect of proclaiming the gospel but as the pathway to eschatological glory for the Gentiles. An illustration of how this works out is found in Philippians 1:12-18, where Paul is imprisoned for the sake of the gospel. His fetters, however, do not hinder the gospel from being proclaimed. In fact, the impact of his mission extends even further because of his incarceration. The gospel has spread among the Praetorian Guard because of his bonds; and fellow believers, seeing the courage of Paul, were emboldened to speak the message of the gospel. The apostolic suffering of Paul is the means God uses to convey his saving message to the world. Some of those proclaiming the gospel, Paul observes, did so with impure motives, hoping to bring grief to Paul. In any case, Paul rejoices because the gospel is being preached. And what precipitated its expansion is Paul's suffering.

Filling up Christ's Afflictions

The previous discussion should help us interpret the controversial text in Colossians 1:24, where Paul says that he fills up in his body the afflictions of Christ on behalf of the church. We can eliminate immediately any notion that Christ's work on the cross was inadequate and that Paul's sufferings play a role in securing forgiveness for human beings. This would contradict one of the major themes of Colossians, for Paul argues that all things were reconciled through the death of Christ (Col 1:20). The Colossian errorists promised divine fullness through mediators other than Christ, but Paul insists that all the fullness of deity dwells in Christ and that believers are full and complete in Christ (Col 2:9-10). In receiving forgiveness of sins in baptism, believers had received all they needed, including victory over angelic powers (Col 2:11-15). Those who suggested that they needed something besides Christ to attain divine fullness, such as abstinence from certain foods or adherence to calendrical observances were losing connection with the head, with Christ (Col 2:16-19). Those who belonged to Christ had died to the elements of the world (Col 2:20) and were raised with him (Col 3:1). It would seriously contradict the theme of Colossians, then, for Paul to even suggest that his own sufferings supplemented those of Christ on the cross. If he advocated such an idea, he would play into the hands of the opponents who denied the sufficiency of Christ. One of the major themes of Colossians is that the death and resurrection of Christ are all believers need. If Paul were putting his sufferings on the same level as Christ's, he could hardly protest against adversaries who trumpeted the importance of angels.

If Paul is not compromising the uniqueness and sufficiency of Christ's death, what does he have in mind when he says he fills up what is lacking in Christ's sufferings? Most scholars detect a reference to the messianic woes or birth pangs that must occur before the end (cf. Mt 24:3-8).[14] This view is much more likely than the view that Paul's sufferings add to Christ's atonement since it does not jar with other teachings in Colossians. Many scholars believe that Paul must be referring to these woes since this was a standard theme in Judaism. Such an interpretation is certainly possible, but another one seems even more likely in context. Paul does not refer to woes in general here but to his own sufferings, which "fill up" *(antanaplērō)* what is lacking in Christ's afflictions (Col 1:24). Nothing is said about other "woes" that contribute to the accession of the end, nor does the text forge a link between Paul's afflictions and the end. The focus is on *Paul's* sufferings, and such afflictions are noted in a passage that refers to his unique apostolic role as the apostle to the Gentiles. Paul is the minister appointed to proclaim the gospel in the whole world (Col 1:23), and it was God's plan that the word be "fulfilled" *(plērōsai)* through him (Col 1:25). The fulfillment of the word is defined in terms of the revelation of the mystery that has been hidden in the past but is now revealed to the saints, and the content of the mystery is identified as "Christ in you, the hope of glory" (Col 1:26-27). The distinctive aspect of the mystery is not merely that Christ resides in his people; it is that Christ resides in the *Gentiles.* Paul received a particular commission to bring the gospel to Gentiles, and thus he labors with intensity to bring every person to eschatological perfection (Col 1:28-29).

Seeing that the passage highlights Paul's unique apostolic commission to bring the gospel to the Gentiles helps us understand how he fills up the afflictions of Christ. We must grasp the link between Paul's "filling up" *(antanaplērō)* Christ's afflictions and his "fulfilling" *(plērōsai)* the word of God (Col 1:24-25). The fulfillment of God's word, as the subsequent verses show,

---

[14]See, e.g., Peter O'Brien, *Colossians, Philemon,* WBC (Waco, Tex.: Word, 1982), pp. 77-80.

relates to bringing the gospel to Gentiles so that they are perfected in Christ and come to "the full assurance [plērophorias] of understanding, to the knowledge of the mystery of God, which mystery is Christ" (Col 2:2). The *means* by which Paul "fulfills" the word of God by bringing the gospel to the Gentiles is suffering. The "filling up" of Christ's afflictions is the pathway by which the gospel is "fulfilled" in the lives of Gentiles. When Paul speaks of what is lacking in Christ's afflictions, he is not suggesting that Christ's death was insufficient inherently. Paul through his sufferings, however, *extends* the message of Christ's all-sufficient death to the Gentiles, for such a message was concealed from the Gentiles during the life of Jesus of Nazareth. The commission to reveal to the Gentiles the message of the gospel has been given to Paul, and Jesus never fulfilled such a role. What is lacking in Christ's afflictions is that the benefit of those afflictions had not yet been proclaimed among the Gentiles. In salvation history the unique privilege of bringing the good news of Christ to the Gentiles belongs to Paul. And like Christ, Paul heralds a message advanced in and through his suffering. Paul's sufferings, in other words, are a corollary of Christ's. They are not of equal importance since the divine fullness is secured through Christ alone (Col 2:9-10). No suggestion that the afflictions of Christ and the sufferings of Paul are equivalent is tolerated. And yet Paul's sufferings mirror and reflect what Christ has done, so that the messenger in this sense replicates the life of the one proclaimed.

Conclusion

It is significant that suffering is the means by which Paul extends the message to Gentiles. Such suffering highlights the weakness of the messenger and points hearers to God as the all-sufficient one. God's work in and through a weak and suffering Paul indicates that the power comes from God rather than Paul. The age to come has invaded this present evil age since God reveals his life in earthen vessels. Suffering also validates the integrity of Paul as a messenger, for his willingness to undergo pain indicates that he does not proclaim the gospel as a way to get rich or to promote his reputation on earth. Paul's sufferings are a corollary to the sufferings of Christ inasmuch as they are the means by which the message is brought to the Gentiles. It is not the case that God desired Paul to bring the message to the Gentiles and afflictions got in the way. Suffering was the intended means by which the gospel would be proclaimed by Paul to the Gentiles. Thereby the focus remains on God and Christ, and glory does not redound to the proclaimer but to the proclaimed.

5

DISHONORING GOD

The Violation of
God's Law

The Pauline mission would be superfluous if this world were paradise. No plausible reason for his gospel exists if the worldm is suffused with goodness. Virtually every human being senses that something has gone wrong in the world. Paul, as an apostle of the gospel, proclaims both the problem with the world and its remedy. The one is inexplicable without the other, and in this chapter and the next we will explore the problem in preparation for examining the remedy in subsequent chapters.

The Fundamental Sin

Sin is often defined as a failure to keep God's commands. Violating what God has ordained is certainly sin, and Paul indicts both Jews and Gentiles for violating God's standards. But we fail to grasp the depth of Pauline theology if we restrict the definition of sin to a violation of what God commands. Instead of viewing sin as a rejection of God personally, we may understand it primarily in terms of failing to live up to a standard. Sin certainly involves the failure to heed God's commands. What must be emphasized, however, is that sin is first and foremost a rejection of the supremacy of God and his lordship over our lives.

Supporting the idea that sin is fundamentally a refusal to honor and praise

God is Romans 1:18-32. It is particularly interesting that Paul's fullest explanation of sin is found in Romans (Rom 1:18—3:20) because this is the only letter written to a church that was not established by Paul or one of his coworkers. In this explanation we see that God's wrath is revealed from heaven because human beings in their ungodliness and unrighteousness suppress the truth about him (Rom 1:18). Identifying the reason for God's wrath is particularly instructive. Paul affirms in both Romans 1:19 and Romans 1:21 that all people have knowledge of God. God has made it clear to all that he exists, that he is God and that he is powerful (Rom 1:20). Human beings perceive these truths about God through the created order, by observing what God has made; and yet they intentionally suppress the truth they know about God through the created world.

A brief aside is necessary here since this text has often been drawn into the orbit of discussions on natural theology. Paul is not suggesting that philosophical arguments for the existence of God are needed. On the contrary, he maintains that all people know that God exists and that he is powerful. The truth of God's existence and power may be suppressed (Rom 1:18), and yet it is still present in *all* human beings. Nor does the text intimate that people come to belief in God's existence and power through a long chain of reasoning. Paul reflects on the experience of *all human beings*, not on the ability of a few gifted philosophers. The belief in God's existence and power is stitched into human beings in such a way that all people inevitably conclude that there is a God when they perceive the created order.

The instinctive response of all human beings to the created world is to acknowledge the existence and power of God. Paul does not attempt to locate *when* people come to the conclusion that there is a God. He asserts *that* they know God. People are not encouraged to ransack their past to identify the time when they came to the knowledge of God. Such an individualistic and psychological reading veers away from the purpose of the text. The idea is not that we should explore our consciousness to specify when we realized God exists. Instead, Paul asserts that all people without exception know that God is, that he is powerful and that they owe him glory and honor (Rom 1:21). However, they have suppressed this knowledge of God (Rom 1:18) and turned deliberately away from serving and worshiping him to serving and worshiping the creature rather than the Creator (Rom 1:18-25). Thus, the knowledge of God that all people have through the natural world is not a *saving* knowledge. They know God's ordinance, and yet they encourage people to practice evil anyway (Rom 1:32). Their thinking about God has become confused and clouded because they have refused to honor and praise him (Rom 1:21-23). No platform is given to natural theology in service of the truth. The knowledge that all people have of God is rejected "so that they are without excuse" (Rom 1:20).

We are now prepared to identify the fundamental reason why God pours out his wrath on the world: even though all people know God as God and perceive his power, they refuse to glorify him as God and give thanks to him (Rom 1:21). The root sin is not lack of knowledge, for human beings *know* God is God; nor is it our finitude since honoring God as God is an acceptance of our creatureliness. The heart of sin is the refusal to worship God and give him the supreme place in our lives. This same view is reflected in Wisdom of Solomon 14:27: "For the worship of idols that are not to be named is the source and cause and end of every evil." Human beings, by rejecting the one true God and turning to idolatry, mirror the sin committed by Adam and Eve in the garden. Eve sinned, as Genesis 3:1-6 indicates, because she failed to trust the goodness of God and because she desired to be like God. Adam and Eve wanted to supplant God with a rival. They were not grateful for God's care for them but suspiciously believed that he was withholding what was best from them. According to Paul, such thoughts indicate the foolishness of human reasoning (Rom 1:21-23). The vanity of human reasoning and the darkness that obscures the mind (Eph 4:17) from truth stem from the rejection of God for idols (Eph 4:18). Once humans' reason is severed from God's lordship, they erect idols. And turning to idols is vanity because idols are not genuine gods (1 Cor 8:4-6). The "truth" about God (see Rom 1:18, 25) is that he is the one and only Lord. The "lie" teaches that worshiping the creature (Rom 1:25) is the path to blessing. Those who abandon the Lord and Creator follow the pathway of Adam and Eve in the garden.[1]

---

[1]Some scholars think Paul refers to Adam in Rom 1, but it is more likely that the experience of all human beings mirrors the experience of Adam. In Rom 1:23 Paul also echoes the experience of Israel (cf. Ps 106:20; Jer 2:11). Some commentators conclude from this evidence that the indictment in Rom 1:18-32 actually includes Israel. See Jouette M. Bassler, *Divine Impartiality: Paul and a Theological Axiom*, SBLDS 59 (Chico, Calif.: Scholars Press, 1982), p. 122; Glenn N. Davies, *Faith and Obedience in Romans: A Study of Romans 1—4*, JSNT-Sup 39 (Sheffield: JSOT, 1990), pp. 47-52. This is doubtful since the polemic found here is typical of the kind of critiques Jews would level against Gentiles (e.g., Wis 11:1—16:4). Nor would homosexuality be a typical vice in the Jewish community (Rom 1:26-27) since Jews universally condemned the practice (Gen 19:1-28; Lev 18:22; 20:13; Deut 23:17-18; Wis 14:26; *T. Levi* 17:11; *Sib. Or.* 3:596-600), whereas the morality of homosexuality was the subject of some debate in the Greco-Roman world. However, the allusion to Israel's idolatry foreshadows Paul's attack against the Jews in Romans 2. Paul follows the pattern of Amos, who begins by indicting the Gentiles (Amos 1:3—2:3) and then turns his criticisms against the Jews. Paul also imitates the surprise tactics of Nathan, whose parable incited David to condemn the man who stole another's precious and only ewe lamb (2 Sam 12:1-14), only

We began our discussion of Romans 1:18-25 by noting that God's wrath is revealed because of the ungodliness and unrighteousness of human beings who suppress the truth. The nature of human unrighteousness and ungodliness is clear from Paul's explanation in Romans 1:19-25. Human unrighteousness and ungodliness consists in the abandonment of the one and only God and the turn toward idolatry. The reason God is so angry, then, is that people refuse to honor, praise and thank him. God is wrathful because his lordship has been denied and human beings have enthroned other lords instead. The fundamental problem is not that people have committed "sins"; it is that they have committed "sin," that is, they repudiated the worship of God and embraced worship of the creature. This is borne out by Romans 1:24, 26, 28. Three times Paul says that God "handed over" (paredōken) people to sin. In each instance the reason for his handing them over is attributed to their rejection of God. All human sins, in other words, have their fountainhead in idolatry. The degradation and blight of sin are a consequence of the failure to honor and praise God.

Paul is not being innovative here, for locating the origin of other sins in idolatry was part of the stock of Jewish tradition (Wis 14:12-14). Nonetheless, it would be a mistake to downplay this theme simply because it exists in Jewish tradition, for it is at the center of Paul's understanding of God. Sin does not primarily consist in violating God's commands; it involves the repudiation and rejection of a person. Paul does not deny, of course, that sin also injures other human beings. The list of vices in Romans 1:28-32 contains many examples in which humans are harmed by one another's sins. What Paul stresses, however, is that the horizontal dimension of sin exists because of the vertical rejection of God. This point is illustrated in 1 Corinthians 8:12: "Thus by sinning against your brothers and wounding their conscience which is weak you sin against Christ." When the strong ignore the consciences of the weak, they sin against them. And yet when they sin against the weak, they also sin against Christ. Ultimately, sin is directed against God and Christ.

The same perspective peeks through when Paul indicts people for coveting in that he links coveting with idolatry (Eph 5:5; Col 3:5). The convergence of the first and tenth commandments of the Decalogue is instructive, especially since the tenth commandment is the only one that forbids *internal*

---

to discover that the parable was a trap that snared David in his sin. In Rom 1:18-32 Paul begins by affirming the Jewish hostility to Gentile vices and then turns the argument against the Jews in Rom 2. Israel is not specifically indicted in Rom 1:23. The Gentiles are targeted because they are committing idolatry, just as Israel did in the Old Testament. Paul is laying a trap for Israel, however, and he will spring it in chapter 2.

desires. All the other commandments proscribe *external* actions. Paul clarifies that coveting, or greed, is idolatry—those who desire anything more than God violate the first and central commandment, which requires devotion to and service of the one and only God. Violating the other commands of the law also involves the rejection of God's lordship and honor. In Romans 2 Paul labors to show the Jews that they face the prospect of judgment since they have transgressed the law. No covenantal advantage accrues to them if they do not keep the Torah, and Paul provides ample evidence of their failure to keep God's commands. Transgressing the law is so heinous because those who disobey the Torah dishonor God (Rom 2:23). God's name is criticized among the Gentiles because of the disobedience of the Jews (Rom 2:24; Is 52:5). Thus, the Jews, despite being God's covenant people, are guilty of the same sin as the Gentiles. The Gentiles dishonored God by rejecting the revelation in nature and turning to idolatry. The Jews brought injury upon God's name by failing to keep his law. In both instances, bringing dishonor on God's name is the fundamental sin.

Sin and the Law

The Jews were convinced that Gentiles dishonored God's name and therefore deserved judgment. On the other hand, God had elected Israel to be his people, had entered into covenant with them and had given them his law.[2] If the Israelites were the people of God, then why did God's saving promises remain unfulfilled? A good place to begin in answering this question is Romans 2. When Paul addresses the Jews here, it is clear that he speaks against the Jewish presumption that their election as God's people will shield them from God's wrath. They believe that the riches of God's kindness will preserve them from judgment (Rom 2:4). A similar sentiment is expressed in Wisdom of Solomon 15:2, "For even if we sin, we are yours, knowing your power." Apparently, some Jews interpreted their election as evidence of

---

[2]It has been suggested that Paul's theology of the law is logically inconsistent and contradictory. See Heikki Räisänen, *Paul and the Law* (Philadelphia: Fortress, 1983). This is not the place to respond in detail to Räisänen, but it is antecedently unlikely that Paul was so confused in his thinking about the law. Before he was a Christian, he served as a Pharisee and lived in utter devotion to the law (Phil 3:6). It is likely, therefore, that he carefully reflected on the role of the law when he became convinced of Jesus' messiahship. Those who think that Paul's view is "shot through" with contradictions have probably not posed the right questions or located the right "map" by which to read Paul. In defense of consistency in Paul's view of the law, see Thomas R. Schreiner, *The Law and Its Fulfillment: A Pauline Theology of Law* (Grand Rapids, Mich.: Baker, 1993); Frank Thielman, *Paul and the Law: A Contextual Approach* (Downers Grove, Ill.: InterVarsity Press, 1994).

God's partiality toward them (Rom 2:11), expecting—because they possessed the law—preservation from God's wrath on the last day (Rom 2:12-20). The covenantal sign of circumcision (Rom 2:25) was understood as an indication of God's favor, protecting them from God's judgment.

Paul punctures their presumption by appealing to God's impartiality in judgment in Romans 2. Those Jews who pass judgment on Gentiles will face condemnation themselves (Rom 2:1). Condemnation is not threatened simply because the Jews *judged* others. Otherwise, Paul would face judgment for condemning both Jews *and* Gentiles in Romans 1—3! Paul expects all to agree (i.e., to pass judgment) that the Gentiles warrant judgment for their behavior. The line of thought in Romans 2:1 explains why the Jews will experience judgment. Even though they condemn Gentiles for evil, *they practice the same things* (cf. Rom 2:2-3). The Jewish judgment of Gentiles would be legitimate if the Jews had repented from their own evil and trusted Jesus Christ. Instead, they were judging Gentiles despite the fact that their own hearts were hard and unrepentant (Rom 2:4-5). In essence Paul argues that the Jews have come no further than the incident of the golden calf (Ex 32—34), for they are still "stiff-necked" (*sklērotēs*, Rom 2:5). The idolatry of the Israelites at Horeb is attributed to their being a stiff-necked people (cf. Ex 32:9; 33:3, 5; 34:9; Deut 9:6, 13). Just as the golden-calf incident severed the covenant, so too Israel's sin in Paul's day invalidates their claim to salvation. Nonetheless, Israel expected God in his kindness to save them from his wrath on the day of judgment. Paul emphatically rejects such an idea, insisting that God impartially judges everyone by his or her works (Rom 2:6-11). If one practices evil, whether one is a Jew or a Gentile, then God's wrath will be one's portion. If one does what is good, then one's reward will be eternal life.

The Jews ought not to think that possessing the law is itself inherently salvific, for merely hearing the law does not preserve them from God's judgment (Rom 2:12-13). Paul argues that even Gentiles know the moral norms of God's law, and their occasional obedience of those norms does not spare them on the day of judgment (Rom 2:14-16). Thus, the Jews should hardly think that mere knowledge of the law is salutary, for even Gentiles, despite lacking the written Torah, are aware of the moral norms disseminated in the law. Paul does not deny that knowledge of the law is a privilege that belongs to the Jews (Rom 2:17-20); he charges them with transgressing the law that they proclaim to be their guide (Rom 2:21-24). The Jews cannot wrap themselves in the mantle of election, using circumcision as a magical talisman to ward off judgment (Rom 2:25), for circumcision is meaningless if not accompanied by obedience. The true Jew and true circumcision are matters of the heart and the result of the Spirit's work (Rom 2:28-29).

Some have denied the credibility of Paul's argument by pointing out that Paul's charges against the Jews in Romans 2:21-22 are wildly exaggerated.[3] The notion that all Jews rob pagan temples, commit adultery and steal seems impossible to believe. Some commentators have tried to resolve the problem by suggesting that Paul imitates Jesus' teaching in the Sermon on the Mount; it is adultery in the heart and the desire to steal that are criticized. This solution is untenable since Paul gives no hint that *internal* attitudes are the issue. The Jews are condemned for their behavior—behavior that is visible and obvious to all. We do not have to concede that Paul's words are wildly off the mark. He does not say, in fact, that *all* Jews actually steal, commit adultery and rob temples. What he does maintain is that they have transgressed the law in which they boast (Rom 2:23). The specific sins named are colorful examples to illustrate the general principle that the Jews violate the very law they proclaim. Paul does not intend to say that *every* Jew commits the particular sins itemized. They serve as examples for the theme that Paul's Jewish contemporaries have disobeyed the law.

Nor would Paul's argument necessarily be rejected by his Jewish peers. The argument in Romans 2 is informed by Paul's understanding of the Old Testament scriptures. God threatened the people with the covenant curses of Deuteronomy (Deut 27:15—28:68; cf. Lev 26:14-39) if they violated Torah, and he threatened them with exile if they persisted in disobedience. These threats became a reality in both the Assyrian (722 B.C.) and Babylonian exiles (586 B.C.) in which the people of God were deported from their land. A reference to exile is strengthened by the citation of Isaiah 52:5 ("continually, all day long, my name is despised," NRSV) in Romans 2:24, for the Gentiles' reviling of God's name occurs because Israel suffers oppression. The Jews during Paul's day were not substantially better off, for they were under the authority of Rome. Submission to Rome was a reality because the nation had fallen short of what the Torah demanded. If Israel had kept God's law, they would be free from the yoke of Rome (cf. 4 *Ezra* 9:5-9). Thus, when Paul charges the Jews with sin, his argument is plausible, though it is not clear that all Jews would agree that they were in exile. In any case, the promises of the Old Testament regarding Israel had not yet become a reality, and the Old Testament teaches that such promises

---

[3]See esp. Räisänen, *Paul and the Law*, p. 101; E. P. Sanders, *Paul, the Law, and the Jewish People* (Philadelphia: Fortress, 1983), p. 125.

will be fulfilled when the Spirit comes (Is 44:3; Jer 31:31-34; Ezek 11:19-20; 36:26-27) and softens people's hearts so that they are enabled to keep the Torah. Paul's indictment of his fellow Jews was not baseless, nor was it marked by reckless overstatements; it followed the pattern of the Old Testament prophets. The Jews are judged because of their failure to obey the Torah.

Works of Law

The idea that all are sinners and all transgress the law is also supported by Paul's statements about works of law. What Paul means by the phrase *works of law (erga nomou)*, however, is sharply disputed, and thus we will need to investigate the meaning of the term in some detail.[4] Paul only uses the term on eight occasions, and it only appears in "negative" contexts. In Galatians 3:10 those who rely on works of law are said to be under a curse, while in Galatians 3:2, 5 receiving the Spirit by works of the law is excluded. The Spirit was given by hearing with faith and not by works of law. In the remaining five instances Paul denies that righteousness can be obtained by works of law (Rom 3:20, 28; three denials in Gal 2:16) and maintains that righteousness comes through faith in Jesus Christ. The curse in Galatians 3:10 is the antithesis of the blessing of Abraham (Gal 3:9, 14), and the blessing of Abraham is marked by the promise of the Spirit (Gal 3:14). The question that must be asked is why people cannot receive the Spirit or obtain righteousness by works of law.

We begin by determining the proper definition of the term *works of law*. Some identify works of law with a legalistic attitude. Those who rely on the works of the law believe that they can earn favor with God by keeping the law. Rudolf Bultmann, in particular, has exerted tremendous influence in the dissemination of this view.[5] He argues, in fact, that even if people kept the law perfectly, they would still be cursed since the *very desire* to keep the law is sin. The reason such an attitude is sinful is because it springs from a desire to earn favor with God. A very different understanding of the term has been proposed by James Dunn, in what has come to be called "the new perspective" on Paul.[6]

---

[4] For a more detailed study of the term *works of law*, which also refers the reader to the work of the various authors mentioned here, see my discussion in *The Law and Its Fulfillment*, pp. 41-71.

[5] Rudolf Bultmann, *Theology of the New Testament* (New York: Scribner, 1951, 1955), 1:264; 2:52-53.

[6] See James D. G. Dunn, "The New Perspective on Paul," *BJRL* 65 (1983): 95-122; "Works of the Law and the Curse of the Law (Galatians 3.10-14)," *NTS* 31 (1985): 523-42; "Yet Once More—'the Works of the Law': A Response," *JSNT* 46 (1992): 99-117; *The Theology of Paul the Apostle* (Grand Rapids, Mich.: Eerdmans, 1998), pp. 354-71.

Dunn, influenced by the work of E. P. Sanders, claims the notion that Judaism is legalistic is a myth imposed on the Pauline material by those who read Paul through the lens of the Reformation. *Works of law* is not shorthand for *legalism*, according to Dunn. The term focuses instead on the parts of the law that separate Jews from Gentiles, particularly circumcision, sabbath and food laws. Paul's rejection of works of law in Galatians occurs immediately after the incident at Antioch where the proper stance toward food laws was debated (Gal 2:11-14, 16). We also know from both Galatians and Romans that the necessity of circumcision was the subject of intense controversy. When we put Paul in his first-century context, says Dunn, we see that he denied righteousness by works of law because such works separated Jews from Gentiles. Paul objected to the idea that Gentiles had to become Jews to enter the people of God. Practices like sabbath, circumcision and food laws were the main "identity markers" or "badges" for Judaism in Paul's day. According to Dunn, we should not think that self-achievement or legalism was the problem with those who touted works of law. Paul objected to their *nationalism*, their *ethnocentricism*, their *particularism*—not to their *legalism* or *activism*. What troubled Paul was that some Jews excluded Gentiles on racial and ethnic grounds. Paul, as the missionary to the Gentiles, desired to *include* Gentiles in the people of God without imposing Jewish ethnic and cultural requirements on them.

Over against the views sketched in above, I argue that *works of law* refers to the deeds or actions demanded by the law. The term *works of law* is not used often in Jewish literature previous to or contemporaneous with Paul. In the texts in which the term appears, the reference is to the entire law. For example, in the Dead Sea Scrolls the phrase *works of the law* refers to the whole law (4QFlor 1:7), for there is no contextual indication of any limitation or focus on part of the law (cf. also *2 Bar.* 4:9; 57:2). The similar phrase *in his works of the law* (1QS 5:21; 6:18) also broadly designates the whole law. We find support for this in 1QS 5:8, where the adherents pledge to "return to the law of Moses according to *all* which he commanded." Joseph Fitzmyer rightly concludes from these and other texts in the Qumran literature (cf. 1QpHab 7:11; 8:1; 12:4; 11QT^a 56:3; 4QMMT^a) that *works of law* in Paul designates the law in its entirety.[7]

Nor is there any persuasive evidence that Paul departed from his Jewish contemporaries when he used the phrase *works of law*. The word *works (erga)*

---

[7]Joseph A. Fitmyer, "Paul's Jewish Background and the Deeds of the Law," in *According to Paul: Studies in the Theology of the Apostle* (New York: Paulist, 1993), pp. 18-35. For another perspective, see James D. G. Dunn, "4QMMT and Galatians," *NTS* 43 (1997): 47-53.

is defined generally in Romans 9:11-12 as "doing anything good or evil." Indeed, *erga* in Paul invariably refers to actions done, whether good or evil (Rom 2:6; 4:2, 6; 9:32; 11:6; 13:12; 2 Cor 11:15; Gal 5:19; Eph 2:9-10; 5:11; Col 1:21; 1 Tim 2:10; 5:10, 25; 6:18; 2 Tim 1:9; 4:14; Tit 1:16; 2:7, 14; 3:5, 8, 14). Even if one were to place Ephesians and the Pastorals in the post-Pauline category, it is telling that in these epistles the term *works* is used in the broadest sense. One could object that the term *works of law* must be distinguished from the word *works*; and thus even if *works* is a broad and general term, *works of law* still focuses on certain parts of the law. Such a theory, though plausible, is not borne out by the evidence, as we shall see.

It is instructive to see in Romans 3—4 that Paul glides from the idea that righteousness is not by "works of law" (Rom 3:20, 28) to the notion that right-eousness is not by "works" (Rom 4:2, 6). Paul uses the word *works* rather than the phrase *works of law* in Romans 4:2 because he speaks of Abraham, who did not live under the Sinai law (but cf. Gen 26:5). The "works" in Abraham's case cannot be confined to sabbath, food laws and circumcision. Similarly, the works that David lacked and for which he needed forgiveness (Rom 4:6-8) can scarcely be restricted to laws that erect barriers between Jews and Gentiles, for David was circumcised, observed sabbath and adhered to the food laws. It is much more likely that Paul understood David to be asking for forgiveness for his sins of adultery and murder (2 Sam 11—12). Convincing evidence that "works" in Romans 4 focuses on the areas of the law that segregate Jews from Gentiles is lacking. The close thematic connection between Romans 3—4 leads us to the further conclusion that the phrase *works of law* should not be defined in a way radically different from the term *works* in Romans 4:1-8.

This is not to say that *works of law* is identical in meaning with the term *works*; nor should we deny that issues of inclusivism and exclusivism were important in Pauline theology. Dunn rightly sees that the issue of boundary markers precipitated the debate on "works of law" (Gal 2:11-21). Nevertheless, *works of law* should be defined as the deeds or actions *demanded by the law*, whereas the term *works* refers to all deeds or actions that are done (including deeds and actions not mentioned in the law). Thus, the terms *works of law* and *works* are not absolutely equivalent. The two terms overlap in that both refer to actions or deeds performed by human beings. It would be a mistake to assume the phrase *works of law* in Romans 3 refers specifically to food law, circumcision and sabbath, given that the parallel term *works* in Romans 4 has a broader connotation. In both texts Paul denies that one is justified by any human works, whether those written in the law or human works generally. Once again the evidence of the later Pauline writings is instructive, for when Paul summarizes his theology later in his life, he excludes salvation by means of works (Eph 2:9; 2 Tim 1:9; Tit 3:5).[8] Nothing is said about works of law. Even if we have a post-Pauline writer in Ephesians and the Pastorals, this writer, one of the earliest interpreters of Paul, understood his rejection of "works of law" in terms of "works" generally, suggesting that Dunn's understanding of "works of law" was not shared by Paul's earliest interpreters. The term *works* can replace *works of law* in the later letters since the latter is a subset of the former. The most convenient way to summarize Paul's teaching is to speak against salvation by works. But such a summary would be ineffective if "works of law" focused on ethnocentricism and nationalism, for these ideas are lacking in the term *works* in the later Pauline writings. By referring to "works" in a general way, the later Pauline writings furnish evidence that the term *works of law* designates all the deeds or actions commanded by the law.

The flow of thought in Romans also supports the idea that *works of law* refers to the deeds required by the law. Romans 1:18—3:20 constitutes Paul's accusation against Jews and Gentiles. In Romans 3:19-20 he summarizes the case he has made, concluding with the assertion that no one "will be justified by works of law, for through the law comes the knowledge of sin." Paul provides a reason (note the *gar* translated "for") why works of law will not justify: that is, through the law people are exposed as sinners. People are condemned through works of law because they fail to keep the law; they do not practice the law's demands and requirements. The exegesis of Romans 2 presented above supports such a reading. The Jews are charged in Romans 2 for failing to keep the law. They are not liable to judgment because of their ethnocentricism or exclusivism, though they believe that their special status before God exempts them from judgment. Nowhere in Romans 2 does Paul suggest that the Jews will be condemned because they *exclude Gentiles*. He maintains that they will be judged because they violate the very law in which they boast. Romans 3:23 nicely sums up Paul's main point, "All have sinned and fall short of the glory of God." Failure to practice God's requirements is the reason for God's judgment.

---

[8]The view that the later writings in the Pauline corpus support the view of "works of law" argued for here is cogently defended by I. Howard Marshall, "Salvation, Grace and Works in the Later Writings in the Pauline Corpus," *NTS* 42 (1996): 339-58. My own view is that Paul wrote both Ephesians and the Pastorals.

Galatians 3:10 supports the same conclusion. Paul asserts that those who are of works of law are under God's curse. The reason he gives *(gar)* stems from Deuteronomy 27:26—"Cursed is everyone who does not abide by all things written in the book of the law to do them." The curse falls if one does not keep "all things" *(pasin)* written in the Torah.[9] It is interesting to note that the word *pasin* is lacking in the MT but is supplied by the LXX. Despite some scholars' reservations, Paul's argument is most naturally understood if an implied proposition is supplied. He assumes that no one can do all things written in the law. The flow of thought in the verse can be set forth as follows: (1) Those who do not keep the whole law are cursed; (2) no one keeps the whole law; and (3) therefore, those who are of works of law are cursed. The fundamental reason for the curse is that people do not and cannot keep the law.

Paul expresses the same thought elsewhere in Galatians. The Galatian opponents are following the wrong path in trying to impose circumcision on Gentile converts, for "they themselves do not keep the law" (Gal 6:13). Paul also reminds the Galatians that if they accept circumcision, then they are obligated "to keep the whole law" (Gal 5:3). The threat is only forceful if keeping the whole law is deemed to be impossible by Paul, for the opponents could have easily replied, "Keeping the entire law is precisely what we intend to do and should do." What Paul suggests, though, is that such law keeping is doomed to failure because no one can keep all that is demanded. Thus, those who endeavor to keep the law to obtain righteousness will be cursed on the last day since they disobey the law's commands.

Restricting (or even focusing) the term *works of law* to apply to those parts of the law that distinguish Jews from Gentiles, therefore, does not satisfactorily account for the evidence from contemporaneous Jewish usage, from the Pauline usage of the term and from the context in which the term is used. Nor is the Bultmannian notion that people are condemned *even if they desire to keep the law* found in Paul. Paul does criticize those who wish to *boast* in their works, but it is confusing and misleading to say that even the desire to keep the law is sinful. We have seen, particularly in Romans 1:18—

---

[9]Paul's interpretation of Deut 27:26 is shared by Justin Martyr in his *Dialogue with Trypho.* Indeed, the statements uttered by Trypho in the dialogue suggest that Paul does not distort the Jewish point of view. For an instructive comparison between Paul and Justin, see Graham Stanton, "The Law of Moses and the Law of Christ—Galatians 3:1—6:2" in *Paul and the Mosaic Law: The Third Durham-Tübingen Research Symposium on Earliest Christianity and Judaism (Durham, September, 1994),* ed. by James D. G. Dunn, WUNT 89 (Tübingen: J. C. B. Mohr, 1996), pp. 99-116.

3:20, that both Jews and Gentiles are condemned *for failing to keep God's commands*—not for desiring to keep them.

Paul's insistence that righteousness and the Spirit are not received by works of law fits with what we have seen in Romans 1—2. People cannot obtain righteousness or the Spirit by works because of human sin. All people violate the law, and thus instead of being pronounced righteous via the law, they are found to be guilty and answerable before God for their evil deeds (Rom 3:19).

Boasting and the Law

Pride in 1 Corinthians. The desire to keep the law is not sinful per se, and yet the Bultmann school rightly puts its finger on a central human problem in seeing a Pauline polemic against boasting. The root problem with the divisions over ministers in Corinth was pride. The Corinthians were entranced with the wisdom of the world and had forgotten that God uses the foolish message of the cross to save (1 Cor 1:18-25). God chose the foolish, weak and disreputable so that no one would boast before him and so that people would boast only in God (1 Cor 1:29, 31). Relying on human wisdom is perilous because then one's faith rests on such wisdom rather than on the power of God (1 Cor 2:5). Boasting in ministers is folly since they are mere human beings and the Corinthians have all things in Christ (1 Cor 3:21-23). Paul writes so the Corinthians will not be puffed up with pride (1 Cor 4:6). Apparently they have forgotten that everything they have is a gift; otherwise, they would not boast as if they themselves, apart from grace, had obtained something significant (1 Cor 4:7). Their pride contributed to the view that they were already reigning in the kingdom (1 Cor 4:8-13). Paul will come with severity against those who are puffed up with pride (1 Cor 4:18-21) and is amazed that pride exists when incest is being practiced (1 Cor 5:1-2, 6).

The pride of those who eat food offered to idols manifests itself in the debate over such food (1 Cor 8:1—11:1). Those who feel free to eat are impressed with their theological acumen, and they dismiss the weak as mere novices in the faith. They have forgotten that knowledge without love leads to pride (1 Cor 8:1-3) and are in danger of being destroyed by their arrogance (1 Cor 10:19-22). Pride is also evident in the debate over the proper attire and behavior of women (1 Cor 11:2-16; 14:33b-36). Some refuse to accede to the customs practiced by all other churches and instead contravene the good order established in the churches. The rich display their arrogance toward the poor by despising the church and using the Lord's Supper as an occasion to satisfy their own desires (1 Cor 11:17-22). The Corinthians' overheated spirituality came to a climax in their use of spiritual gifts (1 Cor 12—14). Apparently they believed that the gift of tongues transported them to angelic levels (1 Cor 13:1) and were tempted to disdain those who had less-flashy gifts.

Pride in a diversity of contexts. Pride is the very core of sin, for people boast in themselves rather than God (1 Cor 1:29, 31). They estimate themselves as the origin of good instead of attributing everything they have accomplished to God (1 Cor 4:7). It is unsurprising, then, that pride often surfaces as a problem in the Pauline epistles. The adversaries in 2 Corinthians 10—13 are consumed with pride. They indulge in comparisons to boast in their accomplishments (2 Cor 10:13-18). Paul boasts as well in his work, but contrary to the opponents' boasting, his boast is ultimately in the Lord (2 Cor 10:17). The opponents, on the other hand, boast in the flesh (2 Cor 11:18) and proclaim themselves as superior ministers of Christ (2 Cor 11:22-23). Paul emphasizes the weakness of his own new-covenant ministry so that the Corinthians will grasp that God works most powerfully through weakness (2 Cor 12:7-10). The errorists in Colossae are also suffused with pride. They propose a way to the divine fullness that circumvents Christ (Col 2:9-10). Their ascetic regime, devotion to angels and observance of the calendar stems from a mind puffed up by the flesh (Col 2:18). The severity of the imposed regimen appears religious, but in actuality it panders to pride and exalts human beings. The false teachers in the Pastorals suffer from the same fault: they want to be known as teachers with authority in the law, and they promote recondite teachings that are useless (1 Tim 1:3-7; 4:1-5; 6:3-10, 20-21; 2 Tim 2:14-18; 3:1-9; Tit 1:10-16; 3:9-11). They promote their teachings out of arrogance (1 Tim 6:4; cf. 2 Tim 3:2).

Pride and the new perspective. Most scholars have focused on boasting and pride relative to the law. Debate over this topic has raged since the publication of E. P. Sanders's *Paul and Palestinian Judaism*, for Sanders argues that Palestinian Judaism was not legalistic, that is, that Judaism did not teach that one could earn favor or merit with God by doing good works.[10] The discussion of legalism and Judaism will never be the same because Sanders's work has "exploded like a bombshell" in the field of New Testament studies. We can all be grateful to Sanders because his work compels us to return to the texts to see what is truly there. The Judaism of the Second Temple period did

---

[10]E. P. Sanders, *Paul and Palestinian Judaism: A Comparison of Patterns of Religion* (Philadelphia: Fortress, 1977).

not believe that one could merit righteousness by good works, says Sanders, nor did it teach that one must weigh good works to see whether the good exceeds the bad in determining if one will enter the kingdom. The standard belief among Jews, Sanders claims, was that one becomes part of the people of God by God's covenantal grace. He describes the theology of Palestinian Judaism as "covenantal nomism." One enters the covenant by God's grace, and keeping the law is the means by which one stays within God's covenantal mercy. Such obedience to the law, Sanders maintains, is not legalism; it is the proper and grateful response to God's covenantal work. If Sanders is correct, and Judaism was not legalistic, then how do we understand Paul's polemic against the law in his letters? Since the time of the Reformation, scholars have detected a polemic against legalism and boasting in works in the Pauline letters. Sanders's work forces us to reexamine Paul's letters to determine whether there is actually a critique of works-righteousness in them, or whether this has been imposed on the letters by scholars reading the text with presuppositions derived from the Reformation. Any challenge to the consensus is salutary in that it provokes us to interpret afresh the Pauline writings. Such a study, however, must not be conducted in a vacuum. The evidence compiled above demonstrates that pride was a problem often confronted by Paul in writing to his churches. However one construes the relationship between law and boasting, it is clear that arrogance manifested itself in a number of ways in Pauline communities.

I have argued above that in Paul's understanding, people are condemned if they attempt to be righteous by works of law since they fail to keep the law. The term *works of law* does not refer to an attempt to earn merit from God; it simply denotes the requirements demanded by the law. Judgment results because human beings fail to practice what the law says. And yet the Pauline critique of the law as a way of salvation is multifaceted. We shall see shortly that the law is set aside for redemptive historical reasons: the covenant with Moses has come to an end, and the new covenant is now in force. What we want to highlight here, however, is the connection between the law and boasting. Works of law are excluded as the way to righteousness since human beings cannot and do not keep the law. But why did some think that the law was the path to righteousness in Paul's day? The Old Testament itself does not teach that human beings merit righteousness before God by keeping the law, nor does the Old Testament conceive of the law as a *source of life or power*. First God redeems Israel from Egypt, *and then* he gives the law, so obedience to the law is a response to God's grace, not an attempt to gain righteousness by works (see Ex 19—20).[11] The notion that the Old Testament teaches salvation by keeping the law and that Paul teaches salvation by grace is misguided and unfortunate, producing a Marcionite view of the Old Testament. Paul does not contradict the Old Testament in rejecting righteousness by "works of law," for the Old Testament teaches salvation is by God's grace. If some Jews had fallen into legalism in Paul's day, such an error must be ascribed not to the Old Testament itself but to a misunderstanding of the Old Testament. Similarly, Christians have often fallen prey to legalism during the last two thousand years. Such legalism is not the fault of the New Testament itself but must be ascribed to a faulty reading or an inconsistent application of the New Testament.

Other scholars maintain that some of Paul's Jewish contemporaries suffered from redemptive-historical ignorance; they did not understand that faith in Jesus Christ displaced Torah. They did not realize that what the law pointed to has now been fulfilled in Christ. They still desired to live in the old era, even though the new age had dawned. Paul's complaint with Judaism, according to this view, had nothing to do with legalism. Paul simply wanted the Jews to understand that now that Christ has come, salvation is through him rather than through Torah. Sanders insists that Paul argues from *solution to plight*.[12] Since Christ is the solution to human malfeasance, then the law must have exacerbated the problem. Paul reasoned backward that since salvation comes through Christ, it cannot be obtained through the law. If Sanders is right, Paul's rejection of the law stems only from theology and not from anthropology. That is, inability to keep the law or legalism had nothing to do with Paul's rejection of the law. The law is set aside solely because salvation is through Christ alone. Sanders's solution is partially correct, for salvation history is part of the answer. Now that Christ has come, the Mosaic covenant is no longer in force. Those who fail to see the covenantal shift between the Old Testament and the New Testament are blind to one of the major themes of Pauline theology. What is less convincing is the either-or position advanced by Sanders. We need not, nor should we, place salvation history and anthropology at loggerheads. We cannot wave the wand of salvation history and make anthropology invisible. Frank

---

[11]The view I am proposing here is a commonplace in Old Testament theologies. See Paul R. House, *Old Testament Theology* (Downers Grove, Ill.: InterVarsity Press, 1998), pp. 109-10.

[12]This is essentially the view of Sanders in *Paul and Palestinian Judaism* and *Paul, the Law, and the Jewish People*.

Thielman, for example, persuasively shows that Paul argued from plight to solution.[13] Failure to obey the Torah was a long-standing problem in Israel. The Israelites were deported to Assyria (722 B.C.) and Babylon (586 B.C.), according to the Prophets, because the people failed to keep the law. The Pharisaical movement and the Qumran community arose, at least in part, as responses to Israel's failure to abide by the Torah. We cannot dispense with the anthropological critique that informs Paul's writing relative to the law.

Evidence of legalism in Romans. In Romans 3:27 Paul affirms that boasting is excluded when the Torah is understood as a law that teaches faith rather than works. Conversely, boasting would be legitimate if works were the path to righteousness. Paul affirms this truth in Romans 4:2, "For if Abraham was justified by works, he has a reason for boasting, but not before God." Some mistakenly understand this to say that Abraham could boast before human beings because of his works, whereas he could not boast before God. In other words, they think Paul says here that Abraham did works so remarkable that they elicited praise from human beings but that God is not impressed by human works, no matter how remarkable they are. This is a serious misreading of the verse, and the grammar of the text is the key to reading it. Paul does not intimate that Abraham *was* righteous by works in the presence of human beings. He says, *if* Abraham were justified by works, then boasting would be fitting. It is not implied or even suggested that Abraham was in fact righteous in the sight of human beings. Whether the if-clause is a reality is not communicated by the if-then construction. Nor is it at all plausible that the term *was justified (edikaiōthē)* relates to Abraham's status before human beings. Paul invariably uses the term to refer to one's status *before God.*

We should interpret the if-then statement in a straightforward way. Paul affirms that boasting would be fitting *if* Abraham did good works. This is where the Bultmann school goes astray, for Paul does not say that even if Abraham performed the necessary works, he sinned anyway because the very desire to keep the law is sinful and betrays pride. Paul maintains that if Abraham did the good works, he would have a valid reason to boast before God! We must remember, however, where this paragraph stands in the flow of the argument in Romans. Paul has already demonstrated that all are sinners (Rom 1:18—3:20). When Paul says, then, in Romans 4:2 "not before God," his point is that Abraham was not righteous before God by his works.

---

[13]Frank Thielman, *From Plight to Solution: A Jewish Framework to Understanding Paul's View of the Law in Galatians and Romans,* NovTSup 61 (Leiden: Brill, 1989).

Why? Because he failed to do the necessary works. Abraham was not right-eous by *doing* but by *believing* (Rom 4:3). Indeed, Abraham is classed in the category of the "ungodly" (Rom 4:5), who are righteous not by "working" but by "believing." This reading of the text is verified by Romans 4:6-8, where David is adduced as a second example. David rejoices over the blessing of righteousness apart from works. David does not speak of a situation in which he does the necessary works and God dismisses his good works. Instead, David was a sinner who failed to practice the works demanded, and thus he needed forgiveness from God.

The illustration of the employee in Romans 4:4-5 makes the situation plain: "Now to the one who works, wages are not considered as grace but as a debt, but to the who does not work but believes upon the one who justifies the ungodly, his faith is counted as righteousness." If Abraham did the required works, then righteousness would belong to him not as a gift but as a debt to be paid by the employer. The problem with Abraham (and all people), how-ever, is that they are "ungodly," and so they cannot do the work required. Thus, they will never receive the payment of righteousness by works. Since righteousness is by faith instead of works, all boasting and pride are excluded (Rom 3:27-28; 4:2, 4-5). Abraham did not work as an employee to receive a reward from God. Instead, he let God *work for him* and trusted that God would vindicate him. Why did Paul raise the issue of boasting and pride relative to works in this section? It seems likely that the issue of boasting arises because it was a genuine problem in the lives of human beings. Paul, as a pastoral and missionary theologian, does not typically bring up issues unrelated to the lives of his readers. But *why* would people boast in works of law if their works were insufficient and they were sinners? We have already noted that Paul does not criticize boasting if the required works are actually performed. What he emphasizes, though, is that all without exception fall short of God's glory (Rom 3:23). People boast, then, because they are deluded. They somehow think that their works demonstrate their righteous-ness, even though they fall short of God's standard. People are prone to such delusion because they are eager to ascribe glory to themselves for the good works done. Human beings are inclined to view themselves as morally noble and righteous, even when they fall significantly short of the required stan-dard. In other words, human nature has not changed dramatically since Paul's day! Paul reminds his readers that pride and boasting have no founda-tion since all are sinners. Indeed, the message that righteousness is obtained by *believing* rather than *doing* demonstrates that righteousness is a gift given to the ungodly (Rom 4:5). Since it is a gift, it is undeserved, and the proper response is grateful thanks instead of arrogance.

Recognizing a polemic against legalism in Paul does not mean that we reject the new perspective totally. We should not deny that Jewish ethnocentricism and nationalism were part of the problem. It is likely that the Jews were proud of their covenantal advantage and their separation from unclean Gentiles. The best solution here involves a "both-and" instead of an "either-or." Some Jews were attempting to be right with God on the basis of works, but they also practiced exclusivism, insisting that Gentiles could only be righteous in God's sight if they joined the Jewish people. It is not the case that Jews believed that they were better than the Gentiles solely because they were Jewish. They also thought their adherence to the law made them morally superior to Gentiles. Of course, it would also be an error to conclude that the problem of boasting is unique to Jews. Human boasting takes many forms, whether it consists in the ability to speak in tongues (1 Cor 12—14) or the wisdom to choose the most gifted minister (1 Cor 1—4). It is only to be expected, knowing human nature, that we are disposed to boast in our works—even if they are not as good as we suppose! Thus, Paul's critique here is hardly confined to the Jews.

The contrast between believing and doing informs Romans 9:30—10:8 as well. Gentiles who did not pursue or seek righteousness have obtained it, while Israel—though pursuing the law for righteousness—has been frustrated in its quest (Rom 9:30-31). No critique of Israel's pursuit of the law for righteousness is implied as if pursuing the law is an inferior goal. Racing imagery is employed in Romans 9:30-33, and thus when Paul says that Israel did not attain the law, the idea is the Israelites did not keep the law, they did not attain to the standard required, they fell short of the goal. Israel's failure to obey the law is also implied in Romans 10:5—"For Moses writes concerning the righteousness that is from the law that the person who does the commandments will live by them." Moses promises righteousness to those who keep the law's requirements (Lev 18:5), but no one becomes right with God through the pathway of the law since human sin intervenes. Paul emphasizes in Romans 10:6-8 that righteousness is by faith—by believing and not by doing. Nor is Paul commending faith in faith. The faith that saves is faith in Jesus Christ as the crucified and risen Lord: "If you confess with your mouth that Jesus is Lord and believe in your heart that God raised him from the dead, you shall be saved" (Rom 10:9). Paul does not confine himself in this section to the thought that all people transgress the law. He inquires in

Romans 9:32 as to why Israel did not attain righteousness. He replies that
they did not seek the law "from faith but as from works." The phrase *as from
works (hōs ex ergōn)* indicates that Israel's subjective attitude is also a problem.
Israel did not respond to God by trusting his promises but by attempting to
do the necessary works to gain his favor.

Romans 10:2-4 confirms this interpretation of Romans 9:32. Israel's zeal for
God is commendable. Unfortunately, their zeal is plagued by ignorance about
God's righteousness. The Jews failed to submit themselves to God's saving
righteousness because they tried to establish their own. Instead of gratefully
receiving righteousness as a gift and submitting themselves to God's saving
righteousness, Israel attempted to secure righteousness by keeping the stat-
utes of the law. Paul remarks that "Christ is the end of the law, resulting in
righteousness for all those who believe." By "end" *(telos)*, Paul probably
means that the law points toward Christ and culminates in him.[14] Believers in
Christ cease using the law as a means to establish their own righteousness,
for the law itself points toward faith in Christ.

Some scholars claim that the issue in Romans 10:3 (Israel "sought to establish its own righteousness") is not works-righteousness but ethnocentrism.
Israel was clinging to its own national righteousness, these scholars claim,
over against the Gentiles. Such an interpretation is unconvincing, for Paul
does not say a word about circumcision, food laws or sabbath in this context.
The text provides a fundamental contrast between *believing* and *doing*. Israel
is criticized for its unbelief in Jesus as Messiah (Rom 9:33; 10:1, 4, 6-13). Israel
has failed to see that Jesus is the fulfillment of salvation history; and by clinging to the law, they have been blinded to its fulfillment. Israel's failure to
believe in Jesus as Messiah is not merely an intellectual oversight; it finds its
roots in self-worship, the desire to be righteous by their own works. We must
say again that this tendency is not restricted to Israel. The passion to be like
God hearkens back to Genesis 3, and thus the problem is a human one—not
just a Jewish one.

Evidence of legalism in Philippians. A similar text on boasting and the law is
Philippians 3:2-11. Opponents, probably Judaizers, are on the horizon and
want to impose circumcision and the law on the Philippians. Paul castigates
them as dogs, evil workers, and the "mutilation" *(katatomē)*. The true circumcision is spiritual, produced by the Spirit of God: "For we are the circumcision, who worship in the Spirit of God and boast in Christ Jesus and do not

---

[14]This represents a change of view on my understanding of Rom 10:4.

put confidence in the flesh" (Phil 3:3). Those who promote circumcision boast in the flesh and in what human beings can accomplish, but believers boast in Christ Jesus rather than in the flesh. Paul does not criticize the adversaries as an outsider, for he matches them and exceeds them as far as confidence in the flesh is concerned. Paul was not only circumcised, from the tribe of Benjamin and a Hebrew of Hebrews, he also was from the sect of the Pharisees, known for his zeal as a persecutor of the church and blameless in his extraordinary devotion to the law. All these advantages, however, Paul has repudiated to gain Christ and to be found in him. He had to choose between "having my own righteousness which is from the law" and "righteousness through faith in Christ, the righteousness from God on the basis of faith" (Phil 3:9). The text establishes a connection between boasting in the flesh and one's own right-eousness on the basis of the law (Phil 3:3, 9). The problem with law-right-eousness is that it is "mine" *(emēn)* and is accompanied by boasting and pride in the accomplishments of the flesh. One looks in vain for any indication that Paul's fundamental problem was excluding Gentiles. The problem was a fixation on his own accomplishments and righteousness. He was devoted to the law as a means to buttress his own ego and his own glory. The unbelief of the Judaizing opponents stems from a desire for self-glory, a glory that is promoted through devotion to the law.

Evidence for legalism in later Pauline literature. The interpretation proposed here is vindicated by Ephesians 2:9. Many interpreters, mistakenly in my judgment, assign Ephesians to a post-Pauline writer. Assuming for a moment that this position is true, Ephesians 2:9 affirms that salvation is "not by works so that no one should boast." It is difficult to imagine the text being much clearer. Works are excluded as the basis of salvation so that people cannot boast that their deeds contributed to their inclusion in the people of God. Apparently the "post-Pauline" writer did not understand Paul's previous letters as indictments of exclusivism.[15] He summarizes the Pauline teaching in general terms: human works of any kind are ruled out because people may exercise pride if works are the basis of their salvation. In my judgment, the apostle Paul himself summarizes his own teaching here. When he considers his teaching on salvation, human deeds are excluded as the foundation for salvation. We see clearly, then, that human works are dangerous precisely because they may provide the platform for human pride. People are not saved "by the works which we have done in righteousness, but according to

---

[15]See Marshall, "Salvation, Grace and Works."

his mercy" (Tit 3:5). Salvation is based on God's gracious call and not human works, on his grace and not human effort (2 Tim 1:9). Thereby God receives the praise for the transformation of human beings.

Some concluding observations on Jewish legalism. It is not the case that all Jews without exception were legalists, though a tendency to boast in our works is a common human problem. Yet some of Paul's Jewish opponents fell prey to it. Neither is it the case that the Old Testament taught such legalism yet now Paul opposes it. Nor was legalism formally enshrined in the teaching of the Judaism of Paul's day. Scholars recognize that Judaism was diverse in the Second Temple period, and thus some segments of Judaism probably emphasized grace more than other segments. Some of the evidence Sanders compiles with respect to rabbinic Judaism certainly could be interpreted as a recipe for legalism.[16] For instance, in rabbinic literature the covenant is rarely mentioned, and detailed instructions are given as to how the law should be carried out. Those who are consumed with how to abide by every facet of the law face the dangers of ritualism and legalism. At the very least Paul maintains that some Jews were captivated by legalism, and Romans 9:30—10:8 seems to suggest that the problem was a common one. This is hardly surprising—human pride is one manifestation of the root sin, the failure to give God the lordship and glory he deserves. Furthermore, serious questions have been raised about Sanders's reading of Second Temple Judaism. Mark Elliott argues that Judaism during this period did not envision the salvation of all Israel but of only a faithful remnant, a remnant that kept the Torah.[17] If Elliott is correct, and he amasses a significant amount of evidence supporting his conclusion, then Paul's critique of the Judaism of his day, or at least some sectors of Judaism, makes good sense. Friedrich Avemarie also shows that Sanders's depiction of Judaism is one-sided.[18] Statements that emphasize God's grace exist, but so do statements that emphasize the contribution of human beings. The tension between these competing statements is not clearly resolved in the literature, suggesting that at least some Jews did not assign the same priority to grace as did Paul, in the sense that they conceived of human works as contributing to salvation.

---

[16]See, e.g., Thomas R. Schreiner, " 'Works of Law' in Paul," *NovT* 33 (1991): 217-44; Robert H. Gundry, "Grace, Works and Staying Saved in Paul," *Bib* 66 (1985): 1-38.

[17]Mark A. Elliott, *The Survivors of Israel: A Reconsideration of the Theology of Pre-Christian Judaism* (Grand Rapids, Mich.: Eerdmans, 2000).

[18]Friedrich Avemarie, "Erwählung und Vergeltung: Zur optionalen Struktur rabbinischer Soteriologie," *NTS* 45 (1999): 108-26.

Paul does not proscribe all boasting. Boasting in the Lord and his work in and through believers is fitting (e.g., Rom 5:2-3, 11; 1 Cor 1:31; 2 Cor 5:12; 10:13-18; 11:30; 12:9; Gal 6:4, 14). But any boasting in the ability, wisdom, strength or righteousness of human beings is rejected. Such boasting is the heartbeat of sin since it robs God of his glory and instead extends it to human beings.

Conclusion

Human beings stand under God's judgment because they worship the creature rather than the Creator. They exalt themselves over God. Even though we fall short of God's moral standards, we are still inclined to boast about our morality. The Pauline gospel indicts us as sinners, uncovering our failure to do God's will and exposing our pride for what it is.

6

DISHONORING GOD

The Power of Sin

In the last chapter we considered the relationship between the law and sin and, particularly, how easily human beings used the law (and other gifts of God) to boast in themselves. In this chapter we continue to investigate how human beings dishonor God. The depth of sin is disclosed in this chapter, for we see that human beings are in bondage to sin, are subject to the flesh and come into the world as descendants of Adam.

Bondage to Sin

Sin as a power. We have seen that the fundamental sin is the failure to honor God as God, that all people disobey God's law and that people boast in themselves rather than in God. When Paul considers the human condition, however, he does not merely describe what people actually do (sin, fail to glorify God and boast). He also explains the nature of human beings. Those who are born in Adam do not merely sin; they are also slaves to sin. Sin, as an alien power, dominates them. They are under its rule and authority.

It is vital to understand that sin is a power that exerts control over those who are in Adam. Sin, as we have seen previously, consists in failure to keep God's law. But sin is also a tyrannical power that exercises its dominion over those in Adam. It enters the world through Adam's sin and exercises its sway over all people (Rom 5:12-19). Sin manifests its reign *(ebasileusen)* in the dominion of death (Rom 5:21). Apart from Christ people are "slaves" to sin *(douleuein,* Rom 6:6), whereas believers have been freed from the sin that enslaved them and are now enslaved to righteousness (Rom 6:16-18, 20, 22). The image of slavery is not overstated since unbelievers cannot liberate themselves from sin's grip. Sin exercises control over them so that they are in bondage to it. Believers must not let sin "reign" *(basileuetō)* over them (Rom 6:12), nor should they present their bodies "to sin" (Rom 6:13) since sin no longer "rules" *(kyrieusei)* over them. The power of sin over those in Adam indicates that the present evil age still exists (Gal 1:4).

Under the power of sin. The grip of sin over those in Adam is conveyed by the *under (hypo)* phrases in Pauline literature, designating that human beings are under sin's control. Those who are of the works of the law are "under a curse" *(hypo kataran,* Gal 3:10). They are under a curse because they do not keep the requirements of the law. Scripture has confined all people "under sin" *(hypo hamartian,* Gal 3:22). Paul explains that righteousness would, in fact, be by the law if the law could produce life (Gal 3:21). The problem, in other words, is not with the content of the law (Rom 7:12), for the law requires what is holy and good. The law is inadequate in that it lacks any power to transform a person's existence. Those who see the law as a source of life are badly mistaken, and instead of enjoying life, such people are in bondage to the power of sin.

Under the rule of the pedagogue. When contemplating the *under* phrases in Paul, it is imperative that one grasp the redemptive-historical force of these expressions. "Faith" entered salvation history through the coming of Jesus Christ (Gal 3:23-25). Before the coming of Christ and faith, people were held in custody "under the law" (Gal 3:23). The Mosaic law served as a *paidagōgos* (person in charge of minors) "until the time of Christ" (Gal 3:24). The word *eis* (until the time of Christ) should be understood as temporal here. The Mosaic law was intended to be in force for only a certain period of salvation history, until the coming of Christ. Now that "faith" has come with the arrival of Christ, believers are "no longer under the pedagogue" (Gal 3:25). They are now full adults (i.e., "sons") in Christ Jesus by faith (Gal 3:26). Some scholars understand the custody under the law and the role of the pedagogue to teach that the law functioned to *restrain* sin before the coming of Christ.[1] It is doubtful, however, that this is a correct reading of

---

[1]For example, David J. Lull, " 'The Law Was Our Pedagogue': A Study of Galatians 3:19-25," *JBL* 105 (1986): 481-98. For further discussion on the pedagogue and this issue, see Thomas

Paul's intention. It is certainly possible that guardianship under the law was designed to limit sin, and some emphasize that the role of the pedagogue in the Greco-Roman world was to curb unmannerly behavior in children. Nonetheless, the notion that the law was instituted to restrain sin is unconvincing in the context of Galatians 3. Paul has already emphasized that no one can keep the requirements of the law (Gal 2:17-18; 3:10). The idea that no one keeps the law sits awkwardly with the idea that the law actually restrains sin. Even more decisive is the near context, for Galatians 3:21-22 reveals that the law does not produce life and that, instead, Scripture documents that all are under the power of sin.

Some appeal to the pedagogue in defending the idea that the law was given to limit sin, since the pedagogue was certainly not appointed to foment bad behavior in children. The pedagogue has also often been understood as an instructor (cf. 1 Cor 4:15), and the law, on this basis, functions as a teacher or tutor leading people to Christ. What we must determine is the function of the appeal to the pedagogue in Galatians. Defining the pedagogue in educational terms is mistaken, for Paul does not assign the law a positive preparatory role elsewhere in Galatians. Even more telling, such a reading violates the salvation-historical character of the text and transforms it into an individualistic pattern for salvation. Nor is it likely that Paul refers to the pedagogue because it limits sin. Such an assertion is out of place in a letter that attacks the Judaizers for imposing the law on the Galatians. The Judaizers maintained that the law was needed to restrain sin. Paul would play into their hands if he maintained the law was given by God to restrain sin in Israel. The Judaizers would probably reply, "The Mosaic Torah must continue to be enforced so that sin will continue to be restrained." They would likely go on and say, "Why does Paul want to do away with the law when even he admits that the law *limits* sin? The reason Paul wants to abolish the law is that he is an antinomian." The notion that Paul refers to the law as a pedagogue because it restrained sin is, therefore, historically and contextually implausible. It is also rather doubtful that Paul would ascribe a positive function to the law in Galatians 3—4 since this is the very section in which he argues for the temporary role of the Mosaic Torah.

To conclude, Paul uses the illustration of the pedagogue *for its temporal significance.* That is, he does not appeal to the pedagogues because they func-

---

R. Schreiner, *The Law and Its Fulfillment: A Pauline Theology of Law* (Grand Rapids, Mich.: Baker, 1993), pp. 74-81.

tioned as teachers or curbed unsuitable behavior. He introduces the pedagogue for one reason only: pedagogues had charge over people during their minority years. Pedagogues are assigned to children, and when one becomes an adult a pedagogue is unnecessary. Thus, Paul uses the pedagogue as a metaphor for the law to make the point that the law was in force for only a certain period of salvation history. The temporal markers in the text powerfully support this interpretation. The Mosaic law was introduced 430 years after the covenant with Abraham (Gal 3:15-18). The law was added "*until* the seed should come" (Gal 3:19). "*Before* faith came, we were guarded under the law, being shut up to the faith *which was about to be* revealed" (Gal 3:23). The law was "our pedagogue *until Christ*" (Gal 3:24). "*Now* that faith has come, we are *no longer* under the pedagogue" (Gal 3:25). The illustration from the guardians and managers in Galatians 4:1-7 communicates the same thesis. When children are minors *(nēpios),* they cannot receive their inheritance but are under the supervision of guardians and managers. This status remains in force "*until the appointed time* of the father" (Gal 4:2). Paul remarks that "*when we were minors,* we were under the elements of the world" (Gal 4:3). But now that the fullness of time has come, we have been redeemed from the law and are no longer minors but sons (Gal 4:4-5). The word *sons (hyioi)* stands in this context (just as in Gal 3:26) for "adulthood." When one becomes a son, one is no longer a minor but an heir (Gal 4:6-7). The days of being under the pedagogue are over and believers are now "sons of God" (Gal 3:26). The illustration of the pedagogue is not introduced, therefore, to indicate that sin was restrained under the Mosaic law. Paul uses the illustration to describe the era in salvation history before the coming of Christ, when believers did not yet have access to their inheritance.

Enslaved under the elements. We have already investigated evidence supporting the notion that the law actually stimulated sin instead of restraining it. This interpretation is confirmed by Galatians 4:3, which says, "when we were minors, we were enslaved by the elements of the world." It is unnecessary to decipher the specific idea intended by "elements of the world" *(stoicheia tou kosmou).* What is plain is that being "under the elements" (Gal 4:3) is parallel to being "under the law" (Gal 3:23; 4:5). Neither should we forget that being "under law" is also described as being "under the curse" (Gal 3:10) or "under sin" (Gal 3:22). Paul argues that those who were under Torah were "enslaved under the elements of the world" (Gal 4:3). In other words, those who were under Torah were enslaved to sin, held in dominion under its power. Christ, by his redeeming work, liberated believers from this dominion and granted them the privilege of becoming sons (Gal 4:4-5). Paul does not conceive, in Galatians, of life under the law neutrally. He describes it as an era in salvation history when the people of God were enslaved.

Does such an idea do justice to the Old Testament? After all, there were believers like Joseph and Daniel who were remarkably righteous, and one thinks of the remnant that followed the ways of the Lord. Despite such counterexamples, Paul's reading of the Old Testament is eminently defensible, for Paul reads the main story line of the narrative. From the time of its calling, Israel quickly fell into sin. Almost immediately after God entered into covenant with his people they abandoned him and worshiped the golden calf (Ex 32—34). The wilderness generation, which again and again strayed from God's commands, foreshadows those who are unbelievers (cf. 1 Cor 10:1-11). Short periods of obedience blossomed under Joshua and David and Solomon. Otherwise, Israel's history was stained by apostasy (see Judges), and punishment was meted out with the Assyrian and Babylonian exiles. When one scans Israel's history as a whole, its failure to keep God's law and the resulting punishment are the focus. Paul would not deny that there were exceptions to this rule. Joseph, Caleb, Joshua and the remnant all testify to the presence of faithful people in Israel, but Paul's point is that generally speaking the Israelites failed to keep the law. They were enslaved to the elements of the world.

The Mosaic Torah was not the means by which God would free his people from sin, for the law was not the source of life. The Mosaic covenant, contrary to the Judaizers, was not the climax of redemptive history; it was an interim arrangement that pointed forward to the coming seed of Abraham. The sin of Israel was not restrained but rather it increased under the tutelage of the law (Rom 5:20; Gal 3:19). The nation under the domain of the law had not yet received the promises of freedom and glory promised in the scriptures. It was still under the dominion of Rome, and the promises of a new world of righteousness and peace (Is 11:1-9) had not yet been realized.[2] Remarkably, Paul draws a parallel between the slavery that was characteristic of Israel under the law (Gal 3:10, 22; 4:3-5) and the Gentiles' slavery to idols (Gal 4:8, 10). In both instances, sin reigned as a tyrannical power. Paul does not represent pre-Christian existence as one characterized by libertarian freedom, that is, the power to choose the contrary. People instead are under the thrall of sin, sub-

---

[2]Supporting a reference to the exile in Paul is James M. Scott, "Paul's Use of Deuteronomic Tradition," *JBL* 112 (1993): 645-65. Whether *exile* is the best term to use is debated, nor is it clear that all would admit they were under exile. We can be confident, however, that all Jews would admit that the promises of a glorious future were not yet realized.

jugated and mastered by alien power. The earthly Jerusalem that resists the Pauline gospel is not only misguided, "she is in *slavery* with her children" (Gal 4:25) and her inhabitants are in bondage (Gal 4:31). The Torah had not brought freedom, nor were the Old Testament promises realized under Torah.

Under sin in Romans. We have already seen in Romans that Paul describes those outside of God's saving righteousness as being in slavery to sin. He also continues to describe being "under law" as equivalent to being under the power of sin. In Romans 6:14 he promises that believers will not be under the rule or dominion of sin. The reason they can be confident of triumph is that they are "not under law but under grace." Paul does not mean by this that believers are liberated from all ethical norms. His letters are full of exhortations and admonitions. Instead, he continues to use "under law" in a redemptive-historical sense. To be under law is to be under the Mosaic covenant, the old era of salvation history. Those who lived in that era, generally speaking, were enslaved to sin. This interpretation is confirmed by Romans 7:5, "For when we were in the flesh, the passions of sins were aroused in our members through the law to bear fruit for death." The flesh, which shall be examined in more detail shortly, should be interpreted in redemptive-historical terms as well. It refers to the time before believers received the Spirit (Rom 7:6; 8:9)— before they became part of the people of God. When the law is given to people without the Spirit, their desire to sin is increased rather than reduced. The law becomes an unwitting ally to the power of sin and ends up producing death rather than life.

Paul steers between Scylla and Charybdis. He does not want the readers to think that the law is sinful (Rom 7:7, 12), since the stipulations of the law are from God himself. His major aim, however, is to prove that the law itself provides no power to overcome sin. For those in the flesh the law becomes an ally of sin. Sin uses the law as its bridgehead of operations to attack and kill human beings (Rom 7:7-11). The same theme is at the heart of the famous passage in Romans 7:14-25. Paul's primary purpose is not to explain whether the experience relayed is Christian or pre-Christian. His intention is to show that the law without the Spirit provides no power to keep the commandments. No person in his or her own strength can keep God's law. It is surely a mistake to argue that the text is a straightforward reference to Christian existence (more on this later), for the person in question is "sold under sin" (Rom 7:14) and is sin's captive (Rom 7:23). It is unlikely that Paul would describe believers in such a way, given what he says about their freedom from sin in Romans 6 and 8. For those who are in the flesh, a desire to keep the law is not powerful enough to be translated into action. The flesh has neither the capacity nor ultimately the will power to resist sin's enslaving force. When Paul says, essentially, "I am not the one practicing sin," he is not absolving the "I" of responsibility. He communicates in a powerful way that the "I" is in bondage. Sin sweeps in as a force and controls one's life.

The contribution of 1 Corinthians 15:56. Paul's negative reflections on the law in Romans 7 are verified by 1 Corinthians 15:56, "The sting of death is sin, and the power of sin is the law." This verse is illuminating because the topic under consideration is death rather than the law. Paul's comment on the law is not addressed to the particular situation in Corinth, since the law does not surface as a subject anywhere else in 1 Corinthians 15 and does not receive any sustained attention elsewhere in the letter. The Pauline aside regarding the law, then, is best explained as one of his central convictions with regard to the law.[3] Apparently he inserts his comment without further explanation and without preparing the reader for it because he assumes the Corinthians will understand and agree with him. The sudden insertion relative to the law indicates that Paul communicates—as a part of his gospel—a piece of his theology that has been thoroughly worked out and that is now passed along without discussion. When Paul says "the power of sin is the law," he means that sin is so forceful that it co-opts the law and uses it to produce more sin in the lives of those in the flesh.

Once again, Paul's understanding of the history of Israel is implied here. Any careful reading of Israel's history reveals that the law was not the means by which the promises given to Abraham became a reality. The story of the Israelites reveals that when they were under Torah, they were also under the power and dominion of sin. Jews typically argued that the law restrained the passions of sin. Paul shocked Jewish sensibilities by maintaining that the law actually multiplied sin (Rom 5:20). The inherent liability of the law is detected in its inability to curb the power of sin. Indeed, sin grasps hold of the law and presses it into its service by provoking the passion to sin in and through the law (Rom 7:5). How sin uses the law to advance itself is illustrated by the relationship between sin and coveting (Rom 7:7-11). Discerning precisely what Paul has in mind is difficult. The idea may be that the prohibition against coveting stirs up the desire to covet under the principle that forbidden fruits are the sweetest. Such a notion is probably conjoined with the

---

[3]On 1 Cor 15:56, see Thomas Söding, " 'Die Kraft der Sünde ist das Gesetz' (1 Kor 15,56): Anmerkungen zum Hintergrund und zur Pointe einer gesetzeskritischen Sentenz des Apostels Paulus," ZNW 83 (1992): 74-84.

rebellion and independence that bristles against prohibitions. The law, Paul insists, is not sinful, and yet the nefariousness of sin is displayed in its ability to co-opt the law to produce sin.

The letter-Spirit contrast. That the law in itself is ineffectual is confirmed as well by the letter-Spirit contrast in Paul. The contrast occurs three times in Paul's letters (Rom 2:29; 7:6; 2 Cor 3:6). In the history of interpretation the letter-Spirit dichotomy has often been understood hermeneutically to designate two different approaches to the Old Testament. According to this construction one should not interpret the Old Testament according to the letter but according to the Spirit. Most scholars today, however, understand the contrast between the letter and the Spirit in terms of redemptive history.[4] This latter view is borne out by the contexts in which the contrast occurs. In Romans 2 the disjunction between the letter and the Spirit is explained in terms of the Jews, who have the advantage "of the letter and circumcision" (Rom 2:27) and yet fail to keep the law. On the other hand, Gentiles who are uncircumcised keep the ordinances of the law by the power of the Holy Spirit (Rom 2:26, 29). The letter designates those who possess the law but lack the power to keep it; the Holy Spirit is the gift of the new age, enabling people to keep God's law.

Such an interpretation is confirmed by Romans 7:6: "But now we have been released from the law, dying to that by which were bound, so that we serve in newness of the Spirit and not oldness of letter." Those who are "in the flesh" (Rom 7:5) and who possess the letter of the law are unable to keep the law because they are unregenerate and live in the old eon (Rom 7:5-6). The parallel in Romans 7:5-6 indicates that those who are "in the flesh" serve "in oldness of letter." Those who have the Spirit, on the other hand, are empowered to "bear fruit for God" (Rom 7:4). The eschatological gift of the Spirit enables them to keep God's requirements (Jer 31:31-34; Ezek 11:19-20; 36:26-27).

Similar results are produced by 2 Corinthians 3:6: "The letter kills, but the Spirit gives life." The letter of the law designates the commands of the Mosaic covenant, which is a "ministry of death" (2 Cor 3:7), a "ministry of condemnation" (2 Cor 3:9) and a temporary ministry (2 Cor 3:11). It is unconvincing to maintain that the "letter" *(gramma)* should be defined as legalism, for the letter is defined as that which is engraved on the stony tablets (2 Cor 3:7). The

---

[4]For a thorough discussion of the letter-Spirit contrast in Paul, see Scott J. Hafemann, *Paul, Moses and the History of Israel: The Letter/Spirit Contrast and the Argument from Scripture in 2 Corinthians 3*, WUNT 81 (Tübingen: J. C. B. Mohr, 1995), pp. 156-86.

letter is not legalism but the demands and requirements of the Mosaic law written on the tablets Moses brought down from the mountain (Ex 32—34). Designating the law as "letter" is no criticism of the content of the law. Paul uses the metaphor of the letter to communicate the law's inability to transform one's life. The law without the Spirit produces death and condemnation because people fail to keep what it says (2 Cor 3:7, 9). The Spirit, on the other hand, grants life to human beings (2 Cor 3:6) and produces righteousness (2 Cor 3:9). Those who have the freedom of the Spirit have the ability to keep God's requirements (2 Cor 3:17), unlike the Israelites who, in their hardheartedness, sinned in making the golden calf (2 Cor 3:14; Ex 32).

What Paul says about the letter, then, fits with our understanding of the law in Romans 7. Those who have the law but lack the Holy Spirit cannot and will not keep what the law says. Only those who have the Spirit will obey God's demands. Such a varying response to the law is explained in terms of salvation history. God withheld his Spirit from most of those who lived during the old covenant era, but in the age of the new covenant he grants the Spirit to his people so that they can obey his commands. The law alone, then, is not the prescription for solving the human dilemma, for it prescribes but does not enliven. Indeed, sin uses the prescriptions of the law to foster more sin when the law is addressed to the unregenerate.

Human inability. The sorry condition of human beings relative to the law is described in Romans 8:5-8. These verses do not constitute an exhortation; they simply delineate the state of affairs that exists for those in the flesh and those in the Spirit. Those who are "in the flesh"—those who are unregenerate and live under the dominion of the old era—inevitably think about the things of the flesh. The "mindset of the flesh," because it is fixed on sin, "results in death." Those who are in the flesh are "hostile toward God," and this hostility is evidenced by their refusal and inability to keep God's law (Rom 8:7). Romans 8:7 is a crucial verse, "For the mindset of the flesh is at enmity with God, for it is not subject to God's law, for neither can the flesh obey it." Paul does not merely say that those in the flesh refuse to keep God's law; he also teaches that they *cannot* observe his law. Or, as he says in Romans 8:8, they are "unable to please God." Paul did not believe disseminating the commands of the law would lead to redemption. The law's commands were given to people who had no inclination or capability to keep the Torah. Those in the flesh are enslaved to sin. Once again, the history of Israel testifies to what Paul says. Israel was thoroughly instructed by the Torah, but they had no inclination to keep it. Those who believe that the law itself is transformative have not thought through Israel's own history, for the prophets proclaimed that the promises of the new covenant would become a reality only when the Spirit was poured out on God's people (Is 44:3; Jer 31:31-34; Ezek 11:19-20; 36:26-27; Joel 2:28). Only then would the age of salvation arrive.

Blindness of human beings. Paul does not speak of the impotence of human beings only when considering the law. He describes those who are under the dominion of the old age as being unreceptive to the things of God: "The natural person does not receive the things of the Spirit of God" (1 Cor 2:14). The person born in Adam does not welcome or assent to the truths given by the Holy Spirit (1 Cor 2:14). He or she rejects such teachings because they appear to be foolish. Paul's point is not that they cannot comprehend mentally the statements made about God and Christ. They "understand" the propositions that Christ died for sins and was raised from the dead. But they believe that such teachings are silly fables and that they are not in accord with reality. They are convinced that the word of the cross (1 Cor 1:18) is untrue because it lacks wisdom and signs (1 Cor 1:22). Not only do unbelievers repudiate the things of the Spirit as foolish, but also they *"cannot* know" these things "because they are spiritually discerned" (1 Cor 2:14). Paul does not hold out hope that unbelievers may be able to understand the gospel if they are impartial and objective and strive to comprehend its teachings. No neutral criterion exists by which unbelievers can assess the gospel, for they cannot welcome it as truth since it contradicts the very heart of their existence. The message of the cross is not perceived as a message of life but as one of death and despair (2 Cor 2:16). Only those who have the Holy Spirit are able to assess and welcome the things of God (1 Cor 2:12-16), for only those who have Christ's mind can grasp spiritual things.

A parallel text to 1 Corinthians 2:14 is 2 Thessalonians 2:9-12. Here Paul speaks of the deceit that accompanies the work of Satan, whose support propels the man of lawlessness into prominence. The deception of unrighteousness exists in those who are perishing, those who, as 1 Corinthians 1:18 indicates, reject the message of the cross as folly. Such people are condemned because "they did not welcome the love of the truth so as to be saved" (2 Thess 2:10). The verb *welcomed (dechomai)* is the same verb that is used in 1 Corinthians 2:14. Unbelievers do not welcome "the love of the truth." Paul could have easily said that unbelievers do not welcome the truth, but he refers to "the love of the truth" to emphasize that unbelievers do not have any affection for or inclination to believe in the truth. Rejection of the gospel is not rooted in a rational decision but in a deep-seated loathing of its message.

They do "not believe in the truth but take pleasure in unrighteousness" (2 Thess 2:12). The truth of the gospel is repudiated because the message appears to be gloomy and world denying. The message of the cross is a scandal to unbelievers (1 Cor 1:23). As a consequence of their rejecting the truth, God sends a delusion on those who resist so that they believe error (2 Thess 2:11). Their intellectual and philosophical errors are rooted in their failure to delight in the truth.

Does this text contradict 1 Corinthians 2:14? Paul says there that unbelievers *cannot* accept the things of the Spirit, whereas in 2 Thessalonians 2 he says merely that they *do not* accept the truth. In 1 Corinthians 2:14 their inability (cf. also 2 Cor 4:4 below) seems to exist *before* they hear the truth, whereas in 2 Thessalonians 2:10-12 delusion is a *consequence* of their forsaking the gospel. Those who are wont to see contradictions will surely detect one here, but the difficulty is only apparent. Paul consistently maintains both that people *cannot* respond to the gospel and that they *do not* respond to it. No logical contradiction exists between these passages. We must also see that 1 Corinthians 2:14 and 2 Thessalonians 2:10-12 contemplate two different situations. The former text emphasizes one's initial inability to welcome the truth, while in 2 Thessalonians Paul emphasizes the consequences of one's rejecting the truth. The two different perspectives are not contradictory but complementary. Supporting the idea that Paul has not abandoned his teaching in 1 Corinthians 2:14 are the immediately following verses in 2 Thessalonians. Those who do receive the love of the truth and take pleasure in righteousness do so because they are elected by God and effectually called through the gospel (2 Thess 2:13-14). Paul does not attribute their positive response to any innate love for the truth. Love for the truth was begotten by God, and this explains their response to the gospel. Thus, *God* is to be thanked for their conversion.

Human beings' resistance to the gospel is also attributed to Satan: "The god of this age has blinded the minds of unbelievers so that they do not see the light of the gospel of the glory of Christ, who is the image of God" (2 Cor 4:4). In this verse, which fits neatly with 1 Corinthians 2:14, Paul informs us that the god of this world, who is almost certainly Satan, impedes unbelievers from grasping the beauty of Christ revealed in the gospel. Paul is not denying that unbelievers can mentally comprehend the proposition "The beauty of Christ is revealed in the gospel." What unbelievers deny is that such a proposition is true. They are blinded from perceiving and sensing that Christ is glorious and full of splendor. They "know" that the gospel proclaims the glory of Christ, but they have no sense or taste of his glory. Instead of perceiving this message as one of life, they are filled with the gloom and darkness of death (2 Cor 2:16). The god of this age obstructs their vision so that they do not perceive Christ as beautiful, lovely and the source of all happiness. Such bondage to the devil is also described in 2 Timothy 2:26, where unbelievers are "held captive by him to do his [the devil's] will." Unbelievers are not portrayed as neutral, having the ability to pursue or reject God. Rather, they are held in captivity under the devil's power, prevented by him from seeing the glory of Christ.

Ephesians 2:1-3. Ephesians 2:1-3 is one of the most comprehensive passages in describing the state of unbelievers since it weaves together the influence of the world, the devil and the flesh. The utter impotence of human beings is relayed by the metaphor of death. Paul tells the Ephesians, "you were dead in your trespasses and sins" (Eph 2:1; cf. Eph 2:5; Col 2:13). Paul does not depict unbelievers as merely disinclined to the gospel. He says that they have no capacity at all to respond to the gospel, for they are engulfed in trespasses and sins and find their delight in the realm of sin and death rather than in doing the will of God. They are powerless to respond to God because they are dead in their sins. Unbelievers live in the realm of death, indulging in sin "according to the age of this world" (Eph 2:2). The "age of this world" designates this present evil age that will be displaced by the coming age (Gal 1:4; Eph 1:21). We have already noted that Paul maintains that the age to come has been inaugurated while the present evil age continues. Unbelievers live in accordance with the present evil age, that is, they are molded and shaped by the conventions and beliefs of this world (Rom 12:2). The structure of the society in which they live exerts a determinative influence on their behavior and worldview.

The text in Ephesians also attributes living within the realm of sin to "the ruler of the authority of the air, the spirit that is now working in the sons of disobedience" (Eph 2:2). The reference here is surely to the devil or Satan. Unbelievers, then, are not merely held in tow by the social forces of this world; they are also under the dominion of spiritual forces, namely, the devil's authority. Paul does not exempt believers from these influences as if believers and unbelievers were different species. Believers lived in the same fashion *before* they were made alive by God (Eph 2:3). Unbelievers, of course, are completely unaware that they are subjugated to the world and the devil. They perceive themselves as "free" because they partake in "the desires of the flesh" (Eph 2:3). Unbelievers are under the dominion of the *social* forces of the world and the *spiritual* authority of the devil, but they are also enslaved *psychologically.* Those in psychological servitude are not compelled to do what they hate. Unbelievers live by carrying out the desires of the flesh and the mind. They do—insofar as it is physically possible—precisely what they want to do. We should not conceive of bondage to sin as if unbelievers are forced or compelled to sin against their will. People manifest their captivity to sin when they do precisely what they wish to do. The dominion of sin is so complete that unbelievers are unaware of their servitude to sin. They believe that they are "free" because they do what they wish and follow the inclinations of their mind. Such desires, however, stem from people who are dead in trespasses in sins, who are actually under the tyranny and dominion of sin.

This passage is also instructive in that the world, the devil and the flesh work in concert in the lives of unbelievers. Paul does not carefully differentiate the influence of the world, the devil and the flesh so that one can distinguish which influence is predominant in particular cases. The state of unbelievers is only explained adequately when all three forces are taken into account. Because unbelievers are dead in trespasses and in sins, are under the dominion of the world and Satan and are indulging the desires of the flesh, they are "by nature children of wrath" (Eph 2:3). They are destined for the wrath of God because of their sin and hostility to him, and such a condition exists from birth. Paul does not conceive of human beings as buds that will blossom into beautiful flowers if left alone. They are by nature and from birth polluted by the power of sin and therefore subject to the wrath of God.

We have already noted that Paul does not place believers in a different class when he describes unbelievers in Ephesians 2:1-3, for he specifically says that believers were formerly under the dominion of this age, the ruler of the air and the desires of the flesh. Titus 3:3 serves the same function, reminding believers that "we were *formerly* foolish, disobedient, deceived, enslaved to various desires and pleasures, living in malice and envy, hateful, hating one another." The reference to being enslaved by desires is particularly interesting because it confirms what we noted previously: unbelievers live out their bondage to sin by indulging in their desires and pleasures. Their slavery does not consist in being forced to do certain things against their will. On the contrary, they live as captives to sin in doing precisely what they wish to do.

Paul's gloomy assessment of the human condition apart from Christ is nothing less than astonishing, especially once we perceive that such a theme is emphatic and sustained. We have noted that unbelievers are portrayed as disobedient to the Torah, incapable of receiving the things of God, blind, dead, proud, enslaved to sin and refusing to honor God. Paul also says that unbelievers are in "darkness" (Eph 5:8; 1 Thess 5:4-5), destined for wrath (1 Thess 1:10, 5:9) and under the dominion of idols (1 Thess 1:9). The sharp separation between believers and unbelievers emerges in 2 Corinthians 6:14-16, where contrasts between righteousness and lawlessness, light and darkness, Christ and Beliar, believers and unbelievers, and the temple of God and idols are stated. The text in Ephesians 2:11-12 is particularly interesting, where Paul communicates his view of Gentiles who had not heard the gospel and were not part of Israel. He does not say that they were innocent because they had not heard the gospel or because they did not possess the privileges of Israel. He describes them as "without Christ, alienated from the commonwealth of Israel, and strangers of the covenants of promise, having no hope and without God in the world" (Eph 2:12). They were "far" from God (Eph 2:13), separated from him and lacking any objective hope for the future. Righteous Gentiles apart from the gospel do not appear on Paul's radar; he concludes that if they are not believers in Christ, then they are alienated from God (Eph 4:18).

The Flesh

Designating human beings. One of the fundamental terms used by Paul to describe the condition of unbelievers is *flesh (sarx).*[5] In keeping with his treatment of most terms, Paul does not use the word *flesh* with only one definition. Sometimes *flesh* is simply a designation for human beings. "No flesh" will be vindicated by works of law before God (Rom 3:20; Gal 2:16), nor should any "flesh"—human beings—boast before God (1 Cor 1:29). When Paul received his revelation of Christ on the way to Damascus, he did not consult with "flesh and blood" (Gal 1:16). On the other hand, the spiritual forces with which believers struggle are not "flesh and blood" (Eph 6:12).

Designating the physical body. The term *flesh* also refers to the physical body or substance with which a person or thing is composed. One of the more interesting passages in this regard is 1 Corinthians 15:39, where human beings, beasts, birds and fish are all said to have a different kind of flesh. The substance with which they are composed varies so that they have distinct physical characteristics. When Paul refers to "the life I live in the flesh" (Gal 2:20), the prepositional phrase *in the flesh* should not be equated with *in the*

---

[5]For a survey of the various understandings of the term *flesh* in Paul, see Herman Ridderbos, *Paul: An Outline of His Theology* (Grand Rapids, Mich.: Eerdmans, 1975), pp. 64-68, 100-107; and James D. G. Dunn, *The Theology of Paul the Apostle* (Grand Rapids, Mich.: Eerdmans, 1998), pp. 62-73.

flesh in Romans 7:5, where the context clearly indicates a reference to the unregenerate state. In Galatians 2:20 Paul merely speaks of his life in the body, a life that he lives by faith. Similarly, Paul's "walking in the flesh" in 2 Corinthians 10:3 does not mean that he lives according to this present evil age, for Paul is careful to say that he does not fight "according to the flesh" (2 Cor 10:3). In this context, *walking in the flesh* designates life in the body. Similarly, in Philippians 1:22, 24 living and remaining "in the flesh" refer to life in the physical body. Paul completes Christ's afflictions in his "flesh" (Col 1:24), which clearly means that Paul experiences these afflictions in his body. The Colossians have not seen Paul's face "in the flesh" (Col 2:1), and he rejoices over their progress in the faith even though he is absent "in the flesh" (Col 2:5). In other words, he is not present bodily. Sexual union means that the couple becomes "one flesh" (1 Cor 6:16; Eph 5:31), which at the least signifies the physical union between a man and a woman. The life of Jesus is displayed through the suffering of Paul's "mortal flesh" (2 Cor 4:11). Similarly, when he says that "our flesh had no rest" (2 Cor 7:5), he probably means that he was physically exhausted. It is likely that the "thorn in the flesh" (2 Cor 12:7) was some kind of physical affliction, for this seems to be the most reasonable way to understand the addition of the words *in the flesh*. Similarly, Paul's "weakness" and "testing" in the flesh were probably some physical ailment (Gal 4:13-14). Jesus' physicality is also emphasized. He was descended from David "according to the flesh" (Rom 1:3). Believers were reconciled "in the body of his flesh" (Col 1:22; cf. Eph 2:16). He "was manifested in the flesh" (1 Tim 3:16).

Focus on physical descent and relationships. Closely related to the previous category are those passages that focus on physical descent, kinship or earthly relationships. For example, we have already noted that Christ was descended from David according to the flesh (Rom 1:3), and Romans 9:5 indicates that the Christ is descended from the fathers—the Jewish patriarchs—according to the flesh. A similar usage is found where Abraham is designated "as our forefather according to the flesh" (Rom 4:1). Paul refers to his fellow Jews as his kinsmen in the flesh (Rom 9:3) and hopes to save some of his "flesh" (Rom 11:14), his fellow Israelites. One's mere physical descent from Abraham does not constitute one's salvation, and thus Paul argues that "the children of the flesh" (Rom 9:8) are not necessarily the children of God. Perhaps 1 Corinthians 10:18 also suggests the inadequacy of physical ancestry in referring to "Israel according to the flesh." In Ephesians 2:11 Paul says the Gentiles "in the flesh" were outside the circle of salvation until the coming of Christ. *Flesh* also refers to earthly relationships. Slaves are to obey their masters "according to the flesh" (Eph 6:5; Col 3:22), and Philemon is to receive Onesimus as a brother "both in the flesh and in the Lord" (Philem 16).

Weakness and the flesh. In the examples catalogued above, the term *flesh* does not denote evil, and yet the notion of weakness is almost invariably present. Because believers are in Adam and have sinned in him (see below), their bodies are destined to die. The bodily flesh of this age is subject to weakness and death. This explains why Paul says that "flesh and blood will not inherit the kingdom of God" (1 Cor 15:50), for the corruptible earthly body cannot enter the future kingdom. We have seen a number of texts that link the flesh with suffering, and such suffering, of course, is only possible during this present evil age. Though Jesus' lineage from David according to the flesh does not suggest in the least that he is sinful (Rom 1:3), the idea of weakness is certainly present, for his physical descent from David is contrasted with his being appointed Son of God with power at the resurrection (Rom 1:4). Jesus did not enter into the world with flesh that was impervious to suffering, but he suffered "in the body of his flesh through death" to reconcile sinners to God (Col 1:22). God "sent his Son in the likeness of sinful flesh" to remove the condemnation that was imposed because of sin (Rom 8:3). The phrase *likeness of sinful flesh (homoiōmati sarkos hamartias)* indicates that Jesus participated in the sin of this age by taking on himself bodily flesh that was weak and subject to death. The word *likeness,* however, guards against the notion that Jesus himself was a sinner. He willingly endured the weakness and sin of the present evil age without being stained with sin himself. The limitations of the flesh are also communicated when Paul explains that he uses a particular illustration "because of the weakness of your flesh" (Rom 6:19).

The flesh and the present evil age. Paul's distinctive use of the term *flesh* is the subject of much controversy. On first glance the correlation of *flesh* with evil and sin suggests the body-mind dualism characteristic of Greek thought. On this construction the flesh is evil because it is *physical.* Some scholars in the history of interpretation have drawn this conclusion about Paul's use of the term. The error of this view becomes apparent when we realize that Paul believed in a future physical resurrection of the body (1 Cor 15). A Hebrew who envisions future existence with a resurrected body does not equate the physical with evil. It is also clear that the "sins of the flesh" are not restricted to physical sins in Paul. "The works of the flesh" (Gal 5:19-21) include sins like idolatry, sorcery, enmity, strife, jealousy, anger, selfish-ambition, dissension, factions and envy. It is scarcely plausible to say, for instance, that envy has a physical source. Romans 13:13-14 leads to the same conclusion, for sins that are identified with the flesh are not only drunkenness and sexual sin but also strife and jealousy. Similarly, in Romans 7:7-25—where the power of the flesh is featured—the sin that is given prominence is not sexual sin (such as adultery) but coveting. The prohibition against coveting in Romans 7 is generalized to include coveting in all its manifestations. In several texts the negative impact of the flesh focuses especially on pride (2 Cor 11:18; Gal 6:12-13; Phil 3:3-4). The notion that the flesh designates only the physical dimension of human beings, given the evidence adduced here, can be safely set aside.

Others focus on the ontological dimensions of the "flesh." Such a perspective is reflected in the NIV translation that renders *flesh* as "sinful nature." Such a rendering is unfortunate since it introduces ontological language precipitously into the Pauline materials and compels readers to understand the flesh solely in ontological categories. A more satisfying approach understands flesh in redemptive-historical categories.[6] Paul's disjunction between the first and second Adam (see below) reflects his view of salvation history. The present evil age was introduced into the world via the sin of Adam, while the coming age has been inaugurated but not consummated through the death and resurrection of the second Adam—Jesus Christ. Thus, the age to come overlaps with the present evil age. The "flesh" designates human beings who are under the dominion of the evil era. In Romans 7:5 Paul says, "when we were in the flesh," referring to the pre-Christian experience of his readers. Being "in the flesh" involves the inability to keep the law so that death is the inevitable result. On the other hand, those who have the Spirit are freed from the power of sin and the law so that they can please God (Rom 7:6). The redemptive-historical dimension is supported by the contrast between the flesh and the Spirit because the Spirit is a gift of the coming age (Is 44:3; Jer 31:31-34; Ezek 11:19-20; 36:26-27; Joel 2:28).

The dichotomy between the flesh and Spirit receives sustained attention in Romans 8:5-13. An emphatic contrast exists between those who think according to the flesh and those who think according to the Spirit. The mindset of the flesh leads to death; the mindset of the Spirit results in life and peace. The mindset of the flesh is hostile to God and does not and cannot keep his law.

---

[6]Walter B. Russell has also effectively argued that *flesh* in Paul must be understood in terms of redemptive history, though he underestimates the anthropological dimension of the term. See his two essays, "Does the Christian Have 'Flesh' in Gal 5:13-26?" *JETS* 36 (1993): 179-87; "The Apostle Paul's Redemptive-Historical Argumentation in Galatians 5:13-26," *WTJ* 57 (1995): 333-57.

Indeed, believers are not "in the flesh but in the Spirit, if the Spirit of God dwells in you" (Rom 8:9). Paul does not define believers as being "in the flesh" or as having a "sinful nature." Those who are in the flesh are unbelievers, but believers are indwelt by the Holy Spirit and live in the age to come. They have been freed from the tyranny of the flesh by the death of Christ (Col 2:11), whereas unbelievers are subjugated to the flesh (Rom 7:18, 25). Those who indulge the desires of the flesh are unbelievers (Eph 2:3). The opposition between the flesh and Spirit is pronounced in Galatians as well (Gal 5:13-24; 6:8). The polarization again is best accounted for in salvation-historical categories. Those who have the Spirit are freed from the dominion of the former eon and now live in the new age that has begun with the death and resurrection of Jesus. They have definitively "crucified the flesh with its passions and desires" (Gal 5:24).

The "wise according to the flesh" (1 Cor 1:26) will be rejected at the judgment because their wisdom is of this world (1 Cor 1:20; 3:18-20) and in accordance with "the rulers of this age" (1 Cor 2:6, 8). The redemptive-historical backdrop for the term *flesh* emerges clearly here: "debater of *this age*" (1 Cor 1:20), "the wisdom of *the world*" (1 Cor 1:20), "wisdom not of *this age*" (1 Cor 2:6), "rulers of *this age* who are coming to an end" (1 Cor 2:6), "rulers *of this age*" (1 Cor 2:8), "if anyone thinks to be wise *in this* age" (1 Cor 3:18), "the wisdom *of this world*" (1 Cor 3:19). Paul is worried about the Corinthians precisely because they are beginning to view the world in terms acceptable to unbelievers. Similarly, in 2 Corinthians 5:16 Paul refuses to estimate anyone "according to the flesh," even, or perhaps especially, the Christ. The reason for this is that the "new creation" has dawned, so that the old things have passed and new things have arrived (2 Cor 5:17). Those who estimate Christ according to the flesh are submerged in the old era, despite the inception of the new one. The many who "boast according to the flesh" (2 Cor 11:18) are sham Christians, claiming to be apostles and ministers of Christ when actually they are servants of Satan (2 Cor 11:13-15). By warring according to the flesh (2 Cor 10:3), unlike Paul, they show their true identity. Thus, Paul emphatically repudiates the notion that he makes promises "according to the flesh" (2 Cor 1:17), for such an approach would compromise the faithfulness of the gospel and the reliability of God's promises (2 Cor 1:18-20).

Paul's stance in Galatians and Philippians is similar to his response to opponents in 2 Corinthians. The Galatian agitators lobby for circumcision because they "want to make a good showing in the flesh" (Gal 6:12-13) and to avoid persecution by boasting in the flesh of the Galatian converts. Perhaps

Paul even coined his distinctive use of the term *flesh* in the midst of his controversy with the Galatians, for they identified "perfection" with circumcision *in the flesh* (Gal 3:3), and the good showing in the flesh is circumcision.[7] Paul may have picked up on this usage to contrast circumcision "in the flesh" with life in the Spirit. The Philippian opponents were probably Judaizers— like the adversaries in Galatia. The "dogs" insist on circumcision, which to Paul is nothing less than "mutilation" (Phil 3:2). They do so in order to boast in the flesh (Phil 3:3-4). In both Galatians and Philippians, Paul sees only eschatological destruction awaiting those who promulgate or receive such teaching (Gal 5:2-6; Phil 3:17-21). Those who follow the dictates of the flesh will not inherit the kingdom of God (Gal 5:21). The false teachers in Colossae were probably of a different stripe, but Paul's conception of the flesh is the same. Those who are dead in trespasses are "in the uncircumcision of the flesh" (Col 2:13), which is a metaphorical way of saying that they are unregenerate. Nor does Paul estimate the philosophy being advocated (Col 2:8) as having any value. It is in accord with human traditions (Col 2:8). Those who champion it are "puffed up by the mind of the flesh" (Col 2:18), and their ascetic regimen has no value in restraining the indulgence of the flesh (Col 2:23).

Those who are in the flesh cannot please God, honor him or keep his commands, for those who have not been inducted into the age to come will invariably resist God. Readers of Paul will inevitably think of the many texts where believers are called on to resist the flesh, texts that we will explore in more detail in due course (e.g., Rom 8:4, 12-13; 13:14; 2 Cor 10:2-4; Gal 3:3; 5:13, 16-17, 19; 6:8). What must be said here is that the threat of the flesh to believers indicates that the age to come has not been *consummated.* The overlap of the ages explains how believers can be in the Spirit and yet must struggle against the flesh. It is crucial also to see that anyone who lets the flesh have dominion will not receive eternal life (Rom 8:13; Gal 6:8). Paul does not think anyone will enter into the kingdom of God if the flesh rules in his or her life (Gal 5:19-21). The redemptive-historical contrast between the flesh and the Spirit, therefore, is ultimately absolute. Believers struggle against the flesh only because they have not yet obtained the fullness of redemption (Rom 8:10-11, 23). Submitting to the flesh is to subjugate oneself to the present evil age. That is why Paul is so concerned about the Galatians' temptation to

---

[7]For the suggestion that the term *flesh* originated from "circumcision in the flesh," see Robert Jewett, *Paul's Anthropological Terms: A Study of Their Use in Conflict Settings,* AGJU 10 (Leiden: Brill, 1971), pp. 96-101.

embrace circumcision (Gal 5:2-4), for they somehow think that perfection can be accomplished by the flesh even though their life in Christ was initiated by the Spirit.

The Old Adam

Paul does not maintain that human beings were originally created as sinners. He traces the origin of sin to Adam (Rom 5:12-19), who transgressed God's commandment. The formative influence on his thinking is clearly Genesis 3, though Jewish tradition also locates the origin of sin to Adam and Eve, with some writers emphasizing the culpability of Eve more than Adam (cf. Wis 2:24; Sir 25:24; 2 Esd 7:21-24, 118; *2 Bar.* 17:3; 48:42-43; 54:18; *Apoc. Mos.* 32:2). Human beings, as originally created by God, do not reject God's lordship, according to Paul. Sin entered the world through Adam's choice (Rom 5:12), and the consequence of Adam's sin was death (Rom 5:12, 15, 17, 21; 1 Cor 15:21-22). The evil age commenced with Adam's sin, and death has exercised its dominion over all human beings since all have sinned (Rom 5:12). Even those who did not violate a revealed commandment died (Rom 5:13-14), revealing that they too were judged for their sin. The evil age inaugurated by Adam will not terminate until death is destroyed as the last enemy (1 Cor 15:26).

Romans 5:12-14. One of the most debated issues in the history of interpretation is the relationship between Adam's sin and the sin of his descendants. Augustine interpreted Romans 5:12 to say that "in" Adam we all sinned. He based his interpretation on the Latin phrase *in quo,* but the Greek wording is *eph hō,* which is more plausibly rendered as "on the basis of which." Dismissing Augustine's grammar does not necessarily invalidate his exegesis of the text. Many interpreters understand Romans 5:12 to say that death spread to all people because all people sinned in Adam. They do not derive such an interpretation from the prepositional phrase in Romans 5:12. They maintain that the parenthetical comments in Romans 5:13-14 compel such an interpretation.[8] The argument goes like this: In Romans 5:13-14 Paul considers the situation of those who lived in the interval between Adam and Moses. Such people did not have the law, and thus their personal sin was not reckoned against them by God since there was no law. Nonetheless, all these people

---

[8]One of the best expositions of this view is John Murray, *The Imputation of Adam's Sin* (Grand Rapids, Mich.: Eerdmans, 1959); see also S. Lewis Johnson Jr., "Romans 5:12—An Exercise in Exegesis and Theology," in *New Dimensions in New Testament Study,* ed. Richard N. Longenecker and M. C. Tenney (Grand Rapids, Mich.: Zondervan, 1974), pp. 298-316.

without exception died, even though they did not transgress against a commandment specifically revealed by God. Why did they die? Not because of their own personal sin, for the text specifically says their sin was not reckoned against them. The reason they died, then, was Adam's sin. When Paul says in Romans 5:12 that "death spread to all people because all sinned," he means that all sinned in Adam.

Although the interpretation presented above is attractive, it should be rejected. Some who espouse this interpretation argue that this view explains why infants, who have not consciously violated any law, die. Paul's intention, however, is not to speak to the issue of infants. The period in question in Romans 5:13-14 is specifically limited to the time between Adam and Moses. If Paul's focus were on infants, such a temporal designation would be unnecessary since infants *always* (not just in the period between Adam and Moses) die without consciously violating the law. Our interpretation of the text must explain why Paul focuses on the period of time between Adam and Moses. The reason is not hard to find, for Paul lands on the period in history before the law of Moses was given. These people died even though they did not violate a specific injunction in the law. Paul is scarcely suggesting at this point, however, that they died solely because of Adam's sin and that their own sin was not a factor in their death. Such a view would blatantly contradict Romans 2:12, where Paul says that "those who sin without the law perish without the law." The subsequent verses in Romans 2 clarify that they perish because they violate the law written on their hearts, and Paul's point here is that such a law is written on the hearts of *all* Gentiles. It would be inconsistent for Paul to assert in Romans 2:12 that Gentiles without the law perish because they transgress the unwritten law and then to say in Romans 5:13-14 that sin is not charged to the account of those without the Mosaic law.[9] Moreover, Paul was well aware of the early chapters of Genesis in which the world was destroyed by a flood and those building the tower of Babel were judged. Such punishments would be indefensible if judgment was only valid after the law of Moses was disseminated. The judgment of the flood generation and Babel fits with the Pauline principle that those who sin without the law will perish without the law (Rom 2:12).

The weaknesses of the interpretations presented above indicate that

---

[9]Heikki Räisänen (*Paul and the Law* [Philadelphia: Fortress, 1983], pp. 145-47) thinks Paul is guilty of such an inconsistency. For a rebuttal of many of Räisänen's arguments, see Jeffrey A. D. Weima, "The Function of the Law in Relation to Sin: An Evaluation of the View of H. Räisänen," *NovT* 32 (1990): 219-235.

another explanation of Romans 5:13-14 is necessary. I understand Romans 5:12 to say that "on the basis of death" *(eph hō)* all people sinned individually and personally.[10] That is, the reason all people sin individually is that they enter the world spiritually dead, and they enter the world spiritually dead because they are descendants of Adam. Some might object that Paul can scarcely say that sin is the result of death since he usually teaches that death is the consequence of sin (cf. Rom 6:23). There is no need, however, for an either-or here. Believers experience death because of personal sin, and yet it is also true that they sin because they enter into the world spiritually dead. Paul's understanding of death is rooted in the Genesis narrative, for Adam is warned that he will die in the very day he eats from the forbidden tree. And yet when we read the narrative we see that Adam did not immediately die—at least he and Eve did not drop dead the moment they ate of the fruit. Nonetheless, they died in the sense that their relationship with God was severed upon eating. Death is fundamentally and ultimately separation from God. What Paul teaches in Romans 5:12 is that all people sin because they enter the world spiritually dead, separated from God.

Romans 5:13-14 explains how it is that people could be judged for sin before the law was enunciated. Paul remarks that sin committed before the Mosaic law was established is not *technically* reckoned as sin. There was not a technical register of sin; sin was present, just like heat and cold are present whether we have a thermometer or not. But one could not, in a sense, *measure* sin before the giving of the law. People who sinned in the interval between Adam and Moses should be distinguished from Adam in that they did not violate a revealed commandment. Paul is *not,* however, claiming that those who lived between Adam and Moses were not held responsible for their sin. He merely remarks that their sin could not be measured as sin without the violation of written commands. Such people were still sinners—as the text says, "sin was in the world until the law" (Rom 5:13)—and they died because of their sin. "Death reigned from Adam until Moses" (Rom 5:14). Paul has already informed his readers that death is the consequence of sin, and here he observes that this principle holds true even for those who lacked the law. Death reigned over those living between Adam and Moses because these people personally sinned.

Romans 5:15-19. Romans 5:15-19 confirms that it is a serious mistake to iso-

---

[10]For a careful lexical study of *eph hō* that fits with my understanding of the verse, see Joseph A. Fitzmyer, "The Consecutive Meaning of *eph hō* in Romans 5.12," *NTS* 39 (1993): 321-39.

late personal sin from the sin of Adam. Sin and death entered the world as powers that reign (cf. Rom 5:14) over people through Adam. Adam's sin introduced death in the world, so that all people enter the world separated from God and, on that basis, they sin. Adam's sin, therefore, is the fountainhead for those that follow. Romans 5:15-19 explains the relationship between Adam and his descendants by emphasizing five times that sin, death and condemnation all stem from Adam. "The many died by the transgression of the one" (Rom 5:15). People do not only die because of their personal sin; they also die because of the sin of Adam. Death began its reign over all people through the one transgression of Adam—"by the transgression of the one death reigned through the one man" (Rom 5:17).

Paul does not restrict the sway of death over all people to personal sin only. Death's rule over all humanity was inaugurated by Adam's sin. It could be the case that death reigned over all people, but they are only condemned for their own personal sin. Such a perspective is certainly *not* Paul's. Condemnation is the portion of all people because of the one transgression of Adam—"the judgment from the one sin resulted in condemnation" (Rom 5:16). Romans 5:18 is quite clear in this regard: "through one transgression resulted condemnation for all people." All human beings are implicated in Adam's sin. Paul, of course, does not deny that condemnation is the result of personal sin. Yet he also traces the roots of human sin back to Adam: "Through the disobedience of the one man the many were made sinners" (Rom 5:19). Notice that many have become sinners on the basis of Adam's sin, so that the sin of all humanity is rooted in the sin of Adam. It would be simpler if Paul taught that people died solely because of their own personal sin. But it is clear that he also attributes their sin, condemnation and death to Adam. Human beings do not enter the world in a neutral state or slightly inclined to evil, according to Paul. They are polluted by the sin of Adam and enter the world as sinners, condemned and destined for death. The parallel between Adam and Christ in these verses supports the interpretation offered here. Christ is the head of the new humanity, and Adam is the head of the old. Those in Christ are righteous and vindicated, and they reign in life. Paul does not explain in as much detail as we might wish the relationship between Adam and his descendants, but the parallel between Adam and Christ suggests that Adam is the head or representative of the old humanity, just as Christ is the representative of the new.

The Adam-Christ contrast should also be understood in redemptive-historical terms. Adam introduced the age of sin and death through his sin, while Christ inaugurated the new age of righteousness and life through his death and resurrection. All human beings are either in Adam or in Christ. They belong to this present evil age or to the age to come. Paul does not explain sin and death solely or finally in terms of individual decisions. Human beings enter the world destined for death because they are in Adam, and only through Christ can they participate in the blessings of the coming age. The "old person" *(palaios anthrōpos)* that was crucified with Christ refers to what people are in Adam (Rom 6:6; cf. Eph 4:22; Col 3:9). The verse indicates that those who are in Adam are slaves to sin and, as such, are loyal servants to its mastery.

Conclusion

We have seen in the last two chapters that human beings apart from Christ are in a bleak state. They dishonor God, fail to keep his law and boast in their works anyway. Even if they tried to observe God's commands, they could not because they are slaves to sin. They are under the dominion of the world, the flesh and the devil. As children of Adam, they are born into the world separated from God and as sinners. The plight of human beings is such that a solution is needed, and Paul finds the solution in his gospel, as we shall see in subsequent chapters.

7

THE PERSON OF
JESUS CHRIST
The Exaltation of Christ
for the Glory of God

The redemption of the world has been achieved by Jesus Christ. As the Christ of God he is reclaiming human beings and all creation for his glory. God desires to bring human beings under his rule so that they will honor and praise his name and experience the joy of salvation. By bringing the good news of God's saving righteousness to all people, the apostle Paul, as Christ's chosen instrument, plays a crucial role in fulfilling God's promises. Those who have dishonored God can become part of his family through faith and repentance. Paul invites all people, both Jews and Gentiles, to enjoy the redemption accomplished by Christ. The tyranny of sin and death is so pervasive, however, that liberation from their grip cannot be accomplished by human beings born in Adam. Paul proclaims in his gospel that God has fulfilled his saving promises in bringing Jesus, the Christ, into the world. Those who exercise faith in him are liberated from the power of sin and restored to peace with God.

Paul must explain in his gospel *how* Jesus Christ has accomplished redemption. Human beings are freed to honor and praise God because Jesus in his person and work has vindicated God's honor. He has succeeded where

Adam and Israel failed. He is the promised seed of Abraham and David, the Lord of heaven and earth, and he even shares in the divine nature. He fulfills the promises of the new covenant, and through him the promise made to Abraham that all nations would be blessed is inaugurated.

Jesus as the Second Adam

Adam introduced sin and death into the world by transgressing God's command. All human beings as descendants of Adam are under the dominion of sin and death. The promises of salvation made to Israel were not yet fulfilled, and the nation continued to live under Roman control because of its sin. The pattern of sin that permeated Israel's history demonstrated that the glorious promises of deliverance and salvation were not yet a reality. The history of Israel shows that for God's promises to be fulfilled, a new humanity is necessary; and for a new humanity, we need a new Adam. Paul proclaims that Jesus the Messiah is the new Adam. The old age of death was introduced by Adam, but the new age of resurrection and life was introduced by Christ (1 Cor 15:21-22). The resurrection was one of the future promises that Israel yearned to see fulfilled, for at the day of resurrection the present age with its evil and futility (Gal 1:4; cf. Rom 8:18-25) would end and a new age of life and joy would dawn. Paul asserts that the new age has arrived because the resurrection is now a reality, for Christ has been raised from the dead (Rom 1:4). The resurrection of Christ signals that the end time resurrection promised in Ezekiel (Ezek 37) had arrived. The "already but not yet" flavor of Paul's eschatology emerges here since believers in Christ still die and await a future resurrection. Believers are not resurrected immediately upon believing; they "all shall be made alive (*zōopoiēthēsontai*) in Christ" (1 Cor 15:22). The future tense of the verb indicates that the resurrection of believers is in view, that is—contrary to what the Corinthians believe—still awaited. Nonetheless, the age to come has penetrated this age because Christ has now been raised. Those who "are in him" (cf. 1 Cor 15:23), those who belong to him as the new Adam, will triumph over death.

The argument of 1 Corinthians 15:44-49 is remarkably similar. The main purpose of the text is not to introduce an abstract discussion on christology, nor is the intention to discuss the *origin* of Adam or Christ in terms of the former being from the earth and the latter from heaven.[1] Nor is Paul counter-

---

[1] For a canvassing of different views and a sober exegesis of these verses, see Gordon D. Fee, *God's Empowering Presence: The Holy Spirit in the Letters of Paul* (Peabody, Mass.: Hendrickson, 1994), pp. 261-69.

ing either Gnostic or Philonic conceptions of the heavenly man. His aim is to show the Corinthians that their resurrection is still future, in that the spiritual body is subsequent to the earthly body. He punctures their overrealized eschatology by reminding them of the interval between Christ's resurrection and theirs. The "life-giving Spirit" of the last Adam (1 Cor 15:45) does not refer precisely to the resurrection that awaits the Corinthians. Jesus poured out the life-giving Spirit when he was exalted to the right hand of God.[2] A new era in salvation history dawned with the gift of the Spirit, and the gift of the Spirit guarantees that the resurrection will occur in the future (Rom 8:21, 23-25; Eph 1:13-14; cf. 2 Cor 1:21-22). Meanwhile, believers live with the weaknesses and flaws of the earthly body, knowing "we shall bear the image of the heavenly" Adam (1 Cor 15:49) when the end arrives. The future resurrection of believers is grounded on the resurrection of Jesus as the last Adam and is certified by the gift of the Spirit. Since believers are "in Christ" (1 Cor 15:22), their rejection of a future bodily resurrection (1 Cor 15:12-19) also involves a repudiation of Christ's resurrection. The resurrection of Christ and believers is logically inseparable, but temporally an interval comes between the resurrection of the last Adam and the resurrection of his people. By virtue of belonging to the last Adam, believers will surely triumph over death on the last day; death as the last enemy will be destroyed (1 Cor 15:26).

The contrast between Adam and Christ is most pronounced in Romans 5:15-19. Sin, death and judgment were introduced into the world through Adam. Paul emphasizes, however, that Christ's work is even greater than Adam's. Adam's influence in the world was exclusively negative in that he brought death and devastation into the cosmos. Jesus Christ, by bringing life and by triumphing over sin, counteracted and reversed the downward pull of Adam's sin. Paul emphasizes the lavishness and superabundance of the work of Christ when he writes, "much more the grace of God and the gift in grace abounded for the many" (Rom 5:15) and "much more those receiving the abundance of grace and the gift of righteousness will reign in life through the one Jesus Christ" (Rom 5:17). Sin reigns in the domain of death through Adam, but now grace also reigns, and the result is eternal life through the saving righteousness of Jesus Christ (Rom 5:21). His grace is so powerful that righteousness is given to all those who belong to him despite the fact that "many trespasses" blocked his gift of righteousness (Rom 5:16). Why does

---

[2]For this view, see Richard B. Gaffin Jr., " 'Life-Giving Spirit': Probing the Center of Paul's Pneumatology," *JETS* 41 (1998): 573-89.

Paul emphasize the astonishing plenitude of Christ's grace by contrasting it with Adam's sin? He does so because the power of grace shines brighter against the dark backdrop of sin. Seeing the havoc, grief and despair engendered by Adam's sin helps us to realize that grace is no small thing. Grace is so powerful that it cleans up the mess produced by Adam and produces the wholeness God intended in creating human beings in the first place. Everyone knows that cleaning up a mess is much harder than creating one in the first place. The grace of Christ is so powerful that it reverses the downward spiral initiated by Adam and makes human beings whole and holy persons. Grace inducts people into life and righteousness so that they can enjoy God's presence forever, so that they will reign in life instead of serving sin as slaves. Those in Adam are condemned and dead, but those in Christ are righteous and reign in life (Rom 5:17). Adam's sin made many sinners, but Christ's obedience made many righteous (Rom 5:19). The two decisive figures in human history are Adam and Christ. Adam brought into the world the great enemies of human happiness—sin and death. These twin powers reign over all those in Adam, and only those in Christ conquer sin and death and become righteous and live.

God's intention for humanity has been realized in Jesus Christ, the second Adam. He is the "one new man" of whom Jews and Gentiles become a part through faith (Eph 2:15).[3] The "new man" whom believers are to put on (Eph 4:24) is the second Adam, while the "old man" whom they are to put aside is the first Adam (Eph 4:22). The "old man" who was crucified with Christ was the first Adam (Rom 6:6). Paul summons believers to live new lives since they have "put off the old man" (Col 3:9) and "put on the new" (Col 3:10). The "new man" in the lives of believers is being renewed by God into the image Adam was intended to have at the original creation. Colossians 3:11 clarifies that the "new man" is Christ himself. The new man is the place "where" (*hopou*) being a Greek or Jew, circumcised or uncircumcised, Barbarian or Scythian, slave or free is insignificant. One's ethnic background, religious ritual and social class are trivial because "Christ is all and in all." What matters is whether one belongs to the second Adam.

Another indication that "putting on the new man" refers to "putting on Christ" as the last Adam is Romans 13:14, for here instead of being exhorted to "put on" the "new man," believers are commanded to "put on [*endysasthe*]

---

[3]The literal wording "new man" is maintained instead of the "new person" or the "new self" so that the parallel between Adam and "the new man" is clearly perceived.

the Lord Jesus Christ." The verb translated here as "put on" is the same verb used in Ephesians 4:24 *(endysasthai)* and Colossians 3:10 *(endysamenoi),* which suggests that putting on the "new man" is nothing other than putting on the second Adam, the Lord Jesus Christ.

Christ as the Image of God

Jesus Christ is not only the second Adam but also "the image of God" (2 Cor 4:4; Col 1:15; cf. Rom 8:29).[4] Such a formulation hearkens back to Genesis 1:27, where Adam (and Eve) is made "according to the image of God" *(kat eikona theou).* We often think of an image as an imperfect or lifeless copy of the original, but the biblical writers understand the image to partake of the reality and the nature of the original. The clearest example supporting this idea is found in Hebrews 10:1, where the law is a mere "shadow" *(skia)* of the "good things to come" and not the "image" *(eikona)* of these good things. The contrast between "shadow" and "image" indicates that the former is used to convey an imperfect replica of the original whereas the latter shares the nature of the original. We shall not enter into the debate as to the meaning of the image of God in Genesis 1. The writer is probably somewhat vague so that the readers would not unduly restrict the notion of being made in God's image. Part of the image consists in the call to rule over the created world (Gen 1:26), but the beneficent rule of Adam and Eve was ruined by the Fall. Instead of bringing joy and peace to the world, they introduced thorns and thistles (Gen 3:17-19), and the created world was subject to frustration and vanity (Rom 8:19-22). Human beings born in Adam would never bring about a world of joy and goodness since they too have sinned (Rom 5:12-19). Jesus the Messiah, however, succeeded where Adam failed. Through him God's plan to bring the world under his lordship will succeed.

Paul does not only identify Jesus as the second Adam, nor does he equate Adam and Jesus in every respect. Adam was created "according to the image of God" (Gen 1:27), but Jesus *"is* the image of God" (2 Cor 4:4; Col 1:15). Christ as the image of God surpasses Adam because the word *image* suggests that he shares the very nature of God. He represents God himself to the world

---

[4]For a helpful study of christology, see James D. G. Dunn, *Christology in the Making: A New Testament Inquiry into the Doctrine of the Incarnation,* 2nd ed. (Grand Rapids, Mich.: Eerdmans, 1996). Dunn's work is seriously flawed, however, in restricting the notion of preexistence to John. It is fair to say that most scholars have not been convinced by such a thesis. Nonetheless, Dunn's work is very useful for tracing some of the antecedents of Paul's christology, and Dunn rightly rejects the idea that Paul's christology is shaped by Gnosticism.

because he partakes in the very essence of God. Jesus is not only the second Adam; he is also the agent of creation and the goal of creation: "All things were created through him and for him" (Col 1:16). These expressions clarify that the Son of God was preexistent. Adam was created at a certain point in history, but the Son is God's image and the means by which the world came into being. He was not created but is the Creator. We are reminded of wisdom's role in the creation of the world in Proverbs 8:22-31. Wisdom is also identified as God's image in Jewish literature: "For she is a reflection of eternal light, a spotless mirror of the working of God, and an image of his goodness" (Wis 7:26 NRSV).

Only through Jesus Christ, the one and only image of God, can human beings attain what God intended in making Adam according to his image. It is interesting to see, therefore, the close conjunction between "the new man" and being restored to "knowledge according to the image" in Colossians 3:10. People are restored to the fullness of God's image through a saving knowledge of God, and such saving knowledge becomes a reality through Jesus (cf. 2 Cor 3:18; Eph 4:24). Indeed, those who are "conformed to the image of his Son" (Rom 8:29) are predestined by God to share in this joy.

In Christ

One of the most common designations in the Pauline letters is "in Christ."[5] The formula cannot be confined to the places where "in Christ" itself occurs. For example, Ephesians 1:3-14 speaks of being "in Christ" (Eph 1:3, 10, 12), "in him" (Eph 1:4, 9, 10), "in the beloved" (Eph 1:6) and "in whom" (Eph 1:7, 11, 13 [2x]). The diversity of expressions to describe being in Christ in this one long sentence (Eph 1:3-14) is astonishing, and the sheer repetition of the formula indicates that it is crucial in Pauline thought. In fact, some scholars such as Albert Schweitzer and E. P. Sanders have maintained that the mystical doctrine of being in Christ or participation in Christ is the nerve-center of Pauline theology.[6] Schweitzer says, "The doctrine of righteousness by faith is therefore a subsidiary crater, which has formed within the rim of the main crater—the mystical doctrine of redemption through the being-in-Christ."[7] Certainly

---

[5]For a helpful study of the "in Christ" formula in Paul, see Mark A. Seifrid, "In Christ," in *Dictionary of Paul and His Letters*, ed. Gerald P. Hawthorne, Ralph P. Martin and Daniel G. Reid (Downers Grove, Ill.: InterVarsity Press, 1993), pp. 433-36.

[6]See Albert Schweitzer, *The Mysticism of Paul the Apostle* (New York: Henry Holt, 1931), pp. 219-26; and E. P. Sanders, *Paul and Palestinian Judaism: A Comparison of Patterns of Religion* (Philadelphia: Fortress, 1977).

[7]Schweitzer, *Mysticism*, p. 225.

participation in Christ is of tremendous importance in Paul's thinking. But we do not need to conclude from this that righteousness is a minor theme in the Pauline literature. Participation in Christ and righteousness are by no means mutually exclusive. Both are prominent and significant in Paul's thinking.

Nor does the word *mystical* provide the best inroad for understanding Paul's "in Christ" theology. Since *mystical* is a vague term with a diversity of connotations, it is too imprecise to prove useful in defining Paul's theology. In particular, during the course of New Testament scholarship some have attempted to forge a connection between Paul and the mystery religions of his day. Paul's indebtedness to the mystery religions was forcefully argued for in the earlier part of the twentieth century.[8] Few scholars today would accept such a thesis. Scholars have carefully sifted through the evidence, and most have rightly concluded that the parallels between Paul and the mystery religions are superficial.[9] Some scholars uncritically used sources later than the Pauline writings and then proceeded to argue that Paul borrowed from these later sources. Paul's faith is rooted in historical events—the death and resurrection of Jesus the Messiah. This is a far cry from the ahistorical and experiential character of the mystery religions. Paul's theology is grounded in and is a reflection on the Old Testament scriptures, not on pagan mystery religions, which Paul would have dismissed as idolatrous and part of the elements of the world. For this reason alone the term *mystical* should be avoided as misleading in explaining Paul's use of the phrase *in Christ*. Others have taken the phrase *in Christ* too literally, even to the point of understanding Christ to be akin to a fluid that permeates our existence. This realistic conception, which was advocated by Adolf Deissmann among others, has been vigorously challenged and most scholars now doubt its accuracy.[10]

---

[8]The influence of mystery religions on Paul was advocated by Richard Reitzenstein, *Hellenistic Mystery-Religions: Their Basic Ideas and Significance* (Pittsburgh: Pickwick, 1978); cf. Wilhelm Bousset, *Kyrios Christos: A History of the Belief in Christ from the Beginnings of Christianity to Irenaeus* (Nashville: Abingdon, 1970). Few scholars today would accept such a thesis. For example, those studying the history of religions were disposed to think that the Pauline doctrine of baptism was influenced by the mystery religions.

[9]For a decisive and careful refutation of this notion, see A. J. M. Wedderburn, *Baptism and Resurrection: Studies in Pauline Theology Against Its Graeco-Roman Background*, WUNT 44 (Tübingen: J. C. B. Mohr, 1987); cf. also Günter Wagner, *Pauline Baptism and the Pagan Mysteries: The Problem of the Pauline Doctrine of Baptism in Romans VI.1-11 in the Light of Its Religio-Historical "Parallels"* (Edinburgh: Oliver & Boyd, 1967).

[10]G. Adolf Deissmann, *Paul: A Study in Social and Religious History* (New York: George H. Doran, 1927), pp. 135-57, esp. pp. 138-42; cf. also Bousset, *Kyrios Christos*, pp. 154-63.

It is fruitful to explore Paul's use of the term *in Christ* by beginning with Adam christology. Paul does not use the phrases *in Christ, in Christ Jesus* or *in the Lord* in only one fashion. The expression oscillates between the ideas of manner, locality and instrumentality. Sometimes the idea of manner seems prominent—"I speak the truth in Christ" (Rom 9:1). In many instances "in Christ" denotes both means and locality. Both of these notions fit under the rubric of Adam Christology, though we must be careful not to force every use of the phrase under this category.

We have observed that all people are either in Adam or in Christ in Paul's thought. Adam and Christ are the two representative heads for humanity. When Paul says believers are "in Christ," he means that they are incorporated in Christ rather than in Adam. Christ, not Adam, is now their representative and head. Some scholars raise doubts about whether such representative or corporate christology can be sustained by examining the evidence. They object that the whole notion of "corporate personality" is imposed on the evidence instead of being vindicated by careful study.[11] Doubtless some have gone too far when they speak of corporate personality. But the contrast between Adam and Christ supports the representative character of Paul's christology, and it is clear that they are the heads of humanity. Such an idea is also found in the Old Testament where the king functions as the representative of his people (e.g., 2 Sam 19:40-43; 20:1). The term *Son of Man* in Daniel 7 also supports such a view, for though the term itself is the subject of intense debate in Daniel 7, it seems likely that the "Son of Man" functions as the representative of the "saints." The Son of Man is the one who receives the kingdom from the Ancient of Days, and all people are subservient to him (Dan 7:13-14). As we read on in Daniel 7, the kingdom is given to the saints (likely the people of Israel rather than angels). Israel, though oppressed and persecuted for a time, will eventually rule the world (Dan 7:21-22, 27). The use of the term *Son of Man* in the gospels cannot be examined here since the controversy over its meaning and usage is enormous. But we can confidently say that the early Christians understood it to refer to Jesus himself. If they also spied in Daniel 7 a reference to the dominion of the saints, it seems likely that the representative role of Jesus was acknowledged in this text. The argument is not that Paul understood the phrase *in Christ* in terms of Son of Man christology since Paul avoids referring to Christ as the "Son of Man." Son of Man

---

[11]See John W. Rogerson, "The Hebrew Conception of Corporate Personality: A Re-examination," *JTS* 21 (1970): 1-16; Stanley E. Porter, "Two Myths: Corporate Personality and Language/Mentality Determinism," *SJT* 43 (1990): 289-307.

christology suggests that that the representative and corporate dimensions of the phrase *in Christ* would not be surprising.

Those who are in Adam experience all the liabilities of being descended from him. Similarly, those in Christ experience all the blessings that accrue to those who belong to God. Every spiritual blessing belongs to believers in Christ (Eph 1:3). Those who are in Christ are a new creation (2 Cor 5:17); they are redeemed (Rom 3:24; Eph 1:7) and made sons of God (Gal 3:26). What marks out Christian communities or assemblies, then, is that they are in Christ (Gal 1:22; Col 1:2; cf. 1 Thess 1:1). Both Jews and Gentiles have been brought near to God in Christ (Eph 2:13). God has reconciled the world to himself in Christ (2 Cor 5:19). The blessing of Abraham is available to Jews and Gentiles in Christ (Gal 3:14). Thus, believers from every social class, ethnic group and gender are one in Christ Jesus (Gal 3:28). Believers have been chosen before the world began in Christ (Eph 1:4), and it is only by virtue of God's work that they are in Christ (1 Cor 1:30). No condemnation comes to those in Christ (Rom 8:1), and believers are alive to God in Christ Jesus (Rom 6:11). Believers are seated in the heavenlies with Christ (Eph 2:6) and experience freedom in him (Gal 2:4). When we see the comprehensive blessings that belong to those in Christ, it is clear that the promise to reclaim the world for God is inaugurated through Christ. The church is a new society that expresses in part what God intended when he made Adam and Eve. The saving promises made to Abraham are becoming a reality in Christ since he reverses the curse and devastation imposed on the world through the first Adam.

Jesus as the Seed of Abraham

One of the distinctive features of Paul's theology is that Jesus is the seed of Abraham (Gal 3:16). The promise to bless all nations was given to Abraham and his descendants (Gen 12:3), and the blessing to all nations would be obtained *through* Abraham. Promises of blessing for both the sons and daughters of Abraham and the nations are contained in the Prophets (see below). The Jews of Paul's day, however, had not yet experienced the fulfillment of these prophecies. Rome still reigned over Israel, and they longed for the day of the Lord when the enemies of God would be judged and his people would be blessed. On the day of the Lord the promises to Abraham would be fulfilled. We know that Paul thinks along the same lines because he refers to the promise that Abraham will be "heir of the world" (Rom 4:13). There are reasons to think, then, that Abraham now fulfills the role of

Adam in reclaiming the world for God. To say that Abraham will be "heir of the world" is astonishing because the Old Testament narrative restricts the promise to the land of Palestine (Gen 12:7; 13:14-17; 15:7, 18-21; 17:8). Nonetheless, we should not conclude that Paul's statement violates the intention of Genesis since the promise to Abraham also involves descendants (Gen 12:2; 13:16; 15:5; 17:4-6, 16-20; 18:18; 22:17) and blessing for all peoples (Gen 12:3; 18:18; 22:18). The notion that Abraham is "heir of the world" is valid if one merges together all three elements of the original promise made to Abraham. That is, the promise cannot be restricted to the land of Palestine since Abraham is also the agent by which the whole world will be blessed. Other Jewish writers in Paul's day drew a similar conclusion and maintained that ultimately Abraham will rule over the world (cf. *Jub.* 22:14; 32:19). And, even more significantly, the Old Testament psalmists and prophets conceived of Yahweh's saving rule as extending over the whole world (Ps 2:7-12; 22:27-28; 47:7-9; 72:8-11, 17; Is 2:1-4; 19:18-25; 49:6-7; 52:15; 55:3-5; 66:23; Amos 9:11-12; Zeph 3:9-10; Zech 14:9).

The genuinely novel element in Paul's argument is the claim that the worldwide blessing promised to Abraham is now in the process of fulfillment. Not only is the promise being fulfilled, but it is coming to fruition through the single seed of Abraham—Jesus the Messiah (Gal 3:16). Paul's argument may seem exceedingly strange to readers of the Old Testament, as we noted earlier, because it is obvious that the term *seed* is a collective noun and embraces many people. Paul himself knows this since he uses the same noun *seed (sperma)* to refer to all the children of Abraham in Galatians 3:29, just thirteen verses later! What do we make of Paul's interpretation of the Old Testament in Galatians 3:16? It is impossible for us to have certainty, but a promising line of investigation is in the Old Testament itself. Even in Genesis there is evidence that the promise of Abraham will come to fruition through a single seed—a descendant of Judah (Gen 49:10).[12] In the Old Testament the Davidic king represents the people of God, and the promises of future salvation will be obtained through an anointed one of David's line. Paul likely merged the idea of Abraham's seed with the promise of a Davidic heir.

In addition, the history of Israel was one in which God's promises were not yet fulfilled, and though there was a small remnant that was faithful, most had violated the covenant to the extent that Israel's sovereignty was

---

[12]See T. D. Alexander, *From Paradise to the Promised Land: An Introduction to the Main Themes of the Pentateuch* (Carlisle: Paternoster, 1995), pp. 39-45, 55-56.

removed and handed over to Rome. Both the Old Testament scriptures and Jewish tradition maintain that a ruler from David's line will bring in a new era (cf. other texts on a Davidic ruler noted above; *Pss. Sol.* 17—18). I am not suggesting that there was only one messianic view in Judaism in Paul's day, for it is well known that diverse views of the Messiah were in the air.[13] The point is merely that Paul retained the idea that the Messiah would be a son of David. When Paul identifies Jesus as the seed of Abraham, he conceives of Jesus as fulfilling this role. He is the sole seed of Abraham because he is the authentic descendant from David. The only means to the blessing of Abraham is by being united to Christ, "the blessing of Abraham comes to the Gentiles in Christ Jesus" (Gal 3:14). In other words, Paul does not neatly separate the various roles of Jesus in his writings: Jesus is the second Adam, the Messiah, the faithful seed of Abraham and God's Son.

Since Jesus is the only legitimate seed of Abraham, only those who believe in Jesus are true sons and daughters of Abraham (Gal 3:7, 26). Paul's argument in Galatians 3:26-29 is particularly instructive along these lines. Sonship is obtained in Christ Jesus through faith. "In Christ Jesus" refers to incorporation into Christ, and this is supported by Galatians 3:27, where those baptized "into Christ" *(eis Christon)* "have been clothed with Christ." The metaphor of baptism pictures submersion into Christ, so that one is incorporated into him as the last Adam. Paul argues along the same lines in Romans 6:3-5. Believers have died to the power of sin because they were baptized into Christ, and baptism into Christ by definition involves baptism into his death and resurrection. Believers have been so incorporated into Christ that they have died and been raised with him in baptism. The "old person," the old Adam, was crucified with Christ (Rom 6:6), and now believers walk in newness of life. Since believers have been baptized into Christ, they are now clothed with Christ (Gal 3:27). The old categories of gender, class and ethnic background are not decisive (Gal 3:28). Paul rounds off this discussion by asserting that "if you belong to Christ, you are the seed of Abraham, heirs according to promise" (Gal 3:29). Incorporation into Christ is the means by which people become the seed of Abraham since Jesus is the true seed of Abraham.

Jesus as Lord

Paul often refers to Jesus as Lord *(kyrios)* in his letters. The centrality and per-

---

[13]For conceptions of the Messiah in Paul's day, see Jacob Neusner, William Scott Green and Ernest F. Frerichs, *Judaisms and Their Messiahs at the Turn of the Christian Era* (Cambridge: Cambridge University Press, 1987).

vasiveness of this designation is signaled by its regular use in greetings and farewells (e.g., Rom 1:7; 16:24; 1 Cor 1:2-3; 16:23; 2 Cor 1:2; 13:13; Gal 1:3; 6:18; Philem 3, 25) and the sheer number of times in which the title is used with reference to Jesus Messiah. The liturgical cast of the term is conveyed in the sonorous phrases that are used: "Jesus Christ, our Lord" (Rom 1:4; 1 Cor 1:9), "Lord, Jesus Christ" (Rom 1:7; 13:14; 1 Cor 1:3), "our Lord, Jesus Christ" (e.g., Rom 5:1, 11; 15:6, 30; 1 Cor 1:2, 8, 10), "our Lord Jesus" (Rom 16:20; 1 Cor 5:4; 2 Cor 1:14) "the Lord Jesus" (Rom 14:14; 1 Cor 11:23; 16:23; 2 Cor 11:31), "Jesus our Lord" (Rom 4:24; 1 Cor 9:1), "our Lord Christ" (Rom 16:18), "Jesus as Lord" (Rom 10:9), "Jesus is Lord" (1 Cor 12:3), "Jesus Christ as Lord"(2 Cor 4:5), "Christ Jesus as Lord" (Col 2:6), "Jesus Christ is Lord" (Phil 2:11), "Christ Jesus, our Lord" (e.g., Rom 6:23; 8:39; 1 Cor 15:31) and "Christ Jesus, my Lord" (Phil 3:8). The frequency with which Paul uses such expressions indicate that the lordship of Jesus was a central part of his theology. The constant collocation with the term *Christ* indicates that the lordship of Jesus was closely associated with his messianic status.

In the tradition. It is also likely that the lordship of Jesus was no Pauline innovation. Paul's use of the title in his greetings and farewells indicates that it was part of the common confession of early Christians. The lordship of Jesus is also expressed in a number of confessional or hymnic statements in Paul, some of which may have been handed down to Paul via the tradition (Rom 1:3-4; 10:9; 1 Cor 8:5-6; 12:3; Phil 2:11).[14] This strengthens the thesis that before Paul the church commonly declared Jesus' lordship. Wilhelm Bousset defended the thesis that the Hellenistic churches were the first to confess Jesus as Lord and that such a confession did not originate in Palestinian churches.[15] The creedal statements noted above, however, have led most scholars to reject Boussett's thesis because the earliest traditions from Palestinian churches acknowledge the lordship of Jesus. Moreover, the firm disjunction between Hellenism and Judaism, which was well accepted in Boussett's day, is no longer accepted by most scholars. Martin Hengel has demonstrated that Palestinian Judaism was significantly influenced by Hellenism, and thus drawing hard and fast distinctions between Palestinian and Hellenistic Judaism is questionable.[16]

The word *maranatha* (1 Cor 16:22) is also significant in this regard. This

---

[14]I have reservations, however, about these texts being pre-Pauline.

[15]Bousset, *Kyrios Christos*, pp. 121-29, 136.

[16]Martin Hengel, *Judaism and Hellenism: Studies in Their Encounter in Palestine During the Early Hellenistic Period* (London: SCM Press, 1974).

Aramaic term should probably be rendered "Our Lord, come," and thus it is clearly a reference to Jesus Christ. The Aramaic form of the word is best explained if the term came to Paul through the earliest Palestinian Christian communities. Paul was no innovator in hailing Jesus Christ as Lord; he was faithful to the confessional tradition of the early Christian churches.

The importance of Jesus' lordship emerges in a number of creedal statements. To be saved one must acknowledge Jesus as Lord (Rom 10:9). The believer's initial submission to Jesus as Lord is reflected in Paul's exhortation in which he reminds the Colossians that they "received Christ Jesus as Lord" (Col 2:6). Pagans bow to many gods and lords, but believers worship only one God—the Father—and only one Lord—Jesus (1 Cor 8:5-6). This last text is particularly illuminating, for it likely contains an early reflection on Deuteronomy 6:4, where the oneness of God is proclaimed. The doctrine of God's oneness is a cornerstone of the Hebrew scriptures and would not be compromised by any faithful Jew. Paul also trumpets God's oneness in contrast to the polytheism that was rampant in the Greco-Roman world (cf. Rom 3:29-30). The lordship of Jesus in Paul's estimation does not jeopardize monotheism but must be explained within the context of monotheism.[17] On the other hand, the lordship of Jesus for Paul (see below) indicates that Jesus is to be worshiped. And yet the deity of Jesus is not such that he is all there is to God. Paul reconceptualizes monotheism so that it includes a divine status for Jesus Christ without denying the oneness of God. Paul distinguishes between God as the source of all things and Jesus as the agent for God's gifts: "God the father" is one "from whom" *(ex hou)* all things come, whereas Jesus Christ is the one "through whom" *(dia hou)* God's gifts are ours (1 Cor 8:6; cf. Col 1:16).

Lord of the whole of life. The lordship of Jesus cannot be confined to an initial decision where one submits to his lordship. Paul often appeals to the lordship of Jesus in his exhortations, showing that the lordship of Jesus carries through all of life. For example, in Romans 14:1—15:13 believers manifest their glad submission to the lordship of God and Christ by refusing to judge fellow believers who differ from them on the matter of foods and the observance of various days. The word *kyrios* in these verses oscillates between God and

---

[17]Scholars have pursued the Christian variation on Jewish monotheism in some detail. For some antecedents to the Christian view, see Alan F. Segal, *Two Powers in Heaven: Early Rabbinic Reports About Christianity and Gnosticism*, SJLA 25 (Leiden: Brill, 1977); Larry Hurtado, *One God, One Lord: Early Christian Devotion and Ancient Jewish Monotheism* (Philadelphia: Fortress, 1988). For a view that differs from Hurtado's in some respects, see Loren T. Stuckenbruck, *Angel Veneration and Christology: A Study in Early Judaism and in the Christology of the Apocalypse of John*, WUNT 2/70 (Tübingen: J. C. B. Mohr, 1995).

Christ (Rom 14:4, 6, 8, 11, 14), so that in some verses it is difficult to discern which is in view. In Romans 14:8, 14 the reference is certainly to Christ, whereas Romans 14:11 most likely refers to the Father. The alternation reveals Christ's high status in Paul's thinking, so high that distinguishing between God's and Christ's lordship in these verses is difficult. In any case, believers reveal their compliance to Christ's lordship by desisting from passing judgment on fellow believers. The lordship of Christ is no abstract teaching for Paul; it penetrates to Christians' everyday existence.

Those who acclaim Christ as Lord need to acknowledge his lordship over their bodies by not giving reign to sexual immorality (1 Cor 6:12-20; 1 Thess 4:3-8). Having Christ as Lord is no idle matter, for those who eat in the temple of an idol cannot also drink "the cup of the Lord" (1 Cor 10:21). By doing so one provokes the Lord to jealousy and becomes prey to his fierce judgment (1 Cor 10:22). Believers manifest their devotion to the Lord in a multitude of ways: by giving thanks in all things (Eph 5:20), by doing all in the Lord's name (Col 3:17), by living in harmony (Phil 4:2), by resisting the wiles of the devil (Eph 6:11), by keeping apostolic instructions (1 Thess 4:2), by respecting their leaders (1 Thess 5:12), by supporting themselves financially instead of being lazy (2 Thess 3:12), by turning away from false teaching (1 Tim 6:3) and by not being ashamed of the message of the gospel (2 Tim 1:8). Wives are to submit to their husbands "in the Lord" (Eph 5:22; Col 3:18), and children are to obey their parents "in the Lord" (Eph 6:1; Col 3:20). Similarly, slaves are to obey their masters with the motivation of pleasing the Lord Christ instead of their earthly masters (Eph 6:5-8; Col 3:22-25). Conversely, masters must beware of abusing and mistreating their slaves, for they too have a Lord in heaven who will pass judgment on them (Eph 6:9; Col 4:1).

Once we grasp the pervasive nature of the lordship of Christ the significance of 1 Corinthians 12:3 becomes clearer: "no one is able to say Jesus is Lord, except by the Holy Spirit." Obviously, Paul does not intend to say that no one can utter the mere words *Jesus is Lord* except by the Holy Spirit. Anyone can pronounce the words. What he means is that no one can acclaim Jesus as Lord *and live under his lordship* apart from the work of the Holy Spirit. The Holy Spirit so works in the heart that people gladly submit themselves to the lordship of Christ.

Lordship and salvation history. The lordship of Jesus entered a new phase at his resurrection and exaltation. This is apparent in the Philippian hymn (Phil 2:6-11). Christ Jesus refused to exploit the advantages of being equal with God and humbled himself by becoming a human being and enduring a degrading death on the cross. Because of his self-humbling, "God exalted him" (Phil 2:9) and bestowed the name Lord Jesus on him. All creatures in the universe will bow and acknowledge the lordship of Jesus. It is apparent that a new dimension in Jesus' lordship became a reality upon his resurrection and exaltation. The confessional statement in Romans 1:3-4 communicates a remarkably similar truth. Jesus was the Messiah during his earthly sojourn by virtue of his birth as a descendant of David (Rom 1:3). But at his resurrection he was "appointed as the Son of God in power by the Spirit of holiness" (Rom 1:4). The participle *appointed (horisthentos)* should not be rendered "declared" (NASB, NIV), as if the resurrection merely vindicated what Jesus already was. The verb clearly has the meaning "appoint," and the idea is that a new phase of salvation history has begun with the enthronement of Jesus as Messiah. It does not follow from this, contrary to some commentators, that Jesus' Davidic lineage is disdained (cf. 2 Tim 2:8), nor is there any intimation that Jesus only became the Messiah after his death. The point is that the earthly sojourn of Jesus was marked by weakness, in that he was David's son "according to the flesh" (Rom 1:3; cf. Rom 9:5). He came "in the likeness of sinful flesh" (Rom 8:3) and was subject to death. As a human being, entering into the world of the first Adam, Jesus was subject to the *rule (kyrieuei)* of death (Rom 6:9). At his resurrection, however, he was installed as God's Son with power. The new age had arrived in his resurrection from the dead and his enthronement as the messianic king. Christ can no longer die since "death no longer rules over him" (Rom 6:9). As the exalted Lord, Jesus became the life-giving Spirit (1 Cor 15:45) who grants the Spirit to his own.

The connection between Jesus' enthronement and his lordship is evident in Romans 10:9 as well. Salvation belongs to those who acknowledge Jesus as Lord *and* believe that he was raised from the dead (Rom 10:9). The collocation of these two ideas suggests that his resurrection vindicates his claim to lordship. The Old Testament teaches that Israel's rule over the world will be theirs at the resurrection (Is 26:19; Ezek 37:1-14; Dan 12:1-3; Hos 5:15—6:3; cf. 2 Macc 7), and the resurrection is the inauguration of the new age. Paul argues that the promised resurrection has begun in the resurrection of Jesus (Rom 1:4), and thus the new age has arrived and Jesus is Lord. First Corinthians 15:23-28 should be understood on the same lines. The reign of the Lord Jesus Christ commences with his resurrection and concludes with the defeat of death at the last day. The resurrection of Jesus in the midst of the present evil age has introduced a surprising wrinkle in the whole system. While the present evil age continues (Gal 1:4), the age to come has penetrated the old age of evil and suffering. The resurrection of Jesus assures believers that the victory over the old world order has been won, for Jesus has conquered death. Believers live in the interval between the resurrection and coming of the Lord, and when he returns death will be destroyed forever. Israel's lordship and rule over the world and the fulfillment of God's saving promises will become a reality at the resurrection. What Paul confesses is that the resurrection of Jesus shows that he is the Lord. He fulfills the resurrection that was promised to Israel. If any wish to join in his resurrection victory and in ruling over the world in righteousness and peace, then they must place themselves under the sovereignty of Jesus as Lord. At the conclusion of the present evil age, death will be vanquished and the Son will submit himself to the Father so that the Father "will be all in all" (1 Cor 15:28). The supremacy of the Father indicates that the lordship of Christ does not diminish the Father's glory.

The enthronement of Christ over all powers is also communicated in Ephesians. The resurrection of Christ necessarily involves his being seated at God's right hand in the heavenlies (Eph 1:20). The heavenly reign of Christ fulfills the messianic prophecy in Psalm 110:1, where David's son reigns until all enemies are subject to him. The Davidic king is Israel's representative, and he is the means by which the promises of deliverance from their enemies will be accomplished. Psalm 110 also informs 1 Corinthians 15:23-28, where we read that Christ's reign extends until death is subjugated and that God's sway over the whole world will become a reality when death is vanquished. In Ephesians, Christ's enthronement involves his installation to God's right hand where he rules over all angelic powers (Eph 1:20-22). The text in Ephesians emphasizes the *present* subjection of all things under Christ (Eph 1:21), whereas 1 Corinthians 15:26-28 focuses on the fact that not all things are yet under subjection. The reason for this difference is likely the overrealized eschatology of the Corinthians. Some were advocating the view that no future resurrection awaited believers. Paul struck back by reminding them that not all enemies had yet capitulated to Christ.

Adam christology is linked to Jesus' lordship in Ephesians. Paul alludes to Psalm 8, a psalm that features the significance of human beings. Human beings, despite their apparent "smallness," are magnificent because God has given us rule over the world. Paul cites the relevant words from the psalm: "He subjected all things under his [humanity's] feet" (Eph 1:22). Interestingly, Paul (like the author of Hebrews in Heb 2:5-9) applies the psalm to Jesus. He has succeeded where Adam, Israel and the rest of humanity have failed. He is

Lord both of angelic powers and of the church. When Paul says in this context that Christ is the "head" *(kephalē)* of the church, the term *head* denotes Christ's authority over the church. Since Christ is Lord and head of the church, the church is to subject herself to him in all things (Eph 5:22-24).

That Christ entered into a new stage of lordship at his resurrection is confirmed in Colossians. Christ "is the head of the church" (Col 1:18). Once again the term *head* refers to his lordship and supremacy and should not be translated "source" here since the Colossian hymn emphasizes the supremacy of Christ over all things (Col 1:18), including his sovereignty over the church. Paul also emphasizes Christ's rule over angelic powers. He "is the head of all rule and authority" (Col 2:10). The idea here is not that Christ is the "source" of angelic powers, for apparently the errorists were advocating submission to angels in order to obtain the divine fullness (Col 1:16; 2:10, 15, 18). Paul counters that Christ created angels and that he *rules* over them (Col 1:16; 2:10). The interpretation suggested here is strengthened by Colossians 2:15, where Christ's death and exaltation are depicted metaphorically. Jesus stripped the rulers and authorities of their power, publicly humiliated them and led them in a triumphal procession *(thriambeusas)* in which they were put to death. The triumphal procession was used by the Romans to portray their lordship and sovereignty over conquered peoples. Similarly, Jesus defeated angelic powers that opposed him and thus began his heavenly reign. The fascinating point is that Jesus conquered his opponents not by destroying them through a show of military might but through his death on the cross. Victory has come through suffering.

Triumph over angelic powers is also communicated in Ephesians 4:8-10. When Jesus ascended, he "led captivity captive" (Eph 4:8). This probably means that demonic powers were routed and shackled due to Christ's death and resurrection. Spiritual gifts were then distributed to the saints, and Christ as the one who "ascended above all the heavens" began to "fill all things" (Eph 4:10). Fullness here designates his ruling power, by which he is beginning to bring all things under the sphere of his dominion. Jesus Christ as the son of David was the Messiah on earth, but he entered into a new dimension of power and lordship at his resurrection. He was installed at God's right hand as the Son of God with power, and the result of his exaltation was the gift of the Holy Spirit.

Lordship and Yahweh. Paul often uses the term *kyrios* in his letters.[18] When he

---

[18]For this section I am dependent on David B. Capes, *Old Testament Yahweh Texts in Paul's Christology,* WUNT 2/47 (Tübingen: J. C. B. Mohr, 1992).

alludes to or quotes from the Old Testament, *kyrios* usually translates the divine name Yahweh. Often *kyrios* functions as the translation of Yahweh when God himself is the referent (Rom 4:7-8 = Ps 32:1-2; Rom 9:27-29 = Is 10:22-23; 1:9; Rom 11:34 = Is 40:13; Rom 15:9, 11 = Ps 18:50 or 2 Sam 22:50; 1 Cor 3:20 = Ps 94:11; 2 Cor 6:18 = 2 Sam 7:8). More significantly, in a number of texts Paul identifies the *kyrios* as Jesus Christ, even though the Old Testament allusion or quotation clearly refers to Yahweh (Rom 10:13 = Joel 2:32; Rom 14:11 = Is 49:18; Jer 22:24; and Is 45:23; 1 Cor 1:31 = Jer 9:24; 1 Cor 2:16 = Is 40:13; 1 Cor 10:22 = Deut 32:21, 26; Phil:2:10-11 = Is 45:23-24; 1 Thess 3:13 = Zech 14:5; 2 Thess 1:8 = Is 66:15).[19] Some of the texts ascribed to Christ might possibly refer to God, but most of those cited clearly have Christ in view. Hence, there is no doubt that texts that referred to Yahweh in the Old Testament are applied to Jesus Christ. The significance of such a move is staggering because Paul as a Pharisee and a Jew was nurtured in Jewish monotheism. He knew that he was identifying Jesus himself as God in assigning Yahweh texts to him.

David Capes rightly summarizes the significance of Jesus' lordship in six statements.[20] First, Jesus Christ was the object of devotion in creedal statements (Rom 1:3-4; 10:9-10). Second, believers prayed for Christ's return (1 Cor 16:22) and identified themselves "as those who call upon the name of the Lord Jesus Christ" (1 Cor 1:2). Third, hymns focusing on the person and work of Christ were composed (Phil 2:6-11; Col 1:15-20). Fourth, during worship early Christians gathered in Jesus' name (1 Cor 5:4). Fifth, new believers were baptized in Jesus' name (Rom 6:3; Gal 3:27). Sixth, early Christians celebrated a meal honoring Jesus, called the Lord's Supper (1 Cor 11:20). Capes is correct, then, in concluding that Jesus' lordship involved worship and that this necessarily implies that Paul and early Christians thought of Jesus "in the way that one thinks of God." And yet God the Father is still distinct from Jesus, and Paul retains his belief in monotheism (1 Cor 8:6). Apparently, Paul did not believe honoring and worshiping Jesus as God compromised his monotheistic belief, but neither did he collapse God and Jesus together into a kind of modalism.

Philippians 2:6-11

Two of the most important texts for discerning Paul's christology are Philippians 2:6-11 and Colossians 1:15-20.[21] Most scholars agree that these passages

---

[19]For the texts referring to Christ, see ibid., pp. 115-60.
[20]Ibid., p. 164.
[21]My understanding of both the Colossian and Philippian hymns has been influenced espe-

are hymnic; probably a majority believe that they are pre-Pauline hymns that have been adapted by Paul. The latter conclusion is debatable, and arguments can be advanced for Pauline authorship.[22] It is not crucial to resolve the original authorship of these hymnic passages since in any case Paul now endorses the confessional statements in the texts before us. Our task is not to unearth the alleged pre-Pauline meaning of these hymns but to determine Paul's meaning. To reach this goal we interpret the text in its present form. Controversy rages, as well, over virtually every word in both of these texts. It is not my intention here to chronicle the history of debate or to consider in detail the various interpretations suggested. I will sketch in briefly my understanding of these central texts and try to defend the interpretation presented with some supporting evidence.

The Philippian hymn occurs in a context in which Paul exhorts the Philippians to unity (Phil 1:27—2:4; cf. also 4:2-3). Traditionally the hymn has been understood as a call to imitate Christ. In recent years this view has been fiercely contested, although it is making something of a comeback.[23] The traditional interpretation is reflected in the translation of Philippians 2:5 by the NRSV, "Let the same mind be in you that was in Christ Jesus" (cf. NIV, NASB). Some scholars dispute this rendering for various reasons. One of the more significant is that imitation of Christ is impossible because human beings, even if they humble themselves, will never be exalted as Lord (as Christ was, Phil 2:9-11). The call to imitate Christ, these scholars maintain, would only be sensible if the reward for imitation were the same as Christ's. Supporting the newer interpretation is also the infrequency with which Paul summons his readers to imitate Christ. A theme that is rarely found in Paul, according to these scholars, is not to be detected in one of his most important christological texts.

Despite the appeal of the newer interpretation, it is difficult to exorcise the theme of imitation in this text. The main verb in Philippians 2:5, *think (phroneite)*, joins Philippians 2:5 to the preceding context because the same verbal form appears twice in Philippians 2:2. It is most natural, then, to detect a link between the exhortation to unity in Philippians 2:1-4 and the example of

---

cially by the outstanding essays by N. T. Wright in *The Climax of the Covenant: Christ and the Law in Pauline Theology* (Minneapolis: Fortress, 1992), pp. 56-119. The literature on those two texts is never-ending, and readers should consult Wright for bibliography.

[22]Ibid.

[23]Contesting any notion of imitation is Ralph P. Martin, *A Hymn of Christ: Philippians 2 5-11 in Recent Interpretation and in the Setting of Early Christian Worship*, rev. ed. (Downers Grove, Ill.: InterVarsity Press, 1997); earlier editions appeared under the title *Carmen Christi*.

Christ in the succeeding verses. Indeed, the traditional interpretation is the most satisfying precisely because it supplies the most natural reading of the hymn in the flow of the argument of Philippians. The objection—that believers will not be exalted in the same way as Christ—demands too strict an analogy between followers of Christ and Christ himself, between what we are called to do and what only God in Christ can do. Believers, of course, will not be exalted as Lord by virtue of their obedience. The argument Paul uses, however, is analogous: just as Christ was exalted as Lord because of his obedience, so too will believers be rewarded for their humility. They will be rewarded precisely because they are in Christ. The reward in the case of believers will not mean that they reign over creation in the same way as Jesus the Messiah. What Paul emphasizes in Philippians is that believers will be rewarded with a glorious resurrection body and leave behind the body that suffers degradation because of sin (Phil 3:20-21). Verbal links between Philippians 2:6-8 and Philippians 3:21 suggest that the two texts are joined in Paul's mind: *form* (*morphē*, Phil 2:6-7) and *conformed* (*symmorphos*, Phil 3:21); *form* (*schēma*, Phil 2:7) and *transform* (*metaschēmatizō*, Phil 3:21); *humble* (*tapeinoō*, Phil 2:8) and *humble* (*tapeinōsis*, Phil 3:21); *glory* (*doxa*, Phil 2:11) and *glory* (*doxa*, Phil 3:21). Conceptually the notion of the subjection of all things to Christ is found in Philippians 2:9-11, and the word *subject* (*hypotassō*) is used in Philippians 3:21. A thematic connection between Philippians 2:6-11 and Philippians 3:21 is hard to deny, yielding the conclusion that the believers' reward in Philippians 3:21 is analogous to Christ's reward in Philippians 2:9-11.

The admonition in Philippians 2:5 *in context*, then, is a call to imitate Christ. The second part of this verse, however, should not be understood as a call to imitate Christ. The words *ho kai en Christō Iēsou,* contrary to most English versions, should not be rendered "which was also in Christ Jesus." The phrase *in Christ Jesus* designates what is true of believers in light of their union with Christ. Thus, the phrase should be translated "which is also yours in Christ Jesus."[24] When we put the whole verse together, the admonition can be paraphrased as follows: "Adopt the mindset of humility, because this mindset is yours by virtue of your union with Christ Jesus." The imperative call to unity is grounded in the indicative of believers' union with Christ.

The remainder of the Philippian hymn can be divided into two segments:

---

[24]For this interpretation, see Moisés Silva, *Philippians,* BECNT (Grand Rapids, Mich.: Baker, 1992), pp. 107-11.

the emptying of Christ (Phil 2:6-8) and the exaltation of Christ (Phil 2:9-11). Some have explained the hymn in terms of Adam christology, but the discontinuity with Adam christology is as significant as the continuity in this text. To say that Jesus "was in the form of God" (*en morphē theou hyparchōn*, Phil 2:6) emphasizes the splendor and glory of his position. Conversely, to be in "the form of a slave" (*morphēn doulou*, Phil 2:7) calls attention to Jesus' lowly status. Scholars have debated interminably whether the phrase *form of God* suggests deity in reference to Jesus. The safest way to resolve this debate is to confine ourselves to the existing context instead of attempting to import the meaning of *form* from other passages. The following line in the hymn (Phil 2:6) is crucial, therefore, in determining its meaning. The debate centers on the word *harpagmon*. The usual rendering, conveyed by the RSV, says "[Jesus] did not count equality with God a thing to be grasped." The words *a thing to be grasped* are offered as the translation of *harpagmon*. The notion of grasping could be understood in two different ways. First, the idea may be that Jesus *already possesses equality with God* and willingly surrenders his position of equality for the sake of the salvation of human beings. Or, second, the idea may be that *even though Jesus is not equal to God*, he does not make it his goal to grasp after such a position. He abandons any quest for equality with God. Scholars have debated the merits and demerits of these options at length. One recent proposal, however, suggests that both of these alternatives should be rejected. Roy Hoover, in a careful lexical study, maintains that the word *harpagmon* should be rendered "take advantage of."[25] The relevant clause would then read, "[Jesus] did not consider equality with God as something to be taken advantage of." This proposal by Hoover has been adopted by quite a few scholars and is reflected in the NRSV translation: "[he] did not regard equality with God as something to be exploited." I believe Hoover's proposal is convincing, and it has recently been supported by N. T. Wright as well.[26]

The implications for christology are immediately obvious. Equality with God is something Jesus possessed before his incarnation, and thus the verse clearly teaches (contra James Dunn) the preexistence of Christ.[27] The parallelism of the text also indicates that "being in the form of God" involves "equal-

---

[25]For Roy Hoover's view, see "The Harpagmos Enigma: A Philological Solution," *HTR* 64 (1971): 95-119.

[26]For Wright's agreement with Hoover, see Wright, *Climax of the Covenant*, pp. 68-82.

[27]For Dunn's view of Phil 2:6, see his *Christology*, pp. 114-21. For a robust defense of preexistence in Pauline christology, see Martin Hengel, "Präexistenz bei Paulus?" in *Jesus Christus als der Mitte der Schrift: Studien zur Hermeneutik des Evangeliums*, ed. H.-J. Eckstein and H. Lichtenberger, BZNW 86 (Berlin: Walter de Grutyer, 1997), pp. 479-518.

ity with God" *(isa theō)*.[28] Christ Jesus, before his incarnation, was equal to God and displayed the splendor of God's glory. When he came into the world, however, he did not take advantage of these privileges. He subjected himself to humiliation for the sake of human beings (cf. 2 Cor 8:9). The contrast of Jesus with Adam is striking since Adam in the garden strove to be equal to God and thus rejected God's lordship in eating of the fruit of the tree. Christ, on the contrary, though possessing equality with God (in this respect he differs from Adam), did not use his status as a means of enriching himself. Indeed, precisely because he was in the form of God and was equal with God, he refused to use his position as a means of self-aggrandizement. He used his status as a platform for giving and self-surrender, not as a bridgehead for praise and self-exaltation. The cross, not the crown, was his path to glory.

The nature of Christ's humiliation is also the subject of controversy. What does Paul have in mind when he says that "Christ emptied himself"? Some have understood this to mean that he surrendered himself completely of his deity in becoming a human being. Close attention to the text is necessary to discern Paul's meaning. The main verb *he emptied (ekenōsen)* is modified by two participles: *taking (labōn)* and *becoming (or being made—genomenos)*. Both of these participles should be understood instrumentally, in that they describe the manner in which Christ emptied himself. That is, he emptied himself *by taking* the form of a servant and *by being made* in the likeness of human beings. The *emptying* of Christ, then, consisted of an *adding*. He emptied himself by becoming fully human. The text does not say that he emptied himself by surrendering his deity; it says that he humbled himself by adding humanity. We have already seen in Philippians 2:6 that he did not exploit or take advantage of his deity in becoming human, and thus the privileges of his divinity were not exercised on earth. But the text nowhere says that he surrendered his divinity or left it behind in the incarnation. The idea is that he did not exploit the advantages of deity, which were his by nature. As a man he lived in dependence on the Holy Spirit, in the same way other human beings do. He did not use the prerogatives of deity but depended on the Spirit to strengthen him.[29] Contrary to Adam, he lived for the sake of the glory of God and surrendered himself for others. This self-giving reached its climax in the cross. The humiliation of Christ did not end with the assumption of human nature. We can easily imagine someone lowering himself to

---

[28]So Hengel, "Präexistenz," p. 488.

[29]This is the view of Gerald F. Hawthorne, *The Presence and the Power* (Dallas: Word, 1991), pp. 207-11, 215-19.

live with those beneath him on the condition that he be treated as royalty. The most exquisite comforts, pleasures and honor must be given to one who humbles himself. But Jesus the Messiah did not follow the expected pattern. Not only did he empty himself by becoming human, but Paul proceeds to inform the reader that he willingly endured death, the most degrading death imaginable in the Greco-Roman world—death on the cross.[30] Death on the cross was not only physically torturous but also deeply embarrassing: the victim was crucified naked, and even his bodily excretions were on public view. As a result of his humiliating death and obedience Christ Jesus was exalted as Lord by the Father (Phil 2:9-11). We have already noted the new stage in salvation history inaugurated by Jesus' resurrection, for at his resurrection he begins to reign as the Son of God in power (Rom 1:4).

Colossians 1:15-20

We have already discussed the phrase *image of God* in Colossians 1:15, and so this phrase will not be analyzed in detail here. The structure of the Colossian poem, or hymn, is the subject of considerable debate. I agree with those who see the poem as having a twofold theme: Christ is the Lord of creation (Col 1:15-17), and he is Lord of the church (Col 1:18-20). Wright explains clearly and persuasively the structure of the hymn.[31]

Colossians 1:17 serves as the middle term of the argument, summing up the theme of the text as a whole: "And he is before all things, and in him all things cohere." The poem is structured with an ABBA chiastic pattern. The middle portion of the chiasm (Col 1:17) summarizes the major thrust of the text, so that the reader will not miss its central theme. There is also a prolonged debate on the background of the passage. Some have postulated a Gnostic background, but this is increasingly questioned today since full-fledged Gnosticism is a second-century phenomenon. It is probable that the antecedents to the poem can be traced to wisdom and creation traditions. Just as wisdom was with God "in the beginning" (Prov 8:22; Gen 1:1) and played a mediatorial role in the creation of the world, so too Christ is now the agent of creation. Ascribing the background of the hymn to wisdom and creation traditions is scarcely surprising given Paul's heritage as a Pharisee. A wisdom background seems to be confirmed as we continue to read Colossians, since

---

[30]For the degradation of the cross in the Greco-Roman world, see the classic work by Martin Hengel, *Crucifixion in the Ancient World and the Folly of the Message of the Cross* (Philadelphia: Fortress, 1977).

[31]See Wright, *Climax of the Covenant*, p. 104.

Paul identifies Christ as the wisdom of God (Col 2:2-3), suggesting that themes relating to wisdom informed his thinking in Colossians.

Paul's dependence on creation traditions emerges with the first line of the poem, where Christ is identified as the image of God. We have already noted that this hearkens back to Genesis 1:26-27, where Adam (and Eve) is created according to God's image and likeness. Some have restricted the notion of image to the humanity of Jesus, insisting that any connotation of preexistence or deity cannot be read out of the term. The linkage with Adam supports this way of looking at the evidence, and so does the reference to Christ Jesus or Jesus Christ (e.g., Col 1:1, 3-4), which refers to the man Christ Jesus. It would be a mistake to rule out any reference to Adam christology here, for it surely undergirds the poem. But the subsequent context also reveals that though Jesus is the second Adam, he also surpasses Adam. His preeminence is communicated by the assertion that Jesus "is the image of God" (Col 1:15) and not merely made "according to the image of God" (Gen 1:27). As we saw earlier, Jesus, by being in the image of God, shares in God's nature. The statements in Colossians 1:16-17 confirm the interpretation proposed for *image*. Jesus is said to be mediator of creation: "in him all things were created," and "all things were created through him and for him" (Col 1:16). Adam was hardly the agent by whom the whole world was created! The language comes from wisdom traditions, where wisdom is the mediator of creation (Prov 8:22-31; Wis 9:2). The author of the Wisdom of Solomon also forges a connection between creation via wisdom and creation via the word:

> O God of my ancestors and Lord of mercy,
> who have made all things by your word,
> and by your wisdom have formed humankind
> to have dominion over the creatures you have made. (Wis 9:1-2 NRSV)

Perhaps the author combined the themes of Genesis 1 and Proverbs 8 here, for what is created by the word of the Lord in Genesis 1 (cf. Ps 33:6) is attributed to wisdom in Proverbs 8.

The wisdom background of Colossians 1 is unmistakable, and on this ground some scholars (especially Dunn) have suggested that this text does not proclaim Christ's preexistence.[32] Wisdom, after all, was not conceived of as a personal being at the creation of a world; the reference to wisdom in the Old Testament and Second Temple Jewish literature is almost certainly an example of personification. Restricting Jesus Christ, however, to wisdom

---

[32]For Dunn's view of Colossians 1, see his *Christology*, pp. 187-94.

categories is unpersuasive, even though wisdom themes inform the text. Colossians 1:16 clearly teaches that he is the *agent* by which the world was brought into being. Such language can scarcely be used of a *person* without implying that this person existed when the world was created. The wisdom theme anticipates and foreshadows the work of Christ, but Christ surpasses wisdom in that, unlike wisdom, he is a person who has always existed. Colossians 1:16 does not merely say that creation was brought into being *for the sake of Christ*—which would be compatible with the idea that he did not exist when the world was formed—it also says that the world was brought into existence *through* Christ. This latter statement demands the personal preexistence of Christ. Some may protest that the designation "Christ Jesus" or "Jesus Christ" itself speaks against this since he was obviously not the "Christ" or "Jesus" in his preexistent state. This objection is not ultimately compelling, for the Son is designated by the name or title by which he became known to believers. We can speak of President Reagan's life as a boy, even though during that frame of life he was not yet president. Similarly, Jesus Christ is described with the name and title by which he accomplished salvation for believers.

The poem also describes Jesus as the "firstborn *[prōtotokos]* of all creation" (Col 1:15). The word *firstborn* reminds readers of Israel, for Israel was God's son *(hyios)*, God's firstborn *(prōtotokos,* Ex 4:22). Because of primogeniture, the firstborn male in the Old Testament had sovereignty over his younger brothers and all his sisters. The exceptions to this, in the cases of Jacob and Esau and of Manasseh and Ephraim, were noted precisely because they were so remarkable (Gen 27:18-46; 48:8-22; Rom 9:10-13). Designating Israel as the firstborn is a way of saying that Israel will receive the inheritance that God has promised for his own. They are his special people and will be the means by which God extends his kingdom over the whole world. The sovereignty and rule involved in being the firstborn is also communicated in Psalm 89:27, where God promises David, "I will appoint him as the firstborn, the highest of the kings of the earth." The Hebrew parallelism is instructive where "firstborn" is further explained in terms of being "the highest of the kings of the earth." Indeed, David was not the firstborn in the sense that he was the oldest in his family, nor was he the first legitimate king in Israel. The term *firstborn* indicates that he was appointed to rule. Interestingly, this draws us back to the role that Adam was designed to play in the garden because he and Eve were commissioned to rule over the world (Gen 1). This was the unique task of the human race according to Psalm 8. Israel and then David, as the representative of Israel, were to reclaim humanity's lordship over the world in the name of the God of Israel. By designating Jesus as the firstborn Paul indicates that he is the fulfillment of the commission originally given to Adam. This view is strengthened when we see that the words *eikōn* and *prōtotokos* are parallel in Colossians 1:15. Israel was appointed to reclaim what Adam had lost, and the Davidic king played a representative role in this reclamation project. What Paul suggests here is that Jesus Christ is the fulfillment of what both Israel and David were called to be. In other words, Jesus Christ is the true Israel and the true Davidic king precisely because he is God's sovereign ruler over the world. He fulfills the task of ruling over the world in God's name as Lord and Christ. His lordship over the world is scarcely surprising since he is the agent of creation (Col 1:16) and also the one who continually sustains the created order (Col 1:17). The one who rules over the created world is also the one through whom the creation came into being.

It should also be noted that the word *prōtotokos* could be construed to say that Christ was the first person who was created. Such an interpretation should be set aside on two counts. First, as we have seen, the term *prōtotokos* emphasizes the sovereignty and rule of Jesus. It may be the case since Colossians 1:18 uses the phrase "firstborn of the dead" that temporal priority is intended as well. If so, the idea is that Jesus existed from all eternity. Second, Colossians 1:16 provides the *reason* why Jesus is the "firstborn over all creation," and the reason given is "because all things were created in him." He is Lord because he is the agent of all that has been created. The text specifically teaches that "all things" *(ta panta)* have been created through Christ, and this comprehensive designation shows that the Son himself is not part of the created order. He is the agent of creation, the sustainer of creation, and its Lord. When the hymn arrives at Colossians 1:17, the internal segment of the chiasm, the lordship of Jesus is featured. He is "before all things"—he is the sovereign over all the created order. In addition, the world that has been created "stands together" *(synestēken)* or coheres through him. His superiority over Adam is evident, for Adam was a creature in the world and yet Jesus is the means by which the physical world coheres and persists. The physical universe would lose its order, cohesion and very existence apart from its sovereign Lord, Jesus Christ.

The second part of the poem features Jesus' lordship over the new creation, the church. The main point is summarized in Colossians 1:18, where Jesus is designated as "the head of the body, the church." The word *kephalē* is understood by some to denote source, although this view has been called into question by some thorough studies of the term.[33] The meaning of *kephalē* must be sought in the particular context in which it occurs. In Colossians 1:18 Paul is not merely suggesting that Jesus is the source of the church; he is emphasizing Jesus' lordship and preeminence over the church. This understanding of "head" is confirmed by Colossians 2:10, where Jesus is said to be the "head over all rule and authority." The terms *archē* and *exousia* refer to angelic powers in both Colossians 2:10 and Colossians 2:15 (cf. Col 1:16). The meaning "source" for *kephalē* is ruled out by Colossians 2:15, since Christ's subjugation over evil powers is featured, not the fact that these powers have their origin from Christ. Colossians 1:16 does say that such powers came into being in and through Christ, so the idea of source is not inherently mistaken. It is likely that the word *kephalē* has the meaning "source" in Colossians 2:19, but such a definition is contextually unlikely in Colossians 1:18 and Colossians 2:10. Paul emphasizes Jesus' lordship and superiority over these powers so that the Colossians will not fall prey to "worship of angels" (Col 2:18). Submitting to angels is unthinkable, for the Son, Jesus Christ, rules over them.

The supremacy of Jesus in the church is witnessed to by his being the "beginning" *(archē)*, the source, of the new people of God. The close connection between "source" and "head" perhaps suggests that authority belongs to that which is the source. The people of God are no longer defined in terms of Israel but in terms of Jesus. Salvation history has taken a decisive turn with his coming since he is the firstborn *(prōtotokos)* of the dead (Col 1:18). In Genesis 49:3 the words *beginning (archē)* and *firstborn (prōtotokos)* are used to designate Reuben as the founder and origin of the twelve tribes. The phrase *firstborn of the dead* signals that the age to come has penetrated the present evil age, in that the resurrection of the dead has become a reality in and through Jesus. Israel longed for the resurrection as a token of the coming age. The resurrection, Paul affirms, has become a reality in and through Jesus. Since he is the founder of a new humanity and the inaugurator of the new age, he is "preeminent" *(prōteuōn)* over all (Col 1:18).

Jesus is not only the agent by which God's promises are fulfilled. He is also exalted and honored as God's agent in the world. Colossians 1:19 explains

---

[33]Wayne Grudem, "Does *Kephalē* ('Head') Mean 'Source' or 'Authority Over' in Greek Literature? A Survey of 2,336 Examples," *TJ* 6 (1985): 38-59; Grudem, "The Meaning of *Kephalē* ('Head'): A Response to Recent Studies," in *Recovering Biblical Manhood and Womanhood: A Response to Evangelical Feminism*, ed. John Piper and Wayne Grudem (Wheaton, Ill.: Crossway, 1991), pp. 425-68, 534-41; Grudem, "The Meaning of *Kephalē* ('Head'): An Evaluation of New Evidence, Real and Alleged," *JETS* 44 (2001): 25-65; Joseph A. Fitzmyer, "*Kephalē* in 1 Corinthians 11:3," *Int* 47 (1993): 52-59.

why *(hoti)* the supremacy of Jesus is no threat to the dignity and honor of God: it is because God himself was pleased to have all of his fullness reside in Jesus. The parallel text in Colossians 2:9 is of immense importance: "all the fullness of deity dwells in him [Christ] bodily." Both Colossians 1:19 and Colossians 2:9 counter any attempt to sever functional from ontological christology. Jesus' reconciling work on the cross is functionally effective because God's fullness dwells in him ontologically. Believers are "full" *(peplērōmenoi)* in him (Col 2:10) because God's fullness *(plērōma)* dwells in him. The good pleasure *(eudokēsen)* of God (Col 1:19) denotes his election, his choice to have the fullness reside in Jesus. For example, in Psalm 68:16 (68:17 LXX) Mount Zion is described as the one mountain on which God was pleased to reside. He chose it above all other dwelling places. So too, God in his sovereignty chose to have all his fullness reside in Jesus, and thus the supremacy of Jesus does not threaten the greatness of God since God himself has exalted Jesus and was pleased to endow him with his fullness. God himself willed that Jesus be supreme in all things.

Jesus as God

The lordship of Jesus Christ does not annul the dignity of God the Father. On the contrary, the Father raised Jesus from the dead and crowned him as Lord to bring glory to his name (Phil 2:9-11). We have also seen that Paul ascribes deity to Jesus, without denying monotheism (1 Cor 8:6). Does Paul ever refer to Jesus Christ as "God"? Such a designation, whatever one's conclusion, is exceedingly rare in Paul's letters, presumably because such an attribution could lead to the conclusion that Jesus is God without remainder. Paul emphatically rejects such a conclusion in 1 Corinthians 8:6. Whether Jesus is specifically called "God" *(theos)* in Paul is confined to two texts: Romans 9:5 and Titus 2:13.[34] In Romans 9:4-5 Paul itemizes the blessings of the Jewish people, culminating with the truth that the Messiah comes from them. He concludes with the words, "the one who is over all, God blessed for the ages, Amen" *(ho hōn epi pantōn theos eulogētos eis tous aiōnas, amēn).* This last phrase is the subject of ongoing controversy, for scholars debate whether Jesus or the Father is called "God" in this verse. The verse can be punctuated in various ways. If the reference is to Christ, then the options are either "Christ . . . who

---

[34]Scholars have long debated whether Paul identifies Jesus Christ as God. A recent and thorough defense of the interpretation adopted here is presented by Murray J. Harris in his work *Jesus as God: The New Testament Use of Theos in Reference to Jesus* (Grand Rapids, Mich.: Baker, 1992), pp. 143-85.

is over all, God blessed forever, Amen" or "Christ . . . who is God over all, blessed for ever, Amen." If the reference is to God, the phrase *who is over all* could be understood as referring to Christ, with Paul breaking off and saying with reference to the Father, "God be blessed for ever, Amen." More likely if the whole phrase refers to God, then it should be translated, "God who is over all be blessed for ever, Amen" or "He who is over all, God, be blessed for ever, Amen." A number of reasons are adduced to support a reference to God the Father:

■ *Blessed (eulogētos)* is always used with reference to God in the New Testament (Mk 14:61; Lk 1:68; Rom 1:25; 2 Cor 1:3; 11:31; Eph 1:3; 1 Pet 1:3).

■ Nowhere else in the Pauline corpus does *God (theos)* refer to Christ, and therefore, some scholars insist that Paul does not break the pattern here.

■ The unusual word order—with *blessed* following *God*—can be explained by Paul's desire to highlight God's lordship over all, a typical Jewish theme (cf. Ps 67:19-20 LXX).

■ No other doxologies to Christ exist in the indisputable Pauline letters.

■ The closest parallel text is Ephesians 4:6, and there the Father is said to be "the one who is over all" *(ho epi pantōn).*

■ A closing reference to God is typical in Jewish literature.

■ The doxology in Romans 11:33-36 refers to the Father, suggesting that the same is true in Romans 9:5.

The above arguments, although diverse, enshrine one fundamental objection: namely, it is thought to be quite improbable that Christ would be designated "God" *(theos)* since this is uncharacteristic of Paul elsewhere. Despite the strength of that argument, there are various reasons for believing that Paul departs from his normal practice and refers to Christ as *theos* here:

■ The phrase *according to the flesh,* even though it does not require an explicit contrasting phrase, fits more smoothly if a contrasting phrase is included. The series of benefits belonging to Israel comes to a stunning conclusion, for though Christ descended from Israel ethnically, he transcends that identity because he also shares the divine nature.

■ The natural antecedent to *ho hōn* (the one who is) is "Christ" since doxologies are almost always attached to the preceding word and asyndetic doxologies do not exist (cf. Rom 1:25; 11:36; 2 Cor 11:31; Gal 1:5; Eph 3:21; Phil 4:20; 1 Tim 1:17; 2 Tim 4:18; Heb 13:21; 1 Pet 4:11; 2 Pet 3:18). A particularly striking parallel is found in 2 Corinthians 11:31, "the God and father of the Lord Jesus knows, who is blessed for ever." The participle *ho hōn* (the one who is) in this case naturally refers back to "the God and Father," and the same principle applies in Romans 9:5 with the result that *ho hōn* refers to Christ.

■ If this were an independent doxology to God the Father, the word *blessed* would occur first as it does in every other instance in the LXX and New Testament (cf. in the LXX Gen 9:26; 14:20; 24:27, 31; Ex 18:10; Ruth 4:14; 1 Sam 25:32; 2 Sam 6:21; 18:28; 1 Kings 1:48; 8:15, 56; 2 Chron 2:11; 6:4; Ezra 7:27; Ps 17:47; 27:6; 30:22; 40:14; 65:20; 67:20, 36; 71:18; 88:53; 105:48; 123:6; 143:1; Dan 3:28; Zech 11:5; Tob 11:17; 13:2, 18; 1 Esd 4:40; cf. also Lk 1:68; 2 Cor 1:3; Eph 1:3; 1 Pet 1:3). The only apparent exception is Psalm 67:19-20 (LXX), but even in this instance it is doubtful that a real exception exists.

■ It would be awkward for Paul to break off and utter praise to God in a context in which he is grieving over Israel. Ascribing blessedness to Christ, after identifying him with God, fits more naturally because the Messiah, who shares the divine nature, is the consummation of Israel's privileges. Paul's ascribing deity to Christ heightens the profundity of his grief. Not only have the Jews rejected Jesus as Messiah, but they also are spurning one who shares the divine nature with the Father.

■ That Paul would call Christ "God" is not totally surprising since, as we have seen, in Philippians 2:6 Jesus is said to be "in the form of God" and "equal to God," and in Colossians 1:15 he is said to be "the image of the invisible God" (cf. also 1 Cor 8:6; Col 1:19; 2:9). When we add to this Paul's application to Christ of texts in the Old Testament that refer to "Yahweh" (cf. Rom 10:13; Phil 2:10-11), the case becomes quite strong. The idea that calling Christ "God" is incompatible with Pauline thought should, therefore, be rejected. Paul does not say that Christ is God without remainder, for the distinction between Christ and the Father must also be maintained (1 Cor 8:6; 15:28; Phil 2:11). Nevertheless, the implication here is that Christ shares the divine nature with the Father.

The attribution in Titus 2:13 is similarly disputed, so that scholars debate whether *theos* refers to God or Christ. The relevant part of the verse reads *epiphaneian tēs doxēs tou megalou theou kai sōtēros hēmōn Iēsou Christou* (literally, "appearance of the glory of the great God and our savior, Jesus Christ"). Lexically the strongest arguments favor the claim that Jesus Christ is called "the great God." I will not reduplicate, however, the detailed arguments of Murray Harris for this view, and readers should consult him for a thorough discussion of the possible alternatives.[35] Two reasons cited by Harris indicate that Paul designates Jesus Christ as God here. First, the phrase *God and savior*

---

[35]Ibid., pp. 173-85.

(theos kai sōtēr) was a common formula in the Greco-Roman world, and it regularly refers to a single deity in such formulas. There is no reason to think Paul departs from standard practice here, and thus the most natural way to take the expression is to conclude that Paul identifies Jesus Christ as God. Second, the one article *tou (the)* is best explained as introducing both the nouns *God* and *savior (theou* and *sōtēros)*.[36] If Paul had wanted to distinguish *God* and *savior*, he would likely have inserted a second definite article before the noun *savior*. By omitting the article before the second noun, Paul indicates that both nouns refer to the same person—Jesus Christ.

The main objection to this reading of the text is theological, while its primary support is grammatical. The theological objection centers on the improbability of designating Jesus as God since the attribution was rare in Pauline writings. The theological objection can be answered in a satisfying way. Paul seldom refers to Christ as God because this title could be confusing, given his monotheism. Believers could wrongly conclude that Jesus was God without remainder. Thus, Paul stresses the distinction between the Father and the Son. Paul's view, however, cannot be so neatly categorized, for he also believed that Jesus was deity, without denying monotheism. The one who accomplished salvation and inaugurated the new age is more than a human being, though he is certainly not less than human. Attributing deity to Jesus does not compromise Jewish monotheism because Paul was not suggesting that there was more than one God. He was maintaining rather that there was more complexity in the being of God than some may have thought. Scholars have recently investigated the antecedents for the theology of early Christians in Judaism and have demonstrated that the view of the early Christians did not arise in a vacuum. Space forbids entering into this arena with any detail here, but scholars such as Alan Segal and Larry Hurtado have carefully traced traditions that posit "two powers" in heaven.[37] Antecedents clearly exist, but it cannot be denied that there is an explicit leap forward in the acclamation of Jesus the Messiah as God.

Conclusion

We are not surprised to see Jesus Christ featured in Paul. He is the one through whom God accomplishes his redemptive plan and brings salvation to the world. He is to be praised, for he succeeded where Adam failed. He is

---

[36]This is the famous Granville Sharp rule. For the best contemporary explanation, see Daniel B. Wallace, *Greek Grammar Beyond the Basics: An Exegetical Syntax of the New Testament* (Grand Rapids, Mich.: Zondervan, 1996), pp. 270-90.

[37]For the antecedents to Pauline christology in Judaism, see n. 17 above.

God's exalted Lord and Christ, and he should be worshiped just as the Father is worshiped. Those who truly honor God also honor Christ, for God intended that his glory would be magnified in Christ.

An Excursus on Universalism in Paul

We have seen in this chapter and the previous one that all of humanity are either in Adam or Christ. The Adam-Christ polarity and other texts in Paul raise the question of universalism. We begin with Romans 5, where the contrast between Adam and Christ is central. In reading Romans 5:15-19, the import of the words *all* and *many* is raised. Clearly both Adam and Christ are conceived as having a universal impact. The question is whether the parallel between Adam and Christ is established at every point, so that we can say that as all are condemned in Adam so too all are saved in Christ. The word *many* is virtually a synonym for *all* in Romans 5:15-19 and does not indicate a lessening of the pervasive influence of Adam and Christ. Similarly, in 1 Corinthians 15:22 "all" die in Adam, whereas "all" shall be granted life in Christ. The formulation in 2 Corinthians 5:14 runs along the same lines. When Paul says "one died for all, therefore, all died," he means that all died in Christ since he is the one who died "for all" *(hyper pantōn)*. Christ Jesus, as the second Adam, is the "one" who died for "all" so that the many would live.

First Timothy 2:6 affirms that Christ Jesus "gave himself as a ransom for all." This confessional statement is interesting because it appears in a context in which Paul exhorts his readers to pray "for all people" (1 Tim 2:1), even kings and other secular authorities (1 Tim 2:2), since God "desires all to be saved and to come to the knowledge of the truth" (1 Tim 2:4). The universal language employed leads some to the conclusion that all people without exception are in Christ (cf. Col 1:20). They maintain that this is the most natural way to understand the contrast between Adam and Christ in Romans 5:15-19 and 1 Corinthians 15:22. They believe that it is special pleading to restrict "all" in the case of Christ to some people but to understand "all" in Adam to all people without exception. Paul's contrast between Adam and Christ should, they allege, be accepted at face value.

The notion that "all" without exception are in Christ can only be sustained if Paul's teaching is contradictory. Of course, some believe that Paul is unconcerned about contradictions and that he uses arguments in one place that do not fit with what he said elsewhere.[38] Scholars often appeal to Paul's pastoral

---

[38]See, e.g., M. E. Boring ("The Language of Universal Salvation in Paul," *JBL* 105 [1986]: 269-

intentions to explain such disjunctions. On the contrary, Paul's teaching would not have been as influential in the early church if it were inconsistent, especially in major areas of his theology. Thus, it is quite unlikely that Paul asserts that all people without exception are in Christ, since he often teaches that judgment, condemnation and death are in store for those who refuse to obey the gospel. The evidence supporting such a statement will be considered in the last chapter, but virtually all agree that such statements are common in Paul. If one posits a contradiction, then we are free to choose which teaching we prefer—universal salvation for all or judgment for those who refuse the gospel. Only those who are resolutely cranky would opt for the latter. But if Paul is a consistent theologian, then he can scarcely be teaching that all without exception will be in Christ.

We do not have to defend our thesis merely by asserting that no contradiction can be accepted in Paul. When we examine the text closely, other evidence that rules out universalism emerges. Paul does affirm in 1 Corinthians 15:22 that all shall be made alive in Christ. The subsequent context clarifies, however, that such a gift is restricted to some. First Corinthians 15:23 says that "those who belong to Christ" will be raised at his coming. The phrase *those who belong to Christ (hoi tou Christou)* suggests that not all are "in Christ." Only those who have believed in the gospel and stay faithful until the end will be raised on the last day (1 Cor 15:1-2). Paul protests against those who deny the resurrection, saying that if their teaching were true, then suffering, danger and persecution would be vanity (1 Cor 15:30-32). Better to eat, drink and be merry, since this world is all there is. The same argument applies if all without exception are in Christ. If all without exception are in Christ, then why does Paul engage in his mission? His suffering seems rather pointless since all will be rescued from God's wrath anyway, particularly when it is the case that those who embrace Paul's gospel may experience *more suffering now* because of the persecution that comes with accepting the gospel.

The text in Romans 5:15-19 also contains a hint that not all are in Christ since Romans 5:17 refers to those *receiving* God's saving gift of righteousness—"how much more shall those receiving the abundance of grace and the gift of righteousness reign in life through the one man, Jesus Christ." Not all "receive" the gift, and therefore only some are in Christ. Sufficient evidence exists to deny that texts like Romans 5 teach universal salvation, but why does Paul use

---

92), who says that both images are present in Paul and that they cannot be resolved on the propositional level.

extravagant language like *all* in the first place? The issue would not even arise, we might say, if Paul were more circumspect in his terminology. As an author, however, Paul deliberately used the word *all* to describe the work of Christ as the second Adam. Our task as readers is to ferret out the significance of this decision. Two reasons for the terminology are possible. First, Paul did not want to use a less-inclusive term because he wanted to emphasize that Christ was as great as Adam. The use of the word *all* reminds the reader that the grace of Christ is so powerful that it supersedes what Adam did.

Second, one of the prominent themes of Paul's theology, and of Romans in particular, is the inclusion of the Gentiles. We have seen that the folding of the Gentiles into God's saving purposes was the distinctive element in Paul's call to the apostleship. He often emphasizes in Romans that God has called the Gentiles, not just the Jews, to be his people (Rom 1:5, 7, 13-14, 16; 2:11, 26-29; 3:23, 29-30; 4:9-12, 16-17; 9:24-26, 30; 10:11-13, 20; 11:12, 15, 17, 19-20, 30; 15:9-12; 16:26). Recognizing this assists us in comprehending Romans 11:32, "God has enclosed all under disobedience, so that he should show mercy to all." The first *all* must include all people without exception, for Paul leaves no room for the idea that some people are obedient and hence need no mercy from God! But if the second *all* is of the same breadth as the first, then Paul is a universalist, teaching that God's saving mercy will be poured out on every single human being. The interpretation is doubtless attractive, but the context reveals its improbability. Romans 9—11 often speaks of the future punishment of those who are unsaved (Rom 9:3, 6-7, 13, 18, 21-22, 31-33; 10:2-4; 11:7-10, 20-23, 28). These chapters oscillate between the salvation promised for the Gentiles and the salvation pledged to the Jews. Any attentive reader of Romans 11 is aware that it features God's saving plan relative to both Gentiles and Jews. When Paul says, therefore, that God shows mercy on "all," the idea is that God's mercy extends to both Jews and Gentiles. Thus, we need not conclude that "all" refers to all people without exception. More likely, when Paul considers Christ's work, the referent is all people without distinction. Both Jews and Gentiles are recipients of Christ's gracious work.

The interpretation proposed here is also supported by the context of 1 Timothy 2, where Paul emphasizes the ransom being made for all. Much remains uncertain about the false teachers in 1 Timothy since Paul dismisses their teaching instead of refuting it. It may be that they were consumed with genealogies because they restricted salvation along certain ethnic lines (1 Tim 1:4). Thus, Paul reminded them to pray for the salvation of all, including governmental authorities whom they considered outside the pale of salvation (1 Tim

2:1-2). When Paul says that God desires all to be saved (1 Tim 2:4) and that Christ was the ransom for all (1 Tim 2:6), he may be responding to some who excluded Gentiles from salvation for genealogical reasons. Such an interpretation is supported further by 1 Timothy 2:7, where Paul appeals to his call to apostleship and particularly to his status as a "teacher of the Gentiles." We are apt to forget how shocking the inclusion of Gentiles was to many in the first century because of our historical distance from the text. It seems quite likely that Paul responds to opponents for he pledges that he is not lying (1 Tim 2:7). Such adversaries may have criticized Paul's Gentile mission, and Paul reminds his readers that God includes all, both Jews and Gentiles, in his saving purposes. Perhaps one motivation for including the account of his own conversion (1 Tim 1:12-16) was to remind his readers that God saves the most unlikely, even one of the chief opponents of the gospel of Christ.

Titus 2:11 should be interpreted along similar lines. When Paul says "the grace of God has appeared bringing salvation to all people," the text could be read in universalist terms. Some fend off universalism by saying that *potential* salvation is in view. The objection to such a reading is that the text refers to actual salvation, not to potential salvation. Paul probably has in mind a salvation that is both accomplished and applied. Nonetheless, a universalist reading misfires, if universalism means the salvation of every single person. Paul counters Jewish teachers (Tit 1:10, 14-15; 3:9) who construct genealogies to exclude some from salvation. He affirms that God in his grace brings salvation to all peoples without distinction. No people group is excluded from his saving intentions. The language of 1 Timothy 4:10 is more difficult, for there Paul declares that God "is the savior of all people, especially believers." The text could be read to teach absolute universalism, but this is contextually unlikely. Why engage in rigorous training for godliness if salvation is assured regardless of one's behavior (1 Tim 4:7-8)? Nor should Timothy concern himself with his teaching and behavior if every single person, including himself, will be saved (1 Tim 4:11-16). We should probably read this along the lines already proposed. God is the Savior of all people groups without exception. The words *especially believers* specify more precisely who is saved. In this instance the word *malista* could be translated "that is." The verse would then read, "God is the savior of all people, that is, believers."

Some object to the interpretation proposed here, arguing that "all" must include all people without exception. Good reasons exist, however, to think that *all* or *world* must be interpreted carefully. For instance, the hymnic statement in 1 Timothy 3:16 says that Christ "was believed by the world." The word *kosmos* here cannot mean that every person without exception has trusted in Jesus Christ, for it was obvious to Paul that many in the world disbelieved. Paul almost certainly means that the whole world, comprising both Jews and Gentiles, believes. In other words, *world* here denotes all without distinction and not all without exception. Colossians 1:6 and Colossians 1:23 should be interpreted similarly. Affirming that the gospel bears fruit and increases "in all the world" (Col 1:6) is simply to say that it is expanding among both Jews and Gentiles. The meaning of Colossians 1:23 has often been discussed. Is Paul indulging in hyperbole when he says that the gospel has been proclaimed "in all the creation under heaven"? When the letter was written, Paul knew that Spain and Britain had not yet been reached with the gospel. Obviously, he is not suggesting that every person in the world has heard the gospel! When we consider Paul's Gentile mission, however, the text yields a sensible meaning. Paul's unique call to the Gentiles receives special emphasis in the subsequent verses (Col 1:24—2:3), so we are hardly reading into the text to see such a theme here. Paul has proclaimed the gospel "in all the creation" in the sense that he has proclaimed the gospel to both Jews and Gentiles. Paul is not engaging in hyperbole but reflecting on his Gentile mission.

Such an interpretation is also a sensible reading of 2 Corinthians 5:14-15. The love of Christ controls Paul, and he concludes that "one died for all, therefore, all died" (2 Cor 5:14). The "all" for whom Christ died are not all without exception but all without distinction, including both Jews and Gentiles. Such an interpretation would explain how "all died" when Christ died for them. One could understand this to say that all died "potentially" when Christ died for them. But the wording of the text actually fits the interpretation proposed here better. All those for whom Christ died "actually" died— they died in the death of Christ to the power of sin. Nothing is said in the text about their potentially dying. Instead, Paul asserts that those for whom Christ suffered actually died. Second Corinthians 5:15 seems to support this view as well: "he died for all so that those living should no longer live for themselves but for the one who died and has been raised for them." When Paul uses the phrase *those living* (*hoi zōntes*), he does not mean those that are physically alive. A reference to physical life would be superfluous and banal, so it is more likely that *those living* refers to those who are spiritually alive. Those who are spiritually alive are the "all" for whom Christ died in 2 Corinthians 5:14. In dying to the power of sin in Christ, they also came to life in Christ.

The parallel between Adam and Christ in Romans 5 also supports this view. Adam did not just make possible the death and destruction of his descendants; he guaranteed their death and destruction. Similarly, Christ as the second Adam did not merely make possible the life and righteousness of his people; he effectually brought them life and righteousness. His grace was so powerful that he overcame the power of death and sin and produced life and righteousness in his people. The contrast between Adam and Christ, then, is crucial for defining the word *grace (charis)* in Paul. Often people define grace only in terms of an unmerited gift. Such a definition is certainly fitting. But grace is more than an unmerited gift in Paul, for the word *gift* could convey the idea that one may choose to open the gift or, conversely, that one may choose to reject the gift. Grace in Paul is also a *power* that effects what is demanded. The gift of righteousness is not merely offered to human beings; it is secured through the work of the second Adam. The last Adam does not merely offer life; he grants life.

One of the more difficult texts relating to universalism is Colossians 1:20— "and through him to reconcile all things to himself, having made peace through the blood of his cross." The reconciliation achieved by Christ includes all things, both "on earth and in heaven." On first glance salvation for all, including demons and Satan, seems to be guaranteed by the death of Christ. A more careful analysis of the context, however, points to a different conclusion. In the immediately succeeding verses Christ's reconciling work is conditional (Col 1:21-23). The Colossian believers will be presented holy and without blemish before God "if you remain in the faith" (Col 1:23). Paul does not promise eschatological salvation regardless of what a person does. Perseverance is necessary to obtain the eschatological reward. Similarly, Colossians 3:6 threatens sinners with God's eschatological wrath, a threat that is superfluous and misleading if no wrath will be dispensed in the future. Nor is there any suggestion elsewhere that demons will be rescued from judgment. In Colossians 2:15 they are stripped of their authority, publicly embarrassed and led on a triumphal procession that concludes with their execution. It is likely, therefore, that the reconciliation described in Colossians 1:20 does not involve universal salvation. What Paul has in mind is the "universal pacification" of all things. Through Christ's work on the cross, everything that opposes God in the universe is subdued. His saving plan has been completed, and no enemy will frustrate his will. Even Satan, who remains God's enemy, has been pacified, subdued and confined. The victory of Christ, as the second Adam, is complete. The first Adam was defeated by Satan, but the second

Adam has triumphed over Satan forever.

Another text that is often adduced to support universalism is Philippians 2:10-11, where Paul writes that every knee "in the heavens and on earth and under earth" bows to the lordship of Jesus and every tongue confesses his lordship. Does this not explicitly teach that every individual, without exception, will be saved? But if universal salvation is taught in Philippians, why does Paul suffer imprisonment for the sake of the gospel (Phil 1:12-26)? All will be saved regardless of his preaching. The motive for accomplishing salvation with fear and trembling (Phil 2:12) seems pointless since salvation is assured even if human beings are evil. That Paul did not envision future salvation for all is evident from Philippians 3:19, where he asserts that the end is "destruction" *(apōleia)* for those who are enemies of the cross. We must also recognize that Isaiah 45:21-26 forms the backdrop for Philippians 2:10-11. Isaiah proclaims that there is only one God and all idols are a delusion. All nations will be saved only through Yahweh, the God of Israel. Every knee will bow and every tongue will confess that Yahweh alone is God. The acclamation with the tongue and the subjugation with the knee do not signal, however, a glad acknowledgment by all of Yahweh's rule. Isaiah 45:24 says "all who were incensed against him shall come to him and be ashamed" (NRSV). On the other hand, "In the LORD all the offspring of Israel shall triumph and glory" (Is 45:25 NRSV). Isaiah envisions a twofold response to Yahweh's lordship. Some people are angry and shamed, while those who belong to Israel are victorious and rejoicing. Nonetheless, *all* acknowledge Yahweh's lordship with their knees and their mouths. Some bow before him gladly and with rejoicing; others bow because they are compelled to do so. It is evident that Paul draws on this text in Philippians 2:10-11, and there is no solid reason to think that his meaning differs from Isaiah's. All will acknowledge Jesus as Lord, but it does not follow from this that all will be saved. Some will bow to his lordship with joy, while others, though bowing to his lordship, will be shamed and disgraced because they resisted his rule.

We conclude that the evidence presented to defend universalism is unpersuasive and that repentance and faith are necessary to enjoy eschatological salvation.

8

GOD'S SAVING RIGHTEOUSNESS

The Basis of a Right Relationship with God

Paul's aim as a missionary was to preach the gospel to all peoples. The gospel he preached centered on the person and work of Jesus Christ. The primacy of Jesus is expressed not only in his person but also by his work on behalf of his people. In this chapter and the next we shall examine God's saving work on behalf of his people. In this chapter the focus will be on God's saving righteousness and forgiveness, and in the next we will focus on other dimensions of God's saving work in Christ.

The work of Jesus is supremely manifested in the cross and resurrection. Those who fail to understand the cross are seriously at odds with the Pauline gospel since Paul preaches nothing "except Jesus Christ and him crucified" (1 Cor 2:2). The gospel is "the word of the cross" (1 Cor 1:18), and those who rely on human rhetoric and artistry undercut the powerful message of the cross (1 Cor 1:17-18), which accomplishes salvation for those who are called (1 Cor 1:24). Thus, Paul heralds the cross of Christ because he knows it is both the wisdom and power of God (1 Cor 1:18, 21, 24, 25). The gospel is God's saving power that results in salvation (Rom 1:16), and this gospel centers on the atoning death of Jesus. His death is the means by which believers have been delivered from the "present evil age" (Gal 1:4) and inducted into the new age. The saving righteousness of God has been revealed now in salvation history (Rom 3:21), and God's saving righteousness centers on the cross-work of Jesus (Rom 3:22-26).

The cross and resurrection are woven into the fabric of Paul's letters. Jesus' resurrection from the dead (Rom 1:4) signals the inauguration of the new age in which Jesus is enthroned as Lord. Romans 4:25 draws on Isaiah 53:12 in declaring that Jesus "was handed over for our trespasses," and Jesus' work on the cross is inseparable from his resurrection, for the verse immediately notes that "he was raised for our justification." The reference to the resurrection may be partially dependent on Isaiah 53, for both the LXX and the Qumran edition of Isaiah 53:11 say that the righteous servant will see "light," and this was most likely understood by the early church to refer to the resurrection. The death and resurrection of Jesus are the heart of the gospel, they induct believers into the new age, and they are the basis for justification.

In 1 Corinthians 15:3-4 Paul reminds the Corinthians of the tradition that was transmitted to him and that he passed along to them, saying, "For I delivered to you of first importance that which I also received, namely, that Christ died for our sins according to the scriptures and that he was buried and that he was raised on the third day according to the scriptures." The death and resurrection of Christ constitute the fulfillment of the Old Testament promises, and they are central to Paul's understanding of the gospel. God desires all to be saved (1 Tim 2:4), and this saving purpose of God becomes a reality through Christ Jesus since he functions as the mediator between God and all humanity (1 Tim 2:5). His redemptive work on the cross is the means by which human beings are reconciled to God (1 Tim 2:6). This fits with the claim in 1 Timothy 1:15 that "Christ Jesus came into the world to save sinners," and the means by which this is accomplished is his death and resurrection.

The Colossians were attracted by innovations and regulations that Paul deemed to be contrary to the gospel. Paul reminds them that in Christ they have all they need. He is the fullness of God (Col 1:19; 2:9), and in him they are full and complete (Col 2:10). The fullness that believers enjoy is based on the cross-work of Christ. The true circumcision became theirs through his death, in which he was "cut off" by God (Col 2:11). Through baptism they have been both buried and raised with Christ, participating in both his death and his resurrection (Col 2:12; cf. Rom 6:3-5). Their sins have been forgiven, their IOU's have been erased and nailed to the cross (Col 2:13-14), and spiritual powers have been decisively defeated (Col 2:15).

The cross is central for Paul because in it God's love is revealed and his righteousness is manifested. The uniqueness of God's love becomes evident when we realize that Christ died for those who are weak and ungodly, for sinners and for his enemies (Rom 5:6-10). Nor does Paul wrench apart the Father and the Son, for the *Father* is the one who sent the Son to die for the ungodly. Jesus does not win over an angry Father, for God himself is the one who sent Jesus to appease his own wrath (Rom 3:25). God sent his Son to deliver his people "at the right time" (*kata kairon*, Rom 5:6), at "the fullness of time" (*to plērōma tou chronou*, Gal 4:4). God's saving love has invaded human history through the cross of Christ, delivering those who were captive "to the present evil age" (Gal 1:4). The new age of life and victory has arrived in and through the cross and resurrection of Jesus Christ. Those who were previously alienated from God (Eph 2:11-20) have now been brought near. The enmity between God and humanity has been healed through Christ's atoning death, and this reconciliation with God also involves reconciliation with others who were at enmity with God. Thus, Jews and Gentiles in Christ are reconciled both to one another and to God. The blood of Christ is the means by which peace is attained in the human community.

Indeed, the new humanity—what Adam was intended to be—is now in the process of becoming a reality through Christ. All human beings are born into the world as the sons and daughters of Adam (Rom 5:12-19). The old Adam (*ho palaios anthrōpos*, Rom 6:6), however, has been crucified together with Christ. Believers, therefore, are no longer in Adam but "in Christ." By virtue of baptism (Rom 6:3-10; Gal 3:26-29; Col 2:12), they are submerged into Christ and are part of him (1 Cor 12:13). They are summoned, therefore, to "put on the Lord Jesus Christ" (Rom 13:14). And since Christ has been raised, believers can indeed live in a new way because the age to come has penetrated this present age (Rom 6:4-10). The believer has crucified the flesh with its desires (Gal 5:24), for the old "I" has died with Christ (Gal 2:20), and a new life in the second Adam has commenced. Believers have died once for all in Christ (2 Cor 5:14-15), and thus they are now free to live for the second Adam, who "died and was raised on their behalf" (2 Cor 5:15). It is interesting to note that in both Galatians (Gal 6:14-15) and 2 Corinthians (2 Cor 5:14-21), the assertion that believers are a new creation (Gal 6:15; 2 Cor 5:17) is linked with the cross-work of Christ. This new creative work of God involves the transformation of his creatures, for now we, unlike Adam, will do good works

(Eph 2:10) because God's creative work results in "righteousness and holiness of the truth" (Eph 4:24). Paul clarifies in both Romans 4 and Galatians 3—4 that those who believe in Christ are the true family of Abraham. They are the heirs of the promise God gave to Israel, and they are the true circumcision. Thus, believers are the sons of God (Rom 8:14-17; Gal 3:26; 4:5, 7) and his "beloved children" (Eph 5:1), inheriting the privilege that belonged to Israel (Ex 4:22).

The work of Jesus the Messiah on behalf of his people is represented through a variety of expressions in the Pauline writings. No single idea captures the whole of what Christ accomplished, and thus a number of different expressions are used to depict the work of Christ. None of these descriptions should be elevated as the central theme in Pauline thought, despite the fact that some of them, such as righteousness, are very prominent and important in Paul's thinking. We shall examine the following aspects of Christ's work in the next two chapters: righteousness, the role of faith, forgiveness, sanctification, reconciliation, salvation, redemption, triumph over evil powers, propitiation and election.[1]

Righteousness

Challenges to its importance. One of the most important terms Paul uses to designate Christ's work on our behalf is *righteousness.*[2] Many scholars in the history of interpretation have maintained that justification, or righteousness, is the center of Paul's theology. It is probably fair to say that since the Reformation this has been the majority view in Protestant circles, and this view continues to be defended up to the present day. On the other hand, some have insisted that righteousness is a secondary motif in Paul. We recall Albert Schweitzer's famous statement asserting that righteousness "is a subsidiary crater within the main crater of being in Christ."[3] Schweitzer believed that mystical union with Christ was much more important to Paul than was the legal metaphor of righteousness. William Wrede also demoted justification, observing that the topic only arises in texts where Paul is engaged in a

---

[1]Other themes could certainly be investigated as well.

[2]I am grateful to Bruce Ware and especially Don Carson for personal correspondence in which they responded to my section on righteousness. They persuaded me that righteousness is forensic rather than transformative, and hence what I have written here is an adjustment to the view I expressed in my book *Romans*, BECNT (Grand Rapids, Mich.: Baker, 1998). Of course, any deficiencies in my view remain my responsibility, and there are still areas in which I set forth a different view from the above scholars.

[3]Albert Schweitzer, *The Mysticism of Paul the Apostle* (London: A. & C. Black, 1931), p. 225.

polemic against false teachers; and Wrede goes on to say that Paul's religion can be discussed without even mentioning justification![4] Since justification is central only in polemical contexts—in Galatians, Romans and Philippians, where the inclusion of Gentiles into the church is emphasized—it can scarcely function as the center of Paul's thought. Such an idea has been trumpeted afresh today in the writings of Krister Stendahl, who thinks that the inclusion of the Gentiles is the primary theme for Paul and that justification is brought in to defend such inclusion.[5] E. P. Sanders hearkens back to Schweitzer, arguing that participation with Christ is more central than righteousness, maintaining that Paul's teaching on righteousness is used to defend the inclusion of Gentiles into the people of God.[6] Georg Strecker argues that the fundamental element in Paul's theology is freedom from the power of the flesh and freedom from sin and death, not justification. Justification is not mentioned in Paul's earliest letter (1 Thess), showing that it is not primary.[7]

The contribution of the above scholars is useful, for it compels us to reexamine Pauline theology. In one sense the view of these scholars is correct, for justification should not be accepted as the center of Pauline theology, as I argued in the first chapter. The foundation of his theology is the glory of God in the work of Christ. On the other hand, we also suggested that the gospel was the theme of Paul's theology, and Romans 1:16-17 indicates that God's righteousness is revealed in the gospel. Since Paul's gospel reveals God's righteousness, it is fair to conclude that righteousness and justification are of great importance in Pauline theology. Justification is crucial because it focuses on the basis upon which believers enter into a relationship with God. In that sense righteousness is fundamental to the Pauline gospel and addresses the greatest need of human beings, namely, forgiveness of sins.[8]

---

[4]William Wrede, *Paul* (Lexington, Ky.: American Theological Library Association, 1962), pp. 122-23, 146. Note how Wrede was a precursor of Krister Stendahl here.

[5]Krister Stendahl, *Paul Among Jews and Gentiles and Other Essays* (Philadelphia: Fortress, 1976).

[6]E. P. Sanders, *Paul and Palestinian Judaism: A Comparison of Patterns of Religion* (Philadelphia: Fortress, 1977); and *Paul, the Law, and Jewish People* (Philadelphia: Fortress, 1983).

[7]Georg Strecker, *Theologie des Neuen Testaments*, ed. F. W. Horn (Berlin: Walter de Gruyter, 1996), pp. 148-49.

[8]For the centrality of justification in Paul's theology, see J. Gresham Machen, *The Origin of Paul's Religion* (Grand Rapids, Mich.: Eerdmans, 1925), pp. 278-79; J. I. Packer, "Justification," in *New Bible Dictionary*, ed. J. D. Douglas and N. Hillyer, 2nd ed. (Downers Grove, Ill.: InterVarsity Press, 1983), pp. 637-38; G. Schrenk, "δικαιοσύνη," in *Theological Dictionary of the New Testament*, ed. Gerhard Kittel and Gerhard Friedrich (Grand Rapids, Mich.: Eerdmans,

We can conclude, therefore, that the scholars who have questioned the centrality of justification have gone to an extreme in diminishing its importance. We must remember that Paul was trained as a Pharisee, and thus one of the first issues that he would have tackled in his newfound faith was the relationship of Christians to the law.[9] Any claim that he would have passed over this issue is historical fantasy, ignoring the Pharisaic and biblical foundation on which Paul was raised. Nor should we expect Paul to tackle the issue of the law and justification in every letter since the letters were occasional and were not doctrinal treatises. Apparently the Thessalonians were not struggling with the issues that plagued the Galatians and the problems that surface in Romans and Philippians. Moreover, there are hints even in the Thessalonian correspondence that believers are righteous on the basis of Christ's death alone (1 Thess 1:10; 4:14; 5:9-10; 2 Thess 2:13-14, 16).

Nor is it satisfying to demote righteousness as a mere "subsidiary crater" or as a tool to defend the Gentiles' inclusion. It is probably a mistake to identify righteousness as the center of Paul's theology, but it is also an error to exalt participation in Christ or life in the Spirit so that they become more important than righteousness. Indeed, a right relation with God is the basis on which believers are united with Christ and on which they receive the Spirit. If anything, then, righteousness is more fundamental than life in the Spirit or participation with Christ. Of course, we should not play the various themes off against each other, for such an approach would lead us off the track from the beginning. Some complain that righteousness is merely a "legal fiction" if it is forensic and if it is in a separate category from life in the Spirit. Such an objection is logically flawed, for believers are truly and really in a right relation with God on the basis of Christ's work. This righteous status with God is no fiction but a reality. Further, because believers are right in God's sight, God grants them his Spirit and power to live a new life. Hence, the forensic gift of righteousness becomes the basis (and is the only basis) on which believers receive God's powerful Spirit that transforms their lives.

1964), 2:202; Ronald Y. K. Fung, "The Status of Justification by Faith in Paul's Thought: A Brief Survey of a Modern Debate," *Them* 6 (1981): 4-11; Mark A. Seifrid, *Christ, Our Righteousness: Paul's Theology of Justification* (Downers Grove, Ill.: InterVarsity Press, 2001).
[9]Paul's Pharisaic background inevitably propelled him into a reevaluation of the law. See Martin Hengel in collaboration with Roland Deines, *The Pre-Christian Paul* (Philadelphia: Trinity Press International, 1991), pp. 40-53, 70-71, esp. 79-86; Martin Hengel and Anna Maria Schwemer, *Paul Between Damascus and Antioch: The Unknown Years* (Louisville, Ky.: Westminster John Knox, 1997), pp. 98-101; Peter Stuhlmacher, *Reconciliation, Law and Righteousness: Essays in Biblical Theology* (Philadelphia: Fortress, 1986), pp. 69-71, 124, 134-54.

Nor should we fall prey to an instrumentalist view in which righteousness is upheld only for the sake of including Gentiles. The impression given is that Paul employed the means to attain a certain end, caring little about the legitimacy of the means. Such a view stumbles over Paul's Pharisaic heritage. As a scholar of the scriptures, he needed to resolve, from an exegetical and theological standpoint, the role of the law in terms of justification. We see from both Galatians and Romans that he knew very well that circumcision (Gen 17:9-14) was required to enter the people of God. Contrary to Sanders, Paul needed a better answer than simply saying that since Christ is the way to salvation, the law must be now set aside. We see from Paul's scriptural exegesis in Galatians 3:6—4:31 and Romans 2:1—4:25 (cf. Phil 3:2-11) that he had carefully worked out his understanding of the law. The arguments presented are complex, and it is quite unlikely that they were simply adopted for the needs of the moment, for pragmatic arguments would have hardly persuaded those wavering under the influence of Pauline opponents.

Philippians 3:2-11, not to mention Galatians 1:11-17, suggests that Paul wrestled with these questions soon after his conversion.[10] The pragmatic scenario suggested by Stendahl and others misses the convictional world of Paul. He was not the kind of person who latched onto any argument to defend a course of action, especially in terms of the Torah! He needed to be convinced that a course of action was biblically sustainable before engaging upon it. J. Gresham Machen is much more convincing when he says that the reason Paul was devoted to justification by faith was not because it made possible the Gentile mission but because it was true.[11]

Paul's teaching in his letters is hammered out in controversy with his opponents. His letters were written after years of oral debate with his opponents, so they reflect his mature thinking about God's righteousness. Indeed, Paul suggests in Galatians (Gal 1:11-24) that his distinctive gospel for the Gentiles was given to him at his conversion. The point is not that he would have understood all the implications of that gospel instantaneously. I am suggesting that he would have immediately engaged in a thorough study of these matters. Some scholars write as if Paul did not take righteousness by faith as seriously because it was forged in controversy. One wonders if some of these scholars have reflected on the controversies in which they have been engaged, because in the midst of a debate we redouble our efforts to make

---

[10]For the importance of Paul's conversion in the formation of his theology, see Seyoon Kim, *The Origin of Paul's Gospel* (Grand Rapids, Mich.: Eerdmans, 1981).

[11]Machen, *Origin*, pp. 278-79.

sure our arguments are persuasive and convincing. Paul knew he was departing from Jewish tradition (Gal 1:11-12)—but not the Old Testament!—and thus it was especially important to him to base his views on compelling arguments. He could hardly succeed in his mission if he tacked this way and then the other whenever opponents came along. Paul must have realized that he needed coherent and consistent arguments to defend his new gospel, nor is it likely that he would have adopted it without them. For Paul never resorted to what would have been an obvious solution, namely, dismiss the Old Testament as inspired scripture. He believed that righteousness by faith was taught by the Old Testament scriptures and that his teaching on justification did not contradict but fulfilled the Old Testament. It was an especially important doctrine to him because it is the basis on which human beings become right with God, the foundation of one's relationship with God.

We have noted that since the Reformation righteousness has often been viewed as the center of Paul's theology. Recently some scholars have attempted to defend the centrality of righteousness on a new basis. Its importance has been especially emphasized by Ernst Käsemann and his students Peter Stuhlmacher and Christian Muller.[12] These scholars maintain that righteousness is not merely individualistic but that it also includes all of creation. God's righteousness is manifested when he restores the world to his lordship in the saving work of Christ. Käsemann sees *righteousness* as a technical term derived from apocalyptic literature, denoting God's saving acts. According to this view, righteousness is not confined to the forensic sphere. God's righteousness is defined as a transforming righteousness, so that God both *declares* righteous and *makes* righteous those who are saved. One can understand how righteousness functions as the center of Käsemann's theology since righteousness language is so comprehensive.

When one compares the arguments of Wrede-Schweitzer and Käsemann-Stuhlmacher, the latter are much more convincing than the former. We will temporarily postpone discussing whether righteousness is both forensic and transformative—whether Paul teaches that we are both declared righteous and made righteous. At this juncture two general and

---

[12]Ernst Käsemann, "'The Righteousness of God' in Paul," in *New Testament Questions of Today* (Philadelphia: Fortress, 1969), pp. 168-82; Peter Stuhlmacher, *Gerechtigkeit Gottes bei Paulus*, FRLANT 87 (Göttingen: Vandenhoeck & Ruprecht, 1965); Christian Muller, *Gottes Gerechtigkeit und Gottes Volk: Eine Untersuchung zu Römer 9—11*, FRLANT 86 (Göttingen: Vandenhoeck & Ruprecht, 1964). It is not my purpose here to discuss the differences between these scholars.

brief comments will be made about the Käsemann's school conception of divine righteousness. First, while the Old Testament antecedents for righteousness are well established,[13] the evidence for *the righteousness of God* as a technical term from apocalyptic is simply lacking.[14] Second, it is quite improbable that God's righteousness can be defined as his faithfulness to all of creation. Such a comprehensive definition is difficult to sustain inductively from the Pauline letters.

Covenant faithfulness? We should also note the view that the righteousness of God refers to his covenant faithfulness. A number of scholars support this understanding, but the most prominent and influential supporter of this view is probably N. T. Wright.[15] Wright, like those in the Käsemann school, appeals to the Old Testament to support his understanding of God's righteousness; but he takes his argument in a different direction, maintaining that both the Old Testament background and the Pauline context support the definition "covenant faithfulness." The work of Wright is becoming enormously popular—and no wonder, for his work is truly magisterial, and he writes lucidly and attractively. We cannot analyze Wright's project in detail here, not even his defense of the view that righteousness means covenant faithfulness.[16] Our task in this chapter will be to assess the meaning of righteousness in Paul from the biblical text, and along the way we shall interact with various scholars all too briefly.

Indeed, numerous monographs have been written on justification in Paul, and thus all the issues can hardly be treated in detail here.[17] My goal is to explain from the biblical text why I understand righteousness as I do. The Old Testament background needs to be sketched in briefly. Often righteousness language refers to God's saving activity on behalf of his people. When Deborah celebrates the victory over Sisera, she refers to "the righteous acts of

---

[13]See Scott J. Hafemann, "The 'Righteousness of God,' " in *How to Do Biblical Theology*, ed. Peter Stuhlmacher, PTMS 38 (Allison Park, Penn.: Pickwick, 1995), pp. xv-xli.

[14]Marion L. Soards, "Käsemann's 'Righteousness' Reexamined," *CBQ* 49 (1987): 264-67.

[15]See N. T. Wright, *What St. Paul Really Said: Was Paul of Tarsus the Real Founder of Christianity?* (Grand Rapids, Mich.: Eerdmans, 1997), pp. 113-33.

[16]See Carey C. Newman, ed., *Jesus and the Restoration of Israel: A Critical Assessment of N. T. Wright's "Jesus and the Victory of God"* (Downers Grove, Ill.: InterVarsity Press, 1999); Richard B. Gaffin Jr., "Review Essay: Paul the Theologian," *WTJ* 62 (2000): 121-41. It should be noted that in many ways I stand in agreement with Wright and have profited significantly from his scholarship. Still, some major differences remain between his and my understanding of Paul.

[17]For a helpful introduction to the issues, see John H. P. Reumann, *Righteousness in the New Testament: Justification in the United States Lutheran-Roman Catholic Dialogue, with Responses by Joseph A. Fitzmyer and Jerome D. Quinn* (Philadelphia: Fortress, 1982).

Yahweh" (Judg 5:11), which could be paraphrased as "his saving acts." Samuel employs the same expression (1 Sam 12:7; cf. Dan 9:16; Mic 6:5) in reminding the people of God's saving actions on behalf of Israel. *Righteousness* does not merely denote "justice" but God's salvation on behalf of his people. This view is confirmed by the Psalms and Isaiah, where righteousness language is often parallel with God's salvation. For example, Psalm 98:2-3 (Ps 97:2 LXX) says,

> He [Yahweh] has made known his salvation [*sōtērion*],
>> in the presence of all nations he has revealed his righteousness [*dikaiosynē*].
> He has remembered his loyal love [*eleos*]
>> and his faithfulness [*alētheia*] to the house of Israel.
> All the ends of the earth have seen
>> the salvation [*sōtērion*] of our God.

We can see from this verse that God's righteousness is linked with his salvation, loyal love and faithfulness. Understanding God's righteousness as his judgment of sinners in this context would seriously misapprehend the psalmist's meaning. Isaiah 51:5-8 is also a striking example:

> My righteousness draws near
>> and my salvation has gone forth. . . .
> But my salvation will be forever,
>> and my righteousness will not fail. . . .
> My righteousness will be forever
>> and my salvation to all generations.

In the context of Isaiah, Yahweh's saving work on behalf of his people is obviously in view. These texts are hardly isolated examples, for many others could be cited to the same effect (e.g., Ps 31:1; 36:10; 40:10; 71:2; 88:10-12; 143:1; Is 46:13).

We can see, from these Old Testament citations, why a number of scholars have understood God's righteousness in terms of his covenantal faithfulness.[18] God's righteousness is often parallel to his faithfulness, his loyal love and salvation in the Old Testament scriptures. God's saving activity also fulfills the covenantal promises made to Israel, and thus designating righteous-

---

[18]See n. 15 above and also N. T. Wright, "Romans in the Theology of Paul," in *Romans*, vol. 3 of *Pauline Theology*, ed. D. M. Hay and E. E. Johnson (Minneapolis: Fortress, 1995), pp. 33-34, 39; James D. G. Dunn, *The Theology of Paul the Apostle* (Grand Rapids, Mich.: Eerdmans, 1998), pp. 340-46; Sam K. Williams, "The 'Righteousness of God' in Romans," *JBL* 49 (1980): 241-90.

ness as God's loyalty to his covenant seems especially fitting to these scholars. Surely, God's righteousness expresses his faithfulness to his covenant, and yet this is not the same thing as saying that God's righteousness *is his faithfulness to the covenant*. God's righteousness surely fulfills his covenantal promises, but it does not follow from this that we should define righteousness as covenantal faithfulness. Mark Seifrid has demonstrated that the words *covenant* and *righteousness* are rarely used in the same context in the Old Testament, which seems strange if righteousness is to be defined as God's covenantal faithfulness.[19] Further, we shall see when we examine specific texts in Paul that covenant faithfulness does not accurately convey what Paul intended to say.

Romans 3:5 is often introduced as evidence for defining "righteousness of God" as "covenantal faithfulness," since in Romans 3:1-8 God's righteousness is parallel to his "faithfulness, truth and reliability." Despite some initial plausibility, this text cannot carry the freight laid on it. First, this text is remarkably difficult and opaque—not a good candidate on which to base our definition of the righteousness of God. How one understands these verses is related to how one construes Romans 6 and Romans 9—11. Indeed, on anyone's reading, Romans 3:1-8 does not fully explicate the issues raised. Since other chapters in Romans are vital for interpreting this text, we should not appeal to it to grasp Paul's understanding of righteousness. Second, it is doubtful that *righteousness of God* should be rendered "covenantal faithfulness" in Romans 3:5. Paul's argument here assumes that "our unrighteousness demonstrates God's righteousness." It is quite likely that the righteousness in view here does not refer to salvation but to God's judgment of sinners.[20] If this is the case, then interpreting God's righteousness as his covenantal faithfulness is singularly ill-fitting, for God's covenantal faithfulness to his people does not consist in his judgment of them. It is true that Paul reminds his readers of God's covenantal faithfulness to the Jews in Romans 3:1-8, but he also reminds them of God's righteous judgment of their sins. To argue that the latter is included in the former is unpersuasive. We are not denying that God saves his people out of faithfulness to his covenant; it is also the case that the word *righteousness* in the Old Testament is used to designate the salvation God will accomplish for his people. This is not to say, however, that the righteousness of God *is to be defined as* his covenantal loyalty.

---

[19]See Seifrid, *Christ, Our Righteousness.*
[20]In defense of this view of righteousness in Rom 3:5, see Schreiner, *Romans*, pp. 155-57.

Some scholars have tried to distinguish between "righteousness" as a divine gift and "the righteousness of God," seeing in the latter God's covenantal faithfulness.[21] This is an attractive argument, but it ultimately fails. First, it has already been noted that God's righteousness fulfills his covenant with his people but should not be defined as his covenantal faithfulness. Second, it is difficult to sustain the idea that *righteousness of God* is a technical term in Paul that is to be distinguished from *righteousness*. For example, Philippians 3:9 refers to "the righteousness from God" *(tēn ek theou dikaiosynēn)*. The contrast between "the righteousness from God" and "my own righteousness" in this verse—and Paul's contrast between his devotion to the law and his newfound allegiance to Christ—indicates that "the righteousness from God" here is a divine gift. It is a righteousness that comes *from* God and is accessed by faith. Someone could object that the preposition *from (ek)* is lacking in Romans 1:17 and Romans 3:21-22, and thus the texts should be distinguished. Such an interpretation is possible but unlikely since both texts zero in on the same theme: how people are right with God. Indeed, both texts query whether one can be right with God via the law or faith in Christ. One is guilty of reading Paul far too technically in positing a distinction between these texts. Hence, in the relationship between these verses (Phil 3:9 and Rom 1:17; 3:21-22) we see powerful evidence that righteousness of God is forensic, referring to the gift of righteousness given to all who believe.

Romans 10:3 supports the exegesis suggested here, for the many parallels between the context of Romans 10:1-5 and Philippians 3:2-9 make it quite improbable that *righteousness of God* should be interpreted in a different way in Romans 10:3 from its interpretation in Philippians 3:9. Romans 10:3 says that Israel "did not subject itself to the righteousness of God *[tē dikaiosynē tou theou]* because it was ignorant of the righteousness of God *[tēn tou theou dikaiosynēn]* and tried to establish its own." The context of this section reveals that Israel attempted to secure its own righteousness through keeping the law (Rom 9:30—10:8; note esp. Rom 10:5—"righteousness which is from the law," *tēn dikaiosynēn tēn ek tou nomou*). Paul declares that self-righteousness is the wrong path to righteousness, for one does not gain righteousness on one's own but as a gift of God. That righteousness here involves a gift from God is hard to deny since it is contrasted with trying to establish one's own righteousness. To understand "God's righteousness" as covenantal faithful-

---

[21]See Williams, "Righteousness of God," pp. 255-89; Peter T. O'Brien, "Justification in Paul and Some Crucial Issues of the Last Two Decades," in *Right with God: Justification in the Bible and the World,* ed. D. A. Carson (Grand Rapids, Mich.: Eerdmans, 1992), pp. 75-78.

ness here is not patently contradictory, but it does not suit the context as well as seeing a reference to the gift of God's righteousness. This suggests, of course, that *the righteousness of God* in Romans 1:17 and Romans 3:21-22 (cf. also Rom 10:3; Phil 3:9) should be rendered similarly, for it is quite improbable that Paul would use the term to denote God's covenantal loyalty earlier and now use it to refer to God's gift of righteousness.

The clinching argument is found in 2 Corinthians 5:21.[22] In 2 Corinthians 5:11-21 Paul features his ministry of reconciliation. He summons people to be reconciled to God inasmuch as reconciliation involves "not counting their trespasses against them" (2 Cor 5:19). Such reconciliation is based on the atoning death of Christ because God "made the one who knew no sin to be sin on our behalf, in order that we might become the righteousness of God [*dikaiosynē theou*] in him" (2 Cor 5:21). The notion of Christ's substitutionary death is inescapable here. Because Jesus was a sinless person, there was no warrant for his death. Yet he became a sin-offering on our behalf—a substitutionary, voluntary offering—so that we might become the righteousness of God. This can scarcely mean that we have become the covenantal faithfulness of God. But it makes eminent sense to understand it in terms of God's saving work through Christ by which he declares the believer to be in the right before him. Indeed, the substitutionary focus of the context almost demands such a reading. Again, it seems antecedently unlikely that *the righteousness of God* in 2 Corinthians 5:21 would bear a different meaning from the term in Romans 1:17 and 3:21-22 (cf. Rom 3:25-26).

Before we discuss the parallel between 2 Corinthians 5:21 and Romans 3:21-26, it should be noted that *righteousness* is a forensic term, stemming from the law court. God as the judge of all is a righteous God who enforces his justice as Lord of the universe. Second Corinthians 5:21 demonstrates this clearly. Believers are declared to be righteous before God as the divine judge because Jesus, as the sinless one, bore their sins. God's righteousness, therefore, consists both of his judgment and salvation. He saves those who put their faith in Jesus, and he judges his Son at the cross. If we were to consider all of Romans 1:18—3:26, it is clear that God preserves his justice by judging and condemning all human beings. All human beings have sinned and therefore stand before the divine judge as condemned. Nevertheless, because of the cross of Christ, God both saves and judges at the cross. In other words,

---

[22]Wright's view that 2 Cor 5:21 refers to Paul's apostolic ministry as an incarnation of God's covenant faithfulness (*What St. Paul Really Said*, pp. 104-5) is to my mind a strange and completely implausible interpretation of the verse.

both the saving righteousness of God (by which he declares sinners to be in the right in his sight) and the judging work of God (by which he pours out his wrath on Christ) meet in the cross of Christ. It should be added that God himself sent his Son to satisfy his wrath, and so righteousness is rooted in God's love.

Once we see what has been sketched in above, the parallel between 2 Corinthians 5:21 and Romans 3:21-26 is quite striking. Romans 3:21 indicates that God's saving righteousness has now been manifested at this juncture of salvation history, and this saving righteousness becomes ours through faith in Jesus Christ (Rom 3:22). Such saving righteousness, however, is only secured through the redemptive and propitiatory work of Christ (Rom 3:24-26). Through Christ's death God's wrath is appeased, so that he does not compromise his judging righteousness in offering forgiveness of sins (Rom 3:25-26). Detecting a reference to God's judgment in Romans 3:25-26 ("God set forth Christ as a propitiation through faith in his blood to demonstrate his righteousness, . . . to demonstrate his righteousness in the present time, so that he might be just and the justifier of the one who has faith in Jesus") is crucial since some scholars insist that the term *righteousness* refers to his saving righteousness in Rom 3:25-26.[23] It is a mistake, however, to limit God's righteousness only to salvation, for God is also righteous in condemning sinners in judgment (cf. also Rom 2:5; 3:4; 2 Thess 1:6-10). Some scholars have mistakenly suggested that God's righteousness relates *only* to his saving acts and that no idea of divine judgment should be attached to God's righteousness. This reading of the evidence cannot be sustained, for Daniel acknowledges that God is righteous in punishing Israel with exile (Dan 9:13-14; cf. 2 Chron 12:6; Lam 1:18). It is the Lord's nature to repay people in accord with their righteousness (1 Sam 26:23), and the Lord manifests his righteousness in judging the wicked for their evil actions.

Indeed, the context of Romans 3:24-26 confirms that *righteousness* in Romans 3:25-26 refers to God's judgment of sin, for justification (Rom 3:21-22) is available to sinners through the redemptive and propitiatory work of Jesus Christ. Thereby God shows that he was not denying his own righteousness in passing over sins that were previously committed (Rom 3:25-26). In other words, Paul wonders if God has compromised his righteousness by not inflicting his full punishment on those who had sinned before Christ suffered

---

[23]The details of this text are fiercely contested. See Schreiner, *Romans*, pp. 181, 191-99, for further discussion.

on the cross. He answers that God's righteousness is not besmirched because he was looking ahead to Christ's atonement. Such a line of argument indicates that God's judging righteousness, his holiness, is in Paul's mind. By virtue of Christ's death God has demonstrated his judging righteousness—he does not tolerate sin that was previously committed. In the death of Jesus Christ, therefore, the saving righteousness and the judging righteousness of God meet. God vindicates his judging holiness since God in Christ absorbs his wrath at his crucifixion. And he displays his saving righteousness since he vindicates all those who have faith in Jesus. The line of thought in Romans 3:21-26 is remarkably similar to 2 Corinthians 5:21, suggesting that God's saving righteousness is his gift of righteousness, though both Romans 3:25-26 and 2 Corinthians 5:21 also indicate that God's judging holiness is satisfied in the cross.

Righteousness as forensic. It has already been argued that the term *righteousness of God* is fundamentally forensic in Romans 1:17; 3:21-22; 10:3; 2 Corinthians 5:21; and Philippians 3:9. We must also see that righteousness in the Old Testament is often forensic. The legal sphere is often featured in righteousness terminology. The hiphil of the verb *sadēq* denotes a judicial declaration (Ex 23:7). Judges are to "justify the righteous and condemn the wicked" (Deut 25:1; cf. 2 Sam 15:4; 1 Kings 8:31-32; 2 Chron 6:23; Prov 17:15; Is 5:23). Clearly, this cannot mean that judges "make" people righteous or guilty. Only an evil judge would render justice in such a way. Rather, judges "declare" a defendant guilty or innocent. The nations are challenged to appear before Yahweh as the divine judge to see whether their case can be vindicated ("justified") before him (Is 43:9). Similarly, Yahweh challenges Israel to appear before him in court to determine if Israel can possibly prove its case and be vindicated before him (Is 43:26). We need to remember that in the biblical text there are only two parties in the courtroom—God and human beings. When the psalmist acknowledges his sin and God's judgment, he confesses that "God is justified" in speaking against him in the divine law court (Ps 51:4). Elsewhere the psalmist pleads for God's mercy, admitting that no one is righteous or vindicated before God (Ps 143:2). Job often uses the language of righteousness in reflecting on his own status before the divine judge, contemplating both whether human beings can be right before God and whether God will vindicate him in the divine law court (Job 4:17; 9:2, 14-15, 20; 13:18; cf. Job 40:8). God's righteousness also denotes his judicial decision by which he will vindicate his people or his servant (cf. Is 50:8; 53:11). When the Israelites are saved, they will praise God since he is their righteousness (Jer 23:6).

Righteousness often has a forensic character in Paul, denoting God's gift to his people. This is especially evident when he uses the verb *dikaioō*, but we have seen previously that the phrase *righteousness of God* should be understood forensically.[24] Those who keep the law "will be justified," that is, vindicated in the divine law court on the last day (Rom 2:13). On the other hand, no one who is of the "works of the law" will be justified before God because vindication before God is only available by faith (Rom 3:20, 24, 26, 28, 30; 5:1; Gal 2:16-17; 3:11, 24; 5:4). Since righteousness by faith is contrasted with works of law, these texts almost certainly teach that we are *declared to be right* before God by faith. This rendering is strengthened by Romans 4:5, which speaks of God's "justifying the ungodly," and the verses immediately following link up this righteousness with forgiveness of sins (Rom 4:6-8). To be forgiven means that a new relationship with God is established, and certainly one who is forgiven is not "made righteous" but is "declared to be righteous." The emphasis is on the right-standing before God that is granted to those who put their faith in Jesus Christ.

The indispensable bond between righteousness and forgiveness is also forged in Romans 4:25, "He [Christ] was delivered over for the sake of our trespasses and raised for the sake of our justification." In this sentence, forgiveness of trespasses and justification are again joined together, indicating that justification involves the forgiveness of sins. The forensic sense of the verb *dikaioō* is undeniable in Romans 8:33, "Who will bring a charge against God's elect? God is the one who justifies." Paul queries whether anyone will condemn God's chosen ones in the divine law court in the last day, and he replies that any such charge will be dismissed by the divine judge since the judge has already vindicated the defendants (cf. Rom 5:9; 1 Cor 4:4). We should note here that justification relates to the divine law court on the last day. In that sense it is fundamentally eschatological, but in Christ the end-time gift has invaded history. The judgment of the last day has now been revealed in the cross of Christ, so that those who believe in Christ are declared to be in the right before God even now.

The verb *reckon* or *count* (*logizomai*) also suggests that law-court terminology is in view (Rom 3:28; 4:3-6, 8-11, 22-24; 9:8; cf. Gal 3:6). The word *count* hails from the commercial sphere, but it is fitting terminology for a judge who

---

[24]J. A. Ziesler argues (in *The Meaning of Righteousness in Paul: A Linguistic and Theological Enquiry*, SNTSMS 20 [Cambridge: Cambridge University Press, 1972]) that the verb is invariably forensic. Compare also Richard N. Longenecker, *Galatians*, WBC (Dallas: Word, 1990), p. 85.

determines whether legal "accounts" have been settled. In Paul's mind, of course, such a reckoning could never be made apart from the atoning death of Jesus, who secured forgiveness for sinners (Rom 3:21-26). And yet God's counting sinners as righteous through faith is an act of grace and mercy since God does "not count their trespasses against them" (2 Cor 5:19). The use of the verb *count (logizomai)* with the noun *righteousness (dikaiosynē)* suggests that the noun for righteousness designates our status before God. Romans 5:17 expresses this idea nicely when it says believers have received "the gift of righteousness" *(tēs dōreas tēs dikaiosynēs)*. The word *gift* when aligned with righteousness indicates that a new status is given to believers by God's grace—a right relation with God.

That righteousness has to do with being declared righteous is also suggested by the collocation of righteousness with faith (Rom 1:17; 3:22, 26; 4:3, 5, 9, 13; 9:30; 10:4, 6, 10; Gal 3:6; 5:5; Phil 3:9). The combination of righteousness and faith suggests that the former is a gift given (Rom 5:17) and that a new status before God is involved. The forensic character of righteousness is confirmed by 2 Corinthians 3:9, which contrasts "the ministry of condemnation" with "the ministry of righteousness." The contrast with condemnation indicates that the judge's verdict is involved here. In 1 Corinthians 1:30 the emphasis is on righteousness as a gift, for it comes "from" *(apo)* God. Similarly, in Philippians 3:9 Paul's "righteousness from the law" is contrasted with "the righteousness from God on the basis of faith." Righteousness is conceived as God's gift *(ek theou)*, not as something earned by human beings.

The above evidence has convinced many scholars that God's saving righteousness is forensic and not transformative.[25] In other words, God declares us righteous and does not make us righteous. All would agree that in some texts Paul uses the noun *righteousness* to refer to godly behavior (e.g., Rom 6:13, 16, 18-20; 2 Cor 6:7, 14; 11:15; Eph 4:24; 5:9; 6:14; Phil 1:11; 1 Tim 6:11; 2 Tim 2:22; 3:16). Some scholars argue, however, that God's righteousness is both forensic and transformative, declaring us righteous and making us righteous. The idea that God's righteousness is also transformative has been defended especially by Käsemann and Stuhlmacher.[26] Though I endorsed this view previously, I would argue that the forensic understanding is finally more convincing.[27]

---

[25]For advocates of this view, see Charles E. B. Cranfield, *A Critical and Exegetical Commentary on the Epistle to the Romans,* ICC (Edinburgh: T & T Clark, 1975-1979), 1:95-99; Douglas J. Moo, *Romans 1—8,* WEC (Chicago: Moody Press, 1991), pp. 65-70, 75-86.

[26]For this view, see n. 12 above.

[27]For my previous view see my *Romans,* pp. 63-71.

Arguments against a transformative view of righteousness. We shall proceed here by stating the arguments of the Käsemann school and then explain briefly why these arguments are not convincing.[28] First, God's righteousness is said to be "revealed" (*apokalyptetai,* Rom 1:17) and "manifested" (*pephanerōtai,* Rom 3:21). The verbs *revealed* and *manifested* are apocalyptic terms denoting God's saving activity and intervention, suggesting God's effectual work. In response it can be agreed that God's righteousness is eschatological and effective, but neither of these points demonstrates that God's saving activity is anything other than forensic. God's forensic verdict is certainly effectual since it is based on Christ's death and resurrection, but it is effective in declaring us to be in the right before God. The eschatological character of righteousness does not cancel out its declarative sense, for the end-time verdict of the divine judge has been declared in advance on the basis of the death and resurrection of Christ.

Second, those who support a transformative understanding point out the parallelism between God's "righteousness" (Rom 1:17), his "power" (Rom 1:16) and his "wrath" (Rom 1:18). The genitives in each case can be construed as genitives of possession, but they also have the idea of source: righteousness, power and wrath all come from God. The collocation of terms suggests to some that God's righteousness is transformative. God's power is closely linked to his righteousness in the argument since Romans 1:16 and Romans 1:17 are joined by the word *for (gar),* suggesting that God's righteousness is an instance of his saving power. In responding to this, we have already noted how God's righteousness can be understood as effective without smuggling in the idea of transformation. Furthermore, God's power is certainly demonstrated in his verdict that sinners are not guilty, for it is precisely here that his wrath is turned away from sinners. It should also be pointed out the collocation of the terms *power, righteousness* and *wrath* does not prove that they are all used in the same sense. We must beware of a kind of illegitimate totality transfer in which each word in context bleeds into other terms used. The parallels between Romans 1:17 and Romans 3:21-22; 10:3; 2 Corinthians 5:21; and Philippians 3:9 indicate that a forensic meaning is more likely.

Third, the Old Testament background is adduced as evidence for the transformative view since God's righteousness is often parallel to his salvation, faithfulness, truth and loyal love. But this argument suffers from the point

---

[28]It is here that the comments of Ware and Carson (see p. 192 n. 2) have been particularly helpful.

just made. The collocation of terms does not demonstrate that the words used all bear the same definition. Paul's understanding of righteousness is rooted in the Old Testament, but we have also seen the forensic emphasis in the Old Testament; hence how Paul understood the term *righteousness* must be determined by the Old Testament landscape and the Pauline context.

Fourth, in Romans 3:24 Paul says that we are justified "through the redemption which is in Christ Jesus." Redemption, as we shall see, hearkens back to the Israelites' liberation from Egypt, their freedom from slavery. It signifies that God has liberated and freed his people from sin in Jesus Christ. God's righteousness, according to the Käsemann school, is not segregated from God's transforming work but includes it. It does not follow from this, however, that righteousness is itself transformative. Redemption is based on what God has done objectively in the cross of Christ, where he was sacrificed as the perfect man, the second Adam. What Paul expresses in Romans 3:24 is that those whom God has declared to be in the right are justified by virtue of the redemptive work of Christ on the cross.

Fifth, the merging of the forensic and transformative could be detected in Romans 6, where Paul maintains that those who are in Christ will lead godly lives because they have been baptized into Christ. Part and parcel of Paul's argument is Romans 6:7, "For the one who died has been justified from sin." It is common for translations to render the word *dedikaiōtai* as "freed," whereas the term *dikaioō* is rendered "justify" elsewhere in Romans. The context of Romans 6 could suggest that those who are justified are also transformed. This argument is perhaps the strongest for the transformative view, but it is not compelling. It has already been noted that the verbal form *dikaioō* is almost invariably forensic. Understanding the verb forensically here still yields good sense. Those who are declared to be in the right before God are free from the penalty of sin on the basis of Christ's death. Paul is arguing that the forensic work of Christ is the basis of God's transforming work, but it does not follow from this that the forensic and transforming work are the same thing. What this verse does indicate is that Christ's forensic work is not separated from a changed life but is the basis for such a change. Hence, the old charge that justification undercuts the need for holiness is baseless. The tendency to separate justification from life in the Spirit is not Pauline. The "ministry of righteousness" (2 Cor 3:9) is the basis for the "ministry of the Spirit" (2 Cor 3:8).

The logical relationship between righteousness and the Spirit is set forth in Galatians. Scholars have often pondered Paul's emphasis on righteousness in

the first part of the letter and his call to live by the Spirit in Galatians 5:13—
6:10. To explain the change of theme, some have even postulated that here
Paul addresses a new set of opponents, those of a libertine stripe.[29] A more
promising solution is to see that the Spirit and righteousness are integral to
Paul's argument from the beginning, in which righteousness is the basis of
receiving the Spirit. Those who have received the Spirit by faith (Gal 3:1-5)
are righteous before God (Gal 2:15-21). The *just as (kathōs)* in Galatians 3:6
forges a link between Abraham's righteousness and reception of the Spirit.[30]
The blessing of Abraham is nothing less than the promise of the Spirit (Gal
3:14), and it is precisely those who have the Spirit who are right before God.
Paul did not place righteousness and the Spirit into two rigidly separated
compartments. God gives his Spirit to those who are declared to be in the
right on the basis of Christ's death, and those who have the Spirit live
changed lives. The forensic righteousness of Christ is the basis of the transforming work of the Spirit.

To sum up, righteousness is an end-time gift (Gal 5:5), a verdict from the
day of judgment, which has now been pronounced in the lives of believers on
the basis of the death and resurrection of Jesus Christ. Believers are in a right
relationship with God forensically on the basis of Christ's sinless life and his
atoning death (2 Cor 5:21). The righteousness given is an alien righteousness,
given to sinners by God. Believers cannot do anything to prepare themselves
to receive such righteousness. It is a gift given by God himself to those who
believe in Christ Jesus. Righteousness is not merited by works or awarded to
those who are good enough to warrant God's favor. All without exception
sin, and our only hope is God's grace. Most important, forensic righteousness
is the basis and ground of any transformation that occurs in our lives. This
means that any change in the lives of believers is rooted in the objective work
of Christ by which believers are declared to be right in God's eyes. But for
Paul the work of God is a whole. He never imagined someone who was justified yet who failed to live in newness of life (Rom 6:4). Those who are
declared to be in the right are united with Christ, they enjoy the gift of the
Spirit, and they are empowered to live in a new way. Hence, any attempt to
divide justification and sanctification—so that some could enjoy the former

---

[29]D. W. Lütgert, *Gesetz und Geist: Eine Untersuchung zur Vorgeschichte des Galaterbriefes*
(Gütersloh: Bertelsmann, 1919); James H. Ropes, *The Singular Problem of the Epistle to the
Galatians* (Cambridge: Harvard University Press, 1929).
[30]See Sam K. Williams, "Justification and the Spirit in Galatians," *JSNT* 29 (1987): 91-100. My
understanding of righteousness, however, differs from Williams's understanding.

without experiencing the latter—violates Pauline theology.

Righteous behavior. We have noted earlier that in some contexts the noun *righteousness* refers to the new quality of life lived by believers. Similarly, the adjective *righteous* almost always denotes those who live righteously, in contrast to the wicked (e.g., Gen 6:9; 7:1; 2 Sam 4:11; Ps 1:6; Prov 10:11; Is 3:10; Ezek 3:20-21; 18:20). When we examine Paul, the group of words derived from *righteous* can designate the behavior of human beings. Paul remarks that "there is none who is righteous, not even one" (Rom 3:10) and notes that one will rarely die for a "righteous person" (Rom 5:7). Believers are to live "righteously" (Tit 2:12), and Paul believes he upheld such a standard when in Thessalonica (1 Thess 2:10). The noun *righteousness (dikaiosynē)* describes the righteous behavior demanded of believers (Rom 6:13, 16, 18-20; 2 Cor 6:7, 14; 9:9; Eph 4:24; 5:9; 1 Tim 6:11; 2 Tim 2:22; 3:16). Romans 5:19 contrasts Adam and Christ: many "were made" *(katestathēsan)* sinners through Adam, whereas many "shall be made righteous" *(katastathēsontai)* through Christ. Paul probably intends to say that the forensic work of Christ is the basis of any righteousness in the lives of believers. The forensic and the transformative are not merged together here, but we do see that the legal is the basis of the transformative. Paul never confines the gospel to the idea that we have been declared righteous before God. To be declared righteous without living righteously would be a monstrosity and an impossibility. The cross-work of Jesus Christ, in which he fulfilled the law by offering himself as a sin offering, has as its goal the obedience of the believer (Rom 8:1-4). Still, Martin Luther was correct in emphasizing that we remain sinners. God's grace invades the lives of his people; and significant, substantial and observable changes occur. Nevertheless, given the already-but-not-yet character of Pauline eschatology, we are still stained with sin until the day we die. Luther was on target; we are justified but at the same time we are also sinners.

Faith/Faithfulness and Righteousness

How does a person participate in or gain a share in God's righteousness? Paul emphasizes that the way one becomes right with God is by faith, trusting in God's provision and resting on his promises. Right-standing with God is "from faith to faith" (Rom 1:17)—from first to last, from the beginning to the end of one's life, it is realized by faith. Paul understands the message of Habakkuk similarly, for he summarizes its contribution by citing Habakkuk 2:4, "The righteous shall live by faith" (Rom 1:17; Gal 3:11). In Romans and Galatians the centrality of faith is highlighted, and faith is contrasted with works of law (see Rom 3:21—4:25; Gal 2:16—3:14; cf. Eph 2:8-10). Such a contrast reveals that faith is a gift and that righteousness is not by works, because in the latter case the one who does the necessary works deserves praise for what has been accomplished (Rom 4:4-5; Eph 2:9). In other words, righteousness by faith is inextricably linked with grace since a right relation with God is based not on doing but on believing and trusting (cf. Rom 9:30—10:8; Eph 2:8; Phil 3:2-11; cf. Tit 3:5, 7). Believers are grateful to God alone for their forgiveness, whereas the one who works for salvation would deserve praise for doing what is required. Faith receives and gratefully accepts what God has done in Christ, trusting in his promises for salvation. Righteousness by faith alone fits beautifully with the idea that honor and praise belong only to God since faith trusts him and his work for salvation. If righteousness were based on works, however, then we would merit reward for accomplishing what God demanded. Righteousness by faith fits with the God-centered and Christ-saturated emphasis in Paul's theology. Faith embraces what God has done for us in Jesus Christ as the crucified and risen Lord (Rom 4:23-25). Paul does not commend faith in general; instead he commends trust in what God has done for believers in Christ, so that believers are constantly reminded because of their dead bodies (Rom 8:10) that they have no capacity to obey God and that their only hope is in the gospel of Christ.

Saving faith is not passive. Abraham (Rom 4:17-22) is the paradigm of faith for believers. The circumstances of life conspired to squelch his belief in God's promises, for his old age and Sarah's barrenness seemed to mock the idea that he would have a son and that his descendants would be as numerous as the sand of the sea. Nevertheless, Abraham triumphed in faith, not because he worked hard for God but because he trusted in the promises of God: "He grew strong in faith, giving glory to God and was fully convinced that he was able to do what he promised" (Rom 4:20-21). God is glorified as God when human beings trust in his promises. Trusting the one who makes promises gives honor to that person. If we trust a doctor's prescription, we honor the doctor's wisdom by taking the prescription.[31] If we trust a coach's strategy, we honor him by executing the play drawn up on the sidelines. If we trust God's power and goodness, we honor him by believing that he will accomplish what is promised. Abraham trusted God by believing his promises regarding a seed. Christians honor

---

[31]This illustration comes from Daniel P. Fuller, *Gospel and Law: Contrast or Continuum?* (Grand Rapids, Mich.: Eerdmans, 1980), pp. 117-20.

God by believing that the way to life is through a crucified and resurrected man (Rom 4:23-25).

The notion that trusting in the death and resurrection of Jesus Christ is the path to life and to victory over death seems just as improbable as believing that a barren wife will have a child (Rom 4:23-25). Who can possibly believe that we will triumph over death and receive forgiveness of sins through a crucified man? Faith clings to God's promise, trusting that he will certainly do as he said, assuring itself on the basis of the resurrection of Jesus the Messiah. Everyday life mocks at the idea that we will conquer death since our bodies are dying and groaning (Rom 8:10, 23). Faith casts itself on God alone, believing that as he did the impossible for Abraham, so he can do the impossible for us. Like Abraham we believe in a God who grants life to the dead and summons into existence what is not present (Rom 4:17). Paul himself testifies that the afflictions of life were so overwhelming that he despaired even of living (2 Cor 1:8). But God provided a stunning deliverance so that he would place his trust in God rather than in himself (2 Cor 1:9). God rescued him in the present to remind him that he would rescue him in the future (2 Cor 1:10; 2 Tim 4:17-18). Faith, then, looks to God for the forgiveness of sins and righteousness so that resurrection life will be obtained on the day of the Lord (Rom 5:9-10).

The dynamism of faith is also clear because obedience flows from it. That is why Paul speaks of the "obedience of faith" (Rom 1:5; 16:26).[32] Obedience and faith are not equal partners because obedience flows from and is rooted in faith. This kind of obedience is radically different from trying to be justified by works of law, for in the latter case one tries to be right with God by one's own works. Obedience that is rooted in faith, however, relies on God and his promises for strength and power. Any praise for good works, therefore, goes to God, because the believer in humble trust does what God says. We should understand Paul's phrase *work of faith* (1 Thess 1:3; 2 Thess 1:11) similarly. The "work" done is the product of faith, and it stems from trusting God's promises and fearing his threats. The Pauline emphasis on faith cannot be consigned to the past as if it were a momentary decision. Faith is an ongoing reality in the lives of those who belong to God.

Scholars debate whether we should define *pistis Iēsou Christou* as "faith in Christ." Many scholars understand the genitive as subjective, denoting "the

---

[32]For a study on the obedience of faith, see Don B. Garlington, *"The Obedience of Faith": A Pauline Phrase in Historical Context*, WUNT 2/38 (Tübingen: J. C. B. Mohr, 1991).

faithfulness of Christ."[33] A number of arguments are presented to support the newer reading. For example, some scholars say that the noun *pistis* followed by a genitive of person always refers to the faith of the individual, never faith *in* an individual. Thus, *pistis tou theou* in Romans 3:3 refers to the "faithfulness of God," not "faith in God." In Romans 4 *pisteōs tou patros hēmōn Abraam* and *ek pisteōs Abraam* (Rom 4:12, 16) refer to the faith *of* Abraham, not faith *in* Abraham. The conclusion drawn is that *pistis Iēsou Christou* must be understood as "the faithfulness of Jesus Christ" in Romans 3:21-26 as well. Proponents of this new interpretation also contend that the objective interpretation is superfluous in a number of verses (cf. Rom 3:22; Gal 2:16; 3:22; Phil 3:9). Thus, to say that the righteousness of God is by "faith in Christ for all those who believe" (Rom 3:22; Gal 2:16) is redundant. The idea of personal faith is found in the verb *believe*, but the noun *faith* reveals that our believing is based on the faithfulness of Jesus Christ from whom we receive the gift of believing.

The traditional interpretation must also explain how God's righteousness has been manifested through human faith (Rom 1:17; 3:21-22). The faith of human beings cannot reveal God's righteousness—allege supporters of the subjective genitive—because God's righteousness is independent of human's actions. Similarly, in Galatians 3:22-25 Paul speaks of "faith" as coming at a certain juncture in salvation history. The coming of "faith" suggests that it is an objective reality, not the subjective experience of faith. The redemptive-historical cast of Paul's words indicates that the faithfulness of Jesus Christ is in his mind, not faith in Christ. Those who support the subjective view also argue that faith and obedience are closely related in Paul (Rom 1:5; 16:26). The obedience of Jesus (Phil 2:6-11) cannot be separated from his faith/faithfulness. In Romans 5:19 the gift of righteousness is granted by virtue of the obedience of Jesus, and the obedience of Jesus cannot be separated from his faithfulness.

Despite the strong currents running in favor of the term *faithfulness of Jesus Christ*, there are good reasons for thinking that Paul has in mind *faith in Jesus*

---

[33]For a sampling of those who support a subjective genitive, see Luke T. Johnson, "Rom 3:21-26 and the Faith of Jesus," *CBQ* 44 (1982): 77-90; Sam K. Williams, "Again *Pistis Christou*," *JBL* 49 (1987): 431-47; Richard B. Hays, *The Faith of Jesus Christ: An Investigation of the Narrative Substructure of Galatians 3:1—4:11*, SBLDS 56 (Chico, Calif.: Scholars Press, 1983); and "*Pistis* and Pauline Christology: What Is at Stake?" in *Society of Biblical Literature 1991 Seminar Papers*, ed. E. H. Lovering Jr. (Atlanta: Scholars Press, 1991), pp. 714-29; Ian G. Wallis, *The Faith of Jesus Christ in Early Christian Traditions*, SNTSMS 84 (Cambridge: Cambridge University Press, 1995).

Christis.[34] The argument that the combination of *pistis* and a genitive of person always refers to the faith/faithfulness of the person is not verified by the text. In many instances, the genitive is a personal pronoun that is possessive (e.g., Rom 1:8, 12; 4:5; 1 Cor 2:5). One would naturally expect that the possessive would refer to the faith of the believers in such cases. On the other hand, a number of examples demonstrate that an objective genitive is found with the noun *faith*. An objective sense is clear in Mark 11:22, "have faith in God" *(echete pistin theou)*. An objective interpretation is also supported by James 2:1, "Do not hold your faith in our glorious Lord Jesus Christ with partiality" *(mē en prosōpolēmpsiais echete tēn pistin tou kyriou hēmōn Iēsou Christou tēs doxēs)*.

Grammatically equivalent constructions in Paul reveal that an objective sense does not run counter to Pauline usage. First Thessalonians 1:3 speaks of "hope in our Lord Jesus Christ" *(tēs elpidos tou kyriou hēmōn Iēsou Christou)* where the genitive *Lord (kyriou)* is clearly the object of hope. So too, in Philippians 3:8 we find "the knowledge of Christ Jesus" *(tēs gnōseōs Christou Iēsou)*; the genitive noun *Christ (Christou)* is objective (cf. Rom 10:3; Eph 4:13) as the parallel phrase *to know him (gnōnai auton)* in Philippians 3:10 demonstrates. This last example is particularly important because in the same context *pisteōs Christou* (Phil 3:9) occurs. Since the genitive noun *Christ (Christou)* is objective in Philippians 3:8, there is no grammatical reason for ruling out such a reading in Philippians 3:9. Indeed, the context suggests that faith *in* Christ is in view since he is both the object of knowledge and faith. To conclude, grammar alone cannot decide this question since both the objective and subjective interpretations can be defended grammatically.[35]

The argument from redundancy is also unconvincing. The use of both the noun and verb together indicate that faith in Jesus Christ constitutes *an emphasis*. Moisés Silva suggests, in fact, that the construction which adds the least meaning to a phrase should usually be preferred.[36] If the traditional interpretation is correct, then Paul labors to clarify that righteousness is

---

[34]In defense of the objective genitive, see James D. G. Dunn, "Once More *Pistis Christou,*" in *Society of Biblical Literature 1991 Seminar Papers,* ed. E. H. Lovering Jr. (Atlanta: Scholars Press, 1991), pp. 730-44; R. Barry Matlock, "Detheologizing the *Pistis Christou* Debate: Cautionary Remarks from a Lexical Semantic Perspective," *NovT* 52 (2000): 1-23.

[35]We should also note that the noun *pistis* is connected with an objective genitive elsewhere in Paul. In both 2 Thess 2:13 *pistei alētheias* (faith in the truth) and Col 2:12 *tēs pisteōs tēs energeias tou theou* (faith in the working of God), the genitive noun is obviously objective. If Paul uses the noun *pistis* for faith in the truth and for faith in God's working, it would not be surprising to find that the same construction elsewhere would refer to faith *in* Christ.

[36]Moisés Silva, *Biblical Words and Their Meanings: An Introduction to Lexical Semantics* (Grand Rapids, Mich.: Zondervan, 1983), pp. 153-56.

through *faith in Christ*. If the subjective view is correct, the emphasis shifts to
the faithfulness of Jesus Christ. The traditional reading is to be preferred
since Paul contrasts works of law with faith in Jesus Christ. In both instances
human responses are in view. We do not become right with God through doing
but by believing (cf. Rom 9:30—10:8; Phil 3:2-11).

Nor does the revelation of "faith" at a particular juncture of salvation history necessarily support the subjective genitive. We have already argued that
God's righteousness has two dimensions. On one hand, it refers to God's
work in redemptive history manifested in the atoning sacrifice of Jesus
Christ. On the other hand, the righteousness of God is also subjectively
appropriated by faith. To limit the righteousness of God only to God's action
in history presents us with a false dichotomy. God's righteousness denotes
his saving action in history, but it also is appropriated by faith. The same line
of reasoning applies to Galatians 3:22-25. Paul certainly teaches that redemptive history has reached its crucial turning point with the coming of "faith." It
is an error though to segregate redemptive history and anthropology. It is
only since the coming of Christ that "faith in Christ" has become a reality. Salvation history and personal faith in Christ converge in this instance.

A number of positive reasons also support the reading "faith in Christ."
First, a plethora of texts in both Romans and Galatians refer to the faith of
believers.[37] We learn from this that the faith of believers is often mentioned,
but no indisputable reference to the faithfulness of Christ exists. The most
natural way to read the text is to see a reference to "faith in Christ" instead
of importing an idea that is not clearly stated elsewhere. Second, there is no
instance in the Pauline literature where *pistis Christou* indisputably refers to
the faithfulness of Christ. Those who support the subjective interpretation
point to Romans 5:18-19 and Philippians 2:6-11, where the faithful obedience of Jesus Christ is featured. Doubtless the obedience of Christ is an
important element in Pauline theology. But what is telling is that in both
Romans 5:18-19 and Philippians 2:6-11 Paul makes no reference to Jesus
Christ's being "faithful." Paul does refer to the "obedience" of Jesus Christ,
but he nowhere describes Jesus as "faithful." If Jesus' faithfulness were crucial in Paul's theology, we would expect an indisputable reference to it elsewhere in his writings. Third, there is unambiguous evidence in the Pauline
epistles that Paul called for faith *in* Christ (Rom 3:22; 10:9-14; Gal 2:16; 3:26?;

---

[37]Rom 1:5, 8, 12; 3:27-28, 30-31; 4:5, 9, 11-14, 16, 19-20; 5:1-2; 9:30, 32; 10:6, 8, 17; 11:20; 14:23;
16:26; Gal 2:20; 3:2, 5, 7-9, 11-12, 14, 26; 5:5-6.

Eph 1:15; Phil 1:29; Col 1:4; 2:5; Philem 5).

Fourth, the reading "faith in Christ" makes the best sense of the flow of thought in Romans 3:21—4:12 and Galatians 2:16—3:9. If we tried an experiment in which we inserted *faithfulness of Christ* instead of *faith in Christ*, such an interpretation would make sense in both Romans 3:21-31 and Galatians 2:16-21. But in Romans 4 and Galatians 3 the credibility of such exegesis is called into question. Paul clearly refers to Abraham's faith *in God* in Romans 4, for he uses the verb *pisteuō* (Rom 4:3, 5). It follows that "the faith" *(hē pistis)* counted to Abraham as righteousness (Rom 4:9) could refer only to Abraham's personal faith, not to God's faithfulness. Similarly, "righteousness of faith" in Romans 4:11 (so also Rom 4:12) must refer to Abraham's personal faith (cf. Rom 4:13-14, 16-20, 24). It is difficult to believe that *pistis* in Romans 3:21-31 is Christ's faithfulness, but in Romans 4 it exclusively denotes the personal faith of believers. The Romans would have had a terrible time reading Paul if he switched the meaning of *pistis* from chapter to chapter. Since the noncontroversial uses of *pistis* refer to the faith of believers and since Romans 3—4 are closely related in subject matter, we should understand *faith* to refer to the faith of believers in both chapters.

A similar argument applies to Galatians 2:16—3:14. Understanding *pistis* as the faithfulness of Christ makes sense in both Galatians 2:16 and Galatians 2:20. But in Galatians 3 this interpretation falls apart. Paul contrasts "works of law" with "hearing with faith" (Gal 3:2, 5), and he contrasts two different *human responses.* Galatians 3:6-9 eliminates any reference to the faithfulness of Christ. In Galatians 3:6 Abraham's righteousness is obtained through "believing" *(episteusen)* God. Obviously, Abraham's personal faith *in God* is in view here. Paul draws a conclusion *(ara)* from Abraham's believing in Galatians 3:7, "Know, therefore, that those of faith, these are the sons of Abraham." The phrase *hoi ek pisteōs* (those of faith) must refer to those who exercised personal faith. The logical relationship between Galatians 3:6-7 demands such a reading. Since Galatians 3:7 clearly refers to the faith of believers, it follows that Galatians 3:8—where Paul says, "the scripture foresaw that God would justify the Gentiles by faith" *(ek pisteōs)*—does as well. There is simply no possibility that Paul would say that the Gentiles are sons of Abraham through their own personal faith in Galatians 3:7 and then resort to saying that they are justified by Christ's faithfulness in Galatians 3:8. Similarly, in Galatians 3:9 he contends that those of faith are blessed along with faithful Abraham. Now if Paul specifically argues in a clear text that believers are justified by faith (believing; cf. Gal 3:6) in Galatians 3:8, then it is almost certain that Galatians 2:16 should be interpreted similarly. Paul would confuse the readers if he said in Galatians 2:16 that believers were righteous by the faithfulness of Jesus Christ and then turned around and said that they were justified by personal faith in Galatians 3:8. He communicates the same message in both texts. Believers are justified by faith, but in the first instance he clarifies that they are justified by faith *in Christ,* denoting the object of faith. Such a reading is confirmed by Galatians 3:10-14, for in every instance (Gal 3:11-12, 14) the faith in view is that of believers.

To conclude, the arguments supporting faith *in Christ* are compelling:

■ Paul often refers to the faith of believers.

■ He never refers to the faith of Christ.

■ He writes specifically of Christ as being the object of believers' faith.

■ The flow of thought in Romans 3—4 and Galatians 2—3 supports the idea of faith in Christ.

Forgiveness

A constituent part of justification, although Paul does not refer to it as often, is the forgiveness of sins. Romans 4:6-8 forges a link between forgiveness and justification, for Paul identifies the forgiveness of David's sins as equivalent with "righteousness apart from works" (Rom 4:6). The connection between forgiveness and justification lends support to the idea that justification is a gift by which one becomes right with God.

It is interesting that Colossians also refers to the forgiveness of sins, especially since righteousness language is not predominant in the letter. Both the fullness that believers experience in Christ (Col 2:10) and the new life that is theirs in Christ are predicated on the forgiveness of sins (Col 2:13). Moral failings are at the root of the disruption between human beings and God, and it is only through the "wiping away" *(exaleipsas)* of the IOU *(cheirographon)* that life can be granted (Col 2:14). The finality of forgiveness is expressed in the picture of the IOU being "nailed to the cross" *(prosēlōsas tō staurō,* Col 2:14). Forgiveness is not achieved merely by a word from God that declares a new beginning for his adversaries. Forgiveness is only granted through the crosswork of Jesus Christ. Indeed, the fullness that believers have received through Christ is only available by virtue of the death and resurrection of the Christ (Col 2:10-15).

One of the fascinating elements of forgiveness is that it is linked with other themes besides justification. In Colossians, Paul implies that the triumph over evil powers (Col 2:10, 15) is only secured through the forgiveness of sins. And the reconciling work of Christ, by which Jews and Gentiles are united at the cross (Eph 2:11-20), involves the forgiveness of sins. The enmity that divides Jews and Gentiles is ultimately hostility toward God and the violation of his commands (Eph 2:14-16), for freedom comes only when release from the law and its decrees is realized. So too, the fundamental reason human beings need redemption is their sin, and thus Paul comments that redemption consists of "forgiveness of sins" (Col 1:14; "forgiveness of trespasses" in Eph 1:7). Since forgiveness of sins is conjoined with other vital elements of Christ's salvific work, it is legitimate to see it as a fundamental aspect of the Pauline gospel, despite the few references to it.

Conclusion

The basis of believers' relationship with God is the gift of righteousness, the forgiveness granted to believers by faith. Believers stand in the right before God by virtue of the work of Jesus Christ on the cross, where he absorbed God's wrath for our sin. Righteousness and forgiveness do not exhaust God's saving work on our behalf, and so in the next chapter we shall continue to explore what God has done in Christ for his people.

9

GOD'S LIBERATING
WORK FOR HIS PEOPLE
Divine Transforming Grace

In the previous chapter we began to explore God's saving work in Christ for his people, focusing on God's saving righteousness and the forgiveness of sins, which are available through faith. In this chapter we continue to explore God's work in Christ for his people, and we will examine sanctification, reconciliation, salvation, redemption, triumph over evil powers, propitiation and election.

Sanctification
The term *sanctification*, derived from the cultic sphere, designates Christ's work on behalf of believers. The Old Testament regularly distinguishes between the sacred and the profane, prohibiting Israel from consuming certain foods because they are unclean and allowing only priests and Levites to perform particular cultic functions because the holy is only accessible to those designated by God. Of course, Israel as a whole is God's holy and priestly people (Ex 19:5-6). Paul applies the appellation "holy" *(hagioi)* to all those who believe in Christ, both Jews and Gentiles (e.g., Rom 1:7; 1 Cor 1:2; 2 Cor 1:1; Eph 1:1; Phil 1:1; Col 1:2; 3:12; 2 Thess 1:10). Believers have been transferred from the realm of the profane into the arena of the holy because they belong to God the Father and Jesus Christ. It is not surprising, therefore,

that Paul identifies the community of believers as God's temple (*naos*—1 Cor 3:16-17; 2 Cor 6:16; Eph 2:21; cf. 1 Cor 6:19). As God's holy people, they are the place of his indwelling. What is anticipated and foreshadowed in the tabernacle and the temple—God's abiding presence—is fulfilled in the church of Jesus Christ. The church of God "is sanctified in Christ Jesus" (1 Cor 1:2). The church has moved into a sacred realm because of its union with the second Adam, Jesus the Messiah.

In 1 Corinthians 1—2 Paul labors to persuade the Corinthians that they already possess true wisdom in Christ Jesus. He proceeds to define that wisdom in terms of "righteousness and sanctification and redemption" (1 Cor 1:30). Wisdom centers on what God has done for believers in Christ by justifying, sanctifying, and redeeming them. The creativity of human beings does not constitute wisdom; the work of God is the genuine wisdom. Paul uses three metaphors to describe the saving work of God: righteousness, sanctification and redemption. No evidence exists here that one metaphor is superior to the others. Nor is the order in which the metaphors are listed particularly significant. The three metaphors are correlative, describing together the saving work of Christ. It would be a mistake to conceive of "sanctification" (*hagiasmos*) as subsequent to righteousness in this verse, as if Paul were attempting to chart out the order in which these saving acts occurred. Then we would be compelled to argue that redemption was accomplished *after* sanctification. Three different metaphors set forth the saving work of Christ because no single metaphor captures what he has accomplished on our behalf. In this text, then, Paul conceives of sanctification as a definitive act that is already accomplished for believers.[1]

Our analysis of 1 Corinthians 1:30 is confirmed by 1 Corinthians 6:11— "But you were washed, but you were sanctified, but you were justified in the name of the Lord Jesus Christ and by the Spirit of our God." In this context the Corinthians are exhorted to live godly lives. Paul reminds them of God's work on their behalf. When he says they were washed, he thinks of their baptismal washing by which they were cleansed of their sins. A related metaphor follows when Paul says "you were sanctified" (*hēgiasthēte*). Paul is hardly thinking of something that occurs *after* conversion for he denotes a past event. Indeed, the sanctification in mind here is simultaneous with the baptismal washing. This is confirmed by the following verb, *you were justified.* The

---

[1]For a helpful study on sanctification, see David Peterson, *Possessed by God: A New Testament Theology of Sanctification and Holiness* (Grand Rapids, Mich.: Eerdmans, 1995).

verb *sanctified* precedes the verb *justified*, and thus no *ordo salutis* should be imposed on the text here. Baptismal washing, sanctification and justification are all gifts given at conversion. Believers have been cleansed, inducted into the sphere of the holy and set in the right before God by the Son and the Spirit. Paul is likely thinking of the cross of Jesus Christ as the means of sanctification in 1 Corinthians 6:11. An allusion to the cross is almost certain in 1 Corinthians 1:30, for the wisdom of God is none other than Christ crucified, which is folly to unbelievers but the power of God for those believing (1 Cor 1:17-18, 22-23; 2:2). Christ's love for his bride, the church, is manifested in his offering his life on her behalf, and by means of his sacrifice he secures her sanctification (Eph 5:25-27). In this Ephesian text sanctification is again closely linked with baptism, by which believers are cleansed. The close link between sanctification and baptism is not surprising since both derive from the cultic sphere—the emphasis of the latter being purification and washing, and the emphasis of the former being placement into the realm of the sacred. The Old Testament emphasis on sanctification and holiness, then, anticipates the work of Christ on behalf of his people by which he inducts them into the sphere of the holy.

The sanctifying work of Christ, of course, is not only definitive. Believers are to lead holy lives (Rom 6:19, 22; 1 Thess 4:3-8). The definitive sanctification accomplished at conversion, which is an invasion of the end of history into the present, manifests itself in the lives of believers and will be perfected on the day of the Lord. Indeed, such holiness is imperative to obtain eternal life on the day of the Lord (cf. also Eph 5:27; Col 1:22; 1 Thess 3:13). Those who succumb to sin as its slave will experience not eternal life but death (Rom 6:23). God's vengeance will be inflicted on those who despise his "Holy" Spirit and live unsanctified lives (1 Thess 4:8). Thus, the imperative to live holy lives can never be dismissed as secondary, nor can the indicative of God's grace swallow up the imperative so that it no longer exists. Paul prays ardently that believers will be holy and live up to their calling (1 Thess 3:11-13). Nevertheless, the future sanctification (there is an already-but-not-yet element here as well!) of God's people is sure. The sanctification and holiness of the church is anchored in God's election before the foundation of the world (Eph 1:4). Christ's self-offering on behalf of the church not only rendered her sanctification possible but also certain (Eph 5:26-27). He will present to the Father a beautiful bride, full of glorious radiance and unstained by any spot or wrinkle. That Paul sees no conflict between the indicative and imperative is clear from 1 Thessalonians 5:23-24. In 1 Thessalonians 5:23 he prays that

God will sanctify his people completely at the coming of Jesus Christ. In 1 Thessalonians 5:24 he expresses confidence that God will do so: "The one who called you is faithful, who will also do it." That is, the God who called believers to salvation will most certainly complete the sanctifying work he has begun. The future holiness of believers is assured because it depends on God himself.

Reconciliation

Scholars have occasionally suggested that reconciliation should be considered the center of Pauline theology since it occurs in crucial texts.[2] It is deemed more significant than justification because it involves personal relationships and also because it is envisioned as embracing all of creation. Reconciliation is certainly an important theme in Paul, but to elevate it as the center of his thought or to see it as foundational is mistaken. No single metaphor used to convey Christ's saving work is comprehensive enough to serve as the center or foundation of his thought. Moreover, the theme of reconciliation, though important for Paul, does not surface often in his writings. It is difficult to believe that a theme that is relatively rare could be the foundation of Paul's theology.

The word *reconciliation* has to do with restoring friendship and peace. So Paul exhorts a wife who is estranged from her husband to become reconciled with him (1 Cor 7:11), that is, to restore and resume the marriage. Any gift offered to God at the altar is not acceptable unless the giver first reconciles with the brother with whom he or she is at odds (Mt 5:24; cf. Lk 12:58). Acts 7:26 nicely captures the meaning of reconciliation in recounting the incident in which Moses tried to adjudicate a quarrel between two Israelites: "He tried to reconcile them to peace." A quarrel was in progress, and reconciliation, as the text specifically says, involves the restoration of peace.

Reconciliation comes to the forefront in four texts in Paul: Romans 5:1-11; 2 Corinthians 5:11-21; Ephesians 2:11-22; and Colossians 1:15-20. It is immediately evident that reconciliation is needed because of human sin. More specifically, the breach between God and human beings is characterized by enmity (Rom 5:10; cf. Rom 8:7-8). But Romans 5:1 proclaims that believers have peace with God since we have been justified. The word *peace (eirēnē)* is a synonym for *reconciliation*, and such peace is possible only on the basis of justification:

[2]For example, Ralph P. Martin, *Reconciliation: A Study of Paul's Theology,* rev. ed. (Grand Rapids, Mich.: Zondervan, 1989).

"having been justified by faith, we have peace with God" (Rom 5:1). In other words, reconciliation cannot occur until people are right with God. Similarly, in 2 Corinthians 5:19 reconciliation includes "not counting their trespasses against them," indicating that sin is what separates us from God. The exhortation "be reconciled to God" (2 Cor 5:20) is superfluous unless enmity exists between God and human beings. Paul describes the state of human beings before reconciliation in terms of alienation and enmity in Colossians 1:21.

Ephesians 2 is particularly emphatic and vivid in portraying the stance of human beings toward God before reconciliation. Gentiles who are not reconciled with God are alienated, apart from Christ, aliens from the covenantal promises; they have no hope since they are not rightly related to God (Eph 2:12). Paul speaks of the enmity that exists among human beings and between people and God (Eph 2:14, 16). This state of hostility means that people are "far away" *(makran)* from God (Eph 2:13, 17). A dividing wall—a fence—separates Jews and Gentiles from one another (Eph 2:14), and hence it is clear that the hostility is not only between human beings and God, for it also surfaces in the conflict between Jews and Gentiles. This separation from God is described in the Gentiles' living as aliens and sojourners in God's world (Eph 2:19). Conversely, reconciliation means that people are now "near" *(engys)* to God (Eph 2:13) and united to one another (Eph 2:19), that the wall erected between Jews and Gentiles has been torn down (Eph 2:14), that human sin which created the breach between God and humans has been atoned for (Eph 2:15-16), that those who are in Christ are no longer aliens but are part of God's household and his family (Eph 2:19) and, supremely, that those who know God are now at peace with him (Eph 2:14-15, 17).

Peace with God (i.e., reconciliation) contributes a thought that is probably implicit, though not explicit, in justification. Believers are not only right with God—they are also his friends. A judge may pardon a defendant and still despise him, but God blesses with friendship those whom he forgives: "For if while we were enemies, we were reconciled to God through the death of his Son, then it surely follows that, since we have been reconciled, we shall be saved by his life" (Rom 5:10). The indissoluble connection between justification and reconciliation is established in Romans 5:9-10, for in both texts Paul argues from the greater to the lesser. Since believers are now justified and reconciled through the cross, they will be saved on the day of the Lord. The parallel does not indicate that justification and reconciliation are synonymous, but it does demonstrate that they are constituent parts of the Christ event. What is particularly striking is that reconciliation is "through the death of his son" (Rom 5:10). Friendship with God is accomplished through his initiative in sending his Son. The close relation between righteousness and reconciliation also emerges in 2 Corinthians 5:21. The message Paul proclaims as God's ambassador is this: "Be reconciled with God" (2 Cor 5:20). Such reconciliation is possible because Christ became a sin offering "so that we might become the righteousness of God in him" (2 Cor 5:21). Reconciliation with God is only possible when God's justice has been satisfied in the cross.

Christ's death for sinners is rooted in his love (2 Cor 5:14), showing that God's desire for peace and friendship is rooted in his concern for the welfare of human beings. Nor can the work of Christ be separated from God in this endeavor because it is *God* who accomplished reconciliation through Christ (2 Cor 5:18-19). The breach between human beings and God is so severe that only the death of the Son can accomplish reconciliation. The language of reconciliation overlaps with the language of mediation. Paul describes Jesus as the "mediator" between God and humans (1 Tim 2:5). As mediator, Jesus restores the relationship between people and God that was severed by sin.

The Christ hymn of Colossians 1:15-20 is a carefully crafted composition that focuses on Christ's supremacy as Creator and redeemer. The hymn concludes with a striking statement on reconciliation, for Paul asserts that "all things" *(ta panta)* have been reconciled through Christ (Col 1:20). That Christ is the agent of reconciliation is scarcely surprising since the entire hymn celebrates his preeminence and lordship. Nor is this reconciliation realized in an ethereal manner, for "he made peace through the blood of his cross" (Col 1:20). Reconciliation is earthed in the ground of the Christian gospel, being located in the cross of Jesus Christ and his atoning work. The centrality of the cross in reconciliation is also emphasized in Colossians 1:22, where Paul writes, "he reconciled you in the body of his flesh through death." The concrete and gory means by which reconciliation becomes a reality is underlined. Paul does not merely speak of Christ's "body" or his "flesh" but of "the body of his flesh." He then adds the words *through death* to underscore the means by which reconciliation was achieved. Colossians does not depart from the touchstone of the Pauline gospel, in that it stresses Christ's cross as the only pathway to reconciliation with God. The "making of peace" *(eirēnopoiēsas)* further defines reconciliation here, providing additional exegetical support to the idea that peace and reconciliation are roughly synonymous.

What seizes our attention is the extent of reconciliation. One might want to limit "all things" to those who believe in Christ, but this option is eliminated by the last words in Colossians 1:20, where "all things" are defined as "whether the things upon earth or the things in the heavens." Reconciliation embraces the entire universe, so that nothing is excluded from its orbit. Such universal reconciliation, however, does not translate into universal salvation.[3] In the very next paragraph (Col 1:21-23) Paul insists that one must remain in the faith in order to be savingly reconciled to God. And the defeat of the demonic rulers and authorities in Colossians 2:15 does not involve their restoration of fellowship with God. These authorities, by means of Christ's death and resurrection, are stripped of their power, publicly humiliated and led in a triumphal procession that will conclude with their execution. God's wrath will fall on those who do not obey him (Col 3:6). Thus, universal reconciliation in this context should not be equated with universal salvation. What Paul has in mind here is the restoration of the universe to harmony, so that God's rule is reinstituted over the whole created order. Reconciliation here involves the pacification of the entire universe, but this pacification has two dimensions. For some it involves willful and glad submission to the supremacy of Christ. Others, however (like the demons in Col 2:15), are compelled to acknowledge the preeminence of Christ and the glory of God. God has reconciled all things through the cross-work of Christ: those who oppose him are defeated, and those who acknowledge Christ as Lord are saved.

Salvation

God's work on behalf of his people is often described in terms of deliverance or rescue. The language of salvation or deliverance hearkens back to God's saving acts in the Old Testament where he intervenes on behalf of his people (e.g., Judg 2:16). In Paul such deliverance is fundamentally eschatological. He speaks of the impossibility of escaping from the judgment of God on the last day (Rom 2:3). Those who have been justified through the blood of Christ "shall be saved from his wrath" (Rom 5:9) on the last day; those who have been reconciled "shall be saved by his life" (Rom 5:10). In all three examples the future tense is used, constraining us as readers to think about future deliverance. Jesus is described as the one "who rescues us from the coming wrath" (1 Thess 1:10). The "rescue" here is certainly eschatological since God's anger, from which believers are spared, is future. What strengthens believers now is "the hope of salvation" (1 Thess 5:8) for God "has not appointed us to wrath but to the possession of salvation" (1 Thess 5:9). These texts emphasize that such salvation is not ours now. It is a future gift, a hope

---

[3]See the excursus on universalism in chapter seven.

that we will be spared from God's wrath on the day of the Lord. Thus, we are not surprised to read of some who shall be saved through the fire on the day of the Lord (1 Cor 3:15). What is remarkable about these verses as well is that salvation is conceived of in terms of escape from the anger of God. The salvation God accomplished in Jesus Christ for his people protects believers from the destruction God will inflict on those who refuse his patience.

When Paul speaks of the gospel "which results in salvation" (Rom 1:16), he has in mind eschatological salvation that will be our possession in the coming age. Similarly, the salvation that belongs to those who confess Jesus as Lord and believe on him in their hearts (Rom 10:9-10; cf. Rom 10:13) is fundamentally eschatological. The future tenses refer to the coming age. The future character of salvation is confirmed by Romans 10:11, "Everyone who believes on him will not be put to shame." Paul hardly has in mind the idea that those who believe in Christ will be spared present humiliation. What he means is that those who believe in Christ will not be humiliated on the day of the Lord. God will vindicate those who have put their trust in Christ. The eschatological character of salvation is strikingly confirmed in Romans 13:11, where salvation is said "to be nearer than when we first believed." Paul does not speak here of salvation as something obtained at the moment we first believed but as a gift to be given at the last day (Rom 13:12).

Even though salvation is an eschatological gift predicated on belief, Paul never separates belief from ongoing obedience. Those who long for salvation must renounce the works of darkness and embrace the weapons of the light (Rom 13:11-14). Salvation will be granted only to the one who experiences "the destruction of the flesh" (1 Cor 5:5). One who sins and is not granted repentance (2 Tim 2:25-26) will not be saved. With all urgency Paul exhorts his hearers to produce (katergazesthe) their own salvation (Phil 2:12), knowing that righteous behavior—though not the *ground* of salvation—is utterly necessary to *obtain* salvation. When Paul says in 2 Timothy 4:17 that he was rescued (errysthēn) from the lion's mouth, he does not mean that he was spared death. Such a statement would be trivial indeed since he knew death awaited him. What he means is that God gave him strength so that he did not deny the faith before Caesar. Those who deny Christ will be denied before God (2 Tim 2:12). Such a reading fits well with 2 Timothy 4:18, where Paul affirms that "the Lord will rescue [rhysetai] me from every evil work and will save [sōsei] me into his heavenly kingdom." God did not promise to spare Paul from the sword of Caesar, nor is Paul suggesting that somehow he will be spared from death. The promise is that God will grant Paul the strength to remain faithful to Christ when he stands before Caesar. He will not renounce the gospel and commit apostasy. God will strengthen him so that he will be safely inducted into the heavenly kingdom.

Once we grasp that salvation is not obtained apart from human behavior, though it is not grounded on such behavior, we are not shocked to read that Paul views his ministry as the means by which the elect are saved (2 Tim 2:10). Similarly, Paul exhorts Timothy to live a godly life and to be devoted to ortho-dox teaching (1 Tim 4:11-16). By persevering in these two things, Timothy will "save yourself and your hearers" (1 Tim 4:16). It would be special pleading to understand the verb tense as communicating a timeless truth or to protest that Paul did not have eschatological salvation in mind. The *salvation* word group is prominent in the Pastoral Epistles and invariably denotes spiritual salvation. Indeed, in every instance in Paul the words *sōteria, sōzō* and *sōtēr* denote God's spiritual work of delivering his people. We have already seen that salvation is typically eschatological in Paul, and it always involves preservation from the wrath of God in the Pauline literature. First Timothy 4:16 means, then, that Timothy must live a godly life and adhere to the apostolic deposit to avoid God's wrath on the last day. His godly living and faithful preaching of the word are the means by which both he and other believers are rescued from God's wrath on the day of the Lord. Similarly, women must adhere to their divinely ordained role ("she will be saved through the bearing of children," 1 Tim 2:15) to be saved. This is an example of synecdoche, in that bearing chil-dren is representative of how women fulfill the role intended for them by God. To avoid misunderstanding, Paul remarks that women must persevere in faith and love and other godly virtues to be saved. Salvation is not merited by hav-ing children, nor is Paul suggesting that all women must have children (cf. 1 Corinthians 7)! What Paul is saying is that women's bearing children and liv-ing in their ordained role is one example of living out the godly life that is nec-essary to obtain eschatological salvation. We have already seen in Romans 13 and 1 Corinthians 5 that eschatological salvation becomes a reality through a godly life. God's grace, however, is the foundation and the energy for such a life. He grants both the "desire" *(thelein)* and the "work" *(energein)* that is needed (Phil 2:13), and so all good deeds are ascribed to grace.

It would be misleading, however, to restrict salvation only to the future in the Pauline letters. Paul occasionally speaks of salvation in the past tense: "By grace you have been saved" *(este sesōsmenoi,* Eph 2:5, 8). The liberating work of Christ in Colossians 1:13 is portrayed in that "he rescued *[errysato]* us from the authority of darkness and transferred us into the kingdom of his Son." In

2 Timothy 1:9 the message of the gospel is encapsulated in the phrase *he saved us,* and in another creedal formulation Paul writes, "he saved *[esōsen]* us through the washing of regeneration and renewal from the Holy Spirit" (Tit 3:5). Nor can one assign such sentences only to the later Pauline letters or argue that limiting salvation to the past is a sign that these letters were not written by Paul. We have already seen that the eschatological dimension of salvation is strongly maintained in the Pastorals. Furthermore, salvation is conceived as a past event in Romans: "For in hope we have been saved" (Rom 8:24). These past-tense statements do not cancel out the eschatological character of salvation. Paul most commonly assigns salvation to the future, but he can speak of salvation as past since the age to come has invaded this present evil age. The past dimension of salvation, therefore, should be understood within the eschatological framework of Paul's theology. And Romans 8:24 helps us understand that the reality of salvation in the past does not mean that salvation is now complete. Believers still hope for the future realization of their salvation for they have not yet received the full inheritance. Once we grasp the eschatological tension between the future and the present, it is understandable that Paul also describes salvation as an ongoing process in the present. Through the gospel "you are being saved" (1 Cor 15:2); and the eschatological tension of Paul's view is preserved in that such salvation will only be realized through perseverance. In 1 Corinthians 1:18 the gospel's power has seized "those who are being saved" (cf. 2 Cor 2:15). Indeed, the gospel is the reason for their salvation.

Paul emphasizes, particularly in the Pastoral Letters, that our Savior is Jesus Christ, or God the Father (1 Tim 1:1; 2:3; 4:10; 2 Tim 1:10; Tit 1:3-4; 2:10, 13; 3:4, 6). The eschatological dimension emerges in Philippians 3:20-21, for believers await the return of their Savior, Jesus Christ, by whom their bodies will be transformed. Christ is the Savior of the church (Eph 5:23); and his saving actions are rooted in his epiphany *(epiphaneia),* by which he appeared to help his people—much like the angel of the Lord in the Old Testament (2 Tim 1:10).[4] Titus 2:11-14 is especially instructive by locating God's grace in the appearance of Christ *(epephanō)* in history. Titus 2:14 locates this gracious work in the self-giving of Christ, "who gave himself for us in order to redeem us from all lawlessness and cleanse for himself a chosen people." The cross-work of Christ has brought salvation to all (Tit 2:11), and yet this salvation is not complete since believers await "the blessed hope and the epiphany of the

---

[4]For the epiphany christology of the Pastoral Letters, see Andrew Y. Lau, *Manifest in the Flesh: The Epiphany Christology of the Pastoral Epistles,* WUNT 2/86 (Tübingen: J. C. B. Mohr, 1996).

glory of our great God and Savior, Jesus Christ" (Tit 2:13). Here Jesus is described as the Savior who inaugurates and completes the saving work. The saving work of Christ is not in contradistinction to the saving work of God, for the creedal summary in Titus 3:4-7, which is to be interpreted in concert with Titus 2:11-14, describes God as our Savior (Tit 3:4).

The kindness and love that animated God's saving work is attributed to God, and the agency by which this salvation is accomplished is attributed to "Jesus Christ, our Savior" (Tit 3:6). In the Pastoral Letters, then, both God (1 Tim 1:1; 2:3; 4:10; Tit 1:3) and Jesus Christ (Tit 1:4) are given the title Savior. Such an attribution should not be reduced to simply a counter claim against the ruler cult in the Greco-Roman world. It hails from the Old Testament witness, and in the Pastoral Epistles, Paul emphasizes that God and Jesus Christ are the Savior of all people without distinction. It is likely that the troublemakers appealed to myths and genealogies to restrict some from God's salvific concern (1 Tim 1:4; Tit 1:14; 3:9). Paul countered by emphasizing God's desire (1 Tim 2:4) to save all people without distinction. He emphasizes his call as the apostle to the Gentiles (1 Tim 2:7), reminding Timothy that no people group by some elaborate genealogical argument can be excluded from God's saving purposes. Thus, when 1 Timothy 4:10 says that "God is the Savior of all people, especially believers," it should not be interpreted to say that God actually saves all people without exception because Paul nowhere teaches such universalism. Nor does it plausibly mean that God makes salvation possible for all but this salvation is only realized in the case of believers. When Paul speaks of God as Savior, he has in mind what God has actually accomplished in the lives of believers. The verse, then, should be understood to say that God is the Savior of all kinds of people—no people group is excluded. Then he delimits precisely what he has in mind. The word *malista* ("that is," cf. 1 Tim 5:17; Tit 1:10), means that God *is* the Savior of those who believe from every people group in the world.

Redemption

Jesus Christ liberates his people by his atoning work.[5] Under the concept of

---

[5]For redemption in the New Testament, see esp. I. Howard Marshall, "The Development of the Concept of Redemption in the New Testament," in *Reconciliation and Hope: New Testament Essays on Atonement and Eschatology Presented to L. L. Morris on His Sixtieth Birthday*, ed. R. Banks (Grand Rapids, Mich.: Eerdmans, 1974), pp. 153-69. Compare also B. B. Warfield, *The Person and Work of Christ* (Grand Rapids, Mich.: Baker, 1950), pp. 429-75; Leon Morris, *The Apostolic Preaching of the Cross* (Grand Rapids, Mich.: Eerdmans, 1965), pp. 16-55; David Hill, *Greek Words and Hebrew Meanings: Studies in the Semantics of Soteriological Terms*, SNTSMS 5 (Cambridge: Cambridge University Press, 1967): 53-81.

redemption are included words and topics that involve the setting free of God's people through the cross of Christ. God's redeeming of his people hearkens back to the Exodus, in which he set Israel free from bondage (e.g., Ex 6:6; 15:13; Deut 7:8; 9:26; 13:5; 15:15; 21:8; 24:18). Isaiah promises a second exodus where God will intervene and bring to a conclusion his saving and liberating work (Is 11:15-16; 40:3-11; 42:16; 43:2, 5-7, 16-19; 49:6-11; 51:10). Paul understands the redemption and freedom accomplished by Jesus Christ as a fulfillment of Isaiah's prophecies of a second exodus, for though there was an inaugurated fulfillment of Isaiah's prophecies in the return from Babylon, the promises were not fulfilled in their entirety. It is fitting, therefore, to describe the redemption in Christ as freedom from exile since the promises in Isaiah were not completely fulfilled in his day.[6]

The creedal-type formulation in 1 Timothy 2:6 is important: "he gave himself as a ransom [antilytron] for all." The term antilytron, which occurs only here in the New Testament and the LXX, denotes a ransom. Though a number of early church fathers maintained that the ransom was paid to the devil, most modern scholars insist that the metaphor should not be pressed. The ransom given is the life of the mediator, the man Christ Jesus (1 Tim 2:5). Paul is not merely saying that Jesus is potentially the ransom for all since the idea of a "potential" ransom must be smuggled into the text. Nor should the word all be defined to include all people without exception, for Paul is not claiming that all people universally have had a ransom paid on their behalf. We need to recall that Paul counters teachers who limit, through genealogical legerdemain, salvation to only some people groups. When Paul says that Christ is the ransom for all, the idea is that he is the actual ransom for human beings from every cultural and ethnic group.

Redemption in Paul is linked with freedom from sin and its enslaving power. Paul does not conceive of human beings as victims who are merely held in thrall by external powers from which they long to be free. Human beings are willing slaves to the power of sin and are deeply complicit in their own slavery. In Romans 3:24 redemption (apolytrōsis) is, therefore, linked with justification (cf. 1 Cor 1:30), since redemption fundamentally involves liberation from the power of sin. That redemption involves a price is also implied, for it is a reality "in Christ Jesus," whose atoning death is woven

---

[6]See N. T. Wright, *What St. Paul Really Said: Was Paul of Tarsus the Real Founder of Christianity?* (Grand Rapids, Mich.: Eerdmans, 1997).

into the fabric of this paragraph (Rom 3:21-26). Moreover, justification is said to be "free" *(dōrean)*, suggesting that it is free for believers because a price was paid by Jesus Christ. Ephesians 1:7 confirms our understanding of Romans 8:23. Redemption is defined in terms of "forgiveness of sins," and the price of redemption is also specified—"through his blood" (cf. Col 1:14).

Other terms are used to communicate redemption. "Christ redeemed *[exēgorasen]* us from the curse of the law by becoming a curse for us" (Gal 3:13). The curse of the law is inflicted because people have broken God's law (Gal 3:10). Freedom from the curse of sin, therefore, becomes ours through the substitutionary death of Christ, who became a curse on our behalf. His death is the payment that effects the freedom of believers. The death of Christ (Gal 4:4-5) is the means by which God "redeemed *[exagorasē]* those under the law." We have seen previously that to be under the law is to be under the power and dominion of sin. Indeed, *under law* is a salvation-historical term, denoting the state of Israel in the old age, for being under law and under the power of sin are coterminous. Paul has a similar idea in mind when he says believers "are released" *(katargeō)* from the law (Rom 7:2, 6; Eph 2:15; cf. Gal 2:4; 5:1, 13). Paul is scarcely suggesting that believers have no need of moral norms or exhortations, for his writings are suffused with both. He is thinking in terms of salvation history. Believers are liberated from the old era in which sin and death reigned. By virtue of the death of Christ they are free from the power of sin.

Paul understands freedom, then, as freedom *(eleutheroō)* for righteousness (Rom 6:15-23, esp. Rom 6:18, 22). The Spirit of life in Christ Jesus has liberated us from the law of sin and death by virtue of Christ's death, and thereby it enables believers to fulfill the ordinance of the law (Rom 8:1-4)! Freedom in Christ does not entail freedom from ought (Gal 5:1, 13); it provides freedom to carry out what ought to be done. Thus, 2 Corinthians 3:17 likely means that the Spirit of the Lord gives freedom to keep the law. The old Adam has been crucified with Christ so that the "body of sin" loses its power *(katargēthē)* over believers, and this manifests itself in freedom from the power of sin (Rom 6:6). Those who are "bought *[ēgorasthēte]* with a price" (1 Cor 6:20), therefore, are no longer enslaved to sexual passions and should "glorify God" with their bodies. Because they have been bought with a price, they should not "be slaves of human beings" (1 Cor 7:23). Paul is not thinking of literal slavery in this case. He argues that since believers are free in Christ (1 Cor 7:22), they should not be captivated by a world that assigns significance to one's social status. Christ's redemptive work involves a new way of life. As Titus 2:14 says, "he gave himself for us, in order to redeem [lytrōsētai] us from all lawlessness." This sentiment should not be waved aside as sub-Pauline, for it is evident in the letters generally accepted as authentic that redemption is inextricably linked with a new freedom morally. Paul did not conceive of freedom as liberation from any moral constraints. He envisioned freedom as involving a zeal for good works (Tit 2:14).

In Paul's theology the new exodus has become a reality. Redemption is a present possession in Christ Jesus. Nonetheless, the not-yet dimension of Paul's theology is not surrendered. Paul also acknowledges that redemption is not yet completed. The redemption of the body and the final adoption as sons will not be realized until the day of the resurrection (Rom 8:23). The Spirit is the down payment of the eschatological inheritance, which will involve the redemption of God's possession (Eph 1:14). Believers are sealed for the day of redemption (Eph 4:30), which means that their obtaining eschatological redemption is certain, and yet it is not ours now. The "day of redemption" (Eph 4:30) is not yet here. Thus, believers are already redeemed and freed in Christ Jesus, and at the same time this redemption is not yet consummated or completed.

Triumph Over Evil Powers

Christ's work on the cross not only broke the power of sin but also spelled the defeat of evil and demonic powers.[7] Paul's understanding of these powers will be explored later, but at this juncture we need to see how Christ's death triumphed over the powers of evil. The notion of God triumphing in battle recalls the Exodus in which Yahweh the warrior vanquished the Egyptians (Ex 15:3). And the prophets often proclaim the day of the Lord in which all of Yahweh's enemies will be defeated and his reign of peace will arrive for Israel (e.g., Is 13:6, 9; Ezek 30:3; Joel 2:1, 11, 31; Amos 5:18, 20; Obad 15; Zeph 1:7, 14; Mal 4:5). The prophets warn, however, that Israel will not participate in this day of victory unless they renounce evil and commit themselves to righteousness.

Actually, triumph over evil powers could be put under the theme of redemption in that both concepts focus on liberation. A discrete category is fitting because redemption focuses on liberation from sin, whereas the

---

[7]Tremper Longman III and Daniel G. Reid, *God Is a Warrior* (Grand Rapids, Mich.: Zondervan, 1995).

emphasis here is on victory over evil powers. It must also be said at the outset that the dominion of evil powers is precisely a result of sin. For example, the authority of Satan over unbelievers in Ephesians 2:2 is intertwined with their subservience to sin and to the course of this world (Eph 2:1-3). Victory over Satan and his demonic agents does not come from some sort of mystical experience, according to Ephesians. Triumph comes through the infusion of the resurrection-life of Christ, which is granted on the basis of the work of Jesus Christ (Eph 2:4-10). Believers are made alive with Christ, raised with Christ and seated with him. Not only was Christ raised from the dead, but he was also seated at God's right hand. By definition this means that he now rules over all demonic powers (Eph 1:21). It follows, therefore, that "all things have been subjected under his feet" (Eph 1:22). This statement, based on and rooted in Psalm 110:1, identifies Jesus as the Lord of David, the second Adam, who now exercises his rule over all creation.

Some scholars think that Ephesians is not authentically Pauline because it lacks an eschatological proviso. Ephesians emphasizes the "already," but the "not-yet" theme still informs the letter. The "coming ages" have not yet arrived (Eph 2:7), and the redemption of the body still lies in the future (Eph 1:14). The realization of the "unity of the faith" and the "mature man" (Eph 4:13) will occur on the last day, when the church is presented as holy and blameless (Eph 5:26-27). The day of eschatological reward has not yet arrived (Eph 6:8). Most important, despite Christ's victory over evil powers, believers must still resist their influence (Eph 6:10-17). A conflict between believers and these powers continues until the day of redemption.

Christ's victory over evil powers and the subjection of all things under his feet are also trumpeted in 1 Corinthians 15:24-28. Here the end and the consummation of the kingdom are the time when evil powers will be vanquished (1 Cor 15:24). The fulfillment of Psalm 110:1, therefore, will occur when he places all enemies under his feet. The battle will cease when death, the last enemy, is conquered. What is remarkable in comparing this text to Ephesians is that here the "not-yet" is in the forefront. This difference does not constitute a contradiction, for even in 1 Corinthians 15—as in Ephesians 1—the resurrection of Christ is featured. The not-yet is prominent in 1 Corinthians, however, because Paul counters the overrealized eschatology of some Corinthians.

Perhaps the most important text on Christ's victory over evil powers is Colossians 2:15. However the details of this verse are interpreted it must be seen that the subjugation of these enemies was accomplished in the cross and resurrection of Christ (Col 2:11-15). Believers share in Christ's triumph because their sins have been forgiven, their certificate of debt has been erased, and their sins have been decisively and finally nailed to the cross. Paul refers to the triumph over demonic powers at the cross and resurrection of Christ. Examining this verse at a general level, it is clear that the demonic powers were decisively defeated at the cross. But what does the verse specifically say? Many commentators think that the middle participle *apekdysamenos* is a true middle, indicating that Christ stripped off from himself his flesh or demonic powers at his death. This is certainly a possible reading, but it is more likely that the participle is middle with an active meaning. Four arguments support this view. First, middle participles often have an active meaning in the New Testament. Second, there is no indication in the text that the subject of the participle has shifted from God to Christ. Thus, the verse teaches that God has stripped the rulers and authorities of their power at the cross of Christ. Third, he publicly exposed them and humiliated them *(edeigmatisen en parrēsia)*. Fourth, God has "led the demons in triumphal procession" *(thriambeusas)* in Christ. The triumphal procession was a ceremonial parade through the streets of Rome in which some captive leaders and their wares were displayed. The march concluded with the execution of those conquered. It seems likely that all three metaphors should be interpreted in similar terms. The powers have lost their authority due to the cross of Christ. They have been stripped and humiliated, and they have been led to execution. They no longer exercise any control over those in Christ. In the context Christ's triumph over evil powers is linked with forgiveness of sins, indicating that in receiving the forgiveness of sins, believers have received everything they need.

Propitiation

This section is titled "Propitiation," but whether this is a fitting term is controversial. The word in question is *hilastērion,* which occurs in Paul only in Romans 3:25. C. H. Dodd argued that the term should not be rendered "propitiation" since that would imply a pagan notion of God in which his anger would need to be appeased.[8] The word *hilastērion* in both the LXX and the New Testament is more suitably translated as "expiation," the wiping away of sin. Dodd defends his view by noting that "sins" rather than God are usually the object of words related to *hilastērion.* Many scholars have been

---

[8]C. H. Dodd, *The Bible and the Greeks* (London: Hodder & Stoughton, 1935), pp. 82-95.

persuaded by Dodd, and some have even described the alternate view as "grotesque."[9] I am persuaded, however, that Leon Morris got the better of the argument, for he shows that God's wrath cannot be sheared off from the *hilas* word group in the LXX.[10] And God's wrath also permeates the text in Romans 1—3. Human sin (Rom 1:18; 2:5; 3:5-6) provokes the wrath of God, and the righteous judgment of God involves his wrath (Rom 2:5; 3:5-6). God's wrath is not the capricious wrath of Zeus or an uncontrolled temper tantrum. It is his holy, just and righteous response to human sin. Nor should we conceive of God and Jesus as polarized in this case, so that Jesus persuades the angry God to desist from wrath. Romans 3:25 shows that God himself "set forth" Jesus as a propitiation. God satisfied and appeased his own wrath by sending Jesus to die. We should not ultimately segregate propitiation from expiation. In the death of Jesus, sins are wiped away and God's wrath is satisfied.

The Old Testament background, especially Leviticus 16, is crucial for interpreting *hilastērion*. In fact, it is likely that the term refers to the mercy seat mentioned often in the Old Testament. Some scholars, on the other hand, are persuaded that the term cannot refer to the mercy seat in Romans 3:24. They note that the term has the article in the LXX when it refers to the mercy seat and that the article is lacking in the Romans text. Moreover, the term does not exclusively refer to the mercy seat in the Old Testament, so would the readers of Romans be sophisticated enough to detect an Old Testament allusion? It is also objected that the picture becomes highly confusing if Jesus is the priest, the victim and the place where the blood is sprinkled!

These cautions against accepting a reference to the mercy seat are significant but not decisive. The omission of an article is not telling since it is a predicate construction. And in the vast majority of cases *hilastērion* refers to the mercy seat in the LXX (e.g., Ex 25:17-22; 31:7; 35:12; 37:6, 8-9; Lev 16:2, 13-15; Num 7:89). Nor can it be said that the Romans would be unfamiliar with the Old Testament because Paul refers to the Old Testament scriptures more in Romans than in any other letter, and the readers would likely be quite familiar with the day-of-atonement traditions of Leviticus 16. Finally, the so-called confusing nature of the picture is overdrawn, for Paul's point is that Jesus transcends and fulfills the Old Testament symbolism.

Another debate centers on whether the background here stems from

---

[9]N. H. Young, "C. H. Dodd, 'Hilaskesthai' and His Critics," *EvQ* 48 (1976): 78.

[10]Morris, *Apostolic Preaching*, pp. 144-213; cf. also Hill, *Greek Words*, pp. 23-48; Roger R. Nicole, "C. H. Dodd and the Doctrine of Propitiation," *WTJ* 17 (1954-1955): 117-57.

martyr traditions or the Levitical cult. It is clear that the passage draws on cultic antecedents, but we need not posit an either-or solution here. It is also likely that an allusion to Hellenistic martyr-theology exists (4 Macc 17:21-22; cf. 2 Macc 6:13-16; 7:18, 32-33, 37-38; 4 Macc 6:27-29; 9:20; 10:8). Such martyr theology is ultimately rooted in Isaiah 53.[11] Appealing to martyr traditions does not rule out the substitutionary and sacrificial dimensions of the term, especially when we see the link between martyr traditions and Isaiah 53.

To sum up, a reference to Jesus as propitiation, though it occurs only once in Paul, evokes many Old Testament themes. God himself puts forth Jesus to satisfy his wrath so that he can display his mercy to his people. Jesus also functions as priest, victim and the place where the blood is sprinkled, signifying that full atonement has been accomplished. There is also an allusion to Isaiah 53, for Jesus is the righteous one who has borne the sins of many. Thus, through Jesus' atoning sacrifice, God's judging righteousness (Rom 3:25-26) has been vindicated. God did not besmirch his holiness by passing over sins in the past or by forgiving sin in the present. He manifested his saving righteousness in Jesus the Messiah precisely because his judging righteousness, his holiness, is vindicated in the death of Jesus. God is both just (holy and righteous) and the justifier (the Savior of those who believe)—precisely because of Jesus' propitiatory death. At the cross of Christ the saving and judging righteousness of God embrace, and neither is compromised.

Election

Inclusion of the Gentiles. One of the remarkable features of God's work in Christ on behalf of his people is that the work intended for Israel also embraces the Gentiles, so that the church of Christ is made up of both Jews and Gentiles. The inclusion of the Gentiles in God's saving promises is one of the central themes in Paul's writings. This is hardly surprising since Paul was called as the apostle to the Gentiles and his distinctive mission was to preach the gospel to the Gentiles (Gal 1:16). The Gentiles' inclusion into the blessings of Israel informs the letter to the Romans. When Paul affirms that the Gentiles in Rome are the "called" *(klētoi)* of Jesus Christ (Rom 1:6), he applies to the Gentiles a term reserved for Israel. He emphasizes that the gospel is for the Jew first, but it is also for the Greek (Rom 1:16; 2:10). Gentiles who observe the law are on the same level as circumcised Jews who keep it (Rom 2:25-29).

---

[11]For the martyrological background, see Thomas R. Schreiner, *Romans*, BECNT (Grand Rapids, Mich.: Baker, 1998), pp. 189-90.

And no distinction exists between Jews and Gentiles, in the sense that all are under the power and rule of sin (Rom 3:9-20, 23). Similarly, God's saving righteousness is available "to all who believe, for there is no distinction" (Rom 3:22). All are righteous before God on the same basis, for the one God cannot justify Jews in one way and Gentiles in another (Rom 3:28-30). Nor can it be argued that Abraham was intended to be the father of the Jews only. His universal fatherhood is prophesied in Genesis 17 and Genesis 12:3. Indeed, Abraham is the father of both Jews and Gentiles (Rom 4:9-12). Righteousness is not based on the law, for Abraham is the universal father of all Jews and Gentiles who trust in Christ (Rom 4:13-17); he is not merely the father of Jews who observe the law.

The law is not the decisive criterion for belonging to the people of God. The real question is whether one is in Adam or Christ. Those who are in Christ and who have the Spirit are members of the people of God. Paul argues in Romans 9—11 that it has always been God's plan to graft the Gentiles onto the olive tree of the people of God. This does not mean that he has abandoned Israel— he is the Lord of all, and thus all who call on him, whether Jews or Gentiles, will be saved (Rom 10:9-13). Given the unity in the people of God, Paul does not want either Jewish or Gentile customs to dominate in the church (Rom 14:1—15:13). The church transcends both groups, and the aim is to glorify God together and praise him for his mercy to both (Rom 15:7-13).

A similar theme emerges in Galatians. Judaizing opponents wanted to restrict the people of God to those who had been circumcised. This was tantamount to saying that one must be a Jew in order to belong to the people of God. Such teaching, in Paul's eyes, was a denial of the truth of the gospel. Compelling Gentiles to live like Jews denies the gospel of justification by faith (Gal 2:15-21). Abraham is the father of all by virtue of faith, not the works of the law (Gal 3:1-14). Indeed, the blessing of Abraham belongs to those who receive the Spirit by faith, not to those who keep the law. The Mosaic covenant was never intended to be in force forever (Gal 3:15—4:7), and now the era of salvation has arrived in which both Jews and Gentiles are members of the people of God. The same theme crops up in Ephesians. The wall of partition has been broken down (Eph 2:11—3:13), and now in Christ Jesus both Jews and Gentiles are united into the same people of God. The inclusion of Gentiles into the people of God is a mystery (*mystērion*) that has now been revealed (Eph 3:6).

This brief survey of Gentile inclusion is fitting because when we consider election we must interpret it in light of the Old Testament. Israel was God's elect people (Ex 19:5-6; Deut 7:6-8) on whom God placed his favor and love. Paul does not deny that Israel is still the object of God's love (Romans 9—11). Nonetheless, he clearly argues that Gentiles are also part of the circle of God's electing love. The Gentiles by virtue of being chosen and elect are included in the blessings of Israel.

Known by God. My placing election last in this chapter is intentional, for it provides a retrospective explanation of how believers have come to enjoy the benefits of Christ's work. When believers seek to clarify the reason for their justification, salvation, redemption and so on, they attribute such to God's electing work. Thereby the priority of grace is maintained in the Pauline gospel. Galatians 4:9 is illuminating in this regard: "And now having come to know God, or rather having been known by God." Paul begins by describing the conversion of the Galatians in terms of their knowing God. He feels compelled, however, to qualify this statement. The Galatians' knowledge of God is preceded by and determined by God's knowledge of them. The word *knowledge* here is rooted in the Old Testament, where God's knowledge of people is a manifestation of his covenantal love.[12] Amos 3:2 functions as a good example: "Only you have I known of all the families of the earth. Therefore, I will punish you for all your iniquities." Yahweh certainly knows about all the nations of the earth in the sense that he knows about their existence! What this text means is that Yahweh has set his covenantal favor and love on Israel in contrast to all other nations (cf. Gen 18:19; Jer 1:5). Similarly, the Galatians have genuinely come to know God, and such knowledge is communicated by their decision to know him. And yet they exercised their wills in such a way because God had previously chosen to place his covenantal favor on them. First Corinthians 8:3 is remarkably similar: "If anyone loves God, this one has been known [*egnōstai*] by him." The human decision to love God and to obey him is rooted in being known by God, in God's covenantal love.

This understanding of God's prior knowledge is crucial in explaining Romans 8:28-30, where the chain of terms in Romans 8:29-30 begins with the word *foreknew (proegnō).* Some interpret this to say that God simply knew in advance who would be predestined, called, justified and glorified (cf. Acts 26:5; 2 Pet 3:17). But the Old Testament background, noted above, indicates that the term *foreknow* must also be interpreted in a covenantal framework.

---

[12]In defense of this understanding of foreknowledge, see Steven M. Baugh, "The Meaning of Foreknowledge," in *Still Sovereign,* ed. T. R. Schreiner and B. A. Ware (Grand Rapids, Mich.: Baker, 2000), pp. 183-200.

Not only did God know whom he would predestine, call, justify and glorify, but he also set his electing and covenantal love on certain individuals. There is no basis, therefore, for the notion that human choice is ultimate in salvation. Just as in Galatians 4:9 and 1 Corinthians 8:3, God's decision precedes, undergirds and determines what human beings choose.

Election and grace. God's election of his people is expressed in the verb *he chose* (*exelexato,* Eph 1:4). This election is pretemporal, having occurred "before the foundation of the world." Any notion that human choice or human works are ultimate in God's choosing us is excluded. This is confirmed by Romans 9:11, where God's "purpose according to election" precedes birth and good or evil deeds. Paul concludes from this that God's promise is "not of works but of the one who calls" (Rom 9:12). Second Timothy 1:9 sounds a similar theme: believers are not called "according to our works but according to his own purpose and grace that was given to us in Christ Jesus before the times of the ages." Salvation is due not to human deeds but to God's eternal purpose, and this purpose involves his powerful grace, which turns unbelievers to faith. The contrast between election and grace is pregnantly expressed in Romans 11:6, "But if it is by grace, it is no longer by works. Otherwise, grace is no longer grace." Paul forges an inseparable link between his gospel of grace, apart from meritorious works, and divine election, showing that election is at the very heart of his gospel of grace. If one shears off election, then not much is left of grace. Such grace is effective because it has been promised before history began. Second Thessalonians 2:13 may communicate the same thought when it says, "God chose you from the beginning [*ap archēs*] for salvation." However, the textual evidence is divided and a better rendering may be "God chose you as the first fruits [*aparchēn*] for salvation." In either case the initiative of God in the salvation of his people is celebrated. The means are not excluded because this election becomes a reality "by means of the sanctification of the Spirit and faith in the truth" (2 Thess 2:13).

Ephesians 1:4 also says that "God chose us in him," that is, in Christ. Some have concluded from this that God chose Christ as the elect one and that those who choose to be in Christ are saved.[13] The ultimate cause of salvation on this reading is human choice. The most natural reading of the text is violated by this interpretation because Paul does not say that God chose Christ, but that he

---

[13]So William W. Klein, *The New Chosen People: A Corporate View of Election* (Grand Rapids, Mich.: Zondervan, 1990).

chose "us" (hēmas). We misread the text in focusing on God's choosing Christ when in fact Paul refers to God's choosing believers. Of course, election is "in Christ"—Christ is the means and perhaps also the locality by which believers are elected. Election occurs in and through Christ. God did not choose people to be saved apart from Christ. Any doubt as to how believers come to be "in Christ" is removed by 1 Corinthians 1:30, "And of [ex] him [i.e., God] you are in Christ Jesus." This verse eliminates the option that believers are "in Christ" ultimately because of their individual choices. Rather, believers are in Christ because of what God has done. Nor does this reading wrench this verse out of its context, for three times in 1 Corinthians 1:27-28 Paul clarifies that the foolish, the weak and the disreputable are part of the people of God because God has "chosen" (exelexato) them. Since being "in Christ" and being chosen are God's work, it follows that "no flesh can boast before God" (1 Cor 1:29) and that "the one who boasts should boast in the Lord" (1 Cor 1:31). Paul does not trumpet election to propound a teaching that is controversial or to provoke intellectual debates. His theology of election is undergirded by his view of God, for election preserves the glory of God and eliminates human boasting. Ephesians 1:3-14 drives home the same point. God chose and predestined his people "for the praise of the glory of his grace" (Eph 1:6). God's election is designed to lead to praise and worship.

Ephesians 1:4-5. Election is also designed to lead to holiness: "He chose us . . . so that we should be holy and blameless before him" (Eph 1:4). The church will be presented by Christ to the Father on the last day as holy and blameless (Eph 5:26-27). We ought not to conclude from this, however, that such holiness is separable from salvation—as if it were an optional addition to God's saving work. In Paul's mind such holiness is part and parcel of being saved. The participle *having predestined us to adoption (proorisas)* indicates the means by which God chose his people (Eph 1:5). God elected his people by predestinating them to adoption as sons. Predestination means that God has marked out his people beforehand for salvation. We know that salvation is in mind since "adoption" (hyiothesian) is simply another way of speaking of the eschatological inheritance of believers. Paul similarly connects predestination with salvation in Ephesians 1:11, emphasizing particularly that God "works all things in accordance with the counsel of his will." That predestination is pretemporal is suggested in Romans 8:30, for predestination precedes calling, justification and glorification.

Calling. The power of God's grace is communicated particularly in the word *calling (kaleō)*. In the Pauline literature the word should not be defined as an "invitation" that can be accepted or refused. Calling is performative, in which the call accomplishes what is demanded. This is apparent in reflecting on a number of texts. For instance, in Romans 8:30 Paul says that "those whom he called, these he also justified." In this verse all of those who are called are also justified. No exception intervenes so that only some of those who are called are justified. Every single person who is called is also justified. And yet we know that not everyone is justified. Paul teaches in Romans that justification is by faith (Rom 5:1), and only some have saving faith. We can conclude from this that calling is restricted only to some and that it does not merely involve an invitation to believe. Calling must create faith since *all* those who are called are also justified. Thus, God does not call all people but only some, and those whom he calls are given the power to believe.

The first chapter of 1 Corinthians is illuminating in this regard. Those who are called will obtain the eschatological inheritance on the final day (1 Cor 1:8-9). And yet it is clear that not all who hear the message are called. The gospel is proclaimed *(kēryssō)* to both Jews and Greeks (1 Cor 1:23), but many Jews and Greeks reject the message, considering it to be weak or foolish (1 Cor 1:22-23). And yet the "called" *(klētoi)* among both Jews and Greeks consider the gospel to be "power and wisdom of God" (1 Cor 1:24). Paul, then, summons his readers to reflect on their "calling" *(klēsin,* 1 Cor 1:26). He proceeds to unpack the nature of this calling by stating three times that God "chose" *(exelexato)* those who are his, whether they are foolish, weak or disreputable (1 Cor 1:27-28). Calling is specifically distinguished from the proclamation of the gospel, in the sense that only some of those who hear the gospel are called. The message is broadcast to all, but only some are chosen and called among those who hear the gospel. The call, then, is effective in that it produces the conviction that the gospel is the power and wisdom of God.

This understanding of calling is borne out in the account of Paul's call to ministry and his conversion (Gal 1:15-16). Paul's conversion and call were not merely an invitation to believe. His transformation rested on the good pleasure *(eudokēsen* of God, the God "who separated him from his mother's womb" (Gal 1:15). In other words, God had decided to call Paul before he was born. Not only so, the calling effectively "revealed the Son to me." Paul's call was completely and utterly the work of God. The three accounts of Paul's conversion and call in Acts (Acts 9:1-19; 22:1-16; 26:1-18) match the account in Galatians. Paul was summoned into ministry by a powerful hand. And despite the exceptional nature of Paul's apostolic ministry, he viewed his call as paradigmatic of the conversion of all believers, maintaining that "Christ Jesus showed all his patience to me, the foremost, as an example of those who were about to believe in him for eternal life" (1 Tim 1:16).

The understanding of calling suggested here is confirmed by texts that closely associate God's call with election. God's election is not based on seeing what human beings would do or what in fact they actually perform (Rom 9:11). God's saving promise "is not based on works but on the one who calls" (Rom 9:12). We might expect Paul to say, "It is not of works but of faith," since the contrast between faith and works is common in his writings. He certainly is not denying such an idea here. And yet he reaches back to something that precedes human faith, to God's call, which creates such faith. Similarly, in 2 Timothy 1:9 God's call is opposed to works ("who saved us and called us to a holy calling, not according to our works but according to his own purpose and grace") and is linked with God's eternal purpose and grace, which were given to believers before time began. In 2 Thessalonians 2:14 God's call, which is exercised in history through the gospel, is closely conjoined with his choosing people for salvation (2 Thess 2:13; cf. Rom 9:24-26; 1 Cor 1:9). Nor should we fail to see that the call guarantees the outcome. Those who are called through the gospel will possess eschatological glory (2 Thess 2:13). The one who called believers will see to it that they obtain the sanctification needed to stand before the Lord (1 Thess 5:23-24). Since God is faithful, he will confirm to the end those who are called as blameless (1 Cor 1:8-9).

It is also remarkable how often "love" is associated with God's calling or election. Those who are called are also "beloved [agapētois] by God" (Rom 1:6-7). The choosing of Jacob is described in terms of God's placing his love on him (Rom 9:13; cf. Rom 9:25). The stunning grace that lifts us out of death (Eph 2:4-6; see below) is attributed to God's deep love (Eph 2:4). The "elect" are also designated as "beloved" (ēgapēmenoi) in Colossians 3:12. First Thessalonians 1:4 contains a similar collocation, for Paul explains the Thessalonians' faith, love and hope in terms of their election—"knowing, brothers, loved [ēgapēmenoi] by God, your election [eklogēn]." And in 2 Thessalonians 2:13 those who are chosen (eilato) for salvation are described as "those loved [ēgapēmenoi] by the Lord." In reference to "election" (eklogēn), the Jews are considered "beloved" (agapētoi) "because of the fathers" (Rom 11:28). Paul does not call into question God's justice when election arises. Instead he meditates on his great and merciful love.

The argument of Romans 9:6-29. The most striking text on God's electing grace is surely Romans 9:6-29, where it is abundantly clear that God's election is sure and certain—nothing can overturn it (Rom 9:6). Therefore, he will certainly fulfill his promises to his people Israel. Isaac's birth was a miracle of God's grace in accord with his promise and was not dependent in the least on Sarah and Abraham (Rom 9:6-9). God never promised that all ethnic descendants of Abraham would enjoy his salvation. The promise was given specifically to Isaac. Of course, some Jews may have responded by saying that they never thought the descendants of Ishmael were recipients of God's saving promises. Paul gives a second example to clarify that *a principle of winnowing* has been at work throughout Israel's history (Rom 9:10-13). Thus, God chose Jacob and not Esau. He did not choose Jacob because he anticipated his works; on the contrary, he set his love on Jacob, not Esau, solely because of his electing good pleasure. Such an argument is stunning indeed, and it leads naturally to this question: Is God unjust (Rom 9:14)? Incidentally, raising this question vindicates the line of argument sketched in above because the interpretation proposed naturally raises the question of God's justice. Paul defends God's justice by insisting that he has mercy on whom he wishes and hardens whom he wishes (Rom 9:14-18). He eliminates human effort *(trechontos)* and human choice *(thelontos)* as decisive, assigning both salvation and perdition to God.

Once again the conclusion is a stunning one, and Paul anticipates his opponent's objection. If God is the ultimate cause of both salvation and perdition, then one cannot find fault since his will is irresistible (Rom 9:19). Paul does not escape this charge by appealing to human freedom and choice as fundamental in the universe, nor does he mount a defense on God's behalf (Rom 9:20-23). Rather, he says that God as the sovereign Creator and Potter is free to do what he wishes with his creation, and no finite human being can legitimately question him. God's mercy is grasped and prized against the backdrop of his deserved wrath (Rom 9:22-23). When human beings understand that they genuinely deserve judgment and that their election is God's gracious gift, they treasure their salvation more, contrasting it with the judgment that they should be receiving. People luxuriate in the sunshine of God's grace when they perceive that they have been spared from the bitter cold of his wrath. It must be noted that no philosophical solution to the problem of evil is offered. Paul assumes that the salvation of anyone is due to God's mercy and that all deserve judgment. The text concludes with the calling of the Gentiles (Rom 9:24-29). Just as God surprised Sarah and Abraham by choosing Isaac and as he stunned Isaac by choosing Jacob, so too he now stuns the Jews by choosing the Gentiles. Thereby his mercy is featured, for it is clarified that no one deserves his merciful grace.

Is Romans 9 about salvation? Many scholars object to the exegesis defended here, claiming that the text does not relate to salvation or that the teaching on predestination cannot be applied to individuals because it relates only to groups or nations.[14] In regard to the first objection, those who assign this text to historical destiny rather than salvation misread the context of the passage. What causes Paul to grieve for his fellow Israelites in Romans 9:1-5 is that they are separated from Christ (*anathema apo tou Christou*, Rom 9:3). Paul grieves not simply because Israel lacks national blessings, but because they are unsaved. Indeed, only Israel's cursed condition explains Paul's willingness to be cursed for his kinsmen. The argument in all of Romans 9:6—11:36 explains that God's word cannot be broken (Rom 9:6) and that he will keep his *saving* promises to Israel. Moreover, the specific terms used in Romans 9 show that salvation is the issue. To be "the seed of Abraham" (Rom 9:7) and "the children of the promise" (Rom 9:8) is synonymous with being saved. Furthermore, the term *election* (Rom 9:11) reveals that salvation is at stake. This is even clearer in Romans 9:12, where "works" are opposed to God's "call." Surely, when Paul speaks of God's calling the Gentiles in Romans 9:24-26 he thinks of their salvation. It would be special pleading to mount a different argument in Romans 9:12, especially since "calling" is opposed to "works"! The vessels of "honor" and "dishonor" (Rom 9:21) also relate to salvation in this context, where Paul refers to "vessels of wrath prepared for destruction" (Rom 9:22) and "vessels of mercy which are prepared beforehand for glory" (Rom 9:23). The word *destruction (apōleian)* typically refers to eschatological destruction, and the contrast with vessels of mercy prepared for glory shows that salvation is the issue here.

The argument is strengthened when we realize the unified argument presented in Romans 9—11. That is, Paul is concerned in all of Romans 9—11 with the matter of Israel's *salvation*. Israel's error in erecting a righteousness by works (Rom 9:30—10:8) is a salvation issue, and one must believe in and confess Christ *to be saved* (Rom 10:9-13). In speaking of salvation in Romans 10, Paul has not left the topic broached in Romans 9! Nor is Romans 11 of a

---

[14]For a detailed response to these objections, see Thomas R. Schreiner, "Does Romans 9 Teach Individual Election unto Salvation? Some Exegetical and Theological Reflections," in *Still Sovereign*, ed. T. R. Schreiner and B. A. Ware (Grand Rapids, Mich.: Baker, 2000), pp. 89-106. For a full-length treatment with responses to other views, see John Piper, *The Justification of God: An Exegetical and Theological Study of Romans 9:1-23* (Grand Rapids, Mich.: Baker, 1993).

different character. Israel's hardening means that she is not saved (Rom 11:1-10). Note again the language, which contrasts election with works, revealing that salvific issues are in mind. The grafting in of Gentiles onto the olive tree and the cutting off of Israel also relate to salvation (Rom 11:17-24). The passage climaxes with the promise that "all Israel shall be saved" (Rom 11:26). Any attempt to say that Romans 9 is not about salvation is singularly unsuccessful. We can say that Romans 9 is about the historical destiny of Israel, as long as her historical destiny is not segregated from, and is indeed linked with, the issue of salvation.

Corporate instead of individual salvation? Others try to blunt the force of Romans 9:6-29 by claiming that the text refers only to the salvation of groups and peoples and not the salvation of individuals. Hence, the text is read to say that the Ishmaelites as a group are excluded but Isaac's descendants are included. A similar explanation is proposed for Jacob and Esau and for the case of Pharaoh: that is, the concern is with ethnic groups and tribes—not individuals. This view is correct in saying that Paul has in mind Israel as a group, but it wrongly severs the group from the individual. After all, Paul uses singular forms often in the argument, especially at crucial points in the argument (Rom 9:16, 18-19, 21). He is not at all careful to distinguish the singular from the plural. Such a distinction is imposed on the text and read into it, rather than being a legitimate reading of the text. And it must also be said that the attempt to divide groups and individuals is logically flawed. Groups are made up of individuals, and God's justice is hardly preserved (which is the desire of those proposing the groups-versus-individuals argument) if he chooses one group over another on the basis of his will. No, the scandal of the text must be allowed to remain.

Miracle of conversion. Conversion in Paul is fundamentally a miracle. Human beings are blinded by Satan and hindered from seeing the beauty of the gospel and the beauty of Christ proclaimed in that gospel (2 Cor 4:3-4). Nonetheless, Paul continues to proclaim the gospel as a servant of Jesus Christ because he knows that conversion is ultimately God's work. In 2 Corinthians 4:6 conversion is explicated in light of the creation narrative in Genesis 1. In the midst of darkness God spoke the word and light shone (Gen 1:3). Similarly, God shines his light in the hearts of those who are shrouded in the darkness imposed by Satan. When he shines his light, he begets the knowledge of God's glory. That is, those in darkness now perceive the beauty and goodness of God. This knowledge of God is communicated "in the face of Jesus Christ." It becomes a reality through the proclamation of the gospel.

Conversion is a miracle in the same way that the explosion of light into darkness on the first day of creation was a miracle. The only explanation for the transformation of human hearts is God's supernatural light, which illumines the heart and mind.

Ephesians 2:1-10 witnesses also to God's transforming grace. We have already seen that unbelievers are portrayed as "dead in trespasses and sins" (Eph 2:1). They are subjugated to Satan, the world and the flesh (Eph 2:2-3). Hope for transformation hardly lies in the human will since people take pleasure in doing what the flesh desires. Thus, they are by nature under the sentence of God's wrath. Yet God, because of his indescribable mercy and deep love, has not left all human beings in this state (Eph 2:4). Those who were dead in trespasses and sins, those who had no inclination whatsoever to turn to God, "he made alive together with Christ" (Eph 2:5). Significantly, Paul immediately comments, "by grace you have been saved." This explanation is noteworthy and imperative for defining grace in Paul. Grace is not merely unmerited favor in the sense that one may choose to receive or reject a gift. Grace is the impartation of new life. Grace is a power that raises someone from the dead, that lifts those in the grave into new life. Grace is not merely an undeserved gift, though it is such; it is also a transforming power. Grace imparted life when we were dead, and grace also raises us and seats us with Christ in the heavenlies (Eph 2:6). The wonder of this grace is such that it will be displayed and praised in the coming ages (Eph 2:7).

Once we grasp this notion of grace, it is clear what Paul means when he says "by grace you have been saved through faith. And this is not of yourselves; it is the gift of God" (Eph 2:8). The power of God saved us by raising us from death when we were utterly unresponsive to God. But is faith included in God's gift? Or is faith our contribution to God's saving work? The demonstrative pronoun *this (touto)* is neuter, and thus it cannot be the specific antecedent to *grace* or *faith* since the words *grace (chariti)* and *faith (pisteōs)* are both feminine. Nor can it refer specifically back to *saved*, for the participle *saved (sesōmenoi)* is masculine. Indeed, no word in the preceding context is neuter. What, then, is the significance of the neuter? Paul wanted to communicate that everything said in Ephesians 2:8 is God's gift. That is, if he had used the masculine or feminine form of the pronoun, some might have concluded that some of the elements contained in this verse were not part of God's gift. By using the neuter he emphasizes that the whole is God's gift.

Faith is not ultimately or finally our "part" in salvation. It too is the gift of

God. Such an understanding of faith is also contextually persuasive because Paul describes God's work as raising the dead to life. Human beings who are enslaved to the flesh have no desire or ability to exercise faith. Faith also is the gift of resurrection life. This understanding of the neuter is confirmed by Philippians 1:28. Paul exhorts the Philippians not to be intimidated by their opponents, and he says that their opposition is "a proof of their destruction, and of your salvation, and this from God." Once again, the word *this (touto)* is neuter. As in the Ephesians text, no neuter word in the context serves as the antecedent. What, then, is the antecedent? It is the whole event—the opposition and destruction of the opponents as well as the salvation of the Philippians. The neuter pronoun works precisely as it does in Ephesians. And that faith is a gift is also communicated by the very next verse in Philippians. God has granted believers the gift of both believing on and suffering for Christ (Phil 1:29). The verb *granted* is *echaristhē*, from which we derive our word *grace*. Belief is a gift, granted by his grace, and, surprisingly, so is suffering for his sake.

Ephesians 2:10 confirms that faith is given by God. The salvation of believers is "his workmanship" *(autou poiēma)*. Indeed, it is the result of the "creative" *(ktisthentes)* activity of God in Christ Jesus. As in 2 Corinthians 4:6, here Paul sees God's work in Christ in terms of his original creative work, and we have already noted that such a work of God is fundamentally miraculous and the product of the divine will. Indeed, we must see that believers are not exhorted to do "good works" in this text. Good works are what God has prepared in advance *(proētoimasen)* for believers. Good works are not commanded but ordained. They are the fruit of God's creative work and his workmanship. Thus, both faith and good works in this passage are ultimately the work of God.

That faith is a gift is confirmed by 2 Timothy 2:24-26, where repentance is ascribed to God's activity. Faith and repentance are ultimately inseparable, and they are constituent parts of the saving process. In this context, Paul summons God's servants to be peaceable and patient in correcting and teaching adversaries. They should act in such ways because God may "grant repentance resulting in knowledge of the truth" to those who oppose them (2 Tim 2:25). Such repentance can only come from God, for human beings are anesthetized by the devil; and only God can provide the power to "sober them up" *(ananēpsōsin, 2 Tim 2:26)*. No hope for the transformation of human beings lies in the human will. God must grant repentance and the necessary sobriety. Human beings are snared in the devil's trap and are held captive *(ezōgrēmenoi)* by him, so that they always do the devil's will.

A Final Word on Faith

Having sketched in God's saving work on our behalf through Jesus Christ, it is fitting to conclude the chapter by reiterating the significance of faith. The emphasis on God's work must not be interpreted to dismiss or downplay the necessity of faith for conversion. Salvation, including faith, is God's gift. And yet human faith is essential in order for anyone to be saved. Faith is highlighted as the means by which one becomes right with God instead of by "works of law," or works. Faith *receives* what God gives to us instead of laboring to give something to God. Since faith is fundamentally receptive, it accords with *grace*. Grace is God's powerful work in our lives. In what work of God does faith place its trust? It believes that "God justifies the ungodly" (Rom 4:5). Or, to put it another way, faith believes in a God who forgives our sins on the basis of Christ's death (Rom 3:21-26; 4:6-8). God works for us by forgiving sin, and we enjoy that forgiveness by believing that God really forgives our sins for Christ's sake.

Faith, in other words, is fundamentally humble, for it acknowledges our inability to save ourselves by our works. Doing good works to receive a reward exalts us as moral human beings. Faith is humble in that it acknowledges our evil, our weakness and our inability. It receives forgiveness and cleansing from God. In other words, faith is God-centered whereas works are me-centered. Faith attributes righteousness to God alone; works point to our contribution and effort in gaining righteousness. The one who does the work gets the honor and praise; and thus if salvation is not wholly of God, then we deserve a reward. But since righteousness is from God alone through Christ, the glory and honor of our salvation are his. We receive the help and he receives the praise.

Paul often affirms that righteousness is through faith in Jesus Christ since it is the inception and platform for life in the Spirit. We must also grasp that faith is not an abstraction for Paul. It consists in faith in Jesus Christ and God the Father, believing in and relying on the work that Christ has done on behalf of believers by virtue of the cross. Faith is not merely intellectual assent. It trusts in the God "who gives life to the dead and calls the things which do not exist into existence" (Rom 4:17). Abraham had this kind of vital faith, believing that God would fulfill his promises (Rom 4:18-22), though the circumstances indicated that this was impossible. Since Abraham believed in a God who could raise the dead and call into existence that which did not exist, he believed that God could produce a child through him and Sarah—despite the fact that his body and Sarah's womb were as good as dead (see *nenekrōmenon* and *nerkrōsin* in Rom 4:19). Since God's vivifying power is particularly powerful where death reigns, Abraham trusted that God would fulfill his promise to supply him with a descendant. Abraham's faith calculated carefully the inadequacy of Sarah and himself, but his faith was strong in that he believed God could and would fulfill his promises: "He was fully convinced that what he promised he was also able to do" (Rom 4:21).

Abraham did not postulate that God would do miracles at his every whim, so that life would be a continuous succession of the extraordinary. No, Abraham believed that God would fulfill his specific promise. Faith which believes that God will fulfill his promises gives him glory (Rom 4:20) in that it considers him as sovereign over the world and one's life. Not any kind of faith, therefore, is reckoned for righteousness. Faith that counts before God is faith like Abraham's. Saving faith relies on God to fulfill his promises and entrusts the future to him. Paul specifically applies Abraham's faith to the lives of believers (Rom 4:23-25). They trust that sins are forgiven in the death and resurrection of Jesus (Rom 4:23-25) and therefore believe that the promise of the resurrection will become theirs on the day of the Lord.

10

LIVING TO
HONOR GOD

The Power to Live
a New Life

The work of Christ, the second Adam, reverses and overcomes the sin of the first Adam so that human beings honor God and Christ. Conversion and faith mean that God is praised as the giver of life and the source of all goodness. And yet the saving work of Christ does not immediately produce a completed work of holiness in his people. The tension between the "already" and the "not yet" remains, so that believers groan for the day of redemption (Rom 8:11, 23), the day when they will receive their resurrection bodies. Paul often speaks, therefore, of how the new community, the redeemed of Jesus Christ, comprising both Jews and Gentiles, should honor God in their new life. In this chapter we shall examine Paul's instructions about the Christian life in Romans 12:1-2, the indicative and the imperative, and the role of the Holy Spirit in living the Christian life. In the two following chapters we shall continue to explore the theme of the Christian life, investigating Paul's understanding of perseverance in chapter eleven and the place of exhortations and the law in chapter twelve.

Romans 12:1-2
A succinct summary of the admonitions directed toward believers is found in

Romans 12:1-2: "Therefore, I exhort you, brothers, because of the mercies of God to present your bodies as a sacrifice, living, holy, well pleasing to God, which is your rational service. And do not be conformed to this age, but be transformed by the renewal of your mind, so that you might approve what God's will is, the good and well pleasing and perfect." In the letter to the Romans these verses constitute a turning point, for sustained and direct exhortations in the letter begin here. It is also clear that the exhortation here flows from and is grounded on 1:18—11:36. Moreover, these verses summarize the admonitions that follow in 12:3—15:13. We can affirm with some confidence that these verses encapsulate Paul's understanding of the Christian life.[1]

Paul uses sacrificial language to urge believers to give themselves wholly to God. They are to present their bodies as living, holy and well-pleasing sacrifices to God. The word *bodies (sōmata)* designates the whole person, signifying that every dimension of our lives should be under God's dominion.[2] Believers are a "living sacrifice" because they have died with Christ and will be raised with him (Rom 6:3-5). The sacrifices in the Old Testament, if properly carried out and offered with a pure motivation, were holy and pleasing to God. Here Paul informs us that a holy and pleasing sacrifice to God consists in the giving of our whole selves to him, in utter commitment to his lordship.

The devotion to God urged on believers is not a testimony of the nobility of believers. Such commitment is *a response to* God's mercies, and so Paul characterizes it as "your reasonable service." The word translated as *reasonable (logikēn)* is translated by many as *spiritual.* The latter translation is unlikely in this instance, for Paul does not use the word *pneumatikēn* but *logikēn.* The word selected is an unusual one for Paul, but it refers to what is "reasonable" or "rational." Giving our entire lives to God is eminently reasonable since he has bestowed his mercy on us. The height of irrationality would be to refuse God's lordship after experiencing his merciful grace. The

---

[1] For a useful collection of various essays on the topic of ethics in Paul, see Brian S. Rosner, ed., *Understanding Paul's Ethics: Twentieth-Century Approaches* (Grand Rapids, Mich.: Eerdmans, 1995).

[2] On the significance of the "body" in Pauline theology, see John A. T. Robinson, *The Body: A Study in Pauline Theology,* SBT 5 (Chicago: Regnery, 1952), and Rudolf Bultmann, *Theology of the New Testament,* 2 vols. (New York: Scribner, 1951-1955). Robinson and Bultmann stress that the body denotes the whole person. Robert H. Gundry (*Sōma in Biblical Theology: With Emphasis on Pauline Anthropology,* SNTSMS 29 [Cambridge: Cambridge University Press, 1976]) rightly points out that the physical dimensions of the term cannot be excluded, but he incorrectly denies a reference to the person as a whole.

word *service (latreian)* also hearkens back to Romans 1:25, where idolators are said to "worship and serve *[elatreusan]* the creature rather than the creator." Romans 12:1-2 captures the reversal of such idolatry. Surrendering one's life to God is true worship, and the glory and thanks previously given to idols are now given to God (Rom 1:21). True worship is not confined to cultic acts, nor do cultic acts receive much emphasis in Paul. Worship involves honoring God by submitting to his sovereignty in every sphere of life.[3]

Currently believers live in the tension between the "already" and the "not yet." Pleasing God is not automatic, for the forces of the world conspire to conform believers to its pattern (Rom 12:2). Hence, believers must resist capitulating to the forces of this age. The means by which transformation is attained is "the renewal of the mind." Even though believers have been converted, transformation or utter submission to God occurs as new ways of thinking are adopted. A process is involved in which believers discern the good, pleasing and perfect will of God. After conversion believers do not instantaneously understand what is pleasing to God. Their thinking must be informed by truth so that they can comprehend and carry out God's will. God's will, according to Romans 12:2, is that which is good, pleasing and perfect. Ephesians 5:8-9 portrays Christian existence as walking in the light, and the "fruit of the light" consists "in all goodness and righteousness and truth." Nonetheless, what is good, righteous and true is not always immediately evident to believers, for Paul goes on to say that we must "test what is pleasing to the Lord." A learning curve is involved in which believers attempt to assess what God demands. A connection with Romans 1 emerges again. Those under God's wrath are darkened in their understanding and are plunged into the foolishness of worshiping the creature rather than the Creator (Rom 1:21-23). As the mind is renewed, believers bow to God's rule in their lives.

The Indicative and the Imperative

Romans 12:1-2 introduces us to one of the most profound and difficult areas of Paul's thought: the tension between the indicative and the imperative.[4] The

---

[3]For a helpful study on worship in the scriptures and in Paul, see David Peterson, *Engaging with God: A Biblical Theology of Worship* (Grand Rapids, Mich.: Eerdmans, 1993).

[4]For two insightful essays on the indicative and the imperative, see Rudolf Bultmann's "The Problem of Ethics in Paul" and Michael Parsons's "Being Precedes Act: Indicative and Imperative in Paul's Writing" in *Understanding Paul's Ethics: Twentieth-Century Approaches,* ed. Brian S. Rosner (Grand Rapids, Mich.: Eerdmans, 1995), pp. 195-216 and pp. 217-47, respectively.

indicative refers to what God has done for believers in Christ, while the imperative calls on believers to live in a way that honors God. We have already investigated in some detail the indicative in Pauline thought. For example, believers are righteous, forgiven, redeemed, saved and reconciled, and they have triumphed over evil powers. And yet, even here, the "not yet" emerges, for there is a future dimension to our righteousness, redemption and salvation and to God's other gifts. If eschatological tension did not characterize Christian existence, no imperative would be needed. At the day of redemption, when our bodies are transformed (Phil 3:21), ethical exhortation will be superfluous.

Parenesis (i.e., ethical exhortation) is necessary only in the interval between the "already" and the "not yet." The presence of the imperative signals that our salvation is not yet completed. Those who dispense with exhortations and commands are guilty of overrealized eschatology. We steer between Scylla and Charybdis, for one could also understand the imperative in such a way that the indicative is canceled. The indicative could be wrongly stripped away so that the emphasis rests on the "not yet," which would be grasped through obeying Pauline commands. The eschatological tension between the indicative and the imperative must be maintained. The work of the cross is complete; believers are forgiven, transformed, ransomed and saved. The imperative always flows from and depends on the indicative. Placing the imperative as foundational is a perversion of the Pauline gospel and effectively cancels out the indicative. The indicative of what God has done in Christ ensures that the imperative will become a reality. And yet the indicative does not cancel out the need for the imperative. The imperative is rightly estimated when rooted in the indicative.

All attempts to formulate the relationship between the indicative and the imperative seem to reflect partial truths. If we say, "Be what you already are," we acknowledge what has already been accomplished in our lives by the grace of Christ, but the future dimension of our salvation—the "not yet"—is slighted. Indeed, such a formulation makes one wonder about the need for any imperative, for if all is already accomplished, then what need for the imperative exists? If we say, "Be what you are becoming," we acknowledge that there is a sense in which salvation is incomplete. We still await the redemption of our bodies and the complete extinguishing of sin. This statement is also helpful in that the Christian life is discerned as progressive. We are in the process of being conformed to the likeness of Christ, and the transformation of our minds does not occur instantaneously. But the formulation does not adequately express the sense in which we have already been transformed and changed. The emphasis lies on what we are in the process of becoming, and it does not acknowledge that the decisive turn has already been accomplished. The omission is a serious one since Paul often says that we have become a new creation by virtue of the work of Christ. We could also say, "Be what you will be." This formulation rightly discerns that the work of redemption will not be completed until the day of the Lord, but it has no room for the salvation that is already accomplished.

Such brief statements cannot express the complexity of Paul's understanding. Each one leaves out essential dimensions of his thought, though they all contain some aspects of the truth. The indicative is the basis for the imperative, and the imperative would never become a reality without the indicative. Indeed, the indicative guarantees the actualizing of the imperative. Nevertheless, the imperative must be obeyed in order to obtain the salvation promised and granted in the indicative. The indicative cannot preempt the imperative so that the imperative is jettisoned, but the gospel would be distorted if the imperative, instead of the indicative, is placed in the foreground.

1 Corinthians 5. The indicative-imperative tension surfaces in 1 Corinthians 5. Paul is outraged that a person committing incest is allowed to remain in the church. This person's presence is infectious in that "a little leaven leavens the whole lump" (1 Cor 5:6). So Paul summons the church to expel him, to "clean out the old leaven" (1 Cor 5:7). The imperative is featured since the church at Corinth can hardly function as God's holy people if they allow unrepentant sin to exist in its midst. The purpose for the imperative is equally striking. The old leaven (the person committing incest) must be driven out "so that you will be a new lump" (1 Cor 5:7). This man must be excommunicated so that the Corinthians will be pure and holy. The Corinthians' holiness and purity depends on their obedience to the Pauline admonition. To put it another way, their holiness is conditioned on their obedience. If they fail to expel the man in question, then the lump is contaminated and ruined. Nonetheless, this is not the whole story. Paul goes on to give the rationale for the command: "just as you are unleavened; for even Christ, our Passover, has been sacrificed" (1 Cor 5:7). The imagery from the Exodus is obvious since no leavened bread is eaten on Passover (Ex 12:14-20).

On the one hand, the Corinthians are to clean out the old leaven in order to be an unleavened lump. On the other hand, they already are unleavened. Why clean out any leaven if the church *already is* unleavened? The tension in Pauline thought must be preserved here. The Corinthians' unleavened and pure state depends on their obeying Paul's admonition. They must excommunicate the sinner *in order to be pure*. And yet, the Corinthians are already pure and unleavened because of the Passover sacrifice of Christ. His death has removed the leaven from their lives. The indicative means that the Corinthians *are* a pure and new lump because of his death. The indicative of his death has produced an unleavened and pure lump. Precisely because they are unleavened in Christ (*hōste* in 1 Cor 5:8!), they are to celebrate the Passover by removing the old leaven from their lives. The indicative is the basis for the imperative. What they are in Christ is the basis and foundation for heeding Pauline admonitions. The tension between the "already" and "not yet"—the indicative and the imperative—remains. Even though the Corinthians are unleavened in Christ, they must cast out the old leaven to be a new lump of unleavened dough. The indicative is the foundation of the imperative, but if the imperative is not heeded, then the newness of the lump is destroyed. The indicative of God's work in Christ cannot be used to jettison the imperative of cleaning out the old leaven, but the imperative can only be realized because of the indicative.

Philippians 2:12-13. Philippians 2:12-13 is another classic expression of the tension between the indicative and the imperative. Philippians 2:12 says, "Accomplish your own salvation with fear and trembling." Sometimes the verb *katergazesthe* is rendered as "work out."[5] A look at the Pauline usage, and the evidence in BAGD itself reveals that the verb simply means "work, accomplish" or "do" (Rom 1:27; 2:9; 4:15; 5:3; 7:8, 13, 15, 17-18, 20; 15:18; 1 Cor 5:3; 2 Cor 4:17; 5:5; 7:10-11; 9:11; 12:12; Eph 6:13). The addition of the word *out* softens the verse unduly. The verse is better translated to say, "Work your salvation with fear and trembling." The imperative here is truly astonishing, especially in a letter of Paul. He often emphasizes that salvation is not based on "works of law" (Rom 3:20, 28; Gal 2:16; 3:2, 5, 10), or "works" (Rom 9:11-12; Eph 2:8-9; Tit 3:5), but here believers are urged to "accomplish" their own salvation. The word *salvation* designates future salvation as is usual in Paul. Believers are summoned to accomplish their own eschatological deliverance!

The seriousness of the imperative could scarcely be more weighty. And yet we must not divorce this imperative from the indicative that immediately follows: "For the one working in you both to will and to work on behalf of his good pleasure is God" (Phil 2:13). Believers are to accomplish their salvation,

---

[5]W. Bauer, W. F. Arndt, F. W. Gingrich and F. W. Danker, *Greek-English Lexicon of the New Testament and Other Early Christian Literature*, 2nd ed. (Chicago: University of Chicago Press, 1979); this is abbreviated BAGD.

and yet ultimately it is God who does the work. He gives the strength to do the work. If this were not acknowledged, what Paul says here would seem to teach that believers can merit their own salvation. Further, we must recall that the admonition is given to believers who are already forgiven of their sins. God's foundational work of setting believers in the right before him underlies this exhortation as well.

Recognizing that God is the one who supplies the strength to work does not detract from the force of the imperative. Indeed, it supplies the basis on which it can be carried out. God's work does not cancel our work but establishes and secures it. The extent to which all our working is ultimately due to God is clarified even further in Philippians 2:13. Not only does God provide the strength to work, he also grants believers the desire to do what is right. Actions or works are the consequences of decisions. Human beings ultimately decide on one course of action rather than another because that is what they wish to do. Even a person committing suicide prefers death over life since life is so miserable.[6] Our choices are always in line with our preferences.[7] The key to a changed life, therefore, lies in the transformation of the will since we choose what we prefer. Paul astonishes us here by teaching that God works in believers so that they desire to please him. God does not only work externally in believers, trying to persuade them by circumstances to follow him. He grants the very desire to obey him by transforming the heart. So believers are to accomplish their own salvation. But ultimately the credit goes to God for such a change because he grants the desire and the strength to obey the command in Philippians 2:12. The seriousness of the command is by no means lessened by the above explanation. One must work to be saved! And yet this work is absolutely dependent on God's transforming work, and the latter is the only basis on which the former can be accomplished. In fact, the indicative guarantees the imperative will become a reality.

Romans 6. Romans 6 demonstrates that the indicative is the foundation for the imperative. Those baptized into Christ have shared in his death and will share in his resurrection (Rom 6:3-5). When Paul speaks of being united in Christ's resurrection (Rom 6:5), it is likely that the future resurrection is envisioned rather than a present resurrection with Christ, for the future tense should be understood to denote a future time. Those baptized into Christ, by

---

[6]So Blaise Pascal, *Pensées*, trans. A. J. Krailsheimer (New York: Penguin, 1966), p. 74.

[7]This view of the will is powerfully defended by Jonathan Edwards (*Careful and Strict Enquiry into the Modern Prevailing Notions of That Freedom of Will*, ed. P. Ramsey [New Haven, Conn.: Yale University Press, 1957]) and has never, in my judgment, been refuted successfully.

virtue of sharing his death and the promise of his resurrection, have died to the power of sin (Rom 6:2). The "old person" *(palaios anthrōpos)*, the person we are in Adam, "has been crucified together" with Christ (Rom 6:6; cf. Gal 2:20). Thus, the body dominated by sin has been stripped of its power *(katargeō* in Rom 6:6), and believers are now freed from the dominion that sin exercised over them when they were in Adam.

The image of dying to sin suggests at first glance that it is impossible to sin. A corpse does not commit sins! Once again, however, the "already but not yet" is crucial for discerning Paul's theology. Even though believers have now died with Christ, the resurrection that believers will share with Christ is future (Rom 6:5, 8), signifying that the full inheritance still awaits believers. This is not to say that the power of the resurrection has not invaded the present evil age. Even though the resurrection of believers is future (Rom 8:10-11), Christ has already been raised from the dead (1 Cor 15:12-28), and his resurrection is the guarantee of believers' future resurrection. Moreover, the power of his resurrection has penetrated this age so that believers are now empowered to "walk in newness of life" (Rom 6:4). The future age has invaded the present age, but the future age has not been consummated. So believers have died to the power of sin in the sense that they are no longer under its lordship or dominion (Rom 6:6, 9, 12, 14). A new age of salvation history has dawned so that believers are no longer under the law but under grace (Rom 6:14), and being under grace means that the tyranny of sin has been broken. By the power of God's grace believers have been handed over to a new master so that they now obey him from the heart (Rom 6:17). This obedience from the heart is a fulfillment of the new covenant (Jer 31:31-34; Ezek 11:19-20; 36:26-27), which promises the internalization of the law in the heart. The lordship of sin has been defeated because those who are experiencing the new-covenant work of God now desire to obey him, for what is truly desired in the heart manifests itself in behavior (Rom 6:18, 22).

Believers are set free from the tyranny, lordship and dominion of sin, but that does not mean it is impossible for believers to sin. Conflict with sin continues even though the lordship of sin has been shattered. The indicative proclaims a genuine freedom from the power of sin, and yet the imperative urgently summons believers: "Do not let sin reign in your mortal body so that you obey its desires" (Rom 6:12; cf. Rom 6:13). Since believers have been freed from sin's dominion, they must not let sin exercise its rule in their lives. The truth of the indicative is a vague and meaningless abstraction unless sin's lordship is also dethroned in the everyday lives of believers. The indicative does not eliminate the need for the imperative, for believers must consciously resist desires for sin that arise within them. They must consciously choose "to present" themselves to God (Rom 6:13, 16).

Other texts. Colossians reflects the same tension, although in this letter Paul emphasizes the "already" and downplays the "not yet." The emphasis on realized eschatology does not contradict the earlier Pauline letters, for here the contingency of the letters comes to the forefront. The "philosophy" of the opponents (Col 2:8) trumpeted a path to divine fullness that detracted from the supremacy of Christ, and thus Paul responds by emphasizing the sense in which believers are already complete in Christ (Col 2:9-10). Thus the dominion of "the body of the flesh" has ended with the circumcision (i.e., the death) of Christ (Col 2:11). In baptism believers have died together with Christ (Col 2:11). Unlike in Romans, however, Paul also emphasizes that believers have now been raised with Christ (Col 2:12; 3:1; cf. Eph 2:6). Evil powers have been stripped of their authority through the cross-work of Christ (Col 2:15).

Despite Paul's emphasis on realized eschatology, the tension between the indicative and the imperative remains. Since believers have died with Christ, they should resist the imposition of an ascetic regimen (Col 2:20-23). Indeed, believers who have died with Christ must "put to death" *(nekrōsate)* earthly desires (Col 3:5). The image of putting to death indicates that conquering evil desires is painful, requiring intensity and forcefulness. Evil desires do not shrivel up and depart after conversion. Those who submit to the flesh will die, whereas those who "put to death the practices of the body by the Spirit will live" (Rom 8:13). The metaphor of putting something to death surfaces again here. Obtaining eternal life is conditioned on striking down and destroying evil desires and practices. Such victory over sin, however, is based on the indicative (Rom 8:1-4, 12), and it is accomplished "by the Spirit" (Rom 8:13). Paul is not suggesting that believers can conquer sin in their own strength. Believers have been raised together with Christ (Col 3:1), but this does not mean that they are transported out of this earthly realm. They must renounce the things of the earth and seek the things above (Col 3:1-2). The fullness of glory will be theirs only when Christ appears in glory (Col 3:4).

We have already seen that "the old person" *(ho palaios anthrōpos)* whom we are in Adam has been crucified with the second Adam, Jesus Christ (Rom 6:6). Hence, Paul urges believers to live on the basis of the indicative. Similarly, in Colossians 3:8-9 believers are exhorted to put off *(apothesthe)* evil attitudes and actions, such as anger and evil speech. The basis for this exhortation is that they "have put off the old person with its practices and have put on the new person who is being renewed to knowledge according to the image of the one who created him" (Col 3:9-10). Here the imperative does not take precedence over the indicative but vice versa. Believers are to remove evil from their lives precisely because they have already shed themselves of the old Adam and have clothed themselves with the new Adam. This new clothing becomes theirs at baptism: "For as many as have been baptized into Christ have been clothed with Christ" (Gal 3:27). At conversion believers have stripped off the old Adam and put on the new. And since they are in the new Adam, they should live as members of the new humanity. The indicative is the basis and foundation for the imperative, and yet carrying out the imperative is not automatic. Believers face the danger of living under the dominion of the old Adam, so they must aggressively resist evil and passionately pursue righteousness.

We have seen in both Colossians 3 and Galatians 3 that believers are already clothed with Christ. Yet in Romans 13:14 Paul says, "Put on the Lord Jesus Christ and do not make provision for the flesh with reference to its desires." Believers have already clothed themselves with Christ, and yet Paul summons them to put Christ on! The indicative should not swallow up the call to put on Christ so that the imperative is minimized or explained away. Nor should the imperative be given the place of prominence so that the indicative loses its foundational character. Romans 13:11-14 demonstrates that the Pauline imperatives can be summarized as putting on the Lord Jesus Christ. Believers have put on Christ, and yet they must choose to put him on. Putting on Christ involves removing "the works of darkness" and clothing oneself with "weapons of light" (Rom 13:12). Those who have been grasped by the indicative must also grasp the imperative. The last sentence is a restatement of Philippians 3:12. Paul ardently pursues the eschatological prize (Phil 3:13-14) so that he will grasp (*katalambanō*) it, for he has already been grasped (*katelēmphthēn*) by Christ Jesus. Paul's stretching for the goal and his ardent pursuit of it are rooted in his being grasped by Christ Jesus.

The infinitives in Ephesians 4:22-24 should be understood as the object of the verb *were taught*, and thus they should be construed as imperatives. Even though the "old person" has been crucified with Christ (Rom 6:6) and stripped off at conversion (Col 3:9), the believers in Ephesus must "put away" (*apothesthai*) the "old person" (Eph 4:22) and continue to be renewed in their thinking (Eph 4:23). Believers must "be clothed" (*endysasthai*) with the "new person" (Eph 4:24). Paul articulates in some detail in subsequent verses what is involved in putting off the old and putting on the new (Eph 4:25—

5:21). Concrete and specific attitudes and actions are forbidden (e.g., lying, stealing, bitterness) or mandated (e.g., imitating God, exposing deeds of darkness). The imperatives are not ultimately sundered from the indicative. Being clothed with the new person is rooted in the work of God since the new person "has been created by God in righteousness and holiness of the truth" (Eph 4:24). Nonetheless, believers must put off the old person and clothe themselves with the new. This is not to say that the indicative and the imperative are in cooperation. It is better to say that they are in correlation with one another.

Living Between the Times in the Power of the Spirit

We have seen previously that those who are in the flesh are dominated by the present evil age. Believers, however, are no longer "in the flesh but in the Spirit, if the Spirit of God lives in you" (Rom 8:9).[8] Paul clarifies that only those, and thus all those, who have the Spirit belong to God (Rom 8:9; cf. Rom 8:11). God's church is his temple, which is characterized by the indwelling of the Spirit (1 Cor 3:16; Eph 2:22; cf. 2 Cor 6:16). Christians individually have the Spirit since their bodies are a temple of the Holy Spirit (1 Cor 6:19). And the mark of new life is that God has given his Spirit to believers (1 Thess 4:8). The hallmark of believers is that "we have received the Spirit which is from God" (1 Cor 2:12). And so believers are aptly described as "spiritual" *(pneumatikos)* since it is impossible for anyone who belongs to Christ to be unspiritual (1 Cor 2:15; cf. 1 Cor 2:14-15). Thus, when Paul addresses "the spiritual" in Galatians 6:1, he is not calling on the spiritual elite but on all believers. The reception of the Spirit comes from hearing with faith and not by doing the works of the law (Gal 3:2, 5). God pours out his Spirit on those who trust his promises, not on those who work to merit its reception. The "promise of the Spirit" (Gal 3:14), which is nothing less than the blessing of Abraham, is received by faith. Those who are God's "sons" *(hyioi)* have received the Spirit (Gal 4:6). Or, as Galatians 4:29 says, believers are those who "are born according to the Spirit."

The Spirit is the emblem that the promises of the coming age are realized. Joel promises that God will pour out his Spirit on his people (Joel 2:28-32).

---

[8]For a full-orbed theology of the Holy Spirit in Paul, see Gordon D. Fee, *God's Empowering Presence: The Holy Spirit in the Letters of Paul* (Peabody, Mass.: Hendrickson, 1994); cf. Max Turner, *The Holy Spirit and Spiritual Gifts in the New Testament Church and Today* (Peabody, Mass.: Hendrickson, 1998). See also Volker Rabens, "The Development of Pauline Pneumatology: A Response to F. W. Horn," *BZ* 43 (1999): 161-79.

In Ezekiel the fulfillment of God's promises is coordinated with the outpouring of the Spirit (Ezek 11:19-20; 36:26-27). The new exodus of Isaiah is linked with the pouring out of God's Spirit (Is 44:3). When Paul refers to all of God's promises being fulfilled in Christ, the Spirit is included among those promises (2 Cor 1:20, 22). Indeed, the anointing in 2 Corinthians 1:21 is probably a reference to the Spirit. In any case, the Spirit is clearly in view in 2 Corinthians 1:22: God "sealed us and gave us the down payment of the Spirit in our hearts." The notion that the Spirit is God's "seal" (*sphragizō*) and "down payment" (*arrabōn*) is reiterated by Paul elsewhere (down payment in 2 Cor 5:5; seal and down payment in Eph 1:13-14). The sealing of the Spirit signifies the authenticating work of the Spirit. The gift of the Spirit documents that believers truly belong to God, and the Spirit is the mark of his ownership in the hearts of believers. The seal also verifies the indelible work of God, for the one who is sealed "has been sealed for the day of redemption" (Eph 4:30). The sealing of the Spirit attests that believers belong to God and guarantees that they will be his on the day of the Lord. The down payment of the Spirit expresses the "already but not yet" character of God's work. The Spirit as God's down payment verifies and guarantees that he will complete the salvific process inaugurated. The same idea is communicated in the phrase *first fruits of the Spirit* (Rom 8:23). The context of Romans 8:23 indicates that the first fruits are a prelude to and a promise of final redemption.

The foundational work of the Spirit. In Paul's theology the gift of the Spirit is especially associated with the power to live a new life. This conception also flows from the Old Testament (Ezek 11:19-20; 36:26-27) where the gift of the Spirit empowers people to obey God's law. We have already observed in Galatians that the gift of the Spirit is not predicated on observance of the law. The Spirit is granted to those who respond in faith to the word of the gospel, to the message that Jesus the Messiah is the crucified and resurrected Lord, who was handed over for our transgressions and raised for our justification (Rom 4:25). Paul can summarize the inception of the Christian life as "having begun in the Spirit" (Gal 3:3), or as we saw in Galatians 4:29, being "born according to the Spirit." Those who genuinely, from the heart, confess that Jesus is Lord do so by the Holy Spirit (1 Cor 12:3). Confessing Jesus as Lord is not the product of human devotion or effort; it is the result of the Spirit's supernatural work. Titus 3:5 attributes "regeneration and renewal" to the Holy Spirit, signifying that new life is a result of his work in the heart.

Insight into the true nature of things is a gift of God's Spirit (1 Cor 2:6-16). God hides his wisdom from the rulers of this age, and the inaccessibility of

God's wisdom to them is verified by their crucifixion of Christ. Conversely, God predestined this wisdom for the eschatological glory of believers. Believers do not have a native capacity to grasp the truth about God. The hidden things of God—the mystery of his wisdom and knowledge—are incomprehensible to all without the intervention of God. More specifically, the wisdom of God manifested in the crucified Christ is foolishness without the work of the Spirit. The Spirit is the agent by which believers comprehend "the deep things of God" (1 Cor 2:10), "the things which eye has not seen and ear has not heard" (1 Cor 2:9). Indeed, the only pathway for understanding the truth about God is the work of the Spirit, for *only* the Spirit knows "the things of God" (1 Cor 2:11). The wisdom belonging to believers, therefore, does not produce pride, for such wisdom is the gift of the Spirit, predestined before the world began. Unbelievers *(psychikos anthrōpos)* do not welcome the truth about the crucified Christ, nor can they properly assess it, precisely because they lack the Spirit (1 Cor 2:14). No human means exist by which God's truth can be grasped by those without the Spirit. The Spirit himself begets knowledge of the things of the Spirit.

The continuing work of the Spirit. If the inception of the Christian life is by the power of the Spirit, so is its continuance (Gal 3:3). Paul does not posit a discontinuity between the two so that the Christian life is commenced by the supernatural work of God and completed by self-effort. The Spirit who grants new life strengthens believers so that they live in a way that is pleasing to God. Both the commencement and the continuance of the Christian life are animated by the Holy Spirit. Thus, in Galatians "freedom" *(eleutheria)* and living by the Spirit are intertwined. The gift of the Spirit is given in the fullness of time as a result of the death and resurrection of Christ (Gal 4:4-7). And those who have the Spirit are no longer slaves but sons. Those who still live under the dominion of the old age of salvation history are in slavery—sin dominates their lives. Those who have received the Spirit, on the other hand, now have the freedom of sons.

In Galatians 4:21—5:1 Paul connects being under the law, slavery, the present Jerusalem and the flesh. Conversely, freedom, the heavenly Jerusalem, promise and the Spirit are linked. Paul's idea of freedom is not so much freedom from law (in terms of being freed from commandments). He understands freedom from law as freedom from the old era of salvation history, for to be under law is to be under the power of sin (Gal 5:18). The outpouring of the Spirit signals the commencement of the new era in redemptive history, and freedom involves the ability to practice love (Gal 5:13-15). Walking in the freedom of the Spirit does not grant freedom to sin, for the latter is abject slavery. Those who walk in the Spirit conquer the desires of the flesh (Gal 5:16). They manifest the lovely and attractive "fruit of the Spirit" in their lives (Gal 5:22-23). Envy and pride, the most repellent of all vices, are conquered by those who march in line with the Spirit (Gal 5:25-26).

Similar themes are advanced in Romans 8. "The law of the Spirit of life has set you free in Christ Jesus from the law of sin and death" (Rom 8:2). The freedom celebrated here is based on the atoning work of Jesus Christ, who offered himself as a sin offering and took condemnation on himself, so that "there is no condemnation to those in Christ Jesus" (Rom 8:1-3). We see here that the forensic work of Christ on the cross is the basis for the transformative work of the Spirit. The liberating work of the Spirit is granted only to those who are already justified, to those who are already forgiven by God. Those who walk in the power of the Spirit fulfill "the ordinance of the law" (Rom 8:4), that is, they walk in love through the Spirit. Such a reading is confirmed by Romans 8:5-8, where the character of life in the Spirit is sketched in. Some read these verses as an exhortation, but they are most emphatically not an exhortation but a *description* of life in the Spirit. Paul does *not command* believers to walk in the Spirit in Romans 8:5-8. He *affirms* that those who have the Spirit think on spiritual things. Those who have the Spirit enjoy peace with God, please God and *do what the law commands!*

Freedom of the Spirit. Freedom in the Spirit means that believers are no longer debtors to the flesh (Rom 8:12). The leading of the Spirit described in Romans 8:14 is the same as the leading of the Spirit in Galatians 5:18, and it does not refer to discerning God's will, as if the leading of the Spirit is equivalent to discerning God's directions for one's everyday life. Instead, the leading of the Spirit is equivalent to yielding to the Spirit, to submitting to the Spirit's will. Those who live in submission to the Spirit, who do what he wishes, are God's sons (Rom 8:14). They are no longer slaves to sin and its power; they have become part of the family of God, and the Spirit witnesses to their adoption (Rom 8:15-16).

The freedom wrought by the Spirit is also featured in 2 Corinthians 3.[9] The law of Moses that was written on stony tablets did not change human hearts. The history of Israel reveals the opposite phenomenon. The majority of those in Israel failed to keep the law, and thus both the northern and southern king-

---

[9]For a thorough history of research on 2 Cor 3, see Scott J. Hafemann, *Paul, Moses and the History of Israel: The Letter/Spirit Contrast and the Argument from Scripture in 2 Corinthians 3,* WUNT 81 (Tübingen: J. C. B. Mohr, 1995), pp. 156-86.

doms experienced exile. The Old Testament prophets proclaim that exile is the consequence of sin, of failure to keep God's Torah. They also promise, however, that God will pour out his Spirit so that his people will keep the Torah and experience his blessing (Is 44:3; Jer 31:31-34; Ezek 11:18-19; 36:26-27). The letter of the law—the mere commandment of the law without the power of the Spirit—kills (2 Cor 3:6). The Spirit gives life so that the people of God are able to keep his commands. Paul has such confidence in his ministry because the Spirit is poured out into people's hearts through the preaching of the gospel. The Mosaic covenant was a ministry of death precisely because the law was not accompanied (generally speaking) by the Spirit (2 Cor 3:7). The Israelites could not gaze intently on Moses' face because it reflected God's glory, and in their sinful and stiff-necked state the experience of God's glory brought them judgment rather than freedom. The Spirit now, however, grants freedom; and this freedom, as described in Galatians and Romans, involves the ability to keep God's commands (2 Cor 3:17). If the stiff-necked Israelites could not look on Moses' face without incurring judgment (hence the veil), so that the effects of judgment would not be experienced, then those in the Spirit can gaze on God's glory with unveiled faces without being liable to judgment (2 Cor 3:18). Indeed, as they gaze on the beauty of God's glory, they are transformed "from glory to glory," and this gradual transformation is itself the work of the Spirit (2 Cor 3:18). The new-covenant ministry is superior because it leads to a new quality of life.

A continuing struggle with sin. Paul's emphasis on freedom and the ability to keep God's commands could be interpreted in a one-sided way. At first glance it might suggest perfection in this present age. Once again the "already but not yet" is crucial in formulating Paul's theology. He highlights the newness of the Spirit and our ability to live a new life (Rom 6:4) because the gift of the new age has arrived. Paul emphasizes the eschatological gift of the Spirit since the outpouring of the Spirit is a stunning fulfillment of the promises of the old covenant. Nonetheless, he acknowledges that redemption is not yet completed; he does not fall prey to an overrealized eschatology. Even in 2 Corinthians 3, perhaps the place where Paul emphasizes most sharply the discontinuity between the old and new age, he acknowledges that those who have the Spirit are not completely transformed: "We are changed from glory to glory" (2 Cor 3:18). Absolute and total glory is not yet ours. A gradual process occurs in which we are changed from glory to glory. It follows, then, that sin still exists in the lives of believers.

This is even clearer in Galatians. Paul writes to those who have the Spirit, and yet they are faltering from their calling in Christ! Of course, the same observation could be made regarding the Corinthians. Life in the Spirit cannot be reduced to autopilot or cruise control. And although the believers in Corinth received the Spirit by faith, Paul is concerned that they may depart from their first steps (Gal 3:1-3). Apparently, believers need admonitions to live by the Spirit. This is confirmed by Galatians 5, where believers are urged to "walk by the Spirit" (Gal 5:16). Such an admonition is needed because in the present age, warfare between the Spirit and the flesh exists (Gal 5:17). Even though believers have the Spirit, desires from the flesh still arise within them. This is hardly the state of one who is perfected. Paul expects believers to have such desires; they are treated as part of the warfare of Christian existence. He teaches them that such desires are overcome by walking in the Spirit and being led by the Spirit. Even though believers "live by the Spirit," they must also "march in line [stoichōmen] with the Spirit" (Gal 5:25). They must "sow to the Spirit" in order to obtain eternal life (Gal 6:8). Such exhortations demonstrate that conflict continues for those who have the Spirit. Though the Spirit is the source of every good work and though God sustains his people by his grace, yet believers must heed the admonition to follow the Spirit.

Scholars have long disputed whether Romans 7:13-25 relates to believers or unbelievers. The notion that Christian experience is in view goes back at least as far as Augustine, and it was also advocated by both Martin Luther and John Calvin.[10] The struggle with sin continues, it is observed, as long as believers are in the flesh. The very longing to keep God's Torah ("I delight in the law of God in the inner person" [Rom 7:22]), it is argued, is only true of regenerate persons. Believers are plagued with agony because they aspire to keep the law but find themselves doing what they hate. Such tension in Christian existence is characteristic of those who live between the "already" and "not yet," and believers will continue to battle sin as long as they are in their mortal bodies (Rom 7:24; 8:10, 23). Only at the day of redemption, when the body of sin is removed, will the struggle portrayed in Romans 7 cease.

Scholars bring forward equally powerful arguments for restricting Ro-

---

[10]Eloquent defenders of the view that Christian experience is in view in Rom 7:13-25 include Charles E. B. Cranfield, *A Critical and Exegetical Commentary on the Epistle to the Romans*, ICC (Edinburgh: T & T Clark, 1975), 1:355-70; James D. G. Dunn, "Rom. 7,14-25 in the Theology of Paul," *TZ* 31 (1975): 257-73; Timo Laato, *Paulus und das Judentum: Anthropologische Erwägungen* (Åbo: Åbo Akademi Press, 1991), pp. 137-82; and Don B. Garlington, *Faith, Obedience and Perseverance: Aspects of Paul's Letter to the Romans*, WUNT 79 (Tübingen: J. C. B. Mohr, 1994), pp. 110-43.

mans 7:13-25 to pre-Christian existence.[11] All of Romans 7:7-25 seems to be a commentary on Romans 7:5 ("when we were in the flesh"), whereas Romans 8:1-17 is a commentary on Romans 7:6 ("but now we have been released from the law"). If this is so, then all of Romans 7:7-25 relates to the old era of salvation history. The most powerful argument for seeing the text as pre-Christian is the state of the person under description. Paul is "fleshly, sold under sin" (Rom 7:14), and he is a captive to sin (Rom 7:23). Paul, it is said, could not possibly assert that Christians are still captives to sin and sold under sin, especially since he argues in Romans 6 that believers are no longer slaves to sin. Moreover, in Romans 8:2 he declares that believers are freed from the law of sin and death by the Holy Spirit. My own view is that Paul's purpose in the text is not to delineate whether believers or unbelievers are the subject of the discussion. His purpose is to communicate the inability of the law to transform human beings. Unbelievers, since they are sold under sin, are unable to keep God's law. They may think that they can keep God's precepts, but they are unable to do so since they are in bondage to sin. Paul does not conceive of believers as in bondage to sin, and yet, insofar as believers still live in the flesh, they continue to experience in part what is portrayed in Romans 7:13-25. Believers, when they contemplate their own capacities for moral transformation, are aware of their wretchedness and incapacity to do what God requires (Rom 7:24). They know that they often fall short of God's holy will. The struggle with sin continues until the day of redemption.

The battle with sin is not confined to Romans 7 but also surfaces in Romans 8. Paul celebrates the gift of the Spirit, but he acknowledges that "the body is dead because of sin" (Rom 8:10). Believers have not yet obtained all that is in store for them because they are destined to die, and the mortality of the body indicates the continuing presence of sin. The gift of the Spirit guarantees the promise of resurrection on the last day (Rom 8:11, 23). Believers must be vigilant, for desires from the flesh still strike at us. Thus, Paul warns, "If you live according to the flesh you will die," and conversely, "but if by the Spirit you put to death the deeds of the body, you will live" (Rom 8:13). Life

---

[11]Many scholars argue that pre-Christian experience is intended. Representative of this view are Werner G. Kümmel, *Römer 7 und das Bild des Menschen in Neuen Testament: Zwei Studien* (Munich: Chr. Kaiser, 1974), pp. 57-73, 97-138; Herman Ridderbos, *Paul: An Outline of His Theology* (Grand Rapids, Mich.: Eerdmans, 1975), pp. 126-30; J. Christiaan Beker, *Paul the Apostle: The Triumph of God in Life and Thought* (Philadelphia: Fortress, 1980), pp. 237-43; Douglas J. Moo, *Romans 1—8*, WEC (Chicago: Moody, 1991), pp. 468-96; and Peter Stuhlmacher, *Paul's Letter to the Romans: A Commentary* (Louisville, Ky.: Westminster John Knox, 1994), pp. 114-16.

in the Spirit is not on a plane removed from this world in which one floats above the decisions of everyday existence. Friction continues so that one must kill sinful bodily desires. The word translated "put to death" (*thanatoute*) indicates that such decisions are painful and hard. And yet putting to death sinful desires and actions is accomplished "by the Spirit." That is, believers ultimately do not keep these commands in their own strength but by relying on the Holy Spirit.

But how do believers rely on the Spirit? Perhaps there is a hint to the answer in the comparison between the exhortations in Ephesians 5:18 and Colossians 3:16. Ephesians 5:18 exhorts believers to be filled with the Spirit, and the consequences are joyful singing and thankfulness as well as right relations between husbands and wives, parents and children, and masters and slaves (Eph 5:18—6:9). Colossians 3:16, on the other hand, enjoins believers to "let the word of Christ dwell in you richly," and the consequences are, again, joyful singing and thankfulness as well as right relations between husbands and wives, parents and children, and masters and slaves (Col 3:16—4:1). From the similarities between these two, it is fair to infer that those who are filled with the Spirit are also filled with the word of Christ. Those who attempt to be filled with the Spirit without renewing their minds (Rom 12:2) are prone to fanaticism and irrational enthusiasm. On the other hand, 1 Thessalonians 1:5 at least implies that there can be a proclamation of the word that lacks the Spirit and power. Some may rely on the word and not the Spirit and become arid and intellectualistic, lacking freshness and vibrancy. The Spirit and the word must work together. Such an idea coheres with Ephesians 6:17, for the "sword of the Spirit" is identified as "the word of God." The desires of the flesh are conquered, then, by filling one's mind with the word of God, and one prays that the Spirit will beget faith in the promises and threats of God's word. The Spirit produces such faith through the word, for faith comes from hearing (Rom 10:17; Gal 3:2, 5), and thus the allurements of the flesh are resisted.

The seriousness of the prospect facing believers comes to light in 1 Corinthians 3:1-4. Paul addresses believers who are living as though they were still in the flesh. One should not conclude from this text that there are distinct classes of Christians—some living in the flesh and some in the Spirit. All believers are "spiritual," or they are not believers at all. In the interval between the "already" and "not yet," however, the struggle with the flesh continues. Believers can lapse into behavior that is characterized by the flesh. Such behavior is hardly a middle ground that can continue to be occupied.

Either one repents and obtains the promises of the kingdom (1 Cor 6:9-11), or one pursues the desires of the flesh and faces the prospect of eternal judgment (Rom 8:13; Gal 6:8-9). Those who have the Spirit need to pray (Eph 3:14-19) for power to live a godly life. Paul prays that those who have the Spirit will "be strengthened with power through the Spirit in the inner person" (Eph 3:16). Those who have the Spirit need to be empowered by the Spirit. Christ lives in believers' hearts by the Spirit (Rom 8:9-10), and yet Paul prays that "Christ may dwell in your hearts by faith" (Eph 3:17). Believers need to experience the Spirit they already have. Prayer unleashes the power of the Spirit in us. The "inner person" (2 Cor 4:16), which is renewed daily, is reinvigorated by the Spirit (cf. 2 Cor 3:18). While believers wait for the day of the Lord, they pray for the Spirit's power and strength as they undertake the tasks before them.

The New Creation

Closely tied to the work of the Spirit is the "new creation" theme in Paul. Isaiah, in promising the new exodus in which God's people would be liberated, linked it with the new creation (Is 42:9; 43:18-19; 48:6-7; 65:17; 66:22). The new creation is the fulfillment of God's saving promises, and Paul heralds the passing away of "old things" and the commencement of "new things" (2 Cor 5:17) in the "new creation" *(kainē ktisis)* that has been inaugurated in Christ Jesus. Those who are in Christ are, therefore, no longer to be appraised in terms of the flesh (2 Cor 5:16). The new creation becomes a reality through the cross of Christ, which effects reconciliation and righteousness (2 Cor 5:15-21). The contrast between the new creation and the flesh emerges in Galatians 6:12-16 as well. Those who promote circumcision pander to the flesh and long for praise from others (Gal 6:12-13). Paul's desire to gain praise from others, however, has been severed by the cross of Christ (Gal 6:14). The centrality of the cross is such that both circumcision and uncircumcision are trivial. The cross is central since it is the means by which the "new creation" is inaugurated (Gal 6:14-15). Those who enjoy the new-creation work of God have died to the power of the world through Christ's cross. The Israel of God is no longer composed of ethnic Jews or proselytes. The true Israel consists of those who have been crucified to the world and participate in the new creation (Gal 6:16).

God's creative work also accounts for his work in his people's lives. When Paul ponders grace, he explains it in terms of God's creative act (Eph 2:1-10). Those who are dead in trespasses and sins come alive by virtue of God's grace. God's grace is his creative power by which he imparts new life to those who are dead. The analogy to the original creation is striking. God's word in Genesis 1 spoke into existence that which did not exist. His word was performative. Similarly, where death reigned God spoke his creative word and people came to life. Second Corinthians 4:6, as we have seen, communicates the same truth. God's creative light shone on those who were blinded by Satan and awakened them to the glory of God in the face of Christ. The new Adam "has been created according to God" (Eph 4:24)—it is a miracle of his grace.

Conclusion

Believers are enabled to live a new life by virtue of the work of Christ on their behalf and through the power of the indwelling Holy Spirit. God's work, however, does not cancel out the response of human beings but establishes it. The indicative is the basis for the imperative, and Paul summons his churches to live out the gospel they have embraced.

11

FAITH & HOPE

The Ground of Perseverance

We concluded the last chapter by seeing that believers can only please God by the power of the Holy Spirit. In this chapter we examine the necessity of perseverance in Pauline theology, though such perseverance is itself a result of the power of God.[1]

Hope and Perseverance

One of the marks of authentic faith is perseverance, and faith perseveres because it is sustained by hope. That faith involves hope is apparent from 1 Thessalonians 1:9, which is a classic description of conversion. The Thessalonians "turned" *(epistrephō)* to God and away from their idols in order "to serve" *(douleuein)* "the living and true God." Faith involves a radical turning to the one and only God, and the shift in loyalty signifies a new vision of the future. A new faith always implies a new hope, and this is verified by the next verse in 1 Thessalonians. The Thessalonians renounced their idols and

---

[1]For a study of perseverance and assurance, see Thomas R. Schreiner and Ardel B. Caneday, *The Race Set Before Us: A Biblical Theology of Perseverance & Assurance* (Downers Grove, Ill.: InterVarsity Press, 2001). For an excellent history of interpretation on the matter of perseverance and apostasy, see B. J. Oropeza, *Paul and Apostasy: Eschatology, Perseverance and Falling Away in the Corinthian Congregation,* WUNT 2/115 (Tübingen: J. C. B. Mohr, 2000), pp. 1-34. Oropeza investigates 1 Cor 10:1-13 and argues for an Arminian position.

pledged their service to God, waiting for the return of Christ, confident that
he would deliver them "from the coming wrath" (1 Thess 1:10). Genuine faith
is always a persevering faith because it is animated by the hope that the God
who called believers to himself will save them from his wrath on the day of
the Lord.

When Paul epitomizes the life of faith, he says "we walk by faith not by
sight" (2 Cor 5:7). This statement is nestled in a discussion of the future hope
of believers (2 Cor 5:1-10). We do not presently grasp or see (Rom 8:23-25) the
redemption of our bodies. To the contrary, present existence is marked by
groaning (Rom 8:23; 2 Cor 5:2, 4), by the corruption of the outer person (2 Cor
4:16) and by relentless afflictions (Rom 8:17-39; 2 Cor 4:17). What we see, in
fact, contradicts hope (2 Cor 4:18), for the suffering of present existence suggests that hope is an illusion. Such difficulties are no different from those
Abraham faced, for it seemed that the circumstances of his life would quench
his hope of having a child through Sarah. He was nearly a hundred years old,
and Sarah was too old to bear children (Rom 4:19). His faith persisted, however, because it was animated by hope. He believed that God could do the
impossible and that he would be true to his promise (Rom 4:20-21). Similarly,
the eschatological hope of believers rests on the crucified and risen Lord
(Rom 4:24-25). True hope is grounded on the resurrection of Christ, and with
this hope believers can cast themselves on God in the midst of the vicissitudes of life.

Hope is vital for Christian existence, since both faith in Christ and love for
other believers are grounded in hope: "We have heard of your faith in Christ
Jesus and of the love that you have for all the saints, because of the hope laid
up for you in heaven" (Col 1:4-5 NRSV). Believers will not be able to take risks
in displaying love for others, nor will they continue to exercise faith in the
present unless they have confidence in the future. The indissoluble link
between perseverance and hope is articulated in 1 Thessalonians 1:3, "the
endurance of hope." The word *hope (elpidos)* here is a subjective genitive, indicating that endurance stems from hope. Hope is the root and endurance is the
fruit. Since hope is essential for persistence in the faith, Paul prays that
believers will grasp the hope of their calling (Eph 1:18).

If anything can dampen hope, it is the affliction and suffering that beset
believers. Paul anticipates this obstacle, reminding believers that afflictions
are God's destined pathway (*keimetha*, 1 Thess 3:3) for every believer (1 Thess
3:3-5; cf. Acts 14:22). Relief from afflictions will come only at the revelation of
Jesus Christ from heaven (2 Thess 1:7). In the meantime the pressures of life

are the means by which believers are "made worthy of the kingdom of God" (2 Thess 1:5, 11). Thus, Paul summons believers to "exult" *(kauchōmetha)* in their troubles, for their sufferings are the gateway to endurance, endurance results in tested and approved character, and such character begets further hope (Rom 5:3-5). The sufferings of life are the crucible from which emerges a godly character. In a paradoxical way suffering actually produces more hope, for when believers suffer and manifest godliness they are assured that God is truly working within them. Their hope increases because they become convinced that God is actually working out his plan of salvation in them. This is not to say that danger does not lurk when sufferings strike. Believers are tempted to lose heart because of the severity of their sufferings (2 Cor 4:16). To avert despair they must lift their eyes from the visible to the invisible (2 Cor 4:18), reminding themselves that God is using these very sufferings as the means by which "the inner self is renewed every day" (2 Cor 4:16) and that such afflictions will not last forever. Indeed, such afflictions are producing an "eternal weight of glory" (2 Cor 4:17) for believers. In light of the great reward—hope!—that is promised, the pressures of this age are deemed to be light and momentary (Rom 8:18; 2 Cor 4:17).

Once we grasp that suffering is the means by which believers are made worthy of God's kingdom, we understand why Paul views his imprisonment as resulting in "salvation" on the last day (Phil 1:19). Some interpreters understand this verse to refer to his release from prison, but there is no reason to define *salvation (sōtēria)* in a way that differs from the rest of Paul's writings.[2] Indeed, the succeeding verse demonstrates that eschatological vindication is in mind, for Paul anticipates that he will not be ashamed at God's judgment on the last day (Phil 1:20). His imprisonment is one means by which God's saving work will be accomplished in his life. This fits with Paul's charge to Timothy. He summons Timothy to endure suffering as a partner in the gospel and to continue to preach and teach the gospel in the midst of opposition. Paul continues to preach the gospel fearlessly because he knows that God will "guard my deposit until that day" (2 Tim 1:12). What sustains Paul in the midst of his sufferings is the confidence that God will reward him with eternal life on the day of the Lord. Those like Onesiphorus, who are faithful and share in suffering, will receive mercy from the Lord on the last day (2 Tim 1:16, 18). Only those who endure will reign with Christ, but those who deny Christ will be denied (2 Tim 2:12).

---

[2]Rightly Moisés Silva, *Philippians,* BECNT (Grand Rapids, Mich.: Baker, 1992), pp. 76-78.

Hope and Assurance

Saints are filled with hope during suffering because they are confident that God will complete what he has begun. Paul recognizes the partnership *(koinōnia)* of the Philippians in the gospel from the time of initial gospel preaching to the day he wrote the letter to the community (Phil 1:5). Their partnership was symbolized by their financial support of the Pauline ministry (Phil 4:10-19), though the partnership was more than financial assistance. Such fruit in their lives persuaded Paul that God was truly at work. He was convinced, therefore, that "he who began a good work in you will complete it until the day of Christ Jesus" (Phil 1:6). The Philippians' initial partnership in the gospel was God's work, and Paul does not envision a situation in which a saving work begun by God will default.

God's faithfulness. First Corinthians 1:8-9 is a remarkably similar text. In 1 Corinthians 1:4-7 Paul rejoices over God's grace in the lives of the Corinthians, but he also inserts an eschatological proviso. The "revelation of the Lord Jesus Christ" is still impending (1 Cor 1:7). Nonetheless, the saints at Corinth need not fear the consummation, for God will confirm them until the end as blameless (1 Cor 1:8). The faithful God who called them will sustain them to the end. The Corinthians will be vindicated on the day of the Lord because God will see to it that he will complete what he has started. In 1 Thessalonians 5:23 Paul prays that God will sanctify believers, asking that they will be kept blameless until the coming of Christ. He then adds, "The one who called you is faithful. He will also do it" (1 Thess 5:24). The logic is similar to that in 1 Corinthians 1:9. Since God initially called the Thessalonian saints into fellowship with himself, he will work so that the Thessalonians will truly be sanctified, and thereby saved, on the day of the Lord. The Thessalonians will experience eschatological salvation—not because they are so noble or godly, but because of God's work on their behalf.

The argument in 1 Corinthians 10:13 is illuminating in this regard. Paul warns the Corinthians about the danger of apostasy in 1 Corinthians 10:1-12. (We shall return to the role of such warnings shortly.) Here we notice that Paul follows such a warning with a remarkable promise in 1 Corinthians 10:13. God's faithfulness is such that he will not allow the Corinthians to be tested beyond their ability: "No temptation has beset you except what is common to human beings. But God is faithful. He will not allow you to be tested beyond what you are able, and will provide with the temptation a way of escape, so that you will be able to endure it." In other words, God will give them the strength to resist apostasy.

The faithfulness of God is regularly linked with the perseverance of the saints, indicating that God's faithfulness is the foundation of, and the reason for, their endurance. In 2 Thessalonians 3:2 Paul contemplates his opposition, asking for prayer since he is opposed by many unbelievers. He veers from the faithlessness of human beings to the faithfulness of the Lord who "will strengthen you and guard you from the evil one" (2 Thess 3:3). Almost certainly Paul reflects on the Lord's prayer where believers beseech the Lord "to deliver us from the evil one" (Mt 6:13). In the 2 Thessalonians text Paul is probably thinking of protection from apostasy, asserting that God is faithful and thus believers will not depart from the faith.

The faithfulness of God involves the fulfillment of his saving promises (2 Cor 1:18-20). We recall from 1 Corinthians 1:8 that God will "confirm" *(bebaiōsai)* believers blameless until the end. In 2 Corinthians 1:18-22 he links God's faithfulness to his promises of "confirming" *(bebaiōn)* and "anointing" *(chrisas)*. Those confirmed and anointed are "sealed" *(sphragisamenos)* and given the "down payment" *(arrabōna)* of the Spirit (2 Cor 1:22). The implication is that God will certainly fulfill his saving promises for those whom he has confirmed, anointed and sealed. The down payment of the Spirit guarantees that God will complete what he has begun. The seal authenticates and documents God's people as his own, and the seal is irrevocable and indelible (cf. Eph 1:13-14). In Ephesians 1:14 the down payment *(arrabōn)* of the Spirit is linked with obtaining the eschatological inheritance, namely, the redemption of the body. Similarly, in Ephesians 4:30 the sealing of the Spirit is "to the day of redemption," suggesting that the seal cannot be broken and that the redemption of those so sealed is certain.

The faithfulness of God to his people emerges in a remarkable text in 2 Timothy 2:13. Paul has just warned that those who deny Christ will be denied before God (2 Tim 2:12). How this fits with the irrevocability of salvation will be considered in due course. What concerns us here is the statement in 2 Timothy 2:13—"If we are faithless, he remains faithful. For he cannot deny himself." Some interpreters understand Paul to say that God is faithful to his promises in the sense that he faithfully carries out his threats to judge his people. That is, God is faithful to his own character in judging those who commit apostasy. Though such a reading is possible, it is less likely. We have seen that God's faithfulness elsewhere in Paul is *always* linked (cf. also Rom 3:3) to his faithfulness to the saving promises he has made to his people. Indeed, in many of the texts consulted above, God's faithfulness is linked with his promise to sustain the saints until the day of the Lord. Moreover, the structure of this line departs from the pattern of the previous lines. In the other three lines the word *and (kai)* commences the "then" clause. The departure from this pattern suggests that Paul moves in a different direction here. The difference from the other verses is also apparent because Paul adds a commentary—"for he is not able to deny himself"—indicating again a departure from the normal structure in the confessional statement. When we compare 2 Timothy 2:12-13 ("If we deny him, he will also deny us. If we are faithless, he remains faithful. For he is unable to deny himself"), the following conclusion emerges. Christ will deny those who commit apostasy, but there is sin and faithlessness that is not apostasy. All believers sin, but not all sin is the same thing as apostasy. We know from reading the Pauline letters that sin was quite common in Christian communities, but Paul does not give up on those who are faltering. He is convinced that the Lord in his faithfulness will preserve those that truly belong to God.

Those falling away. Paul proceeds to speak of Hymenaeus and Philetus, who have deviated from the faith and proclaim that the resurrection has already occurred (2 Tim 2:17-18). They have also influenced others since "they have upset the faith of some" (2 Tim 2:18). This last comment would appear to teach that believers can and do commit apostasy. If this is the case, then the promises that God is faithful and that he will sustain his people would indicate what is generally but not always true.[3] However, the subsequent context clarifies what Paul means when he says that the faith of some has been overturned. He immediately adds that "the foundation of God stands secure, having this seal, 'The Lord knows those who are his' " (2 Tim 2:19). In other words, the defections of some do not ultimately cause the house of God (i.e., the church) to falter, for God has known and ordained from the beginning who belongs to him and who does not. God knows those who appeared to have genuine faith but by their defection demonstrated that their faith was never genuine (cf. 1 Jn 2:19). The seal of God, his authenticating mark on believers, is never shattered and remains irrevocable. Of course, Paul immediately adds that those who belong to the Lord demonstrate that they belong to him by their good works. We shall explore this dimension of Paul's message below. Here we merely note that the defection of some does not call into question the faithfulness of God's promises, for there are always some within the house of God who appear to be part of the people of God and are not.

---

[3] This is the view of I. Howard Marshall, *Kept by the Power of God: A Study of Perseverance and Falling Away* (London: Epworth, 1969).

The same basic perspective is found in 1 Corinthians 11:19. Paul comments on the divisions in the church, saying "that there must be divisions among you so that those who are approved might become manifest among you." We shall see below that the word *unapproved (adokimos)* invariably refers to unbelievers. Conversely, *approved (dokimoi* here) refers to believers. The word signifies those who have been tested and have passed the test. Hence, they are approved and acceptable in God's sight in the sense that they are authentic believers. We can see from this that genuine believers in the community are not immediately apparent. Some who "claim" to be believers are not, in fact, believers. The divisions in the church serve to bring forward those who are authentic and inauthentic. They help sift out the chaff from the wheat. Thus, those who abandon the apostolic faith and the Pauline gospel were never genuinely part of the people of God. The approved become "manifest" *(phaneroi)* as tensions boil in the church.

God's unalterable promise. The unalterable character of God's promise is emphasized for those who love God in Romans 8:28, where Paul promises that "all things work together for good." Such a promise is negated if believers could actually apostatize. Romans 8:29-30 ground *(hoti)* the promise in Romans 8:28. The reason all things work together for good is that a chain of events are a reality for those who love God. They are foreknown, predestined, called, justified and glorified (Rom 8:29-30). Nothing intervenes to break the chain so that all those foreknown will also be glorified. Of course, glorification is in the future, but Paul uses the aorist tense to signify that such glorification is a certainty. Glorification in Romans 8:30 is equivalent to being conformed to the image of God's Son in Romans 8:29, and nothing will obstruct the glorification of those foreknown by God. Some commentators insert the condition that believers will be glorified "if they continue in the faith." Such an observation is true in the sense that no one will be glorified if he or she ceases to believe. But the insertion violates the intention of the text, for Paul's purpose is to teach that the God who first instilled love in the hearts of believers will sustain that love until the end. There is no need to insert the idea that believers will be glorified "if," for the "if" will certainly be accomplished by God himself in the life of believer through the enabling of the Holy Spirit.

Assurance of faith is woven into the Pauline gospel. Those who are justified and reconciled will be spared from God's wrath on the day of the Lord (Rom 5:9-10). God has "appointed" *(etheto)* believers to obtain salvation, not wrath, through Jesus Christ the Lord (1 Thess 5:9). Those on whom God has

set his love, those whom he has elected and called, will experience eschatological glory (2 Thess 2:13-14). No condemning charge will be leveled against
God's elect because he has justified them by the death of Jesus Christ (Rom
8:33-34). Condemning those justified would be a renunciation of the atoning
work of Christ on the cross. God has clearly accepted Christ's death on our
behalf because Jesus Christ is risen from the dead and seated at God's right
hand. Not only has Christ been raised and seated at God's right hand but he
also intercedes for believers. The intercession of Christ is based on his death,
and for God to refuse such intercession is unthinkable. If he rejected Christ's
intercession, he would mock the death of his own Son. Finally, nothing will
separate believers from the love of Christ (Rom 8:35-39). Paul reflects on all
the terrible things that could sever us from God's love, and he notes in
Romans 8:36 that frightful things happen to believers. Christians are afflicted,
persecuted, hungry, unclothed, endangered and martyred. Nonetheless, they
are more than conquerors in the midst of these sufferings (Rom 8:37) not
because they are so noble but because the love that comes from Christ and
God is so powerful that it sustains them through these difficulties. No true
believer will ever apostatize because Christ's love will not let them go.

Some scholars object that believers may turn against Christ's love, that
they can choose to separate themselves from Christ's love. Such an objection
fails to comprehend Paul's teaching. He contemplates the worst things that
can happen in life, such as starvation and martyrdom, because these are precisely the circumstances that could propel one to commit apostasy. Paul
stares apostasy in the face by considering what could cause believers to forsake Christ. And he argues that they will not do so because the love of God
and Christ will not let them go. Nothing in the created order can sever believers from God's love. Their assurance is strong and steadfast, resting on God's
unalterable and irrevocable promises.

Paul's confidence in suffering comes to the forefront in 2 Timothy 4:16-18. At
his trial all his friends abandoned him, and he was left alone. The prospect of
denying Jesus was present, but if Paul denied his Lord, then the Lord would
also deny him before God (2 Tim 2:12). When Paul says, "I was rescued from
the lion's mouth" (2 Tim 4:17), he does not mean that he was rescued from
death. He means that he was strengthened to proclaim the gospel and prevented from committing apostasy. This reading is confirmed by 2 Timothy 4:18:
"the Lord will rescue me from every evil work and will save me into his heavenly kingdom." Paul uses the same verb *rescue (rhyomai)* that he used in 2 Timothy 4:17. Second Timothy 4:18 certainly does not mean that God will rescue

Paul from death in the future since Paul knew death was imminent. Paul affirms that God will prevent him from committing apostasy, and *in this way* he will "save" *(sōsei)* him and induct him into the kingdom. Paul does not absolve himself of responsibility in this matter, and yet his faithfulness is ultimately due to God's rescuing and saving work. God fortifies Paul so that he will remain faithful to the gospel no matter what the cost, even if the cost is his own life.

Paul's personal experience fits with his teaching in Ephesians 5:25-27. Paul constructs an analogy between Christ's relationship with the church and a husband's relationship with his wife. Christ displayed his love for the church in giving his life as an atoning sacrifice for her benefit (Eph 5:25). His purpose in doing so is the sanctification of the church, namely, so that the church on the last day would be presented before God as holy and blameless, without spot or wrinkle (Eph 5:26-27). We must see that this text is not an exhortation. Paul elsewhere urges believers to live sanctified and holy lives. Here his purpose is to focus on what Christ secured for the church through his death. Christ's church will be presented as holy and blameless because Christ has obtained this end through his atoning sacrifice. God's church will obtain the eschatological reward not because she is so strong or spiritually committed, but because Christ's death has achieved her sanctification.

The Relationship of Perseverance to Assurance

The role of good works in Romans 2. It would be a terrible mistake to conclude from Paul's emphasis on assurance that perseverance in the faith is unnecessary. One must not cancel out the other pole of the biblical witness in order to sustain assurance. Perseverance in the faith is absolutely necessary to maintain assurance. Paul does not encourage anyone to believe that eternal life will be theirs if they persist in disobedience. The statement that God "will render to each one according to his works" (Rom 2:6) is not hypothetical, nor is the assertion that "the doers of the law will be justified" (Rom 2:13). Some consign these statements to mere hypothesis or even label them as contradictory since elsewhere righteousness is said to be apart from works of law (e.g., Rom 3:20).[4] A contradiction is unlikely inasmuch as Paul did not forget what

---

[4]For a fuller discussion of these issues, see Thomas R. Schreiner, "Did Paul Believe in Justification by Works? Another Look at Romans 2," *BBR* 3 (1993): 131-58. Kent L. Yinger (*Paul, Judaism and Judgment According to Deeds,* SNTSMS 105 [Cambridge: Cambridge University Press, 1999]) demonstrates the pervasiveness of the motif and the improbability of a hypothetical interpretation. His own conclusion, however, falls short in terms of an adequate theological synthesis of the data.

he wrote in chapter 2 when he added chapter 3, especially since the argument of Romans is well organized and sustained. The hypothetical interpretation is more attractive, for how can Paul say that people are not justified by works of law and also say that righteousness is by doing the law? The hypothetical interpretation solves the problem by saying that *if* someone does the required works, he or she will be righteous before God. According to this view, Paul concludes that all fall short (Rom 3:23), that none do what the law requires. Even though righteousness is available, in theory, by doing the law, no one keeps the law; and so the only pathway to a right relation with God is faith in Jesus Christ.

If the hypothetical interpretation is correct (and it may be), nothing central to my understanding of Paul is threatened. On the other hand, the problem with the hypothetical interpretation surfaces at the end of Romans 2. Uncircumcised Gentiles who keep the ordinances of the law (Rom 2:26) and observe the law (Rom 2:27) will judge Jews on the last day. Not only will they judge the Jews, they are also the true circumcision and true Jews (Rom 2:26, 28). One could reply that this illustration is simply introduced as a foil. Paul does not seriously believe any Gentiles actually keep the law. Nor does he literally think the Gentiles will pass judgment on the Jews on the day of judgment. We shall take up the last objection first. Paul probably does not have in mind a court scene in which Gentiles will literally condemn the Jews, but he does have in mind an event in which the Gentiles' right standing with God will condemn the Jews who have squandered their advantages. The point of Romans 2:27 is that the Jews will be condemned by the Gentiles because the latter kept the law, while the former did not. The concept is similar to Jesus' indictment of his contemporaries. The Ninevites and the Queen of the South (Mt 12:41-42) will condemn the Jews on the day of judgment because they responded to God's revelation to them, whereas the Jews rejected the greater revelation given through Jesus. Jesus is scarcely saying that the Ninevites and the Queen of the South will literally stand up at the judgment and condemn the Jews. The argument is that the positive response of such Gentiles will stand in contrast to the negative response of the Jews, and that God will present the Gentiles' positive response to indict the Jews for failing to believe. Paul uses a similar argument here. The Gentiles will condemn the Jews on the last day because the Gentiles observed God's law, whereas the very recipients of God's law transgressed it. On the day of judgment God will use the conversion of the Gentiles as evidence to censure the Jews.

That Paul describes a genuine obedience of the Gentiles is confirmed by

Romans 2:29, where true Jewishness and the circumcision of the heart are from the Spirit but not from the letter. On two other occasions (Rom 7:6; 2 Cor 3:6) Paul contrasts the Spirit *(pneuma)* and the letter *(gramma)*, and the contrast in both instances is between the Holy Spirit and the Mosaic law. There is no substantial reason to doubt the same contrast exists here. What is even more interesting is the context of both Romans 7—8 and 2 Corinthians 3. Paul argues at some length in these texts that the law is not the source of life. Those who rely on the Mosaic law to obtain life are enslaved to sin and experience death since the law—although holy and good—provides no power for obedience. The mere "letter" of the law does not enliven but kills. Power for pleasing God comes not from the law but from the Spirit. Those who have the Spirit are enabled to keep God's law and are transformed from within. Similarly, in Romans 2:29 Paul teaches that the circumcision of the heart, which was commanded and promised in the Old Testament (Deut 10:16; 30:6; Jer 4:4) is only accomplished by the Holy Spirit (cf. Jub 1:23). A true Jew does not necessarily have the marks of circumcision; the real Jew is empowered by the Holy Spirit. The reference to the Holy Spirit suggests that Paul does not argue hypothetically in Romans 2:26-27. The keeping of the law by the Gentiles is a real obedience, but it is one that stems from and is inspired by the Holy Spirit. Paul is, therefore, not contrasting the innate abilities of Jews and Gentiles. Both Jews and Gentiles, when their intrinsic capacities are contemplated, transgress God's law and are under the power of sin (Rom 3:9-20). Those who have the Holy Spirit, however, are strengthened to keep God's commands, and thus the new-covenant promises of Jeremiah (Jer 31:31-34) and Ezekiel (Ezek 11:19-20; 36:26-27) are being fulfilled in their lives.

Therefore Paul means what he says in asserting that "the doers of the law will be justified" (Rom 2:13). Such keeping of the law for justification, however, is to be distinguished from righteousness by works of law (Rom 3:20). The latter—righteousness by works of law—refers to the attempt to be right in God's sight on the basis of keeping the law. In this instance the law is viewed as a means by which people can become right with God. This is impossible because human beings are sinners and violate what God commands. But when Paul says the doers of the law will be justified, he has something else in mind. He contemplates the result of the Spirit's work, not the attempt of human beings to be right in God's eyes by virtue of their own works. Righteousness by works of law is rejected because all people sin, and hence those who attempt to be right in God's sight by doing the law are attempting to earn right standing before God. And yet Paul does not dismiss the idea that our lives must be changed in order to be vindicated on the last day. Such changes, though, are due to the transforming work of the Holy Spirit. No boasting is ascribed to human beings for their autonomous effort (Rom 3:27-28). The good works are produced by the power of the Spirit.

The need of a changed life. It is also imperative to see that Paul cannot possibly be speaking of perfection, as if believers do good works perfectly. Perfection will be ours in the eschaton, but in the "not yet" period it eludes believers. When we examine the texts that demand good works for salvation, they must not be interpreted in a perfectionistic framework. Paul envisions a new direction, a new obedience, a new affection in the lives of believers. He does not expect or demand perfection. He knows that sin afflicts us while we are in our mortal bodies (Rom 8:10, 23). He envisions the Christian life as a fierce struggle between competing desires while we are on earth (Gal 5:16-18). And yet the very reality of faith and the genuineness of the Spirit's work must be expressed in concrete ways. The new-covenant work of the Spirit is not abstracted from everyday existence. Paul's adversaries in 2 Corinthians are assessed and found wanting because their works are deficient (2 Cor 11:15). God will judge the works of these so-called believers and send them to destruction (cf. Phil 3:19; 2 Tim 4:14). Conversely, Paul insists that one must do good works to receive eschatological vindication (Gal 6:4-5; 2 Cor 5:10). The reward in these texts is eternal life itself, entrance into the kingdom of God. Even in Galatians, the letter in which Paul proclaims freedom in Christ from the law, he insists that those who practice the works of the flesh "shall not inherit the kingdom of God" (Gal 5:21).

Galatians 6:8 is also remarkably clear. Those who sow to the flesh will reap "corruption" *(pthoran)*, but those who sow to the Spirit will reap "eternal life" *(zōen aiōnion)*. The phrase *eternal life* in contrast to *corruption* demonstrates that one's eternal destiny is at stake. Paul is not merely saying that sowing to the Spirit will lead to increased rewards. Sowing to the Spirit is necessary to experience *eternal life.* Similarly, in 1 Corinthians 6:9 he asserts that "the unrighteous will not inherit the kingdom of God," and he follows this with a list of vices, indicating the kind of lifestyles that exclude people from the kingdom. Indeed, this threat surfaces because the Corinthians are acting like the "unrighteous" *(adikeite,* 1 Cor 6:8), and so Paul reminds them that the unrighteous *(adikoi,* 1 Cor 6:9) will not inherit the kingdom. The words of Ephesians 5 are strikingly similar. Paul focuses on sexual sin (Eph 5:3-5) and then reminds his readers that people who live in such a manner "have no inheritance in the kingdom of Christ and God. No one must deceive you with empty words. For on account of these things God's wrath comes on disobedient people" (Eph 5:5-6; cf. Col 3:5-6). Paul does not demand perfection, but there must be a remarkable change of direction and a new orientation in the lives of believers.

This same idea is expressed in Romans 6:15-23. Paul exhorts believers to submit themselves to God as slaves to righteousness. The slavery of believers is described with reference to obedience, righteousness (Rom 6:16, 18-20) and God (Rom 6:22). This close association reveals that submission to God is necessarily intertwined with obedience and righteousness. Indeed, those who become slaves of sin are threatened with death, "for the wages of sin is death" (Rom 6:23). The death here is certainly eschatological since it is specifically contrasted with "eternal life" (Rom 6:22-23). Once again, the gravity of the exhortation surfaces. Yielding to sin produces death. Submission to God is necessary for experiencing eternal life. It is not the case, though, that God addresses those who are equally poised between death and life. The new-covenant work of God has invaded the lives of believers so that now they are "obedient from the heart" to the pattern of teaching (Rom 6:17). God has installed new desires into believers so that they long for righteousness and obedience. The initiative of God is emphasized in the word *paredothēte* (you were handed over). Believers were handed over to the pattern of teaching. Who did the handing over? The passive here is a divine passive. God handed over believers to the pattern of teaching. The metaphor stems from the world of slavery. God has handed believers over to a new master, so that their obedience is now from the heart.

Romans 8:14-17 proceeds along the same lines. Paul has already emphasized in the near context that believers are indwelt and empowered by the Holy Spirit (Rom 7:6; 8:1-11). Now he relays that those who "are led by the Spirit are sons of God" (Rom 8:14). The Spirit's leading does not involve guidance for everyday decisions but submission to the Spirit's authority. Those who are part of God's family yield to the Spirit's direction. Subjection to sin is equated with "slavery," for the very mark of the Spirit's presence is liberation from sin and a joyful and heartfelt acclamation of God as Father (Rom 8:15). The Spirit also witnesses with our spirits that we are God's children (Rom 8:16). This witness of the Spirit is ultimately inseparable from a changed life, and yet it is not precisely the same thing as our moral transformation. The Spirit communicates in an ineffable way that we are part of God's family. Such communication from the Spirit cannot be objectively discerned since it is subjectively experienced. Nonetheless, this inner witness of the Spirit can never be divorced from obedience. Believers must not herald a subjective witness that is contradicted by their everyday lives.

Evidence from 1 Timothy. The significance of Christian obedience becomes apparent in an astonishing text in 1 Timothy. Paul exhorts Timothy (1 Tim 4:11-16) to live a commendable life and to be devoted to the public reading of Scripture, exhortation from the Scriptures and teaching the Scriptures. The exhortation is summed up in 1 Timothy 4:16 with the words, "Pay attention to yourself and your teaching. Persevere in them." Both dimensions of what Paul emphasized in 1 Timothy 4:11-15 are present. Timothy is to concentrate on living a godly life and on being faithful to apostolic teaching. The reason for this instruction follows in the last part of 1 Timothy 4:16—"For by doing this you will save yourself and your hearers." What is provocative here is that such actions will "save" *(sōseis)* both Timothy and those who listen to him. Some attempt to swerve away from this statement by maintaining that *save* does not refer to eschatological salvation. Such an endeavor cannot succeed, for Paul regularly (especially in the Pastorals) uses *sōzō* to refer to eschatological salvation. Paul can hardly mean that Timothy is ultimately responsible for his own salvation or the salvation of his hearers. This would contradict Paul's insistence that salvation is of the Lord (cf., e.g., 1 Tim 1:12-17; 2 Tim 1:9-11; Tit 2:11-14; 3:4-7). Nor is it persuasive to argue that Timothy's actions have no role in the salvation of his hearers or himself. In that case the wording of the text is jettisoned altogether! Salvation is ultimately of the Lord, for it is his work. And yet the actions of human beings are significant and crucial as well. Timothy's faithfulness is necessary for him to be saved, and his faithfulness plays a role in the salvation of others. On the other hand, such faithfulness in the life of Timothy is ultimately and finally due to God's work in his life. Both of these strands must be held together and in the right order to grasp Paul's theology.

Paul's statement that a woman "shall be saved through childbirth" should be interpreted similarly (1 Tim 2:15).[5] This verse, of course, is the subject of fierce controversy, and it cannot be examined in detail here. To translate the verb *sōthēsetai* as "preserved" (NASB), so that it refers to physical preservation in childbirth, is attractive since it removes the scandal of the text in question.

---

[5]For a more detailed interpretation of this text, in which I interact with other scholars, see Thomas R. Schreiner, "An Interpretation of 1 Timothy 2:9-15: A Dialogue with Scholarship," in *Women in the Church: A Fresh Analysis of 1 Timothy 2:9-15,* ed. Andreas J. Köstenberger, Thomas R. Schreiner and H. S. Baldwin (Grand Rapids, Mich.: Baker, 1995), pp. 146-53.

Craig Keener tries to sustain such a reading by appealing to extrabiblical literature.[6] Two decisive objections render this view unconvincing. First, such a view ignores the meaning of *sōzō* in Paul, where without exception it refers to eschatological salvation. Second, Christian women are not always preserved in childbirth. Many have died—presumably in Paul's day as well! Andreas Köstenberger offers another view, arguing that the salvation in view is protection from Satan and his wiles.[7] He shows that protection from Satan is often at issue in the Pastoral Epistles. Perhaps Köstenberger is correct in seeing preservation from Satan in this text, although the connection is not as clear as Köstenberger alleges. In any case, even if protection from Satan is involved, such protection involves eschatological salvation. Those who fall under Satan's tyranny will not be saved. So how could Paul possibly say that a woman will be saved through bearing children? The idea seems bizarre, and many protest that this would involve salvation by works. The latter objection is too vague to be of any use in the discussion, for we have already seen that Paul believes good works are essential to be saved on the day of the Lord. What would contradict Pauline theology is if such works were the ultimate cause of salvation or if good works were conceived of as earning salvation. The Paul of the Pastorals decisively rejects any notion that salvation is ultimately due to the work of human beings or that human beings merit salvation by good works (1 Tim 1:12-17; 2 Tim 1:9-11; Tit 2:11-14; 3:4-7). But the Pastoral Epistles also emphasize that good works are an essential part of salvation. They are the *evidence* of genuine salvation and the *means* by which salvation is obtained on the last day. They are the product of the Lord's prior work in believers' lives. That Paul does not think exclusively of childbirth is evident because in the last part of 1 Timothy 2:15 he says that women will be saved "if they remain in faith and love and sanctification with sound judgment." What Paul says here is that women will be saved if they persevere in faith, love and Christian godliness. The idea that perseverance is necessary for salvation is mainstream Pauline teaching.

So why does he mention childbirth? It is not because each and every woman needs to have a child to be saved. Paul's discussion in 1 Corinthians 7 indicates that he actually prefers the unmarried state to marriage. It is not convincing to say that Paul (or even a later Pauline disciple!) jettisons or for-

---

[6]See Craig S. Keener, *Paul, Women and Wives: Marriage and Women's Ministry in the Letters of Paul* (Peabody, Mass.: Hendrickson, 1992), pp. 118-19.

[7]Andreas J. Köstenberger, "Ascertaining Women's God-Ordained Roles: An Interpretation of 1 Timothy 2:15," *BBR* 7 (1997): 107-43.

gets 1 Corinthians 7 at this juncture. Nor is the birth in view in 1 Timothy 2:15 a reference to the birth of the Messiah, for a clear reference to the birth of Jesus is lacking in this text. We must face the starkness of the text. Paul actually says that a woman shall be saved through childbirth; and the word *teknogonia* refers to the birthing of children, not the rearing of them (cf. 1 Tim 5:10). We are thus back to the original question—why does Paul say a woman will be saved through childbirth? Probably because the bearing of children marks off the role of women in distinction from the role of men. When we consider what men and women can do in this world, the one thing men can never do is bear children. This task is specifically and exclusively consigned to women. Paul thus employs the part for the whole here. A woman will be saved by living out her Christian life as a woman, fulfilling her specific and God-ordained calling. Such a calling usually (but not always) involves the bearing of children. Paul is not literally demanding that all women have children. He does insist that in order to be saved they must live out their lives in a manner that is true to their female gender. They should not deny the goodness of marriage—contra the false teachers (1 Tim 4:3)—or the beauty of having children.

The perseverance of Paul and the Corinthians. Paul does not merely exhort other believers, Timothy and women about the need for perseverance to be saved. In 1 Corinthians 9:24-27 he directs a similar exhortation to himself. He uses illustrations from the realms of running and boxing to portray the effort needed to obtain the eschatological prize. Paul does not dismiss the need for strenuous human effort in obtaining salvation, even though both the desire and the activity ultimately come from God himself. For, as he asks in 1 Corinthians 4:7, "what do you have that you have not received?" God's gifts can never be used to eliminate human action and responsibility. Instead, his grace establishes and undergirds perseverance. Some understand the crown here as a reference to rewards above and beyond eternal life. If this is true, Paul's eschatological inheritance is not at stake. There are three pieces of evidence, however, which indicate that eternal life is in view. First, in 1 Corinthians 9:23 Paul says that he undertakes his ministry "in order to be a fellow sharer in the gospel." The term *fellow sharer (synkoinōnos)* demonstrates he refers to participation in the blessings of the gospel, not to a reward above and beyond the gospel. Second, Paul exercises discipline in bringing himself under subjection, so that he would not be "unapproved" *(adokimos)* after preaching to others (1 Cor 9:27). In every instance in Paul the term *adokimos* refers to those who will not pass the test, to those who do not belong to the people of God.

In Romans 1:28 those who reject God's revelation of himself are handed over to an "unapproved mind" by God. Paul informs the Corinthians that Jesus is truly in them unless they are "unapproved" (2 Cor 13:6). If the latter is the case, then they do not genuinely belong to Christ. He hopes that the Corinthians will be assured that he as an apostle is "approved," but even if they think he is "unapproved" (a mistaken judgment, surely!), it is acceptable as long as they persist in well doing. Paul says false teachers are "unapproved with reference to the faith" (2 Tim 3:8), and that they are "unapproved with reference to every good work" (Tit 1:16; cf. Heb 6:8). Since *adokimos* elsewhere in Paul refers to unbelievers, it likely does here as well.

Third, and most important, the context favors this interpretation. In 1 Corinthians 9 Paul becomes Exhibit A for the proper use of freedom. At the conclusion of the chapter he glides over into the topic of the danger of freedom, namely, eschatological judgment. Paul fears that the Corinthians may fall into this very trap. Thus in 1 Corinthians 10 he reminds the "knowers"—who feel free to eat even in idols' temples—that even though the Israelites were freed from Egypt, though they experienced a baptism of sorts at the Red Sea, though they experienced an anticipation of the Lord's Supper in eating manna and water from the rock, though they had Christ's presence in their midst, they were still judged by God. The Old Testament precedents are sobering indeed. Israel's destruction is a type of God's eschatological judgment (1 Cor 10:11) and functions as a warning to the church. The Corinthians ought not to think that they can eat in an idol's temple—sharing in the benefits of the temple—and escape God's judgment (1 Cor 10:14-22). One cannot partake of the benefits of Christ's sacrifice by eating at his table and then proceed to eat at the table of idols and share in the "benefits" of demonic powers. God will not tolerate such idolatry. Those Corinthians who presume that they stand firm, that nothing can ever threaten them, must beware lest they fall and are ruined forever (1 Cor 10:12). It seems quite improbable that the topic here is anything besides eschatological destruction. Believers need severe warnings lest they make the error of thinking that they will be saved regardless of their behavior. And yet Paul pauses to comfort them as well in 1 Corinthians 10:13, reminding them that no testing is so strong that it will overwhelm them. God is faithful, and thus he will provide them with the ability to withstand idolatry and apostasy. He will complete the good work he has begun (Phil 1:6). Ultimately, the preservation of the Corinthians depends on God. And yet they cannot use this promise to strip the warning of 1 Corinthians 10:1-12 (and 1 Cor 10:14-22) of its power. It is precisely by

heeding warnings that they will avoid apostasy. To sum up, the context surrounding 1 Corinthians 9:24-27 indicates that the issue of eternal life is in
view in these verses.

Saved by fire in 1 Corinthians 3. In some circles almost every text adduced as
requiring the need for perseverance for salvation is related to rewards. Probably the text most often cited to defend this notion of rewards is 1 Corinthians
3:10-17 since the person whose work is burned up is saved, even though his
work is useless ("If the work of someone shall be burned up, he shall suffer
loss. But he himself shall be saved, but as through fire," 1 Cor 3:15). Some
conclude from this that good works are optional for eternal life, that people
can live Christian lives that show no evidence of salvation and that some
Christians are like those described in 1 Corinthians 3:1-4—"fleshly." This
interpretation fails to read 1 Corinthians 3:10-17 in context and offers a
flawed understanding of 1 Corinthians 3:1-4. First Corinthians 3:10-17 is not a
description of the life of every Christian believer. Paul conceives of the church
in these verses as a building—God's temple (1 Cor 3:16-17), for the church is
the dwelling place of God himself. The foundation of the building (i.e., the
church) is nothing other than Jesus Christ himself (1 Cor 3:10-11). When Paul
speaks of how one builds on the foundation, he has in mind ministers like
Apollos, who build on the foundation or who water what has already been
planted (1 Cor 3:5-9). He is not thinking of all Christians but of the quality of
materials that ministers use to build on the foundation. Ministers who build
with gold, silver and precious stones will find that their work endures on the
fiery day of judgment; but ministers who build with wood, hay and stubble
will find that their work is consumed and destroyed on the last day. It seems
likely that the ministers' work relates particularly to the teaching with which
they build on the foundation.

On the other hand, there are some ministers who destroy God's temple,
who wreak havoc on a particular church (1 Cor 3:16-17). Such ministers will
be destroyed by God and experience eschatological judgment ("if anyone
destroys God's temple, God shall destroy him," 1 Cor 3:17). Ministers who do
a good work will be rewarded ("If the work of anyone remains which he has
built, he shall receive a reward," 1 Cor 3:14). It may be that this reward
involves a distinct reward above and beyond eternal life, though this is disputed.[8] In any case, those ministers whose work is burned (1 Cor 3:15) will

---

[8]For an illuminating study on rewards, see Craig L. Blomberg, "Degrees of Reward in the
Kingdom of Heaven?" *JETS* 35 (1992): 159-72. I do not concur, however, with all of
Blomberg's conclusions.

find that their ministries did not have a lasting effect. They did not build on the foundation with quality materials. Paul does not suggest that such ministers were themselves dominated by evil, nor does he deny that good works were in their lives. It seems to be the case that the shoddy materials refer to teaching that is inadequate, though not heretical, in building up the Christian church. This text, therefore, does not teach that some will enter the kingdom regardless of their evil lives.

Some appeal to 1 Corinthians 3:1-4, where the Corinthians are indicted for envy and strife because of their attitudes toward Paul and Apollos, arguing from this that some Christians are spiritual and others are fleshly. We must beware of reading into this text. On the one hand, Paul does not categorically label the Corinthians as unbelievers simply because envy and strife are running rampant. In the interval between the "already" and the "not yet," Paul knows that believers will sin, sometimes in remarkably immature and foolish ways. His bracing words are intended to rekindle their devotion to Christ and godly living. The Corinthians must throw off secular attitudes that have snared them. On the other hand, Paul does not assure the Corinthians that they are believers either. He does not suggest that they can be assured of final vindication regardless of their behavior. His intention is not to speculate on their standing with God, for he could scarcely know the answer to such a question. Those faltering are exhorted to pursue righteousness because such righteousness demonstrates the genuineness of faith. To continue to live under the dominion of the flesh, with envy and strife in control, would be serious indeed.

Paul similarly reminds the Galatians that those who practice the works of the flesh (including envy and strife) will not inherit God's kingdom (Gal 5:21). No room is provided here for two classes of Christians, some who are spiritual and others who are dominated by the flesh. And yet the Christian life is marked by struggle and battle. Serious defeats may be experienced along the way. Paul does not engage in speculation in such cases as to the authenticity of initial conversion. What interests him is their *present* response to his exhortations. Do his converts continue to trust in Jesus Christ as Lord? If so, they will respond to his apostolic injunctions. The way forward is not by excavating the past to determine whether conversion was genuine. The way forward is by trusting God in the present. Paul believed, of course, that those who genuinely believed would certainly receive the eschatological prize.

Every church has some members who are true believers and some who only appear to be believers. Both genuine believers and so-called believers may fall into serious sin, making the task of distinguishing them difficult. Paul was not a diviner but an apostle. When members of the church sin, he does not pronounce on their state—unless, like false teachers, they stubbornly resist the apostolic gospel (Gal 1:8-9; Phil 3:2). Paul does warn that the person committing incest (1 Cor 5) is in danger of eschatological destruction. Yet even in this case Paul does not say this person will certainly face judgment, nor does he promise that he will be saved. The church is commanded to expel this man from the community in the hope (but not with the promise) that he will be saved (1 Cor 5:5). The same approach is followed in the case of Hymenaeus and Alexander (1 Tim 1:19-20). They are "handed over to Satan so that they will be instructed not to blaspheme" (1 Tim 1:20). Paul does not guarantee what will happen in the future, since he himself does not know. Even in the case of Demas (2 Tim 4:10), who has abandoned Paul because of love of the present evil age, Paul does not pronounce an eschatological condemnation on him. The peril of Demas's situation is clear. Whether he is doomed permanently remains an open question, depending on Demas's future repentance.

In conclusion, 1 Corinthians 3:1-4 does not warrant classifying believers into the categories of spiritual and fleshly. In the interval between the "already" and the "not yet," believers may fall into some astonishing sins. The Pauline exhortations are designed to provoke believers to renounce sin and to continue following God. When one heeds these exhortations, one averts eschatological danger. In such ambiguous cases, pronouncements regarding the spiritual state of Paul's converts is avoided. Paul addresses the situation at hand instead of excavating the biography of those in question.

Identifying some as unbelievers. If Paul is tentative in such situations, why does he assert in other cases that his opponents are unbelievers? Those who proclaim another gospel in Galatians are called "false brothers" (Gal 1:6-9; 2:3-5; 6:12-13). The Philippian opponents are rejected as "dogs," "evil workers" and "the mutilation" (Phil 3:2). They are labeled as "enemies of the cross"—"their end is destruction," they "glory in their shame" and their mind is fixed on this world (Phil 3:18-19). The teaching of the Colossian opponents is dismissed as "empty deception" and "human tradition" (Col 2:8). It accords with "the elements of the world" instead of Christ. Their asceticism indicates reliance on human means of holiness instead of Christ (Col 2:16-19). Other texts could be added (e.g., 1 Tim 4:1-5; 2 Tim 3:1-9) where Paul categorizes adversaries as unbelievers.

What causes Paul to pronounce eschatological judgment on these people when he avoids doing the same in a text like 1 Corinthians 3:1-4? The answer is that Paul condemns forthrightly those who *teach* a different gospel. The texts cited from Galatians, Philippians and Colossians make this clear. These adversaries proclaim a different gospel, a tradition at variance with the Pauline gospel (cf. 2 Cor 10—13). When the gospel is at stake, Paul issues categorical denunciations in order to protect the boundary between the church and the world. Such denunciations, we should also remember, are addressed not to the opponents themselves but to those whom they are attempting to convert. Paul fences off his territory and protects his converts from evil by hurling invectives at false teachers. This is not to say that Paul proclaims a different message to the false teachers. Perhaps, though, he would use a different strategy or approach if he addressed his adversaries directly. In any case, he warns his churches in the strongest terms about opponents so that they will not capitulate to their teaching.

The role of warnings. Paul does not soften his words to his converts when he considers whether they will submit to the teaching of his adversaries. In Galatians 5:2-6 he addresses wavering believers who are tempted by the prospect of circumcision. He asserts that if they receive circumcision, then Christ will not profit them any longer (Gal 5:2). They will be separated from Christ and will put themselves in the impossible position of trying to be right before God by means of the Mosaic law (Gal 5:3-4). Once again, we see that Paul addresses believers in terms of the situation they currently face. He does not say that they will be saved no matter what they do. Nor does he suggest that they are cursed because they are tottering and influenced by the Judaizers. What is crucial is how they respond to the opponents now. They must not submit to their teaching because to do so would involve a renunciation of the gospel of grace.

Warnings and admonitions are a constituent part of the Pauline gospel. The summary of the gospel in 1 Corinthians 15:1-4 asserts that the Corinthians are saved by that gospel "if you hold it fast, unless you believed in vain" (1 Cor 15:2). Eschatological salvation is conditioned on perseverance in the gospel. Paul never views faith as a static reality that cancels out the need for present and future faith. Faith is dynamic and must embrace each new situation.

The same message is communicated in Colossians 1:21-23. The Colossians have been reconciled to God through Christ's work on the cross, and he will present them as holy and blameless before God "if you remain founded and steadfast in the faith and do not move away from the hope of the gospel which you have heard" (Col 1:23). Some interpreters have maintained that the word *if (ei)* here should be translated "since."[9] It is likely these interpreters are imposing a theological preconception on the text here. Recent work on conditional clauses also demonstrates the grammatical implausibility of such a reading.[10] This is a genuine condition. Believers will be presented as holy before God "if" they continue in faith and hope. Those who abandon faith and hope give God a vote of "no confidence." Paul admonishes his readers to continue to believe in order to enjoy the inheritance promised to them.

A similar phenomenon may be observed in Romans 11. In Romans 11:17-24 the Gentiles are warned not to be proud. They may begin to think that they are actually superior to the Jews since many of the latter were pruned from the olive tree and the Gentiles were grafted in. Paul emphasizes the dynamic nature of faith, reminding the Gentiles that they "stand in faith" (Rom 11:20). Therefore, they should "fear" (Rom 11:20-21), for God will not spare them if they depart from the faith. They will only continue to experience God's kindness if they "remain in his kindness, otherwise you also will be cut off" (Rom 11:22). The seriousness of the admonition is breathtaking. Paul fears that the Gentiles will become lax and presume on God's kindness. By taking the warning seriously they will avoid destruction.

In his last letter Paul was still proclaiming the same message. He insists that "if we shall deny him, he also will deny us" (2 Tim 2:12). This saying almost certainly draws on the words of the historical Jesus (Mt 10:33 and par.). Outright and persistent denial constitutes apostasy, and those who deny Christ will face eschatological judgment. We have already seen that Paul follows this warning about denial with an assurance that God remains faithful if we are faithless. We must put these two sayings together in order to understand Paul's teaching accurately. Not all sin is a denial of Jesus, and God remains faithful to his people even if they stumble and fall. Nonetheless, one cannot contemplate denying Jesus casually as if one will be forgiven regardless. Paul probably would not reject the notion that people could be forgiven after such a public denial. Presumably the story of Peter, found in all

---

[9]So S. Lewis Johnson Jr., "From Enmity to Amity," *BSac* 119 (1962): 147.

[10]For assistance in interpreting conditional clauses, see especially the series of articles by James L. Boyer in the *Grace Theological Journal*: "First Class Conditions: What Do They Mean?" 2 (1981): 75-114; "Second Class Conditions in New Testament Greek," 3 (1982): 81-88; "Third (and Fourth) Class Conditions," 3 (1982): 163-75; "Other Conditional Elements in New Testament Greek," 4 (1983): 173-88. Compare also Daniel B. Wallace, *Greek Grammar Beyond the Basics: An Exegetical Syntax of the New Testament* (Grand Rapids, Mich.: Zondervan, 1996), pp. 679-712.

four Gospels, was well known. Thus, repentance after such denials would issue in forgiveness from God. Relying on such forgiveness *before* a denial, though, is highly dangerous, for such a stance fails to see the transformation that may occur in a person who denies Christ. Such a one may have no desire to repent after a denial because repentance by definition involves both a willingness to affirm Jesus on the next occasion and a willingness to endure suffering. No one knows before a denial whether he or she will have hardened themselves beyond repair, and thus the warning stands in all its starkness.

The dynamic nature of faith is displayed in the way Paul responds to his newly planted churches. When the Thessalonians encountered afflictions and troubles, he worries about the genuineness of their faith (1 Thess 3:1-10). He sends Timothy to investigate how the Thessalonians have reacted to trials because he could not tolerate the suspense any longer. He needed "to know about your faith, lest the tempter had tempted you and our labor was in vain" (1 Thess 3:5). If Paul held to a static view of faith, or if he believed that he could easily assess authentic and inauthentic faith, these latter words are almost incomprehensible. Paul would not worry about their faith, for he could be assured that they were all genuine believers come what may. Instead, Paul was uncertain about their status because the genuineness of faith becomes apparent in and through trials. The response to trials is particularly significant because the authenticity of faith is on display when troubles strike. Indeed, Paul rejoices and is full of confidence, for upon hearing that the Thessalonians have responded well to trials, he is persuaded that they are truly believers.

Paul's checkered history with the Corinthians is comparable. The worldliness of this congregation and their attraction to false teachers fills Paul with doubts about their status. After writing the severe letter, he sends Titus to find out how they responded. Paul is filled with anxiety, worried that the meeting with Titus might turn out badly (2 Cor 2:12-13; 7:5-16). He knows that the Corinthians' response to Titus and to his gospel indicates where they stand relative to God. He exults in 2 Corinthians 7:5-16 because their zeal and longing in response to Paul's letter revealed their authentic faith. They repented at receiving Paul's severe letter. Such repentance was not optional, for "God's grief produces repentance resulting in salvation and does not involve regret" (2 Cor 7:10). The repentance the Corinthians expressed was necessary for salvation, as Paul says specifically. There is no thought that the reaction of the Corinthians is inconsequential. Nor is there any suggestion that since the Corinthians are saved their response to the severe letter does not bear on their salvation. One cannot reify salvation so that it becomes a rigid and static reality, impervious to the situations of life. For Paul salvation is worked out in the circumstances of life. He rejoices over the Corinthians' response because it confirms and establishes their standing with God.

Prayer and Perseverance

On the one hand, God has promised to sustain believers until the end so that their faith will not fail. On the other hand, believers are to persevere until the end, vigilantly maintaining their faith and ensuring that their hearts do not grow cold. Added to this is prayer. Paul often prays that God will fulfill his good promises and sustain believers until the end.[11] In some ways prayer is the middle term between these two poles, for in prayer Paul acknowledges that endurance comes from God. At the same time *he prays* that God will intervene and affect human behavior, human actions. When Paul prays for his converts, both the work of God and the behavior of human beings is taken seriously. Yet it is obvious that God's work is primary, fundamental and decisive, for prayer by definition is the acknowledgment that God can change human attitudes and actions.

1 and 2 Thessalonians. We have seen that in 1 Thessalonians 3 Paul rejoices over the continued faith of the Thessalonians, for this confirms to him that their faith is genuine. Nevertheless, Paul prays that he may have an opportunity to visit them and "to complete what is lacking in their faith" (1 Thess 3:10). Even though their faith is growing and increasing, room for improvement exists since faith is not a static quality. Paul immediately prays in the subsequent verses that God will allow him to visit and strengthen them (1 Thess 3:11-13). More specifically, he prays that they will increase in love for other believers (1 Thess 3:12). Such an increase in love is linked indissolubly with an increase in faith, because faith expresses itself in love (Gal 5:6). Those who are trusting God to meet their needs are liberated to meet the needs of others. Growth in love is the pathway to holiness and acceptance before God on the day the Lord returns. For those who are full of love will have "hearts blameless in holiness before God our Father" (1 Thess 3:13). At first glance this may seem to suggest that we can earn an eschatological reward because Paul says an increase in love is necessary for an eschatological reward. No merit theology exists here, however, because it is *God* who strengthens believ-

---

[11]For a practical and useful study of Paul's prayers, see D. A. Carson, *A Call to Spiritual Reformation: Priorities from Paul and His Prayers* (Grand Rapids, Mich.: Baker, 1992).

ers to love more fervently, and it is *God* who strengthens believers in holy love. And Paul *prays that God* will produce such love in his converts. Thus, Paul would say that love is necessary to enjoy God forever, but such love is his work and the result of his grace.

Our above exegesis is confirmed by 1 Thessalonians 5:23-24. Paul prays for the believers, asking that God would sanctify them and keep them blameless at the coming of the Lord Jesus Christ. It would be a mistake to conclude that sanctification is optional for entrance into God's presence or that sanctification is reserved for an elite circle of Christians. We have already seen in Ephesians 5:25-27 that God has secured the holiness of his people through Christ's death. Still, Paul prays that God will fulfill his promise. Paul never responds to promises by absolving himself of the responsibility to pray that such promises will be fulfilled. His prayers, on the contrary, are the very means by which the promises become a reality. The verse following 1 Thessalonians 5:23 supports the interpretation suggested: "The one who called you is faithful. He will also do it" (1 Thess 5:24). Paul does not doubt whether his prayer will be answered, nor does he merely think it *might be* answered. He is *certain* it will be answered. The certainty of an answer does not hinder Paul from praying; it is the sure foundation for his prayers.

The same tension appears in 2 Thessalonians 3:3, 5. We have seen in 2 Thessalonians 3:3 that God's faithfulness is proclaimed. He will strengthen believers and keep them from the evil one; specifically, he will preserve them from committing apostasy. Such assurances do not preclude the need for action or prayer. In the next verse Paul calls believers to keep his commands. Then a prayer is offered—"May the Lord direct your hearts to the love of God and to the endurance of Christ" (2 Thess 3:5). Paul is probably asking God to work in the Thessalonians so that they will love God more and experience the same kind of endurance until the end that Christ had. Second Thessalonians 3:3 affirms that believers will be strengthened by God so that they will not fall into the trap of the devil and renounce their God. Nevertheless, Paul prays that God will so work within believers that he will preserve their love for God and their endurance. We are apt to think that if a promise exists, then prayer is superfluous. Such a dichotomy reveals a difference between Paul's theology and ours.

Praying for love. One must progress in the faith to receive an inheritance, and Paul often prays for his converts and churches. For instance, in Philippians 1:9-11 he asks that the Philippians will grow in love. For Paul, becoming like God means that our lives are lived more and more for others, and this is nothing other than growing in love. *Love* is a plastic word, however, that can be twisted and defined in numerous ways. So he prays that love will be accompanied by knowledge and discernment. Love without discernment easily becomes sentimentality. Discernment is needed so that love will be channeled into what is best, and in turn people who love this way will be "sincere and blameless" when Christ returns.

The prayer in Colossians is remarkably similar (Col 1:9-11). Paul prays that believers will be fully cognizant of God's will. No spirituality that bypasses the mind is endorsed or contemplated. God's will is not communicated in a mystical way that sidesteps our thinking capacities. Understanding and wisdom are needed to do God's will. Only then will we live lives worthy of and pleasing to the Lord. In both of these prayers God is acknowledged as the giver of love and wisdom. In the Colossian prayer he is the one who strengthens believers to carry out his will (Col 1:11).

Prayer to be made worthy. When Jesus returns, unbelievers will be punished and believers will be stunned with the beauty of Christ (2 Thess 1:5-10). Paul prays for believers in light of this future reality. He asks that God will make them worthy of their calling (2 Thess 1:11). Paul has already communicated that believers are made worthy of God's kingdom through suffering and affliction (2 Thess 1:5). Still, he prays that God's intention will succeed, that believers will be made worthy of the kingdom. What is involved in being made worthy of the kingdom? Certainly Paul is not suggesting that believers can merit or earn access to God's presence. Nor is it persuasive to argue that the words *kataxiōthēnai* and *axiōsē* should be defined as "counted worthy" or "considered worthy" instead of "made worthy." The sufferings and afflictions experienced by believers produce an increase of faith and love (2 Thess 1:3-4), so that there is an observable change in the lives of the Thessalonians (cf. Rom 5:3-5).

This interpretation is confirmed by 2 Thessalonians 1:11. One is made worthy when God "fulfills every desire for goodness and a work of faith in power." Paul prays that desires will become strong enough to be translated into actions. He realizes that desires only result in actions by a miracle of grace, and thus he prays that God will fill believers with a delight in what is good. Paul is not satisfied with desires remaining at an abstract level. Desires must be translated into actions and enter the concrete sphere. Even here, however, Paul qualifies the work that is accomplished as a "work of faith." The genitive *faith (pisteōs)* is a genitive of source: the work that is accomplished flows from faith.

A similar prayer occurs in 2 Thessalonians 2:16-17. The prayer, in fact, is confined to verse 17; verse 16 constitutes the introduction and ground for the prayer. In verse 16 Paul reflects on the benefits that belong to those in Christ. Believers are the recipients of God's love. Since Paul has just spoken of the election and calling of Christians (2 Thess 2:13-14)—even linking such with God's love (2 Thess 2:13)—he surely thinks here of the salvation that is promised to believers and that has been guaranteed through Christ. The love of God has brought "eternal encouragement" and "a good hope in grace" (2 Thess 2:16). The emphasis is on the eschatological inheritance belonging to believers. The promise of such an inheritance brings consolation in the midst of painful trials and pressures, and the confident expectation of a glorious future brings rays of sunshine into the gloomiest circumstances. So Paul prays, in light of these very truths, that God will encourage the hearts of believers and strengthen them "in every good work and word" (2 Thess 2:17). The eschatological hope is the foundation for encouragement in present difficulties and for living righteously in the present evil age.

Two prayers in Ephesians. Two of Paul's most beautiful prayers are found in Ephesians (Eph 1:15-23; 3:14-19). The first of these prayers occurs after Paul recounts believers' spiritual blessings (Eph 1:3-14). Paul begins by praying that his readers will grasp the wonder of what is theirs in Christ. They need a "spirit of wisdom and revelation in the knowledge of him" (Eph 1:17), and, as Ephesians 1:18 says, they need "the eyes of their heart enlightened." The perception for which Paul prays cannot be simply an emotional or rational perception. The whole person is included. Paul asks for God's illumination so that his work on their behalf will grip their entire being. Mentally grasping spiritual blessings is insufficient. Believers must absorb the glory, beauty and loveliness of their spiritual inheritance.

Paul prays that they would understand three things in particular: "the hope of his calling," "the riches of the glory of his inheritance among the saints" and "the surpassing greatness of his power toward those who believe." The "hope of his calling" refers to the hope to which God has called believers. Believers should have a firm confidence that their future is glorious, knowing that God has summoned them to a glorious destiny. The riches of the glory of his inheritance is harder to define, but it probably should not be distinguished too specifically from hope. The text specifically identifies the inheritance as *God's,* but the genitive may be one of source, signifying the inheritance God gives to believers. The inheritance, then, designates the future joy that awaits believers. An inheritance is anticipated as the promise of future joy and rest, and so Paul wants believers to understand that the future is one of incomprehensible joy. Lastly, Paul asks that believers will comprehend the power that is theirs in Christ. This last item receives the most attention (Eph 1:19-23). The power that belongs to believers is the same power that raised Christ from the dead and exalted him to the right hand of God. He is now the cosmic Lord over all angelic powers and the head and ruler of God's church. Believers have nothing to fear, for all their enemies have been defeated and destroyed.

The prayer in Ephesians 3:14-19 comes after Paul has explained the unity and solidarity of Jews and Gentiles in Christ (Eph 2:11—3:13). The Father to whom Paul prays and before whom he bows is the one from which every family receives its name (Eph 3:14-15). Human paternity is derivative and secondary, and it was always God's intention that there would be a diversity of "families," or people groups, worshiping before his throne (cf. Gen 12:3). When Paul utters this prayer he does not fear that resources will be inadequate, for God responds "according to the riches of his glory" (Eph 3:16). Paul asks that God will strengthen each believer's inner person with the Holy Spirit. The Holy Spirit and Christ Jesus already indwell believers (Rom 8:9-10), and yet Paul asks that they may reside in our hearts with power. Faith is the instrument that unleashes the power of Christ and the Spirit. On the one hand, it seems that Paul prays that believers will experience the power of the Spirit and Christ *because* they have been rooted and grounded in love. God's love in redeeming them (cf. Eph 2:1-10) begets faith. On the other hand, faith is the channel by which God's immeasurable love is experienced. Knowing and experiencing the love of Christ means that one is filled with the fullness of God. Being full of God is the goal of the Christian life, and no one experiences God's fullness unless he or she is full of his love. Paul prays for such love and fullness because he knows that it is a miracle. No one can conjure up such an experience. No one can demand it. No one can produce it from his or her own resources. Believers need the power of God to experience the love of God. Believers need the power of God to know the fullness of God. Only God creates in us a love for God. And that is why Paul prays.

Romans 8:26-27. Romans 8:26-27 may be one of the most remarkable texts on prayer in Paul. Here the Spirit's assistance in prayer comes to the forefront. This prayer is situated in a context that features the hope of believers (see esp. Rom 8:28-39). The Spirit's prayers on our behalf fortify our hope. We get a better understanding of the text if we see the chiasm in Romans 8:26.

A The Spirit helps

B in our weakness

B' For we do not know what to pray for

A' But the Spirit himself intercedes with unspeakable groanings

The believers' problem is their weakness, but the chiasm reveals that the weakness is not general but specific. Believers have all kinds of weaknesses, but the weakness in mind here is insufficient knowledge relative to prayer. The text, contra to some commentators and translations, does not say that we do not know *how* to pray, if by "how" we refer to the manner in which we pray. Believers are weak in that they do not know *what* to pray for, in terms of the content of prayer.

Surely Paul does not mean to say that believers are always uncertain in prayer. Often we know what God intends for our lives. We can always pray for patience; for experiencing God's love; for faith, hope and love; and so on. Paul considers here the many situations in which we are ignorant of God's will. Life is full of many circumstances, and often we are unsure about the will of God. Nor does God usually reveal his will to us in these situations. Instead the Spirit comes to the aid of believers in such situations. The chiasm helps us determine how the Spirit comes to our aid. He helps by interceding on our behalf with unspeakable groanings. In other words, when we are perplexed about what to pray for, the Spirit helps us by interceding to God for us. What the text means by "unspeakable groanings" *(stenagmois alalētois)* will be investigated shortly, for though the meaning is controverted, the debate diverges from the main point of the text. Romans 8:27 indicates that God, who searches the hearts of all people, knows the mindset of the Spirit since the Spirit intercedes for believers in accord with God's will. This probably means that God always answers the prayers uttered by the Spirit in the affirmative. They are answered in the affirmative because such prayers are invariably in accord with God's will, and God always fulfills his will. The comfort for believers is inestimable. We are often perplexed regarding what God's will is, and therefore we are uncertain in prayer. But the Spirit always prays in accord with God's will. He always knows what God wants. Since his prayers are in harmony with God's design, God always answers the Spirit's prayers positively. The comfort for believers is that God is certainly fulfilling his will in their lives. He is working all things for their good, conforming them to the image of Jesus Christ (Rom 8:28-29). The answers to such prayers may not fit with what believers consciously want, but they are in accord with what we need. Believers are endued with hope, knowing that God is fulfilling his will in their lives.

The Spirit's intercession is carried out through "unspeakable groanings." What does Paul have in mind? Some insist that the experience only fits with speaking in tongues.[12] Those who detect a reference to *glossolalia* maintain that all prayer in the ancient world was audible and vocalized and that the word *unspeakable (alalētois)* may have the meaning "ineffable" instead of "unvocalized." The most significant objection against this interpretation is that not all Christians speak in tongues. In Romans 8 Paul announces the hope that belongs to *all* Christians. Since 1 Corinthians 12 makes it clear that not all Christians speak in tongues, then if Romans 8:26-27 refers to *glossolalia*, only some believers would receive the help from the Spirit described here. Such a division of Christians at this juncture in Paul's argument is highly unlikely. It would tear the heart out of Paul's argument, sundering believers into different camps at the very place he desires to comfort all. Moreover, it is likely that the word *unspeakable (alalētois)* refers to something that is unvocalized, for this is the most natural way of rendering a word that negates speech. Some scholars think that the Spirit's groanings bypass our consciousness, so that we are entirely oblivious to the groanings of the Spirit. This is certainly possible, and it does not affect the meaning of the text in a major way. It seems more likely, though, that the Spirit's groanings coalesce with our own groanings. This fits with Romans 8:27, where God deciphers the mindset of the Spirit by searching our hearts. Presumably he detects the mindset of the Spirit in and through our groanings. These very groanings are produced by the Holy Spirit, and thus they are his groanings as well. In any case, the Spirit's prayers are answered, and God works out his good purpose in the lives of his people.

Perseverance and Satan

The Christian life is fraught with danger, for spiritual forces attempt to hinder believers' growth. No treatise on Satan or demons appears in Paul, nor is there any philosophical discussion about their existence or reality. Paul *assumes* that Satan and demons exist and that they pose serious threats to both believers and unbelievers. Satan is an angel of light (2 Cor 11:14), masquerading his true intentions and duping people so that they do not adhere to the gospel. He is the god of this present evil order, who blinds unbelievers from seeing the glory and beauty of Christ (2 Cor 4:4). He is the spirit effect-

---

[12]See especially Ernst Käsemann, *Perspectives on Paul* (Philadelphia: Fortress, 1971), pp. 127-37, and Gordon D. Fee, *God's Empowering Presence: The Holy Spirit in the Letters of Paul* (Peabody, Mass.: Hendrickson, 1994), pp. 580-85.

ing his will among the disobedient; he is the ruler of the present sphere (Eph 2:2).[13] Paul detects Satan, then, behind the opponents in 2 Corinthians (2 Cor 11:15). Like Satan they dazzle people so that some actually think the adversaries foster righteousness, when in reality they are in bondage to evil. Satan attempts to deceive believers from the simplicity of faith in Christ, just as he deceived Eve in the garden (2 Cor 11:3; 1 Tim 2:14). In 2 Corinthians the deceptive message is one that denies that believers are weak and destined to suffer. It is a triumphalism at odds with the cross of Jesus Christ and the apostolic ministry of Paul. In 1 Timothy 2:14 readers are reminded that Eve was deceived into thinking that she could be like God, the most fundamental and oft-repeated deception in the history of the human race.

Satan's strategy. Satan's goal is to hinder faith and to promote idolatry, since faith is the converse of idolatry. Thus, he uses the tribulations of the Thessalonians to thwart their faith (1 Thess 3:1-5), tempting them so that they will despair and cease to believe in the gospel. He tries to induce the Corinthians to revenge and hardheartedness so that they will continue to hold a grudge against the person whom they disciplined (2 Cor 2:5-11). God, however, desires forgiveness and restoration now that the discipline is completed. The craftiness of Satan manifests itself, for he is apt to take a good thing (in this case, discipline) and distort it, so that the church goes too far and becomes unforgiving. The same danger crops up in 1 Corinthians 7:5. Devoting oneself to prayer is commendable, but Paul worries that Satan may tempt husbands and wives to sexual sin, when they abstain for too long from sexual relations in order to devote themselves to prayer. Again, Satan takes what is good and tries to use it for evil by propelling people to overact. Not all anger is sin, but Satan wants people to nurture anger so that it festers into a spirit of resentment (Eph 4:26-27). The nurturing of anger gives room to the devil, and a spirit of unforgiveness, which is contradictory to the very nature of Christian commitment, seeps into the church. In the church at Ephesus, Paul laments that some women have turned to sensuality, gossip and deleterious behavior (1 Tim 5:11-15). He concludes that such women have turned aside to Satan and are now fulfilling his purpose. Satan even does miracles (2 Thess 2:9) that confirm unbelievers' hatred of the truth (2 Thess 2:9-12).

God's purposes. Ironically enough, God may use Satan's evil machinations

---

[13]When it says that Satan rules the air and that he is the spirit at work in the disobedient, the word *air* is literal, referring to the realm in which he works. The word *spirit*, on the other hand, is a reference to Satan himself (so Clinton E. Arnold, *Powers of Darkness: Principalities and Powers in Paul's Letters* [Downers Grove, Ill.: InterVarsity Press, 1992], pp. 196-97).

for his good purposes. Satan brings Paul a thorn in his flesh (2 Cor 12:7-10), presumably to inflict misery on him and cause him to doubt God's goodness. God, however, works out his purposes through Satan's devices. The thorn in the flesh becomes the means by which Paul is preserved from pride and the vehicle by which the power of Christ dwells on him. God's power, as the cross of Christ reveals (2 Cor 13:4), is most notably displayed in weakness. Similarly, in 1 Corinthians 5:5 and 1 Timothy 1:20 members are expelled from the church and translated into Satan's realm. Such a realm is dangerous indeed. Paul's hope, however, is that such experiences will provoke sinners to repentance so that they will be saved on the day of the Lord. If this occurs, then Satan becomes a tool for God's purposes.

Spiritual warfare. The battle against Satan and spiritual forces is intense, and Paul is aware of how easy it would be to wage war according to the flesh (2 Cor 10:2-3). Only God is strong enough and wise enough to overcome the flesh, so Paul resorts not to the flesh but to divine power. Divine weapons are imperative in the battle against the fortresses of evil (2 Cor 10:4). Evil wins its victory in the mind, and thus Paul's goal is to "tear down thoughts and every high thing lifted up against the knowledge of God, and to take every thought captive to the obedience of Christ" (2 Cor 10:5). Paul does not conceive of spiritual warfare as a mystical and ineffable struggle that bypasses human beings. The battle is for the mind of human beings. Satan and the flesh are conquered when human beings *think* and live the way God desires. When people come to know God and obey Christ, then Satan is defeated.

The classic Pauline text on spiritual warfare is Ephesians 6:10-17. Clearly the opponents are spiritual powers, for Paul specifically says that the battle is not "against flesh and blood" (Eph 6:12). The adversaries are identified as "rulers," "authorities," "the world rulers of this darkness" and "the spiritual forces of evil in the heavenlies." The last two designations clarify that governmental rulers are not in view. The struggle is against invisible spiritual powers, as confirmed by Ephesians 6:11, where the "wiles of the devil" are noted. How should believers fight against superior and invisible forces? Paul does not resort to magical incantations to ward off evil influences, though magical formulas were often invoked in the ancient world to defeat evil powers.[14] Neither does Paul think that victory over evil powers comes through mechanical means or some kind of superstitious invocation. Such approaches

---

[14]For the pervasiveness of magic in the ancient world, see Clinton E. Arnold, *Ephesians, Power and Magic: The Concept of Magic in Ephesians in Light of Its Historical Setting*, SNTSMS 63 (Cambridge: Cambridge University Press, 1989).

are inherently deficient since they bypass human character and view evil only as an outside intruder instead of as an enemy that strikes within. Paul is not guilty of the reductionism that has been so common in the Western world dominated by the Enlightenment. Such scholars dismiss the reference to spiritual powers and locate the reality of evil exclusively in human beings and the structures our society.[15] Those who adopt this worldview cannot believe that spiritual forces actually exist because such forces are not empirically demonstrable. We can all understand why many modern people doubt the existence of spiritual forces, though with the rise of postmodernity a major cultural shift is underway. What is ironic is when scholars attribute such views to Paul since he was not a product of the Enlightenment. There is little doubt that he believed such forces were real because he did not limit reality to the observable and testable realm.

How can believers defeat forces more powerful than they, and how can they conquer an adversary who is wise and crafty? As we have seen, Paul does not resort to magical incantations or secret formulas, as if victory could be obtained in such abstract ways, separated from ordinary human life. Victory over the devil and his forces comes by being "strong in the Lord and the strength of his might" (Eph 6:10) and by putting on "the full armor of God" (Eph 6:11, 13). When human beings are pitted against spiritual forces, they are destined to be defeated. They are no match for such powers. Believers triumph over these spiritual forces by virtue of the Lord's strength and power. Paul emphasizes again and again in Ephesians that believers have been liberated from the grip of the flesh and Satan through the death, and especially the resurrection, of Christ. Jesus Christ now reigns over all spiritual forces (Eph 1:20-23), and believers have been raised from the dead and now sit with Christ in the heavenlies (Eph 2:1-6). Paul, then, does not summon believers to secure the victory. The battle has already been won through the death and resurrection of Christ. Paul is no dualist, seeing the devil and Christ locked in a mortal and equal combat. The devil and his forces are already defeated in Christ. Believers are to put on God's armor and clothe themselves with the Lord's strength.

Since the victory over the devil and his associates has already been won,

---

[15]So, e.g., Walter Wink, *Naming the Powers: The Language of Power in the New Testament* (Philadelphia: Fortress, 1984); *Unmasking the Powers: The Invisible Forces That Determine Human Existence* (Philadelphia: Fortress, 1986); and *Engaging the Powers: Discernment and Resistance in a World of Domination* (Minneapolis: Fortress, 1992). For a persuasive critique of Wink, see Arnold, *Ephesians, Power and Magic*, pp. 48-51, 129-34.

believers are summoned "to stand" (Eph 6:14). The converse of standing is apostasy, a denial of God and Christ. The "evil day" of Ephesians 6:13 is this present evil age, an era filled with sorrow and temptations. Believers are tempted to deny Christ in the midst of the pressures and difficulties of this present evil age (Gal 1:4). In Christ the victory over evil forces has been achieved, so that the onus is not on believers to triumph over evil powers. And yet it does not follow from this that believers can be passive. They must stand against the devil's methods and hold fast when the onslaught comes.

How do believers resist evil forces? We might expect Paul to communicate some secret information that would help them conquer evil. The whole notion of warfare against spiritual forces conjures up images of exorcisms and specially formulated prayers that will assist believers in their struggle. Paul says nothing at all about exorcisms here, nor does he pass along particular prayers that are guaranteed to drive out evil forces. Instead, he points his readers to the gospel of Christ. Believers stand against Satan and his forces in the same way they resist all sin. It is instructive to note that Paul never says "cast out the demon of anger" or "cast out the demon of sexual immorality." He invariably says, "Since you are in Christ, put away anger" or "put away sexual immorality." Similarly, Ephesians 6 does not contain any "gnostic" admonitions. Paul uses the illustration of battle gear to portray how believers can stand against such evil forces. We might expect him to say something astonishing and mysterious, but he begins by saying that evil powers are resisted "by girding your loins with truth" (Eph 6:14). Perhaps the reference here is to the truth of the gospel, or perhaps it is to the truth that is to characterize believers' lives. Most likely, both are involved. In any case, what is striking is the normalcy of the admonition. Believers do not do anything unusual to conquer the devil and his cohorts. They live in accord with the truth of the gospel.

Believers are also to put on "the breastplate of righteousness" (Eph 6:14). We must beware of seeing any absolute significance in identifying the breastplate with righteousness, for in 1 Thessalonians 5:8 the breastplate is faith and love. In Ephesians righteousness probably refers both to the righteousness God gives and to the resulting life of righteousness believers live. In chapter two I have discussed the significance of having one's feet shod in preparation with the gospel of peace (Eph 6:15). It is likely that Paul admonishes believers to be prepared to proclaim the gospel, to be ready and alert for every opportunity. The shield of faith must be poised and ready since the devil will launch flaming darts, which can only be extinguished by faith (Eph

6:16). Faith trusts in God's promises and threats, and thereby it quenches any evil intimations from the devil. Believers also stand by taking up the helmet of salvation (Eph 6:17). Once again a comparison with 1 Thessalonians 5:8 is instructive, for the helmet there is the "hope of salvation." The last item of the armor is the Spirit's sword, namely, the word of God (Eph 6:17). Believers stand against the devil by wielding God's word against him, believing that God's words rather than the words of the devil are the truth.

There is some debate whether prayer (Eph 6:18-20) should be considered part of the armor. Even though prayer is not related to a piece of armor, the lack of a paragraph break suggests that it should be considered as part of the weaponry by which believers stand against evil forces. Standing against the devil is accomplished through truth, righteousness, the gospel, faith, salvation, the Word of God and prayer. Paul does not offer any novel or strange means to stand against spiritual forces. He does not suggest one needs a mystical knowledge of the demonic world. To conquer the devil, believers must live in accord with the truth of the gospel, with the same admonitions Paul gives elsewhere.

Conclusion

Paul's gospel would not be good news if redemption depended on the strength and ability of human beings. Hence, his gospel emphasizes that God saves his people in and through Jesus Christ. This gospel is also distorted, however, if human beings' response is eliminated. Human beings are called on to stay true to the gospel for the whole of their lives. Such perseverance is itself the result of God's grace, and yet human beings must stay true until the end to be saved.

12

LIFE OF LOVE
IN THE SPIRIT
Exhortations & the
Law in Paul

In the previous two chapters we have considered the power of the Spirit and the need for perseverance. In this chapter we examine what this persevering life in the Spirit looks like. What does it mean specifically to live by the power of the Spirit and to persevere in the faith? In order to understand this we shall examine Pauline exhortations and Paul's view of the role of the law in the life of the Christian—what is often called "the third use of the law."

Pauline Ethics and Exhortations

It would be easy to conclude that the presence and empowering of the Holy Spirit rules out the need for parenesis—ethical exhortation—in Paul. After all, one could say that those indwelt by the Holy Spirit have an inner guide and director for all life situations. When we add to this the danger of legalism and casuistry, the need for exhortations seems to diminish further. Exhortations could easily stifle the freedom that is ours in the Spirit, and believers could become rule-oriented instead of Spirit-directed and life-oriented. When we read the Mishnah (which was compiled around A.D. 200, though many of the traditions surely preceded that date), we note an attention to detailed regulations that must be classified as casuistry. Paul, it is often argued, breathed a new spirit; he freed himself from the choking detail of such regulations. He relied on the Spirit alone for guidance and direction, and if he had any ethic at all, it was the law of love.

Those who believe one needs only the Spirit for ethical living are right in a number of respects. Paul eschews the kind of detailed regulations found in the Mishnah. Instead, he believes the Spirit empowers and strengthens believers so that they can please God. He announces our freedom in Christ, avoiding casuistry and a rule-oriented ethic. He insists that the law of love is the center of his ethic. But none of these truths compel us to say that exhortations and commandments are unnecessary. This same Paul—who celebrates life in the Spirit, freedom in Christ and the centrality of love—fills his letters with commands and exhortations. Apparently he did not believe that exhorting believers contradicted the reality of the Spirit in their lives.[1]

Exhortations for spiritual people. Spiritual people need exhortations, as is apparent from Galatians 6:1, where Paul addresses spiritual ones *(pneumatikoi)* about brothers or sisters who have fallen into sin. He does not say that the Spirit will guide the spiritual ones in their response. He instructs them to restore fallen believers in a spirit of gentleness and humility. Paul did not believe that the presence of the Spirit ruled out the need for exhortations. Indeed, a very specific and concrete exhortation is given to those who are spiritual. Similarly, no one could deny the presence of the Spirit in the Corinthian congregation. In 1 Corinthians 6:19 Paul specifically reminds the Corinthians that their bodies are temples of the Holy Spirit. Nevertheless, the reality of the Spirit does not prevent Paul from giving commands to the Corinthians. Probably some of them were engaging in sexual immorality, perhaps excusing it with the saying "all things are lawful" (1 Cor 6:12). Perhaps they even drew a parallel between hunger and sexual desire (1 Cor 6:13), arguing either that both desires should be satisfied whenever they arise or that the body is of no consequence, so it does not matter what we do. Noting what Paul does *not* say is illuminating. Nowhere does he counsel the Corinthians to listen to the voice of the Spirit, to seek an internal word to resolve the problem. On the contrary, he presents them with a crisp and authoritative external word: "Flee immorality" (1 Cor 6:18). Once again, it is evident that

---

[1]For studies that are very helpful in understanding parenesis in Paul, see Wolfgang Schrage, *Die konkreten Einzelgebote in der paulinischen Paränese: Ein Beitrag zur neutestamentlichen Ethik* (Gütersloh: G. Mohn, 1961); T. J. Deidun, *New Covenant Morality in Paul,* AnBib 89 (Rome: Biblical Institute Press, 1981).

Paul does not believe that specific commands stifle life in the Spirit. On the contrary, he believes that they promote and enhance life in the Spirit. They are the means by which life in the Spirit is carried out.

Exhortations for the Thessalonians. The first letter to the Thessalonians is most instructive in this regard. Paul was proud of this young church, convinced that they were doing well in their newfound faith (1 Thess 1:6-10; 2:13; 3:1-10). He believed that they were pleasing God and were full of love (1 Thess 4:1, 9-10). No matter how well a church is doing, however, Paul is persuaded that it can always do better (1 Thess 4:1). What is particularly interesting is that instructions on how they should live and please God were transmitted from the beginning (1 Thess 4:1). These instructions are designated as "certain commandments we gave to you through the Lord Jesus" (1 Thess 4:2). A vibrant and growing church still needs specific commands and instructions about how to please God. This is confirmed in the exhortations that follow in 1 Thessalonians 4:3—5:22. Paul continues to affirm, of course, that God's work precedes and establishes obedience to specific commands. In 1 Thessalonians 4:9 he says the Thessalonians do not need to be instructed about brotherly love since they are taught by God to love one another. The new-covenant work of God proclaimed in Jeremiah 31:31-34 and Ezekiel 11:19-20; 36:26-27 is almost certainly in view here. God enables his people to love one another. Paul is not introducing a new legalism. When he says the Thessalonians have no need for such instruction, we have an example of hyperbole since Paul exhorts them in the very next verse (1 Thess 4:10) to abound even more in love for one another! Evidently being taught by God to love one another does not circumvent an exhortation to love one another. The command does not hinder God's internal work but secures it even further.

Exhortations and the "not yet." In 1 Corinthians 4:17 Paul informs the Corinthians why he has sent Timothy to them. Timothy will remind the Corinthians of all Paul's "ways" *(hodous)* in Christ. Paul's "ways" must include his ethical teaching, for he proceeds to say "just as I *teach [didaskō]* everywhere in every church." Paul's ways are communicated in and through Paul's *teaching*, suggesting that he gave definite instructions as to how they should live.

Christians need exhortations because, even though they are indwelt by the Spirit, the threat of sinning remains (Rom 6:12-14). They must not let sin gain dominion in their lives. Believers should not consider themselves as immune to the dangers of sin. They must constantly be on the alert, knowing that those who think they stand are the most prone to fall (1 Cor 10:12). They need exhortations because they have not yet been perfected (Phil 3:12-16).

When believers have entered fully into their inheritance, exhortations will be superfluous and unnecessary. Those who are completely transformed stand in no need of commands. But we have not yet obtained the resurrection or moral perfection. Like Paul we keep striving to receive the goal, the eschatological prize that has been promised to us. Those who are "perfect" (*teleioi*, Phil 3:15) know that "perfection" still awaits them. Anyone who thinks that perfection can be ours in this present evil age is self-deceived. In the interval between the inauguration and consummation of our salvation, therefore, we need exhortations and commands so that we will continue to pursue the call of God in Christ Jesus.

Exhortations and life in the Spirit. Some scholars have unfortunately communicated the impression that external words or commands are not in accord with Paul's conception of life in the Spirit. We have already seen that this conclusion is mistaken. Sexual immorality is ruled out for believers (1 Cor 6:19; 1 Thess 4:3-8). Paul appeals to Jesus' ruling, which prohibits divorce (1 Cor 7:10-11). And he adds his own ruling to the situation of a believer who is married to an unbeliever (1 Cor 7:12-16). Paul does not believe that commands or exhortations quench life in the Spirit. The Spirit and the word work together in conforming believers to the likeness of Christ. The parallel between Ephesians 5:18 and Colossians 3:16 is very illuminating in this regard. It is apparent to all that the latter sections of Ephesians and Colossians are remarkably similar. The near context in both Ephesians and Colossians speaks of joy in worship, of thankfulness and of right relations between husbands and wives, parents and children, and masters and slaves (cf. Col 3:16—4:1; Eph 5:18—6:9). Before listing these qualities Paul exhorts believers in Ephesians to "be filled with the Spirit" (Eph 5:18). In Colossians, on the other hand, he summons believers to "let the word of Christ dwell in them richly" (Col 3:16). The parallel reveals that being filled with the Spirit and being filled with the word of Christ are complementary. There is no such thing as being filled with the Spirit if one is not filled with the external word of Christ. Focusing on the external word without relying on the Spirit can easily lead to rigidity, harshness and formalism. On the other hand, devotion to the Spirit that leaves out the word can easily lead to fanaticism, an obsession with spiritual phenomena and a blind zealotry. For Paul the Spirit and the word are not contrary. The word and the Spirit work together. The external word is one of the primary means by which believers realize life in the Spirit.

Those who walk in the Spirit do not transgress the law but fulfill it (Gal 5:13-15; Rom 8:4; cf. Rom 2:26-29). When Paul mentions the law of Christ, he gives a specific admonition to bear one another's burdens (Gal 6:2). Clearly, the law of Christ involves specific commands and injunctions. Indeed, Paul proceeds in the same context to enjoin believers to support their teachers with their finances (Gal 6:6) and to be generous to all believers and even unbelievers who are in need (Gal 6:9-10). Such admonitions are not contrary to life in the Spirit but are woven together with the call to sow to the Spirit (Gal 6:8). The importance of an external word is evident when we consider Paul's emphasis on knowing God's will. Love must be conjoined with knowledge and discernment *(epignōsis, aisthēsis)* so that the Philippians can discern *(dokimazō)* what is pleasing to God (Phil 1:9-10). The Colossians must be filled with "the knowledge" *(epignōsis)* of God's will "in all spiritual wisdom and understanding" *(en pasē sophia kai synesei pneumatikē)* to live in a way that is worthy and pleasing to God (Col 1:9-10). Believers escape being shaped by this world as they are transformed "by the renewal of their mind" *(tē anakainōsei tou noos)* so that they assess what is good, pleasing and perfect (Rom 12:2). Ephesians 4:23 contains a similar admonition "to be renewed in the spirit of your mind." Romans 8 is famous for its discussion of life in the Spirit. Paul does not conceive of life in the Spirit apart from the life of the mind. Those who are spiritual "think" *(phronousin)* on spiritual things (Rom 8:5-6). There is no room in Paul's theology for segregating the Spirit and knowledge into separate compartments. The supernatural work of the Spirit occurs in and through the thinking process of human beings, and thus exhortations and commands are one of the means by which God's will is communicated to believers. Paul does speak of freedom from law (more on this below); but this freedom from law does not involve freedom from *ought*.

The occasional nature of the letters and exhortations. When considering Pauline parenesis, we must take into account the situation he addresses. We expect less-detailed exhortations to be addressed to the believers in Galatia, where agitators tried to impose circumcision and the Old Testament law. In such a situation we expect Paul to proclaim freedom in Christ from the constraints of the law. Similarly, the opponents in Colossae were attempting to impose an ascetic regimen on believers, demanding that they abstain from certain foods, observe the sabbath and follow other human traditions (Col 2:16-23). Paul emphasizes that no one can bind the consciences of believers with such regulations. However, when Paul wrote 1 Corinthians the church had inclinations toward libertinism. We are not surprised, therefore, to find more specific commands and exhortations in this letter. Paul corrects a misunderstanding about life in the Spirit. Pauline exhortations receive their accent from the situation addressed. This does not mean, of course, that specific commands are lacking in Galatians or Colossians, nor does Paul ignore entirely the message of freedom in 1 Corinthians. Nevertheless, the circumstances of the churches do color Paul's letters, so that the emphasis on commands differs according to the situation addressed.

General exhortations. Though Paul often casts his exhortations in light of specific circumstances, we would be hard pressed to conclude that all his exhortations address specific situations. The parenesis in Romans 12:9-21 and Romans 13:8-14 seems to consist of general exhortations of the sort that Paul would give to any believing community. No compelling evidence exists that these commands are given in light of circumstances in Rome. Similarly, it is difficult to see how the parenesis in Colossians 3 addresses any direct problem in Colossae. The exhortations seem to be general, for they contain the kind of directives that would be given to any group of believers. The exhortation to refrain from sexual immorality in 1 Thessalonians 4:3-8 does not necessarily indicate that believers in Thessalonica had a severe problem with sexual sin. Paul may have included these words because he knows human nature; sexual drives are incredibly powerful, and thus Paul warns the Thessalonians about sexual sin. The string of exhortations near the end of 1 Thessalonians (1 Thess 5:12-22) are harder to assess. The admonition against laziness seems to address a genuine problem in the community (1 Thess 5:14; cf. 1 Thess 4:11-12; 2 Thess 3:6-13). Perhaps the church was also in danger of overestimating or quenching prophecy (1 Thess 5:19-22). We cannot be certain whether some problems with church leaders were the occasion for the word to respect and honor them (1 Thess 5:12-13). On the other hand, some of the exhortations are almost certainly general admonitions, reflecting common, garden-variety instructions for Christian churches (1 Thess 5:15-18).

A number of vice and virtue lists also occur in the Pauline letters (Rom 1:29-31; 13:13; 1 Cor 5:10-11; 6:9-11; 2 Cor 6:6; 12:20; Gal 5:19-23; Eph 4:31-32; 5:3-5; Phil 4:8-9; Col 3:5, 8, 12; 1 Tim 1:9-10; 4:12; 6:4-5, 11; 2 Tim 2:22; 3:2-4; Tit 3:3). Scholars have proposed that these lists are indebted to Stoicism, Iranian religion or Jewish sources.[2] It is not my intention to delve into each one of

---

[2]See C. G. Kruse, "Virtues and Vices," in *Dictionary of Paul and His Letters,* ed. Gerald F. Hawthorne, Ralph P. Martin and Daniel G. Reid (Downers Grove, Ill.: InterVarsity Press, 1993), pp. 962-63. Supporting a Jewish background are Eduard Schweizer, "Traditional Ethical Patterns in the Pauline and Post-Pauline Letters and Their Development (Lists of Vices and House Tables)," in *Text and Interpretation: Studies in the New Testament Presented to Matthew Black,* ed. E. Best and R. McL. Wilson (Cambridge: Cambridge University Press, 1979), pp. 195-209; and Peder Borgen, "Catalogues of Vices: The Apostolic Decree and the Jerusalem Meeting," in *The Social World of Formative Christianity and Judaism: Essays in Tribute to Howard Clark Kee,* ed. J. Neusner, E. S. Frerichs, P. Borgen and R. Horsley (Philadelphia: Fortress, 1988), pp. 126-41.

these lists in detail here. Some of the lists are probably shaped by the specific situation. On the other hand, many of the lists reflect general exhortations intended for all Christians. The Pauline household codes are probably also general parenesis (Eph 5:22-6:9; Col 3:18—4:1), for the directives found there do not seem to counter any problem in the churches. What is relevant for the topic at hand is that these admonitions demonstrate that all Christians, no matter how godly, need specific instructions both on what to avoid and on what to pursue in the Christian life. Some of the instructions in the household codes and in the vice and virtue lists are rather self-evident and could be described as prosaic. Still, Paul was convinced that believers indwelt by the Spirit needed such concrete and practical directives. Once again, we see that specific commandments are not extraneous to Paul's understanding of the Christian life but intrinsic.

The centrality of love. External commandments and exhortations are part and parcel of Paul's theology. Emphasizing the importance of specific exhortations may lead to an overreaction. We must still insist that love is the heart and soul of the Pauline ethic: All the exhortations are expressions of love. All the commandments of the law can be summed up in loving one's neighbor (Rom 13:8-10; Gal 5:14). Colossians 3:14 ("Above all things is love, which is the bond of perfection") suggests that love is the supreme virtue, and perhaps Paul is saying here that all of the other virtues are bound together with love, finding their origin and foundation in it. The whole Christian life can be summed up in the admonition to "walk in love" (Eph 5:2), a love that is patterned after Christ's love for his people, which is demonstrated in the giving of his life. When Paul thinks of the supreme duty of husbands to wives, he summons them to love their wives (Eph 5:25, 28-29), and again the model for such love is the atoning death of Christ on behalf of the church. It is instructive that the long list of exhortations in Romans 12:9-21 commences with the words, "Let love be sincere" (Rom 12:9), suggesting that all the virtues that follow are summed up by love.

The controversy over spiritual gifts is interspersed with the beautiful and poetic description of love (1 Corinthians 13), indicating that love is superior to any spiritual gift or ability. All the other virtues to be pursued are rooted in love; all the vices to be avoided are rooted in a lack thereof (1 Cor 13:4-7). Similarly, it is instructive that the fruit of the Spirit begins with love (Gal 5:22-23), suggesting that the remaining items in the list are comprehended in this one virtue. Another controversy in 1 Corinthians relates to food offered to idols (1 Cor 8:1—11:1). Paul lays the foundation for the whole discussion by making love, rather than knowledge, primary (1 Cor 8:1-3). Those who insist on their freedom to eat any and all foods will do the right thing if they are filled with love; and they should not wield their knowledge to damage the weak and thereby fail to love them.

The centrality of love is confirmed by its close association with faith and hope. The three virtues that remain are faith, hope and love (1 Cor 13:13). Paul thanks God for the Colossian believers because he hears that faith, love and hope are in their lives (Col 1:3-5), and he remarks especially on the reality of their love (Col 1:8). The Thessalonian church is commended for the work that stems from faith, the labor that derives from love and the steadfastness that comes from hope (1 Thess 1:3). In 2 Thessalonians they are commended for growing in faith and love (2 Thess 1:3). Thanks are offered to God for Philemon's love and faith (Philem 4-5). The close connection between faith and love is confirmed by Galatians 5:6, where faith is said to express itself, or manifest itself, in love. The centrality of love is communicated by 1 Timothy 1:5, where Paul says "love is the goal" of his instruction. When Paul prays for the Philippians, he begins by asking that their love will grow (Phil 1:9).

The primacy of love is also attested in texts where the word *love* is omitted but the concept is present. Some members of the Thessalonian church (2 Thess 3:6-13; cf. 1 Thess 4:11-12; 5:14) had ceased working—perhaps because they believed the end was at hand—and wanted to sponge off others. Paul demands that they work to support themselves. A reference to love is unstated, but we can legitimately conclude that laziness is indicted because it is contrary to love (cf. 1 Cor 13:5). According to Romans 14—15, the Roman church was divided over the issue of whether to eat unclean food. Paul does not specifically appeal to love to solve the dispute, but we do no injustice to the text to say that the dissension would be dissolved by love. Paul asks both the strong and the weak to refrain from judging each other. He implores the strong to help the weak in their failings, to avoid placing a stumbling block before their brothers and sisters, and to live to please others rather than themselves. Though the word *love* is not used, such actions capture the essence of love.

First Corinthians 6:1-8 serves as another example. Lawsuits over trivial matters are dividing the Corinthian church. Paul never says, "You should love each other instead." Instead he says, "Why not rather be wronged? Why not rather be cheated?" (1 Cor 6:7). To be wronged and cheated instead of insisting on one's own rights is an expression of love, even though the term *love* is lacking in the text. Or we can think of the Lord's supper in Corinth (1 Cor 11:17-34), where the rich were consuming a sumptuous meal and even getting drunk while the poor were lacking food. Paul is outraged at such a lack of concern for the poor in the community. Once again, though the word *love* is lacking, it is obvious that the Corinthian church is plagued by a lack of love. In the letter to the Philippians the believers are called to unity and to put others before themselves (Phil 1:27—2:30). Christ Jesus is the supreme model of such sacrificial living (Phil 2:5-11), though Timothy (Phil 2:19-24) and Epaphroditus (Phil 2:25-30) also function as models for the Philippians. The word *love* is not used to describe their lives, but putting others before oneself and living so that others will be strong in the Lord are apt portrayals of love.

We could continue with other examples, but the point is obvious: Love is the heart and soul of the Pauline ethic. It does not follow from this that commandments and exhortations are superfluous, for love is expressed in definite and concrete ways. Love goes beyond the calculable demand since there are countless situations in which the loving course of action cannot be prescribed in advance. In some circumstances what is done is a matter of indifference *(adiaphora)* per the discussions in 1 Corinthians 8—10 and Romans 14—15. A specific course of action cannot be commended in every circumstance, for some situations are too complex to chart out beforehand a clear mandate. Here one must test what is pleasing to the Lord (Eph 5:10) and pray that love will be accompanied by discernment (Phil 1:9-10). Though love goes beyond specific demands, it never transgresses or goes around such demands.

The Pauline exhortations give some parameters as to what is "loving." If specific commands were unnecessary, then there would be no need for exhortations. All Paul would need to say is, "Be loving." Further specifics are given because it is extraordinarily easy to deceive ourselves about how loving we are. Particular commands give shape and substance to the call to love. No one can claim to be loving and still be lazy, full of bitterness, harsh, selfish, a thief, and so on. But still, love cannot simply be collapsed into "doing the right thing." In 1 Corinthians 13:3 Paul says that one can lack love and yet give all one's possessions to the poor and even sacrifice his or her life![3] If love is merely acting correctly, then one could claim that sacrificing one's life or giving all one's belongings to the poor are sure signs of love. What could be more loving than these two actions? Apparently, Paul believes that motives

---

[3] I think the superior textual reading is *kauthēsomai* instead of *kauchēsomai*.

are crucial in defining love. We may give up our possessions so that we will be praised as generous. Perhaps we will even dare to give up our lives to enhance our reputations. But for Paul true love is rooted in a desire to honor and thank God in whatever we do (Rom 1:21). Genuine love must be rooted in faith, for whatever is not of faith is sin (Rom 14:23). Therefore one's actions may not issue from love even though they conform externally to what is good. Love also involves the motives and affections of the heart. We see from this that the primacy of love is connected with the heart of Pauline theology, for love is not genuine unless it flows from a heart that longs to bring God glory in all that is said and done.

The power of the Spirit. In any discussion of Pauline parenesis we must emphasize that Paul never proclaims that human ability is sufficient to keep God's commands. Believers are not summoned to love or live a life worthy of God on the basis of their own abilities. The power of the Holy Spirit is the only means by which believers can do what God commands. In Pauline letters, commands are often given after Paul has detailed what God has accomplished in Christ for his people. In other words, the indicative precedes the imperative. A godly life is the fruit of the Spirit (Gal 5:22-23), the result of the Spirit's work and power in the life of the Christian. Believers overcome the flesh and the power of the law by walking in, and being led by, the Spirit (Gal 5:16, 18). Triumphing over envy and pride comes by keeping in step with the Spirit (Gal 5:26). Those who are generous and give to help others are those who sow to the Spirit (Gal 6:6-10). Those who walk in the Spirit fulfill the law (Rom 8:4). Those who are filled with the Spirit are characterized by joy, praise and singing, and they have right relations with their families and in society (Eph 5:18—6:9). It is only by the Spirit that the deeds of the body can be slain and conquered (Rom 8:13). It would be a complete distortion of Pauline theology if one understood his exhortations as appealing to human potential and ability. Only through the work of the Spirit can the believer keep what is commanded; and in this life such obedience, though significant, will always be partial and incomplete.

Shared moral norms? Does Paul in his ethic draw on ethical norms from the Greco-Roman world?[4] We see from Romans 2:14-15 that Paul believes each human being has a conscience, so that even without a written law all are aware, at least to some extent, of right and wrong. Thus it would not be sur-

---

[4]For an informative study of early Christians' moral world, see Wayne Meeks, *The Moral World of the First Christians*, LEC 6 (Philadelphia: Westminster Press, 1986).

prising if in some arenas Paul shared moral norms with his contemporaries. In Romans 1:32 he describes human beings as those "who know the ordinance of God" in the sense that they are keenly aware that some actions are deserving of death. We can conclude from this that unbelievers are aware of moral norms—they know certain things are right and others are wrong. When Paul says certain things are "not fitting" (Rom 1:28), he uses language similar to the Stoics'. The ethical exhortations in Philippians 4:8 would not be at all surprising to those who lived in the Greco-Roman world. The same judgment could be articulated regarding the vice and virtue lists in the Pauline letters.

Paul's ethic is distinctive not necessarily because its content is new but because the motivation and power that undergird obedience are new. This is not to say that there is complete identity between the Pauline ethic and that of the Greco-Roman world. Humility was despised by the Greek world but exalted by Paul. The difference here is not accidental, for humility emphasizes human weakness and dependence on God, whereas Greek morality highlights the nobility of human beings in doing what is right. Even where the same ethical ideals are prized, the fulfillment, realization, motivation and foundation distinguish Paul's thought from the Greco-Roman worldview.

Paul, like the Stoics, believes that some things are contrary to nature. Yet unlike the Stoics, he does not believe nature is an all-embracing norm. He does appeal to it, though, as a confirming argument to establish an ethical norm. We must also note the different understanding of "nature" in Paul and the Stoics. For the Stoics, nature is in accord with reason, and it functions as the norm in a pantheistic worldview. For Paul, on the other hand, nature is rooted in a theistic worldview. That which is in accord with nature fits with what God, the Father of the Lord Jesus Christ, ordained for human beings from the creation of the world.

Homosexuality. Paul critiques homosexuality because it is contrary to nature (Rom 1:26-27).[5] In the past such a judgment on Paul's part was accepted as a matter of course, but today homosexuality is a fiercely debated subject. Before delving further into this issue, we should observe the context. Paul has just argued that human beings depart from what is "natural" (i.e., intended by God) in that they worship the creature rather than the Creator (Rom 1:18-25). Human beings were made to thank, glorify and worship the

---

[5]For a discussion of homosexuality that also includes a bibliography, see Thomas R. Schreiner, *Romans*, BECNT (Grand Rapids, Mich.: Baker, 1998), pp. 93-97.

one and only God, but instead they have turned to idolatry and self-worship. Self-worship is fundamentally unnatural in that creatures are made to worship the Creator. Similarly, homosexuality is introduced because it is fundamentally unnatural. From Genesis 1—2 it is apparent that God made men and women to have sexual relations with one another. The desire to have sexual relations with someone of the same sex is, in Paul's mind, akin to worshiping the creature rather than the Creator. It inverts what God intended, turning the world upside down in the social sphere. Paul raises the issue of homosexuality not because he is so interested in this particular sin but because its presence attests to a world that has turned its back on God. Sexual relations are distorted because the relationship between God and human beings has gone awry.

Some have attempted to argue, of course, that Paul limits his critique of homosexuality to only some forms of it. A number of different explanations have been offered in defense of the legitimacy of some same-sex unions. For instance, some have said that only pederasty, a sexual relationship between an older man and a young boy, is criticized here. On this construction no criticism of homosexuality per se is criticized but only an exploitative relationship in which an older man takes advantage of a boy or teenager. Others have suggested that Paul speaks only to heterosexuals who are acting unnaturally in indulging in homosexual behavior. That is, Paul thinks it is wrong for those who have heterosexual desires and inclinations to engage in same-sex unions. It follows that those who are naturally born as homosexuals are not criticized since when they pursue same-sex unions they live in accord with their own homosexual nature and inclinations. Others affirm that homosexuality per se is not wicked; they hold that Paul is bothered by unions that are not monogamous or that in the context of Romans 1 homosexuality is stained by idolatrous associations. Doubtless the variety of interpretations will increase since the issue is hotly controversial, and to some the apparent meaning of the text violates our own sense of justice and love.

Nevertheless, there is little doubt that Paul condemns all forms of homosexuality. Some in the Greco-Roman world defended and even celebrated homosexuality. But the Jewish tradition is unanimous in condemning it (cf. Gen 19:1-28; Lev 18:22; 20:13; Deut 23:17-18; Wis 14:26; *T. Levi* 17.11; *T. Naph.* 3:3-4; *Sib. Or.* 3:596-600; *Ag. Ap.* 2.24, 37; *Spec. Laws* 3.7). No evidence exists to the contrary. The most natural way of interpreting Paul is to interpret him in continuity with his Jewish tradition. The burden of proof certainly lies on those who see some window for the acceptability of homosexuality in Paul.

To read the text as if some exceptions exists is eisegesis. The text contains a general condemnation, with no indication that some forms of homosexuality are acceptable. Nowhere else in Jewish tradition, in the New Testament or in Paul is there any hint that the practice would ever be admissible. Nor are the attempts to evade the meaning of the text persuasive. Paul does not limit himself to pederasty, for he specifically indicts sexual relations between women in Romans 1:26, even though there is no evidence that older women exploited and engaged in sexual relations with younger women. So to see a focus on pederasty violates the parallel between women and men in the text since older women did not exploit younger girls sexually. Nor is there any evidence that a different kind of homosexuality is criticized in Romans 1:27, when men are addressed. In Paul's description of the sin in Romans 1:27, the words *men with men (arsenes en arsesin)* occur. Instead of saying "men with boys," Paul directly refers to "men with men." Any idea that only pederasty is condemned is an invention of modern exegetes.

Similarly, we can reject the idea that those who are "naturally" homosexual are excepted. The problem with this reading is that the word *nature (physis)* is interpreted in a modern psychological sense, so that Paul reflects on the internal psychological state of individuals. Reading Paul in this way imposes modern psychological categories on him. *Nature (physis)* refers here to what God intended when he made human beings. Paul is not reflecting on the "natural" sexual inclinations of human beings, in the sense that he probes their internal desires. Instead, he uses *nature* to designate God's paradigm for human sexuality as it is revealed in creation. Genesis 1—2, not modern psychology, is in Paul's mind when he writes these words. There is no room, then, for differentiating between people who are "naturally" homosexual and "naturally" heterosexual in this text.

The attempt to limit the prohibition to idolatrous homosexual unions or to unions that are not monogamous is no more convincing than the previous argument. Not a word is breathed about such ideas, nor is there any contextual warrant for inserting them into the text. If one were to say that Paul proscribes idolatry in Romans 1, we could simply respond by saying that for Paul *all homosexuality (indeed all sin)* is a consequence of idolatry. Some interpreters have argued that the norm of love justifies loving homosexual relationships. But the same Paul who wrote so eloquently about love also proscribes homosexual behavior. If we use his definition of love, and not ours, then any defense of homosexuality on the basis of "love" vanishes. Other scholars contend that homosexuality is permissible and conclude that Paul is mistaken. They are correct in their estimation of *Paul's theology*, but they feel free to substitute their own wisdom as a norm. At least in such cases the text is not distorted or twisted in favor of a particular agenda, and Paul's own verdict continues to be sounded, even if such scholars dissent from Paul.

Some might object that Paul's indictment of homosexuality cannot apply to today since he also appeals to nature in saying that men should wear short hair and women long (1 Cor 11:14-15). Surely the length of hair is not an issue of profound moral importance. Or perhaps some might say that Paul's criticism of homosexuality is on the level with his disapproval of long hair on men and short hair on women. Paul's opinion on homosexuality should be given the same respect as his view on the length of hair. In other words, in both cases Paul's cultural limitations manifest themselves, and these texts are mainly interesting as windows into Paul's worldview.

All would agree that 1 Corinthians 11:2-16 contains a nest of difficulties, and we will explore these further when we consider Paul's view of women. Here it must be said that it is a mistake to conclude that Paul's instructions regarding hair length are trivial. The adornment of women arises as an issue because the distinction between the sexes must be preserved according to Paul.[6] One way in which the differences between the sexes manifested itself in Paul's day and culture was the length of hair. What is considered "long" hair or "short" hair is relative, of course. What animates Paul is not some prescribed length that has been written on heavenly tablets. He is concerned about the issue of hair length because in the Greco-Roman world it spoke to differences between males and females. Paul does not think that masculinity and femininity are merely social constructs. They are rooted in the created order, and Paul is concerned about hairstyle not because it is itself a crucial issue but because he does not want the differences between males and females to be erased. More needs to be said about this text, but enough has been said to suggest that similar concerns motivated Paul in both texts. In both instances, distinctions between the sexes are to be preserved. Hence, Paul appeals to the created order to support the differences between the sexes. Of course, the texts are also distinct because in 1 Corinthians 11:2-16 Paul appeals to a cultural convention (length of hair) to remind readers of the differences between the sexes.

---

[6] In this respect Gordon Fee is on target in his exegesis of 1 Cor 11:2-16. See his *The First Epistle to the Corinthians*, NICNT (Grand Rapids, Mich.: Eerdmans, 1987), pp. 491-530.

New Obedience and the Law

It is fitting to examine general Pauline exhortations before examining Paul's view of keeping the law. Some scholars, when they write about the law, give the impression that any observance of the law robs believers of freedom in Christ, destroys life in the Spirit and is contrary to the Pauline gospel. We can see why scholars mount such a case, for Paul does proclaim freedom from law and life in the Spirit. Surely there is a danger of exalting the law over the Spirit. Otherwise, the letter to the Galatians is quite superfluous. Still, the way some scholars write about freedom in the Spirit gives the impression that any commands or moral norms stifle life in the Spirit. Confident declarations about freedom from law seem to suggest freedom from all moral norms. Whatever one makes of Paul's view of the ongoing authority of the law, we cannot and must not conclude that all moral norms are jettisoned. The numerous Pauline exhortations demonstrate that moral norms do not necessarily violate life in the Spirit or the freedom of the Pauline gospel. Similarly, if some of the moral norms come from the Mosaic law, nothing essential in Paul's gospel is violated. We must be careful to understand precisely what Paul has in mind when he proclaims freedom from law so that we do not draw the conclusion that Paul's gospel teaches freedom from *ought.*

The law and redemptive history. We have already seen that Paul proclaims freedom from law in a salvation-historical sense. The Mosaic covenant was instituted 430 years after the covenant with Abraham (Gal 3:17) and is subsidiary to the Abrahamic covenant. Contrary to the opponents in Galatia the covenant with Abraham—not the covenant with Moses—is primary in God's purposes. The Mosaic covenant was never intended to be in force forever. It was designed for the interval before the arrival of the seed (Gal 3:19). Now that faith in Christ has come, the era of the law as a pedagogue has expired (Gal 3:23-25). The law is compared to stewards and guardians who impose their rule over minors until they reach maturity (Gal 4:1-7). In Christ the fullness of time has arrived, and believers are liberated from the domain of the law. Believers are no longer minors but full-fledged sons and heirs.

Paul often uses *under (hypo)* phrases to designate the old era when the Mosaic covenant was in force. Those who are of works of law are "under a curse" (Gal 3:10). The Scripture has confined all "under sin" (Gal 3:22). This is equivalent with being "under the law" (Gal 3:23), or "under the pedagogue" (Gal 3:25). As we have already said, Paul compares this to being "under stewards and managers" (Gal 4:2), which is equivalent to being "under the elements of the world" (Gal 4:3). Jesus, the Messiah, was born "under the law"

(Gal 4:4) to redeem those "under the law" (Gal 4:5).

Amazingly the Galatians want to be "under law" (Gal 4:21), but Paul proclaims that those who are led by the Spirit are not "under law" (Gal 5:18; Rom 6:14-15). When he uses the various *under* phrases, he has in mind the time period when the Mosaic law was in force. When we consider Israelite history, however, the promulgation of the law was concurrent with the spread of sin (Rom 5:20). Those who live in the new era inaugurated by Jesus Christ's death and resurrection are liberated from the dominion of law and sin (Rom 6:14-15; Gal 4:4-5). Those who are led by the Spirit are free from the dominion of the law and the sin that inevitably accompanies it. Paul describes the Mosaic covenant as a "ministry of death" (2 Cor 3:7) and "a ministry of condemnation" (2 Cor 3:9) and one that is temporary (2 Cor 3:11). The problem with the Mosaic covenant is not the content of the law; the commandments are holy, righteous and good (Rom 7:12). In the era of the law, though, desire to sin was stimulated through the law (Rom 7:5, 7-25). We see in Romans as well that the letter of the law (Rom 2:29; 7:6) is associated with the advance of sin, while those who are no longer under the law but are empowered by the Spirit (Rom 7:1-6; 8:1-4) do God's will.

Freedom from law. Freedom from law seems to be a feature of Paul's teaching elsewhere. He proclaims that "all things are lawful" (1 Cor 6:12; 10:23). Sabbath regulations are no longer in force since in Colossians 2:16-17 Paul says that the sabbath is merely a shadow, anticipating the coming of Christ. In Romans 14:5-6 observing days is considered a matter of indifference. Most commentators agree that the sabbath is included here since the sabbath is the most prominent day in the Jewish calendar (cf. Gal 4:10).

Food laws also are no longer binding, according to Paul. The dispute between the weak and strong in Rome centered on food (Rom 14:1—15:13). We can be almost certain that foods prohibited by the Old Testament were the center of the controversy. Paul proclaims in Romans 14:14 that "nothing is common in itself." The word *common (koinos)* is never used in the Greco-Roman world to designate unacceptable food. It is only used by Jewish writers to refer to food that is unclean. Romans 14:20 confirms this reading, for Paul says that "all things are clean" *(kathara).* Those who desired to keep the Mosaic law were scrupulous about what they ate, for the Old Testament clearly demarcates acceptable and unacceptable food (Lev 11:1-47; Deut 14:3-20). We have already seen in Romans 14—15 that Paul believes all foods are clean. He is only worried about injuring believers who feel bound to observe food regulations.

The same attitude toward food manifests itself in 1 Corinthians 8:1—11:1. Paul does not believe that food offered to idols is inherently tainted, for idols are a figment of the imagination and God is the Creator of all (1 Cor 8:4-6; 10:26). Believers may freely eat food sold in the meat market, even if it has been offered to idols (1 Cor 10:23—11:1). Paul does not believe that the origin of the meat disqualifies it. Here he seems far from purity rules that see food tainted by that with which it has been in contact. Again in 1 Corinthians he is concerned about hurting the brother or sister who would be scandalized by eating food offered to idols. He also warns against idolatry, which would occur when the food was consumed in a cultic meal that involved a worship setting (1 Cor 10:19-22).[7] No inherent defect is located in the food itself, though, and the freedom with which Paul approaches the issue is somewhat astonishing.

Identifying the opponents in Colossae is remarkably difficult.[8] Some Jewish influence seems likely, since the Jews were propagating the sabbath (Col 2:16). They also advocated food regulations (Col 2:16, 20-23), apparently as part of some ascetic regimen. Once again, food regulations are dismissed by Paul, here more strongly than in either Romans or 1 Corinthians. Demands that certain foods be avoided are part of the shadow, and now that the substance, Christ, has been revealed, the shadows can be left behind. Foods are part of the "elements of the world" that have been superseded by Christ's death (Col 2:20). Such regulations are fundamentally anthropocentric (Col 2:22), and they ignore the fact that foods are eliminated through ordinary bodily processes. Those who continue to promulgate diet as important exalt the shadow over the substance. They live on the basis of the old after the new has come. They fail to see what the shadow pointed to, and they reify the shadow. The opponents in 1 Timothy banned certain foods as well, though we are uncertain about the rationale for their prohibition. Paul appealed to creation to justify eating all things (1 Tim 4:3-4). Any notion that certain foods are defiled is excluded (cf. Tit 1:14-15).

---

[7]On food offered to idols, see Gordon D. Fee, "*Eidōlothyta* Once Again: An Interpretation of 1 Corinthians 8—10," *Bib* 61 (1980): 172-97; Bruce N. Fisk, "Eating Meat Offered to Idols: Corinthian Response and Pauline Response in 1 Corinthians 8—10 (A Response to Gordon Fee)," *TJ* 10 (1989): 49-70; David Horrell, "Theological Principle or Christological Praxis? Pauline Ethics in 1 Corinthians 8.1—11.1," *JSNT* 67 (1997): 83-114.

[8]Scholars continue to debate the identity of the opponents in Colossae. For a recent summary of research, see James D. G. Dunn, *The Epistles to the Colossians and to Philemon: A Commentary on the Greek Text*, NIGTC (Grand Rapids, Mich.: Eerdmans, 1996), pp. 23-35. See also Clinton E. Arnold, *The Colossian Syncretism: The Interface Between Christianity and Folk Belief at Colossae* (Grand Rapids, Mich.: Baker, 1996), esp. pp. 1-7.

Not only are food laws passé, but circumcision is also no longer obligatory. Paul responds in the strongest possible terms to those who want to impose circumcision on Gentiles (Gal 2:3-5; 5:2-6, 11-12; 6:12-13). Those who demand Gentile circumcision proclaim a false gospel, and God's curse is on them (Gal 1:8-9). This is all the more surprising when we realize that the Old Testament demanded circumcision for membership in the covenant people (Gen 17:9-14). Nor was Paul's response to the Galatian crisis a temporary judgment. In Philippians he upbraids the purveyors of circumcision as "evil workers" and describes their view of circumcision as "mutilation" (*katatomē*, Phil 3:2). In Romans true circumcision is the circumcision of the heart (Rom 2:28-29), and literal circumcision is unnecessary for righteousness since Abraham was righteous by faith *before* receiving circumcision (Rom 4:9-12).[9]

The Mosaic covenant is temporary, according to Paul. Hence, sabbath, food laws and circumcision are no longer in force. The "new perspective" on Paul rightly discerns part of the rationale lying behind this judgment. In Paul's mind the gospel of Christ fulfills the promise to Abraham that the gospel would be proclaimed to all nations (Gal 3:6-9). The gift of the Spirit is the blessing promised to Abraham (Gal 3:1-5, 14). The Mosaic covenant was intended to be in force only until the seed arrived, and the Gentiles were included in God's saving promises (Gal 3:15-4:7; Rom 4:9-17). Sabbath, food laws and circumcision come to the forefront in Paul's letters because such practices distinguished Jews from Gentiles in the Greco-Roman world. When Greco-Roman writers considered Judaism, such boundary markers were prominent and often criticized. James Dunn is correct in labeling these practices as "boundary markers" and "badges" that separated Jews from Gentiles.[10] Now that the covenant with Abraham is being fulfilled in Christ, such boundary markers are no longer in force. To insist on them is to deny that Christ is the fulfillment of the promise to Abraham. Adhering to these boundary markers would say that Gentiles had to become Jews to enter the people of God. The exclusivism that was characteristic of the old covenant has ended, and now all peoples can participate in Abraham's blessing through Christ Jesus. The wall of partition between Jews and Gentiles is razed (Eph 2:11-22), and now all those who belong to Christ Jesus are equal members in God's household, fellow citizens in God's church (Eph 3:6).

---

[9]For the difference between Paul and Philo on circumcision, see John M. G. Barclay, "Paul and Philo on Circumcision: Romans 2.25-29 in Social and Cultural Context," *NTS* 44 (1998): 536-56.

[10]James D. G. Dunn, "The New Perspective on Paul," *BJRL* 65 (1983): 95-122.

The fulfillment of the law. It is fitting, in one sense, to speak of the Mosaic covenant as being abolished in Christ. Yet even Old Testament commands that are no longer binding are also fulfilled in Christ. Circumcision anticipates the circumcision of the heart (Rom 2:28-29), the work of the Holy Spirit within (Phil 3:2-3) and the cross work of Christ (Col 2:11-12). It is not as clear what the food laws and the sabbath were pointing to, but the fact that they are called "shadows" *(skia)* suggests that they anticipate the fulfillment in Christ in some way. Second Corinthians 6:17; 7:1 hints that purity regulations point to purity of life. Passover anticipates Christ's sacrifice on the cross (1 Cor 5:7), and the removal of leaven signifies that believers should dispense with all evil (1 Cor 5:6-8). Paul communicates no concern about the literal temple, although the temple was central to the Jews. He teaches instead that believers are the new temple (1 Cor 3:16; 2 Cor 6:16).[11]

Describing Paul's view of the law merely in terms of abolition is unsatisfying, for we also find the motif of fulfillment in Pauline writings. The whole Mosaic law is fulfilled in terms of love (Rom 13:8-10; Gal 5:14). Are any specific commands from the Mosaic law in force? When Paul says that love fulfills the law in Romans 13:8-10, he includes the prohibitions against adultery, murder, stealing and coveting as part of the law of love. All of these commands, of course, come from the Ten Commandments (Ex 20:13-17; Deut 5:17-21). He proceeds to add the injunction that one must love one's neighbor as oneself (Lev 19:18). Elsewhere murder (Rom 1:29), adultery (1 Cor 6:9) and stealing (1 Cor 5:10-11; 6:10; Eph 4:28) are indicted, and the prohibition against coveting receives extended treatment in Romans 7 (Rom 7:7-25; cf. 1 Cor 10:6; 2 Cor 9:5; Eph 4:19; 5:3; Col 3:5). The command to honor one's father and mother (Ex 20:12; Deut 5:16) is repeated in Ephesians 6:2 (cf. Rom 1:30; 2 Tim 3:2). Paul does not mention lying in Romans 13:9, but he does speak against it in Ephesians 4:25 and Colossians 3:9 (cf. Rom 9:1; 1 Cor 5:8; 13:6; 2 Cor 4:2; 6:7). Idolatry, which is proscribed by the first two commandments, is prohibited by Paul as well (1 Cor 5:10-11; 6:9; 10:7; Gal 5:20; Eph 5:5;

---

[11]Adolf von Harnack ("The Old Testament in the Pauline Letters and in the Pauline Churches," in *Understanding Paul's Ethics: Twentieth-Century Approaches*, ed. Brian S. Rosner [Grand Rapids, Mich.: Eerdmans, 1995], pp. 27-49) argues that the Old Testament does not play a formative role in Pauline ethics. For the contrary view, see Traugott Holtz, "The Question of the Context of Paul's Instructions" in the same volume (pp. 51-71). Brian S. Rosner rightly traces the pervasive influence of the Old Testament on Paul's ethics, even though I would not subscribe to all his conclusions; see his *Paul, Scripture and Ethics: A Study of 1 Corinthians 5—7* (Grand Rapids, Mich.: Baker, 1994). See also Peter J. Tomson, *Paul and the Jewish Law: Halakah in the Letters of the Apostle to the Gentiles* (Minneapolis: Fortress, 1990). In my judgment Tomson overplays the theme of *halakah* in Paul.

Col 3:5). The almost unreflective way Paul includes these commands in some of his vice lists suggests that he simply assumed that some commands found in the Old Testament continued to be authoritative.

It is also suggestive that when Paul indicts his Jewish contemporaries, commands relating to stealing, adultery and idolatry take center stage (Rom 2:21-22). Infractions relating to sabbath, circumcision and food laws are not mentioned. Instead their failure to observe moral norms of the law is highlighted. Scholars have often observed that the vice list in 1 Timothy 1:9-11 seems to be patterned, to some extent, after the Decalogue. "Lawless, rebellious, ungodly, sinners, unholy, and profane" (1 Tim 1:9) may reflect the first four commands of the Decalogue. The connection is inexact, and it is telling that the sabbath is not particularly noted. The first four commands of the Decalogue, however, focus on honoring God, and those who are ungodly and profane bring dishonor to his name. Violation of the command to honor parents is particularly egregious here—"patricide and matricide" (1 Tim 1:9). The list continues with murder, sexual immorality and homosexual relations (1 Tim 1:9-10), which correspond to the commands proscribing murder and adultery in the Decalogue. Kidnapping is a blatant example of stealing, and perjury violates the command not to bear false witness (1 Tim 1:10).

One feature in both 1 Timothy 1:9-11 and Romans 13:8-10 must also be observed. After Paul cites several commands of the Decalogue in Romans 13, he adds "and if there is any other commandment" (Rom 13:9). In other words, he is not providing an exhaustive list. Other commands from the Mosaic law are included in the law of love as well. Similarly, in 1 Timothy 1:10 Paul says "if there is anything else opposed to sound teaching," suggesting that other commands could be cited. Surely love receives the priority in both Romans and 1 Timothy (1 Tim 1:5). The affections of the heart are the essence of love, for what is in the heart will flow into one's life. That is probably why Paul speaks of anger and bitterness more than murder. Still, love must not be separated from external commands, even commands that come from the Mosaic law. No one can claim to be "loving" and at the same time commit adultery, murder, steal or covet. Commands give some texture to love so that it does not float in an airy-fairy sphere. People may feel very loving in their hearts, but their lives contradict their feelings. Paul believed that some elements of the law were still normative for believers since the prohibitions against idolatry, adultery, murder, stealing, lying and coveting are still in force, as is the injunction to honor one's parents.

Further evidence supports the notion that some of the commands from the

Old Testament are normative for Paul. He says, "Circumcision is nothing and uncircumcision is nothing, but keeping the commandments of God is everything" (1 Cor 7:19). The commandments could possibly be those of the historical Jesus, but more likely Paul has in mind commands from the Old Testament. In Romans 7—8 Paul begins by speaking of the alliance between sin and the law. The law is manipulated by sin, resulting in death. Liberation from the nexus of sin and the law comes through the work of Jesus on the cross. He accomplishes what the law was unable to do (Rom 8:1-4). By the power of the Holy Spirit believers are set free from the law of sin and death. The net result is that believers fulfill "the ordinance of the law" (Rom 8:4). Some interpreters understand this fulfillment to be forensic, so that nothing is said here about actual obedience in the lives of believers.[12] But it is highly unlikely that Paul consigns keeping the law to the forensic sphere. The law is fulfilled in those "who do not walk according to the flesh but according to the Spirit" (Rom 8:4). This is most naturally taken to refer to the concrete working out of the law in the lives of believers. The subsequent verses strengthen such a view. Those who are in the flesh do not and cannot submit to God's law (Rom 8:7). Conversely, it follows that those who are in the Spirit do submit to God's law per Romans 8:4! Such theology hardly exalts the ability of human beings because Paul emphatically teaches in Romans 8 that such obedience only comes from the enabling of the Holy Spirit. Such a view of Romans 8:4 fits with Romans 7. In Romans 7 Paul proclaims human beings' inability to keep God's law. Conversely, in Romans 8 Paul tells the other side of the story: by the power of the Spirit believers keep God's law. Of course, we are not talking about perfection here, and I have indicated earlier that believers, insofar as they inhabit the "not yet," have not left Romans 7:14-25 behind.

A related text is Romans 2:26-29. I have argued previously that Paul speaks of Christian Gentiles here, for their obedience is traced to the work of the Holy Spirit. What is remarkable is that Paul refers to their obedience as "keeping [phylassō] the ordinances of the law" (Rom 2:26). In Romans 2:27 such Gentiles are said to "observe [telousa] the law." When we remind ourselves that the Jews have just been criticized for committing adultery, stealing and robbing temples, it seems clear that some Gentiles are commended for keeping the moral norms of the law. The soundness of this conclusion is confirmed when it is noticed that Paul insists that "uncircumcised" (akrobystia)

---

[12]The most effective defense of a forensic interpretation of Rom 8:4 is provided by Douglas J. Moo, Romans 1—8, WEC (Chicago: Moody Press, 1991), pp. 514-17.

Gentiles keep the law. Anyone like Paul, nurtured and raised in the Torah, would immediately spot the oxymoron. Uncircumcised people cannot possibly keep the law since the law requires circumcision—unless there is an implicit reduction of the law and matters like circumcision are now excluded. First Corinthians 7:19 seems to drive us to this very conclusion: "Circumcision is nothing and uncircumcision is nothing, but keeping the commandments of God is everything." Once again circumcision is excluded from God's commands.

It seems that some of God's commands in the Torah continue to be binding for the people of God: prohibitions against idolatry, murder, adultery, stealing and lying as well as the command to honor one's parents. However, some commands—such as circumcision, the observance of sabbath and the practice of purity laws—are no longer to be literally obeyed. How do we put all this together? We must see that the Mosaic covenant qua covenant is no longer in force but that this covenant is fulfilled in Christ. Thus, all the commands of the law, including circumcision, point to something, even if they are not literally practiced today. Circumcision anticipates circumcision of the heart, Old Testament sacrifices anticipate the sacrifice of Christ (Rom 3:24-26) and so on. Some of the laws in the Old Testament, however, are fulfilled in a rather straightforward way. The prohibition against adultery passes over into the new era intact, without any change in content, though Paul emphasizes that the Spirit provides the strength to obey the command.

Children must continue to honor their parents as well (Eph 6:2-3). The command to honor our parents is one of the most helpful in trying to put together what Paul says, for he goes on to add the promise that those who obey their parents will live long on the earth. Surely in the Old Testament this promise relates to a long life in the land of promise that God gave Israel. But the church has no specific real estate that it can call its own. Nor is Paul promising that obedient children will live until old age. The latter hardly fits with the prospect of suffering that is the lot of the children of God. Does it follow from this that Paul sees no significance in the promise to live long in the land? No. If we understand Paul's theology, we know that the inheritance promised to Abraham has become the world (Rom 4:13)! Paul does not restrict the inheritance to the land of Palestine. He understands the inheritance to refer to the future glory awaiting believers (Rom 8:17). The promise of long life in the land, in Paul's view, relates to our heavenly inheritance. In other words, those who obey their parents will receive an eschatological reward—the inheritance promised to Abraham, Isaac and Jacob. They will not receive that reward in this life but the next. We have here not an earning of salvation but the evidence of God's saving work.

How Paul handles the command to honor one's parents is paradigmatic. The injunction to honor parents is fulfilled rather straightforwardly in the new covenant, but the promise to live long in the land no longer relates in the same way. The land now becomes the future world that belongs to the people of God, the heavenly Jerusalem (Gal 4:26). The land promised in the Old Testament anticipates and is fulfilled in the eschatological inheritance awaiting the people of God. Understanding the law in Paul, therefore, requires a broad understanding of his theology, involving detailed exegesis of many texts. Those who categorically eliminate any obedience of the law in the new covenant fail to understand Paul. Keeping the law by the power of the Spirit is not legalism, nor does it quench freedom. On the contrary, it is the highest expression of freedom (2 Cor 3:17).

Conclusion

Freedom from the law for Paul does not imply freedom from exhortations or commands. Life in the Spirit and the freedom of the Spirit are not quenched by commands. Instead, commands are compatible with life in the Spirit. Paul recognizes that believers still fall short of perfection, that they still inhabit the "not yet" until the day of the resurrection. He does not overestimate the ability of believers and advocate some kind of perfectionism. We have seen, however, that a changed life constitutes evidence that one belongs to God's people. For those who are justified and have received God's Spirit, commands and exhortations chart out the pathway in which believers should walk. These commands are not a summons to self-effort. They remind believers of their inability, casting them onto the power of the Spirit and summoning them to faith alone.

13

THE CHURCH &
SPIRITUAL GIFTS
The Unity of God's People

As a missionary Paul was not satisfied merely by individual conversions. His goal was to plant churches in specific localities. Only when such churches were established (1 Thess 3:1-10) did he feel his work was not in vain. The majority of his letters were addressed to the needs of such churches, instructing and exhorting them to stay true to the faith. In this chapter we shall examine the unity of the church and spiritual gifts; in the subsequent chapter, baptism, the Lord's Supper and the Pauline concept of ministry shall be explored.

Church

The term Paul uses most often to designate the new communities he established is *ekklēsia* (church). The term *ekklēsia* derives from the Old Testament, where the people of Israel were the *qahal Yahweh* (e.g., Num 16:3; 20:4; Deut 23:1, 8; 1 Chron 28:8) or *qahal Israel* (e.g., Ex 12:6; Lev 16:17; Num 14:5). The former was typically translated in the LXX as the *ekklēsia kyriou*. Paul often uses the phrase *church of God* (e.g., 1 Cor 1:2; 10:32; 11:22; 2 Cor 1:1; 1 Thess 2:14), perhaps to avoid the confusion between the Father and Christ that would be precipitated by the word *Lord*. The constant use of this term with

reference to Paul's converts indicates that he conceived of the church as the
new Israel, the new people of God, the fulfillment of what God intended with
Israel. This does not mean, of course, that there is no role or future for ethnic
Israel. We need not opt for an either-or, but we can affirm that the church is
the new Israel *and* that a future exists for ethnic Israel—a subject we shall
return to in due course.

One of the remarkable features of Paul's theology is that the local assembly is conceived of as a church in its own right. Often local assemblies and
gatherings are designated as churches: "the church in Cenchrea" (Rom 16:1),
the church in the house of Prisca and Aquila (Rom 16:5; 1 Cor 16:19), Gaius as
the host of the whole church (Rom 16:23), "the church of God in Corinth" (1
Cor 1:2; 2 Cor 1:1), the church in Nympha's house (Col 4:15), the church in
Laodicea (Col 4:16), "the church of the Thessalonians" (1 Thess 1:1; 2 Thess
1:1) and the church in Philemon's house (Philem 2). Most scholars believe
that at least four or five house churches existed in Rome (Rom 16:5, 10, 11, 14,
15). We do not know how many persons constituted a house church. Scholars
estimate anywhere from fifty to seventy-five. In any case, the local assembly,
usually meeting in houses, is considered a full-fledged church. Sometimes
Paul uses the plural *churches*, but a locality is given, suggesting a number of
local churches in a certain geographical setting: "churches of Galatia" (1 Cor
16:1; Gal 1:1), "the churches of Asia" (1 Cor 16:19), "the churches of Macedonia" (2 Cor 8:1) and "churches of Judea" (Gal 1:22). Paul does not suggest
that the church is somehow deficient or not authentically a church because it
is limited to one locality.

Paul also uses the plural *churches* of the various local assemblies (Rom
16:4, 16; 1 Cor 11:16; 14:33-34; 16:1, 19; 2 Cor 8:1, 18-19; 11:8, 28; Gal 1:2, 22;
1 Thess 2:14; 2 Thess 1:4). This does not detract from the authenticity of local
assemblies, but the plural does emphasize the interrelationship between various churches. Perhaps Paul mentions that all churches give thanks for the
work of Prisca and Aquila to emphasize this couple's devotion to Paul and
the solidarity between Paul and the other churches. In this way, Prisca and
Aquila attest to the validity of the Pauline gospel. It is also possible that such
a greeting simply communicates the solidarity among various churches (cf.
Rom 16:16; 1 Cor 16:19). Paul also appeals to the plurality of churches when
he feels that a particular church is misled. He reminds the Corinthians that
the other churches follow the custom regarding the adornment of women (1
Cor 11:16) and that in all other assemblies the women keep silent (1 Cor
14:33-34). His instructions about abiding in one's calling are not unique to

Corinth but represent what he says in "all churches" (1 Cor 7:17). Even though Paul does not technically use a plural in 1 Corinthians 4:17, the expression *every church* is obviously plural in conception: the "ways" of Paul are what he teaches in every assembly. The churches' mutual responsibility to care for one another provokes Paul to remind the Corinthians of the plurality of the churches when he asks and exhorts them to contribute to the collection (1 Cor 16:1; 2 Cor 8:1, 18-19, 23; 11:8; 12:13).

The word *ekklēsia* also emphasizes the church gathered, just as the term in the Old Testament is used when Israel gathered together (e.g., Ex 12:6; Lev 16:17; Num 14:5; Deut 31:30; Josh 8:35; 1 Kings 8:14, 22, 55). Paul mentions gathering for the Lord's Supper (1 Cor 11:18) or for the use of spiritual gifts (1 Cor 14:19, 23, 28). The meaning of the term *church,* of course, implies gathering together even when such an idea is not specifically stated. The assembly of God in Christ Jesus is God's new community, his new people.

Many scholars, who believe that Colossians and Ephesians were written by a disciple of Paul, doubt that Paul ever referred to the universal church. The distinction between the universal and local church can be pressed too hard.[1] Some evidence, even in the letters commonly acknowledged as Pauline, suggests that Paul moved somewhat fluidly between the ideas of a local and universal church. For instance, Paul sometimes uses the plural *churches* to communicate the unity among God's people. In 1 Corinthians 10:32 Paul urges the Corinthians to give no offense "to the church of God." It is just possible that only the local church is in view, given the specific situation addressed. The generality of the phrase suggests, however, that the universal church is intended.

First Corinthians 12:28 almost certainly focuses on the universal church: "God appointed in the church first apostles, second prophets, third teachers." James Dunn argues that only the church of Corinth is in mind here.[2] More likely, Paul communicates what is generally the case, not limiting himself just to Corinth but discussing the pattern evident in the church as a whole. We have already noticed that the plural *churches* is employed on a number of occasions in the Corinthian letters, presumably because the church was inclined to go its own way and needed to be reminded that they were not the

---

[1]See the illuminating essay by Peter O'Brien, "The Church as a Heavenly and Eschatological Entity," in *The Church in the Bible and the World: An International Study,* ed. D. A. Carson (Grand Rapids, Mich.: Baker, 1987), pp. 88-119, esp. pp. 93-98.

[2]James D. G. Dunn, *The Theology of Paul the Apostle* (Grand Rapids, Mich.: Eerdmans, 1998), pp. 578-79.

only church in the world. Paul reminds the Corinthian church in 1 Corinthians 12:28 that God has established a certain priority of gifts in the church as a whole. Again, the lines are somewhat fluid between the local and universal church, for what applies to the latter also applies to the former. Twice Paul says he persecuted "the church of God" (1 Cor 15:9; Gal 1:13), and in Philippians 3:6 that he persecuted "the church." Certainly local churches are included in Paul's persecution, but Paul also conceives of his persecution of the church in general terms to convey his opposition against the church as a whole.

The oscillation between the universal and local church appears in 1 Timothy. Paul clearly refers to the local church when he says that widows should be helped by others so that the church will not be burdened (1 Tim 5:16). The work of an overseer in caring for the church must also refer to the local church (1 Tim 3:5), for Paul does not conceive of the overseer caring for the universal church! It is likely in 1 Timothy 3:15, though, that he thinks of the church more generally or universally. The church is "the house of God, the pillar and support of the truth." Again some fluidity is likely. Paul does not play off the universal church against the local church.

The emphasis on the universal church is most evident in Colossians and Ephesians. We have already seen that the notion of local churches exists in Colossians (Col 4:15-16), but references to the universal church are also found in this letter. Christ is said to be "the head of the body, the church" (Col 1:18; cf. Col 1:24). One could just possibly restrict these sayings to the local church, but the phrase *the body, the church* suggests the universal church. And yet we must admit that the fluidity of usage continues, for no disjunction between the universal and local church is intended, even if the emphasis is on the universal church.

The focus on the universal church is most evident in Ephesians, perhaps because this letter is an encyclical. Jesus is the head of the church (Eph 1:22). Through the church, God's wisdom is disclosed to angelic powers (Eph 3:10). Glory redounds to God in the church (Eph 3:21). The parallel between husbands and wives and Christ and the church receives extended attention in Ephesians 5:22-33 (see esp. Eph 5:32). Christ is the head of the church (Eph 5:23), and the church is subject to Christ (Eph 5:24). Christ demonstrated his love for the church through his death and nurture, and he cherishes it (Eph 5:25, 29); and his intention is to preserve a pure church (Eph 5:27). Though Paul's focus here is on the universal church, the boundary lines between the universal and local church still remain somewhat indistinct. He concentrates his discussion on the church as a whole. This is not so remarkably different from the other Pauline letters where occasionally he considers the churches as a plurality. On the other hand, in Colossians and Ephesians the emphasis falls on the church as a whole—the church as a unity throughout the world.

The Body and the Unity of the Church

The most famous metaphor for the church in Pauline writings is the "body of Christ." Scholars have been fascinated with the origin of the metaphor.[3] It used to be popular to derive its origin from the primal-man myth of Gnosticism, but this theory has been abandoned by nearly everyone. Some think that it stems from the Damascus Road revelation, where Jesus discloses that Paul's persecution of the church involves persecuting Jesus himself (Acts 9:4-5). Or perhaps it comes from Paul's Adam christology, his "in Christ" theology, corporate personality, sacramental theology or the conception that the city or state is like a body. No theory can be proved, and in the end *where* Paul got the idea is less important than *how* he used it. The former can never be more than a hypothesis, but the latter can be explored from Paul's letters.

In Paul's earlier letters the body metaphor is used to emphasize the unity of the church. We can understand why some trace its origin to communion, for in 1 Corinthians 10:16-17 an analogy is forged between the one loaf shared at communion and the body of Christ. Sharing the cup involves sharing in the benefits of Christ's blood, and sharing in the loaf involves sharing in the benefits of Christ's death (1 Cor 10:16). Paul detects significance in the fact that there is "one loaf" (1 Cor 10:17). The unity of the loaf demonstrates that believers are one body, that they are united in Christ. The unity stems from the source of their life since all believers partake of the same loaf. The life of believers comes from their feeding on the crucified and resurrected Lord; their new life derives from believing in the crucified and risen Christ. Only by partaking in the benefits of his death are believers made members of Christ's body.

Unity in 1 Corinthians 12 and Romans 12. An extended discussion on the church as a body ensues in 1 Corinthians 12. Divisions over spiritual gifts were creating havoc in Corinth (1 Cor 12-14). Paul attempts to provide perspective, without quenching the use of such gifts in the community. His main theme is unity in diversity. Some might want to say the theme is diversity in unity, but then the accent is placed on diversity when the emphasis is on unity. Diversity is a given, for it is obvious that various spiritual gifts are

---

[3]For a survey of the discussion, see ibid., pp. 549-51.

being used. Paul reminds the Corinthians that such diversity does not cancel out unity but is instead an expression of it. The metaphor of the body dominates 1 Corinthians 12:12-27. The body is one and yet it has many different members, but the variety of members does not nullify the fact that there is one body. The presence of two legs, two arms, two eyes and two ears does not prove that there is more than one body. First Corinthians 12:12 says, "For just as the body is one and has many members, and all the members of the body, though many, are one body, so also is Christ." What is surprising in this verse is that instead of saying "so also is the church," Paul says "so also is Christ." Why does Paul insert *Christ* instead of *the church?* It seems that the idea is similar to what we saw in 1 Corinthians 10:16-17. The church is one body because it eats of the one loaf, Christ. The individual members of the church, in other words, are the body *of Christ.* Christ, not the church, has priority. The fundamental reality in the people of God is Christ, not the diversity of gifts. Paul wants the Corinthians to take their eyes off their so-called dazzling gifts and focus on Christ.

The unity of the body is realized at baptism, where believers are baptized into one body (1 Cor 12:13). Baptism fundamentally involves being baptized "into Christ Jesus" (Rom 6:3), in which believers are plunged into his death (Rom 6:3-4). "Those who are baptized into Christ have been clothed with Christ" (Gal 3:27). To be baptized into one body, then, is to be baptized into Christ. He is the one body. But by definition the one body is characterized by diversity (1 Cor 12:14), for bodies are made up of many members. No member of the body should feel inferior (1 Cor 12:15-16), for every member is needed. The foot and ear may appear less useful than a hand or an eye, but they are just as crucial to the body. Indeed, if the body were composed of only one member it would be grotesque. It would be a monstrosity if the body were a giant eye or a giant ear (1 Cor 12:17). The variety of the body is "appointed" *(etheto)* and determined by God (1 Cor 12:18). The diversity of the church is not contrary to his will but is an expression of it. By definition a body is composed of not one but many members (1 Cor 12:19-20). If some members of the church are tempted to exalt themselves, thinking that they are superior to other members, they are sadly mistaken (1 Cor 12:21). The eye cannot dispense with the hand, nor can the head dispense with the feet, for without the so-called inferior parts there is no body. The various parts of the body are needed for the body to function properly (1 Cor 12:22-24), and God has constituted the body as a unified whole (1 Cor 12:24-27). This unity manifests itself in caring for one another, so that all participate in another's joy or sorrow (1 Cor 12:25-26). So Paul reminds them at the end of the discussion that they are Christ's body and therefore members of one another (1 Cor 12:27). The text ends with the emphasis on unity ("you are the body of Christ") and diversity ("and members individually").

The body is portrayed in the same way in Romans 12:4-5. The human body by definition has many members, and thus it is marked by diversity of function. Believers similarly are one body in Christ, but they belong to one another and are individually members of the same body.

Unity in Colossians and Ephesians. Some scholars doubt that Paul wrote Colossians and Ephesians because in these letters the body metaphor changes. Now Paul speaks of Christ as being the *head* of the body (Eph 1:22-23; 4:15-16; 5:23; Col 1:18; 2:19). The argument against Pauline authorship on this basis is unpersuasive. Understanding the church as Christ's body is a metaphor, and it is common to change a metaphor to make a different point. Those who object to such a shift understand metaphors too rigidly. Why does the metaphor shift in Colossians and Ephesians? Because Paul wants to emphasize Christ's lordship over the church. Christ at his resurrection was exalted over all angelic powers and seated at the right hand of God, and presently he reigns over the church (Eph 1:19-23). Similarly, the Colossian hymn (Col 1:15-20) features Christ's supremacy in creation and redemption. Since Christ is the Lord of the church, the church must submit to him as Lord and Master (Eph 5:23-24). There is no doubt here that the word *kephalē* refers to Christ's authority over the church.[4] Yet there is also the idea that the head is the source from which the body derives its strength, nourishment and growth.[5] Paul uses a twofold metaphor of "head." Those who are swept away by the asceticism of the "philosophy" (Col 2:8) are "not holding fast to the head" (Col 2:19). And it is from the head that growth comes (Col 2:19), suggesting that the head is the source of nourishment. Perhaps Paul conceives here of food entering the body through the head. Similarly, in Ephesians 4:15 the church is exhorted to grow up into the head, clearly an example of mixing

---

[4]On *kephalē*, see esp. Wayne Grudem, "Does *Kephalē* ('Head') Mean 'Source' or 'Authority Over' in Greek Literature? A Survey of 2,336 Examples," *TJ* 6 (1985): 38-59, and "The Meaning of *Kephalē* ('Head'): A Response to Recent Studies," in *Recovering Biblical Manhood and Womanhood: A Response to Evangelical Feminism*, ed. John Piper and Wayne Grudem (Wheaton, Ill.: Crossway, 1991), pp. 425-68, 534-41; Wayne Grudem, "The Meaning of *Kephalē* ('Head'): An Evaluation of New Evidence, Real and Alleged," *JETS* 44 (2001): 25-65; Joseph A. Fitzmyer, "*Kephalē* in I Corinthians 11:3," *Int* 47 (1993): 52-59.

[5]Clinton E. Arnold, in *Jesus of Nazareth: Lord and Christ: Essays on the Historical Jesus and New Testament Christology*, ed. Joel B. Green and M. Turner (Grand Rapids, Mich.: Eerdmans, 1994), pp. 346-66.

metaphors! And from the head comes the growth that is necessary for a well functioning body.

Another theme in Colossians and Ephesians is unity. Believers must let Christ's peace have dominion in their corporate life, for they were called to such harmony as the body of Christ (Col 3:15). In Ephesians 2:11—3:13 Paul emphasizes the unity of Jews and Gentiles in Christ. By virtue of the work of Christ on the cross, Jews and Gentiles are no longer estranged from one another, nor are they estranged from God. They have been "reconciled to God in one body through the cross" (Eph 2:16). The inclusion of Gentiles is high-lighted since they were formerly cut off from the covenant people and sepa-rated from the promises of Israel. Christ has come and broken down the barrier that separated Jews and Gentiles. The peace established between Jews and Gentiles, expressed in the "one body" they now share, is rooted in the gospel, namely, the message of the crucified and risen Lord (Eph 2:16-17). This gospel proclaims peace to those who are near and far. On the basis of this gospel, both Jews and Gentiles have access to God through the Spirit. Paul exults in the fact that Gentiles are no longer strangers and aliens but fel-low citizens with Israel and members of God's household. The mystery revealed to him is that Gentiles are "fellow heirs and members of the same body [syssōma] and fellow sharers of the promise through the gospel" (Eph 3:6). The unity of the body of Christ, both Jews and Gentiles together, is the major theme in Ephesians 2:11—3:13.

Paul's focus on the unity of the body is not surprising, for the church is at center stage in Ephesians. God has chosen and predestined a people for his glory (Eph 1:3-14). After saying that Christ is the head of the church (i.e., his body), the church is said to be "the fullness of the one who fills all things" (Eph 1:23). Although the meaning of this is debated, the participle plēroumenou should probably be construed as a middle that functions like a verb in the active voice. This judgment is supported by the theology of Ephe-sians as a whole, where the church receives its fullness from God, Christ and the Spirit (Eph 3:19; 4:10, 13; 5:18). The power of the church is not inherent but comes from God himself, who has filled the church on the basis of Christ's death, resurrection and exaltation.

Since the church is so extraordinary, we are not surprised to learn later that it is "through the *church* that the manifold wisdom of God" is displayed (Eph 3:10). Paul was not a Western individualist who indulged in a privatized Christianity. Nor did he conceive of the church as an embarrassment or a nec-essary evil. The church enshrined God's plan for history, revealing to all creation the wisdom and depth of God's saving plan. The church is the locus of God's glory, the theater in which he displays his grace and love. The church features God's wisdom, declaring to the whole universe that the outworking of history is not arbitrary but fulfills God's plan.

Since the church is at the center of God's purposes, Paul summons it to live up to its calling (Eph 4:1-3). When the church follows its Lord, it brings honor to God and to the Lord Jesus Christ. The church fulfills its calling in particular when it maintains "the unity of the Spirit in the bond of peace" (Eph 4:3). We have already seen from Ephesians 2:11—3:13 that the unity of the church was established through the blood of Christ. The church is not called on to create unity but to preserve the unity that already exists. The basis of this unity is proclaimed again in Ephesians 4:4-6: "There is one body and one Spirit, just as you were also called in one hope of your calling. There is one Lord, one faith, one baptism, one God and Father of all, who is over all and through all and in all." Paul does not summon people to unity who are fractured by irreconcilable differences. He calls the church to peace because enmity and hatred ended at the cross of Jesus Christ. He summons the church to enjoy the peace and harmony already won. The imperative, as always, is grounded in the indicative.

The unity of the body continues to be a theme in the discussion of spiritual gifts (Eph 4:7-16). Various gifts are given to the church so that the body will be edified (Eph 4:12). This edification is defined further as "unity of the faith" (Eph 4:13). Such unity is realized when believers attain the knowledge of God's Son, when they grow up into maturity and reach the full stature of Christ (Eph 4:13). This vision for the church will not be fulfilled perfectly until the day of redemption, but Paul expects that it will be attained in some measure in this age. The church will be stabilized so that it will not be rocked by every new and devious teaching (Eph 4:14). The unity that Paul envisions, therefore, cannot be described merely as feelings of harmony and love, as important as the expression of love is. The unity demanded is rooted in truth and is jeopardized by deviant teaching. Unity will be realized only if the church is faithful to the truth of the gospel and avoids teachings contrary to this gospel. Hence, the church will grow up into its head only through the proclamation of the truth of the gospel (Eph 4:15). This verse is not simply saying that we should speak the truth in love—as right as that thought is— but that the truth of the gospel should be heralded with love. The unity of the body, then, coincides with the growth of the body. And the body grows when it is rooted in the truth of the gospel. Paul would have no place for those who proclaimed unity but disparaged truth, nor for those who prized truth but overlooked the importance of unity.

Survey of texts on the unity of the church. The theme of the church's unity is so pervasive that we must survey some texts briefly to demonstrate its presence. In Romans, for instance, Paul writes to rally the Roman churches around his gospel so they will support his venture to Spain. The section on the weak and strong (Rom 14:1—15:13) indicates that the church was polarized over unclean food and the observance of days. Paul could hardly convince the church to support the furtherance of the gospel if the Romans were quarreling over various matters. We will not linger at this point to explore Paul's argument, but his aim was to bring the church together "so that with one mouth they would glorify God" (Rom 15:6). He wants them to praise God together as Jews and Gentiles (Rom 15:7-13). Paul tolerates different views on foods and the observance of days, but he explains that the attitude toward those with whom we differ should be loving and not censorious. Believers should think of ways they can minimize offending others instead of scandalizing the weak. The Corinthian church also experienced divisions over food (1 Cor 8:1—11:1). The text differs in a number of respects from Romans 14:1—15:13, but Paul's essential message of unity is parallel to Romans 14—15.

The Corinthians were also divided over their estimation of church leaders (1 Cor 1:10—4:21): some followed Paul, some followed Apollos, others followed Cephas, and apparently others said they followed Christ. Paul was intensely troubled by their factions because personality cults nullify the cross of Christ. He desperately wanted the church to unite, but he wanted unity on the basis of the cross, a cross that undercuts human pride. Factions existed not because Paul and Apollos had different theologies (otherwise Paul would scarcely encourage Apollos to visit Corinth; see 1 Cor 16:12) but because the Corinthians pandered to their egos by attaching themselves to one leader rather than another. Paul reminds them of the message of the cross—for the cross scuttles human wisdom—and that boasting should only be in the Lord. We have already seen how the Corinthians were also plagued by dissension over spiritual gifts, so that the bulk of the letter can be described as Paul's attempt to bring them to a united acceptance of his gospel.

Significant evidence exists that the Philippian church was plagued by disunity. Paul specifically exhorts Euodia and Syntyche to come to peace (Phil 4:2-3), asking other believers to help them do so. His sustained exhortation to unity (Phil 1:27—2:4) suggests that a serious problem needed to be remedied in the church. Once we perceive the problem as disunity, the rest of the letter fits together nicely. Paul writes about the divided response he has received from other believers, probably located in Rome, to his preaching and his imprisonment (Phil 1:12-18) because it functioned as an example for the Philippians. Some believers proclaimed the gospel out of envy and strife, hoping to bring grief to Paul during his incarceration. Other believers heralded the gospel and had good will toward Paul. Paul rejoices in either case, despite the problematic motives of some fellow believers, because in both instances Christ is being preached. Paul tells this story to instruct the Philippians. Even if other believers have poor motives, we should continue to live for the gospel and overlook the sins of others. Believers proclaiming Christ with impure motives are still preaching the gospel. No evidence exists that they were promulgating false teaching, and it would be a mistake to identify these preachers with the false teachers of Philippians 3:2—4:1. These preachers apparently proclaimed the correct gospel. Their motives, not their message, was problematic. Perhaps they were jealous of Paul's prominence, hoping to demote him in the eyes of other believers. As we saw earlier, Paul does not countenance a unity that dismisses the importance of truth. He does, however, overlook the petty jealousies of others, prizing the spread of the gospel over his own reputation.

In Philippians 2 Paul sets forth three examples of lives committed to the glory of God. Christ Jesus is the supreme exemplar of one who sacrifices his own interests for the good of others. He did not exploit his advantages and was willing to suffer the most degraded and despicable death imaginable for the sake of others (Phil 2:5-8). As a result God rewarded and exalted him (Phil 2:9-11). Unity is preserved when believers live like Jesus Christ and set the cause of the gospel over and above their private interests. Timothy and Epaphroditus (Phil 2:19-30) are also set forward as men who were willing to live for the sake of the gospel. Paul knows no one else like Timothy who is genuinely concerned with what is happening in the lives of believers (Phil 2:20). Others seek their own interests, but Timothy seeks the things of Christ Jesus (Phil 2:21). Similarly, Epaphroditus risked his life for the cause of the gospel while visiting Paul and ministering to his needs. Unity comes not by prizing unity for its own sake; it comes when people live to spread the gospel of Christ, when believers imitate people like Timothy and Epaphroditus. Divisions spread when believers take their eyes off their mission and become embroiled in personal disputes. Paul, Christ Jesus, Timothy and Epaphroditus function as models because they all lived for the glory of

God and the spread of the gospel of Christ.

Of course, a competing gospel is vying for the Philippians' attention (Phil 3:2—4:1). Paul warns the Philippians about the dogs, the evil workers and the mutilation. They should follow Paul's example and disavow the "gospel" that demands circumcision. The only gospel that deserves their loyalty calls for faith in Christ and not righteousness through the law. Some might espouse perfection in this world, but perfection is only available on the day of resurrection. Paul, therefore, summons the church (Phil 3:17—4:1) to join in imitating him and others who walk according to his pattern. Enemies of the cross lurk nearby, but their destination is destruction. Those who follow Paul and Paul's like-minded colleagues will receive, on the other hand, an eschatological reward. The present body, weakened by sin, will be replaced by a resurrection body. This all-too-brief summary of Philippians 3 serves as a reminder of how important the truth is to Paul. Those who claim to believe in Christ, like the Judaizers, who proclaim a gospel that demands circumcision, receive the sharpest of rebukes from Paul. He engages in a fierce polemic against them, dismissing them as unbelievers and warning of their future destruction.

More could be said about this theme, but it is apparent that the unity of the church was precious to Paul and worth contending for. The unity for which he strives, though, is the unity demanded by the gospel. Unity is not to be pursued at all costs, however, if it contradicts the truth of the gospel (e.g., Gal 2:3-5). Even where theological agreement exists, harmony is difficult to sustain. Believers must work to maintain it. Paul exhorts his readers to sustain such harmony, for this too is a witness to the gospel.

Temple and People

Paul does not often call the church God's temple *(naos)*. Still, such an attribution (1 Cor 3:16-17; 2 Cor 6:16; Eph 2:21) is significant because the temple was so central to Judaism; it was one of the pillars on which Judaism rested. For Paul, by contrast, the Jerusalem temple no longer holds any importance. Paul does not make any reference to priests serving as cultic functionaries, nor does he recommend offering sacrifices, since the one definitive sacrifice was the sacrifice of Christ. To have a "religion" without a temple, priests or sacrifices would have seemed quite strange in the Greco-Roman world. The newness of the gospel emerges at this very point. God's new building cannot be confined to a physical structure but is the church (1 Cor 3:9): the people of God are his dwelling place. The foundation of this building is Jesus Christ, and ministers build on this superstructure either with quality materials or with materials that will perish on the day of judgment (1 Cor 3:10-15). The Spirit dwells in believers, not the temple in Jerusalem (1 Cor 3:16). In 1 Corinthians 3:16 the focus is not on the Spirit's indwelling believers individualistically. What Paul emphasizes is the Spirit's dwelling in believers corporately. The Jerusalem temple pointed to and anticipated the church of Jesus Christ, which fulfills what the former temple envisioned.

Second Corinthians 6:16 makes it abundantly clear that the temple imagery of the Old Testament is fulfilled in God's dwelling in his people corporately. The only uncleanness to worry about now relates not to food or other Levitical regulations, but to the uncleanness of sin (2 Cor 7:1). Temple imagery is also found in the word *access (prosagōgē)*. Access to God is available not through some cultic process but through faith in Christ (Rom 5:2). Believers now have access to God—not through the sacrificial system and the temple in Jerusalem, but in the Spirit on the basis of the cross of Christ (Eph 2:18). Since Gentiles are now part of God's temple, they must be members of his household (*oikeioi*, Eph 2:19). In the temple, the Court of Gentiles was segregated from the Court of Israelites, and a famous sign proclaimed that any Gentile who entered forbidden precincts in the temple would be slain. Perhaps Paul refers to this notion when he says that in Christ the dividing wall of partition has been removed (Eph 2:14). In God's new temple Jews and Gentiles are no longer alienated from one another but are equal members of the same house.

In Ephesians the church is said to be built on the foundation of the apostles and prophets (Eph 2:20) instead of on Christ. On first glance, this seems to contradict 1 Corinthians 3:10-11, where the foundation of the house is restricted to Jesus Christ alone. Those who believe Paul is contradicting himself read metaphors too rigidly, expecting that Paul will always use the same metaphor for the same purpose. In actuality, the Ephesians text makes the same point as 1 Corinthians 3:10-11 does. Jesus Christ is the cornerstone of the building (Eph 2:20): he is the crucial element in the whole building. The entire building takes its shape and structure from him. Such a statement communicates the same truth that is articulated in 1 Corinthians 3:10-11, where Jesus Christ is announced as the only foundation for the church. To say that the apostles and prophets are the foundation of the church is not a genuine contradiction, for the teaching of the apostles and prophets must adhere to the gospel of Jesus Christ to be authoritative. Paul assumes here that the apostles and prophets are faithful to the cornerstone of the building, the decisive stone in the entire building—Jesus Christ.

Believers are God's temple in Christ and are "built up together as God's dwelling place in the Spirit" (Eph 2:21-22). The theology here is similar to what we have seen in 1 Corinthians 3:16 and 2 Corinthians 6:16—the church is God's temple. Ephesians does not represent an advance over the Corinthian letters in this respect. Nor do the Pastoral Letters deviate from genuine Pauline teaching when they say in 1 Timothy 3:15 that the church is "God's house." Temple imagery is probably still present here, but Paul is also probably suggesting that the church is structured after the household (cf. 1 Tim 3:4-5, 12). To say that the church "is the pillar and support of the truth" (1 Tim 3:15) does not deny the priority of the gospel, nor does Paul conceive of the church as foundational and the gospel as dependent on the church. The gospel, after all, created the church. The preached word brought it into existence, as the Pastorals themselves suggest (1 Tim 1:12-17; 2:1-7; 2 Tim 1:9-11; Tit 2:11-14; 3:4-7). What Paul acknowledges here is that if the church goes astray, the witness of the gospel will be damaged, for the gospel that first created the church is also disseminated by the church. If the church deviates from the gospel, the message proclaimed will be distorted. Paul does not intend here to answer the question of how the gospel is recovered if the church strays from the path. He wants to emphasize how important it is for the church to stay true to the gospel it proclaims (1 Tim 3:15-16) since it bears that message in the world.

The Old Testament often refers to Israel as God's "people" (laos). It is somewhat surprising how little Paul employs this term to refer to the church of Jesus Christ (Rom 9:25-26; 2 Cor 6:16; Tit 2:14). The use of the term indicates, however, that the blessings of Israel are now fulfilled in the church of Christ. The church is the new people of God.

Unity and Food

The unity of the church in Paul's day was tested severely over the issue of food. Believers had sharp differences of opinion as to whether it was legitimate to eat food offered to idols (1 Cor 8:1—11:1). Contention also surfaced over the eating of unclean foods (Rom 14:1—15:13). Some scholars are convinced that 1 Corinthians 8:10—11:1 and Romans 14:1—15:13 address the same basic situation, suggesting that in Romans Paul summarizes and rewrites the exhortations in 1 Corinthians 8—10. If this view is correct, then Romans 14—15 is not addressed to particular circumstances in Rome but contains general instruction.[6] The common elements in the two passages are remarkable. Paul addresses the "weak" in both texts (Rom 14:1-2; 15:1; 1 Cor 8:7, 9-12). Even a cursory reading of both chapters reveals that believers debated whether they should eat certain foods. In both texts Paul encourages believers to edify and build up one another instead of engaging in behavior that causes a brother or sister to stumble or to be destroyed (Rom 14:13, 15, 19, 21; 15:2; 1 Cor 8:1, 9, 11, 13; 10:23-24, 32-33). We are not surprised that in both sections Paul emphasizes that believers are to honor God and give him glory in whatever they do (Rom 14:6-9; 15:6; 1 Cor 10:30-31).

Despite the remarkable similarities between the two texts, it is quite likely that Paul addresses different situations in 1 Corinthians 8—10 and Romans 14—15.[7] For example, food offered to idols takes center stage in 1 Corinthians (1 Cor 8:1, 4, 7, 10; 10:19, 28), but the matter of idols is never even raised in Romans. The propriety of abstaining from meat and wine for the sake of others emerges as an issue in Romans (Rom 14:2, 21), whereas this matter is not broached in 1 Corinthians. The weak in 1 Corinthians come from a pagan background and feel defiled by food offered to idols since the reality of idols is still all too real (1 Cor 8:7, 10, 12). The weak in Romans, on the other hand, reject food that is unclean and impure in accordance with the Levitical food laws (Rom 14:14, 20). The terms *common (koinos)* and *clean (katharos)* reflect a typical Jewish concern about the purity of foods (Rom 14:14, 20 respectively). The noun *koinos* and the verb *koinoō* often refer to the issue of clean and unclean foods in Jewish literature (1 Macc 1:47, 62; 4 Macc 7:6; Mk 7:2, 5; Acts 10:14-15, 28; 11:8-9; Josephus *Ant.* 11.8.7). So too, the *katharos* word group designates foods that are pure or impure (in the LXX, see Gen 7:2-3, 8; 8:20; Lev 11; Deut 14:7-8, 10, 19; Ezek 4:13; Hos 9:3; see also Mt 23:25-26; Mk 7:19; Lk 11:39, 41). There is no evidence, in other words, that the weak in Romans had any past associations with idols. They abstained

---

[6]For example, Robert J. Karris, "Romans 14:5—15:13 and the Occasion of Romans," in *The Romans Debate*, ed. Karl P. Donfried, rev. ed. (Peabody, Mass.: Hendrickson, 1991), pp. 65-84; Wayne Meeks, "Judgment and the Brother: Romans 14:1—15:13," in *Tradition and Interpretation in the New Testament: Essays in Honor of E. Earle Ellis for His Sixtieth Birthday*, ed. Gerald F. Hawthorne with O. Betz (Grand Rapids, Mich.: Eerdmans, 1987), pp. 290-300.

[7]For this view, see Karl P. Donfried, "False Presuppositions in the Study of Romans," in *The Romans Debate*, ed. Karl P. Donfried, rev. ed. (Peabody, Mass.: Hendrickson, 1991), pp. 102-125; Mark Reasoner, *The Strong and the Weak: Romans 14:1—15:13 in Context*, SNTSMS 103 (New York: Cambridge University Press, 1999); Joseph A. Fitzmyer, *Romans: A New Translation with Introduction and Commentary*, AB 33 (New York: Doubleday, 1993), pp. 68-84; Christoph Heil, *Die Ablehnung der Speisegebote durch Paulus: Zur Frage nach der Stellung des Apostels zum Gesetz*, BBB 96 (Weinheim: Beltz Athenäum, 1994), pp. 254-55.

from foods that were declared unclean by the Mosaic law.

The connection with idols explains why "conscience" comes to the forefront in 1 Corinthians (1 Cor 8:7, 10, 12; 10:25, 27-29), but it is not even mentioned in Romans 14—15, although this point should not be pressed too hard since the idea of conscience seems present in Romans 14—15. Paul addresses the question of whether it is fitting to eat in a pagan temple in 1 Corinthians 10:19-22, but once again such a subject is lacking in Romans. The call to mutual acceptance rings through Romans (Rom 14:1, 3; 15:7) but is found nowhere in 1 Corinthians. Finally, the controversy in Romans is not restricted to dietary issues, for the matter of observing certain days also arises (Rom 14:5-6). The commonalities between Romans 14—15 and 1 Corinthians 8—10 cannot be denied, but the differences are such that the texts cannot be merged together in every respect.

We have already noted that the issue in 1 Corinthians 8—10 is the eating of food offered to idols. The weak, convinced of the reality of idols, feel defiled if they indulge in eating idol food (1 Cor 8:7). The weak may be temporarily emboldened by observing the "knowers" eating idol food, but in actuality they will be destroyed *(apollymi, skandilzō)* by participating because they violate their conscience (1 Cor 8:10-13; 10:28-33).[8] The same danger emerges in Romans. Paul fears that the weak will stumble (Rom 14:13, 21) and be destroyed *(apollymi*, Rom 14:15; *kataluō*, Rom 14:20) at the behest of the strong. What does Paul have in mind when he uses terms such as *destroy, obstacle* and *cause to stumble (apollymi, proskomma* and *skandalizō)*? Some scholars suggest that eternal ruin is not in view since Paul speaks of believers being grieved (Rom 14:15), which suggests subjective pain rather than future judgment.[9] Further support for this interpretation is found in the word *edification* (Rom 14:19; 15:2; cf. 1 Cor 8:1, 10; 10:23), for this term suggests a failure to grow as a believer, not eternal damnation. Understanding the threat to be less than eternal judgment is attractive, but the argument is not persuasive. Paul regularly uses the term *destroy (apollymi)* for eschatological destruction (Rom 2:12; 1 Cor 1:18-19; 10:9-10; 15:18; 2 Cor 2:15; 4:3; 2 Thess 2:10), and there is no reason to depart from a similar definition here. Similarly, the terms *stumbling block (skandalon)* and *obstacle (proskomma)* often designate future ruin (Mt 13:20-21; 18:6-7; Lk 17:1; Rom 9:32-33; 11:9; 16:17; 1 Cor 1:23; Gal 5:11; 1 Pet 2:8; 1 Jn 2:10). Defin-

---

[8]Paul never calls those who feel free to eat idol food "strong" in 1 Corinthians. In light of 1 Cor 8:1-6 a better term is *knowers*. Nevertheless, I will use the term *strong* for both in a few instances for the sake of convenience.

[9]See especially Judith M. Gundry Volf, *Paul and Perseverance: Staying In and Falling Away* (Louisville, Ky.: Westminster John Knox, 1990), pp. 85-97.

ing the threat as future judgment does not cancel out the word *grief;* it merely demonstrates that the grief is everlasting. We also see that the term *edification* (*oikodomē*) is contrasted with *destroy* (*kataluō*) in Romans 14:19-20, indicating that the tearing down envisioned is irrevocable. The use of the word *condemned* in Romans 14:23 also points to eschatological judgment.

Why would the weak perish simply by eating food that they considered to be defiled? Paul's answer is that they are no longer living by faith (Rom 14:23) because they are living in violation of their conscience (1 Cor 8:7, 9-12). Those who violate their own consciences and do not live within the orbit of their own faith have no foundation on which to live. By living on the basis of another's conscience, they lose any individual moral axis and depend on the whim of others. They are thereby susceptible to the convictions of any outsider who claims to know the truth. Those who have surrendered their own convictions are destined for destruction since they are at the mercy of any charlatan who arrives on the scene, for the Christian life cannot be sustained when people begin to transgress what they believe are moral norms. Eternal destruction is at stake not because eating suspect food is inherently harmful, but because those who derive their moral standards from others are cast adrift, having no anchor by which to secure their own lives. Therefore, they are blown about by every new view that arrives.

We are not surprised to learn, therefore, that Paul encourages the stronger believers to tolerate the weak ones and to accept their opinions (Rom 14:1; 15:1). In particular, the strong should beware of causing the weak to stumble and thereby ruin their faith (Rom 14:13; 1 Cor 8:9). Love seeks what edifies and pleases others (Rom 14:19; 15:2-3; 1 Cor 8:1-3). Only the immature flaunt their freedom, insisting on their rights despite the convictions of those who are weaker (cf. 1 Cor 9:1-23). Love seeks a way by which those who are fragile will be supported and sustained, not ruined and harmed. Those with robust consciences are tempted to despise and scoff at the restrictions of the weak (Rom 14:3, 10), mocking and scoffing at the restrictions that limit their behavior. The way of love, however, desists from scorn and ridicule and seeks to build up and accept those who are weak. Love does not demand agreement on every controversy but accepts different opinions on matters that are negotiable. The weak abstain from food because they think such abstention is pleasing to God, just as they observe certain days to honor him (Rom 14:5-6). They ought to be embraced as brothers and sisters precisely because they desire to honor God in what they do.

Conversely, the weak are tempted to judge the strong, convinced that the strong are licentious and displeasing to God (Rom 14:3-4, 10). The weak must also learn to be more tolerant and realize that their opinions are not the same as God's. God himself has accepted the strong and is pleased with them because they live to honor him (Rom 14:3-6). Both the weak and the strong are granted the freedom to stay true to their own convictions on these matters (Rom 14:5). In fact, all must live on the basis of faith since living contrary to one's faith is sin (Rom 14:23). Many interpreters think that Romans 14:23 is limited to the specific context of Romans 14 and cannot be interpreted as a universal statement. This view is likely mistaken. The universality of the statement is communicated in the way the saying is formulated, "Everything that is not of faith is sin." The verse, of course, could be reduced to absurdity by asking if brushing one's teeth should always be done with conscious faith in God. We are not to ask every moment of our lives, "Does faith truly exist in me?" Obviously, no one would get anything done! We could breed an unhealthy introspection that would paralyze us. But Paul is saying that trust in God and dependence on him is the very air that a believer breathes. If believers do something in which they are *not* trusting God, then such an action is sin. People are not living in faith if they violate their own convictions or conscience in any matter. That is why faith in Romans 14:23 is contrasted with doubting. Faith means that one lives in the confidence and assurance that one's behavior is pleasing to God.

Paul does not expect an undifferentiated unity in the assembly in which everyone agrees on every matter. He does not expect or even desire unanimity of opinion. All believers are expected to live in accord with their conscience and to grant freedom to others to disagree. Most importantly, both the strong and the weak need to realize that they live under the sovereignty of God and Christ. Christ, not other believers, is the Lord of the conscience (Rom 14:7-9). The life and the death of believers are subsumed under the lordship of Christ. Believers belong to the Lord and live unto the Lord, whether they live or die. In other words, Paul has not abandoned the center of his theology in the section on foods. Everything is to be done for the glory and honor of God and Christ. Believers should not worry about what other believers think, nor should they stand in judgment over others. All their activities are to be done unto the Lord. Every realm of life falls under his lordship. The oscillation between God and Christ in Romans 14 (see esp. Rom 14:6-12) reflects the centrality of both in Paul's theology. Paul summons believers to live as servants of God and Christ, recognizing that they will give an account on the day of judgment. Unity is to be pursued in service to Christ *(douleuōn)* and to please *(euarestos)* God (Rom 14:18). Paul comes to a similar conclusion in 1 Corinthians 10:31. Whether believers are eating or drinking, they should do everything for God's glory. Pursuing God's glory is closely linked in both Romans and 1 Corinthians with a desire to please others instead of ourselves, a desire to build up others instead of satisfying our own interests, and a passion to see others saved instead of destroying their faith.

Paul grants believers remarkable liberty to come to their own conclusions in the matter of foods. At the end of the day, however, he agrees more with the strong than the weak, though he desires them to accept the weak and to live in a way that does not offend them. The "knowers" are correct in thinking it does not matter what food we eat (1 Cor 8:8), for idols are nonexistent and there is only one true God (1 Cor 8:5-6). Similarly, Paul emphatically states, "I know and am persuaded in the Lord Jesus that nothing is defiled in itself" (Rom 14:14). Such an assertion supports the conclusion that Paul had departed from his Jewish roots, for the Paul who adhered to the ancestral traditions could never utter such a statement (Gal 1:13-14). It also reveals that Paul sided theologically with the strong in Romans, for the weak held a very different opinion. Even though the strong are exhorted to be gentle with the weak, Paul does not conceal his own convictions on the matter.[10] Paul no longer feels bound by Levitical food laws.

Buying food offered to idols in the local market is permitted, as long as one does not feel contaminated in conscience (1 Cor 10:25-27), for such food is God's gift to his people. Nevertheless, if another reveals that the food has been offered to idols, then the believer should abstain for the sake of the other's conscience (1 Cor 10:28). It has been argued that Paul forbids the eating of all idol food, permitting it only if the eater is unaware of the fact that the food has been offered to idols.[11] Supporting this interpretation is the consistent rejection of idol food in Jewish sources and other early Christian writers. According to this view, Paul thought eating food offered to idols was idolatry both inside and outside the temple if the eater was informed that the food was offered to idols. Despite the attractiveness of this solution, it is more likely that Paul permits

---

[10]John M. G. Barclay argues insightfully that Paul's advice on the matter of foods demonstrates that Paul disagrees with the weak and guarantees the eventual dissolution of their point of view (" 'Do We Undermine the Law?' A Study of Romans 14.1—15.6," in *Paul and the Mosaic Law: The Third Durham-Tübingen Research Symposium on Earliest Christianity and Judaism (Durham, September 1994)*, ed. James D. G. Dunn, WUNT 89 [Tübingen: J. C. B. Mohr, 1996], pp. 287-308).

[11]See Alex T. Cheung, *Idol Food in Corinth: Jewish Background and Pauline Legacy*, JSNTSup 176 (Sheffield: Sheffield Academic Press, 1999).

believers to eat idol food sold in the market (in both 1 Cor 8:7-13 and 1 Cor 10:23—11:1), forbidding it only if someone else informs the believers it is idol food. To say that eating idol food is idolatry if one knows it is idol food but that it is permissible otherwise is the kind of rabbinic distinction that seems unlikely for the apostle Paul. If he were convinced that consuming meat offered to idols was idolatry, he would advise believers *to ask* whether the food was offered to idols so that they could avoid idolatry. Indeed, believers would be careful to ask such a question, for if eating such food constituted idolatry, they would want to avoid any suggestion of doing evil. In conclusion, Paul did not discourage believers from eating idol food sold in the market place, unless consuming such food would cause others to stumble.[12]

On the other hand, he is also worried in 1 Corinthians that the "knowers" will become idolators, presuming on God's grace as the Exodus generation did (1 Cor 10:1-13). It is difficult to decipher what concerns Paul about the "knowers." First Corinthians 10:14-22 suggests that they were participating in cultic meals in pagan temples. Does Paul prohibit believers from consuming food offered to idols in the temple? This is the view advocated by Gordon Fee.[13] Others scholars think that believers may go to pagan temples on social occasions, but they must never participate in a temple feast in a worship or a cultic context.[14] Discerning what Paul prohibits is difficult, for in 1 Corinthians 8:10 eating in a pagan temple is mentioned but not explicitly criticized. In 1 Corinthians 10:19-22, on the other hand, eating in a pagan temple seems to be absolutely prohibited since those who do so become sharers with demons. Fee thinks that Paul delays his criticism of the practice in 1 Corinthians 8, for Paul wants to concentrate on the obligation of the "knowers" toward the weak. Then in 1 Corinthians 10 the mortal danger of sharing in demons that the "knowers" face by eating in temples is revealed.

---

[12]For some other helpful studies on food offered to idols, see Wendell Willis, *Idol Meat in Corinth: The Pauline Argument in 1 Corinthians 8 and 10,* SBLDS 68 (Chico, Calif.: Scholars Press, 1985); Peter D. Gooch, *Dangerous Food: 1 Corinthians 8—10 in Its Context,* Studies in Christianity and Judaism 5 (Waterloo, Ont.: Wilfrid Laurier University Press, 1993); Derek Newton, *Deity and Diet: The Dilemma of Sacrificial Food at Corinth,* JSNTSup 169 (Sheffield: Sheffield Academic Press, 1998); Chuck Lowe, "Cult and Culture: A Christian Response to Idol Food in Chinese Popular Religion," unpublished; Coye Still, *The Rationale Behind the Pauline Instructions on Food Offered to Idols: A Study of the Relationship Between 1 Corinthians 4:6-21 and 8:1-11* (Ph.D. diss., The Southern Baptist Theological Seminary, 2000).

[13]Gordon D. Fee, *The First Epistle to the Corinthians,* NICNT (Grand Rapids, Mich.: Eerdmans, 1987), pp. 357-92, 463-91.

[14]Bruce N. Fisk, "Eating Meat Offered to Idols: Corinthian Behavior and Pauline Response in 1 Corinthians 8—10 (A Response to Gordon Fee)," *TJ* 10 (1989): 49-70; David Horrell, "Theological Principle or Christological Praxis? Pauline Ethics in 1 Corinthians 8.1—11.1," *JSNT* 67 (1997): 83-114.

Others think that Paul makes no criticism of eating in the temple in 1 Corinthians 8 because some eating in the temple (for social or noncultic reasons) is permitted, whereas a temple feast is prohibited if worship is involved.

It is extraordinarily difficult to decide which view is correct. At the very least we can say that Paul prohibits any participation in the temple that involved worship. Such eating is tantamount to idolatry and exposes people to God's judgment. It is probably the case, though, that any attempt to distinguish social settings from worship settings in the temple falls prey to the kind of casuistry that Paul would avoid. Trying to discern whether temple meals were social or whether they involved worship introduces a dichotomy that is likely foreign to the ancient world, where the religious and social were intertwined. The solution of Fee, then, is most satisfying. Eating idol food sold in the market is permissible, if no one is caused to stumble. Eating idol food in the temple, however, is always wrong, since such constitutes idolatry.

In both 1 Corinthians 8—10 and Romans 14—15 Paul hopes that his advice will unify the church and minimize divisions. Thereby believers will be edified and no one will take offense at what is happening. In Romans, Paul envisions believers worshiping God together in unity (Rom 15:6). Such united worship is the goal of Christ's ministry for both Jews and Gentiles, for Paul understands a number of Old Testament texts to proclaim a united worship in the Christian assembly (Rom 15:7-12).

Spiritual Gifts

In the last century spiritual gifts have emerged again as a controversial topic. When we read 1 Corinthians 12—14 it is evident that contention over spiritual gifts divided the Corinthian church. Perhaps it will help our discussion if we begin by providing a list of the various gifts and the verses in which they appear.

Rom 12:6-8	1 Cor 12:8-10	1 Cor 12:28-30	Eph 4:11
Prophecy	Word of wisdom	Apostles	Apostles
Serving	Word of knowledge	Prophets	Prophets
Teaching	Faith	Teachers	Evangelists
Exhortation	Healing	Miracles	Pastor-teachers
Giving	Miracles	Healings	
Leading	Prophecy	Helps	
Mercy	Distinguishing of spirits	Administration	
	Tongues	Tongues	
	Interpretation of tongues	Interpretation of tongues	

The terminology for spiritual gifts is enlightening. Paul uses the following terms:

- *spiritual things* (*pneumatika,* 1 Cor 12:1; 14:1)
- *spirits* (*pneumata,* 1 Cor 14:12)
- *manifestation of the Spirit* (*phanerōsis tou pneumatos,* 1 Cor 12:7)
- *gifts* (*charismata,* Rom 12:6; 1 Cor 12:4, 31)
- *gift* (*charis,* Eph 4:7)
- *gifts* (*domata,* Eph 4:8)
- *ministries* (*diakoniai,* 1 Cor 12:5)
- *results* or *effects* (*energēmata,* 1 Cor 12:6)

The words *charisma, charis* and *doma* emphasize the gracious character of the gifts. They are *gifts*—given by God for the good of his people. The words *pneumatikos* and *pneuma* and the phrase *phanerōsis tou pneumatos* stress that these gifts are the result of the Spirit's work. In this sense all the gifts are supernatural endowments from God. *Diakoniai* features the service-character of the gifts. These gifts are given to help others in the faith, while *energēmata* indicates that concrete results are seen in everyday life because of the gifts.

Gifts and lordship. The emphasis on *charisma* and the Spirit brings to the forefront an important Pauline theme. Gifts are not an indication of greater spirituality: the Corinthians were apparently inclined to believe that a gift like tongues demonstrated the Spirit's presence in a more remarkable way than the other gifts did. Paul utterly rejects any such idea. Any ability one has comes from God and is the result of his grace. Behind the diversity of gifts stands the same Spirit (1 Cor 12:4). Behind the diversity of ministries stands the same Lord (1 Cor 12:5). Behind the diversity of results stands the same God (1 Cor 12:6). The focus is on God and his work, not on the person exercising the gift. That is why Paul calls gifts "a manifestation of *the Spirit*" (1 Cor 12:7). In 1 Corinthians 12:8-9 the recurrence of *the Spirit* is strikingly redundant. The word of wisdom is "through the Spirit," the word of knowledge is "according to the same Spirit," faith is by "the same Spirit" and gifts of healings are by "the one Spirit." Not even a millimeter of human boasting is permitted. "All these things are effected by one and the same Spirit who distributes to each one just as he wills" (1 Cor 12:11).

The gift one has is attributed to the sovereignty of the Spirit and cannot be ascribed to one's own spirituality. God is the one who has "appointed" (*etheto,* 1 Cor 12:28) whether one will be an apostle, prophet, teacher, and so on. He has "appointed" (*etheto*) the members of the body according to his will (1 Cor 12:18). Or as Ephesians says, "Grace is given according to the measure of the gift of Christ" (Eph 4:7). Nearly every word of that verse communicates the gracious quality of gifts. Ephesians 4:11 says, "He *gave* some to be apostles and prophets" and so on. In Romans 12, before discussing gifts, Paul warns believers against pride, reminding them to think sensibly because *"God has apportioned* to each one a measure of faith" (Rom 12:3). And when he begins the list of gifts, he introduces them with the words "and having gifts according to the grace that is given to us" (Rom 12:6). Again, practically every word heralds God's grace and generosity. Under no circumstances should believers exalt themselves for their gifts. They are the result of God's grace, and comparisons with others—even comparisons that thank God (see Lk 18:9-14!)—are odious if they put down other believers for lacking the gift one has.

Since gifts are the result of God's grace and sovereignty, it follows that all gifts are exercised under the lordship of Christ. Paul begins his discussion of spiritual gifts in 1 Corinthians 12:1-3 on this very note. No one can confess from the heart that "Jesus is Lord" except through the work of the Holy Spirit (1 Cor 12:3). The banner over all gifts is the acclamation of the lordship of Christ, and the inspiration for all gifts comes from the Holy Spirit. It is God's intention, therefore, that a diversity *(diaireseis)* of gifts exist (1 Cor 12:4-6). Any notion that all believers would exercise the same gift is rejected (1 Cor 12:27-30). Nor *should* all believers exercise the same gift. It would be a strange body indeed if everyone were an eye or an ear (1 Cor 12:17). A body by definition comprises diverse members (Rom 12:4-5; 1 Cor 12:12, 14). No one should feel inferior because of the gift he or she exercises, for every member of the body has a gift (or gifts) assigned by God (1 Cor 12:14-18). Nor should anyone feel superior on account of one's gift since each member of the body is important (1 Cor 12:21-24). The variety of gifts, services and results was instituted by God (1 Cor 12:4-6). The gift possessed is not to be ascribed to one's own spirituality but to the sovereignty of God (1 Cor 12:11, 18, 27).

Gifts and edification. Gifts were not given for narcissistic purposes but "for the common good" (1 Cor 12:7). Therefore, no schism should injure the body, but instead members should care for one another (1 Cor 12:25-26). Paul labors in 1 Corinthians 14 to communicate that gifts are intended to edify others. He has no use for uninterpreted tongues in the assembly because they do not build up others (1 Cor 14:1-5). Prophecy is preferable to tongues because others will be edified, encouraged and consoled (1 Cor 14:3). One of the remarkable features here is that edification is closely conjoined with *the mind.* An interpreted tongue is equivalent to prophecy because in such a case a person can understand what is said (1 Cor 14:5). Unintelligible words are like harps or flutes that are so off key that one cannot even discern the melody (1 Cor 14:7). Tongues without interpretation are like a trumpet blast meant to warn of war but which is unintelligible instead (1 Cor 14:8). One might as well shout words to the sky for all the good they do for others (1 Cor 14:9) because edification occurs when others *understand* what is being said (1 Cor 14:10-12). One must pray with the Spirit (or spirit) and the mind for others to be strengthened (1 Cor 14:13-15). Paul does not believe that others are edified when what is going on in the assembly—no matter how emotionally gripping—bypasses rational faculties (1 Cor 14:16-19). Paul is, of course, not a philosopher who conceives of the spiritual life as rational comprehension of truth. He desires his converts to be emotionally gripped by the truth of the gospel; but the path to the emotions is *through* the mind, not around it. Edification and understanding are indissolubly connected for Paul. When the community gathers and gifts are exercised, "all things are to be done for edification" (1 Cor 14:26). Encouragement *(parakalōntai)* and learning *(manthanōsin)* are intertwined (1 Cor 14:31).

In Ephesians 4 Paul explains that God has placed gifted persons in the church "to equip the saints for the work of the ministry, for the edification of the body of Christ" (Eph 4:12). Such maturity or edification is again defined in terms of the understanding. Unity in the faith, that is, the doctrinal truth of the gospel, indicates that edification is a reality (Eph 4:13). Of course, edification is more than understanding, though it is certainly not less. It involves personal and experiential knowledge of Jesus as the Son of God (Eph 4:13). Once again, no conflict between the intellectual and experiential is involved—they work together. Nevertheless, Paul's focus on understanding is remarkable. Being carried away by new and dangerous teaching is evidence of a believers' immaturity (Eph 4:14). Mature believers, on the other hand, receive the truth about Christ and thereby grow. Edification becomes a reality through proper teaching and comprehension (Eph 4:15-16). Paul's emphasis on learning is not surprising for the gifted people listed are apostles, prophets and evangelists, as well as pastors and teachers (Eph 4:11). This is not to say that only some Christians play a role in building up the body of Christ. The body grows through the contribution of each and every individual part (Eph 4:16, *en metrō henos hekastou merous*). The smallest ligament and tendon makes a difference, as anyone who has injured one knows!

Spiritual gifts and love. Perhaps the most important perspective on spiritual gifts appears in 1 Corinthians 13. This chapter is inserted intentionally in the midst of the discussion on spiritual gifts. It must not be explained as a digression or as extraneous to the main purpose of 1 Corinthians 12—14, as if the passage is unrelated to the content of chapters 12 and 14. Showing love for one another is vastly more important than exercising any gift. Speaking in the tongues of humans or angels without love is merely irritating noise (1 Cor 13:1). Knowledge of the future is impressive and mountain-moving faith remarkable, but without love those with such gifts are nothing (1 Cor 13:2). The love Paul celebrates involves the affections, but it cannot be restricted to sentimentality. Love manifests itself in specific and concrete ways (1 Cor 13:4-7). It is eternal, but spiritual gifts are temporary (1 Cor 13:8-12). Such gifts are part and parcel of this present age; and when this age comes to an end at the second coming of Christ, then spiritual gifts will cease. Exalting gifts over love places primacy on the temporal instead of on the eternal, the superficial and partial over against what is lasting and complete.

The nature of gifts. People often ask whether gifts are supernatural or natural talents. In one sense the question is flawed, for all gifts are from God and in that sense are *supernatural:* "What do you have that you have not received?" (1 Cor 4:7). Nor is any gift exercised apart from the animating work of the Spirit. There is no room in Paul for a gift that has an impact because of the native talent or ability of human beings, no place for honor to belong to those with such remarkable abilities. Any good effect from gifts comes from God, "who works all things in all" (1 Cor 12:6). On the other hand, it is difficult to deny that some gifts are more overtly miraculous than others. The Corinthians became entranced with the gift of tongues, not the gift of helps! Some gifts, such as tongues, interpretation of tongues, healing, miracles and prophecy, are striking manifestations of God's presence in a community. Gifts such as teaching, helps, leading, giving, mercy and exhortation are not as remarkable to the human eye, though they are still supernatural in the sense that they are animated by the Holy Spirit and that any good effect is also from the Spirit. It seems likely that some of the latter gifts are stitched into one's personality in a way that a gift like tongues cannot be. The supernatural character of the gift is not thereby denied, for even in this case the gift comes from God.

Another question that arises is whether gifts are permanent possessions or whether people can exercise a gift that is not normally theirs. Paul does not specifically answer this question, so we must content ourselves with reading the clues from his writings. The emphasis seems to lie on gifts as permanent possessions. In 1 Corinthians 12 the text moves from the gift manifested (e.g., prophecy) to gifted persons (prophets), suggesting that no dichotomy is envisioned between them. The fact that Paul speaks of prophets, teachers, evangelists and pastor-teachers indicates that some gifts were a regular feature in the lives of some persons. However, Paul does not refer to anyone as a healer, miracle-worker, tongue-speaker or interpreter of tongues. He only refers to the gift itself. It does not follow from this that no one regularly exercised gifts like tongues or healings, but we cannot rule out the idea that someone might speak in tongues or do a miracle only once or on rare occasions.

Closely related to the previous discussion is whether Paul speaks of offices in using terms like *apostles, prophets, teachers* and so on. The English word *office* suggests an appointment to a certain position. It is doubtful, though, that such an idea is intended in Paul's listing of these various gifted persons. When Paul describes someone as a prophet, he does not envision the appointment to a definite prophetic office. The person is called a prophet because he or she regularly functions as a prophet. Of course, a teacher or a prophet may still have an office in the church. Still, the terms *teacher* or *prophet* do not specifically designate an office but a regular function. The issue becomes even more complicated in the case of "apostles." It seems hard to deny that Paul viewed apostleship as an office, though some understand *apostles* in 1 Corinthians 12:28 to refer to apostles in local churches. Even if those who are called apostles inhabit an office, which is likely, Paul's purpose in using the term is not to focus on office but function.

Another question emerges from Paul's discussion of spiritual gifts. If Paul says that the Spirit gives all gifts and that the possession of one gift rather than another does not imply inferiority or superiority, then why does he say to desire the greater gifts (1 Cor 12:31; 14:1)? This question really has two parts. First, what does Paul mean when he says that some gifts are greater than others? Does that contradict his assertion that one's gift does not demonstrate inferiority or superiority? It would seem that those who have "greater gifts" might be more important in the church than those who have lesser gifts. Yet no contradiction is involved when we understand what Paul actually means. First Corinthians 14 is the key to understanding what Paul means by "greater gifts." Prophecy is greater than tongues in the sense that prophecy edifies the church more than the gift of tongues does (1 Cor 14:1-5). When Paul says that "the one who prophesies is greater than the one who speaks in tongues" (1 Cor 14:5), he is speaking functionally and not ontologically. Prophecy is a more significant gift in the community because the church is edified by the exercise of this gift, whereas an uninterpreted tongue does not build up the church. Paul is not saying that one who prophesies is spiritually superior to the one who speaks in tongues. Prophecy is only greater in that it helps the church more than uninterpreted tongues. When Paul speaks of some gifts as being greater than others, he thinks of function, not essence. Nor does he confuse the gift exercised with the spirituality of the person bearing the gift. An intelligible prophetic word is more helpful to the church than an uninterpreted tongue. In that sense the gift of prophecy is a greater gift. Paul is not saying that the one who prophesies is a better Christian or is closer to God than the one who speaks in tongues.

The second part of the question is, why should we seek gifts if they are sovereignly given? Some feel this tension so sharply that they interpret the verb "be zealous" (*zēloute*) in 1 Corinthians 12:31 as an indicative, detecting a note of reproach in the statement that the Corinthians are zealous for spiritual gifts. This reading might work in 1 Corinthians 12:31, but it is difficult to sustain in 1 Corinthians 14:1, for in the latter instance Paul most naturally says "be zealous for spiritual gifts, especially in order that you may prophesy." In both instances Paul likely summons the church to be zealous for spiritual gifts. There is certainly a tension between the teaching that God sovereignly gives gifts and the summons to seek them earnestly. But such a tension is a common characteristic of Paul's teaching. People should repent and believe, but such repentance and belief are God's gifts. God has given us all good gifts in Christ (the indicative), and yet people should live out the new life in Christ (the imperative). We should not be surprised, then, that Paul says that the gifts are due to God's sovereignty and that we must seek them earnestly. Such a message is typical in Paul.

Defining the gifts. We have been discussing gifts in general but the specific gifts identified by Paul have not been defined. Most scholars agree that the lists are not exhaustive but representative, though any additional gifts could probably be placed under one of the categories found in Romans 12:6-8. In some cases, defining the gift is extraordinarily difficult. For instance, "the word of wisdom" and "the word of knowledge" in 1 Corinthians 12:8 are frustratingly vague. In some circles "the word of knowledge" is understood to be a supernatural understanding of, for example, another person's sin, problem or disease.[15] If this is accurate, the word of knowledge is almost indistinguishable from prophecy, but it seems unlikely that these two gifts are the same since prophecy occurs in the same list (1 Cor 12:10). On the other hand, the gifts in the list do overlap in some respects, and thus this argument

---

[15]John Wimber, *Power Healing* (London: Hodder & Stoughton, 1986), p. 278.

is not decisive. On any scheme, distinguishing between the word of wisdom and the word of knowledge is difficult. In popular circles some say that wisdom is applied knowledge, suggesting that knowledge involves the possession of mere intellectual content. But it is doubtful that Paul ever confines knowledge to the intellectual sphere alone as if it were theoretical information that has no practical value, so the suggested distinction should be dismissed. Perhaps Graham Houston is correct in saying that both the word of wisdom and the word of knowledge refer to teaching.[16] In every other list the gift of teaching is mentioned, but it is lacking here—unless wisdom and knowledge refer to teaching. In 1 Corinthians 1:18—2:16 wisdom is identified as the message of the crucified Christ, so perhaps such teaching is intended here as well. The phrase *word of* may also signify the transmission of tradition, for elsewhere Paul speaks of the "word of God" (Rom 9:6; 1 Cor 14:36; 2 Cor 2:17; 4:2; Phil 1:14; Col 1:25; 1 Thess 2:13; 1 Tim 4:5; 2 Tim 2:9), "word of faith" (Rom 10:8), "word of truth" (Eph 1:13) and "word of life" (Phil 2:16). Knowledge is also intimately wedded with the truth of the gospel (cf. Rom 15:14; Eph 3:17-19; Col 1:9-10; 2:2-4; 3:9-10). Identifying the word of wisdom and the word of knowledge with teaching is plausible, but we cannot assert this with certainty.

The gift of "faith" (1 Cor 12:9) is not the same thing as saving faith, for the latter is the province of all Christians, and here Paul speaks of something that only some believers possess. In 1 Corinthians 13:2 Paul speaks of a faith that moves mountains, and thus the gift of faith likely relates to a faith that believes that God can do the extraordinary. This may be confirmed by James 5:15, where the prayer of faith may be the conviction that God will heal the sick. The gifts of miracles and healings (1 Cor 12:9-10, 28) overlap. All healings are miracles, but not all miracles are healings. The gift of healing obviously relates to being healed from sickness or some infirmity (cf. Acts 3:1-10; 14:8-11). An example of a miracle that does not involve healing is the temporary blindness of Elymas (Acts 13:11), the casting out of the spirit by Paul (Acts 16:18) and the raising of the dead by Peter (Acts 9:38-43).

Before delving into gifts that are more controversial, we will explore those that are relatively easier to define. The gift of "helps" (*antilēmpseis*, 1 Cor 12:28) refers to practical assistance of every kind. This is probably the same thing as the gift of "service" (*diakonia*) in Romans 12:7. This is an eminently

---

[16]Graham Houston, *Prophecy: A Gift for Today?* (Downers Grove, Ill.: InterVarsity Press, 1989), pp. 98-107.

practical gift that is not flashy but is indispensable for the life of the church. The gift of leadership is conveyed by the word *administrators* (*kybernēseis*, 1 Cor 12:28). The related word *kybernētēs* is used of a pilot of a boat (Acts 27:11; Rev 18:17) and of Christ as the pilot or master of our bodies *(Mart. Pol.* 19:2). There is little doubt, then, that leaders in the community are designated by this term. Such leaders may be the equivalent of *ho proistamenos* in Romans 12:8. Some scholars believe that Paul has in mind a caregiver rather than a leader since the word bears both meanings. It is pointed out as well that the term is sandwiched by sharing and giving mercy. Nevertheless, the term probably indicates leadership. In parallel texts (1 Thess 5:12; 1 Tim 3:4-5; 5:17) the reference is clearly to leaders. Probably the same notion applies to Romans as well. The list of gifts in Romans 12:6-8 is not clearly organized, so adjoining terms do not necessarily cast light on one another. One practical gift in the life of the church, then, is leadership and guidance, by which the church is given direction and assistance in its everyday affairs.

The gifts of giving and mercy are also easily comprehensible. Giving in Romans 12:8 *(metadidous)* relates to giving financially. Those who give are to do so "generously" *(haplotēti)*, or perhaps "sincerely." Others have a special gift of exercising mercy and compassion to those in need (Rom 12:8). Those with such a gift are to exercise mercy "cheerfully." They are never to be grudging and meager in showing mercy, for such a spirit would belie the good work. Others are evangelists (Eph 4:11), being specially endowed by God for the dissemination of the gospel. Those who have such a gift should "do the work of an evangelist" (2 Tim 4:5).

It has already been noted that the word of wisdom and the word of knowledge may relate to the gift of teaching. Teaching is an important gift, mentioned specifically in Romans 12:7 and 1 Corinthians 12:28. The same gift is also likely in view when Paul refers to "pastors and teachers" in Ephesians 4:11. Teaching differs from prophecy in that it is rooted in and dependent on previously transmitted tradition. It does not involve a spontaneous word but an explication of a word already given. The tradition probably included the Old Testament scriptures, the words and works of Jesus, and catechetical material. In 1 Corinthians 4:17 a relationship between Paul's "ways" and his "teaching" is forged. A number of texts in Paul suggest that "teaching" focuses on Jesus Christ (Eph 4:21; Col 1:28; 2:7). Paul also emphasizes on more than one occasion (not just in the Pastorals!) that the churches are to conform to handed-down traditions (Rom 6:17; 16:17; 2 Thess 2:15; 1 Tim 4:11; 6:2; 2 Tim 2:2; Tit 1:11). Such traditions would need to be taught and explained. The gift of "exhortation" *(paraklēsis)* is closely related to teaching. In Romans 12:8 the gift of exhortation immediately follows the gift of teaching. The close relationship between exhortation and teaching surfaces in 1 Timothy 4:13 as well, where Timothy is exhorted to "pay attention to the public reading of scripture, to exhortation, to teaching." Similarly, in 1 Thessalonians 2:3 the word *paraklēsis* is practically equivalent to teaching. It does not follow from this that the gifts are exactly the same. Exhortation concentrates on the practical implications of what is taught and how it relates to everyday life. Teaching highlights the content of the tradition whereas exhortation applies it, summoning and stirring the hearers to action. Good preaching is a combination of teaching and exhortation. The former alone could descend to the level of the lecture, while the latter may contain heat without light.

The gift of prophecy. The hardest gifts to define are probably prophecy, tongues and apostleship; we will look at them in this order. Some define prophecy as preaching. One thinks of 1 Corinthians 14:24-25, where the words of prophecy reveal the secrets of the heart and cause the visitor to acknowledge God's presence. Or, in 1 Corinthians 14:3 prophecy results in edification, encouragement and consolation. But this verse hardly helps us define the gift of prophecy, for all the gifts rightly used would edify, encourage and console. Such results are not the exclusive province of prophecy. Surely teaching would edify, encourage and console as well. Nor does 1 Corinthians 14:24-25 demonstrate that prophecy is preaching. This text informs us that the person visiting the community is convicted by the prophetic words, but it does not specify that these words constitute preaching. Indeed, there is a hint that some kind of oracular revelation is involved, for in the case of the visitor "the secrets of his heart become clear" (1 Cor 14:25). A spontaneous word spoken by the prophet brings to light what lies deep in the heart of the unbeliever.

Prophecy is better defined as communicating revelations from God in a spontaneous utterance.[17] In 1 Corinthians 14:6, for example, the words *revela-*

---

[17]For similar understandings of prophecy, see David E. Aune, *Prophecy in Early Christianity and the Ancient Mediterranean World* (Grand Rapids, Mich.: Eerdmans, 1983); Wayne A. Grudem, *The Gift of Prophecy in 1 Corinthians* (Washington, D.C.: University Press of America, 1982); Max Turner, *The Holy Spirit and Spiritual Gifts* (Peabody, Mass.: Hendrickson, 1998), pp. 185-220. See also Christopher Forbes, *Prophecy and Inspired Speech in Early Christianity and Its Hellenistic Environment,* WUNT 2/75 (Tübingen: J. C. B. Mohr, 1995), pp. 218-21, though Forbes distinguishes in some respects the Lukan and Pauline conceptions of prophecy.

tion and *prophecy* are probably overlapping terms. Similarly, in 1 Corinthians 14:26 believers are encouraged to participate in a church meeting in various ways. The term *prophecy* is not found in this verse, though it dominates the discussion of chapter 14. But prophecy is likely included in the phrase "each has a revelation." The close relationship between prophecy and revelation is cemented by 1 Corinthians 14:29-33. Paul mandates how the gifts should be exercised in these verses. 1 Corinthians 14:30 is especially instructive since it describes prophecy in terms of a revelation granted suddenly to one who is sitting down: "But if a revelation is given to one sitting, the first one should be silent." Again we note the connection between revelation and prophecy. The notion that prophecy involves spontaneous revelations is also confirmed, for the revelation comes to a person while he or she is sitting in the assembly. No previously prepared message is contemplated here. First Corinthians 13:2 suggests that prophets through revelation have access to mysteries and knowledge that are otherwise unknown, though hyperbole is certainly involved since Paul speaks of comprehending "*all* mysteries and *all* knowledge."

A few examples in Acts confirm that prophets receive spontaneous revelations from God. Luke informs us that prophets and teachers were worshiping God in Acts 13:1-3. The formula "the Holy Spirit said" (Acts 13:2) is likely a prophetic formula, and what the Spirit communicated is that Paul and Barnabas were to be commissioned for the missionary enterprise. It is likely that this word of the Spirit was received spontaneously by one or more of the prophets during worship and that then this revelation was communicated to the assembly. Agabus communicates two prophecies in Acts. In Acts 11:28 he prophesies that a famine is about to come on the world. He obviously did not work from a prepared text in sharing this word, but he must have received this revelation spontaneously from God. Similarly, in Acts 21:10-11 he utters an oracle about Paul's fate in Jerusalem, saying that the Jews will bind him and hand him over to the Gentiles. The formula "these things says the Holy Spirit" is a prophetic formula, and prophetic symbolism is also employed since Agabus took Paul's belt and bound his own hands and feet in delivering the prophecy. The parallel to Old Testament prophets is unmistakable, for they often used symbolism. To sum up, New Testament prophets received immediate revelations from God and shared such revelations with their hearers.

Some scholars, most notably perhaps Wayne Grudem, have argued that New Testament prophecy is to be distinguished from inscripturated Old Testament prophecy. Old Testament prophecy is without error and flawless, but New Testament prophecy is mixed with error and thus must be discerned and evaluated.[18] Grudem thinks the apostles are the successors of Old Testament prophets, while New Testament prophets are in a distinct category from the apostles since their teaching is not infallible but contains a combination of truth and error. New Testament prophets may be from God and yet still have errors in their prophecies because (1) their prophecies are judged (1 Cor 14:29; 1 Thess 5:19-22); (2) some prophecies are disobeyed (Acts 21:4); and (3) Agabus's prophecy was in error.

In Acts 21:11 Agabus said that the Jews "would bind" Paul "in Jerusalem and hand him over to the Gentiles" (Acts 21:11). But, in fact, the Jews did not bind Paul and deliver him over to the Romans. Instead the Romans rescued Paul when the Jews were about to slay him. On first glance Ephesians 2:20 would seem to counter Grudem's interpretation since the church is said to be built on the foundation of the apostles and prophets, suggesting that his distinction between infallible apostles and fallible prophets cannot be sustained. Grudem contends, however, that since both apostles and prophets are governed by one Greek article they refer to one group. In other words, the church is built on the foundation of apostles, and these apostles are also prophets. Ephesians 2:20, according to Grudem, does not refer to ordinary prophets who are fallible but only to the New Testament apostles who also functioned as prophets.

Grudem's interpretation is certainly possible, but it should be rejected as unlikely. Ephesians 2:20 more plausibly refers to two different groups, apostles *and* prophets, instead of to apostles who are prophets. That the apostles and prophets are distinct groups is suggested by Ephesians 4:11, where the two are clearly distinguished: God "gave some as apostles and some as prophets." Apostles and prophets are two distinct categories in 1 Corinthians 12:28 as well ("God appointed in the church first apostles, second prophets"), suggesting that it is more natural to see two groups in Ephesians 2:20. If Grudem is incorrect on this point, it casts doubt on the notion that though the apostles are infallible, the New Testament prophets are fallible. It is quite unlikely that Paul suggests in Ephesians 2:20 that the church is built on the foundation of infallible apostles and fallible prophets, so that the former are without error whereas the latter utter both truth and untruth. The burden of proof is on those who wish to drive a wedge between Old Testament and

---

[18]Grudem, *Gift of Prophecy*, pp. 54-74, esp. pp. 58-67. Turner (*Holy Spirit*, pp. 213-17) agrees with Grudem in a qualified way.

New Testament prophets, for we would expect that such prophets would function in the same way. Both were judged on the same basis, and accuracy was demanded of both.

Grudem rightly notes that the prophecies of the New Testament prophets were evaluated (1 Cor 14:29; 1 Thess 5:19-22). This is no different from the Old Testament standard because the legitimacy of the prophet was discerned by the accuracy of the prophecies (Deut 18:20-22). To say that Agabus erred in Acts 21:11 is to read the prophecy too literally and woodenly. We have already seen that Agabus used prophetic symbolism and a formula typical of Old Testament prophets. Luke does not drive a wedge between Agabus and Old Testament prophets. Instead he builds a bridge between them by referring to the introductory formula ("these things says the Holy Spirit") and the prophetic symbolism (Agabus's binding his own hands and feet), suggesting that Agabus functioned like an Old Testament prophet. As mentioned above, Grudem points out that the Jews "in Jerusalem" did not actually "bind" (*dēsousin*) and "hand over" (*paradōsousin*) Paul "into the hands of the Gentiles" (Acts 21:11). But Paul himself borrows this very language later in describing the incident that led to his incarceration. He says, "I was delivered over [*paredothēn*] into the hand of the Romans" (Acts 28:17). Apparently, Luke believed that Agabus's prophecy was fulfilled, even to the extent of using the very verb Agabus employed. Grudem makes the mistake of pressing the details of the prophecy, so he sees an error where Luke sees none.

Grudem appeals to Acts 21:4, where Paul is instructed through the Spirit not to go up to Jerusalem, but Paul is convinced that it is the Lord's will that he should go. This text is the best support for his view, and it is possible, of course, that he is correct. I would suggest that the text is too ambiguous to support Grudem's reconstruction since elsewhere there is no evidence that both truth and error were combined in the prophecies of New Testament prophets. Probably Luke merges together two themes here. The prophets prophesied that Paul would face trouble in Jerusalem, and they concluded from such prophecies that he should not go. The conclusion was not part of the prophecy proper but was an inference drawn from it. Paul believes the prophecy is true (Acts 21:13), but he rejects the inference drawn from it. To sum up, there is no compelling evidence that New Testament prophets spoke both truth and error. Like the Old Testament prophets, they spoke the word of the Lord accurately.

"Distinguishing of spirits" (*diakriseis pneumatōn*, 1 Cor 12:10) fits nicely after a discussion of prophecy, and it immediately follows prophecy in the list in 1 Corinthians 12:10. We have already seen that prophecies were judged and evaluated (1 Cor 14:29; 1 Thess 5:19-22). Those who had the gift of distinguishing spirits were able to discern whether the prophecies and interpreted tongues were truly from God. Such a gift was practical for the community indeed, since many false prophets threatened the young churches.

The gift of tongues. Probably the most controversial gift Paul discusses is the gift of tongues. Apparently the Corinthians believed that tongues were a mark of greater spirituality, and perhaps the Corinthians supported their overrealized eschatology by referring to their ability to speak in tongues, and thus Paul had to place tongues in proper perspective. We are reminded of 1 Corinthians 12, where Paul labors to teach that believers are not inferior or superior if they lack or possess a certain gift. A discreet reference to tongues is probably intended. Paul also clarifies that God never intended for all to speak in tongues (1 Cor 12:30). The very diversity of the body rules out the idea that all believers should exercise all the gifts. Sometimes interpreters point to 1 Corinthians 14:5 ("Now I want you all to speak in tongues") and 1 Corinthians 14:18 ("I thank God that I speak in tongues more than you all") to say that all *should* speak in tongues. Such statements must be interpreted contextually and not in isolation. Both statements appear in the course of an argument in which Paul minimizes the importance of tongues and exalts the gift of prophecy. He makes these statements to remind the readers that speaking in tongues is still a good thing and so he can avoid the charge that he denigrates speaking in tongues. He is hardly suggesting, though, that all believers *should* speak in tongues. He merely states it would be a good thing if all did. If some want to argue that all should speak in tongues on the basis of 1 Corinthians 14:5, then they should also argue that all Christians *should* be single because Paul wishes all had that gift in 1 Corinthians 7:7!

Tongues are a good gift from God and should not be forbidden (1 Cor 14:39), and yet they should not be confused with entrance into a heavenly existence. Tongues, prophecy and knowledge belong to what is partial, and they shall cease when the perfect comes at the second coming of Christ (1 Cor 13:8-12). Spiritual gifts are blessings from God, and they are needed in this present evil age, when our perception of truth is partial. Gifts are needed during the age of childhood (this present age); but when adulthood ("the perfect") comes, then the gifts will be needed no more because we shall see Christ face to face. Paul here strikes a blow against the overrealized eschatology of the Corinthians.

Tongues without a corresponding interpretation are unedifying (1 Cor 14:1-19) because no one understands what is being said. We saw earlier that rational and comprehensible words are linked with edification. One of the more difficult paragraphs in Paul's writings is 1 Corinthians 14:20-25. Paul counsels against uninterpreted tongues in the assembly, citing Isaiah 28:11-12 to support his assertion. The text in Isaiah refers to God's judgment on Israel, a judgment meted out when the Assyrians invaded Israel and sent them into captivity (722 B.C.). Israel was unable to understand the language in which the Assyrians spoke, and thus the presence of the Assyrians speaking in a foreign tongue was a sign of judgment. Paul draws an analogy between speaking in tongues and the foreign language of the Assyrians. Just as the presence of the Assyrians in Israel was a sign of judgment, so tongues are a sign of judgment—on unbelievers. How are tongues a sign of judgment? Because when unbelievers enter the assembly and believers speak in tongues, unbelievers will think that Christians are out of their minds and reject the gospel. But Paul's argument is that believers should *not* be the agent of judgment on unbelievers. So instead of speaking in tongues and driving unbelievers away, they should prophesy and bring them to faith. Paul is not contradicting himself when he says tongues are a sign for unbelievers and prophecy is a sign for believers, and then turns around and says that prophecy brings unbelievers to faith. Prophecy is a sign for believers because it brings *unbelievers* to belief, and uninterpreted tongues should be avoided in the assembly because they will spook unbelievers and drive them away.[19]

Paul's overriding concern in his discussion of tongues and prophecy is the edification of the church. Confusion reigned in the church at Corinth, so he limited the number of people speaking in tongues to two or three (1 Cor 14:27-28) and told them not to speak at the same time! And if no interpreter is present, then the one speaking in tongues should be silent. It is interesting to note that a similar order is prescribed for prophecy (1 Cor 14:29-33a). Paul wants all to participate and be edified, but in an orderly and comprehensible manner. He rejects the idea that the gift takes over so that believers lose control. The "spiritual gifts of the prophets are subject to the prophets" (1 Cor 14:32). Believers can and must control what they are doing. Once again, we see that Paul does not forbid tongue speaking, but he demands that it be done in an orderly way.

Perhaps just a word should be said about the baptism of the Spirit (actually only the verbal phrase is used). Some have identified speaking in tongues as the baptism of the Spirit (1 Cor 12:13). The discussion actually cen-

---

[19]On the interpretation of 1 Cor 14:20-25, see Grudem, *Gift of Prophecy,* pp. 185-201; J. P. M. Sweet, "A Sign for Unbelievers: Paul's Attitude to Glossolalia," NTS 13 (1966-1967): 240-57.

ters on Acts, so we can be quite brief here. Paul conceives of the baptism of the Spirit as occurring at conversion for *all* believers. He does not breathe a word about it being connected to the gift of tongues or to any other spiritual gift. Paul is quite emphatic in saying that all believers have been "baptized into one body," for he uses the words "we all" (*hēmeis pantes*) and then says "whether Jews or Greeks, whether slaves or free"; and finally he says again that "all" (*pantes*) have been irrigated with the one Spirit. The baptism of the Spirit is something all believers experience at conversion—no one is left out.

Paul excludes tongue speaking in the assembly without an interpreter, but does he rule out speaking in tongues in private? We must admit that this was not the burden of Paul's discussion, so it does not receive any extended treatment. Nor can it be considered at all important for the Christian life since nowhere do the Scriptures speak directly to this issue! It seems, though, that Paul does not exclude speaking in tongues in private. Speaking in tongues edifies oneself (1 Cor 14:4). The intention of believers should be to edify others, but presumably Paul has no objection to self-edification in private. He also advises that one who lacks an interpretation should speak to oneself and God, suggesting that private tongue speaking is permissible (1 Cor 14:28).

We have not yet discussed the nature of the gift of tongues. What exactly is it? Does tongue speaking in Paul involve foreign languages, or is some kind of ecstatic utterance involved?[20] In Acts 2 the gift seems to be in human languages because people from all over the world hear the apostles "speaking in their own language" (Acts 2:6). They say they hear "each of us in our own language *in which we were born*" (Acts 2:8) and "in our own tongues" (Acts 2:11). We find no evidence elsewhere in Acts that speaking in tongues is different in character (Acts 10:44-48; 19:6). It seems unlikely that a different kind of tongues is intended in subsequent chapters in Acts since Luke gives no indication of a variance from the first occurrence.

Many scholars, however, believe that Paul differs from Luke, and this is certainly possible. We must dismiss the idea, however, that tongues are simply an ecstatic utterance without any underlying code at all, for in Paul there is also the gift of interpretation.[21] Interpretation of tongues cannot occur

---

[20]On the nature of speaking in tongues, see the convincing arguments of Forbes, *Prophecy and Inspired Speech*, pp. 44-74; cf. also Robert H. Gundry, " 'Ecstatic Utterance' (N.E.B.)?" *JTS* 17 (1966): 299-307.

[21]For an alternate view, see Anthony C. Thiselton, "The 'Interpretation' of Tongues: A New Suggestion in the Light of Greek Usage in Philo and Josephus," *JTS* 30 (1979): 15-36. For a convincing refutation of Thiselton, see Forbes, *Prophecy and Inspired Speech*, pp. 65-72.

unless tongues have some kind of decipherable code. There must be something to interpret, for one cannot interpret gibberish or ecstatic babbling. Even the word *tongue (glōssa)* suggests some kind of language, some kind of code. Many scholars contend that the tongues in view are the languages of angels (1 Cor 13:1). In this instance the tongue would qualify as a language, and yet the code of the language would not be discernible to us.[22] Some scholars hold that the Corinthians believed they were now transported to a heavenly state because they spoke in the tongues of angels. Reading so much out of 1 Corinthians 13:1, though, is quite difficult. The reference to the tongues of angels could just as easily be a rhetorical flourish on Paul's part. Certainly he engages in hyperbole in 1 Corinthians 13:2 when he speaks of a gift of prophecy that grasps *"all* mysteries" and *"all* knowledge." Similarly, adding "tongues of angels" to "human tongues" may be hyperbolic.

The strongest argument for tongues being some kind of ecstatic prayer language is found in 1 Corinthians 14:2. Those who speak in tongues do not speak to "people but to God. For no one understands but he speaks mysteries by (or 'in') the Spirit." In Acts 2, on the other hand, those who speak in tongues proclaim to *people* "the mighty works of God" (Acts 2:11) and those present *understand* what is being said. First Corinthians 14 describes a tongue that is incomprehensible and addressed only to God, whereas Acts 2 involves a tongue that people understand and that speaks *about* God.

Despite the fact that most interpreters now seem to favor this view, I remain unconvinced, for both passages must be read in context—not as isolated proof-texts. In 1 Corinthians 14:1-5 Paul argues that prophecy is superior to tongues because it is comprehensible. Interpreted tongues, on the other hand, are equivalent to prophecy since people can understand what is being said. Paul's comment about tongues in 1 Corinthians 14:2 must be understood carefully. The reference here is to *uninterpreted tongues.* If no interpreter is present, then no one can understand what the one speaking in tongues says. He utters mysteries that are incomprehensible to all who are present. He speaks "to God" in the sense that only God understands what is being said. Such a statement about tongues does not contradict Acts 2. The tongues are comprehensible in Acts 2 only because those who understood the languages spoken happen to be present. The tongue speakers themselves were speaking mysteries, for presumably they did not understand the mean-

---

[22]For this view, see Fee, *First Epistle to the Corinthians,* pp. 597-98; D. A. Carson, *Showing the Spirit: A Theological Exposition of 1 Corinthians 12—14* (Grand Rapids, Mich.: Baker, 1987), pp. 77-88.

ing of their utterances. Even in 1 Corinthians 14:1-5 Paul agrees that tongue speaking is no longer a mystery if an interpreter can translate what is being said. There is no compelling evidence, therefore, that Acts and 1 Corinthians refer to two different gifts of tongues. In both instances, languages with a discernible code are in view. Because tongues are in languages, they can be interpreted. First Corinthians 14:2 does not counter this idea, for here Paul simply describes the nature of tongues without an interpreter. In such a case no one understands what is being said except God. However, if an interpreter is present (either someone who understands the language from birth or someone to whom the gift of interpretation is granted), then the tongue is no longer mysterious.

A word about contemporary tongue speaking should be said. It can be concluded from the discussion above that most tongue speaking today does not match the biblical depiction of tongues since most people do not speak in discernible languages. It does not follow from this that such tongue speaking is necessarily evil or demonic. J. I. Packer is probably correct in suggesting that most contemporary tongue speaking is a form of psychological relaxation that is helpful to the one engaging in it.[23] Packer compares it to singing to oneself in the shower. Those who contend that such an experience is crucial or even important in the Christian life are, of course, mistaken. Still, the experience itself is not damaging and is indeed relaxing and freeing for those who enjoy it.

Apostles. Paul mentions those who are gifted as apostles in 1 Corinthians 12:28-29 and Ephesians 4:11. As we have seen earlier, Paul usually uses the word *apostolos* of his own authoritative ministry. The word is not always a technical term. For instance, in 2 Corinthians 8:23 and Philippians 2:25 it is best defined as messenger, with no suggestion of special authority. If Andronicus and Junia (or Junias) are called apostles (Rom 16:7), the term probably designates them as missionaries and is not used in the technical sense. It is possible in 1 Corinthians 12:28-29 that Paul uses the term *apostles* in this secondary sense as well. If so, he refers to apostles here as missionaries, and the kind of authority that belonged to Paul and the remaining apostolic circle is not implied. It is probable, though, that the term *apostles* in both 1 Corinthians 12:28-29 and Ephesians 2:20; 3:5; 4:11 has the same referent. In these texts the distinctive authority of the apostles is in view, and the apostolic circle is a closed entity. Nor does Paul expect any more apostles after his

---

[23]J. I. Packer, *Keep in Step with the Spirit* (Old Tappan, N.J.: Revell, 1984), pp. 207-11.

tenure, for he asserts that he is the last of the apostles (1 Cor 15:8), and a freak apostle at that (1 Cor 15:9). The distinctiveness of the apostles emerges in the affirmation that the church is built on the foundation of the apostles and prophets (Eph 2:20). Once the foundation has been laid, such authoritative apostles and prophets are superfluous. Indeed, God's revelation as to the nature of the church (Eph 3:5) has been uniquely revealed to the apostles and prophets. Thus, when Paul says in 1 Corinthians 12:28 that first there are apostles and then prophets, the thought is similar to Ephesians 2:20, where the distinctive foundational role of the apostles and prophets is taught.

Cessation of gifts. Some interpreters, especially in the dispensational tradi-tion, argue that Paul teaches that the gifts, at least the supernatural ones, cease with completion of the canon. First Corinthians 13:8-12 certainly teaches that gifts will not last forever. Indeed, 1 Corinthians 13:10 says that they will pass away when "the perfect" *(teleion)* arrives. In some circles "the perfect" is understood to refer to the New Testament canon. This reading is impossible since Paul had no conception that he was contributing to a com-pleted canon of writings that would function together as an authority for the church in its history. Paul was keenly conscious of his authority as an apostle, and he expected churches to submit to his authority. But he did not have any notion that history would last a long time. To see "the perfect" as referring to the New Testament canon is an example of anachronism. It has also been sug-gested that "the perfect" here refers to spiritual maturity and that such matu-rity is possible once the canon is completed.[24] But the objections to this view are equally strong.[25] Instead of referring to spiritual maturity or to the canon of the New Testament, "the perfect" most likely refers to the second coming of Christ, the end of the age. The perfect is equivalent with seeing God face to face (1 Cor 13:12), which most naturally refers to the coming of Christ. "Face to face" often refers to theophanies in the Old Testament (Gen 32:30; Deut 5:4; 34:10; Judg 6:22; Ezek 20:35), and thus seeing a reference to Christ's return is most probable. What makes the spiritual maturity view even more unlikely is the reference to knowledge. When the perfect comes, the partial will pass away (1 Cor 13:10). Presently Paul sees imperfectly, but when the perfect arrives, he will see face to face (1 Cor 13:12). Partial knowledge will give way to complete knowledge (1 Cor 13:12). If the "perfect" refers to the New Testa-ment canon or spiritual maturity, we no longer have partial knowledge.

---

[24]Robert L. Thomas, "Tongues . . . Will Cease," *JETS* 17 (1974): 81-89.
[25]See, e.g., the arguments of Forbes, *Prophecy and Inspired Speech,* pp. 85-91.

Those who have the canon or those who are mature would know all things fully. Indeed, they know more than Paul! But any notion that our knowledge is perfect now is overrealized eschatology and should be rejected.

Another word should be said about apostles, prophets and the cessation of gifts.[26] Ephesians 2:20 affirms that the church is built on the foundation of apostles and prophets. No more authoritative apostles of the likes of Paul or the Twelve are to be expected. Paul is the last of the apostles (1 Cor 15:8). The foundation of the church has been laid, and the distinctive revelation relative to the Christ event has been transmitted. Nor is there any room for prophets, if they were infallible, since the church was built on the foundation of the apostles and prophets. The prophetic gift continued in the church for some time, but it slowly disappeared. We should not expect such prophets today, since prophets spoke the word of God infallibly. If the word *apostles* is used derivatively in terms of missionaries, then they still exist today, but not with the authority of the founding apostles. Similarly, people receive impressions about God's will today, and such impressions may be from God, but such impressions do not have the same authority as those of the founding prophets. Paul nowhere explicitly teaches the cessation of gifts, but it is legitimate to infer that both apostles and prophets have ceased. Have any other gifts ceased? Paul does not say. Healings, miracles and tongues (per my definition) seem to be rare, but we cannot definitively say that they have passed away. Perhaps we should say that in certain situations these gifts are granted by God but that this is the exception rather than the rule.

Conclusion

God's intention was not merely to save individuals but to create a new community, a new people for his glory. When the church is united and growing, it is an emblem of God's grace and goodness, inviting others thereby to embrace God's grace in Christ. The unity of the church is important to Paul because then the church attests to the love of God and to the saving message of the gospel, and hence the promise to bless all peoples through Abraham becomes a reality through the church. Spiritual gifts are given to the church so that believers can minister to one another and to the world. Love is expressed in service, and hence spiritual gifts, when used rightly, pattern themselves after the self-giving of Jesus Christ, for he lived for the good and salvation of others.

---

[26] A view that is similar to mine relative to apostles and prophets is found in Richard B. Gaffin, *Perspectives on Pentecost: Studies in New Testament Teaching on the Gifts of the Holy Spirit* (Phillipsburg, N.J.: Presbyterian & Reformed, 1979).

14

THE ORDINANCES
OF THE CHURCH
& ITS MINISTRY
The Building Up of the Body

In the previous chapter we saw Paul's emphasis on the unity in the church. Unity is never to be achieved by sacrificing truth but is to be established on the basis of the truth. The church is Christ's body and the means by which God's saving message is proclaimed to the world. In this chapter we shall continue to investigate the theme of the church, examining the Pauline view of baptism, the Lord's Supper and the ministry of the church. In our discussion of ministry shall be included leaders in the church and their offices, church discipline and the Pauline view of women in ministry.

Baptism
Background. No extended discussion or defense of baptism occurs in Paul. Presumably, he received the tradition of baptism from those who were believers before him and practiced it accordingly. We see from Acts that those who believed in Jesus Christ and repented of their sins were baptized immediately (Acts 2:38, 41; 8:12-13, 36, 38; 9:18; 10:47-48; 11:16; 16:15, 33; 18:8; 22:16), even if a church was not gathered (Acts 8:36, 38; 9:18; 16:33). In the early part of the twentieth century it was quite popular to trace the practice of baptism in Paul

to the mystery religions.[1] Few scholars would espouse such a theory today. Our knowledge of the rites of mystery cults is frustratingly vague, and there is no decisive evidence that some kind of washing was a requirement for initiation.[2] We should not be surprised, actually, if many different religious cults had some kind of washing ritual for entrance since cleansing with water is an obvious way to depict the beginning of a new life. Such parallels, however, do not establish dependence of one movement on another. In any case, clear parallels are lacking in regard to Paul and mystery religions.

Scholars have also been inclined to focus on baptismal and catechetical traditions in Paul, identifying many texts as liturgical baptismal texts (e.g., Gal 3:26-28; Phil 2:6-11; Col 1:15-20). We must be careful here of imposing later sacramental teaching on Paul. It is easy to associate any text that has to do with the initiation of the Christian life or that has a creedal formula with baptism. Baptism is linked with a whole complex of initiation events in Paul: receiving the Spirit, confessing Christ as Lord, believing in Christ, being justified and so on.[3] We would be mistaken, however, to read baptism into all of these texts, even though Paul never conceived of a believer who received the Spirit and refused baptism. Even though those who are anointed and sealed with the Spirit (2 Cor 1:21-22; Eph 1:13) received such a seal or anointing at baptism (i.e., at conversion), we would transcend the evidence to identify these metaphors with baptism. The approach here will be to limit the discussion to texts in Paul that specifically refer to baptism or that contain a clear allusion to it—a more debatable matter of course!

One baptism. Probably the best place to begin is with Paul's assertion that there is "one baptism" (Eph 4:5). Some query whether Spirit or water baptism is intended. Certainly Paul associated the reception of the Spirit with baptism (1 Cor 12:13; Tit 3:5), so he never envisaged people *who had not received* the Spirit being baptized. Nevertheless, water baptism was probably at the forefront of his mind here, for baptism in water, as we have seen from Acts, was invariably the rite of entrance into the new community. Water baptism sig-

---

[1]So Richard Reitzenstein, *Hellenistic Mystery Religions: Their Basic Ideas and Significance* (Pittsburgh: Pickwick, 1978); Wilhelm Bousset, *Kyrios Christos: A History of the Belief in Christ from the Beginnings of Christianity to Irenaeus* (Nashville: Abingdon, 1970).

[2]Günter Wagner, *Pauline Baptism and the Pagan Mysteries: The Problem of the Pauline Doctrine of Baptism in Romans VI.1-11 in the Light of Its Religio-Historical 'Parallels'* (Edinburgh: Oliver & Boyd, 1967); A. J. M. Wedderburn, *Baptism and Resurrection: Studies in Pauline Theology Against Its Graeco-Roman Background*, WUNT 44 (Tübingen: J. C. B. Mohr, 1987).

[3]See Robert H. Stein, *Difficult Passages in the Epistles* (Grand Rapids, Mich.: Baker, 1988), pp. 116-26.

naled to all that one had joined the Christian church. Paul can appeal to baptism as a mark of unity in Ephesians 4:5 because it was a given that all his converts were baptized at conversion. No one debated the necessity of baptism, for it was unheard of for any believer to *refuse* baptism. The historical debates on baptism that continue to this very day were unknown in the early church. Paul did not have to debate with Christians who wanted to dispense with baptism. By referring to one baptism he appeals to the initiation rite shared by all believers, the plunging under the water that was part of the commencement of the Christian life. Most scholars now agree that baptism by immersion was practiced in the New Testament. What they debate is whether the same pattern is required today.

The common experience of baptism is communicated in 1 Corinthians 12:13—"For indeed in one Spirit we were all baptized into one body, whether Jews or Greeks, whether slaves or free, and we all were made to drink of the one Spirit." The antecedent for Paul's statement here, as James Dunn rightly maintains, is the tradition stemming from John the Baptist: "I baptize you in water, but he will baptize you in the Holy Spirit" (Mk 1:8; cf. Mt 3:11; Lk 3:16; Jn 1:33; Acts 1:5; 11:16).[4] The word *en* in 1 Corinthians 12:13 should not be translated as "by" but "in," for elsewhere in the New Testament the agent of baptism is regularly designated by *hypo* (e.g., Mt 3:6, 13-14; Mk 1:5; Lk 3:7; 7:30) and the element with which they are baptized by *en* (Mt 3:6, 11; Mk 1:8; Lk 3:16; Jn 1:26, 31, 33; Acts 1:5; 11:16). Baptism in 1 Corinthians 12:13 is linked especially with incorporation into the body of Christ so that baptism involves induction into the people of God. Here we see the close association between baptism and the Spirit, demonstrating that the reception of water baptism and the reception of the Spirit occur at the same time. There is no need to disassociate water from the Spirit in this text. Paul emphasizes twice in the verse that believers were plunged into and irrigated by the Spirit at conversion.

What is distinctive about baptism, then, is that believers received the Spirit. Still, we should not make the mistake of eliminating the reference to baptism in water. Baptism in the Spirit and in water are closely associated, and they should not be divorced from one another. All believers were baptized in the Spirit when they were inducted into the church. No believers are excepted. Baptism is the badge of entrance into the Christian community. It

---

[4]James D. G. Dunn, *Baptism in the Holy Spirit: A Re-examination of the New Testament Teaching on the Gift of the Spirit in Relation to Pentecostalism Today* (Philadelphia: Westminster Press, 1970).

functions as a boundary marker between believers and unbelievers. Thus all Christians received baptism upon their entrance into the people of God. If one asked Paul, "Are we baptized in water or in the Spirit at conversion?" His reply would be, "Both."

Baptismal washing. That baptism is an initiation rite is confirmed by texts like 1 Corinthians 6:11 and Ephesians 5:26. In the 1 Corinthians text Paul says, "you were washed . . . in the name of the Lord Jesus Christ and by the Spirit of our God"; and in Ephesians text he says that Christ died to sanctify the church "cleansing it by the washing of the water by the word." Titus 3:5 is a comparable text: "He saved us through the washing of regeneration and renewal of the Holy Spirit." None of these verses specifically mentions baptism, but the words *washing* and *cleansing* are obvious references to the practice. Some scholars downplay any reference to water baptism, maintaining that the focus in these texts is only on the Spirit. Such an interpretation is a classic case of "either-or" exegesis where a "both-and" solution fits better. The focus on the Spirit is evident in Titus 3:5 and 1 Corinthians 6:11, and even in Ephesians 5:26. The background to these verses is probably Ezekiel 36:25-27 (quoted here from the NRSV):

> I will sprinkle clean water upon you, and you shall be clean from all your uncleannesses, and from all your idols I will cleanse you. A new heart I will give you, and a new spirit I will put within you; and I will remove from your body the heart of stone and give you a heart of flesh. I will put my spirit within you, and make you follow my statutes and be careful to observe my ordinances.

Here the sprinkling of clean water is coterminus with receiving a new heart and a new Spirit (or spirit). Cleansing comes when God's Spirit comes into one's life.

In Titus 3:5 the words *regeneration (palingenesia)* and *renewal (anakainōsis)* both modify *washing* and function as synonyms. The washing involves regeneration and renewal. It does not follow from this that the washing is understood mechanically, as if the water magically transforms people. Both the "regeneration" and "renewal" come from the Holy Spirit. The words *the Holy Spirit (pneumatos hagiou)* function as the genitive of source for both the nouns *regeneration* and *renewal.* Regeneration and renewal are the product of the Spirit's work in the life of a believer. On the other hand, it is hard to believe that early believers would not think immediately of water baptism when reading the words *washing* and *cleansing.* Baptism in water was a major event in the lives of new believers, functioning as a boundary between their old and new life. They would naturally look back to their baptism as a time when their sins were washed away. Once again, we are faced with the issue that we treated formerly. The Spirit is fundamental in Paul's theology, for the reception of the Spirit preceded baptism in water. Still, Paul linked washing with water and with the Spirit. Both occurred at conversion. The two ideas can be conceptually distinguished, but Paul often merges them together in his writings; and we do an injustice to Paul if we segregate them in such a way that any reference to water baptism is deleted from the above texts.

Immersed into Christ. Baptism designates conversion another way, in that it is associated with being plunged into or immersed in Christ. In Galatians 3:26 Paul affirms that believers are God's children in Christ Jesus through faith. The ground for this assertion *(gar)* is that all believers were clothed with Christ when they were baptized into Christ: "For as many as were baptized into Christ are clothed with Christ" (Gal 3:27). The fundamental reality for believers is not their ethnic background (Jew or Greek), gender (male or female) or class (slave or free). What is fundamental is whether they are in Christ, since all those in Christ are Abraham's seed (Gal 3:28-29). One becomes part of Abraham's family not through circumcision but through faith. Induction into Abraham's family is accomplished in Christ because he is the true seed of Abraham (Gal 3:16). Being plunged into Christ at baptism is the rite by which believers enter into the family of Abraham. It is the badge for entrance into the people of God. Paul does not view baptism alone as sufficient. All those who are baptized have exercised faith (Gal 3:26)! In baptism, though, they have been transferred from the first Adam to the second, from the old era of redemptive history to the new.

Romans 6 also emphasizes that in baptism believers are incorporated into Christ. In 1 Corinthians 12:13 the emphasis is on induction into the people of God, Christ's body. Baptism in Romans 6:3 is explained as being plunged into Christ Jesus, being immersed into him as the second Adam. Those who are baptized into Christ have shared in his death: "Don't you know that those who were baptized into Christ Jesus were baptized into his death? Therefore, we were buried together with him through baptism into death" (Rom 6:3-4). Debate exists over whether Romans 6:3-5 also communicates sharing in Christ's resurrection. If so, baptism pictures being plunged underneath the water with Christ (dead and buried) and then rising again from the waters. Paul does not explicitly portray resurrection with emergence from the baptismal waters, though such an idea seems to be implied in Romans 6:4-5. Some object that burials were often above ground, so that the idea of emerging from the water cannot signify coming up out of the grave. But this requires more than we should expect from a metaphor. Paul is not trying to depict literally where people are buried, whether it is below the ground or in caves. On the contrary, baptism is a portrayal of death since human beings will die if they are submerged under water long enough. They have been overcome by the waters of death. Death is defeated, not by avoiding it but by being united with Christ in his death and resurrection. It is at baptism that the old Adam died with Christ—"our old self was crucified together with him," that is, with Christ (Rom 6:6).

That believers have died and been raised with Christ in baptism is suggested by Colossians 2:12, "having been buried together with him [i.e., Christ] in baptism, in which you were also raised together with him through faith in the work of God who raised him from the dead." Again Paul affirms that believers have been buried together with Christ in baptism. If *in which (en ho)* refers to baptism—and baptism is the immediate antecedent—then this verse also asserts that "in baptism you have also been raised together with him."[5] We must notice again that baptism is not understood mechanically. It is inevitably linked with faith (Col 2:12). Paul uses water baptism as a shorthand for conversion since a whole series of events is associated with baptism: trust in Christ, reception of the Spirit, confessing Christ as Lord, justification, adoption and so on. It never entered Paul's mind to separate baptism from any of these other realities, but he naturally refers to their baptism as a boundary marker since it represents the transfer from the old life to the new.

Magical views of baptism? The importance of baptism for early Christians is communicated by 1 Corinthians 15:29, where at least some Corinthians were being baptized on behalf of the dead. We must admit that the details in this text are obscure. Paul's purpose was not to explain or defend the practice, but to use it as an argument to support the reality of the resurrection. Scholars cannot identify with certainty why the Corinthians were conducting baptisms for the dead. I would suggest that occasionally believers died in the interval between faith and baptism. Baptism was considered so important by the Corinthians that they went ahead and conducted a baptism on behalf of the person who died. Probably the Corinthians overemphasized the significance of baptism. 1 Corinthians 10 suggests that some understood baptism and the Lord's Supper in a magical sense, thinking that by partaking in these they were preserved from any harm so that they could sin with impunity. Perhaps some believed that baptism and the Lord's Supper protected them,

---

[5]The Greek could also be translated "in whom."

so that even if they ate a meal devoted to an idol no harm could come to them (1 Cor 10:19-22). To counter their view Paul constructs an analogy between the experience of Israel and that of believers. The Israelites were baptized in a sense in that they were baptized into Moses when they entered the water (1 Cor 10:2). Perhaps the idea is that they were plunged into the water, so to speak, because they were poised between the cloud and the sea. Israel also ate something like the Lord's Supper, for they enjoyed the manna and the water flowing from the rock (1 Cor 10:3-4). Such experiences, however, did not shield them from God's wrath. He destroyed them in the wilderness because of their sin (1 Cor 10:5-12). Thus, the Corinthians should not think that they are somehow magically protected from God's judgment by virtue of their baptism or participation in the Lord's Supper. Paul never separates baptism from the rest of the Christian life, as if it alone could prop up believers.

First Corinthians 1:10-17 is also instructive in discerning Paul's view of baptism. The Corinthians had split into different factions, some adhering to Paul, others to Apollos, others to Peter and still others to Christ. Perhaps some converts were choosing sides on the basis of who baptized them, for Paul reminds them forcefully that they were not baptized into his name (1 Cor 1:13, 15). He recounts whom he baptized in Corinth, indicating that he cannot even remember all those who were baptized by him (1 Cor 1:14-16). Paul's mission was "not to baptize but to preach the gospel" (1 Cor 1:17). This text is misinterpreted if it is understood as a denial of baptism. Certainly all Pauline converts were baptized. It was inconsequential to Paul *whether he personally baptized them.* We should not conclude from this that he thought baptism itself was immaterial. Still, baptism is clearly subordinated here to the preaching of the gospel. We receive a hint that baptism could be unduly exalted and could function in opposition to the gospel Paul preached. Baptism was important for Paul. It must be understood, however, in light of the gospel, so that the gospel (and not baptism) receives priority. Advocates of baptismal regeneration exalt baptism over the gospel, failing to see that the former must be understood on the basis of the latter.

Infant baptism. Did Paul believe in infant baptism? The text gives no explicit answers, hence the debate. The clues we have, though, suggest that he did not. The adversaries in Galatia insisted that Gentile believers had to be circumcised to be saved. It would have been easy for Paul to reply, "You do not need to be circumcised. Baptism has replaced circumcision." Seeing such a correspondence between baptism and circumcision is attractive, and it is part of the reason that many believers today support infant baptism. A one-to-one correspondence between baptism and circumcision would imply that baptism, like circumcision, could be administered during infancy for the children of believers. It is instructive, however, that Paul never argues that baptism replaces circumcision in Galatians. Some appeal to Colossians 2:11-12 to defend the idea that baptism replaces circumcision: "In him [i.e., in Christ] you were also circumcised with a circumcision performed without hands, in the removal of the body of the flesh, in the circumcision of Christ, having been buried together with him in baptism, in which you were also raised together with him through faith in the work of God who raised him from the dead." This interpretation misplaces the analogy between baptism and circumcision. Colossians 2:11 refers not to physical circumcision but *spiritual circumcision*, which occurs when believers in Christ put off the old person. In addition, baptism in Colossians 2:12 is associated with faith, so it is difficult to see how it could apply to infants.

The most significant argument against infant baptism stems from Paul's theology as a whole. One of the primary reasons he dispenses with circumcision is that it marked a person as a Jew, a member of a certain ethnic and nationalistic community. Circumcision signaled one's affiliation with the Jewish people. Circumcision is no longer fitting as a badge of entrance into the people of God because the church transcends all ethnic and nationalistic boundaries. In addition, circumcision only applied to males, whereas baptism applies to males and females. We have seen that in Paul baptism is linked with faith, with incorporation into Christ, with confessing Christ as Lord, and so on. Paul does not envision people being part of the church on the basis of family or ethnic ties. The idea that the children of believers are "holy" (1 Cor 7:14) does not invalidate what is being said here. Paul does not mean that these children are part of the people of God, for he similarly argues that the unbelieving spouse "is sanctified" (1 Cor 7:14). He is not implying that unbelieving spouses are saved and belong to the people of God. First Corinthians 7:16 confirms that the "sanctification" of unbelieving spouses is not equivalent to salvation, for Paul remarks that believers cannot be sure that unbelieving spouses will be saved. When Paul speaks of children being holy and unbelieving spouses sanctified, he likely means that the presence of believers in a family places the family in a holy sphere, which gives unbelievers the *possibility* of salvation.

Any initiation rite that links membership in the community to birth or ethnic background is a reversion to the old covenant. That is why baptism is parallel to the circumcision of the heart instead of to physical circumcision. In the old covenant one could be a member of the covenant community by virtue of circumcision and yet lack a circumcised heart (cf. Deut 10:16; 30:6; Jer 4:4). We must remember that Israel was both a nation and the people of God. Not all of those who were part of Israel as a nation were truly believers, but all male Israelites were inducted into the community during infancy. Paul teaches that the new community is made up of all baptized members—those who have confessed that Jesus Christ is their Lord and placed their faith in him. Membership in the new community is open to all who believe in Jesus Christ. The church of Jesus Christ is not a political or nationalistic entity as Israel was. The church comprises people from every ethnic and cultural group. Paul did not envision the church as a theocratic entity. Therefore, the moral norms of the church would not necessarily be enforced also at the state level. The newness of the people of God and their distinction from Israel as a political entity helps us understand why baptism was applied only to believers, whereas in Israel circumcision was applied to those who were part of the nationalistic entity.

The Lord's Supper

One of the remarkable features of the Lord's Supper in Paul is that we would not even know it was practiced in Pauline communities if it were not for 1 Corinthians. This serves as a reminder that the Pauline letters are occasional letters addressed to specific situations. The Lord's Supper was part of the tradition that was passed on and accepted in the churches (cf. Mt 26:26-29; Mk 14:22-25; Lk 22:19-20; Acts 2:42, 46; 20:7). It is likely that Paul communicated the tradition about the Lord's Supper when he established the various churches. The Lord's Supper was regularly practiced in his churches, and in most cases no definite problems emerged, so nothing is said about it except in 1 Corinthians. Some scholars have argued that the Lord's Supper is dependent on mystery religions, as they have argued with baptism. But the same objections leveled against baptism's being derived from the mystery religions apply here. We have little knowledge of the rites of mystery religions, and although meals are a common feature in religious cults, analogy does not prove dependence. It is much more likely that Paul's understanding comes from the historical Jesus, per his own explanation in 1 Corinthians 11:23-26. When we compare Paul's wording with the accounts in the Synoptic Gospels, it is immediately evident that the Pauline account is closest to what we find in Luke 22:19-20.

1 Corinthians 10:14-22. The first text in which Paul discusses the Lord's

Supper focuses on idolatry (1 Cor 10:14-22). Paul warns the Corinthians against participating in meals devoted to idols. According to Paul such an activity is idolatry because eating in an idol's temple was a cultic act of worship—even if the person participating in the temple meal claims that he or she only attended the temple meal for social purposes. Paul draws an analogy between participating in the Lord's Supper and partaking of idolatrous meals to provoke the readers to abstain from such meals in the temple of idols. He reflects on the significance of the cup and the bread in 1 Corinthians 10:16: "The cup of blessing which we bless, is it not participation in the blood of Christ? The bread which we break, is it not participation in the body of Christ?" The cup is a symbol of blessing, of praise to God. God is praised for supplying sustenance for his people and for delivering us through the work of Christ on the cross. The cup involves "participation" *(koinōnia)* in the blood of Christ. "Participation" here denotes the benefits of Christ's blood. Those who drink of the cup are partaking of the benefits of Christ's death on their behalf. Similarly, those who consume the broken bread share in the benefits of Christ's body. The broken bread symbolizes the body of Christ given for his people in his death; the cup symbolizes Christ's blood that has been shed for his people. Those who sit at the Lord's table enjoy the benefits of his death on their behalf.

Paul makes a distinct point in 1 Corinthians 10:17 when he writes, "Because there is one bread, we the many are one body. For we all share of the one bread." All believers share of the one bread, and it follows from this that there is one body—one church. The one bread, per 1 Corinthians 10:16, must refer to the broken body of Christ given for his people. All believers share in the benefits of his death. The ingesting of this one bread symbolizes that believers are one body, the one people of God. The church draws its sustenance from one source, and so it is one people. The church lives on the basis of the death and resurrection of its founder. Paul goes on to say that no believer may eat a cultic meal to honor an idol (1 Cor 10:19-22), for demons lie behind idols, and such meals mean that believers derive "benefit" from demons. No one, though, can benefit both from the Lord's table and from the table of demons. No one can drink from the Lord's cup and from a demon's cup. Again we are reminded that Israel had spiritual food (manna) and drink (water) in the wilderness (1 Cor 10:3-4). This food and drink functioned as an anticipation and type of the Lord's Supper. No magical benefit accrued to the Israelites simply because they ate spiritual food and drank spiritual drink. Nor should the Corinthians think that participating in the Lord's Supper shields them from demonic powers. The Lord's table does convey a benefit, but only for those who are devoted to the Lord.

1 Corinthians 11:17-34. The second text in which the Lord's Supper is addressed is 1 Corinthians 11:17-34. The precise problem in the church is difficult to identify, but the general nature of the situation is clear enough. Paul is dismayed because divisions among the members surface when they gather for the Lord's Supper. The divisions in this instance are not theological but social. The Lord's Supper in Paul's day was celebrated as part of a regular meal. Apparently rich members in the community were eating and drinking sumptuously during these meals, while the poor were not even getting enough to eat. Probably the rich came to the supper before the poor and were eating and drinking the food before the poor arrived. By the time the poor arrived there was little or nothing left to eat. By treating the poor in this way the rich were preserving class distinctions characteristic of secular society. Paul is incensed that such a callous disregard of poorer brothers and sisters in Christ occurs at the Lord's Supper. Indeed, the behavior exhibited indicates that what is being celebrated is not truly the Lord's Supper (1 Cor 11:20). To allege that they are meeting in honor of the Lord when the poor are despised and some of the rich are even getting drunk is a contradiction in terms. Such behavior amounts to a despising of God's church and the humiliation of the poor (1 Cor 11:22). Perhaps Paul has in mind the nature of the church when he says that believers who eat unworthily bring judgment on themselves if they "do not discern the body" (1 Cor 12:29). Does the term *body* refer to Christ's death or the church? It is difficult to be certain. Perhaps both could be defended. One who treats fellow believers poorly fails to discern that they are members of Christ's church, his body. One may also fail to discern the significance of Christ's death since by his death he created a people; and therefore one who mistreats fellow believers at the Lord's Supper reveals that he has little understanding of why Christ died.

Paul emphasizes in 1 Corinthians 11:23-26 that in the Lord's Supper they commemorate Christ's self-giving on behalf of his people. The rich Corinthians are hardly remembering his death if they oppress the poor at the very time the supper is celebrated. Genuinely remembering the Lord's death makes a difference in one's everyday life. Paul has no place for "sacramental devotion" that coexists with social oppression. Proclaiming the Lord's death (1 Cor 11:26) in the supper must be matched by the self-giving modeled by the Lord Jesus. Paul counsels the community, therefore, to wait for one another when eating (1 Cor 11:33). The Lord's Supper is only genuinely in honor of the Lord when the members share the meal together and the poor are not ignored. If some protest that they are so hungry that they cannot wait to eat, then Paul advises them to eat *before* coming to the Lord's Supper (1 Cor 11:34). In this way they will avoid God's judgment and will cease mistreating the poor.

This text reminds us that Paul does not separate the theological and the social. Those who eat the Lord's Supper in an unworthy manner—in this context, by mistreating the poor—are guilty of sinning against the "the body and blood of the Lord" (1 Cor 11:27). They contradict the very essence of the Lord's Supper by using it as an occasion to pander to their selfish interests. Paul calls on believers to test (*dokimazetō*, 1 Cor 11:28) themselves before eating the bread and drinking from the cup, for those who are oppressing the poor and not examining themselves bring judgment on themselves. Indeed, Paul suggests that some in the community are not "approved" (*dokimoi*, 1 Cor 11:19), meaning that they are not genuine believers. The "judgment" that afflicts those in the community in 1 Corinthians 11:29, however, is not the same thing as the judgment inflicted on those who are not genuine believers. In 1 Corinthians 11:30 the judgments fall short of eternal punishment. The Lord is disciplining some through sickness and illness, and others are even dying. Paul views such "judgments" as merciful, for they prevent sinning believers from receiving the condemnation that the world experiences at the last judgment (1 Cor 11:31-32). We should note here that it is difficult to discern between those who are "unapproved" and those who merely experience temporal judgment. Apparently a line is crossed in which it becomes evident, at least to God, that some in the community are not genuine believers at all.

The terms *I received (paralambanō)* and *I handed down (paradidōmi)* suggest that Paul received the tradition of the Lord's Supper from believers who preceded him (1 Cor 11:23). We have already noted that the Pauline tradition is closest to the Lukan form. For Paul the Lord's Supper is a commemoration of the heart of the gospel. The bread represents Christ's body, which was broken in death for sinners. We have already seen that the remembrance of such is not merely a mental act but that it involves the transformation of one's life, for Paul links it with genuine concern for poorer members in the community. Those who have truly experienced God's grace as it is mediated in Christ's death long to bless others, just as they themselves have received the blessing of forgiveness through Christ's self-giving on their behalf. The cup represents the inauguration of the new covenant promised in Jeremiah (Jer 31:31-34). The shedding of Christ's blood inaugurates a new era when the new covenant becomes a reality. The new covenant involves both forgiveness of sins and the indwelling Spirit (Ezek 11:19-20; 36:26-27), who enables the fulfillment of God's law. Paul also adds a forward-looking word about the Lord's Supper: those who share in it proclaim the death of the Lord until he comes again (1 Cor 11:26). Perhaps Paul reflects here on Jesus' saying that he will eat the Passover meal again in the kingdom of God (Lk 22:16). The Lord's Supper also communicates the "already but not yet" character of Paul's theology. The new covenant has arrived but it is not yet completely fulfilled. It will reach its consummation when the Lord returns, when the kingdom is fulfilled.

Anyone who has read church history knows that interpreting the Lord's Supper has been a matter of much controversy. Most of the debate has centered on what the text means when Jesus says of the bread, "this is my body" (1 Cor 11:24). Martin Luther and Ulrich Zwingli argued ardently over the meaning of the word is *(estin)*, coming unfortunately to no agreement. How literally should we take it? I would suggest that we have another clue that is often overlooked. Paul says in 1 Corinthians 11:25 that "this cup is the new covenant in my blood." Obviously the word is cannot be taken literally here, for no one believes that the cup actually is the new covenant. Paul means that the cup *represents* the new covenant inaugurated by Christ's blood. Similarly, to say that the bread "is my body" means that it represents what Christ has done on behalf of the church through his sacrifice.

Church Leaders

In discussing church offices and leaders in the church, it should be noted at the outset that scholars have often posed the "authentic" and "charismatic" Paul against the "inauthentic" and "structured" Paul.[6] For example, Ernst Käsemann says, "For we may assert without hesitation that the Pauline community had no presbytery during the Apostle's lifetime."[7] According to this view, the genuine Pauline churches were spontaneous, open, free and Spirit-directed, while the post-Pauline churches became institutional, rigid and leadership-oriented, so that the freedom of the Spirit was no longer the norm. This portrait in which the "charismatic" Paul is posed against the "struc-

---

[6]For example, Ernst Käsemann, "Ministry and Community in the New Testament," in *Essays in New Testament Themes* (Philadelphia: Fortress, 1964), pp. 63-94; James D. G. Dunn, *Unity and Diversity in the New Testament: An Inquiry into the Character of Earliest Christianity* (Philadelphia: Westminster Press, 1977), pp. 109-16.

[7]Käsemann, "Ministry and Community," p. 86.

tured" Paul is deeply flawed.[8] The Pauline churches were charismatic but they were also structured. *Charisma* and structure are not mutually exclusive. Dependence on the Spirit does not exclude order and structure. Anyone who is familiar with charismatic churches today knows that some churches that blaze with the gifts of the Spirit are structured, ordered and run by highly effective leaders.

Evidence for leaders in the Pauline churches. When we read the Pauline letters carefully, it is evident that leaders and teachers were present in the community from the beginning. The *terminology* used for such leaders varies, showing that normative titles were not in place from the beginning. We cannot argue that structured leadership was nonexistent on the basis of the diversity of nomenclature. The early letters, of course, do not contain any sustained discussion on church leadership. It does not follow from this that such leadership was unimportant or nonexistent, however. Since Pauline letters are occasional, we should not expect them to cover every topic, and thus it is not surprising that leadership was more of an issue in some letters than others (i.e., the Pastorals). We must remember again that we would not even know that the Lord's Supper was practiced in the Pauline churches apart from 1 Corinthians.

Interestingly, there is evidence of church leaders in the early and acknowledged Pauline letters. The situation of the churches addressed in the Pastoral Letters differed from all of Paul's previous letters, so that in them a fuller exposition regarding the structure and leaders in the church was deemed fitting. Perhaps Paul expressed himself more fully on this subject in the Pastorals because he recognized that he was near the end of his life. When a powerful leader like Paul becomes aware that the end of his ministry is near, he naturally thinks of communicating how the work he has accomplished may be maintained in the future.

It is wrong to presume that we have no evidence of structured leadership in the earlier Pauline letters, although we lack a full-orbed discussion of the matter. The presence of church leaders is evident from what may be Paul's earliest letter. In 1 Thessalonians 5:12 believers are charged to respect those who labor *(tous kopiōntas)* among them, lead *(proistamenous)* them and admonish *(nouthetountas)* them. The combination of these three words and the exhortation to regard such in love "because of their work" indicates that

---

[8]Rightly R. A. Campbell, *The Elders: Seniority Within Earliest Christianity* (Edinburgh: T & T Clark, 1994). See also the persuasive work of Ben Merkle, *The Elder and Overseer: One Office in the Early Church* (Ph.D. diss., The Southern Baptist Theological Seminary, 2000).

leaders in the community are in view. The community as a whole is to show extraordinary love and respect for those who labor so diligently. Their authority is evident in the words for leadership *(proistamenous)* and instruction *(nouthetountas)*.

We also see from 1 Thessalonians 5:19-22 that charismatic gifts were operative in the community but that no disjunction between the exercise of gifts and the presence of leaders is suggested. Perhaps this is the place to mention a possible objection. Paul typically addresses the congregation as a whole, not the leaders. Some scholars use this as leverage to downplay the authority of leaders. There is some truth in this analysis, but one could exaggerate its significance. The congregation as a whole is addressed because the congregation ultimately determines the direction of the church. Leaders are not autocratic or dictators in the Pauline churches. Those who are led, after all, must voluntarily submit themselves to leadership. We see from reading the Corinthian letters that Paul attempts to persuade (not coerce) the Corinthians to obey him. If the Pauline letters were addressed only to leaders, we might conclude that leaders were to enforce their will on congregations. There are instances in which authority must be brought to bear on churches, but Paul believed that each member of the community was indwelt by the Spirit and played a significant role in the life of the church. Too much focus on leaders could obscure the equality of all believers in Christ. Paul maintained a delicate balance between the role of leadership and the contribution of each member in the church. Leaders were important in the Pauline churches, but they did not operate in such a way that individual members' contributions were quashed; they led mainly by example and persuasion, not by coercion.

First Corinthians is a prime example of the preceding discussion. The divisions and issues that rocked the congregation are well known. Paul addresses all believers in adjudicating the situation, not just the leaders. Nonetheless, at the end of the letter he acknowledges that leaders exist—for instance, the house of Stephanas (1 Cor 16:15-16). The Corinthians are urged to submit to the household of Stephanas and to every coworker *(synergeō)* and laborer *(kopiaō)* in the gospel. This text is like 1 Thessalonians in that the specific tasks carried out by leaders are vague. To be told that they "work," "labor" and "minister" *(diakonia,* 1 Cor 16:15) gives us little idea of what leaders did. First Thessalonians 5:12-13 is a bit more specific, for besides using the word *labor,* Paul writes that some "led" and "admonished." It is certainly impossible to derive any detailed picture of the function of leaders from these texts. Paul's purpose was not to describe such functions here, for presumably their tasks were well known or at least being worked out in the life of the community. The Corinthian congregation is summoned to "submit" *(hypotassō)* to such leaders. The call to submission is not an example of authority being enforced from above. Paul does not say that the leaders are to compel the congregation to submit. He urges the congregation to submit voluntarily and gladly to leadership. The congregation takes it upon itself to follow the leadership. Paul does not instruct leaders to compel the congregation to submit.

Galatians 6:6 indicates that there were teachers in the earliest churches. Those who are instructed in the word are to provide financial support for those who do the teaching *(ho katēchoumenos)*. Financial support for teachers suggests a regular teaching ministry supported by the community (cf. 1 Cor 9:14). Those teaching presumably also exercised a leadership role in the congregation. One of the most interesting texts with reference to leadership is Philippians 1:1, where Paul addresses "the overseers and deacons" *(episkopois kai diakonois)*. Nowhere else does Paul identify leaders by title in the introduction to his letters, and even in Philippians those who bear such titles do not appear explicitly elsewhere. Perhaps the leaders are addressed because they are being summoned to live a life of humility and servanthood, following the example of Paul (Phil 1:12-26), Christ (Phil 2:5-11), Timothy (Phil 2:19-24) and Epaphroditus (Phil 2:25-30). Scholars have often labeled such "offices" as early catholic, which means that the church is beginning to take on an institutional form that culminated in and found its full expression in Roman Catholicism. It is unpersuasive to argue that Philippians is early catholic since virtually all scholars agree the letter is authentically Pauline. The reference to leaders is almost casual, and no definite instruction regarding their functions is passed on. What is striking is that leaders with specific offices existed, and presumably they exercised a definite role in guiding the community. We must admit that if Philippians were our only letter, our knowledge of the tasks of leaders would be frustratingly vague.

Leaders in the Pastoral Epistles. What is striking in reading the rest of the New Testament—without entering debates about historicity and date—is that leaders, particularly elders, are an essential part of the life of the churches. When someone is severely ill, James instructs believers to summon "the elders of the church" (Jas 5:14). Peter's letter, which is addressed to churches in several provinces in what is now Turkey, contains a significant exhortation to "the elders" (1 Pet 5:1-4; cf. 1 Pet 5:5). According to Acts, Paul and Barnabas appointed elders in the churches established during the first missionary journey (Acts 14:23). The Jerusalem church was constituted with elders as well, according to the witness of Acts (Acts 11:30; 15:2, 4, 6, 22-23; 16:4; 21:18). Most instructive is Acts 20:17-38, where Paul addresses the leaders of the Ephesian church. In Acts 20:17 they are called "elders" (presbyteros), but in Acts 20:28 the same people are called "overseers" (episkopos), suggesting that the two terms are different names for the same function.

The Pastoral Letters seem to confirm the above observation. Titus is instructed to appoint "elders" in every city (Tit 1:5), but two verses later the term overseer appears (Tit 1:7). The singular overseer is sometimes seen as distinct from the plural elders, but it is more likely that overseer is a generic term here.[9] No clear evidence exists to distinguish "elders" from "overseers," for it is most natural to presume that the same persons are addressed and that two different titles are used for the same role. The singular for overseer is likely generic. The same state of affairs obtains in 1 Timothy. In 1 Timothy 3:1-7 qualifications for the "overseer" are listed and nothing is said about elders. In 1 Timothy 5:17, however, those who labor in preaching and teaching are called "elders" (cf. 1 Tim 5:19). It is possible that two distinct offices are in view, but again it seems more likely that Paul glides from one term to the other. The term elder (presbyteros) derives especially from the Jewish background, designating those who were respected leaders in the community. Discerning their precise role in both the Old Testament and later Jewish literature is difficult. The background to the term overseer (episkopos) is more difficult. Some have emphasized a Greco-Roman background, and others have seen parallels or influence in the Dead Sea Scrolls.[10] In any case, the term seems to stress function—the task of superintending and watching over the health of early Christian congregations.

The parallel between Philippians and 1 Timothy is especially interesting since both refer to overseers and deacons (diakonoi, Phil 1:1; 1 Tim 3:1-13). Often the term diakonos is used in a general way to refer to the ministry in which Paul and others are engaged (1 Cor 3:5; 2 Cor 3:6; 6:4; 11:23; Eph 3:7; 6:21; Col 1:7, 23, 25; 4:7; 1 Tim 4:6). In these texts no specific office is designated by the term. An office does seem to be intended, though, in some texts (Rom 16:1; Phil 1:1; 1 Tim 3:8, 12). It is likely, for instance, that Phoebe was a deacon of the church at Cenchrea (Rom 16:1). Delineating the distinction

---

[9]Contra Campbell, Elders, pp. 182-205; Frances M. Young, "On Episkopos and Presbyteros," JTS 45 (1994): 142-49.

[10]For a survey of backgrounds, see Hermann W. Beyer, "ἐπίσκοπος," in Theological Dictionary of the New Testament, ed. Gerhard Kittel and Gerhard Friedrich (Grand Rapids, Mich.: Eerdmans, 1964), 2:608-20.

between overseer-elders and deacons is not easy, but two requirements for overseers are not repeated for deacons: overseers and elders must have an ability to teach, and they must also possess leadership abilities (1 Tim 3:2, 4-5; 5:17; Tit 1:9). These requirements are never stated for deacons, suggesting that deacons engaged in a ministry of assistance and service rather than teaching and ruling.

Many scholars are persuaded that the Pastoral Letters are later documents, even dating them in the second century, since attention is focused on the structure of the church and leaders. Evidence exists, however, to distinguish the Pastorals from the structures found in the second century. For example, in the Ignatian letters the monarchial episcopate takes center stage, and exhortations to submit to the bishop percolate through virtually all Ignatius's letters. No monarchial episcopate is found in the Pastorals. The leaders function in a collegial fashion as a group, and no one has an office above another. The leaders certainly have a significant role in the Pastorals, but constant appeals to their authority by virtue of their office is lacking. Paul emphasizes the authoritative teaching, not the authoritative person. We could make the mistake of positing too great a disjunction between authoritative teaching and teachers, and yet the difference is important, for the gospel itself is the authority rather than the teacher or elder per se. Some leaders in the churches addressed in the Pastorals have gone astray and are promulgating false doctrine (1 Tim 1:3-11, 18-20; 4:1-5; 6:3-10, 20-21; 2 Tim 2:14-18, 24-26; 3:1-9), and thus Paul is careful to locate authority in the message rather than in the messenger. The messenger is subordinated to the message. In this respect the Pastorals are in the same orbit as Galatians, for Paul emphatically subordinates his apostleship to the gospel (Gal 1:8-9).

The idea that the Pastorals are church manuals must also be resisted. We must remind ourselves that both Titus and 1 Timothy were addressed to specific circumstances in the churches in Crete and Ephesus. Issues relating to ordering the church and leaders were doubtless a major part of Paul's instructions. What we do not have, though, are comprehensive treatises that explicate and order the life of the church. Remarkably little is actually said about the activities of those who serve as overseer-elders and deacons. If these are church manuals, they are quite vague. In every instance some kind of false teaching, rather difficult to pin down, threatens the churches, and Paul gives advice to counter such teaching. This is not to deny a shift in focus in the Pastorals. Paul does speak more about the structure of the church and the transmission of doctrine here than in his earlier letters. Presumably he is aware that the torch is passing from him to the next generation. Paul's circumstances differ, therefore, from those he faced when writing his earlier letters. What we do not have, though, is a systematic exposition of the function of the church. Various instructions are communicated to Paul's trusted assistants—Timothy and Titus—which are deemed particularly crucial for the problems besetting the churches. Many things are not discussed, probably because Paul left the details to Timothy and Titus and to the churches themselves. The letters still bear the imprint of the circumstances that called them forth.

Another problem emerges if the letters are seen as later church manuals. If an author desired to write a church manual for his day, then it is difficult to see why three letters are needed; this is particularly the case with Titus, since it does not seem to add much to the so-called manual in 1 Timothy. A much more effective way to write a manual would be to compose *one* treatise in which everything is explained thoroughly. Three partial letters is a rather confusing way to write up a manual. Another feature, mentioned previously, distinguishes the Pastorals from church manuals: practically nothing is said about the specific functions of the leaders. Virtually all of the attention is devoted to the character of those appointed (1 Tim 3:1-13; Tit 1:5-9). One hardly writes a church manual and then leaves so much about the leaders' specific functions up in the air. Details were probably not filled in because Paul left it to individual churches to work out the concrete circumstances of church life. He did not intend to prescribe everything but left much up to the spiritual wisdom and good sense of the congregation. Perhaps some of the differences may be accounted for by the specific situations addressed. New converts are prohibited from serving as overseers in 1 Timothy 3:6, but no such requirement exists in Titus. It would be nearly impossible to fulfill such a mandate in Crete since the church was newly planted, whereas the church in Ephesus had been established for a number of years. Perhaps the omission of deacons in Titus can be explained similarly. As a new church, it simply did not have enough qualified people to have both overseers and deacons.[11]

Teaching function of overseers. We have noted that two distinct functions are prescribed for the overseer-elders: they are to teach and lead. These two functions are, of course, rather general. Still, they provide the superstructure under which overseer-elders do their work. Their primary calling is to pass on the tradition and truth of the gospel. Their leadership, in other words, is

---

[11] I owe this insight to Boyd Luter of Criswell College.

not primarily bureaucratic, as the case in so many denominations today. Overseer-elders exert their leadership through their teaching ministry and by their adherence to the gospel (1 Tim 5:17). The importance of tradition and teaching in the Pastorals is undeniable. Paul often contrasts unhealthy teaching with that which is healthy (1 Tim 1:10; 6:3; 2 Tim 1:13; 4:3; Tit 1:9, 13; 2:1-2). The truth that must be safeguarded is the gospel (1 Tim 3:16). False teachers veer away from the truth (1 Tim 1:3-11; 4:1-5), and so teaching centered on the faithful word is crucial (1 Tim 1:15; 3:9; 4:9; 2 Tim 2:11; Tit 3:8). It seems that in every case the faithful saying has to do with "salvation," indicating again that the saving message, not the leaders themselves, is the focus.

In addition, the Pastorals are punctuated by confessional statements that emphasize the saving work of God in Christ (1 Tim 1:12-17; 3:16; 2 Tim 1:9-10; 2:11-13; Tit 2:11-14; 3:4-7). Paul exhorts Timothy to live in accord with God's saving work in Christ and to be diligent in teaching such truth (1 Tim 4:11-16; cf. 1 Tim 6:2, 11-14, 20-21). The deposit must be guarded because of the threat of false teachers (2 Tim 1:14), and it must be passed on to the next generation (2 Tim 2:2). Paul's emphasis on the truth that Timothy must preserve is a counterpoint to what the false teachers promulgate (2 Tim 2:14-18). The call to preach the word (2 Tim 4:1-5) is urgent because false teachers are at work. Elders, who will be faithful in preserving the truth and resisting what is evil, are needed in the community because others are spreading teaching that will destroy the community (Tit 1:9-16). We also see in the Pastorals that right teaching is consistently linked with right living. The teaching of God as Savior is inseparable from a transformed life (1 Tim 1:3-11; 4:1-16; 6:3-12; 2 Tim 2:14—3:17; Tit 2:1-14; 3:4-11). Some see this as "stuffy" orthodoxy and a bourgeois ethic. Paul says very little, though, about specific false teachings; and even the call to godly living is quite general. Apparently the false teachers were ascetics (1 Tim 4:3) who proclaimed a form of overrealized eschatology (2 Tim 2:18). Apart from these two features it is difficult to discern what they were teaching. If Paul is interested in transmitting a systematic and codified theology, he does not succeed, for what he emphasizes is the gospel as the message of salvation and living in accord with it. Some may perceive this as a rigid orthodoxy that focuses on tradition and does not comport with the authentic Paul. But in the Pastorals detailed creedal statements are missing, which indicates that the traditional statements found here do not reflect the later history of the church, where doctrinal statements become more comprehensive.

Many scholars think that the emphasis on tradition demonstrates that the

Pastorals are not authentically Pauline. Yet Paul is not averse to tradition in his letters. He pronounces a curse on all those who proclaim a different gospel (Gal 1:8-9). Traditions regarding women's adornment (1 Cor 11:2-16), the Lord's Supper (1 Cor 11:17-34) and the gospel itself (1 Cor 15:1-11) were prized and transmitted by Paul. The Thessalonians are exhorted to stand true to the traditions (2 Thess 2:15) and to live in accordance with the tradition passed down to them (2 Thess 3:6). Many scholars believe that a number of creedal statements and hymns were handed down to Paul by Christians that preceded him (e.g., Rom 1:3-4; 3:25-26; 4:25; Phil 2:6-11; Col 1:15-20). Verifying this last claim is difficult, though it is probable that some creedal statements were received and transmitted by Paul. We cannot say that the interest in traditional teaching in the Pastorals shows that they are inauthentic. The increased emphasis on tradition may be traced to the situation addressed and to Paul's realization that his life on earth was drawing to a close.

In the Pastorals the overseer-elders are responsible to transmit the tradition faithfully. What is truly remarkable is how little Paul says about the responsibilities of these leaders. Paul focuses on the character needed to fill such offices (1 Tim 3:1-7; Tit 1:5-9). Some scholars complain that the requirements are mundane and even shockingly low. (One cannot be a drunkard!) Several things can be said in response. Both lists begin with the requirement to be "without reproach." Paul was concerned that leaders have a good reputation both in the church and the community. "Without reproach" functions as a generalization so that readers would recognize that no comprehensive list follows. The ethical requirements are not a comprehensive, computer-generated questionnaire designed to determine whether one is qualified for the job. One reason that the character qualities listed have occasionally been described as mundane or even inferior is because we judge them from our own cultural setting. The United States, for instance, with all its faults, has been significantly influenced by the gospel from its inception; and the moral norms of the gospel have been essentially the moral norms of Western European societies. But as the twenty-first century dawns, dramatic changes have occurred. The morality accepted by our ancestors is now the subject of fierce debate. And even where there is no debate, more and more people are now plunged into moral defeat and disaster. The leaders described in the Pastorals may have seemed mundane to cultures shaped by Christian values—even up to the latter part of the twentieth century. Finding such faithful leaders today is not such an easy task. Perhaps we are in a better position to see the distinctiveness of such people in the Greco-Roman world, for like Paul's readers, we live in a world of moral confusion. Leaders who live solid, faithful, though unspectacular lives may not have stood out forty years ago. Those who have experienced life in the church and have watched the moral collapse of Western society realize that faithful and godly leaders are at a premium. Luke Johnson rightly observes:

> Fidelity to one spouse, sobriety, and hospitality may seem trivial virtues to those who identify authentic faith with momentary conversion or a single spasm of heroism. But to those who have lived longer and recognize how the administration of a community can erode even the strongest of characters and the best of intentions, finding a leader who is truly a lover of peace and not a lover of money can be downright exciting.[12]

Supporting leaders. Apparently, Paul believed that at least some elders should be paid. The information we have is partial, but 1 Timothy 5:17-18 enjoins payment: "Those elders who rule well should be considered worthy of double honor, especially those who labor in the word and teaching. For the scripture says, 'You shall not muzzle the ox while it is threshing,' and 'The worker is worthy of his wages.' " Verse 18 confirms that "double honor" (1 Tim 5:17) refers to payment, for there Paul cites Deuteronomy 25:4 and a word from Jesus (cf. Lk 10:7) to support paying elders. The idea of paying those who teach is not native to the Pastorals. In Galatians 6:6 those who are taught "must share in all good things with the one who is teaching." This almost certainly means that some measure of material support should be provided. First Corinthians 9 contains the most developed defense of providing material support for those who proclaim the gospel, though the focus is on supporting Paul as an apostle. Paul provides a number of examples from everyday life to demonstrate that one who works is deserving of financial support (1 Cor 9:7). Paul also invokes the Mosaic law in support of such a conception, appealing again to Deuteronomy 25:4. Paul argues from the lesser to the greater here. If oxen are free to eat while they work, then those who are involved in the work of the gospel should be supplied with necessary provisions. Those who have sown in the spiritual realm should be provided for in the material realm (1 Cor 9:11). Just as those who work in the temple share in the material benefits of what is offered in the temple (1 Cor 9:13), so too those who proclaim the gospel should make a living from the gospel (1 Cor 9:14). In this latter text Paul appeals to the command of the

---

[12]Luke Timothy Johnson, *Letters to Paul's Delegates: 1 Timothy, 2 Timothy, Titus* (Valley Forge, Penn.: Trinity Press International, 1996), pp. 148-49.

Lord, and apparently the tradition found in Luke 10:7 (and par.) is in view.

Primacy of the gospel. Leaders in the churches exercised authority, but their authority is always subordinate to the gospel. Paul pronounces a curse on himself or anyone else who preaches a different gospel (Gal 1:8-9; cf. Gal 6:12-13). Any teachers who promulgate a different message are "false brothers" (Gal 2:4). The adversaries in 2 Corinthians 10—13 are not given the benefit of the doubt. Paul is convinced that they are false apostles and Satan's ministers (2 Cor 11:13-15). These so-called apostles contradict the heart of the gospel, which teaches that Christ "was crucified in weakness but he lives by the power of God" (2 Cor 13:4). Similarly, those who espouse circumcision are dismissed as "evil workers" and "enemies of the cross," and they are destined for destruction (Phil 3:2, 18-19). The "philosophy" advanced in Colossae is to be rejected because it is "not according to Christ" (Col 2:8). The Colossian errorists are propounding a teaching that denigrates Christ and advocates a means of fullness that diminishes what Christ has accomplished. Even Peter (and Barnabas!) are to be resisted and rebuked if they "do not live in accord with the truth of the gospel" (Gal 2:14). Authority ultimately resides in the gospel, not the ministers themselves.

We know that the Corinthians were entranced with Paul and Apollos. Paul reminds them that he and Apollos are merely servants—God is the one who provides the growth (1 Cor 3:5-9). What Paul says about himself in 1 Corinthians 4:1-5 applies to all those who have some kind of official ministry. Those who have positions of authority are "servants" (*hypēretas*, 1 Cor 4:1), not masters. They are "stewards" (*oikonomous*) of God's mysteries, responsible to the Lord for carrying out their tasks. Their call is to be "faithful" (*pistos*, 1 Cor 4:2) as stewards, subordinate to the will of the master. In 1 Corinthians 3:10-17 he reminds the Corinthians of the minister's responsibility. He describes himself as the builder who lays the foundation, but he does not ascribe preeminence to himself as the builder but to Jesus Christ as the foundation. The test of any ministry is whether it builds on the foundation of the gospel of Jesus Christ and him crucified (1 Cor 2:2).

Some ministers build with quality materials that will survive the winnowing fire of the day of the Lord; others use materials that will perish quickly on the day of assessment (1 Cor 3:12-13). Building with quality materials refers to teaching that is in accord with the gospel of Christ. Some ministers do quality work and will be rewarded; others build shoddily on the foundation, and their work will be destroyed (1 Cor 3:14-15). Those in the latter category will be saved, but their work of ministry will not be preserved. Another category of ministers exists—those who destroy God's temple (i.e., God's church; 1 Cor 3:17). Such ministers will be destroyed: they will not be saved but will face eternal destruction. Part of what Paul says here teases us with its difficulty. How do we distinguish between shoddy work on the foundation of the church and work that destroys the church? Those who destroy are themselves destroyed, while those who build poorly at least escape with their lives. Perhaps some teaching is defective but not ultimately destructive. Some teaching makes the building totter but does not cause it to crash. Other teaching veers off the foundation and wrecks the building. Any teaching that deviates from the foundation is dangerous, but Paul recognizes that some teaching is more destructive than others. In any case, the foundation—Jesus Christ—is the norm for all teaching, and he functions as judge over all teachers.

Discipline of leaders. Since Jesus Christ and the gospel are the highest norm, those in positions of leadership are subject to a greater responsibility. Hence Paul is constrained to rebuke Peter when he strays from the gospel (Gal 2:11-14). Hymenaeus and Alexander are evicted from the church and placed in Satan's realm because they have rejected the faith (1 Tim 1:19-20). The purpose of such discipline is remedial, for Paul hopes that these teachers will return to a life and teaching that is honoring to God. Elders must sustain healthy teaching and refute those who contradict it (Tit 1:9), for rebellious teachers threaten to plunge the community into confusion. Since the gospel is the highest norm, charges may be brought against elders in sin. Such charges, though, must be warranted (1 Tim 5:19). The community does not receive wild accusations, but only those that are substantiated with sufficient evidence to make the charge credible. If elders have not lived up to their calling, then they are to be reproved as sinners before the whole congregation (1 Tim 5:20). It is possible that Paul means that the elders are to be reproved before the other elders, but it is more likely that he intends for them to be rebuked before the whole congregation. Since elders must have a public reputation of probity (1 Tim 3:1-7), the failure to live up to such standards must be publicly exposed. Paul recognizes that favoritism may incline Timothy to be less rigorous with those toward whom he feels special affection (1 Tim 5:21), and thus he warns him to be impartial, to maintain the same standard for all. Since standards for such leaders are high, Paul cautions that Timothy must be cautious about placing one into leadership too soon (1 Tim 5:22). We recall here his words about not installing someone who is a new convert since such a person is apt to become proud (1 Tim 3:6). To sum up, Paul believes that leaders are crucial in the churches and that they do exercise authority, especially in their teaching. Such leadership, though, is always dependent on the gospel.

Discipline in the Congregation

Discipline does not apply exclusively to leaders but to anyone in the community who needs correction. The case of the man committing incest in 1 Corinthians 5 is instructive. Probably he was having sexual relations with his stepmother: Paul says "he has his father's wife" instead of saying "he has his mother" (1 Cor 5:1). Scholars have attempted to discern why the Corinthians were tolerating such behavior. Were they libertines, believing that ethics were unimportant? Is this another example of their overrealized eschatology? Whatever the reason, Paul is outraged at their pride, observing that even Gentiles find such behavior reprehensible. He mandates that this man be evicted from the church, and once he is severed from the church he enters Satan's sphere (1 Cor 5:3-5). The motive behind such discipline is love, so that the man's "spirit will be saved on the day of the Lord" (1 Cor 5:5). Such salvation will not occur without "the destruction of the flesh" (1 Cor 5:5). What incenses Paul about such laxity in the church is that "a little leaven leavens the whole lump" (1 Cor 5:6). In other words, tolerating such sin inevitably means that sin will spread further in the church. The purity of the church is at stake, for once a sin of such magnitude is tolerated, other sins will seep into and be accepted by the church.

Censorious judgment of others is itself censured by Paul (Rom 2:1), but it does not follow from this that all evaluation and judgment of others is banned. The judgment of unbelievers is to be left to God, for unbelievers are not part of the Christian community (1 Cor 5:12-13), but Paul specifically commands believers to judge one another in 1 Corinthians 5:12—"Should you not judge those inside the church?" The beauty of the church is preserved by mutual accountability and responsibility. Those who are tripped up by sin are to be restored by others in the community who are walking in the Spirit (Gal 6:1). Believers must use their discernment to detect those who have fallen astray into sin. Does such judgment fall under the strictures of Romans 2:1, where Paul condemns those who judge others? Not if it is exercised "in a spirit of gentleness, looking to yourself lest you also be tempted" (Gal 6:1). Judging that is supercilious, censorious and proud is castigated by Paul, yet there is a kind of evaluation of others that is gentle but firm, loving but strict, humble but severe. Hatred should never coexist with discipline. Associating with or even eating with a person under discipline is banned

(1 Cor 5:9, 11), for such fellowship would communicate that nothing serious has happened. Treating the person as usual would display one's lack of love, betraying one's apathy about the person's salvation.

Paul's advice in 2 Thessalonians matches the text in 1 Corinthians 5. Those who ignore the instructions in the letter are to be isolated so that they will be shamed into repentance: "But if anyone does not obey our instruction through this letter, take special notice not to associate with him, so that he will be ashamed" (2 Thess 3:14). Such an exhortation may seem horribly cruel to moderns, but shame here is the path to wholeness. Nor is any room allowed for personal vindictiveness. Refusing to fellowship with the recalcitrant must flow from love. So Paul immediately adds, "Do not consider him as an enemy but admonish him as a brother" (2 Thess 3:15). There is a kind of admonition that is brotherly and family-oriented, not rooted in enmity and hatred, and yet that still administers discipline.

Once we comprehend this paradigm Paul's instructions regarding those who have ceased to work is clear (2 Thess 3:6-13). In his first letter to the believers in Thessalonica, Paul told them to avoid laziness, especially since it is a poor recommendation of the Christian faith to unbelievers (1 Thess 4:11-12; 5:14). Paul's own labor to support himself financially (2 Thess 3:7-9) functions as an example of the kind of diligence the Lord requires, even though Paul himself, strictly speaking, deserves financial support. The Thessalonians should rouse the lazy by withholding food from them until they are willing to work (2 Thess 3:10). Those who are idle inevitably get into trouble, usually with their mouths (2 Thess 3:11; cf. 1 Tim 5:13). Such advice is fundamentally loving, even though judgment is involved, for it provokes the lazy person to become a productive citizen and, at the same time, it enhances the witness of the community. Those who refuse to help the idle, on the other hand, could fall into the error of thinking that everyone is lazy, that no one needs help. After inflicting some discipline we could think that discipline is what everyone needs, and we could become cold-hearted toward those truly in need. Paul closes his instructions, therefore, by reminding believers "not to lose heart in doing good" (2 Thess 3:13). Believers should be inclined to help others, with generous hearts and lives, while at the same time discerning what is best for each person.

Discipline is especially directed toward the recalcitrant who refuse to repent. Apparently this is the case with the man committing incest (1 Corinthians 5). The argumentative person who ferociously enters debates and is immune to correction falls into the same category (Tit 3:9-11). Even in this case a first and second warning are to be given, but if the stubborn ones continue to resist, then they are to be left to their own devices. Paul warns the Corinthians that he will be forced to exercise discipline if they do not respond suitably (2 Cor 12:19—13:3; cf. 1 Cor 4:18-21). He emphasizes, though, that using such disciplinary authority is deeply unpleasant (2 Cor 10:8; 13:10; cf. 2 Cor 2:1-4). Paul will discipline if he must, but he hopes and prays it is unnecessary. Judgment is only exercised after an opportunity for salvation is given. Anyone who enjoys wielding discipline, in other words, is not following the Pauline pattern! Disciplining another is grievous and painful, like the sorrow felt by the parent who, in love, needs to discipline a child.

An obstinate person must have been the object of discipline in 2 Corinthians 2:5-11. A few scholars believe that this is the same person who committed incest in 1 Corinthians 5:1-13. Most think that he is not the same person as the one who committed incest, but that this man was involved in some kind of rebellion against Paul himself. We must confess that our certainty is frustrated by the paucity of information. What we do know is that this man has been the object of the Corinthians' discipline. Apparently he has responded well, for now Paul is worried that the community will overreact and fail to shower love and forgiveness on him now that he has repented. Forgiveness, love and encouragement are to be bestowed on the repentant man lest he be overwhelmed with sorrow and lose heart. This account helps us to see that restoration is the ultimate aim of discipline in Paul. Love is the final goal, even in the case of discipline; but love is sometimes tough and even severe, like surgery that cuts out an invading cancer.

Does this mean that discipline should be applied every time a believer sins? The early Christian community was one in which encouragement and correction were part and parcel of church life. The church functioned like a family in which loving exhortation and correction were interwoven into its daily existence. Formal discipline, however, was not instigated casually or quickly. We have seen that discipline seems to be applied to severe cases in which there was no repentance. The man committing incest is disciplined because he is not willing to change his actions. Protracted warnings are given to the Corinthian adversaries (2 Cor 10—13) so that discipline can be averted. We saw in Titus (Tit 3:9-11) that warnings preceded any formal discipline. A chance to repent is granted to the lazy before any specific action is taken against them (2 Thess 3:6-15). Paul recounts some of the sins deserving of discipline, and they include sexual immorality, coveting, stealing, idolatry, slander and drunkenness (1 Cor 5:9-11). The list is representative instead of exhaustive. Paul is not advising expulsion of a person who gets drunk once or who slanders another person. In such cases, however, normal Christian correction would be part of community life. The community would not bypass such actions as insignificant, but a member who repented would be welcomed to stay in the church. Any sin that is committed and defended would become the object of discipline, since in such cases the health and purity of the church are at stake. When Paul mentions a sin like coveting, he presumably limits discipline to situations where coveting manifests itself. One hardly knows if another is coveting internally! Sufficient evidence must exist, of course, to warrant discipline (2 Cor 13:1). Church expulsion is limited to cases of unrepentant sinful behavior or to deviant teaching that transgresses the standard of the gospel. It is the gospel itself that is the norm for discipline, and those who are being transformed by the gospel long to love, encourage and strengthen others. Part of this strengthening occurs in mutual admonition and correction that occasionally even reaches the point of expelling an unrepentant member.

Women and Ministry

One of the most sensitive and controversial issues today relates to women in ministry. Since the most contested texts relating to this issue are in Paul, it is not surprising that his writings are in the forefront of the discussion.[13] If we ask the question, are women to be involved in ministry? Paul's answer is clearly yes. If we ask the question, are women invited to be in *every* ministry? the answer is more nuanced.

Women deacons. Romans 16 is a surprising source of information on the contribution of women in the ministry of the early church. We begin with Phoebe (Rom 16:1-2) who is designated as a "deacon *[diakonos]* of the church in Cenchrea." Possibly the word *diakonos* here simply refers to service of a general kind and should not be defined in terms of office. It seems more likely, though, that Phoebe actually served as a deacon since she is described as the deacon of a particular church—"of the church in Cenchrea." Some

---

[13]The literature on this issue is unending. See esp. Craig S. Keener, *Paul, Women and Wives: Marriage and Women's Ministry in the Letters of Paul* (Peabody, Mass.: Hendrickson, 1992); Stanley J. Grenz with Denise Muir Kjesbo, *Women in the Church: A Biblical Theology of Women in Ministry* (Downers Grove, Ill.: InterVarsity Press, 1995); John Piper and Wayne Grudem, eds., *Recovering Biblical Manhood and Womanhood: A Response to Evangelical Feminism* (Wheaton, Ill.: Crossway, 1991); Andreas J. Köstenberger, Thomas R. Schreiner and H. S. Baldwin, eds., *Women in the Church: A Fresh Analysis of 1 Timothy 2:9-15* (Grand Rapids, Mich.: Baker, 1995).

have suggested that Phoebe was a leader of the church since she is called *prostatis* in Romans 16:2. But given the patriarchal nature of the ancient world, we should beware of seeing the term as carrying the same status as was the case when describing male patrons *(prostatēs)*. Moreover, it is doubtful that Paul would describe Phoebe as his "leader" or "president," especially since he is reluctant to grant that kind of authority even to the "pillar" apostles (Gal 2:1-10). It is likely that Phoebe is commended here as a "patron"; that is, she rendered significant financial assistance to the church in Cenchrea. Paul calls on the Roman churches to render assistance *(parastēte)* to Phoebe since she herself has been the helper *(prostatis)* of many, including Paul.

What is striking about the case of Phoebe is that she served in the office of deacon. It is likely that Paul refers to women deacons in 1 Timothy 3:11 as well, though the word *gynaikas* is ambiguous and could possibly refer to the "wives" of deacons. Several lines of argument suggest that women deacons are in view in 1 Timothy 3:11. First, the word *likewise* introduces the discussion on women, and this is the same linking word that introduces men who serve as deacons in 1 Timothy 3:8. No indication of a change of subject is given, and thus we should presume women deacons are intended. Second, if Paul intended wives of deacons, he could have made this clear by adding the words *of deacons* or the pronoun *their (autōn)* to say they were "their wives." Using the word *women* alone suggests that he discusses the qualifications a woman must possess to serve in a deaconal role. Third, the qualifications required for women in 1 Timothy 3:11 are quite similar to those required for men who serve as deacons (1 Tim 3:8-10, 12-13), indicating most probably that qualifications for an office are in view. Fourth, if wives of deacons are intended, why does Paul say something about the wives of deacons but not the wives of overseer-elders? The wives of the latter would seem to be equally, or even more, important. It is more convincing, therefore, to see women deacons in view instead of wives of deacons.

Women laborers and coworkers. The ministry of women is also described in the verb *labor (kopiaō)*. Four women are designated as "laborers": Mary (Rom 16:6) and Tryphaena, Tryphosa and Persis (Rom 16:12). We know nothing about these women apart from these all-too-brief descriptions. The word *kopiaō* designates both Paul's ministry (1 Cor 15:10; Gal 4:11; Phil 2:16; Col 1:29; 1 Tim 4:10) and the ministry of others (1 Cor 16:16; 1 Thess 5:12; 1 Tim 5:17). Many scholars maintain that the term denotes missionary service, and this is as good a guess as any, though certainty eludes us. The term itself does not mean that one served as a leader. Better evidence must be adduced to establish that thesis. What is clear, however, is that women served in significant ministries and labored with intensity.

Paul also calls three women "coworkers" *(synergoi):* Prisca (Rom 16:3) and Euodia and Syntyche (Phil 4:3). One of the most striking texts is Philippians 4:2-3, where Euodia and Syntyche are exhorted to harmony in the Lord. Paul says that they "labored together with him in the gospel" and goes on to call them "coworkers" *(synergoi).* Probably they labored with Paul in spreading the gospel, functioning as missionaries by proclaiming the word. Urbanus (Rom 16:9), Timothy (Rom 16:21; 1 Thess 3:2), Titus (2 Cor 8:23), Epaphroditus (Phil 2:25), Philemon (Philem 1) and various others (Col 4:11; Philem 24; cf. the verbal form in 1 Cor 16:16; cf. also 1 Cor 3:9; 2 Cor 1:24) are also called coworkers. Prisca and Aquila, according to Acts 18:2, were expelled from Rome circa A.D. 50-51 by Claudius's decree. They met Paul in Corinth and ministered with him there. They instructed Apollos more accurately about the gospel (Acts 18:26), and according to 2 Timothy 4:19 they resided in Ephesus near the end of Paul's life. It may be significant that Prisca is typically named first. Certainly she was vitally involved in the Christian movement. Paul clearly believed women played a crucial role in the ministry of the church. They functioned as both laborers and coworkers, fulfilling significant roles in the early Christian movement. Once again, however, we cannot establish that women functioned as overseer-elders from the term *coworker* alone. The term broadly designates ministry in general, but it cannot be used to determine whether women filled every ministry position.

Women apostles? A text that continues to be debated is Romans 16:7, where Andronicus and Junia (or Junias) are saluted as distinguished in the eyes of the apostles. The debate centers on whether the person Paul compliments along with Andronicus is male (Junias) or female (Junia).[14] If the person in question is male, then the name is contracted from Junianus. Most scholars, however, now agree that the person in question was female. The contracted form of this name appears nowhere in Greek literature, so it is difficult to believe that in Romans we have the only example of such a contraction. Moreover, the name Junia for a woman was quite common. Finally, until the thirteenth century virtually all writers understood this person to be a woman. The evidence for the person in question being a woman is, therefore, rather impressive. Many scholars also believe that Andronicus and Junia were hus-

---

[14]For a more detailed survey of scholarship, see Thomas R. Schreiner, *Romans,* BECNT (Grand Rapids, Mich.: Baker, 1998), pp. 795-97.

band and wife, and this is indeed probable.

What is striking here is that Paul says Andronicus and Junia are "distinguished among the apostles." The Greek phrase could also be translated "outstanding in the eyes of the apostles," but most agree that this is an unlikely way of rendering the phrase. Michael Burer and Daniel Wallace, however, have recently conducted an intensive search and analysis of the phrase, compiling significant evidence to support the idea that "noteworthy in the eyes of the apostles" is the best translation.[15] If the research of Burer and Wallace stands the test, then Andronicus and Junia are not identified as apostles at all, removing any idea in this verse that women served as apostles. Even if Andronicus and Junia are identified as apostles, we should not conclude that they were apostles in the same sense as were Paul, the Twelve, Barnabas and James, the brother of Jesus. The term *apostle (apostolos)* is not always a technical term (2 Cor 8:23; Phil 2:25), and Andronicus and Junia were likely itinerant missionaries if they are called apostles here. The word *apostolos* is used of such traveling missionaries in the Apostolic Fathers (*Did.* 11.3-6; Herm. *Vis.* 13.1; Herm. *Sim.* 92.4; 93.5; 102.2). Such apostles did not have the same kind of authority as did Paul, the Twelve, Barnabas or James, the brother of the Lord. Given the patriarchal nature and the practical necessities of life in the ancient world and given our interpretation of 1 Timothy 2:11-14, Junia probably exercised her ministry particularly toward other women.

Galatians 3:28. One of the most stunning statements in the Pauline corpus is Galatians 3:28—"There is neither Jew nor Greek; there is neither slave nor free; there is neither male nor female. For you are all one in Christ Jesus." Many scholars insist that this declaration must be paradigmatic in assessing Paul's statements on women in ministry. Any word that appears to limit women is transcended by this ringing declaration of equality. Using Galatians 3:28 as Paul's manifesto on women's rights is appealing to moderns but it is not authentic *Pauline* theology. We must beware of reading Paul as if he were a modern-day feminist. What Paul says here is stunning enough. He relativizes one's ethnic background, social status and gender. The decisive reality for Paul is whether one belongs to Christ Jesus. Union with Christ is the means by which one becomes part of Abraham's family. No one qualifies as Abraham's child simply because he is Jewish, free or male. One's social status

---

[15]Michael H. Burer and Daniel B. Wallace, "Was Junia Really an Apostle? A Re-examination of Romans 16:7," *NTS* 47 (2001): 76-91.

is irrelevant to Paul (1 Cor 7:17-24), for matters like marriage (1 Cor 7:29-31) are part of this temporary age, which will soon be over. Galatians 3:28 is a soteriological statement, heralding equal access to salvation through Christ Jesus. It does not follow from this that there are no social consequences from the declaration.[16] The union of Jew and Gentile in Christ influences dramatically table fellowship (Rom 14:1-15:13; 1 Cor 8:1—11:1; Gal 2:11-14). One cannot place soteriology and social relations in hermetically sealed compartments so that the one never touches on the other. Yes, there are social consequences to the Pauline declaration, but the decisive point is this: How does Paul himself articulate the social consequences? Moderns can use this statement in a variety of ways—as a trumpet call to raise feminist consciousness and even in defense of the legitimacy of homosexuality. Paul himself never understood Galatians 3:28 to cancel out all distinctions. He continued to believe that there were differences between Jews and Greeks; otherwise the whole argument in Romans 9—11 is superfluous. He continued to believe that there were differences between slaves and masters; otherwise, his advice to both is contradictory (Eph 6:5-9; Col 3:22—4:1). He continued to believe there were differences between males and females. Otherwise, his indictment of homosexuality is inconsistent (Rom 1:26-27), his commands to husbands and wives incomprehensible (Eph 5:22-33; Col 3:18-19) and his restrictions on women a relapse from his better days (1 Cor 11:2-16; 14:33b-36; 1 Tim 2:9-15). The value and worth of all human beings is proclaimed by Paul, but this verse must not be served up so that it fits with modern ideologies. We must hear Paul's own word—be it ever so foreign to us.

1 Corinthians 11:2-16. One of the more difficult texts regarding men and women is 1 Corinthians 11:2-16. Scholars debate virtually every aspect of the text.[17] Apparently Paul enforces a cultural practice on the women in the community so that they are distinguished from the men. Scholarship has not clearly resolved what the custom is: Paul may be requiring women to wear a veil or a shawl, or perhaps he requires women to wear their hair tightly bound on their head instead of letting it fall loosely over their shoulders. Even though we cannot identify precisely the cultural practice, it is clear that

---

[16]This is rightly emphasized by Klyne Snodgrass, "Galatians 3:28: Conundrum or Solution?" in *Women, Authority and the Bible*, ed. A. Mickelsen (Downers Grove, Ill.: InterVarsity Press, 1986), pp. 161-81. But Snodgrass, unfortunately, draws social consequences outside Pauline parameters.

[17]See Thomas R. Schreiner, "Head Coverings, Prophecies and the Trinity: 1 Corinthians 11:2-16," in *Recovering Biblical Manhood and Womanhood: A Response to Evangelical Feminism*, ed. John Piper and Wayne Grudem (Wheaton, Ill.: Crossway, 1991), pp. 124-39, 485-87.

Paul maintains cultural distinctions between men and women. The differences between the sexes must not be erased but preserved. When Paul appeals to "nature" *(physis)* to support different hair lengths between men and women, he reflects on the creation order that reflects God's will that men and women be distinct (1 Cor 11:14-15).

Even though we cannot locate the custom enforced with certainty, we are able to learn much about Paul's understanding of the relations between men and women from this text. It is already evident that distinctions between men and women are preserved. Thus, no one can legitimately appeal to Galatians 3:28 to support homosexuality. On the other hand, Paul encourages and permits a woman to pray or prophesy if her head is properly adorned (or her hair is displayed appropriately, 1 Cor 11:5). We see from this that Paul does not limit the prophetic gift to men, nor does he suggest that women can only prophesy when men are absent. Women exercise the prophetic gift when both men and women are gathered together (cf. Acts 2:17-18; 21:9). Some, finding this incredible, want to limit this to informal meetings—such as those taking place in homes. But this is an anachronism. Many early churches met only in homes, and there is no evidence that some meetings in the early church were considered to be "unofficial." Paul believed that God had gifted women to prophesy authoritatively in the assembly.

That women could prophesy is not the whole story, for Paul devotes considerable attention to adornment or hairstyle because he is concerned about *the manner in which they prophesy.* The language of "shame" dominates this text, indicating that if women did not present themselves suitably, they would be dishonored. Paul also desires the women to conform since the practice enjoined is in accord with the traditions transmitted in other churches (1 Cor 11:2, 16). What is at stake here? We have already suggested part of what concerns Paul. Distinctions between men and women must be preserved. Paul will have nothing to do with an overrealized eschatology that misinterprets declarations like Galatians 3:28 so that men and women become indistinguishable from one another. Paul is even more specific about what concerns him. Women must prophesy in a suitable manner so that the headship and priority of men is preserved. He begins the text with the assertion that Christ is the head of man, man the head of woman, and God the head of Christ (1 Cor 11:3).

Does Paul mean by "head" *(kephalē)* that man is the "source of" or the "authority over" women? The matter is keenly debated, but the latter meaning is more common in Paul. Indeed, 1 Corinthians 15:28 strikingly supports this notion, for Paul argues that Christ will be subject to the Father when the end arrives. The authority of God over Christ is not defended with an argument but is assumed by Paul. Similarly, women are under the authority of men. In other words, Paul wants women to prophesy with a head covering or a proper hairstyle because such adornment communicates that women are submissive to male headship. Even if the word *kephalē* should be defined as "source," the thrust of Paul's argument does not change dramatically. For if the term means "source," women must still wear their hair a certain way or have a head covering because their origin lies in Adam. The woman must show that she is "the glory of the man" (1 Cor 11:7). Indeed, Paul unambiguously uses the "source" argument later in the text. Women should adorn themselves rightly because they come ultimately from Adam (1 Cor 11:8; Gen 2:22-23). Women, after all, were created to help men and not vice versa (1 Cor 11:9; Gen 2:18). Paul encourages women to prophesy, but they must do so in a way that preserves the difference between the genders and the priority of men.

What Paul says in the previous verses strikes many of us today as a violation of justice and equality, but we must also see that 1 Corinthians 11:11-12 add a crucial dimension to Paul's argument. The different functions between men and women could be overplayed. Paul does not believe women are inferior—women are equal in worth, essence and dignity with men, just as Christ is equal in worth, essence and dignity with the Father. Men and women share their life in the Lord. All men since Adam come into the world through women, yet the differences between men and women can be pressed too far, and men have too often in history used texts like this to mistreat women.

Some scholars take a different tack on this passage, arguing that proper adornment on women actually gives them authority over men. First Corinthians 11:10 says that "a woman ought to have authority upon her head because of the angels." No one really knows what the reference to angels means (the best guess is that angels are superintending the order and worship of the church), but it has often been argued recently that *authority (exousia)* is an active, not a passive, term. Paul does not refer to the sign of authority, then, but to authority itself. Women properly adorned, on this scenario, have as much authority as men. I have argued in some detail against this view elsewhere.[18] The most fundamental objection to this reading is contextual. The words *for this reason (dia touto)* in 1 Corinthians 11:10 link the

---

[18]See ibid.

argument back to 1 Corinthians 11:8-9, where the priority of the man is emphasized. Verse 11 begins with the word *nevertheless (plēn)*, suggesting a *qualification* from what has just been said. Paul proceeds (in 1 Cor 11:11-12) to qualify what he said about the priority of man in the previous verses. Such a qualification only works if 1 Corinthians 11:10 emphasizes the authority of men while permitting women to prophesy and pray if they adapt to such leadership. Words take their meaning in context, and in this verse Paul recommends the proper attire for women as a symbol of male authority.

1 Corinthians 14:33-36. Another very difficult text is 1 Corinthians 14:33-36. A few scholars suggest that the verses are a later interpolation, but the evidence for such a view is really not strong.[19] A few manuscripts in the Western tradition place these verses subsequent to 1 Corinthians 14:40. The shift makes sense since the rearrangement completes the discussion on prophecy and tongues before addressing the question of women at worship. What is decisive is that *all manuscripts* have these verses, and the weight of the manuscript tradition supports the idea that they belong where they are now placed in our English Bibles. The burden of proof in situations like these lies heavily on those advocating inauthenticity. It is evident that women were disrupting worship in some way, but it is much more difficult to discern what was happening. Some, noting that the problem was native to Corinth, question the wider relevance of the verses. But Paul begins by appealing to the rule that was practiced *in all the churches* (1 Cor 14:33). He concludes by rebuking the Corinthians for thinking that they possess the authoritative word on such matters, when instead they should submit to the authoritative word that transcends their local community (1 Cor 14:36). In 1 Corinthians 14:34 the women are enjoined to submit in accord with the law. The law is almost certainly the Mosaic law, and Paul probably has Genesis 2 in mind as part of the Mosaic law, as he did in 1 Corinthians 11:8-9 and 1 Timothy 2:13-14. The appeal to the law and the practice of all the churches suggests that what follows is a word that applies to all cultural situations.

---

[19]Supporting an interpolation is Gordon D. Fee, *The First Epistle to the Corinthians*, NICNT (Grand Rapids, Mich.: Eerdmans, 1987), pp. 699-708. For a convincing rebuttal of Fee, see D. A. Carson, " 'Silent in the Churches': On the Role of Women in 1 Corinthians 14:33b-36," in *Recovering Biblical Manhood and Womanhood: A Response to Evangelical Feminism*, ed. John Piper and Wayne Grudem (Wheaton, Ill.: Crossway, 1991), pp. 140-53, 487-90. The evidence adduced by Philip B. Payne ("Fuldensis, Sigla for Variants in Vaticanus, and 1 Cor. 14.34-5," *NTS* 41 [1995]: 240-62) for an interpolation is not persuasive. See Curt Niccum, "The Voice of the Manuscripts on the Silence of Women: The External Evidence for 1 Cor 14.34-35," *NTS* 43 (1997): 242-55.

Some have argued that Paul requires women to be absolutely silent in the community, revealing a restriction not apparent in 1 Corinthians 11:2-16. In other words, Paul does not permit women to pray or prophesy after all! It is hard to believe anyone has seriously advocated this view, for why would Paul bother to spend fifteen verses in 1 Corinthians 11 specifying the adornment of women when they prophesy if he does not believe they should do it at all? Others have suggested that women were disrupting worship by asking questions during the meetings and that Paul commands them to ask questions of their husbands at home instead of introducing chaos into worship. Others have said that Paul forbids women to speak in tongues. Still others think women are forbidden to pass judgment on the prophecies uttered (cf. 1 Cor 14:29). Such passing of judgment assumes a kind of authority that Paul thinks is inappropriate for women to have. Certainty eludes us, though on balance it seems most likely that women were disrupting worship by interrupting meetings with questions.

1 Timothy 2:11-15. The text that has drawn the most attention is probably 1 Timothy 2:11-15. Many scholars, of course, omit this text since they believe it was not written by Paul. Some attempt to play off the liberated Paul against the restrictive post-Pauline disciple. The paradigm is historically suspect, for it reads Paul through feminist glasses. Nor is the evidence compelling for a "liberated" Paul in the authentic letters. We have seen that restrictive statements on women exist in 1 Corinthians 11:2-16 and 1 Corinthians 14:33b-36. In my view, the Pastorals are authentically Pauline, and what Paul says here coheres with his instructions in 1 Corinthians. A number of scholars maintain that the restriction in 1 Timothy 2:12 ("I do not permit a woman to teach or exercise authority over a man, but to be silent") is culturally limited.

Before we explore that point we should say something about the meaning of the word *authentein* (exercise authority) in 1 Timothy 12:12. The verb only occurs here in the New Testament and never in the LXX, and thus it has been the subject of considerable controversy. Alternate suggestions range from the bizarre (a reference to sexual fertility practices!) to the possible (the word has the negative connotation "domineer" instead of the positive notion of "exercise authority").[20] The translation "domineer" is unlikely since it has been established that the verb *authentein* typically has the positive meaning "exer-

---

[20]For a summary of the history of research, see H. Scott Baldwin, "A Difficult Word: *authentein* in 1 Timothy 2:12," in *Women in the Church: A Fresh Analysis of 1 Timothy 2:9-15*, ed. Andreas J. Köstenberger, Thomas R. Schreiner and H. S. Baldwin (Grand Rapids, Mich.: Baker, 1995), pp. 65-80, 269-305.

cise authority."[21] It is possible, of course, that in the existing context "exercise authority" has a negative nuance. But when we explore the context it is clear that "exercise authority" fits well. The matching infinitive *teach (didaskein)* does not have a negative meaning here.[22] There is nothing intrinsically negative about teaching. In the same way, exercising authority has no inherent problem. Women are not banned from teaching men or from exercising authority over them as if either of these activities are themselves blameworthy; they are prohibited from these functions because women should not exercise such functions over men. This brings us afresh to the question, why does Paul prohibit women from such actions?

A dizzying array of alternatives are proposed to explain the Pauline prohibition, though today many say that women are forbidden from teaching or exercising authority over men because women were uneducated or because they were promulgating heresy. The lineaments of the heresy differ according to the reconstruction posited by the scholar. Some detect a Gnostic heresy, others the invasion of first-century feminism through the influence of Artemis worship, others a combination of Jewish-Gnostic influence and so on.[23] One can hardly doubt that false teaching at least partially provoked the writing of 1 Timothy (1 Tim 1:3-11; 4:1-5; 6:3-10, 20-21). And it is not crucial for our purposes to discuss the precise features of the heresy. What counts for this interpretation is that women are banned from teaching in the public assembly because they were disseminating the heresy. Women who are properly instructed and teaching the truth, according to this view, are free to teach in the assembly like any man.

This explanation of the text is enormously attractive—especially since it comports with modern notions of equality—but it is doubtful. The most obvious problem with the proposed solutions is that they leap over the actual wording of the text. Paul says nothing about women being uneducated or

---

[21]See ibid.

[22]See the definitive study of Andreas Köstenberger, "A Complex Sentence Structure in 1 Timothy 2:12," in *Women in the Church: A Fresh Analysis of 1 Timothy 2:9-15*, ed. Andreas J. Köstenberger, Thomas R. Schreiner and H. S. Baldwin (Grand Rapids, Mich.: Baker, 1995), pp. 81-103.

[23]For Gnosticism see Bruce Barron, "Putting Women in Their Place: 1 Timothy 2 and Evangelical Views of Women in Church Leadership," *JETS* 33 (1990): 451-59. For the influence of the Artemis cult, see Sharon Hodgin Gritz, *Paul, Women Teachers and the Mother Goddess at Ephesus: A Study of 1 Timothy 2:9-15 in Light of the Religious and Cultural Milieu of the First Century* (Lanham, Md.: University Press of America, 1991). For a general Jewish-gnostic influence, see Werner G. Kümmel, *Introduction to the New Testament*, rev. ed. (Nashville: Abingdon, 1975), pp. 378-79.

untrained. It is not hard to imagine Paul writing, "I do not permit a woman to teach or exercise authority over a man . . . because women are uneducated." Nor would it be difficult for Paul to say that women cannot teach "because they are spreading false teaching." Nothing close to either of these two points is communicated. Catherine Clark Kroeger and Richard Clark Kroeger have devoted an entire book to the situation that provoked the writing of these verses, contending that Ephesus was a feminist enclave and that Paul is responding to such feminism.[24] The notion that Ephesus was any more feminist than other cities in the Greco-Roman world has been decisively refuted by Steven Baugh.[25] As we would expect, careful research reveals that men exercised most of the power in ancient Ephesus. The patriarchal character of society was not seriously challenged in any of the cities in which Paul ministered. The admonition in 1 Timothy 2:11 is probably a response to an overrealized eschatology in which women were insisting that they were free to teach and exercise authority over men. But there is no evidence that Ephesus itself was a feminist stronghold. It is not credible to suppose that women were actually teaching that they were superior to men, nor can it be established that Ephesian women were influenced by Artemis worship.

Paul himself gives two reasons to support his ban on women teaching and exercising authority over men: the priority of Adam in creation (1 Tim 2:13) and the fact that Eve was deceived and Adam was not (1 Tim 2:14). The appeal to creation in 1 Timothy 2:13 indicates that Paul located his prohibition in a transcendent norm. We have seen earlier that his fundamental criticism of homosexuality was that it violated the created order (Rom 1:26-27), and Jesus himself criticized divorce as a transgression of God's created intention (Mt 19:3-12 and par.). The prohibition is not grounded in the curse or the Fall, but in God's creation *before the Fall.* Paul apparently believes (cf. 1 Cor 11:8-9) that the order in the creation narrative (Gen 2:18-25) instructs us on the relationship between men's and women's roles. Some respond by saying that Paul's reasoning is faulty. After all, animals were created before humans! Such a view at least has the virtue of *understanding what Paul says,* even though Paul's own worldview is rejected. In response, we should note that

---

[24]Catherine Clark Kroeger and Richard Clark Kroeger, *I Suffer Not a Woman: Rethinking 1 Timothy 2:11-15 in Light of Recent Evidence* (Grand Rapids, Mich.: Baker, 1992).

[25]See Steven M. Baugh, "A Foreign World: Ephesus in the First Century," in *Women in the Church: A Fresh Analysis of 1 Timothy 2:9-15,* ed. Andreas J. Köstenberger, Thomas R. Schreiner and H. S. Baldwin (Grand Rapids, Mich.: Baker, 1995), pp. 13-52. See also Baugh's review of the Kroegers' book (which is referred to in n. 24), "The Apostle Paul Among the Amazons," *WTJ* 56 (1994): 153-71.

Paul was an intelligent man. He knew animals were created first, but he also believed that the account of the creation of Adam's being created before Eve was a narrative signal as to how the story should be interpreted. That animals were different from human beings was apparent to any Jewish reader, and hence their creation before human beings is irrelevant.

Paul also argues that it was not Adam but Eve who was deceived (1 Tim 2:14). The argument here is much tougher to assess. Many who see false teaching or lack of education as the real reason behind the prohibition in 1 Timothy 2:12 appeal to this verse. The argument is not convincing. Paul says Eve was *deceived*, not uneducated. How was she deceived? Did Adam wrongly communicate what God said about not eating from the tree of the knowledge of good and evil? Then the fault lies with Adam, and Paul would hardly use this as an example of why women should not teach! Was Eve unable to understand Adam when he told her what God said about not eating from the same tree? If so, Eve is close to being a dunce since the instruction was rather simple: "Don't eat from that tree!" Genesis is rather clear (Gen 3:1-6) that the serpent deceived Eve into thinking that she could become like God by eating what was forbidden. So what is Paul's argument here? He may be saying that Eve is forbidden from teaching because she was deceived first. Or perhaps the emphasis is on how Satan tempted Eve and inverted the created order in bypassing Adam. Many in church history have believed Paul suggests that women are inherently gullible and more apt to be deceived than men. Nevertheless, Paul is not saying women are intellectually inferior, for if he believed that were the case, he would not counsel Titus to have women teach other women (Tit 2:4). The most likely view is that Paul is criticizing the inversion of the created order—that Satan took the initiative with Eve rather than Adam.

It is interesting to observe that the two activities forbidden to women (teaching and exercising authority) are the two distinctive roles of the overseer-elders (1 Tim 3:2, 4-5; 5:17; Tit 1:9). I conclude from this that women are prohibited from the office of overseer-elders. Women can serve as deacons because that office focuses mainly on serving and assisting in the practical affairs of the congregation. Women are permitted to prophesy because such a gift is passive in nature and does not constitute a settled and permanent authority. The long-term and sustained leadership of the congregation comes through the teaching office. This role is limited to the men.

Conclusion

In this chapter we have seen that conversion was inevitably accompanied by baptism, which was the boundary marker representing new life in Christ. Those baptized celebrated the Lord's Supper together in remembrance of Christ's death on their behalf, and Paul reminds them that their participation in the supper is a symbol of the unity of the church. Baptism and the Lord's Supper both point believers to the saving work of Christ and to the salvation he accomplished for his people. They herald the joy of salvation and look forward to the day of resurrection.

We then investigated the issue of ministry in Paul, noting that a charismatic and structured ministry belong together in the Pauline letters. The Spirit works in a diversity of ways, and order and spontaneity coexist together in the church. Ministry is the responsibility of all believers, for the new life in Christ manifests itself in the joy of giving. The equality of all believers in Christ and in ministry, however, does not exclude some kind of hierarchy as well. Some members of the church have a special responsibility to lead, and the office of overseer-elder was apparently not open to women, though they did serve as deacons and in many other ministries.

15

THE SOCIAL WORLD OF THE NEW COMMUNITY

Living as Christians in the Culture

In previous chapters we have explored various dimensions of the church in Pauline writings. In this chapter we examine the social world in Paul's writings. That is, what does Paul say about marriage, singleness, divorce, parents and children, masters and slaves, helping the poor, and government?[1] Many other topics could be explored, but we are restricting our study to issues addressed in *Paul's writings*, not to concerns that may be ours in the twenty-first century.

Introduction

It must be emphasized at the outset that Paul does not abandon his eschatology in addressing the issues noted above. In fact, his eschatology is determi-

---

[1]On Paul's social world, see Bruce Malina, *The New Testament World: Insights from Cultural Anthropology*, rev. ed. (Louisville, Ky.: Westminster John Knox, 1993); Jerome Neyrey, *Paul in Other Worlds: A Cultural Reading of His Letters* (Louisville, Ky.: Westminster John Knox, 1990); Bruce Malina and Jerome Neyrey, *Portraits of Paul: An Archaeology of Ancient Personality* (Louisville, Ky.: Westminster John Knox, 1996); Ben Witherington III, *The Paul Quest: The Renewed Search for the Jew of Tarsus* (Downers Grove, Ill.: InterVarsity Press, 1998), esp. pp. 18-51.

native for his approach to all these issues. First Corinthians 7:29-31 is fundamental for understanding Paul's social worldview:

> Now this I say, brothers, the time has been shortened. From now on, those who have wives should live as those not having them. And those who weep should live as those who do not, and those who rejoice should live as those who do not, and those who buy should live as those who do not possess, and those who use the world should not make full use of it. For the form of this world is passing away.

Naturally this text, taken out of context, could be severely misunderstood. Paul does not disavow specific responsibilities of husbands to wives (cf. 1 Cor 7:8-16; Eph 5:25-33; Col 3:19). Neither is he suggesting that husbands should behave as if they were unmarried. Nor is he dismissing weeping and rejoicing, so that believers who are grieved or happy are simply told, "Get over it!" Paul himself counseled, "Rejoice with those who rejoice; weep with those who weep" (Rom 12:15), and he viewed the sparing of Epaphroditus's life as a great mercy that spared him from "grief upon grief" (Phil 2:27).

Paul takes seriously the joys and sorrows of life, but he emphasizes that all experiences in this world are temporary. The present evil age does not go on forever. Those who are married must remind themselves that marriage is transitory. The existing social order is ephemeral, and thus husbands and wives should not devote themselves to their marriages and children as if they will last forever; instead they must prepare themselves for the world to come. Similarly, experiences of joy and sorrow, as significant as they are, are not indelible. No earthly grief or earthly joy is permanent. In the same way, possessions are fleeting—lasting, at best, only as long as one lives. Paul's advice is not to forsake this present world or to flee from it. He expects believers to be commendable citizens, good husbands and wives, loving parents and obedient children, just masters and devoted slaves. Those who understand that the present evil age is fleeting, however, will have a new perspective on all events. They will avoid trying to make earth into heaven. They will not fall prey to overrealized eschatology but will set their hopes on the future, on the consummation of all things, on the day when moral perfection will be theirs. They will not become consumed with roles and stations in this world, even though they will seek to do as much good in this world as possible. The present world order will never be perfectly cleansed of evil, and thus any utopian schemes will be jettisoned.

How does Paul's social worldview work out in practice? First Corinthians 7:17-24 is helpful, though often it receives very little attention in Pauline theologies. From the chapter as a whole we can glean that the Corinthians were wondering whether they could be more useful to God if they abandoned their current social roles.[2] Some husbands and wives, therefore, desired to abstain from sexual intercourse while married (1 Cor 7:1-5). Perhaps others insisted that believers should be single (1 Cor 7:8-9, 25-38), while still others may have even wondered if it is advisable to disband current marriages (1 Cor 7:10-11). Those married to unbelievers were tempted to abandon such "defiled" unions and be devoted wholly to the Lord (1 Cor 7:12-16). Those engaged to be married wondered whether God preferred that they live as singles (1 Cor 7:25-40).

We shall return to Paul's specific advice on these questions shortly, but his fundamental answer appears in 1 Corinthians 7:17-24. He reiterates three times in these verses that each person should remain in the calling in which he was called (1 Cor 7:17, 20, 24). The structure of the paragraph is significant, for the admonition to remain in one's calling commences the paragraph, concludes the paragraph and is at the center of the paragraph. Not only so, but 1 Corinthians 7:17-24 appears in the middle of chapter 7 as a whole, signifying that this section is the central theme of the entire chapter. Paul teaches that marital status, position in society and external circumstances are insignificant. Human beings tend to believe, especially in modern societies, that changing and improving their social station is important, but Paul disagrees. Our social status is unimportant before God. The fundamental principle is this: our social status is irrelevant to God, and hence we should not seek to change our status in order to become more pleasing to God.

It follows, then, that whether one is circumcised or uncircumcised is unimportant (1 Cor 7:18-19). No one should bother to go to the trouble of removing the marks of circumcision. Such a painful operation was sometimes endured by those who wanted to hide their ethnicity from their contemporaries, especially if they competed athletically, for athletic contests were performed in the nude. Nor should anyone be concerned about his uncircumcision and undergo the operation of circumcision. Human beings may think that circumcision is necessary to be in a right relation to God (Gal 2:3-5; 5:2-6), but what is vital in his sight is not circumcision but keeping his commands (1 Cor 7:19). Even more surprisingly Paul discounts the significance of slavery (1 Cor 7:21-23). He urges slaves not to worry about their status as

---

[2]See esp. the exegesis of Gordon D. Fee, *The First Epistle to the Corinthians*, NICNT (Grand Rapids, Mich.: Eerdmans, 1987), pp. 267-70.

slaves. What really matters is that slaves are free in Christ—and conversely free people are slaves of Christ! The slavery that damages is slavery to sin, a total enmeshment in the fashions and worldview of the present order. The difference between Paul's worldview and the modern worldview is striking. Many would tend to think that Paul's advice here fosters oppression and leads to disconnection from life in the here and now. We must remember that Paul is not addressing masters. Such a text is dislodged from its context if it is employed to support the status quo by those who are in positions of leadership. But the difference between Paul's worldview and ours still comes to center stage. One's station in life is inconsequential in God's eyes. No believer should worry about a change in status, for God has called believers to the particular circumstances of their lives. Those who worry about social status reveal that they are banking on the present world for happiness, but Paul summons them to remember that the world we live in is temporary.

Paul does not apply the principle articulated in 1 Corinthians 7:17-24 rigidly. The last part of verse 21 is debated: does Paul counsel slaves who are able to gain their freedom to avail themselves of freedom or to remain as slaves? Some opt for the latter, thinking that only this course fits with the context as a whole. I am convinced by those who think that Paul advises slaves to gain their freedom if they can.[3] Such advice does not contradict the overall principle of these verses. Believers should not worry about their social status, but they are not prohibited from moving in a new direction if circumstances permit. Such new possibilities are also from God. Paul recognizes that some people will change from being single to being married or from being married to being single. Similarly, slaves should avail themselves of freedom if the opportunity to do so presents itself. Even in this case, however, the change in circumstances should not be overestimated. Freedom for slaves is not to be despised, and yet they only have a few years to enjoy such freedom before they, like the rest of us, will die. No one should think that new opportunities in this world are of great consequence. Faithfulness in one's present calling is what God demands.

Singleness and Marriage

One of the most surprising elements of Paul's theology is his view of being

---

[3] S. Scott Bartchy (*Mallon Chrēsai: First-Century Slavery and the Interpretation of 1 Corinthians 7:21*, SBLDS 11 [Missoula, Mont.: Society of Biblical Literature, 1973], pp. 155-59) thinks the verse means that slaves who are manumitted should live as free men and women in accord with God's calling. I think Fee (*First Epistle to the Corinthians*, pp. 315-18) is correct in saying that slaves are advised to choose freedom.

single. The typical Jewish view, informed by Genesis 2:18-25, was that being alone was not good and that living as a single person was to be avoided. This conviction is attested in Sirach:

> He who acquires a wife gets his best possession,
> a helper fit for him and a pillar of support.
> Where there is no fence, the property will be plundered;
> and where there is no wife, a man will become a fugitive and a wanderer.
> For who will trust a nimble robber
> that skips from city to city?
> So who will trust a man that has no nest,
> but lodges wherever night overtakes him?" (Sir 36:29-31 NRSV)

The same sentiment is reflected in the *Genesis Rabbah* on Genesis 2:18, "It has been taught on Tannaite authority; whoever has no wife lives without good, without help, without joy, without blessing, without atonement" (*Gen. Rab.* 17:2). What is remarkable and undeniable in Paul's theology, given his Jewish background, is that he thinks singleness is "better" than marriage (1 Cor 7:7-8, 26, 28, 32-35, 37-38, 40). Paul's verdict seems strange even to many today, and to his Jewish contemporaries it must have been shocking as well. This is not to say that asceticism did not exist in the ancient world. In fact, in 1 Corinthians 7 Paul responds to Corinthians inclined toward asceticism, and we must take this into account in assessing Paul's own view of singleness. To classify Paul as an ascetic is misleading. He believes that some are gifted by God to live as singles and some to live as married (1 Cor 7:7). Those who are gifted by God to marry should do so. In fact, even though singleness is "better" and a greater blessing (*makariōtera*, 1 Cor 7:40), it is "better" for those with strong sexual desires to get married (1 Cor 7:9, 36). Apparently believers can discern in part whether or not they are called to singleness by evaluating how strong their sexual desires are. Paul also labors to say that those who do marry have not sinned (1 Cor 7:28, 36, 38-39). Marriage is one of the good gifts God gives to human beings. Absolute asceticism—a fundamental denial of marriage—is rejected by Paul as demonic and as a rejection of the goodness of the created order (1 Tim 4:1-4). He celebrates the beauty of marriage in Ephesians 5:22-33, seeing it as an analogy of Christ's relationship to the church. And in 1 Timothy 5:14 he advises young widows to marry since they still have powerful sexual desires and are becoming ensnared by idleness, spending their time gossiping (1 Tim 5:11-13). Apparently by "young" widows he means women of childbearing age because the advice to marry is immediately followed by the advice to bear children (1 Tim 5:14; cf. 1 Tim

2:15). Despite the emphasis in 1 Corinthians 7, Paul likely viewed marriage and children as the calling for the majority of believers. Those who marry should celebrate marriage as their distinctive calling.

Despite the high regard for marriage, however, Paul prizes the single state as the better one and as a calling that should not be denigrated or forsaken lightly. God has gifted many for singleness as well (1 Cor 7:7). Those who have a firm grip on their own will and are able to resist the power of sexual desires should stay single (1 Cor 7:37), for to abstain from sexual relations is a good thing (1 Cor 7:1). This is contrary to some moderns who believe that persons can only be complete if they have sexual relations and who sometimes suggest that people who refrain from sexual intercourse are abnormal! Paul does not impose his own distinctive calling on others (1 Cor 7:25), though he insists his words are inspired by the Spirit of God (1 Cor 7:40). He is not suggesting in 1 Corinthians 7:12 and 1 Corinthians 7:25 that the Corinthians can ignore his advice, for his words are prophetic and accurate (1 Cor 7:40). He merely distinguishes his words from those of the historical Jesus (1 Cor 7:10), not wanting to suggest that all should live a single life as he does. Still, singleness is to be preferred for a number of reasons. First, Paul advises singleness because of "the present distress" (1 Cor 7:26). It is doubtful that a specific problem in Corinth is intended. Likely Paul refers to the distress of living in the present evil age, when the time has been shortened and the end of the age has arrived (1 Cor 7:29; 10:11). Second, those who marry will have trouble (1 Cor 7:28, 32-35). Those who are married must be concerned about the specific needs of their spouses, and this detracts from their focus on the things of the Lord. Paul does not think that being concerned about how to please one's husband or wife is evil, but those who are single have fewer distractions and a freedom to fulfill the Lord's will. Paul is scarcely suggesting that single people are free from all concerns or difficulties. Those who are single must live in the present evil age as well; no paradise on earth is envisioned for those who are single. The single state is recommended because those who are unmarried are more available for ministry and they can be more devoted to the things of the Lord.

When we consider Paul's estimation of the single state, it is clear that he does not view social relations according to the standards of the existing society. Singleness is prized because the single person can live exclusively for the Lord. The single state is not imposed on anyone, but the Jewish expectation of marriage for all is radically relativized. Marriage is a gift of God, intended for many, probably most. But many are also called to singleness, for the things of the Lord are the most important; and relationships, like marriage, though not denigrated, are subordinate to the glory of God, the centrality of Christ and the spread of the gospel.

Marriage

We have already seen that marriage is a gift of God (1 Cor 7:7), which is not to be despised. Paul firmly resists any asceticism that would rule out marriage (1 Tim 4:1-4), for sexual relations and marriage are part of the good order of creation (Gen 2:18-25). Paul's hard-headed practicality relative to marriage emerges in 1 Corinthians 7. One way to discern whether marriage is one's gift is by judging the strength of one's sexual desires. Those who burn with sexual desires should marry if the opportunity avails itself (1 Cor 7:9, 36). They should not think that repressing such strong desires for one's whole life is necessarily God's will for them. Paul does not espouse a false spirituality that attempts to overcome one's inherent sexual desires and inclinations. He thinks singleness is preferable, but he recognizes that human beings must live according to the specific gift granted them by God. Those who are given a gift for marriage are not to deny God's work in them and try to be what they were never intended to be. We must be careful, on the other hand, not to exaggerate the recommendation of marriage for those with strong sexual desires, because Paul realizes that one may go without sexual intercourse for long stretches of time, perhaps years, even though one has powerful sexual urges. Nor is he advocating that one should marry the first person available to satisfy one's desires! He writes to a specific situation in which some of the Corinthians were inclined to pursue the single life. Some of the Corinthians wanted to abstain from sexual relations to show their devotion to the Lord. Paul commends such an aspiration, but he warns that it may violate what God intends and that one should not try to transcend nature.

1 Timothy 5 and 1 Corinthians 7. Paul's advice to the younger widows suggests that marriage is God's will for the majority (1 Tim 5:11-15). These words are addressed to widows who likely made a vow to stay single after the death of their husbands. Paul is distressed because powerful sexual desires led some of these widows to violate their vows and because some of the widows were meddling in the affairs of others and engaging in gossip. Paul exhorts such widows to marry, raise children and superintend their households. In this way their sexual desires will be satisfied, and they will employ their skills usefully instead of frittering away their time.

Some might think that Paul's advice to widows in 1 Timothy 5 contradicts the call to singleness in 1 Corinthians 7. In actuality, when we take into account the situations addressed, the counsel is remarkably consistent. The single state is to be preferred, for one can devote oneself in a more undistracted way to the Lord. Nevertheless, each person must assess his or her gift. In both 1 Corinthians 7 and 1 Timothy 5 the strength of sexual desires function as one indication of whether one is called to be single. If 1 Corinthians 7:32-35 informs us that the extra time afforded to an unmarried person provides opportunities to be more devoted to the Lord, 1 Timothy 5:11-15 reminds us that some people use such "extra time" in less-than-helpful ways. In the latter instance, marriage will provide a disciplined pathway to prevent the widows from getting involved in evil activities. Some may believe that Paul's view of marriage is rather pessimistic or even crude since he counsels marriage for those who have strong sexual desires and for those who are wasting their time. We must beware of thinking that such practical advice is *all* that Paul has to say on the subject of marriage, for he addresses specific circumstances in his churches. On the other hand, we must acknowledge that Paul is a realist. He does not view marriage as some romantic fairy tale far removed from the vicissitudes of everyday life. Paul knows that sexual desires are powerful and that they are helpfully channeled in marriage. He is aware that people with leisure time are liable to waste it, engaging in activities that are not profitable. He summons people to live responsibly before God in practical and concrete ways.

Since we have been focusing on 1 Corinthians 7, we will explore further what that chapter says about marriage. We have already seen that one must not automatically pursue marriage. All should consider whether they are called to be single. The unmarried *(agamois)* and widows *(chōrais)* are addressed in 1 Corinthians 7:8. Perhaps the "unmarried" here are actually widowers, since the term *unmarried* is parallel to *widows.* Or perhaps general advice is delivered to the unmarried and widows here. In any case, the goodness of the single state is celebrated. People are not to think that marriage or remarriage should be pursued as quickly as possible. Similar advice is given to those who are virgins and those who are unmarried in 1 Corinthians 7:25-38. Those who are bound to a wife through an engagement (1 Cor 7:27) should not feel compelled to break off the engagement. Marriage is a good gift to be celebrated. However, those who are not engaged should not actively seek marriage (1 Cor 7:27). If marriage occurs in the sovereignty of God, then it should be celebrated (1 Cor 7:28), but seeking it actively is discouraged. Believers are free to marry whomever they wish (1 Cor 7:39). The dignity of the person choosing a spouse is preserved, for he or she determines the Lord's will. The only limitation Paul lays on them is that they should marry "in the Lord" (1 Cor 7:39). This means that believers should only marry other believers, for it is inconceivable to join together with those who do not live to glorify God.

We can also glean from 1 Corinthians 7 some of Paul's positive advice regarding marriage. His commentary on why the single state is preferable reveals something of his view of marriage (1 Cor 7:32-34). Husbands and wives are both mentioned, showing something of the mutuality that characterizes the Pauline view of marriage. Both husbands and wives are to be concerned with *(merimnaō)* pleasing their spouses. The aim in marriage is not to advance one's happiness but to promote the well-being and spiritual maturity of the spouse. Marriage exists to glorify God by pleasing and serving one's spouse, so that spouses become more and more like Christ.

The first six verses of 1 Corinthians 7 are also a window into the Pauline view of marriage. The quote "it is good for a man not to touch a woman" (1 Cor 7:1) is probably a citation from the Corinthians' letter to Paul, meaning that it is good for a man not to have sexual relations with a woman. Apparently some of the Corinthians, even though they were married, believed that sexual abstinence in marriage was preferable. Perhaps they believed that such abstinence signaled greater devotion to God. If Paul were fundamentally ascetic, he would agree with such a stance. The subsequent verses reveal that Paul emphatically rejects the idea that married couples should abstain from sexual intercourse. He says in 1 Corinthians 7:2 that each one should "have" *(echetō)* a husband or wife because of "immoralities" *(porneias)*. Many in the past interpreted this verse to say that men and women *should get married* because of immoralities. But the word "have" *(echetō)* probably does not refer here to obtaining a spouse but to *sexual intercourse*. For instance, in 1 Corinthians 5:1 the man committing incest is said "to have" *(echein)* his father's wife. The word *have* refers here to sexual relations with his stepmother. Similarly, in 1 Corinthians 7:2 Paul advises that sexual intercourse between spouses is needed to prevent sexual immorality. Perhaps some were even visiting prostitutes (1 Cor 6:12-20) because sexual relations were denied in marriage.[4] What Paul says in 1 Corinthians 7:2 is not a full-fledged view of sexual relations; Paul does not think such relations are only necessary to curb sexual sin. But Paul is also realistic, knowing how powerful sexual desires

---

[4]Compare Brian S. Rosner, *Paul, Scripture and Ethics: A Study of 1 Corinthians 5—7* (Grand Rapids, Mich.: Baker, 1994), pp. 127-28.

are. He counsels regular sexual intercourse in marriage because such will limit temptation (1 Cor 7:5).

The mutuality of Paul's advice is also striking here. Both wives and husbands have a debt to pay to the other (1 Cor 7:3). The debt Paul has in mind is a sexual debt. Their bodies are no longer their own, and thus no spouse can say to other, "God has told me that we should abstain from sexual intercourse from now on!" More specifically, both husbands and wives no longer have authority (exousiazō) over their own bodies. The wife has authority over the husband's body and vice versa. We again see a fundamental feature of Paul's view of marriage: Once a couple is married, each spouse is obliged to live for the good of the other. Their own authority and will is no longer determinative. A couple may abstain from sexual relations by mutual consent and for the purpose of prayer, but only for a short time (1 Cor 7:5). Long periods of abstention will foster immorality and should be rejected. When Paul writes in 1 Corinthians 7:6 that what he has said is a concession and not a command (1 Cor 7:6), he is not speaking of the *permission to have sexual relations, nor is he thinking of the permission to marry.* Unfortunately, Augustine interpreted this verse in such a way and hence believed that sexual intercourse was inherently sinful. But the concession, as a closer examination of the context reveals, is the permission *to abstain from sexual relations for a limited time of prayer.* In other words, Paul does not demand that married people refrain from sexual intercourse for the sake of prayer. If couples mutually agree to do so, then Paul grants his permission. Nevertheless, Paul does not see any inherent virtue in times of abstinence.

Ephesians 5:22-33. The most sustained and perhaps controversial discussion on marriage is found in Ephesians 5:22-33. The mutuality of marriage was emphasized in 1 Corinthians 7, but now we see that wives should submit to husbands and husbands should love their wives. The responsibility of wives to submit is repeated in Colossians 3:18. A similar exhortation surfaces in 1 Peter 3:1-6, and thus there is every reason to think that these exhortations were a typical part of the early church. Most scholars now agree that this subject (including the instructions given to parents and children as well as to masters and slaves) stems from the household-management instruction deriving from Aristotle, though the material is shaped and transformed by the gospel.[5]

---

[5]See David L. Balch, *Let Wives Be Submissive: The Domestic Code in 1 Peter,* SBLMS 26 (Chico, Calif.: Scholars Press, 1980). See also Andrew T. Lincoln, "The Household Code and Wisdom Mode of Colossians," *JSNT* 74 (1999): 93-112. Lincoln has a lucid survey of previous proposals on pp. 93-102.

Many today wonder whether the gospel had enough influence in Paul's instructions, for he says husbands have authority over wives. We must notice, first of all, the kind of authority that husbands possess. In Paul's mind such authority is worked out in terms of responsibility instead of privilege. Paul dismantles any notion that husbands can boss their wives around to satisfy their own selfish pleasures. The authority husbands have is a servant-model of authority, similar to Christ's self-giving for the church (Eph 5:25-29). This is not to deny the authority delegated to the husband; for he is to be like Christ, who, though he lived as a servant, was always the authority in the apostolic circle. Christ's self-giving on the cross, however, is the paradigm for husbands; their love for their wives is to have the same quality of self-giving and sacrifice as Christ's love for the church (Eph 5:25). The love of Christ, of course, is distinctive. Husbands cannot sanctify and cleanse their wives; Christ did this for both husbands and wives at the cross (Eph 5:26). Husbands cannot ensure that wives will be holy and without blemish on the day of judgment (Eph 5:27). Christ secures such holiness and blamelessness for both husbands and wives. Still, what Paul says here relates to husbands. The love husbands have for their wives is a love that longs for and promotes their sanctification, holiness and perseverance. This is not just any kind of love—it is a Christian love that makes a husband long for his wife's happiness and holiness in God.

The controversy over who has authority is misunderstood if husbands arrogate their authority in such a way that wives are treated as slaves. Nor does Paul think it is honoring to wives if husbands erase their wives' dignity, scorn their intellect and ignore their wishes. Love prizes the good of another, and godly love for a wife is tender, caring and strong. If Christian husbands had lived out the Pauline ethic throughout history, women would not be as liable to view Paul's words with suspicion. Husbands, unfortunately, bear a significant part of the blame for the attack on Paul's authority, for they have too often used his words as a pretext for selfishness instead of as a platform for love.

The mystery of Christ's relationship with the church casts light on love in marriage. Believers in Christ become members of his body (Eph 5:30), joined with Christ Jesus by virtue of faith in him. Similarly, husbands and wives are united as one by marriage. The most important verse on marriage in the Scriptures, Genesis 2:24, is cited here by Paul: "For this reason a man shall leave his father and mother and cleave to his wife, and the two shall become one flesh" (Eph 5:31; cf. Mt 19:5 and par.). Marriage consists of leaving one's family, cleaving to one's wife and becoming one flesh with her. Every element is important. In marriage a new family is formed, and thus both husband and wife leave the old family unit behind to constitute a new one. Marriage is a covenant in which the husband and wife cleave to one another. And in marriage the husband and wife become one flesh in sexual union. The one-flesh character of marriage becomes a reality at sexual union, but it transcends sexual union. A deep and ineffable unity is established between husbands and wives when they leave, cleave and become one flesh. Just as believers are united with Christ and become part of his body, so husband and wife are now united in marriage. Because of this unity between husbands and wives, husbands should love their wives as they love their own bodies, for since they are one, the husband who loves his wife loves himself (Eph 5:28). Husbands are to nourish and cherish their wives as Christ does the church (Eph 5:29).

Paul's words are not abstract. Any husband knows that if he has not treated his wife well, then both he and his wife are miserable. Paul calls on husbands to live with the kind of self-giving love characteristic of Christ and to care tenderly for and cherish their wives. The same responsibility to love is sounded in Colossians 3:19, where Paul adds that husbands should "not become embittered against" their wives. Bitterness contradicts love, for it thinks selfishly and exclusively of one's own interests and hurts. The bitter husband forgets that he and his wife are now united. Paul sees a husband as the authority over his wife, but there is no room in his theology for selfishness, privilege, abuse or mistreatment. Husbands are to treat their wives as Christ did the church—with a self-giving love that is beyond any husband's grasp but should never be beyond his reach.

Many scholars think that Paul was particularly radical in his call for mutual submission between husbands and wives. The household code in Ephesians 5:22—6:9 is introduced with the words "submitting to one another in the fear of Christ" (Eph 5:21). Some conclude from this that both husbands and wives are to submit to one another. This particular reading of the text is doubtful. The command "to be filled with the Spirit" in Ephesians 5:18 is followed by five participles: speaking, singing, making melody, giving thanks and submitting (Eph 5:19-21). These participles are probably instrumental, conveying how one is to be filled with the Spirit. The call to submit to one another is directed to the community as a whole. Believers are not to insist on their own way. This includes, of course, men who may have to submit to women in the church. One of the watchwords of the Christian community in its everyday existence is restraining desires for the sake of others.

It is doubtful, though, that mutual submission can be read into the exhortations to husbands and wives. Nowhere in Paul, or the rest of the New Testament, are husbands ever asked to submit to their wives. The exhortations are consistent: men are to love and care for their wives, and wives are to submit to their husbands (Eph 5:22-33; Col 3:18-19; Tit 2:5; 1 Pet 3:1-7). Another problem with reading Ephesians 5:21 as the introduction to the section surfaces when we apply it to parents and children. It is doubtful that Paul would think that parents should submit to children. He summons children to obey their parents, but never the converse (Eph 6:1-3; Col 3:20). Some people today believe that mutual submission between parents and children is commendable, but it is quite unlikely that such an idea ever entered the mind of the apostle Paul. We must beware against reading our own cultural values into the biblical text. Any reference to mutual submission is also questionable given the analogy constructed in Ephesians 5:22-33. Paul maintains that the marriage relationship between husbands and wives is patterned after Christ's relationship to the church. Wives submit to husbands just as the church submits to Christ (Eph 5:22-24). Paul is hardly suggesting that Christ and the church should mutually submit to one another!

We must be exceedingly careful in describing Paul's thought here. We saw above that 1 Corinthians 7:3-4 teaches mutuality in the marriage relationship, and certainly this includes the idea of yielding to the wishes of one's spouse and living to please one's spouse. Some husbands conceive of their relationship with their wives in militaristic terms, with the husband serving as the general. They wrongly eliminate the genuine mutuality that should permeate the marriage relationship. At the same time, it seems that Paul carves out distinct roles for husbands and wives. Such distinctions are increasingly foreign to our culture, but it is precisely here that an imposition of modern categories and notions must be avoided. Paul does summon wives to submit (*hypotassō*) to their husbands. This certainly does not mean that husbands should try to make their wives submit. The directive is to wives, summoning them to submit voluntarily and graciously.

The close connection between submit (*hypotassō*) and obey (*hypakouō*) is evident in 1 Peter 3:5-6. Peter speaks of the holy women of old who "submitted" and then compares them to Sarah ("as Sarah obeyed"). The semantic overlap between *submit* and *obey* is undeniable. Even the most cursory investigation of the term *hypotassō* in Paul indicates that the notion of obedience is present in the term:

■ submission to God's law (Rom 8:7)

- submission to God's righteousness (Rom 10:3)
- submission to the government (Rom 13:1, 5; Tit 3:1)
- submission to leaders (1 Cor 16:16)
- submission of spiritual powers to Christ (Eph 1:22)
- subjection of all things to Christ (1 Cor 15:27; Phil 3:21)

Nor should we read into the concept of submission the lessening of a person's dignity. Christ submits to the Father at the end of history (1 Cor 15:28), and yet he continues to be worshiped and adored as Lord forever. The submission of wives signifies not the inferiority of wives but the different roles between husbands and wives.

Ephesians 5:24 says that wives are to submit "in everything," and yet Paul is not writing an exhaustive code here. Certainly he would make an exception if a husband commanded a wife to sin. We can imagine how horrified Paul would be if a husband asked a wife to murder or commit adultery. Paul emphasizes that wives submit to husbands "as to the Lord" (Eph 5:22). Submission to the husband is grounded in and flows out of the wife's relationship to Christ; it does not come about because the husband is intrinsically superior. Any rigid notion of a chain of command that suggests that women relate to the Lord only through their husbands should be dismissed.

It is occasionally suggested that submission for wives is only enjoined because of the culture of the day. Paul says such submission is "fitting in the Lord" (Col 3:18), and he commands it so that "the word of God is not reviled" (Tit 2:5). Paul, it is claimed, suggests submission for wives (and slaves) because equality would be rejected and misunderstood in his culture. Living out full-fledged equality in Paul's day would impede the progress of the gospel. In our culture, on the other hand, following the Pauline restrictions hampers the spread of the gospel. This line of thinking is more attractive than persuasive. Paul did believe in a fundamental equality between men and women, as our study of Galatians 3:28 in the previous chapter revealed. Such equality, however, did not cancel out the distinctions in men's and women's roles.

Nor is any convincing evidence set forth that Paul counseled submission to fit in with the culture. Saying that submission is "fitting" (Col 3:18) cannot resolve the issue one way or the other. Nothing in Colossians suggests that it is fitting for temporary cultural reasons. Neither does the context from Titus imply that the admonition was given for cultural reasons. At first blush this argument appears strong because Paul enjoins women to be workers at home (Tit 2:5). And yet carving out what is culturally limited in this text is by no means easy, for wives are also commanded to love their husbands and children and to be sensible and pure (Tit 2:4-5). Presumably no one would say that these injunctions have been culturally transcended. No clear contextual evidence warrants the limitation of the call of wives to be submissive to the first century. In Ephesians the responsibility of the wife to submit to the husband is analogous to the church's call to submit to Christ. Indeed, Paul argues that marriage is a mystery that represents Christ's relation with the church (Eph 5:32). Paul labels marriage a mystery after citing Genesis 2:24 in Ephesians 5:31. What he means by "mystery" is that human marriage represents a truth that was not immediately evident when instituted. With the arrival of Jesus Christ and the new covenant, the mystery is now revealed. Human marriage points to something more fundamental than the relationship between man and wife. Christ's relationship with the church is not patterned after human marriage. Rather, the relationship between husband and wife mirrors Christ's relation with the church. Christ's relationship with the church is the primary and fundamental reality. When God instituted marriage, he did so precisely because it would picture Christ's relation with the church. If marriage mirrors Christ's relationship with the church, the call on the wife to submit like the church and the summons for the husband to love like Christ are not temporary injunctions. Paul grounds his admonitions in a reality that transcends culture, for the relationship between husband and wife reflects the deeper truth of Christ's relationship to the church.

Scholars also debate what Paul means when he calls the husband the "head" *(kephalē)* of the wife (Eph 5:23). Typically scholars have defined this to mean that the husband is "the authority over" the wife, though some have recently suggested the idea of "source." In our previous discussion of this term it was noted that the bulk of the evidence, as Wayne Grudem and Joseph Fitzmyer have demonstrated, favors the definition "authority over."[6] Context is determinative in defining words, and we can confidently say that the term means "authority over" in Ephesians 5:23. Wives are called on to "submit" to husbands "as to the Lord" (Eph 5:22); and just as the church is subject to Christ, in the same way wives are to submit to husbands in all things (Eph

---

[6]On *kephalē*, see esp. Wayne Grudem, "Does *Kephalē* ('Head') Mean 'Source' or 'Authority Over' in Greek Literature? A Survey of 2,336 Examples," *TJ* 6 (1985): 38-59, and "The Meaning of *Kephalē* ('Head'): A Response to Recent Studies," in *Recovering Biblical Manhood and Womanhood: A Response to Evangelical Feminism,* ed. John Piper and Wayne Grudem (Wheaton, Ill.: Crossway, 1991), pp. 425-68, 534-41; Wayne Grudem, "The Meaning of *Kephalē* ('Head'): An Evaluation of New Evidence, Real and Alleged," *JETS* 44 (2001): 25-65; Joseph A. Fitzmyer, "*Kephalē* in I Corinthians 11:3," *Int* 47 (1993): 52-59.

5:24). The reason for the command in Ephesians 5:22 is introduced by the word *because (hoti)* in Ephesians 5:23. The logic of the verse is as follows: wives are to submit because husbands are the head. It makes much more sense to say that wives are to submit because husbands are the authority over wives, than to say wives are to submit because husbands are the source of their wives. We should not fail to note, however, that even if *kephalē* were defined as "source," wives are still to *submit* because husbands are the source. Defining the word as source hardly removes the scandal of the text. Clinton Arnold defends the idea that authority and source are both communicated in the word *kephalē*. The notion of source does seem to be primary in some texts (Eph 4:15; Col 2:19). If we were to adopt both meanings in Ephesians 5, Christ is both the authority over the church and the source of its life and purity. Similarly, husbands would bear the responsibility for leadership and provision in the family.[7] Nevertheless, the context in Ephesians 5 (i.e., the use of the word *submit* with *head*) suggests that authority rather than source is intended here.

Divorce

We intentionally discuss Paul's view of divorce after addressing his view of marriage, for the former is best understood in the light of the latter. The sacrificial and servant character of marriage demonstrates that marriage is not primarily for one's own fulfillment. Covenantal love—the kind of love and obedience that exists between Christ and the church—is to mark a marriage. Since Paul wrote to specific situations, we lack a full-fledged treatment on the topic of divorce. We can probably say that in most instances Paul believed that divorce and remarriage constituted adultery. Both men and women are bound *(deō)* to the marriage contract while the spouse lives (Rom 7:2; 1 Cor 7:39). The illustration, actually, is limited to women, but Paul certainly would have applied the same principle to husbands (1 Cor 7:10-11). If a husband or wife remarries while the former spouse is still alive, he or she commits adultery (Rom 7:3). Only if the spouse dies is one free to marry again (Rom 7:3; 1 Cor 7:39). Why is remarriage adultery? Because the first marriage is intact until one of the partners dies. Those who are already married cannot and must not marry another partner.

The most extensive discussion on the subject appears in 1 Corinthians 7:10-16. Two different situations are addressed. First, should Christians

---

[7]Clinton E. Arnold, "Jesus Christ: 'Head' of the Church (Colossians and Ephesians)," in *Jesus of Nazareth: Lord and Christ: Essays on the Historical Jesus and New Testament Christology,* ed. Joel B. Green and M. Turner (Grand Rapids, Mich.: Eerdmans, 1994), pp. 346-66.

divorce their spouses (1 Cor 7:10-11)? And second, should Christians married to nonbelievers divorce their unbelieving spouses (1 Cor 7:12-16)? We must recall the circumstances that provoked these issues in Corinth. Some of the Corinthians were convinced that their lives would be more pleasing to God if they abstained from sexual relations (1 Cor 7:1), even in marriage (1 Cor 7:2-5). It is not surprising that some may have concluded that divorcing one's partner would be pleasing to God. In this way they could devote themselves exclusively to the Lord (1 Cor 7:32-35). Even though Paul prizes the single life, he emphatically rejects the idea that believers should get divorced.

We begin with his advice to those who are married to fellow believers (1 Cor 7:10-11). Paul indicates that his instruction on this topic does not come from himself, but from the Lord Jesus. In other words, Paul cites the words of Jesus himself on the subject of divorce—words that come from the Jesus tradition (cf. Mt 5:31-32; 19:1-12; Mk 10:2-12; Lk 16:18). Explicit citations from the Jesus tradition are quite rare in Paul, and thus the appeal to it here is significant. Paul summarizes the tradition, presumably because the Corinthians (cf. 1 Cor 11:23-26; 15:1-5) were already familiar with the tradition via oral instruction. A preliminary statement should be made about the words for divorce used here. Occasionally scholars have attempted to distinguish between *separate* (*chōrizō*, 1 Cor 7:10-11, 15; cf. Mt 19:6; Mk 10:9) and *leave* (*aphiēmi*, 1 Cor 7:11-13). The alternation between the two terms reveals, however, that they are basically synonymous. Nor was there any period of formal separation in Paul's day as we have in Western societies. Indeed, divorces regularly occurred without any paperwork at all. Spouses would simply leave their partners. Paul's words to Christian married couples derive from Jesus' teaching in the Gospels. Wives and husbands are both addressed, and they are enjoined not to leave, not to divorce their spouses. Jesus taught that remarriage after divorce is adultery (Mt 5:31-32; 19:1-12; Mk 10:2-12; Lk 16:18), and Paul agrees.

In addressing the wife Paul adds a comment, "But if she separates, she must remain unmarried or be reconciled to her husband" (1 Cor 7:11). Paul addresses a situation where a wife violates Jesus' command and divorces her husband. When a wife (or husband) transgresses Jesus' command, she must either remain single or reconcile to her husband. If this interpretation is correct, we have no discussion by Paul of the exception clause contained in the Matthean tradition (Mt 5:32; 19:9), though my reading assumes that remarriage would be permissible in the case of a spouse's sexual immorality (*porneia*). Some scholars read this verse in a very different manner, arguing that the woman leaves her husband here because *he has committed sexual sin*. In other words, the woman leaves in accordance with the exception clause in Matthew. According to this interpretation, Paul compresses the Jesus tradition, noting that the woman legitimately leaves her husband since he has been unfaithful. According to this view, we have an early interpretation of the exception clause in Matthew from the apostle Paul. Husbands or wives who divorce their spouses under the auspices of the exception clause cannot marry someone else. Divorce is permissible in the case of sexual infidelity, but remarriage in any circumstance (while the husband lives) constitutes adultery.

It is more likely that Paul does not address the Matthean exception clause in 1 Corinthians 7:10-11. Spouses who *unjustifiably* opt out of the marriage are denied the possibility of remarriage. In other words, Paul does not address in these verses spouses who divorce for valid reasons. He speaks to those who wish to leave their spouses, even though there are no legitimate grounds to do so. In such instances the one who initiates the divorce has only two options: reconciliation to one's spouse or remaining single.

Paul also addresses believers married to unbelievers (1 Cor 7:12-16). The key to understanding the background of the text is probably the word *sanctified (hēgiastai)* in 1 Corinthians 7:14—"For the unbelieving husband is sanctified by the wife, and the unbelieving wife is sanctified by the husband." Some of the Corinthians, desiring to be pure and to follow the Lord ardently, probably concluded that sexual intercourse with unbelievers was defiling. We can easily understand that believers might think sexual intercourse with unbelievers would always be wrong. We can imagine them saying, "How can someone who has the Holy Spirit have sexual intercourse with those who are God's enemies? One who has sexual relations with unbelievers is polluted and tainted by joining together with those who hate God." Perhaps they even appealed to Ezra's practice where those involved in marriages to non-Israelite wives had to send their foreign wives away (Ezra 9:1—10:44; cf. Neh 13:23-29). On this matter, Paul has no specific word from the Jesus tradition (1 Cor 7:12), and thus he relays his own advice on the whole question. Paul does not view his own advice to be inferior to the words of the historical Jesus. He merely indicates that no word of the historical Jesus exists on the matter of whether to divorce unbelievers. As an authoritative apostle (1 Cor 7:40), Paul believes his words are accurate and from the Holy Spirit.

Paul's response to the problem of staying married to unbelievers is illuminating. Typically Jews believed that the unclean contaminated what was clean. So if that which was clean came into contact with something unclean, the clean item became unclean. If this were applied to marriage between believers and unbelievers, the believers would be defiled by the unbelievers. Paul argues to the contrary, maintaining that the clean believer sanctifies (*hēgiastai*) or cleanses the partner who is unclean (1 Cor 7:14). The newness of Paul's gospel and his rejection of Old Testament injunctions regarding cleanness are quite evident here. As a Pharisee, Paul would have repudiated the view he recommends here, but the old cleanness rules no longer apply. Indeed, the clean exerts power over the unclean, as in the life of Jesus himself (cf. Mk 1:40-45). Ezra's injunction to put away pagan wives does not apply in the same way to the new covenant people of God, presumably because the era in which the Jews were God's people is over and that which distinguished the Jews from the Gentiles is passé. Ezra was trying to maintain a nation that was separate from the Gentiles and trying to preserve a distinct culture. In Paul's mind the call to purity and cleanness is fulfilled in living a godly life while living in the present evil age (2 Cor 6:14—7:1). Paul probably addresses a situation in which one spouse became a believer after the marriage was consummated. He would probably say that the lesson from Ezra is that believers should not marry unbelievers (1 Cor 7:39). But once the marriage has been consummated (here the difference from Ezra emerges), believers should not worry about being unclean because of sexual intercourse with unbelieving spouses. Instead the unbeliever becomes sanctified via marriage to a believing spouse. The practical outcome is that believers should not initiate divorce with unbelieving spouses (1 Cor 7:12-13). If unbelievers are willing to remain in the marriage, believers should work at maintaining the marriage.

What if unbelievers desire to leave and break off the marriage (1 Cor 7:15)? In such circumstances believers should not try to coerce unbelievers to remain in the marriage. When Paul says that believers "are not enslaved" (*ou dedoulōtai*) in such circumstances, he means that they are not required to devote all their efforts to preserving their marriage. They could be robbed of peace and instead be filled with anxiety and despair over losing their spouse. They might think they have failed God when the marriage falls apart. Paul assures them that this is not the case. Believers should not initiate divorce, but if the unbelievers insist on ending the marriage, then believers should not be dismayed.

Scholars have often discussed whether the closing statement in 1 Corinthians 7:16 is optimistic or pessimistic: "For how do you know, O wife, if you will save your husband? Or how do you know, O husband, if you will save your wife?" Many scholars think it is optimistic, given the context as a whole, for the major theme is the reason why believers should remain married to unbelievers. According to this interpretation, 1 Corinthians 7:15 is a parenthesis and 1 Corinthians 7:16 is linked with the argument in 1 Corinthians 7:12-14. Believers should stay married to their spouses because they may play a role in the salvation of their unbelieving spouses. Such a reading is certainly possible. When Paul says that unbelieving spouses are "sanctified" in 1 Corinthians 7:14, he probably means that unbelievers are in a holy sphere in which their salvation is more likely than if they were married to an unbeliever. He does not mean by "sanctified" that they are part of the people of God, nor does he promise that they will be saved. The presence of believing spouses inducts unbelievers into a holy sphere where salvation is possible. If 1 Corinthians 7:16 is an optimistic word, it would fit this paradigm nicely. It seems more likely, however, that 1 Corinthians 7:16 is pessimistic and that the verse is a ground *(gar)* of the immediately preceding verse. One should not be robbed of one's peace if an unbelieving spouse divorces because God never promised that the unbeliever would certainly be saved. If the salvation of one's spouse were certain, then divorce would be a disaster. But God never promised the salvation of unbelieving spouses, and thus if the unbeliever desires to end the marriage, the believer should leave that person and the whole situation in God's hands.

Does Paul permit a believer to remarry after he or she is divorced from an unbeliever since he says the believer "is not enslaved" (*dedoulōtai*, 1 Cor 17:5) to the previous marriage if the unbeliever leaves? Finding an answer to this question is extraordinarily difficult. Some scholars say no for three reasons. First, Paul has already prohibited remarriage in 1 Corinthians 7:10-11. It is unlikely a different course is permitted now. Second, the context addressed is not one in which remarriage was sought. The Corinthians were asking Paul whether abstaining from sexual relations within their current marriages was advisable. They were not inquiring about the grounds for remarriage but were asking whether the single life (or at least the sexually abstemious life) was preferable. Third, when Paul speaks of the binding character of marriage, he uses the term *deō* ("bind," Rom 7:2; 1 Cor 7:39; cf. 1 Cor 7:27), and this word should be distinguished from *douloō*. Freedom to remarry is not granted. Paul simply says that believers are not enslaved to anxiety about preserving the existing marriage if their spouse leaves.

I am inclined, however, to think Paul permits remarriage. First, 1 Corinthians 7:10-11 may be interpreted to say that remarriage is prohibited if a believer is responsible for the divorce. But if the believer did not initiate divorce or commit sexual infidelity to precipitate divorce, then he or she is the innocent party. In such cases freedom to remarry exists. Second, a comprehensive treatment of divorce and remarriage is lacking here—hence the debate over Paul's meaning! But it seems likely, given human nature and the strong sexual desires that Paul himself speaks of (1 Cor 7:2, 9), that some of those who were left by their spouses would long for remarriage. Third, the attempt to separate *deō* from *douloō* is semantically suspect, for the verbs are in the same semantic range. Part of the peace and relief for the spouse left behind is freedom to remarry. Remarriage after divorce, after all, was the standard Jewish view, and Paul would have needed to make it very clear if he departed from his heritage. Such a clarification is lacking, suggesting that remarriage after a legitimate divorce was permitted.

Parents and Children

No extended discussion exists on parents and children, presumably because the issue was not a matter of controversy. Instruction from the Pentateuch and the wisdom literature of the Old Testament was likely deemed sufficient. Children are enjoined to obey their parents (Eph 6:1; Col 3:20). The authority of parents over children is evident. When Paul adds "in the Lord" (Eph 6:1), he does not mean children must only obey if their parents are believers, for the prepositional phrase attaches to the verb. Children are to obey parents because of their union with Christ. The Christian motivation emerges in Colossians 3:20—"for this is well pleasing to the Lord." In Ephesians 6:1 the inherent rightness of such obedience is communicated in the phrase *for this is right*. The totality of the parents' authority is contemplated in the call to obey parents "in all things" (Col 3:20), though once again any injunction to sin would constitute an exception.

Such obedience is seen as the fulfillment of the command to honor father and mother (Ex 20:12; Deut 5:16). In the Old Testament this command has attached a promise of long life in the land. Paul, by appending the promise, is not guaranteeing that children will live a long life if they obey their parents. As we noted earlier, the land promise for Paul is now the eschatological inheritance pledged to those in Christ Jesus. The future inheritance is not merely the land of Palestine but the world (Rom 4:13). What Paul teaches here, therefore, is that believing children who obey their parents will receive an eternal inheritance. They will possess the promise of Abraham. Is Paul teaching that children earn salvation by good works? Or does he demand that they obey their parents perfectly in order to receive the promise? Hardly. He has already argued that salvation is by faith rather than works (Eph 2:8-9). Works are not the basis of salvation. And yet God has preordained certain works in the lives of believers (Eph 2:10). Those who have been raised with Christ (Eph 2:1-7) have been transformed so that they live new lives—not perfectly, of course, but substantially and significantly. Such works are the result of being filled with the Spirit (Eph 5:18), displaying evidence that believers are filled with God's fullness and power (Eph 1:19-23; 3:14-19).

In addressing the responsibility of parents, Paul only addresses fathers, perhaps because he viewed them as having ultimate responsibility for the welfare of the family. It is just possible that the word *pateres* refers to parents (cf. Heb 11:23; 12:9) and that both fathers and mothers are addressed here. Presumably the command applies to both parents in any case. As in his instructions to husbands, Paul is primarily concerned about the fathers' abuse of authority. Children are not little "slaves" who live to satisfy the whims of parents. Those in authority can easily provoke their children (Eph 6:4; Col 3:21) through excessive correction. Paul assumes, of course, that children need correction and training. They must be nurtured "in the admonition and instruction of the Lord" (Eph 6:4). Paul was not like some in our culture who believe that children are naturally beautiful and that they will naturally grow up into lovely flowers. Children need to be trained, shaped and disciplined by parents. The danger, however, is that parents will get out of balance, constantly harping on the weaknesses of children so that they become disheartened and discouraged. Such a balanced perspective on child rearing is remarkable indeed.

Slaves and Masters

The Pauline perspective on slavery. One of the most disconcerting elements of Paul's theology for readers today is his apparent acceptance of slavery. We wonder why he did not criticize the institution as inhumane and contrary to the will of God. It is imperative, since our task here is to explicate *Paul's* theology, that we grasp his viewpoint on the matter of slavery. It is tempting to impose our own conceptions in this arena. We must begin by reminding ourselves of the discussion on 1 Corinthians 7:17-24. In Paul's mind one's social standing or class was rather insignificant. The present age is temporary and will soon pass away, and thus whether one is slave or free is of little importance (1 Cor 7:29-31). Indeed, Paul believes that God has "apportioned" (*emerisen*, 1 Cor 7:17) the calling (1 Cor 7:17, 20, 24) for each person. Hence slaves should not worry about their status as slaves (1 Cor 7:21). What really matters is that slaves are free in Christ (1 Cor 7:22). Conversely, citizens who are free need to remember that they are slaves of Christ (1 Cor 7:22). Social status is not to be prized; what is crucial is whether believers live out their redemption in Christ (1 Cor 7:23).[8] Believers are not to become slaves to the people of this world. As Romans 6:15-23 emphasizes, they are to be slaves of righteousness instead of slaves of wickedness.

When Paul asserts in Galatians 3:28 that there is neither slave or free, he is not denying the social realities of the Greco-Roman world. His instructions to slaves and masters in Ephesians (Eph 6:5-9) and Colossians (Col 3:22—4:1) and the letter to Philemon reveal that he was no revolutionary—the social pattern of Greco-Roman society is maintained. At the same time the Pauline gospel transforms the social world, in that slavery was viewed in a new way. In Christ Jesus it is irrelevant whether one is slave or free. Belonging to Christ is the fundamental and decisive reality. We should not conclude that Paul's view of slavery was bereft of concrete social consequences. Recognizing that a slave is a brother or sister in Christ would certainly transform how one treated slaves. The social stratification of this world is only temporary. Hence believers should not live as if it were ultimate, as if it says anything of great significance about a fellow believer. If believers disdained and scorned slaves because of their social standing, they would reveal that they had capitulated to the present evil age instead of setting their hopes on the age to come. Christ has immersed both slaves and free in the Spirit (1 Cor 12:13). In the new Adam it is irrelevant whether one is a Gentile or a Jew, circumcised or uncircumcised, a member of the lower social classes like Barbarians or part of the despised Scythians, or even slave or free (Col 3:11). The new Adam, Jesus Christ, encompasses all. In the believing community there are two defective ways of thinking, and both flow from the same mistaken mindset: some might think highly of themselves because of their distinguished social class; others might rue their fate because they are slaves. Paul rejects both of these conclusions. What matters is the gift of the Spirit and belonging to Christ as the second Adam. Those who belong to Christ are members of the new humanity, the new man—Christ. The old humanity is part of the evil age that is passing away.

It does not follow from this that life in this world is irrelevant or a mirage.

---

[8]Contra Dale B. Martin, *Slavery as Salvation: The Metaphor of Slavery in Pauline Christianity* (New Haven: Yale University Press, 1990), pp. 63-68. Martin contends that Paul actually says that slaves have a higher status in Christ than those who are free.

Paul encourages slaves to avail themselves of freedom if this is possible (1 Cor 7:21).[9] He fears, though, that those who are enslaved (and those who are free!) will latch onto the idea that their social position is important in God's sight or that it is decisive for their ministries. The social implications for the church are evident. No one in the church is to be slighted because of his or her social status. All are members of Christ's body and are indwelt by the Spirit. Indeed, Paul reminds the Corinthians that God typically bypasses intellectuals, the powerful and the elite (1 Cor 1:26-28). God has chosen those who are intellectually inferior in the eyes of the world, those who are socially powerless and those who are from the lower classes. The reason for this is to undercut any pride in one's own abilities (1 Cor 1:29). The radical reevaluation of persons in Christ is easy for us to overlook because we wonder why Paul did not lead a social revolution. Paul's conception of social standing is itself revolutionary. Whether one is slave or free is a secondary matter to him. Those who concentrate exclusively on such issues reveal that they are still caught up with the life of this present world.

Philemon. In Paul's letter to Philemon we see how he works out the relationship between a master and his slave. The evidence that Onesimus served as Philemon's slave is compelling. The exhortation to receive Onesimus back "no longer as a slave but more than a slave, a beloved brother" (Philem 16) most naturally suggests that Onesimus was his slave. That Philemon exercised authority over Onesimus is apparent from a number of other clues: the latter was formerly "useless" to Philemon but now a change is envisioned (Philem 11); Paul needs Philemon's consent regarding the future of Onesimus (Philem 14); and Paul promises to repay any debt incurred because of Onesimus (Philem 18-19). What is more difficult, probably impossible, to resolve are the circumstances that brought Philemon to Paul.[10] Was he a fugitive running from Philemon who accidentally ran into Paul? Or was he fleeing from Philemon and intentionally going to Paul for help? Some think Philemon sent him to Paul, but if this is the case, he was apparently reluctant to return home. As is so often the case in Pauline letters, we must admit that we do not, and ultimately cannot, know the answers to these questions. Paul and Philemon were well aware of the situation, and thus Paul does not elaborate.

---

[9]This verse (1 Cor 7:21) is fiercely debated. I believe Fee rightly argues that slaves are encouraged to gain their freedom (see n. 3 above).

[10]For the view that Onesimus was not a fugitive, see James D. G. Dunn, *The Epistles to the Colossians and to Philemon: A Commentary on the Greek Text*, NIGTC (Grand Rapids, Mich.: Eerdmans, 1996), pp. 301-7.

We do know that Onesimus was Philemon's slave, that he encountered Paul, that he was converted under Paul's ministry (suggesting, at the least, that he sought out Paul; Philem 10), that he ministered to Paul in prison and that Paul felt that he should send him back to Philemon.

Abolish slavery? What leaps out at readers today is that Paul nowhere explicitly asks Philemon to liberate Onesimus, though some see this as implied in the letter. Similarly, 1 Timothy 6:2 is most plausibly read as an injunction for slaves to obey believing masters precisely because such masters are part of the family of God. Any public campaign by the fledgling Christian movement to eradicate slavery would have been superfluous. The political wherewithal to accomplish such an aim was totally lacking. Neither did Paul advise Christian masters to free their Christian slaves. He exhorts masters and slaves to comport themselves well as Christians in their respective stations of life. We must recognize that Paul was not nurtured in the political traditions of the Western world. Ending an institution like slavery, even in the Christian community, probably never entered Paul's mind, for evidence is lacking that people in Paul's day considered ending slavery.[11] We should also note that slavery in the Greco-Roman world was remarkably different from slavery in the American experience. Slavery was not racially based, many slaves could look forward to manumission, and they could hold positions that required intellectual acumen and business skill as doctors, merchants and teachers. This is not to say that slavery was pleasant, but we should not confuse recent history with ancient facts. Some slave conditions, naturally, were horrible. Some slaves were required to work in the mines, and the conditions were abominable enough to provoke revolts. But many of these slaves were criminals, and such revolts occurred more than a hundred years before Paul was born, so these revolts likely had little affect on his thinking; and even during the revolts no thought was given to abolishing the institution.

Is slavery mandated by God? Did Paul think slavery was a "good" institution? He never addresses this question directly in his letters. We have a hint in 1 Corinthians 7:21, for he exhorts slaves to obtain their freedom if possible. The Old Testament frowns on enslaving a fellow Hebrew (Ex 21:2-11; Neh 5:5), and Paul would naturally conclude from this that the state of slavery was not ideal for any brother or sister in Christ. Contrasting Paul's perspec-

---

[11]For slavery in the ancient world, see Bartchy, *Mallon Chrēsai*, pp. 37-120; S. Scott Bartchy, "Slave, Slavery," in *Dictionary of the Later New Testament and Its Developments*, ed. Ralph P. Martin and Peter H. Davids (Downers Grove, Ill.: InterVarsity Press, 1993), pp. 1098-1102; Martin, *Slavery as Salvation*, pp. 1-49.

tive on slavery with his view of marriage and the family is instructive. Paul locates the role differences between men and women in the created order, in the good world God initiated before the Fall into sin. The different functions of men and women are not ascribed to sin. He traces their different functions back to God's intention in creation, just as he rejects homosexuality because it violates the created order. Similarly, the relationship between parents and children is rooted in creation. God intended Adam and Eve to be fruitful and multiply (Gen 1:28), and thus from the inception of the world the responsibility of parents to nurture children is enforced. The entrance of sin, of course, impinges on the relationship between men and women and between parents and children. Abuses and distortions are now introduced that did not exist in the world before the Fall of Adam. When Paul addresses husbands and wives and parents and children, he particularly warns those with "more power" to beware of abusing their leadership responsibility, for he is keenly aware of how those with power are liable to mistreat those under their responsibility. Nevertheless, nowhere does Paul suggest that marriage or the family as an institution is inherently defective. He grounds them in the created order, seeing them as a fitting and good part of life in this world.

On the other hand, Paul nowhere locates the institution of slavery in the created order. Nothing in Genesis 1—2 suggests that slavery is God's intention for some human beings. Indeed, if one were to argue from Genesis 1—2, the contrary conclusion should be drawn. Paul never criticizes slavery directly, but neither does he ground it in creation as he does the relationship between men and women and the institutions of marriage and the family. He does not recommend the elimination of slavery, but neither does he endorse it. Paul could not possibly foresee that other cultures in later centuries would tackle this question afresh and that such societies would have different political systems—systems that were shaped at least to some extent by Pauline ethics. I think it is fair to say, however, that if the question were posed to him today, he would say that the institutions of marriage and the family are fundamental and permanent. Husbands and wives should exist in every society, and parents should always exercise particular responsibility for their own children. Slavery, however, is quite different. Nothing in the Scriptures requires its existence, nor does it reflect God's creational intention. Paul does not commend slavery as he does marriage and the family. He regulates and reshapes how masters and slaves relate to one another in the Christian community. The institution is dealt with as it exists in the Greco-Roman world. Paul is more interested in the personal character and response of believing masters and slaves than he is with a generalized treatise on the institution.

Advice to slaves and masters. At this juncture we return to Paul's letter to Philemon. We have no direct word regarding Paul's oral instructions to Onesimus, but we can conclude from the letter that he exhorts him to return to Philemon, to submit to the latter's authority and to be a useful and helpful slave. These instructions fit with the exhortations given to slaves elsewhere. The exhortations for slaves in Ephesians and Colossians are remarkably similar (Eph 6:5-8; Col 3:22-25). Paul calls on slaves to obey their masters. Not only are slaves to submit to masters (cf. Tit 2:9), but they are to do their work in a wholehearted way, doing the best job that they can. In Titus, Paul fills out what doing a good job entails (Tit 2:9-10). They should not contradict their masters, nor should they misappropriate funds from them, but they should be slaves whom their masters can trust. By doing so they would show unbelieving masters the beauty of the gospel. Similarly in 1 Timothy 6:1 slaves are summoned to honor their unbelieving masters so that God's name and the gospel will not be besmirched in the eyes of the world.

In Ephesians and Colossians (Eph 6:5-8; Col 3:22-25), slaves are commanded to obey their masters out of fear of the Lord, because they have a wholehearted desire to please and honor him in whatever they do. We see that the central theme of Paul's theology emerges in his admonition to slaves. They are to glorify and honor God in all that they do. Slaves who obey their masters are promised an eternal inheritance (Col 3:24; cf. Eph 6:8), and this inheritance is nothing less than eternal life (Eph 1:18). It is doubtful that a particular reward beyond eternal life is promised to slaves. We have here Paul's regular and mainstream message that genuine salvation is accompanied by and attested with good works. Slaves are reminded that their faithful work, even under unjust and cruel masters, will be repaid in the world to come.

Admonitions for masters are notable for their brevity (Eph 6:9; Col 4:1). Paul warns masters against abusing their authority. He is well aware that those who possess authority are prone to use their social position to oppress those beneath them. Masters must desist from threatening in a domineering and imperious way, as if they are the ultimate authority in their slaves' lives. For masters too have the same Lord in heaven, and he is impartial and will judge them if they mistreat their slaves. Thus, masters must do what is right and grant what is fair to their slaves, and like slaves they are to conduct their work as masters out of reverence for Christ.

Helping the Needy

Galatians 6 and 1-2 Thessalonians. Early Christians cared for the needy in their midst. Concern for the poor permeates the teaching of the Gospels and is also evident in Acts. Paul is no exception in this regard. The importance of generosity informs Galatians 6:6-10, where believers are enjoined to pay teachers (Gal 6:6). Although sowing to the flesh and sowing to the Spirit in Galatians 6:8 probably transcend giving, they still include giving. Part of what it means to sow to the Spirit is to give generously, whereas sowing to the flesh means living for oneself. Generosity is not optional. God will not be deceived by those who worship money and restrict their giving (Gal 6:7). Sowing to the Spirit results in eternal life, but sowing to the flesh leads to destruction (Gal 6:8). Believers who live generously will "reap" eternal life on the final day (Gal 6:9). Some worry that this language compromises the gospel of grace, suggesting that salvation can be earned by good works. But Paul has labored to explain in Galatians that all fall short of the requisite works. No one obeys to the extent that he or she warrants eternal life. The extent to which one gives does not merit salvation, but it does reveal what one worships and, hence, constitutes evidence that one has new life. Those who have money as their god hoard it and keep it from others. Those who genuinely entrust their future to God are free to use their material resources to help others.

"Doing good" *(kalon poiountes)* in Galatians 6:9 also focuses on helping those in need. Those supplying the needs of others may grow tired of helping others, and thus Paul exhorts them not to lose heart in such an endeavor. Similarly, in 2 Thessalonians 3:13 Paul admonishes the Thessalonians not to tire of doing good. This admonition in 2 Thessalonians balances the previous instruction, for the Thessalonians are not to provide food for those who are lazy (2 Thess 3:6-12). Those who are unwilling to work should not be supported with food (2 Thess 3:10; cf. 1 Thess 4:11-12; 5:14). The generosity of early Christians is not blind, nor is it severed from responsibility. Handouts are not to be given willy-nilly to anyone who makes a request. Support is for those who are genuinely needy and cannot find a way to support themselves, not for those who are dissolute and slothful, refusing to work and support themselves. We can easily grasp why the summons to persist in helping the needy follows after the lazy are admonished. When thinking about how some are indolent and desire to live off the riches of others, believers may be tempted to conclude that *everyone who is needy* is lazy, and so they might begin to close off their hearts from helping anyone. The hearts of believers must always be inclined toward generosity and helping those in financial straits. They must not let the lassitude of a few quench their desire to support those who are lacking. On the other hand, giving is always to be accompanied with wisdom. Biblical giving constantly has the good of the recipient in view. Believers long to give to those who are hurting financially, but they must not give to those who are indolent, for in that case they are actually hurting the recipients. The basic rule is that believers should be ready and eager to help all financially (Gal 6:10). In particular, they are to support those who are fellow believers (Gal 6:10).

Supporting widows. The importance of financial support is indicated by Paul's insistence that godly widows receive support in 1 Timothy 5:3-16. The church, however, should not be the first line of support for widows. Family members of the widows are obligated to provide for the widows' needs before turning to the church (1 Tim 5:3-4, 16). Circles of responsibility are established, so that a family with sufficient funds cares for widows instead of absolving themselves of responsibility and transferring the widow to the church's care. The extraordinary importance of the whole matter surfaces in 1 Timothy 5:8: those who do not provide for widows "have denied the faith and are worse than an unbeliever." That is, refusal to help a widow in the family is equivalent to denying Christ. It is a repudiation of the Christian faith. There is no reason to think that one who behaves in such a way is a Christian at all.

Not all widows can depend on family members for assistance. If widows are devoted to the things of God and in need of daily provisions, the church should step in and render aid. It is difficult to discern whether Paul is addressing two different categories of widows in 1 Timothy 5:3-16. Some believe that needy widows are discussed in 1 Timothy 5:3-8 and that a special order of widows, those who were involved in ministry, are in view in 1 Timothy 5:9-15.[12] The widows in verses 9-15 are even seen by some as wealthy widows, who function as patronesses. Arguments supporting an order of widows are as follows:

■ An age limit is prescribed in 1 Timothy 5:9-15 but not in 1 Timothy 5:3-8, suggesting a distinction between the two groups. Would Paul really deny support to widows who were under sixty years of age? But it makes sense if only those who had reached such an age could belong to the ministering order of widows.

---

[12]Against seeing an order of widows, see Luke Timothy Johnson, *Letters to Paul's Delegates: 1 Timothy, 2 Timothy, Titus* (Valley Forge, Penn.: Trinity Press International, 1996), pp. 179-83. In favor of such a notion, see Reggie Kidd, *Wealth and Beneficence in the Pastoral Epistles: A 'Bourgeois' Form of Early Christianity?* SBLDS (Atlanta: Scholars Press, 1990), pp. 104-6.

■ The terms *let her be enrolled* (*katalegesthō*, 1 Tim 5:9) and *refuse* (*paraitou*, 1 Tim 5:11) may refer to a voting procedure by which qualified widows are placed on a list.

■ The qualifications for widows in 1 Timothy 5:9-10 are similar to the qualification for elders, suggesting some kind of official ministry.

■ Younger widows are prohibited (1 Tim 5:11-15) because they are unable to sustain their vows of celibacy, and such vows were required to enter the order.

Detecting a separate order of widows is quite attractive, and it solves some problems in the text. It seems on balance, however, that the same group of widows is in view in 1 Timothy 5:3-16, so that a separate order of widows is not in view. Here are several arguments supporting this reading:

■ Evidence for a break between the widows of 1 Timothy 5:3-8 and 1 Timothy 5:9-15 is difficult to discern. It is scarcely clear that a new category of widows is addressed in 1 Timothy 5:9.

■ The words *enroll* and *refuse* (1 Tim 5:9, 11) more likely refer to being put on the list to receive financial support. Some kind of official action of the church is contemplated, but these words in themselves do not necessitate a reference to an official order of widows devoted to ministry.

■ The age limit probably indicates an age in which the energy of women was decreasing and their need for support was increasing. Before most women reach the age of sixty, presumably, they may find other sources of support. Paul is not absolutely prohibiting helping any woman younger than sixty; he sets this limit because women sixty years old and older have diminishing strength and need greater assistance. Indeed, the age limit speaks against an order of ministry, for older women had less energy for ministry, not more.

■ The reference to character qualities (1 Tim 5:9-10) does not necessarily suggest an office, for 1 Timothy 5:5 already indicates that widows worthy of support must be constantly devoted to prayer and to have set their hope on God. Verses 9-10 simply elaborate the character requirements already suggested in verse 5.

■ The strongest argument for seeing an order of widows is the vow of celibacy pledged by the younger women (1 Tim 5:11-15). But it is also possible that by remarrying, such women gave up a life of prayer enabled by the financial resources of the church. Paul has learned that these younger women are devoting themselves to activities other than prayer, so he counsels that they remarry and raise children (1 Tim 5:13-15).

If the reference is to needy widows throughout, we see how important such support was for Paul. Older widows, who are godly, are to be helped financially. We might wonder why Paul does not include all widows who are older and in need. Why the character qualifications? Perhaps to insure that only widows who were genuine believers in Christ received the assistance. Presumably, funds were limited, and the church had to concentrate on meeting specific needs since it lacked the wherewithal to meet all needs. It is not that Paul opposes in principle helping needy unbelievers. He advocates, as we have seen in both Galatians 6:10 and 1 Timothy 5:3-16, circles of responsibility. Believers should first support their own family members and fellow believers. Then if funds permit, believers should support others. Such an approach is not selfish. Any community that does not care for its own will eventually cease caring for anyone.

Philippians. Believers who trust God with their money find contentment (Phil 4:11; 1 Tim 6:6, 8). Paul explains how contentment manifested itself in his own life in Philippians 4:10-19. In these verses he offers thanks for the gift of the Philippians. It has been said that this is a "thankless thanks" because Paul keeps reminding the Philippians that he did not really need the gift! Such a description fails to understand Paul's purpose in these verses. His thanksgiving to the Philippians is genuine and heartfelt (Phil 4:10, 14-16, 18). But he also wants them to know that he has learned to be content in every situation, whether he is poor or rich (Phil 4:11-12). He has learned to be content because he trusts God's provision in every circumstance, knowing that God will strengthen him. Thus the famous verse about being able to do everything through the Christ who strengthens appears in an economic context (Phil 4:13).

Paul is no Stoic, teaching believers that the external world or circumstances do not matter. He is keenly aware of whether he has little or plenty. Nor are believers summoned to steel themselves and overcome calamitous circumstances. What Paul argues is that he was able to triumph by depending on Christ who strengthened him. No testimony to Paul's virtue is celebrated here; Paul exalts God as the one who sustains him in the midst of difficulties. That is why he concludes by reminding the Philippians that God will supply every need they have according to the riches of his glory in Christ Jesus (Phil 4:19). Contentment is a gift of God, a result of his grace and strength, and hence the glory belongs to him for such an experience (Phil 4:20). Paul is so impressed with the gift given (Phil 1:5-6) because it reveals that God has been working in them from the first day, and it provides confidence that God will complete what he has inaugu-

rated. The gift they have given to Paul multiplies in their account before
God and is a fragrant aroma, an acceptable sacrifice and pleasing to God
(Phil 4:17-18). These words could be interpreted as a tribute to the noble
self-sacrifice of the Philippians, an indication of their virtue. Such a reading would stray far from Paul's intention. The reason their gift pleases God
and is a fragrant aroma is that it is rooted in trust in God, believing that he
will provide every need they have. Their generosity cannot be attributed to
their virtue; it comes from their childlike trust that believes God will
secure their future.

1 Timothy 6. The call to contentment in 1 Timothy has a different basis (1
Tim 6:6-8). Paul warns against falling in love with the things of this world
since all will leave the world the same way they entered it: with nothing. In
the present era, therefore, we should be content with food and shelter—the
basic necessities of life. Still, Paul's instructions in 1 Timothy (1 Tim 6:17-19)
are ultimately not different from his discussion in Philippians. The rich are to
beware of arrogance, as if they themselves ultimately had anything to do
with the money they acquired! Riches can lead people to think they are gods
worthy of admiration and worship. They are not to base their joy on uncertain riches, for money may vanish quickly—and *will* vanish when death
arrives. Paul worries that riches will rivet our attention away from God, for
believers are to set their hope on God. The call to set one's hope on God
matches the admonition in Philippians. Paul is no ascetic, for he wants believers to enjoy every good thing God grants, as long as such enjoyment is in the
context of trusting God instead of trusting riches. And yet this is not the last
word. There is no room in Paul for those who selfishly enjoy their riches.
Those who are rich do not really trust God unless they are generous with
their money, helping the needy and eagerly distributing what God has given,
so that they are rich in good works.

Once again Paul links such generosity with eternal life. Only in this way
is a good foundation secured for the future, and that good foundation is
nothing less than eternal life, for Paul specifically says, "that they might
take hold of life indeed" (1 Tim 6:19). In other words, those who are selfish
will not inherit such a life. Paul, of course, is speaking not of perfection or
of a works-righteousness that inherits salvation. A generous heart leads to
good works, showing that such a person puts his hope in God. The obedience that flows from faith (Rom 1:5; 16:26) is what Paul speaks of here. If
those who are rich hope in God, then they do not believe that a happy
future depends on having riches. They are convinced that God is the one

who will sustain them in the future, come what may, and thus they are freed up to love others by contributing to financial needs. This is no contradiction to salvation by faith alone; this is how salvation by faith alone expresses itself, for faith is no cipher.

Conversely, we also see from this why "those who desire to get rich" (1 Tim 6:9) are in such serious straits. The temptation and snare that Paul describes is eternal destruction, for he uses the words *ruin* (*olethron;* cf. 1 Thess 5:3; 2 Thess 1:9) and *destruction* (*apōleian;* cf. Rom 9:22; Phil 1:28; 3:19; 2 Thess 2:3). When Paul says "the love of money is the root of all sorts of evils" (1 Tim 6:10), he speaks of the eternal ruin of those enamored with money. Such sin leads to eternal destruction because the love of money reveals that another god is supreme; it demonstrates that money, not the God and Father of our Lord Jesus Christ, is to be trusted. We see here that faith is still the fundamental reality, for all live in accordance with what they believe. Those who live for riches believe that life in this world and accumulating things are fundamental.

The collection. The financial issue that has attracted considerable attention in Pauline scholarship is the collection for the poor saints in Jerusalem (Rom 15:25-28; 1 Cor 16:1-4; 2 Corinthians 8—9).[13] We must clarify at the outset that this collection was not to sustain the weekly ministries of churches, nor was it intended to support elders or overseers in local congregations. The collection was a contribution to poor believers in Jerusalem from Gentile Christians. We initially learn of the collection in 1 Corinthians 16:1-4, but if we were limited to this text, our knowledge would be quite scanty. From these verses we learn that the collection transcends Corinth, for the role of the Galatian churches is also mentioned. A weekly pattern of giving is encouraged so that the money is available for Jerusalem when Paul arrives in Corinth. We also learn that the gift is destined for saints in Jerusalem, though the specific reason for the collection is not revealed, surely because the Corinthians were already informed on this matter. Displaying probity and integrity in the whole matter is essential, and thus only those who are well qualified and honest should convey the gift to Jerusalem.

The most extended treatment of the collection is in 2 Corinthians 8—9. Some scholars maintain that the chapters represent two separate letters composed at different times, but good reasons exist to see the chapters as a

---

[13]See esp. Keith F. Nickle, *The Collection: A Study in Paul's Strategy,* SBT 48 (Naperville, Ill.: Allenson, 1966).

unity.[14] The scope of the collection is indicated by the reference to the Macedonian churches (2 Cor 8:1-5). Romans 15:26 confirms this reading, for both Macedonia and Achaia are noted as participating in the collection. We saw above (1 Cor 16:1) that the Galatian churches are also included. Probably all the churches of the Pauline mission were contributing, and the text in Romans 15:26 is not intended to be an exhaustive account of contributors.

It is also clear that the collection is for poor believers in Jerusalem. Romans 15:26 confirms this, for the collection is for "the poor among the saints in Jerusalem." Surprisingly, 2 Corinthians 8—9 never mentions the recipients of the collection, but we can fairly infer that the poor in Jerusalem are intended since Jerusalem is the object of the gift in 1 Corinthians 16:1-4 and since these chapters encourage the Corinthians to bring to completion what they have promised.

The main goal in 2 Corinthians 8—9 is to provoke the Corinthians with a number of arguments to give the gift they promised. The genuineness of their repentance celebrated in 2 Corinthians 1—7 will be revealed by their participation in the collection. Hence, the Corinthians' response to Paul's overtures is not inconsequential, for how they respond is an indication of their spiritual state. It is rather astonishing that Paul begins by featuring the generosity of the Macedonians (2 Cor 8:1-6), suggesting not so subtly that the Corinthians should do likewise. The Macedonians, however, are not commended for their own virtue. Their generosity can be traced to God's grace (charis, 2 Cor 8:1). Nor did Paul coerce the Macedonians to give. Their contribution was not enforced but rather was a joyful decision they made on their own. Apparently, Paul did not expect much from them because their own financial situation was rather bleak, but they joyfully gave even more than was thought to be humanly possible. They begged Paul to give them the opportunity to give because in their minds giving was a joy and a privilege, an expression of grace and partnership (koinōnia, 2 Cor 8:4; cf. 2 Cor 9:13; Rom 15:26). That the Macedonians would be devoted to God was expected, but Paul was joyfully overwhelmed by their devotion to him and to the Jerusalem saints.

This is not the first time Paul asked the Corinthians to give. He reminds them of what they have already promised, and he hopes that they will give

---

[14]For the two-letter theory see esp. the thorough defense of this thesis by Hans Dieter Betz, *2 Corinthians 8 and 9: A Commentary on Two Administrative Letters of the Apostle Paul*, Hermeneia (Philadelphia: Fortress, 1985). For a brief response to Betz, see D. A. Carson, Douglas J. Moo and Leon Morris, *An Introduction to the New Testament* (Grand Rapids, Mich.: Zondervan, 1992), pp. 275-77.

with the same joy and desire that the Macedonians have. The pledge of love must be completed by the concrete action of giving, or else the Corinthians' promise to give is an empty gesture: the authenticity of their love is secured by actually giving (2 Cor 8:8). Seeing the sacrifices of others could provoke envy or an unhealthy sense of competition. Generosity, on the other hand, can also be catching, and that is Paul's dream (cf. 2 Cor 9:2). He wants the Corinthians to overflow with the joy of generosity just as they abound in other areas of the Christian life (2 Cor 8:7). Paul is engaged in a very sensitive endeavor, for he believes that God's grace can work through his exhortations, motivating the Corinthians to give. On the other hand, he does not want them to give out of compulsion (2 Cor 9:7) and in that sense mandate their giving (2 Cor 8:8). Paul's teaching is quite nuanced on this matter, for he believes Gentiles stand in debt *(opheiletai, opheilousin)* to the saints in Jerusalem, for they are participating in *(ekoinōnēsan)* Israel's spiritual blessings (Rom 15:27). Conversely, the actual gift should not be the result of compulsion but a deep desire *(eudokēsan,* Rom 15:26) to help others. We should not understand the debt to be a legal one, imposed by the Jews on the Gentiles. The debt is a moral one: the Gentiles should help the Jews because they are enjoying salvific blessings that belong to the Jewish people.

The Corinthians themselves, as noted, had promised to give and had indicated a strong desire to do so (2 Cor 8:6, 8, 10-11; 9:1-2). If the desire was genuine, then it will bear fruit in action, and the reality of their love will be expressed in completing what was begun. Moreover, both the Corinthians and Paul would be embarrassed if no gift is set aside when he arrives, for he had already boasted to the Macedonians about the gift promised by the Corinthians (2 Cor 9:3-5). Paul does not expect the Corinthians to give if resources are lacking (2 Cor 8:12), nor is he advocating poverty for the Corinthians and abundance for others (2 Cor 8:13-15). Paul envisions equality, in the sense that the basic material needs of believers are met. When Israel collected manna those who accumulated more shared with those who gathered less (Ex 16:18). Similarly, those whom God has blessed with riches should share with those less fortunate, so that no one goes hungry.

The injunctions to give could be construed as contradictions of the Pauline gospel of grace. Does Paul erect an ethic of duty that contravenes his emphasis on the grace of God as the root of every moral action? One *could interpret* the Pauline admonitions to give in a way that would exalt duty over love, but such an interpretation would be mistaken. Paul does not summon the Corinthians to give in order to impose an external duty on them. Instead he views

giving as a blessing (*eulogia*, 2 Cor 9:5-6). Giving is the path to joy and blessing, for the one who sows little will reap little, while those who sow a blessing will reap a blessing (2 Cor 9:6; cf. Gal 6:7-8). Moreover, any generosity at
all is due to God's powerful grace at work in his people (2 Cor 8:1), and such
grace produces an abundant joy in giving (2 Cor 8:2), not a sense of duty and
compulsion (2 Cor 9:7). It is remarkable how often Paul describes giving here
in terms of grace (*charis*, 1 Cor 16:3; 2 Cor 8:1, 4, 6-7, 19; 9:8, 14), and thus
thanks are rendered to God for any generosity (2 Cor 9:15; cf. 2 Cor 8:16).
Indeed, God is the one who lavishes riches on his people so that they can
abound in good works (2 Cor 9:8, 10). He grants riches so that we can be generous. Such generosity brings honor and glory to God, for those who are
helped thank God for his goodness as it is manifested through saints (2 Cor
9:11-13). Those who give reveal that they have been captured by the same
grace that rescued them, for grace lifts up people in need. Christ Jesus
became poor in order that we should become rich (2 Cor 8:9), and as a corollary saints should minister to others by using their riches to help the poor.
The Corinthians' generosity is evidence of God's surpassing grace, verifying
that they have received the unspeakable gift of Christ (2 Cor 9:14-15). The call
to give, therefore, is not a contradiction of the gospel but a manifestation of it.

Scholars debate the significance of the collection in Paul. Some have suggested that it was a hidden levy on the Gentiles. Evidence is lacking, however, to verify this interpretation. Others have suggested that the collection
was a temple tax. This suggestion is also unlikely because the temple tax was
collected yearly, whereas the collection was a one-time event. Nor is it persuasive to think that Paul proclaimed the significance of the Jerusalem temple
to Gentiles since his letters nowhere emphasize the temple; in fact, Jewish
distinctives (like circumcision, sabbath and purity laws) are downplayed. In
addition, it is hard to conceive of Paul's agreeing to a tax imposed by the
Jerusalem authorities, given his emphasis on independence from Jerusalem
(Gal 1:11—2:14). What is clear is that the collection was quite important to
Paul. Can we discern why? When we read the Old Testament we see a number of prophecies which predict that the Gentiles would bring their wealth to
Jerusalem (Is 2:2-3 par. Mic 4:1-2; Is 45:14; 60:5-17; 61:6; Mic 4:13; cf. also Tob
13:11; 1QM 12:13-15). These texts were probably interpreted to also teach that
Gentiles would be inducted into the people of God. If this is the case, then
Paul would understand the gifts of the Gentiles to signify their inclusion into
the people of God. The collection, therefore, would verify the authenticity of
the Pauline mission. Perhaps Paul hoped as well that such a gift, verifying the

Gentiles' inclusion into the people of God, would provoke the Jews to jealousy so that they in turn would be saved (Rom 10:19; 11:11, 14). Nevertheless, Paul did not think that the collection guaranteed the conversion of all Israel.[15] Those who teach such a notion run beyond the evidence in drawing this conclusion.

Government

The role of government is not often addressed in the Pauline letters. Because sources are scarce, Romans 13:1-7 is at the center of the discussion since it contains the longest discourse on believers' relationship to governing authorities. The reference to government suddenly erupts in the course of the argument in Romans, leading some scholars to the conclusion that the text is a later interpolation.[16] Despite the doubts of some, the majority of scholars believe the text is authentic. We know that taxes were the subject of controversy in Rome near the time of its composition. Suetonius (*Nero* 6.10.1) reports that taxes were exorbitantly high, and Tacitus (*Ann.* 13.50-51) records complaints over the extortionary practices of tax collectors in A.D. 57 or 58. Nero even considered repealing indirect taxes, though he was dissuaded from this course of action by senators. The passage in Romans concludes by enjoining believers to pay taxes (Rom 13:7), suggesting that subjection to governing authorities was most keenly felt in the pocketbook and that Paul addresses a genuine issue in the Roman churches. We should not overlook the thematic connections to the previous paragraph. Believers are urged not to take vengeance but to leave vengeance to God (Rom 12:17-21). Romans 13:1-7 introduces an important qualification into the argument. Though believers should not exact retribution from those who injure them, the state has a responsibility to punish malefactors so that society is spared from anarchy. A number of linking words attach the two paragraphs together: *good (agathos)* and *evil (kakos)* in Romans 12:17, 21 and Romans 13:3-4; *wrath (orgē)* in Romans 12:19 and Romans 13:4-5; and the concept of vengeance in Romans 12:19 and Romans 13:4. Finally, the burden of proof always lies on one suggesting an interpolation, and there is no reason to doubt the authenticity of the text in this case.

---

[15]Contrary to Johannes Munck, *Paul and the Salvation of Mankind* (Atlanta: John Knox, 1959), pp. 297-308.

[16]For example, see J. Kallas, "Romans xiii.1-7: An Interpolation," *NTS* 11 (1964-1965): 365-74; Walter Schmithals, *Der Römerbrief als historisches Problem,* SNT 9 (Gütersloh: Gerd Mohn, 1975), pp. 175-87.

Before examining the substance of Paul's instructions, we must discern what Paul means by the words *authority* (*exousia,* Rom 13:1-2) and *rulers* (*archontes,* Rom 13:3). A reference to earthly governing authorities is certainly included, but some scholars, most notably Oscar Cullmann, have maintained that both human and angelic powers are the referent, for *authority* (*exousia*) often denotes angelic powers in Paul (1 Cor 15:24; Eph 1:21; 2:2; 3:10; 6:12; Col 1:16; 2:10, 15).[17] Walter Wink also propounds this view, locating the structural evil of human governments in the realm of the demonic, in which the demonic is not understood to refer to spiritual beings but to the evil pervading human structures.[18] The reality of the demonic realm was acknowledged by Paul (cf. Eph 6:10-12), but the context of Romans 13 renders any reference to angelic powers as highly unlikely. First, believers are commanded to submit to the ruling authorities (Rom 13:1-2, 5; Tit 3:1). It is impossible to envisage Paul giving this admonition relative to angelic powers, for nowhere does he counsel subservience to angels or demons. In Colossians 2:8-15 he emphasizes that believers have been freed from the dominion of angelic authorities and rulers. Submission to earthly rulers in Paul is conceivable, but capitulation to angelic powers is unimaginable. Second, we know that Paul intends to discuss earthly powers because the passage concludes with the admonition to pay taxes (Rom 13:7), and taxes can be paid only to earthly authorities, not to heavenly powers. Finally, the call to submit to ruling authorities in Titus 3:1 functions as confirming evidence. Even if Paul were not the author of Titus, we learn from this text how an early Pauline interpreter understood Romans 13:1-7, interpreting it in terms of subjection to earthly rulers. If Titus derives from Paul (as I believe it does), then we see terminology similar to that in Romans 13 applied to earthly authorities.

The believers' fundamental responsibility is to subordinate themselves to ruling authorities. Some have suggested that Paul gave such advice because Romans was written during the genial part of Nero's reign, in which case Paul conceived of Roman rule as beneficial and just. According to this view Paul would not have given the same advice if he had written during or after the horrors of Nero's reign. This proposal should be rejected. First, Paul was already an adult during Caligula's reign (A.D. 37-41), and thus he was almost certainly aware of the emperor's insistence that he be worshiped, which precipitated a threat of war averted only by Caligula's timely death. Second,

---

[17]Oscar Cullmann, *The State in the New Testament* (New York: Scribner, 1956), pp. 95-114.
[18]Walter Wink, *Naming the Powers: The Language of Power in the New Testament* (Philadelphia: Fortress, 1984), pp. 46-47.

Paul knew from the Jesus tradition that Herod and Pontius Pilate were complicit in the death of Jesus. He was all too aware of the venality of human rulers. Third, Paul had endured injustice at the hands of governing authorities in his own missionary work (Acts 16:19-24; 35-40; 17:5-9). Fourth, those who had some knowledge of the Old Testament and of Second Temple literature were familiar with the corruption and evil promoted by ruling authorities (e.g., Ex 1:8-22; Is 10:5-34; 13:1-23:18; Jer 46:1—51:64; Dan 4:1—5:31; Amos 1:3—2:3; 1 Macc 1:10—2:68). As a brilliant Pharisaic student, Paul was well instructed in these stories, and he was thoroughly acquainted with the despotism of earthly rulers. The notion that Paul counseled subservience because Nero's reign had an auspicious beginning, therefore, is naive and insupportable. Paul knew human nature and human structures well enough to know better than that. His teaching on human corruption did not abandon him when he reflected on governing authorities.

Subjection to rulers is commanded because rulers have been ordained by God (Rom 13:1). Thus those who resist authority actually defy God's ordinance (Rom 13:2). Rulers are God's "servants" (*diakonos*, Rom 13:4) and "ministers" (*leitourgoi*, Rom 13:6), ordained by him to praise what is good and to punish what is evil. Some may be startled by the idea that rulers are ordained by God, but the roots of Paul's theology are in the Old Testament. Daniel, living in the midst of an empire that was hostile to Yahweh, the God of Israel, explicitly teaches that God raises up and deposes kings (Dan 2:21, 37-38; 4:17; 5:18-20; cf. Prov 21:1; Jer 27:5-7). Even in the case of the evil Pharaoh, Paul says that God "raised him up" (*exēgeira*, Rom 9:17), indicating God's sovereign control over wicked rulers. Second Thessalonians 2 points to the same conclusion. Paul predicts the arrival of the man of lawlessness, reminding the Thessalonians that he will deify himself and oppose the one true God (2 Thess 2:3-8). Nonetheless, he will not appear until the restrainer is removed (2 Thess 2:6-7). The restraint on evil is imposed by God himself, and hence in this text we are informed that the evil ruler will arrive at a time God has ordained. Even though Paul locates the raising up of Pharaoh and the arrival of the man of lawlessness in the will of God, he does not conclude from this that God is himself responsible for evil, nor does he exempt Pharaoh or the man of lawlessness from responsibility for their evil actions. God sovereignly ordains what occurs, and yet he is not stained by any evil. Moreover, the man of lawlessness and Pharaoh are held responsible for their evil behavior. We see from this that Paul is what we would call a compatibilist. He upholds both divine sovereignty and human responsibility.

Integrating Romans 9:17 and 2 Thessalonians 2 with Romans 13 is imperative, for we see that God ordains the rule of both evil and good leaders. We
can scarcely limit God's ordination to those rulers who are peaceable and
law-abiding. On the other hand, we should not conclude from this that governing authorities should be obeyed even if they pass laws that are evil. After
so many centuries of interpretation we may inadvertently begin to treat
Romans 13:1-7 as if it were a treatise on the Christian's relation to the state.
The text is only seven verses long! It has already been noted that inordinately
high taxes may be one reason for its composition, suggesting that Paul
addresses a specific situation. It follows that we do not have a comprehensive
discussion on the relationship of believers to the state. Paul simply explains
what believers should generally do: namely, obey the laws of the land (cf.
1 Pet 2:13-17). The world is not transformed by revolutionary activity but by
Christians living as good citizens. Even the most oppressive regimes generally punish the evils of fraud, murder, stealing, rape and other forms of indis-
criminate violence and lawlessness. Christians should never engage in any of
these activities but should be known for their devotion to righteousness and
peace. Believers cannot opt out of paying taxes by appealing to the injustice
of the ruling authority, nor should they even parcel out how much they pay,
basing their apportionment on the perceived justice of the regime. Paul was
well aware, as noted above, that all governments are to some extent unjust,
but he did not countenance withholding taxes on the basis of the government's corruption.

Believers should be inclined toward submission to, and compliance with,
governing authorities. Christians should stand out as model citizens and
should not be known as troublemakers in society. Does it follow from this
that the obedience of believers is blind and that there are no instances in
which the rule of law is contravened? We must recall that the admonitions in
Romans 13:1-7 contain the general rule and the normal course of affairs in the
Christian life. The text cannot be wrested from its context to support obedience to the law no matter what the government enjoins. Paul assumes that
believers will refuse to do what is evil. No believer will conform to a state
that demands worship or compromises the centrality of God. No believer will
comply with a government that requires murder or stealing. The man of lawlessness will also have a kingdom (2 Thess 2:3-12), and the Old Testament
background suggests that his kingdom will persecute the people of God (Dan
7:19-25). Paul is hardly suggesting that believers will do everything that the
man of lawlessness mandates!

Paul was aware that the state could go astray. Hence, he summons believers to pray for kings and authorities (1 Tim 2:1-2). A quiet and ordered life is the preferable path for believers, but if governing authorities begin to contravene the will of God, then believers have no recourse but to resist. Such resistance does not involve a call to arms, nor does Paul contemplate any form of violence, for such activities would be foreign to the very nature of the gospel. Believers resist by refusing to do the evil demanded by the state, and they endeavor to persuade ruling authorities about the just and right course. Fundamentally believers pray that God will work in the hearts of kings so that their society will be grounded in that which is true and right and beautiful.

Conclusion

Paul does not expect life in this world to be heaven on earth, but he does expect believers to be good citizens, to give generously to the poor, to live in society in a way that features their Christian faith and to have families that are pleasing to God. Paul does not endorse a private Christianity, where one's individual salvation does not affect public living. New life in Christ embraces and touches every dimension of the life of believers. The blessing promised to Abraham is worked out in new relationships and new attitudes in the social sphere.

16

THE HOPE OF GOD'S PEOPLE
The Fulfillment of God's Saving Purposes

We have seen throughout this book that eschatology pervades Pauline theology, particularly the tension between the "already but not yet."[1] The salvation of believers has already been inaugurated but not yet consummated. The future hope of salvation is an anchor for all of life, for it represents ultimate reality and the certain destination of all believers. The hope for future redemption runs like a thread through all of Paul's theology, and it is woven into every theme in his writings. For instance, in the last chapter we explored Paul's view of human governing authorities. Such authorities, in Paul's mind, were provisional and temporary, functioning as rulers in the interim between the first and second coming of Christ. Realizing this truth prevents Christians from deifying the state or from expecting the kingdom of God to manifest itself in this world. The hope of future glorification, therefore, cannot be shunted aside to the periphery of Paul's thought, nor can we segment it so that it merely represents the last topic when organizing Paul's theology—a topic neatly segregated from all that has preceded it. The hope of

---

[1] The presence of the "already but not yet" theme in Paul is explained well by Oscar Cullmann, *Christ and Time: The Primitive Christian Conception of Time and History*, rev. ed. (Philadelphia: Westminster Press, 1964).

the future permeates every dimension of Paul's theology, reminding his readers that God's purposes will be realized.

When the future promises are realized, God will be glorified, honored and praised as God (2 Cor 1:20). Every knee will bow and every tongue will confess that Jesus Christ is Lord to the glory of God the Father (Phil 2:10-11). All things will be reconciled in Christ (Col 1:20), and God's plan to sum up all things in Christ (Eph 1:10) will be completed. Believers will marvel at and enjoy God's grace for endless ages (Eph 2:7; cf. Eph 3:10; 2 Thess 1:10). The missionary task that animated Paul will be finished, and God's plan of including both Jews and Gentiles (Rom 9—11; Eph 2—3) will have reached its consummation. The suffering of the present era will be just a memory, the glorification promised will be a reality, and the sufferings of the present will seem small compared to the beauty that has dawned (Rom 8:18; 2 Cor 4:16-18). God's saving work in believers will be finished, and any talk of "not yet" will be passé. The structures of the present world order will cease, and a world of endless joy will commence.

The goal in this chapter is not to explain how the future hope is woven into every part of Paul's theology, for to some degree such an interleaving is present in every part of this book. As we investigate certain topics in this chapter, we must resist any notion that only these issues relate to the future in Paul since redemptive history is part and parcel of all of Paul's theology. We could include every topic under Paul's eschatology, but for the purposes of organization it seemed fitting to have a separate chapter where a few matters relative to the future hope are specifically studied.

The Return of Christ

Believers love Jesus Christ and long for his return. Hence, Paul prays in 1 Corinthians 16:21, "Our Lord, come." It is not difficult to see that the eschatological urgency permeating the Pauline letters is intertwined with Christ's future coming. Indeed, even when Christ's coming remains unmentioned, it is probably implied when the consummation of God's purposes is in view. We shall restrict ourselves here to texts where Christ's coming is specifically noted.[2]

Paul teaches a physical return of Jesus to earth: "the Lord himself shall descend from heaven with a shout, with the voice of an archangel and with the trumpet of God" (1 Thess 4:16). The return of Jesus cannot refer here to

---

[2]For a detailed study of the coming of the Lord in Paul, see Joseph Plevnik, *Paul and the Parousia: An Exegetical and Theological Investigation* (Peabody, Mass.: Hendrickson, 1997).

the destruction of Jerusalem in A.D. 70 since the text says he will "descend from heaven," nor can it be reduced to a private event in one's inner consciousness. He will return publicly and visibly from heaven (cf. Phil 3:20), and he will be accompanied by the noise of shouting, an archangel's voice and a trumpet.

Jesus' physical return fits with the notion of his "coming" *(parousia)*. This term is used of the arrival of Stephanas to meet Paul (1 Cor 16:17) or the coming of Titus to meet with the Corinthians (2 Cor 7:6-7). Similarly, in 1 Corinthians 15:23 Paul speaks of the Lord's "coming" *(parousia)*, referring to the future coming of Christ (cf. also 1 Thess 2:19; 3:13; 4:15; 5:23; 2 Thess 2:1, 8). In the New Testament the word *coming* always has the idea of physical presence (cf. 2 Cor 10:10; Phil 1:26; 2:12), confirming the notion of a physical return of Christ. The public nature of the event is confirmed by the presence of angels at his return (1 Thess 3:13; 4:16). Similarly, in 2 Thessalonians 1:7 his coming is described as the "revelation of the Lord Jesus from heaven with his mighty angels." In this latter text the word used is not *parousia* (coming) but *apokalypsis* (revelation). Jesus will be unveiled from heaven in glory to punish unbelievers, and at the same time believers will marvel at his beauty (2 Thess 1:7-10; cf. 1 Cor 1:7).

Another term Paul uses for Christ's future coming is *appearance (epiphaneia)*. In Hellenistic thought the word *appearance* was used for the manifestation or appearance of a hidden divinity. Paul most often uses it of Christ's second coming (2 Thess 2:8; 1 Tim 6:14; 2 Tim 4:1, 8; Tit 2:13), though in 2 Timothy 1:10 the reference is to the incarnation. When Christ appears, he will destroy the man of lawlessness (2 Thess 2:8) and bring in his kingdom. Paul particularly emphasizes that believers must persevere until Jesus appears (1 Tim 6:14; 2 Tim 4:1-2, 8; Tit 2:13) in order to receive their eschatological reward. The term may be used to remind believers that Jesus will come suddenly and without warning, and hence they must be prepared. The verb *manifest (phaneroō)* belongs in the same semantic range. Paul looks forward to the glorification of believers "when Christ is manifested" (Col 3:4). Throughout this chapter we shall see that Christ's future coming is the climax of history. His return will spell the defeat of all spiritual powers that oppose him and the defeat of death as the last enemy (1 Cor 15:23-28; 2 Thess 2:8). When Christ comes again, believers will rejoice (1 Thess 2:19), the sanctification of believers will be completed (1 Thess 3:11-13; 5:23-24), and the dead shall be raised (1 Thess 4:13-18).

Resurrection and Waiting for Christ's Return

In Jewish thought, the resurrection is the inauguration of the age to come. For

Paul and other New Testament writers, the age to come has invaded the present evil age in the resurrection of Jesus Christ (Rom 1:4; cf. 2 Tim 2:8). When Paul proclaims the resurrection, the shared tradition of the church is transmitted by him (1 Cor 15:1-4). Nor does Paul understand the resurrection of Jesus in immaterial terms, so that it can be described as a visionary experience.[3] The resurrected Lord was seen in space-time history by many people (1 Cor 15:5-8). Any notion of a hallucination is excluded, for five hundred people saw him on the same occasion. Some saw him who did not believe in him previously, such as his brother, James, and Paul (cf. 1 Cor 9:1; Gal 1:12). The appearances of the resurrected Lord were persuasive enough to overcome the skepticism of both James and Paul. We are also told that many of those to whom the Lord appeared are still alive (1 Cor 15:6), with the implication that the Corinthians can ask these witnesses if they still have doubts. Some who live today may have a difficult time conceiving of a physical resurrection, but there is little doubt that Paul believed in such.

Resurrection in 1 Corinthians 15. The new age dawned in the resurrection of Christ, and thus Paul conceives of it as the "first fruits" *(aparchē)* of the resurrection to come (1 Cor 15:20, 23). The surprising element in Christ's resurrection is that the resurrection of all believers did not immediately commence, for Christ's resurrection signals that the future age has arrived. It is precisely here that some contemporaries of Paul stumbled. They believed that the future age had arrived in the resurrection of Christ and, therefore, that believers were already raised with Christ. They denied any future physical resurrection for believers. Some apparently taught that believers were resurrected immediately upon conversion (1 Cor 15:12-57; 2 Tim 2:18), but this resurrection was only spiritual, ruling out any future physical resurrection of believers.[4] Perhaps they derived this notion from a one-sided understanding of Paul's teaching that believers at conversion have been raised with Christ (Eph 2:6; Col 2:12; 3:1). Paul emphatically rejects any teaching that denies the future bodily resurrection of believers, identifying it as a departure from the faith (1 Cor 15:12-19; 2 Tim 2:18). The error of Paul's opponents is aptly

---

[3]See William Lane Craig, *Assessing the New Testament Evidence for the Historicity of the Resurrection of Jesus* (Lewiston, N.Y.: Mellen, 1989), pp. 1-159; Robert H. Gundry, "The Essential Physicality of Jesus' Resurrection According to the New Testament," in *Jesus of Nazareth: Lord and Christ: Essays on the Historical Jesus and New Testament Christology,* ed. Joel B. Green and M. Turner (Grand Rapids, Mich.: Eerdmans, 1994), pp. 216-19.

[4]See Anthony C. Thiselton, "Realized Eschatology at Corinth," *NTS* 24 (1977-1978): 519-26; William L. Lane, "1 Tim iv. 1-3: An Early Instance of Over-Realized Eschatology?" *NTS* 11 (1965): 164-67.

described as "overrealized eschatology," for they collapsed the teaching on the resurrection so as to exclude any future dimension to God's promises, with the result that a future physical resurrection was denied.

Paul vigorously contests such an overrealized eschatology in 1 Corinthians 15. We have already seen that in 1 Corinthians 15:4-8 Paul emphasizes the physicality of Jesus' resurrection. Many witnesses attested to its reality, and the bodily resurrection of Jesus is the common confession of the church (1 Cor 15:11). Having established the truth of Christ's bodily resurrection, Paul advances to the next stage of his argument in 1 Corinthians 15:12-19. Four times in this paragraph the indissoluble connection between the resurrection of Christ and the bodily resurrection of believers is stated (1 Cor 15:12, 13, 15, 16). Paul does not *argue for* the connection between the resurrection of Christ and the resurrection of believers. He *assumes* the correlation between the two, affirming that these two events cannot be detached from one another. Hence, he says, "If there is no resurrection from the dead, neither has Christ been raised from the dead" (1 Cor 15:13). The argument is likely constructed in this way because the Corinthians *do believe* in the physical resurrection of Christ. Paul wants to shock them with the internal contradiction in their thinking, and so he states four times that if they deny the bodily resurrection of believers, then they also deny the bodily resurrection of Christ. They cannot have the one without the other. No fissure is allowed between the resurrection of believers and Christ, nor does Paul say that he understands how some may believe in Christ's bodily resurrection but doubt the bodily resurrection of believers. The issue is nonnegotiable for Paul. The consequences of denying Christ's resurrection are massive—for then Paul's preaching is mistaken, their faith is vain, their sins remain unforgiven, and those who have died have perished (1 Cor 15:14-15, 17-19).

Those advocating overrealized eschatology did not understand the "already but not yet" pattern of Paul's eschatology, and an explanation of this matter constitutes the next leg in Paul's argument (1 Cor 15:20-28). Christ resurrection is the first fruits (*aparchē*, 1 Cor 15:20, 23), functioning as the promise and assurance of the future resurrection of believers. Just as the first fruits of the harvest are the prelude to the full harvest, so also the resurrection of Christ anticipates and ensures the resurrection of all those who belong to him. The resurrection of believers occurs at the second coming of Christ, when the end of history arrives. In the meantime believers continue to face the last enemy, death (1 Cor 15:25-26). Overrealized eschatology diminishes the current reality of evil since it claims that we enjoy a heavenly life now and that the end time promises have already arrived. Such claims are contradicted by both suffering and the specter of death, since the former continues to beset us and the latter is still on the horizon for believers.

Not all of God's enemies have been subjected to him and vanquished (1 Cor 15:27-28). The day when God "is all in all" has not yet arrived. Believers groan under a "body of humiliation" (*sōma tēs tapeinōseōs*, Phil 3:21), anxiously awaiting a body that will be conformed to the glorious body of the resurrected Christ. Redemption is not yet fully realized, for "the body is dead because of sin" (Rom 8:10), but the promise that the same one who raised Christ will raise our bodies fortifies us in the interval (Rom 8:11; cf. 1 Cor 6:14; 2 Cor 4:14). Believers groan and sigh as they await "the redemption of our body" (Rom 8:23). The "not yet" of salvation is evident in the corruption of the outer person and the afflictions of the present age (2 Cor 4:16-17). Believers groan in their present bodies, longing to be clothed with their new resurrection bodies (2 Cor 5:1-4). The presence of the Spirit within us ensures that the resurrection body will be ours in the future (2 Cor 5:5).

Those who disavowed a future resurrection apparently questioned even the possibility of a resurrected body in the future, doubting whether anyone could defend coherently a bodily resurrection (1 Cor 15:35). Paul dismisses such skepticism as foolish (1 Cor 15:36), perceiving in their objections a rejection of God's power. The life that springs out of dormant seeds, after all, is completely unanticipated and must be ascribed to God's power (1 Cor 15:36-38). If God is able to accomplish such a transformation in seeds, surely he can transform and raise our bodies. Similarly, the sheer diversity of earthly and astral bodies (1 Cor 15:39-41) signals God's power, for he is able to create whatever he wills. In any case, the temporal interval and the qualitative difference between our present and future bodies must be maintained (1 Cor 15:42-49). The body received from Adam is corruptible, weak and natural, whereas the body we shall receive from Christ will be incorruptible, powerful and spiritual. When Paul uses the word *spiritual* (*pneumatikos*, 1 Cor 15:44) with reference to our bodies, he does not deny the physicality of the future body. The term *spiritual* does not mean the resurrected body is immaterial, for an "immaterial" body would support the view of the opponents. What Paul means is that the body is animated and empowered by the Holy Spirit; it is no longer weakened by the power of sin (1 Cor 15:57; cf. Col 3:4). In 1 Corinthians 15:44-49 the order of the two bodies is emphasized: the natural body precedes the spiritual body, just as the first Adam preceded the last Adam. The body from the last Adam is not ours immediately upon entering the people of God. Glorified bodies will not be ours until the coming of the Lord Jesus Christ.

The present mortal body (1 Cor 15:50-57) cannot enter the kingdom of God. When Paul says "flesh and blood cannot enter the kingdom of God" (1 Cor 15:50), we should not conclude that physical bodies will not inhabit the kingdom. What Paul means is that our present bodies which are "corruptible" *(pthora)* cannot enter the kingdom. Hence our corruptible bodies, which have not been freed from sin, must be transformed and changed. God promises to do this very thing. The dead in Christ shall be raised with incorruptible bodies that are fit for a heavenly existence; and the living, when he returns, will be instantaneously transformed, so that their new bodies meet the standards of heavenly existence. At this time death will be vanquished as the last enemy. Believers must patiently wait and work until the end of the present evil age.

1 Thessalonians 4 and 5. That believers live in the era before the demise of the last enemy is apparent from 1 Thessalonians 4:13-18. The inexperienced believers at Thessalonica were distressed because some of their believing loved ones had died before the coming of the Lord. Apparently they were persuaded that those who were deceased would suffer some disadvantage because they died before the second coming. Identifying the precise reason for their grief is difficult, and the many guesses have not yielded any certainty. We know that they were paralyzed by sorrow and by the feeling that their deceased loved ones were at some disadvantage, but we do not know precisely why they felt this way. Could their confusion stem from Paul himself? Is it possible that Paul had not conceived of the possibility of Christians' dying before the coming of the Lord—and now he had to provide an explanation for the death of believers? Such a view is scarcely plausible. Even though 1 Thessalonians may be his first letter, it was written around A.D. 50 or 51, and Paul was converted at least fifteen years before such a letter. Fellow believers had certainly died during that time period. Moreover, Paul was present when Stephen was stoned (Acts 7:58—8:3), and the death of James, the brother of John, must have been known to him (Acts 12:2). We can dismiss, then, the notion that Paul was caught by surprise and forced to reflect on the death of Christians for the first time. The Thessalonians may have been surprised, and Paul may have been caught off guard by their puzzlement, but what we cannot argue is that Paul never grappled with the death of believers before writing 1 Thessalonians.

The echo of grief produced by death reminds us that death is an enemy (1

Thess 4:13). Death in one sense is preferable to life because those who die are inducted into the Lord's presence (Phil 1:21-23). Yet Paul confesses that he would have experienced "grief upon grief" if God had not spared the life of Epaphroditus (Phil 2:27). The prospect of future joy and a future resurrection does not cancel out the reality of sorrow in the present evil age. Such sorrow, however, is not identical to the grief that strikes unbelievers, for all hope is extinguished at death for those who do not know God (1 Thess 4:13). Conversely, believers' grief is genuine and piercing, but it is mingled with hope and with the confidence that the deceased will be raised from the dead and reunited with their loved ones. Such confidence is grounded in the death and resurrection of Jesus, for—as we read in 1 Corinthians 15:12-19—Paul is confident that since God raised Jesus from the dead, he will also "bring with him those sleeping through Jesus" (1 Thess 4:14). The indissolubility of the resurrection of Christ and the resurrection of believers is again evident. As in 1 Corinthians 15, here the hope of believers still lies before them and is directed to the resurrection. The future is not yet realized since those who have died are "the dead in Christ" (1 Thess 4:16).

Since the Thessalonians were worried that their deceased loved ones would be at some disadvantage when Jesus returned, Paul emphasizes the order of events at Jesus' coming (1 Thess 4:15-17). At Jesus' coming dead believers will arise first, and then the living will be snatched up to join the Lord in the clouds. When Jesus returns, living saints will not precede those who have died. Such words are not written to satisfy eschatological curiosity, nor do they provide a detailed chart of things to come. Paul's words assure believers that they will all be present with the Lord forever. Such words gave comfort to those who were concerned about deceased loved ones (1 Thess 4:17-18).

It is instructive to correlate 1 Thessalonians 4:17 and 1 Corinthians 15:52. In 1 Thessalonians 4:17 we are informed that living saints will be caught up into the air, while in 1 Corinthians 15:52 we discover that when Christ returns living saints will be instantaneously transformed. No one will meet the Lord without a transformed body. In evangelical circles there is much discussion about the time of the "snatching up." Neither 1 Thessalonians 4:13-18 nor 1 Corinthians 15:51-53 is definitive on the matter. No explicit word regarding the time when the Lord will return is given. The only hints given indicate that the "snatching up" and the return of the Lord are coincident, that is, there is not a seven-year interval between "the rapture" and "the second coming." In 2 Thessalonians 1:5-10 the future judgment of unbelievers is described (see below for further discussion). What is instructive is that the "relief" *(anesin)* of believers and the punishment of unbelievers are contemporaneous (2 Thess 1:7-10). Believers will be relieved of their afflictions when Jesus is revealed from heaven and punishes unbelievers. Notice that the relief of believers does not occur seven years before the punishment of unbelievers but *at the same time* that Jesus returns and punishes unbelievers. Since the believers' relief and the unbelievers' punishment occur at the same time, there is no reason to think the "rapture" precedes the second coming by seven years. Such a scenario suggests that the second coming and the rapture are both included in the same event.

Another hint, a bit harder to grasp, is provided in 2 Thessalonians 2. The Thessalonians are persuaded that the day of the Lord has arrived or is imminent. Paul objects to this, saying that such is impossible since the apostasy and the man of lawlessness have not yet appeared. If Paul believed in a rapture preceding the second coming, then he could have appealed to the rapture as proof that the day of the Lord had not arrived. The argument here is from silence and so is not decisive, and yet it should not be dismissed entirely. It seems that the clearest evidence against the Thessalonians' position would be the rapture, for then Paul could say, "The day of the Lord cannot be here. Do you not recall that you will all be gone, snatched away, before the day of the Lord even arrives?" His failure to say this at least suggests that he held no such teaching, that he never separated the snatching up from the second coming.

Some scholars also suspect that Paul was mistaken in 1 Thessalonians 4:13-18, since he seems to think that he will actually be alive when the parousia (i.e., the second coming) arrives, for he speaks of "we who live and remain until the coming of the Lord" (1 Thess 4:15; cf. 1 Thess 4:17). Obviously, Paul died before the Lord returned, and thus it appears that he was mistaken for he speaks of remaining until the parousia. The problem is more apparent than real. Several things need to be said to have a full-orbed picture. First, Paul would probably have been astonished to find that two thousand years have passed since he wrote 1 Thessalonians. He did expect the Lord to return relatively soon. Saying this, however, is not to say that Paul erred in what he said about Christ's coming. Second, nowhere does Paul actually specify a timetable that delimits when the Lord will return. He expected the Lord to come soon, but he had no certainty as to when the Lord would return. No detailed chronology of future events can be teased out of Paul's writings, nor did he intend to provide a chart of what lies ahead for his readers. Third, when Paul wrote 1 Thessalonians he did not know if he would live or die before the second coming. By speaking of "we," he identifies himself with those who will be alive when the Lord returns. Since he did not know the timing of the event, it was possible, when he wrote 1 Thessalonians, that he would still be alive at the return of the Lord. The "we" is defined as "those who are living" *and* "those who remain until the coming of the Lord" (1 Thess 4:15; cf. 1 Thess 4:17). The last clause implies that "we" includes those who live until the Lord returns. When Paul wrote the letter, he was not in a position to say who would still be alive when the Lord returned, since the Lord had not informed him about the precise date of his coming. For pastoral reasons Paul uses the inclusive "we," for to avoid it would imply that he knew who would die before the Lord returns. Paul does not make a definitive pronouncement one way or the other as to whether he would be alive upon the Lord's return. He contemplates, however, the possibility that both he and the Thessalonians will live until the Lord's return. Contemplating the possibility, however, is not the same thing as guaranteeing he will live until the Lord comes. We should not expect Paul to write as a disinterested theologian but as a pastor and missionary who longs for the return of his Lord.

We should remind ourselves that Paul did not provide a detailed chart of future events, and this is evident in 1 Thessalonians 5:1-11. The "times and seasons" are known to his readers through apostolic instruction. Some might conclude that knowledge of the times or seasons means that believers have a precise chronology of what will occur. Such a view misunderstands the import of these verses. Believers do not know the day of the Lord's return, but they do know that his return will be sudden and surprising, like the arrival of a thief at night. Unbelievers will realize too late that destruction is imminent, for the end will arrive without warning, just as birth pangs suddenly seize a pregnant woman. When Paul says believers "are not in darkness so that the day should overtake you as a thief" (1 Thess 5:4), this could be read to say that believers know when the day will arrive. They will not be surprised by its arrival because they are not in the dark about when it will come. But such a reading is unlikely. It seems to contradict 1 Thess 5:2, which posits that the day of the Lord arrives as a thief for believers and unbelievers. When Paul says that the day will not come as a thief in 1 Thess 5:4, he does not intend to say that believers know when the Lord will return. The point is that believers will not experience the negative consequences of the Lord's arrival. That is, for them the coming will not actually be like the coming of the thief in that something precious is stolen. The coming will be like a thief for believers only in the sense that they will be astonished at the time when the Lord returns, but the consequences of his return will be beneficial rather than adverse. If this reading is correct, Paul does not furnish a chronology of events that believers can check off before the Lord comes. He simply reminds them that the Lord's coming will not have negative consequences for them, even though they too will be surprised on the day he arrives.

When the Thessalonians are summoned to sobriety and to alertness (1 Thess 5:6), Paul is not telling them to calculate, through the reading of signs, the day of the Lord's return. The alertness demanded here is moral, not chronological. Believers show that they are alert and prepared for the Lord's coming by living in a way that pleases him every day. First Thessalonians 5:5 confirms this reading when it identifies believers as "sons of light and sons of the day" and distinguishes them from those "of the night" and "darkness." Unbelievers are characterized by moral slumber and lassitude, while believers are fully awake by virtue of their new life in Christ. The illustration of sleeping in 1 Thessalonians 5:7 ("for those who sleep, sleep at night"), therefore, is metaphorical, signifying moral enervation. Such moral enervation is fitting for unbelievers since they live in the realm of darkness.

Similarly, moral drunkenness is typical of those of the night, but it must not invade the lives of those who live in the light. (The illustration of drunkenness in 1 Thess 5:7 is metaphorical as well, standing in contrast to the sobriety demanded in 1 Thess 5:6.) Hence believers are called to live morally sober lives, characterized by faith, love and hope. The hope of salvation (1 Thess 5:9) brings the text full circle, for believers know the times and seasons precisely because they know that Jesus Christ has dispelled the darkness of the present world order through his death and resurrection. They can be assured of future salvation because of the work of Christ. When Paul speaks of "waking" and "sleeping" in 1 Thessalonians 5:10 ("he died for us so that whether we wake or sleep we should live together with him"), the metaphor has changed, for "sleeping" here does not refer to moral collapse. Paul never promises life for those who live morally dissolute lives. Here "sleep" refers to death. Both the dead and the living in Christ will certainly receive the life of the age to come. Being ready for the Lord's coming does not mean calculating the day when he will arrive; it means that believers are to live their everyday lives in a different fashion from unbelievers, with moral alertness and seriousness, because they know that the Lord will return.

2 Thessalonians. Another form of overrealized eschatology surfaces in 2 Thessalonians. The Thessalonians were persuaded that the day of the Lord had arrived *(enestēken)* or was imminent (2 Thess 2:2), drawing this conclusion presumably because of their intense suffering (2 Thess 1:4-7). Paul's warning against deception and caution about other sources of information (2 Thess 2:2-3) suggests that either a prophetic word or an alleged epistle of Paul (or both) advanced the notion that the end was upon them. Paul attempts to douse this eschatological frenzy by calling on the church to regain composure and to think clearly. The day of the Lord cannot be on the horizon just yet since the rebellion *(apostasia)* had not begun and neither had "the man of lawlessness" appeared (2 Thess 2:3). This is the only reference in Paul to the "lawless one" or, as he is also called, "the son of destruction" (2 Thess 2:3), but clearly he is modeled on the person described in Daniel 11:36 (cf. 2 Thess 2:4). The lawless one's distinctive trait is a claim to deity and a demand for worship.

Paul assures his readers that the lawless one had not yet arrived because the restrainer hinders him from appearing. Scholars have devoted much energy to decipher the identity of the restrainer, which is described with both the neuter *(to katechon,* "the restraining thing," 2 Thess 2:6) and masculine *(ho katechōn,* "the restraining one," 2 Thess 2:7) gender. Suggestions have ranged from evil and Satan, to the Holy Spirit, to the presence of missionaries and the apostle Paul, to the Roman government and the Roman emperor, to the archangel Michael, to human government, and so on. Unfortunately, only the Thessalonians and Paul know the identity of the restrainer since it was part of their oral communication (2 Thess 2:5), and thus Paul feels no need to be specific. He never informs us about the identity of the restrainer since he had already communicated the matter orally to the Thessalonians. The main point, in any case, is that the day of the Lord cannot have begun since evil continues to be restrained. At some point the restraint will be removed, and then the full force of evil will be unleashed. Ultimately, then, no matter who the restrainer might be in particular, the one who restrains evil from breaking out with all its fury is God himself. At some point in history he will remove the shackles of evil, and the evil that is bottled up now—the "mystery of lawlessness" (2 Thess 2:7)—will manifest itself. The depth of human evil and its brutality will be evident to all those who have any moral barometer.

Paul betrays little interest in what the lawless one will actually do. He informs us that the power behind the scenes is Satan himself, so that the lawless one has the ability to do signs and wonders and miracles. The miracles are designated as "false" *(pseudous,* 2 Thess 2:9), but this should not be interpreted to say that the miracles are "fake." The signs and wonders are real enough, but they have their origin in evil. Because they have their source in what is evil, they are described as "false." Those who are perishing and hate the truth will find such evidence persuasive, but the doom of evil is sure. Indeed, before Paul explains even a single activity of the lawless one, he says his destruction is promised: "The Lord Jesus will slay him by the breath of his mouth and destroy him by the appearance of his coming" (2 Thess 2:8). The message communicated is that the triumph of evil, though real, is remarkably short. The lawless one will be swept aside summarily when Jesus returns.

Did Paul change his mind? Some scholars have suggested that Paul developed or changed his view regarding the future resurrection. When writing 1 Thessalonians he clearly believed that believers were raised from the dead upon Jesus' return and not at their death. Some scholars maintain that Paul altered his view after experiencing his trial in Asia (2 Cor 1:8-11).[5] He began to realize that he would likely die before the coming of the Lord, and thus he began to think that believers would be resurrected immediately upon death. Such a change seems to be reflected in 2 Corinthians 5:1-10, where upon the dissolution of the earthly body, believers "have" (*echomen*, 2 Cor 5:1)—note the present tense—a new body. Seeing a change in Paul's view of the resurrection, though possible, is not likely.[6] Against it is what Paul wrote in 1 Corinthians 15, for there, as we have seen, the resurrection of believers is located at the return of Christ. The interval between the resurrection of Christ and the resurrection of believers is emphasized to correct the overrealized eschatology of the Corinthians. The resurrection of believers is located at the last trumpet (1 Cor 15:52) or the end (1 Cor 15:24), which is the time when Christ returns. If Paul were to change his view from the time he penned 1 Corinthians to the time he wrote 2 Corinthians, the reader would expect that Paul would clearly signal to the readers such a change. Otherwise, he would be apt to leave the Corinthians confused. The present tense verb *echomen* in 2 Corinthians 5:1 does not qualify as a clear departure from the previous letter. Indeed, recent study of the verb in Greek confirms that the primary significance of the verb is not temporal but aspectual.[7] The present

---

[5]For example, C. F. D. Moule, "St. Paul and Dualism: The Pauline Conception of the Resurrection," *NTS* 12 (1965-1966): 106-23; W. D. Davies, *Paul and Rabbinic Judaism: Some Rabbinic Elements in Pauline Theology* (New York: Harper & Row, 1948), pp. 309-19.

[6]Rightly Ben Witherington III, *Jesus, Paul and the End of the World* (Downers Grove, Ill.: InterVarsity Press, 1992), pp. 204-8.

[7]For recent study on verbal aspect in Paul, see Stanley E. Porter, *Verbal Aspect in the Greek of the New Testament: With Reference to Tense and Mood*, SBG 1 (New York: Peter Lang, 1989);

tense does not necessarily indicate present time, and, in context, it most likely refers to a future event. Thus Paul uses the present tense to convey the certainty of their future physical resurrection.

An investigation of 2 Corinthians 5:1-10 reveals no departure from standard Pauline teaching on the resurrection. Our present body is compared to an earthly house that is slowly becoming dilapidated and will eventually be torn down. Our future body, on the other hand, is heavenly and eternal, for it is from God himself. Because of the weakness of our earthly bodies we groan and sigh, longing for the day when we will be clothed with our new bodies. The gift of the Spirit is the guarantee and assurance that we shall receive such a body. The tension between the "already but not yet" that characterizes Paul's theology is nicely captured in these words: "We walk by faith, not by sight" (2 Cor 5:7) in the interlude between our conversion and resurrection. Believers anticipate the future day when they shall be clothed with their resurrection bodies. No clear evidence exists that Paul dramatically changed his view regarding the time of the resurrection.

The evidence of Philippians is significant here as well. Even if Philippians were written during Paul's Ephesian or Caesarean imprisonment (in both these cases Philippians would be written *before* Paul's Roman imprisonment), the letter would be dated after the writing of 2 Corinthians.[8] It is clear in Philippians 3:20-21, however, that the transformation of our bodies will occur at the time of Christ's return. When Christ returns he "will transform the body of our humiliation to be conformed to his glorious body." Paul gives no indication that our bodies will be changed immediately upon death since the resurrection is reserved for the time of Christ's coming.

Intermediate state. A less important question is whether Paul believed in an intermediate state between believers' death and resurrection. Paul often speaks of the resurrection since that is the goal to which believers are destined. We can understand why a focus on the intermediate state would be lacking, precisely because it is intermediate and temporary. For instance, in 1 Thessalonians 4:13-18, where the believers in Thessalonica are concerned about whether deceased members of the community are at some disadvantage at the Lord's coming, Paul says nothing about an intermediate state. One text seems to indicate a belief in an intermediate existence, and another could

---

Buist M. Fanning, *Verbal Aspect in New Testament Greek* (Oxford: Clarendon, 1990); K. L. McKay, *A New Syntax of the Verb in New Testament Greek: An Aspectual Approach,* SBG 5 (New York: Peter Lang, 1994).
[8]I believe that it was written during his Roman imprisonment.

be interpreted to support such a view. When Paul reflects on the possibility of his death in Philippians 1:19-26, he finds death preferable because then he would be "with Christ" (Phil 1:23). One could possibly say that he anticipates being with Christ at his resurrection. It is more natural, though, to conclude that Paul would be with Christ immediately after his death since he seems to find an instantaneous benefit in death. No other passage speaks clearly to the question of an intermediate state, but some think Paul refers to it in 2 Corinthians 5:1-4, understanding "nakedness" after death to be the intermediate state and "being clothed" to the future resurrection of the body. It is also possible, however, that "nakedness" here refers to the lack of good works at the coming judgment (2 Cor 5:10). Still, when Paul speaks about being "absent from the body and present with the Lord" (2 Cor 5:8), this seems to imply an intermediate state because one who is resurrected is not absent from the body.

Judgment of Unbelievers

2 Thessalonians 1. One of the consistent features of Paul's gospel is that unbelievers will face a future judgment. The decision as to whether one should believe in the gospel is not an idle one; the destiny of human beings is at stake. One of the most developed statements on the judgment of the wicked appears in 2 Thessalonians 1:5-10. The judgment *(krisis)* inflicted on the unrighteous is designated as "righteous" *(dikaios)* in 1 Thessalonians 1:5-6, especially since those who do evil persecute God's people. Postmoderns tend to find any reference to judgment repulsive and unworthy of a loving God. Paul, on the contrary, thinks that God's judgment is righteous, which implies that the failure to inflict judgment would render God unrighteous. The deviation between Paul and contemporary thought is evident precisely here, for many today would not be troubled if God overlooked most human sin and included all in salvation. Paul, on the contrary, thinks God's righteousness is manifested precisely because he inflicts judgment on unbelievers.

The elements of the judgment are sketched in more clearly as the text unfolds. The judgment cannot be assigned to the natural consequences of sin in this world, for it eventuates at the return of Christ, "at the revelation of the Lord Jesus from heaven with his mighty angels" (2 Thess 1:7). Jesus will inflict punishment on those who have persecuted believers, but the judgment will not be limited only to those who engaged in persecution. When Jesus returns, he inflicts "vengeance upon those who do not know God and those who do not obey the gospel of our Lord Jesus" (2 Thess 1:8). This righteous judgment of God is reserved for all those who do not know God in a saving way. It also falls on those who have not submitted to the gospel in obedience. The gospel summons all to believe, and the refusal to believe is not merely an intellectual matter but one that strikes at the heart of who we are as human beings. One's refusal to believe signals a disloyalty toward and a rebellion against the Lord Jesus. What kind of penalty is imposed on those who disobey the gospel and do not know God? The penalty could be temporary, but Paul rules this out in 2 Thessalonians 1:9. The penalty is "eternal destruction" (*olethron aiōnion*) in which a person is excluded "from the presence of the Lord and from the glory of his strength." Unbelievers are excluded from the beauty of Christ's presence forever.

Future destruction. The future judgment threads its way through all of Paul's writings, usually without extended comment. Its pervasiveness, though, signals its importance in his thought. He often speaks of those who are perishing (*apollymi*, 1 Cor 1:18; 15:18; 2 Cor 2:15; 4:3; 2 Thess 2:10). The word *perishing* designates the future destiny of those who reject the gospel. Instead of being saved they are destined for destruction. Those perishing despise the word of the cross and find it foolish (1 Cor 1:18). To them the gospel has a terrible aroma that drives them away, for it is not an aroma of life, joy and peace but carries the stench of death (2 Cor 2:14-15). Satan has blinded the minds of those perishing so that they do not perceive the beauty of Christ in the gospel proclaimed by Paul (2 Cor 4:3-5). Similarly, those perishing "did not welcome the love of the truth so that they would be saved" (2 Thess 2:10). They perish because they find the truth repugnant and odious.

People perish because they repudiate the gospel, and Paul also invokes a curse (*anathema*, Gal 1:8-9) on those who proclaim a different gospel. Those who preach a variant gospel are destined to destruction. Believing the gospel inevitably involves a fervent love for the Lord Jesus Christ, and so Paul pronounces a similar curse on those who do not love the Lord (1 Cor 16:22). Conversely, God's grace rests on those who love the Lord Jesus Christ with an incorruptible or indestructible love (Eph 6:24).

The noun "destruction" (*apōleia*) is also used to refer to those who are destined to receive God's judgment. Opposition to the church is a sign of destruction; and, conversely, suffering as part of the church is a sign of salvation (Phil 1:28). Paul weeps over the presence of opponents in Philippians 3:18-19. He considers them to be enemies of the cross (Phil 3:18). "Their god is their belly and their glory is their shame and they think about the things of the earth" (Phil 3:19). Because of these things, their "end" (*telos*), or outcome, is "destruction" (Phil 3:19). Destruction is reserved for those who do not cling to the cross of Christ (cf. Phil 3:2-11) as their only hope for righteousness and vindication on the last day. Those who have a righteousness that is their own (Phil 3:9) will find that it is insufficient to stave off God's wrath. They are truly enemies of the cross. Those who long to become rich and crown money as their god have the same unhappy destiny, for in their case the end result is "ruin and destruction" (*olethron kai apōleian*, 1 Tim 6:9).

Judgment according to works. We have seen that destruction impends for those who do not believe in the gospel, do not have a love for the Lord Jesus Christ and do not delight in the truth of God. Paul also speaks of judgment on those who do not practice good works. In one sense, of course, all lack the necessary works to be saved—salvation is only through faith in Jesus Christ. On the other hand, as we have seen, good works are necessary to inherit eternal life.[9] It is not surprising, then, that those who experience judgment are those who fail to do good works. The call for good works is not a foreign element in Paul's gospel but a constitutive part of it. God judges those who do what is evil (Rom 2:1-2), repaying each person according to his works (Rom 2:6). We must notice that evil works, according to the previous verse (Rom 2:5), stem from a "hard and unrepentant heart," indicating that the way one lives is a reflection of the heart's disposition toward God.

Those who are disobedient to God have the same problem as those who constructed the golden calf—they are stiff-necked and obstinate (Ex 32:9; 33:3, 5; 34:9). Those who have hard hearts will experience God's "wrath" (*orgē*) on the day of his righteous judgment (Rom 2:5) because they failed to do good works. His "wrath and anger" (*orgē kai thymos*) will be inflicted on those who are dominated by "selfish ambition and who *disobey* the truth and obey unrighteousness" (Rom 2:8). Romans 2:9 states the same truth in another way: every single person who does evil will experience "tribulation and distress." This verse captures the psychological dimension of future judgment, in that those who experience God's judgment will be overwhelmed with distress and sorrow. Romans 2:8 provides the reason for their distress and sorrow—the wrath and anger of God. Notice that God's future judgment and his inflicting of wrath and evil are not merely the outworking of cause and effect, as if judgment is the impersonal effect of doing wrong. God personally and righteously inflicts his wrath on those who have dis-

---

[9]On the necessity of good works for eternal life, see Thomas R. Schreiner, "Did Paul Believe in Justification by Works? Another Look at Romans 2," *BBR* 31 (1993): 131-58.

obeyed him. The whole paragraph (Romans 2:6-11) underscores what the basis for the judgment is, namely, doing what is evil.

In Romans 2:12 the failure to do what the law requires will result in judgment for both Jews and Gentiles. Paul speaks of the destiny of the unrighteous as an experience of "judgment" *(krithēsontai)* and "destruction" *(apolountai)*, indicating that both terms together describe what the disobedient will experience. Paul does not maintain that the works are always evident to human beings, for in the same paragraph we see that "God will judge the secrets of human beings" on the day of judgment and in accord with Paul's gospel (Rom 2:16). Some people, in other words, manage to conceal to some extent the depth of their evil. The final judgment, however, will lift the veil so that the truth is plain to all. Those who worshiped themselves and those who relied on God will become evident. It follows, therefore, that the final judgment is not ethereal or mysterious but that it accords with the concrete realities of everyday life. Those who have done evil cannot plead ignorance, nor will they be able to deny what is done, for how they have lived will be manifest to all. We must also notice that God's judgment accords with the gospel. Some have said that judgment contradicts the gospel, but Paul himself sees judgment as a constitutive part of his gospel.

The need for good works to avert judgment is an integral part of Paul's gospel. The opponents in Corinth are described as "false apostles, deceitful workers, and those who transform themselves as apostles of Christ" (2 Cor 11:13). They advertise themselves as people who do good works and claim to be "servants of righteousness" (2 Cor 11:15), but all of this is subterfuge. The good works are lacking, "and their end shall be according to their works." Similarly, the adversaries in Philippi are "evil workers" (Phil 3:2), and the Judaizers in Galatia do not keep the law themselves (Gal 6:13). Alexander the coppersmith, who resisted Paul so intensely, would face judgment in accord with his deeds (2 Tim 4:14). When Paul speaks of judgment according to works, therefore, it is likely that he has in mind works necessary for obtaining eternal life, not merely a reward above and beyond eternal life (2 Cor 5:10). Paul does not teach that his opponents are sincere and humane people who merely have a difference of opinion. He is persuaded that they are evil when measured by the gospel's standard.

We must say again, however, that the judgment according to works cannot be isolated from the Pauline gospel. Any good works are the fruit and outworking of the gospel itself. They do not constitute an earning of salvation, nor does Paul conceive of anyone attaining perfection in this life (Phil 3:12-

16). Those who practice evil reveal that they have never trusted in Jesus Christ for salvation (Rom 3:21-26), and they have not experienced the transforming work of the Holy Spirit (Rom 2:28-29). Good works in the lives of believers testify to the power of the gospel, and hence those who lack good works reveal that they have never placed their trust in the gospel.

The Future of Israel

What place does Israel play in Paul's theology? This question is being urgently asked today, especially subsequent to the Holocaust, for some believe that Christian theology is at least partially responsible for the horrible evil perpetrated against Jews. Paul's own conception of Israel is quite complex, defying simplistic formulations. At the outset we must remember that Paul himself was a Jew and that he conceived of his faith in Jesus as the Christ as a *fulfillment* of what the Old Testament promised the Jewish people (e.g., Rom 1:1-4). Those Jews who repudiated Jesus, according to Paul, were not true to their heritage. They were like the Jews who strayed from Yahweh and were then exiled by Assyria and Babylon.[10]

Paul's prophetic critique of Israel. Those who are truly sons and daughters of Abraham put their faith in Jesus as the Messiah (Gal 3:6-9). Accordingly, Gentiles become part of the family of Abraham if they believe in Jesus as Messiah. Conversely, those Jews who fail to believe in Jesus reveal that they are not truly sons or daughters of Abraham. A genealogical relationship to Abraham does not automatically qualify one to be part of the people of God (Rom 9:6-13). Paul does not criticize his Jewish contemporaries simply to attack his foes or to win cheap debating points. What he says about some of his Jewish contemporaries can be traced to the Old Testament itself. The history of Israel is marked by a winnowing process. Even in the wilderness a few believed but most failed to trust in God. The days of the judges were ones in which the hearts of many in Israel drifted from Yahweh. The prophets likewise taught that only a remnant truly belonged to God, while most of the nation turned to other gods. In Paul's day a remnant of Israel believed (cf. Rom 9:29), but the majority turned away from the living God.

Paul scarcely saw himself, therefore, as anti-Jewish or as deviating from his ancestors in his invectives against some fellow Jews. Those Jews who did not believe in Jesus as the Messiah were culpable before God and guilty of sin, just

---

[10]For an excellent discussion of the issue of anti-Semitism in the early church, see Craig A. Evans and Donald A. Hagner, eds., *Anti-Semitism and Early Christianity: Issues of Polemic and Faith* (Minneapolis: Fortress, 1993).

as the wilderness generation was judged by God for its idolatry (1 Cor 10:1-12). The problem with Paul's Jewish contemporaries was that they did not keep the very Torah they taught (Rom 2:1-29; 3:9-20; Gal 3:10). Paul did not think their loyalty to Torah exceeded his own. Instead, he believed that genuine loyalty to Torah would lead to faith in Jesus as the Messiah because he fulfills what the Torah promised. Some Jews, despite their failure to keep the Torah, used the Torah as a means of propagating their own righteousness (Rom 9:30—10:8; Phil 3:2-11). Paul rejects such law-righteousness because it is founded on an illusion and it fosters idolatry. It is founded on an illusion because no one keeps the law (Rom 7:7-25). It promotes idolatry, for those who are devoted to Torah begin to think that their righteousness is pleasing to God.

It should be said that Paul follows in the footsteps of Jesus, for Jesus himself warned about the danger of self-righteousness and taught that God justifies sinners who plead for forgiveness (Lk 18:9-14). The Pauline criticisms are not from an outside observer: a singular devotion to Torah characterized Paul's life (Gal 1:13-14; Phil 3:4-6), leading him, perhaps unconsciously and quite subtly, to the idea that he was especially pleasing to God. Subsequent to his conversion Paul embraced the righteousness of God in Christ as a gift, and he disavowed self-righteousness (Phil 3:7-11).

Those Jews who promote Torah and circumcision, therefore, are labeled as "evil workers" (Phil 3:2). A curse *(anathema)* is pronounced on those who proclaim a gospel that demands circumcision (Gal 1:8-9). Those who insist on circumcision for salvation are classified as "false brothers" (Gal 2:4). They promote Torah observance to avoid the scandal of the cross and to curry favor in the sight of others (Gal 6:12-13). Paul's emotions run high when he thinks of some Jews who hinder the proclamation of the gospel. Advocates of circumcision are described as "the mutilation" *(katatomē, Phil 3:2)*, and Paul sarcastically recommends that the Galatian adversaries "castrate themselves" *(apokopsontai, Gal 5:12)*.

1 Thessalonians 2:14-16. Given the texts discussed above, the negative words about the Jews in 1 Thessalonians 2:14-16 are not as surprising as some suppose. Some scholars think the passage is a later interpolation, especially because it contradicts Paul's more positive assessment of the Jews in Romans 9—11.[11] Interpolation theories are notoriously hard to disprove since textual evidence is not necessarily needed to advance them. The burden of proof,

---

[11]Those who support an interpolation include Birger Pearson, "I Thessalonians 2:13-16: A Deutero-Pauline Interpolation," *HTR* 64 (1971): 79-91; D. Schmidt, "I Thess 2:13-16: Linguistic Evidence for an Interpolation," *JBL* 102 (1983): 269-79.

however, surely lies on those supporting the interpolation theory since the verses are well-established in the textual tradition. In any case, harsh words about opponents (cf. 2 Cor 11:13-15), as we have just seen, seem to be characteristic of Paul, so there is no compelling reason to doubt the authenticity of these verses.[12]

Some accept the authenticity of 1 Thessalonians 2:14-16 but think it contradicts Paul's positive assessment of the Jews in Romans 9—11 since in the 1 Thessalonians text Paul consigns Jews to destruction, while in the Romans text he announces that they will be saved in the future.[13] A more sympathetic reading of 1 Thessalonians 2:14-16 and Romans 9—11, however, indicates that no contradiction exists. Impassioned words are wielded against the Jews—for they killed the Lord Jesus and the prophets, they persecuted Paul, they failed to please God, they are hostile to all people and they attempt to prevent Paul from proclaiming the gospel (1 Thess 2:14-16). Paul concludes that they have filled up the full measure of their sins and that wrath has come on them to the end. One element of continuity between the harsh words in 1 Thessalonians 2 and the opponents in Galatia and Philippi must be noted. Paul criticizes the Jews because they hinder the proclamation of the gospel, and the gospel is the means by which people are saved (1 Thess 2:16). Paul's vehemence against the Jews is rooted in his desire to see others rescued from God's wrath. Paul's strong words about some Jews, therefore, flow from his commitment to the gospel. He is convinced that those opposing the gospel are bringing destruction on themselves and others. Identifying 1 Thessalonians 2:13-16 as either unrestrained emotion or as hateful is mistaken, for the invective against the Jews stems from a desire to see others helped, from a desire to see others saved. Paul's words follow in the train of the Old Testament prophets who indicted Israelite leaders because they induced the nation to sin and did not restrain them from transgression (e.g., Jer 4:4-6; 8:8-12; 14:13-22; 20:1-6; 21:1-12; 22:1-30; 23:9-40; 36:27-31; Ezek 13:1-14:11; 19:1-14; 22:6-12, 25-28; Hos 5:1-14; Mic 3:1-12; Zeph 3:3-4). Paul would not have viewed himself as disloyal to his Jewish heritage but as faithful to his apostolic calling, for like the prophets of old he calls his people to account, reminding them of impending judgment.

---

[12]Defending the authenticity of the text is Donald A. Hagner, "Paul's Quarrel with Judaism," in *Anti-Semitism and Early Christianity: Issues of Polemic and Faith,* ed. Craig A. Evans and Donald A. Hagner (Minneapolis: Fortress, 1993), pp. 130-36.

[13]For example, John W. Simpson Jr., "The Problems Posed by 1 Thessalonians 2:15-16 and a Solution," *HBT* 12 (1990): 42-72.

The alleged contradiction between 1 Thessalonians 2:14-16 and Romans 9—11 admits of a plausible resolution. The apparent difficulty in harmonizing the two texts can be resolved only by anticipating my understanding of Paul's view of Israel in Romans 9—11, a matter to which we shall turn shortly. The texts appear to be contradictory because Paul predicts Israel's future salvation in Romans 11:26, whereas a future condemnation of Israel is enunciated here. In actuality, however, Paul does not pronounce a future judgment on all Jews in 1 Thessalonians 2:14-16. First Thessalonians 2:14 introduces a comparison between the Thessalonian Christians and believers in Judea. Both have been subjected to suffering by their fellow citizens. What must be noticed is that virtually all the Christians in Judea who suffered at the hands of their fellow countrymen were Jews. So, when Paul names the Jews in 1 Thessalonians 2:14 and begins his series of indictments that issues with the climax in 1 Thessalonians 2:16, it is imperative to note that 1 Thessalonians 2:14 already indicates that he refers *only to some Jews*. The Jews on whom he pronounces judgment are persecuting *other Jews in Judea who believe in Jesus as the Christ.* There is no warrant, therefore, to understand 1 Thessalonians 2:14-16 as a blanket indictment on all Jews. Paul's harsh words are for those Jews who persecute the church of Jesus Christ and hinder the preaching of the gospel. We need to remember that Paul did not foresee the Holocaust, nor the horrible things that Christians have done to Jews in intervening centuries, when Christians ruled and Jews were mistreated. Paul addresses a situation in which the church was a minority and in which the Jews who opposed the gospel were at the top of the social ladder. Paul's strong words are directed to the oppressors, and they are sadly misused if they are used to justify violence or oppression of Jews in our own day or at any other period of history.

In saying that "wrath has come upon them to the end" (1 Thess 2:16), it is unlikely that the destruction of Jerusalem is anticipated. The language fits with a threat of eternal destruction, a judgment that never ends. Those Jews who oppose the gospel and persecute believers have a grim destiny before them, one in which they will experience God's wrath forever. We have already seen in 2 Thessalonians 1:5-10 that the same sentence is pronounced against Gentiles who afflict and persecute believers. Paul's words here are scarcely novel or astonishing. On the other hand, we must beware of reading these few verses as if they constitute a complete treatise on the Jews. The possibility that some of the Jewish opponents may still be converted and rescued from God's wrath is not eliminated by the finality of the language. Otherwise, it would be hard to see how Paul could explain his own conversion. He himself at one time resisted fiercely those who preached the gospel! What we have here is the language of generalization. Those Jews who oppose the gospel and persecute God's people fill up their sins and will experience God's eschatological wrath. Paul knows that the category of unrepentant opponents will certainly be filled by some, but he is not ruling out the prospect that some who are now opponents may eventually repent.

The seriousness of what Paul says here must not be underestimated since those Jews who oppose the gospel are threatened with judgment. On the other hand, the verses could also be wrongly turned into a treatise, as if they provide a complete and definitive explanation of the future of the Jews. Paul addresses one situation, and his words must be correlated with what he says elsewhere. If the interpretation proposed here is correct, no contradiction between Romans 9—11 and 1 Thessalonians 2:14-16 exists—for Paul does not promise the salvation of all Jews without exception in Romans, and in 1 Thessalonians 2:14-16 he does not pronounce judgment on all Jews without exception. First Thessalonians enunciates judgment on those Jews who persecute the church of Jesus Christ and oppose the gospel. What Romans 11 promises shall now be explored in more detail.

Romans 9—11

What we should notice at the outset is Paul's fervent desire in Romans 9—11 for his fellow Jews to be saved. Romans 10:1 says this explicitly, and in Romans 9:1-3 the same idea is communicated in an indirect and poignant manner. Paul speaks in a manner analogous to that of Moses—almost willing to be cursed for the sake of the salvation of Israel. The harsh words against fellow Jews in 1 Thessalonians 2:14-16 must be integrated with what Paul says here, for the threat of impending judgment does not exclude a desire for future salvation, even when the writer knows that some will never repent.

Much of the content of Romans 9—11 has been explored previously. The litany of Israel's privileges in Romans 9:4-5 serves as a reminder that the Israelites are God's covenant people and the recipients of his saving promises. Such promises are not limited to the past, for God's word to his people cannot be nullified (Rom 9:6). God's saving righteousness is displayed in fulfilling his promises to Israel. Even though every ethnic Israelite is not saved, a remnant belongs to God, for salvation is the result of his grace and is dependent not on human works but on God's call (Rom 9:6-13). If Romans 9 stresses God's faithfulness in fulfilling his promises to his people, Romans 10 (actually Rom 9:30—10:21) denotes Israel's failure to believe in the gospel. Israel attempted to be right with God by working instead of believing. No contradiction exists between chapters 9 and 10, for Paul did not understand divine sovereignty in such a way that it excluded human responsibility. Indeed, divine sovereignty is the orbit in which human responsibility functions. Paul is an heir here to the Old Testament tradition that ascribes all things to Yahweh, including which way the dice lands (Prov 16:33) and even the inclination of a king's heart (Prov 21:1). Such meticulous sovereignty, however, does not absolve humans of genuine responsibility for their actions.

Is Paul's final word on Israel limited to the promise that a remnant will be saved? At the beginning of Romans 11 God's faithfulness to Israel is reaffirmed inasmuch as he has not rejected the Jews, the objects of his covenantal favor (Rom 11:1-6). Paul introduces himself as an example of God's selection of a remnant, for just as Yahweh preserved seven thousand who were devoted to him in the days of Elijah, so in the present era he maintains a remnant by his gracious election. The hardening of the majority of Israel in the present (Rom 11:7-10) is not the final word, nor should it be interpreted as Israel's permanent fate (Rom 11:11-16). God has designed redemptive history to accentuate the wonder of his grace, so that it always seizes people with a surprise that evokes gratefulness and awe. The choice of Isaac rather than Ishmael overturned the expectations of Abraham and Sarah, filling them with joy at God's unexpected mercy (Rom 9:6-9). Similarly, he overturned human calculations in showering his grace and favor on Jacob instead of on the firstborn, Esau (Rom 9:10-13). In Paul's day God continued to upend human expectations. He hardens Israel and bestows salvation on the Gentiles. The Israelites anticipated that they would be the recipients of God's salvation while the Gentiles would be largely excluded or at least be clearly subsidiary. God has overturned human prerogatives to stave off pride, which is disposed to take credit for the good bestowed. The Gentiles are admonished to avoid pride (Rom 11:20-22), for the proud would fall into the same error as Israel in thinking that they are somehow qualified to receive God's mercy. Looking back twenty centuries, we can see how prescient Paul's words were, since Gentiles have often vaunted themselves over against Israel.

The stunning conclusion to salvation history, however, is that God will once again soften Israel and turn the Jews to himself. At the end of history God will surprise Israel, so that those who have disbelieved will perceive that Jesus is the Messiah. Paul anticipates "their fullness" (plērōma, Rom 11:12), that is, their "acceptance" (proslōmpsis, Rom 11:15). This probably means that they will be accepted by God for salvation and again be members of God's people. The olive tree (Rom 11:17-24) represents the people of God throughout history, and God has surprisingly grafted wild branches from the Gentiles onto the tree and removed many of the original Jewish branches. Nevertheless, the removal of many of the original olive branches is not the final word relative to Israel. God will graft many of the original olive branches back onto the olive tree at the conclusion of history.

All Israel will be saved. The explanation of Israel's role comes to a climax with the revelation of the mystery in Romans 11:25-27. The word *mystery* stems from an apocalyptic background (e.g., Dan 2:18-19, 27-30; 1QpHab 7:1-5, 8, 13-14), denoting a secret plan of God that has previously been hidden and now has been revealed. The mystery revealed here is not limited to Israel, though it finds its climax in God's plan for Israel. The mystery has at least three elements: (1) the partial hardening of Israel throughout history; (2) the influx of the fullness of the Gentiles into the church of Jesus Christ; and (3) the future salvation of ethnic Israel. The focal point of the mystery is the timing and manner of Israel's salvation, for all Israel will be saved *after* the full number of Gentiles have entered into the people of God.[14]

Some interpreters, on the other hand, interpret the salvation of "all Israel" to denote the church of Jesus Christ, which is composed of both Jews and Gentiles. Such an understanding of Israel was suggested by John Calvin and has as contemporary representatives scholars like Ralph Martin and N. T. Wright.[15] Paul certainly emphasizes elsewhere that believers are true Jews, the true circumcision, and part of the family of Israel (see below). The context of Romans 11, however, limits Israel to ethnic Israel. In Romans 11:17-24 ethnic Jews and Gentiles are distinguished in the illustration of the olive tree. Even more decisive is Romans 11:25, for hardening is ascribed to "Israel" and salvation to "Gentiles." When salvation is promised to "all Israel" in Romans 11:26, it is difficult to believe that Israel should be defined differently in verse 26 than in verse 25. It is scarcely clear that Paul suddenly lurches to a new definition so that verse 25 refers to ethnic Israel whereas verse 26 refers to spiritual Israel. In both verses Paul refers to ethnic Israel, but verse 25

---

[14]I am not suggesting that *kai houtōs* is temporal, only that the context reveals that Israel's salvation will occur after the salvation of the Gentiles.

[15]Ralph P. Martin, *Reconciliation: A Study of Paul's Theology*, rev. ed. (Grand Rapids, Mich.: Zondervan, 1989), pp. 134-35; N. T. Wright, *The New Testament and the People of God*, vol. 1 of *Christian Origins and the Question of God* (Minneapolis: Fortress, 1992), pp. 236-46; cf. also John Calvin, *The Epistles of Paul the Apostle to the Romans and to the Thessalonians*, ed. D. W. Torrance and T. F. Torrance (Grand Rapids, Mich.: Eerdmans, 1960), p. 255.

describes the hardening of most of Israel during the time when Gentiles are converted, and verse 26 promises the future salvation of ethnic Israel. Is it possible, though, that Paul suddenly shifts the definition of Israel in verse 26? Yes, it is possible, but the succeeding context reveals that it is implausible and unpersuasive. Romans 11:28-29 confirms that ethnic Israel is the subject of Romans 11:26, for they are enemies of the gospel, but they are beloved by God and the recipients of God's irrevocable promises because of God's covenantal promises to the patriarchs. Paul does not restate his argument in Romans 11:28-29 by conceiving of Israel in a spiritual sense, as if Israel comprises believing Jews and Gentiles. Rather, he emphasizes again that ethnic Israel is the object of God's saving and elect love because of God's sovereign and effective grace. No contextual warrant appears for widening the definition of Israel. The climax of the mystery is that God will pour out his grace again on ethnic Israel, the children of Abraham, Isaac and Jacob.

Most scholars agree that Paul has ethnic Israel in mind in Romans 11:26 when he makes the statement "all Israel shall be saved."[16] But what does Paul mean when he says "all Israel shall be saved"? Is he promising that all Jews who ever lived will be saved, regardless of whether they have put their faith in Jesus as Messiah? Or, alternatively, does he intend to say that the remnant of Jews throughout history who have put their faith in Jesus will be saved? Or is he speaking of the salvation of the Jews at the end of history, near the time when Jesus will return? Let us address these questions one at a time, and it will be argued that the last view is the most accurate.

It has become increasingly popular to argue that salvation is envisioned for Israel apart from faith in Christ. Krister Stendahl propounded this view in an important essay, and it has been promoted by scholars who advocate a two-covenant theory of salvation, like Lloyd Gaston and John Gager.[17] The two-covenant theory says that Gentiles are saved through faith in Christ and that Jews are saved by adhering faithfully to the Torah. It is also pointed out that in Romans 11 Paul does not say Jews must believe in Christ to be saved, suggesting that faith in Jesus as Messiah is unnecessary for Jewish salvation. This interpretation certainly comports with postmodern sensibilities, but it is

---

[16]For a more detailed defense of this view, see Thomas R. Schreiner, *Romans*, BECNT (Grand Rapids, Mich.: Baker, 1998), pp. 611-23.

[17]Krister Stendahl, *Paul Among Jews and Gentiles and Other Essays* (Philadelphia: Fortress, 1976), p. 3; Lloyd Gaston, *Paul and the Torah* (Vancouver: University of British Columbia Press, 1987), p. 92-99; John G. Gager, *The Origins of Anti-Semitism: Attitudes Toward Judaism in Pagan and Christian Antiquity* (New York: Oxford University Press, 1983), pp. 252, 261.

exegetically unpersuasive.[18] Romans 11 must be interpreted within the context of Romans 9—11, and the chapters open with Paul's deep sorrow that Israel is separated from *Christ* (Rom 9:3), revealing that the only way they can be right with God is through faith in Jesus as Messiah (Rom 9:5). Israel is criticized for failing to believe in Christ, and salvation for both Jews and Gentiles is explicitly attributed to the proclaimed word of the gospel (Rom 9:31—10:21). Paul's prayer for Israel's salvation is superfluous (Rom 10:1) if Stendahl is correct, because the Israel that Paul has in mind is already zealously devoted to Torah (Rom 10:2-4). If the two-covenant theory were correct, Paul should praise the Jews for their devotion to Torah instead of indicting them. Paul dismisses Israel's zeal for Torah as a false path, insisting instead that the only righteousness that counts before God comes from believing in Christ, not from doing the law (Rom 10:4-13). We should also note that disbelieving Jews are not considered to be part of the olive tree but represent severed branches. In Romans 11:23 the removal of Israel from the olive tree is attributed to "unbelief," and it is almost certain that unbelief in Christ is intended. It is difficult to see why Paul would conceive of the need to graft the original Jewish branches back into the tree if one needed only to observe Torah to be part of God's people. Indeed, the "deliverer coming from Zion" who rescues Israel (Rom 11:26) is probably Jesus himself. No convincing exegetical grounds exist, then, to think that Paul envisioned a salvation for Israel apart from faith in Jesus Christ.

Other scholars take a different tack and maintain that "all Israel" refers to the remnant of Jews throughout history who have been saved.[19] Others have gone farther and have even suggested that those who are hardened by God will eventually be saved.[20] According to this latter opinion, the hardening referred to in Romans 9 (Rom 9:18-22) will eventually be reversed by the grace of God. There is no indication, however, in Romans 9:21-23 that the vessels of wrath will eventually become vessels of mercy. Nor should Romans 11:26 be understood to promise the salvation of all Jews that ever lived.

---

[18]For a view that harmonizes with my exegesis, see Scott J. Hafemann, "The Salvation of Israel in Romans 11:25-32: A Response to Krister Stendahl," *ExAud* 4 (1988): 38-58; Reidar Hvalvik, "A 'Sonderweg' for Israel: A Critical Examination of a Current Interpretation of Romans 11.25-27," *JSNT* 38 (1990): 87-107; E. P. Sanders, "Paul's Attitude Toward the Jewish People," *USQR* 33 (1978): 175-87.

[19]For example, Herman Ridderbos, *Paul: An Outline of His Theology* (Grand Rapids, Mich.: Eerdmans, 1975), pp. 358-59; D. W. B. Robinson, "The Salvation of Israel in Romans 9—11," *RTR* 26 (1967): 94-95.

[20]For example, James D. G. Dunn, *Romans*, WBC (Dallas: Word, 1988), 2:555.

Romans 11:25 clarifies that the salvation of Israel in verse 26 will only occur *after* the fullness of the Gentiles is completed. The manner in which Israel is saved *(kai houtōs)* in context is inextricably intertwined with *the time* in which they are saved (i.e., after the fullness of the Gentiles enter in).[21] Such a reading is confirmed by the Old Testament citation in Romans 11:26. Israel will be saved when "the deliverer comes from Zion" (Is 59:20). The deliverer here is most likely Jesus Christ. He will come from Zion at his second coming and "remove ungodliness from Jacob." The salvation promised to Israel, then, is not a salvation of all Jews that ever lived, but a salvation of the end-time generation *after* the salvation of the Gentiles and associated with the return of Christ.

Romans 11:15 seems to confirm this interpretation, for "life from the dead" follows Israel's acceptance by God. Most scholars agree that "life from the dead" refers to the resurrection. Israel's "acceptance" (i.e., her conversion) in Romans 11:15 is also described as her "fullness" in Romans 11:12 since the two verses are clearly parallel. Paul is likely teaching, then, that the resurrection of the dead, the consummation of history, will follow Israel's conversion. If this is the case, we can conclude that the salvation of Israel occurs at the end of time since her salvation and acceptance will be immediately followed by the resurrection of the dead. During the course of salvation history most of Israel has transgressed the gospel and been removed by God (Rom 11:12, 15). Of course, a remnant of Jews embraced the gospel during the whole period of salvation history. Paul envisions, however, a different state of affairs in which Israel as a whole embraces the gospel, and at that juncture God concludes history and raises his people from the dead.

Those who support the idea that Paul envisions the salvation of Jews throughout all of redemptive history also fail to account for the climactic nature of Romans 11. Paul has already clarified in Romans 9:1—11:10 that a remnant of Jews are saved throughout history. Romans 11:11-32 would add little that is new to the argument if it simply reprised that theme. The language of mystery employed in Romans 11:25 reveals that Paul adds a new, previously concealed truth. The mystery, as already suggested, involves three elements: (1) a partial hardening of Israel; (2) the fullness of Gentiles entering in; and (3) the salvation of all Israel. The first two points, in and of themselves, scarcely constitute a new argument in Romans 9—11. What is decisive is the third point. For Romans 11:25 clarifies that the partial hard-

---

[21]For my discussion of this point, see Schreiner, *Romans*, pp. 619-21.

ening of Israel will not last forever. Israel will only be hardened "until [*achri*] the fullness of the Gentiles enter in." Romans 11:26 specifies the manner *(kai houtōs)* in which all Israel shall be saved, and the logical relation of verse 26 to verse 25 shows that the manner also involves *time*. That is, Israel shall be saved *in this way, after* the fullness of the Gentiles enter in. Such a temporal statement indicates that Paul is not speaking of the salvation of a remnant of Israel throughout history. He contemplates a salvation of "all Israel" *after* the salvation of Gentiles is completed. What Paul has in mind, therefore, is not merely the salvation of a Jewish remnant throughout history but the salvation of an end-time generation of Jews. Indeed, Romans 11:26 also suggests that this salvation will occur near or at the coming of Jesus Christ, for he is likely the deliverer who comes from Zion and removes ungodliness from his people.

Is Paul contradictory? Some scholars think Paul contradicts himself in Romans 9—11 because he begins Romans 9 by saying that God does not choose anyone based on their ethnic background (Rom 9:6), yet in the end salvation is promised to ethnic Israel precisely because of their ethnic background.[22] Is the ethnic principle repudiated in chapter 9 reappropriated in chapter 11? The claim to see a contradiction is unpersuasive.[23] Paul nowhere argues, not even in Romans 11, that all ethnic Jews without exception will be saved. What he does argue is that after a period of time—in which Israel is hardened and Gentiles are being included in salvation—all Israel shall be saved. God's gracious bestowal of his saving mercy on Israel at the end of history does not violate the freedom of his grace, for salvation is not promised to every single ethnic Israelite on the basis of ethnic background. The structuring of redemptive history, in fact, features the freedom and unexpected nature of God's grace. He chooses Gentiles when Israel expects to receive his salvation. And then, when all hope for Israel's salvation seems to be gone, God's grace intervenes afresh, delivering Israel when the hope of its salvation is nearly extinguished. By structuring salvation history in this way

---

[22]Supporting a contradiction here are E. P. Sanders, *Paul, the Law, and the Jewish People* (Philadelphia: Fortress, 1983), pp. 193, 197-99; Hans Hübner, *Gottes Ich und Israel: Zum Schriftgebrauch des Paulus in Römer 9—11*, FRLANT 136 (Göttingen: Vandenhoeck & Ruprecht, 1984), p. 122; Heikki Räisänen, "Paul, God and Israel: Romans 9—11 in Recent Research," in *The Social World of Formative Christianity and Judaism: Essays in Tribute to Howard Clark Kee*, ed. J. Neusner, E. S. Frerichs, P. Borgen and R. Horsley (Philadelphia: Fortress, 1988), pp. 192-96.

[23]See the illuminating article by Frank Thielman, "Unexpected Mercy: Echoes of a Biblical Motif in Romans 9—11," *SJT* 47 (1994): 169-81.

the grace of God is featured instead of the virtue of human beings, whether they be Jews or Gentiles. Nor is God's freedom restricted in fulfilling his promise to the Jews, for the God who first made the promise in freedom wills to fulfill the promise that he freely made.

Another area of tension relates to Paul's understanding of the church of Jesus Christ as the true Israel. In Romans 2:28-29 true Jewishness and true circumcision belong to those who have had the work of the Holy Spirit in their hearts, so that the people of God is not limited to ethnic Jews but includes all those who are beneficiaries of the new-covenant work of the Spirit. Similarly, in Philippians 3:2-3 the true circumcision effected by God's Spirit is contrasted with physical circumcision that is external only. Not only is the church the true circumcision, but believers are also part of the family of Abraham since they are sons of Abraham. Participation in Abraham's family is through faith in Jesus Christ and not circumcision (Rom 4:1-17; Gal 3:6-9, 26-29). Abraham is the father of all who believe, whether Jews or Gentiles. All those who have the Holy Spirit have received the blessing of Abraham (Gal 3:1-5, 14; Is 44:3). Finally, Paul says that believers in Christ are "the Israel of God" (Gal 6:16). Some scholars insist that "Israel of God" is limited to Jewish believers in Galatians 6:16. The grammar of the verse has been studied intensely to decipher whether the Israel of God is separate from, or identified with, the church.[24] The decision cannot rest on the grammar alone, which can be construed in both ways, but must be discerned from the argument of the letter as a whole.

I would suggest that a reference to the church is the most plausible way to read Galatians 6:16. The whole argument of Galatians is that Gentile believers are part of the family of Abraham by faith. They are the true circumcision through the work of Christ on the cross. Segregating the Israel of God from Gentile believers at the close of the letter would send exactly the wrong message to Judaizers, for it would suggest that the Israel of God is distinct from the church. And if this were the case, it would raise the question of circumcision afresh. Should Gentiles become part of God's elite people, the Israel of God, by circumcision? Gentiles would likely feel that they still lack something vitally important if Jewish believers alone are the Israel of God, and hence circumcision and Jewishness would seem to be introduced in a way that would vitiate the argument of the entire letter. Instead, Paul concludes

---

[24]See the discussion in Richard N. Longenecker, *Galatians,* WBC (Dallas: Word, 1990), pp. 298-99.

the letter with a rhetorical flourish. Those who are the recipients of God's new creation work, the work of Christ on the cross, and who do not consider circumcision significant—they are the Israel of God (Gal 6:14-16). Paul impresses on the readers at the conclusion of his letter that all those who belong to Christ are part of the true Israel. Circumcision is not the path by which one becomes part of Israel. In the new era of salvation history, faith in Christ, the work of the Spirit and the new creation work of God are what qualify one to be part of God's people. Paul conceives of the church as the new Israel since he thinks of believers as sons of Abraham, the true circumcision and the Israel of God.

If Paul conceives of the church as the new Israel, does this rule out any future salvation for ethnic Israel? Many opt for such a conclusion, thinking that if one holds to the former then the latter must be surrendered. Or, conversely, if one sees a future salvation for ethnic Israel, it is often thought that the church could never be designated as the true Israel. I have tried to show here that the dichotomy so often suggested cannot be supported in Paul's letters.[25] He teaches that the church is the new Israel *and* that there is a future salvation for ethnic Israel. No contradiction is involved, for there is no transcendent rule requiring that the word *Israel* always has the same meaning in every text. *Israel* can (and does) have different referents depending on the context in which the term occurs. Nor is there any logical contradiction. A promise of salvation for the final generation of ethnic Israel does not violate the truth that the church is the true Israel, for Israel is only saved through faith in Jesus Christ. Ethnic Israel, by believing in Jesus Christ, becomes part of the true Israel, the genuine people of God. Paul sees the inclusion of both Jews and Gentiles in God's redemptive-historical plan as a manifestation of the depth of his wisdom and knowledge (Rom 11:33). His saving plan and the working out of it are the result of his grace alone, and thus to him belongs the glory forever (Rom 11:34-36).

Conclusion

Believers can be filled with confidence about the future because the Lord Jesus Christ will come again. He will vindicate his own and raise them from the dead. His saving work will be completed for those who are his own, and believers from every people group will worship God and Christ. Unbelievers

---

[25]See also Thomas R. Schreiner, "The Church as the New Israel and the Future of Ethnic Israel in Paul," *StudBibT* 13 (1983): 17-38.

and those who practice evil will be judged and punished forever. God will also fulfill the promises he made to Israel, for he is a faithful, covenant-keeping God. God's people will enter a new world full of joy, praising his goodness forever.

EPILOGUE

Magnifying God in Christ

We cannot rehearse the contents of the book here, but we can remind ourselves of the foundation of Paul's theology. Philippians 2:6-11 features the work of Christ and emphasizes his humiliation on the cross and his exaltation as Lord. The centrality of Jesus comes to the forefront in both, for in his self-giving he manifested a love for sinners even though they worshiped the creature rather than the creator. Those who have spurned God and his glory receive forgiveness of sins through faith in Jesus Christ, on the basis of his atoning death. God vindicated the work of Christ by exalting him above every name and crowning him as Lord of the universe. The exalted Christ bestows the gift of the Spirit on his people; and believers by the power of the Spirit are enabled, to a substantial degree, to live in a way that pleases God. Hence, the death and resurrection of Christ have inaugurated a new era in which the promise to bless all people groups, made so long ago to Abraham, is becoming a reality.

Paul, as the apostle of Jesus Christ, was chosen by God to bring the gospel of the crucified and risen Lord to all peoples. Indeed, he was specifically commissioned as the apostle to the Gentiles. Paul grasped that God's promise to bless all peoples was now being fulfilled in Jesus Christ, and in his writings he explicated this promise theologically, explaining how human beings have dishonored God and how they can now glorify him by putting their trust in Christ. He rejects the idea that the blessing is restricted to the Jewish people or to those who live by the Mosaic covenant. With the arrival of the new covenant the distinctions between Jews and Gentiles have been erased. Together Jews and Gentiles form the new people of God—the church of Jesus Christ. As the new people of God, the church becomes the locus of God's glory in the world.

God chose Paul as his ambassador and apostle to the nations, but he also planned that the gospel would be disseminated through Pauline suffering. The suffering of Paul was not atoning, and hence it falls far short of the death of Christ. Nor was Paul's suffering the basis of forgiveness, and hence he did not suffer for the sins of others as Christ did. Still, Paul's sufferings were the means by which the gospel was spread to the Gentiles. In that sense, then, Paul's sufferings were a corollary to the sufferings of Christ. Life comes from the death of Christ, and in Paul's ministry God's power was manifested in his weakness and salvation for all was proclaimed through his suffering.

The connection between salvation and suffering is woven into the hymn in Philippians 2:6-11. Suffering, of course, is not the final story. Jesus, who is equal to God and in the form of God, humbled himself to experience the degradation of crucifixion. On the cross he absorbed God's wrath against sin. As a result, God raised him from the dead and exalted him above all. He is worshiped and adored forever as Lord and Christ. Or, for those who refuse to believe and obey, there is the acknowledgment that he is Lord and the pain of knowing that they refused the message of eternal life.

The exaltation and glory of Jesus Christ does not diminish the glory of God. Indeed, Philippians 2:11 informs us that the humiliation and exaltation of Christ is the means by which God himself is glorified. He is glorified because through Christ he has fulfilled the promise to Abraham to bless all peoples. He is magnified because the love of God is evident in his sending his Son for our salvation. He is honored because his justice was satisfied in Christ's death on our behalf. He is worshiped by those who have tasted the goodness and joy of salvation. He is acknowledged as the God of the universe even by those who rejected his kind offer. God in Christ will be worshiped and adored forever, "because from him and through him and to him are all things. To him be the glory forever, amen" (Rom 11:36).

Author Index

Subject Index

Abraham, 23, 119-20, 141, 152, 243, 478
  blessing of, 38, 73-74, 78-79, 83-85, 110, 152, 159-60, 237, 261, 324, 370, 451, 482
  covenant, 321
  faith of, 29, 78, 80, 248-49, 272
  family of, 54, 79-83, 161, 192, 215, 237, 244, 375, 401, 471, 482-83
  Jesus as "seed of," 159-61
  promises to, 48, 82-84, 159, 324, 328, 431, 485-86
Adam, 31, 80, 105, 127, 142-43, 146-50, 152-56, 172, 174-76, 181, 191, 237, 258-60, 270, 375, 376, 404, 408-9, 436, 458
adoption, 240, 264, 322, 376
Alexander, 394
already but not yet, 20, 33, 92-93, 96-97, 138, 143, 145, 152, 165-66, 191, 209, 221, 228, 232-33, 251, 253-69, 289-90, 310, 327, 383, 453-58, 466
Andronicus, 400-401
angels, 27-28
  victory over, 232-34, 259, 302-3
anthropology, 118-19, 214
  old person, 31, 82, 154, 161, 191, 259-61, 376
  new person, 31, 154-56, 191,

259-61, 270
Apollos, 19, 24, 91-93, 288, 340, 377, 393, 401
apostasy, 274, 276-78, 292-93, 295, 304, 461, 464
apostle, 22, 38-39, 60, 61, 85, 87-88, 91, 94-98, 184, 343, 351-53, 356, 362, 368-70, 388, 393, 400-401, 428
  call to be, 40-49
Aquila, 400
assurance, 274-94
baptism, 80, 161, 190-91, 220-21, 257-60, 287, 336, 371-79, 410
  infant, 377-79
Barnabas, 393, 401
boasting, 24, 32
body, 142, 153, 252, 268, 458-60, 466
calling, 32, 41-49, 84, 137, 184, 222, 239-42, 277-78, 295, 297, 339, 413, 475
center of Pauline theology, 16-18, 22, 192-94, 196, 222
children, 328-29, 378, 413-14, 420, 423, 431-32, 436
church, 84, 279, 331-35
  body of Christ, 335-38, 373, 380-81
  discipline, 255, 290, 301, 394-98
  divisions, unity, 23-26, 335-42, 344-51
  leaders, 312, 340, 383-95, 438
  purpose of, 34
circumcision, 23, 26, 42, 45-46, 50-56, 63, 80-82, 96, 99, 108-9, 111-12, 114, 122-23, 134, 144-46, 190, 192, 195, 259, 269, 280-81, 291, 311, 324-28, 342, 375, 377-79, 393, 413, 446, 472, 477, 482-83

collection, 333, 443-47
conscience, 346-47
covenant faithfulness, 197-201
covenantal nomism, 117
David, 74-75, 120, 141, 152, 160-61, 165-67, 175-76, 233
day of the Lord, 232, 302, 393, 461-64
deacons, 386-89, 398-99, 409-10
death, 133, 135, 138, 142, 146-50, 153, 233, 283, 455, 457-60, 463, 466-67
destruction, 346-47, 394, 443, 455, 457, 460-62, 465, 467-71, 473-75
devil. *See* Satan
distinguishing of spirits, 363-64
divorce, 310, 408, 426-31
edification, 353-54, 356, 366
elders, 334, 383, 386-92, 394, 399, 401, 409-10
election, 32, 84, 137, 159, 222, 236-47, 278, 434, 476, 478
Epaphroditus, 341, 386, 401
Esau, 243, 245
eternal life, 282-83, 286, 288, 438, 442, 469-70, 486
Euodia, 25, 68, 340, 400
evangelists, 351, 354, 356, 359
Eve, 105, 146, 155, 159, 174-75, 301, 408-9, 436
exhortation, 307-17
  gift of, 355, 360
exile, 79, 109, 131, 202, 230, 265
exodus, new, 46, 48-49, 78-79, 230, 232, 262
faith, 128, 240, 242, 246-49, 268, 291, 293-94, 296, 298,

305, 314, 316, 329, 347-48, 375-76, 378, 442-43, 463, 466, 469, 471-72, 479, 482-83, 486
  gift of, 351-52, 355, 358
  nature of, 29
  to receive the Spirit, 78
  relation to hope, 271-79
  relation to right-eousness, 65, 119, 202, 204-5, 209-16
flesh, 132-33, 135, 138-46, 282, 302
food laws, 322, 325-26
food offered to idols, 91, 115, 287, 314, 323, 344-51, 380
foreknow, 238-39, 277
forgiveness, 48, 100, 190-91, 193, 204-5, 210-11, 230, 234, 248, 264, 382-83
Gentiles
  inclusion of, 54-59, 83-85, 184-86, 191, 193-95, 217, 236-38, 298, 324, 338, 343, 446, 483, 486
  unity with Jews, 33-34, 54-59, 61-62, 71-72, 483
giving, 355, 359
glorification, 453-55
God
  Creator, 243
  faithfulness, 274-76
  foundation of all, 20-21, 163
  glory, 20-22, 26, 28-35, 71, 72, 94, 102, 104-7, 124, 177-78, 182, 210, 240, 248, 253, 298, 316, 334, 339, 345, 348-49, 417, 419, 441, 446, 454, 483, 486
  love, 191, 202, 229, 235, 238,

504

3:11, *399*
3:12, *344, 387*
3:12-13, *399*
3:15, *334, 344*
3:15-16, *344*
3:16, *141, 185, 390*
4:1-5, *116, 290, 388, 390*
4:1-16, *390*
4:3, *286, 390*
4:3-4, *323*
4:5, *358*
4:6, *387*
4:6-16, *65*
4:9, *390*
4:10, *185, 228, 229, 399*
4:11, *359*
4:11-15, *284*
4:11-16, *227, 390*
4:12, *312*
4:13, *360*
4:16, *227, 284*
5, *417, 418*
5:3-8, *439, 440*
5:3-16, *439, 440, 441*
5:5, *440*
5:8, *439*
5:9, *440*
5:9-10, *440*
5:9-15, *439*
5:10, *112, 286*
5:11-13, *415*
5:11-15, *301, 418, 440*
5:13, *396*
5:13-15, *440*
5:14, *415*
5:17, *229, 359, 387, 388, 390, 392, 399, 409*
5:17-18, *392*
5:17-25, *38*
5:19, *387, 394*
5:20, *394*
5:21, *394*
5:22, *394*
5:25, *112*
6, *442*
6:1, *437*
6:2, *359, 390, 435*
6:3, *164, 390*
6:3-10, *116, 388*
6:3-12, *390*
6:4, *116*
6:4-5, *312*

6:6, *441*
6:6-8, *442*
6:8, *441*
6:9, *443, 469*
6:10, *443*
6:11, *205, 209, 312*
6:11-14, *390*
6:14, *455*
6:17-19, *442*
6:18, *112*
6:19, *442*
6:20-21, *116, 388, 390*

2 Timothy
1:8, *164*
1:9, *41, 112, 113, 124, 228, 242*
1:9-10, *390*
1:9-11, *284, 285, 344*
1:10, *228, 455*
1:12, *273*
1:13, *390*
1:14, *390*
1:16, *273*
1:18, *273*
2:2, *359, 390*
2:8, *39, 76, 165, 456*
2:9, *358*
2:9-10, *100*
2:10, *84, 227*
2:11, *390*
2:11-13, *390*
2:12, *273, 292*
2:12-13, *276*
2:13, *275*
2:14—3:17, *390*
2:14-18, *116, 388, 390*
2:15, *65*
2:17-18, *276*
2:18, *276, 390, 456*
2:19, *276*
2:22, *205, 209, 312*
2:22-26, *68*
2:24-26, *247, 388*
2:25, *247*
2:26, *138, 247*
3:1-9, *116, 290, 388*
3:2, *116, 325*
3:2-4, *312*
3:8, *287*
3:16, *205, 209*
4:1-2, *455*
4:1-5, *65, 390*
4:3, *390*

4:5, *68, 359*
4:8, *455*
4:10, *290*
4:14, *112, 282, 470*
4:16-18, *278*
4:17, *226*
4:17-18, *211*
4:18, *179, 226, 278*
4:19, *400*

Titus
1:1, *84*
1:2, *58*
1:3, *229*
1:4, *229*
1:5, *387*
1:5-9, *38, 389, 391*
1:7, *387*
1:9, *388, 390, 394, 409*
1:9-16, *390*
1:10, *185, 229*
1:10-16, *116*
1:11, *359*
1:13, *390*
1:14, *229*
1:14-15, *185, 323*
1:16, *112, 287*
2—3, *69*
2, *390*
2:1-14, *390*
2:3-5, *69*
2:4, *409*
2:4-5, *425*
2:5, *423, 424*
2:7, *112*
2:9, *437*
2:9-10, *437*
2:11, *185, 228*
2:11-14, *70, 228, 229, 284, 285*
2:12, *209*
2:13, *178, 180, 455*
2:14, *112, 228, 232, 344*
3:1, *424, 448*
3:3, *139, 312*
3:4, *229*
3:4-7, *229, 284, 285, 344, 390*
3:4-11, *390*
3:5, *112, 113, 124, 210, 256, 262, 372, 374*
3:6, *229*
3:7, *210*
3:8, *112, 390*

3:9, *185, 229*
3:9-11, *116, 396, 397*
3:14, *112*

Philemon
1, *400*
2, *84, 332*
3, *162*
4-5, *314*
5, *84, 215*
10, *66, 435*
11, *434*
14, *434*
16, *142, 434*
18-19, *434*
24, *400*
25, *162*

Hebrews
2:5-9, *166*
6:8, *287*
10:1, *155*
11:23, *432*
12:9, *432*
13:21, *179*

James
2:1, *213*
5:14, *386*
5:15, *358*

1 Peter
1:3, *179, 180*
2:8, *346*
2:13-17, *450*
3:1-6, *420*
3:5-6, *423*
4:11, *179*
5:1-4, *386*
5:5, *386*

2 Peter
3:17, *238*
3:18, *179*

1 John
2:10, *346*
2:19, *276*

Revelation
18:17, *359*